FAMILY LAW AND PRACTICE

FAMILY LAW AND PRACTICE

Nancy Duffield BA (Hons), Solicitor
Jacqueline Kempton BA (Hons), Solicitor
Christa Sabine BA (Hons), Solicitor

CLP

Published by

College of Law Publishing,
Braboeuf Manor, Portsmouth Road, St Catherines, Guildford GU3 1HA

British Library Cataloguing-in-Publication Data

A catalogue record for this book is available from the British Library.

ISBN 978 1 908604 34 7

Typeset by Style Photosetting Ltd, Mayfield, East Sussex

Printed in Great Britain by Ashford Colour Press Ltd, Gosport, Hampshire

Preface

Family law is a dynamic subject, constantly changing, and a challenge to everyone involved with it. We have taken on the challenge in preparing this book. Our main aim has been to prepare a book which provides the legal background for students on the Legal Practice Course. It will be the springboard for students to use to practise the skills learned during the Legal Practice Course. We hope it will also be of use to trainees and newly qualified solicitors who are using these skills for the first time in the real world.

Throughout the book, for uniformity, we have generally referred to the client and the solicitor as 'he'. In reality, it is usually the woman who initiates proceedings on the breakdown of the relationship, and in some places, for example domestic abuse, we have changed the sex of the client to reflect the more usual situation.

In the book the terms 'husband and wife' or 'spouses' should be taken to include civil partners unless the text states otherwise. Similarly 'matrimonial home' includes a civil partnership home.

We would like to acknowledge with thanks the contribution made to this book in the past by Jo Theobald. Our thanks also go to our colleagues at The College of Law who have helped us with this book, and to our long-suffering families and friends who have endured its rebirth.

Unless otherwise mentioned, the law is stated as at 1 September 2011.

NANCY DUFFIELD
JACQUELINE KEMPTON
CHRISTA SABINE
The College of Law

Contents

PREFACE			v
TABLE OF CASES			xi
TABLE OF STATUTES			xix
TABLE OF STATUTORY INSTRUMENTS AND CODES OF PRACTICE			xxiii
TABLE OF ABBREVIATIONS			xxv
Chapter 1	INTRODUCTION: THE FAMILY PRACTICE		1
	1.1	The family client	1
	1.2	The family practitioner	3
	1.3	Support for family clients	5
	1.4	Alternative dispute resolution	6
	1.5	The family courts	7
	1.6	Human Rights Act 1998	8
	1.7	Family law in the future	9
	1.8	Conclusion	9
	1.9	Chapter summary	9
Chapter 2	FUNDING		11
	2.1	Introduction	11
	2.2	Contracting	11
	2.3	Levels of service and fees	12
	2.4	Effect of public funding	14
	2.5	The statutory charge	15
	2.6	Human rights	17
	2.7	Other methods of funding	17
	2.8	Chapter summary	18
Chapter 3	DIVORCE LAW AND PROCEDURE		19
	3.1	Introduction	19
	3.2	One-year rule	20
	3.3	Jurisdiction of the English courts to hear suits for divorce	20
	3.4	The ground for divorce	22
	3.5	Protection of children: Matrimonial Causes Act 1973, s 41	29
	3.6	Nullity	30
	3.7	Judicial separation	31
	3.8	Presumption of death and dissolution of marriage	32
	3.9	Divorce procedure	32
	3.10	Defended divorces	43
	3.11	Costs	43
	3.12	Divorce law and procedure in the future	43
	3.13	Chapter summary	43
Chapter 4	FINANCIAL ORDERS: THE LAW		47
	4.1	Introduction	47
	4.2	The powers of the court	47
	4.3	Income orders	48
	4.4	Capital orders	50
	4.5	Deciding what orders to make	52
	4.6	The clean break	62
	4.7	Pensions on divorce	64
	4.8	Financial cases in the future	66

	4.9	Financial provision during marriage	66
	4.10	Chapter summary	68
Chapter 5	TAX ON MARRIAGE BREAKDOWN		69
	5.1	Introduction	69
	5.2	Tax on marriage breakdown	69
	5.3	Chapter summary	72
Chapter 6	WELFARE AND LOCAL AUTHORITY HOUSING		73
	6.1	Introduction	73
	6.2	Child benefit	73
	6.3	Income support	73
	6.4	Jobseeker's allowance	76
	6.5	Working tax credit and child tax credit	76
	6.6	Housing benefit	79
	6.7	Council tax benefit	79
	6.8	Discretionary housing payments	80
	6.9	The social fund	80
	6.10	Welfare benefits and marriage breakdown	81
	6.11	Local authority housing	82
	6.12	Chapter summary	84
Chapter 7	CALCULATING CHILD MAINTENANCE		85
	7.1	Introduction	85
	7.2	The Child Support Agency and the Child Maintenance and Enforcement Commission	85
	7.3	When does the CSA 1991 apply?	86
	7.4	The jurisdiction of the court	86
	7.5	Maintenance agreements and consent orders	88
	7.6	Calculating the child maintenance	90
	7.7	Further reforms	96
	7.8	Chapter summary	97
Chapter 8	MAINTENANCE FOR A SPOUSE		99
	8.1	Introduction	99
	8.2	High income families	99
	8.3	Middle income families	100
	8.4	Low income families	101
	8.5	Chapter summary	102
Chapter 9	DEALING WITH THE CAPITAL ASSETS		103
	9.1	Introduction	103
	9.2	Selling the home	103
	9.3	Retaining the home	105
	9.4	The interests of third parties	108
	9.5	The rented home	110
	9.6	Protecting the capital assets	110
	9.7	Lump sums	113
	9.8	Pensions	115
	9.9	Bankruptcy	115
	9.10	Chapter summary	116
Chapter 10	PROCEDURE FOR OBTAINING A FINANCIAL ORDER		119
	10.1	Introduction	119
	10.2	Public funding	119
	10.3	Overview of the procedure	119
	10.4	The pre-application protocols	120
	10.5	The application	121
	10.6	Filing and service	122
	10.7	Obtaining the evidence	123
	10.8	Court hearings	125

	10.9	Interim orders	128
	10.10	Costs	128
	10.11	Negotiations	129
	10.12	Consent orders	130
	10.13	Drafting financial orders	130
	10.14	Summary of court procedure	143
	10.15	Maintenance calculations	146
Chapter 11	ENFORCEMENT, APPEALS, SETTING ASIDE AND VARIATION		147
	11.1	Introduction	147
	11.2	Financial orders in the county court	147
	11.3	Enforcement in the family proceedings court	149
	11.4	Collection and enforcement by the Child Maintenance and Enforcement Commission	150
	11.5	Property adjustment orders	152
	11.6	Appeals	152
	11.7	Setting aside	153
	11.8	Variation	154
	11.9	Chapter summary	157
Chapter 12	PRE-MARITAL AGREEMENTS AND SEPARATION AGREEMENTS		159
	12.1	Introduction	159
	12.2	Pre-marital agreements	159
	12.3	Post-nuptial and separation agreements	160
	12.4	Reform	163
	12.5	Chapter summary	163
Chapter 13	CHILDREN		165
	13.1	Introduction	165
	13.2	Parental responsibility	166
	13.3	Section 8 orders	170
	13.4	Welfare principle	181
	13.5	Checklist of factors to be taken into account in applying welfare principle	182
	13.6	The 'no order' presumption	186
	13.7	Avoiding delay	186
	13.8	Procedure for s 8 orders	187
	13.9	Protection of children	197
	13.10	Financial provision and property orders for children	200
	13.11	Chapter summary	202
Chapter 14	CHILDREN: PUBLIC LAW		205
	14.1	Introduction	205
	14.2	Local authority support for children and families (CA 1989, Pt III)	206
	14.3	Preventing neglect or abuse	209
	14.4	Care and supervision orders (CA 1989, Pt IV)	211
	14.5	Contact (s 34)	215
	14.6	Discharge of care orders (s 39)	216
	14.7	Effect of a supervision order	217
	14.8	Care or supervision order	218
	14.9	Interim orders (s 38)	218
	14.10	Emergency protection and assessment (CA 1989, Pt V)	220
	14.11	Procedure for care and supervision orders	223
	14.12	Human rights implications	230
	14.13	Compensation for local authority failings	232
	14.14	Special guardianship order	232
	14.15	Chapter summary	232
Chapter 15	DOMESTIC ABUSE		235
	15.1	Introduction	235
	15.2	Protection under Pt IV of the Family Law Act 1996	236

	15.3	Human rights implications	250
	15.4	Protection from Harassment Act 1997	251
	15.5	The Forced Marriage (Civil Protection) Act 2007	251
	15.6	Chapter summary	252
Chapter 16	THE COHABITING FAMILY		253
	16.1	Introduction	253
	16.2	Setting up home together	254
	16.3	Breaking up	256
	16.4	Children	261
	16.5	Bankruptcy	263
	16.6	Death	263
	16.7	Chapter summary	264

APPENDICES **265**

Appendix 1 – Legislation			267
	(A)	Matrimonial Causes Act 1973	267
	(B)	Inheritance (Provision for Family and Dependants) Act 1975	287
	(C)	Domestic Proceedings and Magistrates' Courts Act 1978	290
	(D)	Child Abduction Act 1984	292
	(E)	Children Act 1989	295
	(F)	Child Support Act 1991	348
	(G)	Family Law Act 1996	359
	(H)	Trusts of Land and Appointment of Trustees Act 1996	373
	(I)	Family Procedure Rules 2010 (SI 2010/2955)	374
Appendix 2 – Code of Practice for Resolution Members			407
Appendix 3 – Court Forms			409
	(A)	Divorce petition	409
	(B)	Statement of arrangements for children	417
	(C)	Form FM1 (Family mediation information and assessment)	423
	(D)	Form A (Application for a financial order)	425
	(E)	Form E (Statement for a financial order)	427
	(F)	Form D81 (Statement of information for a consent order)	455
	(G)	Parental responsibility agreement (1)	461
	(H)	Parental responsibility agreement (2)	463
	(I)	Form C1 (Children Act application)	465
	(J)	Form C100 (Application for a s 8 order)	471
	(K)	Form C1A (Supplemental information)	485
	(L)	Form C110 (Application for a care or supervision order)	491
	(M)	Form FL401 (Family Law Act application)	509
INDEX			515

Table of Cases

A

A (a child) (joint residence: parental responsibility), Re [2008] EWCA Civ 867 171
A (Contact: Separate Representation), Re [2001] 1 FLR 715, CA 183
A (Minors) (Parental Responsibility), Re [1993] Fam Law 464 167
A (Section 8 Order: Grandparent Application), Re [1995] 2 FLR 153 175
A Local Authority v YZ and Others [2006] 2 FLR 41 180
A v A (Maintenance Pending Suit; Provision of Legal Fees) [2001] 1 FLR 377 17
A v N (Committal: Refusal of Contact) [1997] 1 FLR 533 177
A v T (Ancillary Relief: Cultural Factors) [2004] 1 FLR 977 52
A, Re [2009] EWCA Civ 1141 177
AD (A Minor) (Child's Wishes), Re [1993] 1 FCR 573 188
AD and OD v UK [2010] ECHR 340 232
Airey v Ireland (1979) 2 EHRR 305 17
A-J (Adoption Order or Special Guardianship Order), Re [2007] EWCA Civ 55 232
Allington v Allington [1985] FLR 586 184

B

B (a child) (residence order), Re [2009] UKSC 5 171
B (A Child), Re [2006] EWCA Civ 1574 93
B (Contact Application: Costs), Re [1995] Fam Law 650 177
B (Removal from Jurisdiction), Re; S (Removal from Jurisdiction), Re [2003] EWCA Civ 1149, [2003] 2 FLR 1043 173
B v A and others (Parental Responsibility) [2006] EWHC 2 (Fam) 170
B v B [2008] 2 FLR 1627 53
B v B (A Minor) (Residence Order) [1992] 2 FLR 327 186
B v B (Occupation Order) [1999] 1 FLR 715 238
B v M (Child Support: Revocation of Order) [1994] Fam Law 370 89
Bailey v Tolliday [1983] 4 FLR 542 59
Balfour v Balfour [1919] 2 KB 571 255
Bank v Dobson and Dobson [1986] 1 FLR 171 259
Barder v Barder [1988] AC 20 153
Barnes v Barnes [1972] 3 All ER 872 54
Behzadi v Behzadi [2008] EWCA Civ 1070 127
Bernard v Josephs [1982] Ch 391, [1983] 4 FLR 178 261
Birch v Birch [1992] 1 FLR 564 25
B-J (Power of Arrest), Re [2000] 2 FLR 443 237
Bokor-Ingram v Bokor-Ingram [2009] EWCA 412 123
Bradley v Bradley [1973] 1 WLR 1291 26
Brickell v Brickell [1973] 3 All ER 508 28
Browne (formerly Pritchard) v Pritchard [1975] 1 WLR 1366 104
Burns v Burns [1984] Ch 317 258
Burns v Burns [2004] EWCA Civ 1258 154
Burris v Azadani [1995] 4 All ER 802 251
Burrow v Burrow [1999] 1 FLR 508 65

C

C (A Minor) (Interim Care Order: Residential Assessment), Re [1996] 4 All ER 871 219
C (Care Order or Supervision Order), Re [2001] 2 FLR 466 218
C (Change of Surname), Re [1998] 1 FLR 549 170
C (Minors) (Parental Rights), Re [1992] 1 FLR 1 167
C and B (Care Order: Future Harm), Re [2001] 1 FLR 611 218
C v C (Financial Relief: Short Marriage) [1997] 2 FLR 26 57
C v C (Minors: Custody) [1988] 2 FLR 291 184
C v C (Variation of Post-Nuptial Settlement: Company Shares) [2003] 2 FLR 493 114
Chalmers v Johns [1999] 1 FLR 392 238
Charman v Charman [2007] EWCA Civ 503 58, 66
Citro, Re [1991] 1 FLR 71 116

CL v East Riding Yorkshire Council and Others [2006] EWCA Civ 49 212
Clark v Clark [1999] 2 FLR 498 59
Cooke v Head [1972] 1 WLR 518 258
Coombes v Smith [1986] 1 WLR 808 259
Cornick v Cornick [1994] 2 FLR 530 153
Cowan v Cowan [2001] 2 FLR 192 58
Crossley v Crossley [2007] EWCA Civ 1491 160
Crozier v Crozier [1994] 1 FLR 126 154
CT (A Minor) (Wardship: Representation), Re [1993] 2 FLR 278 188
Curley v Parkes [2004] EWCA Civ 1515 257
Curling v Law Society [1985] 1 All ER 705 15
Currey v Currey [2006] EWCA Civ 1338 17

D

D (A Minor) (Child: Removal from Jurisdiction), Re [1992] 1 FLR 637 179
D (A Minor) (Contact), Re [1993] 1 FCR 9 174
D (Care Proceedings: Preliminary Hearing), Re [2009] EWCA Civ 472 213
D (Care: Natural Parent Presumption), Re [1999] 1 FLR 134 185
D (Children) (Shared Residence Orders), Re [2001] 1 FLR 495 171
D (Contact and Parental Responsibility: Lesbian Mothers and Known Father), Re [2006] EWHC 2 (Fam) 168
D (Intractable Contact Dispute: Publicity), Re [2004] EWHC 727, [2004] 1 FLR 1226 177
D (Minors) (Conciliation: Disclosure of Information), Re [1993] Fam 231 393
D v D and B Ltd [2007] EWHC 278 (Fam) 114
D v East Berkshire Community Health NHS Trust, K and Another v Dewsbury Healthcare NHS Trust and Another, K and Another v Oldham NHS Trust and Another [2005] UKHL 23 232
Dawson v Wearmouth [1999] 1 FLR 1167 172, 231
Delaney v Delaney [1990] 2 FLR 457 55
Dixon v Marchant [2008] 1 FLR 665 153, 155
Donohoe v Ingram (Trustee in Bankruptcy of Kirkup) [2006] EWHC 292 116
Dorney-Kingdom v Dorney-Kingdom [2000] 2 FLR 855 96
Dutfield v Gilbert H Stephens & Sons [1988] Fam Law 473 4
Duxbury v Duxbury [1987] 1 FLR 7 114
DW (A Minor), Re [1984] Fam Law 17 183

E

E (Residence: Imposition of Conditions), Re [1997] 2 FLR 638 174
E v E (Financial Provision) [1990] 2 FLR 233 58
E v E (Premature Remarriage) [2008] 1 FLR 220 121
Edgar v Edgar [1980] 3 All ER 887 162
Evans v Evans [1989] 1 FLR 351 59
Evans v Evans [1990] 1 FLR 319 125
Ever's Trust, Re [1980] 1 WLR 1327 261
Eves v Eves [1975] 1 WLR 1338 258

F

F (A Minor) (Blood Tests), Re [1993] 1 FLR 598 167
F (Child: Surname), Re [1993] 2 FLR 837 172
F (children) (internal relocation), Re [2010] EWCA Civ 1348 174
F (Contact: Child in Care), Re [1995] 1 FLR 510 216
F v F (Clean Break: Balance of Fairness) [2003] 1 FLR 847 114
F v F [2008] Fam Law 182 59
F v G (Child: Financial Provision) [2005] 1 FLR 261 201
F v Kent County Council and Others [1993] 1 FLR 432 216
Flavell v Flavell [1997] 1 FLR 353, [1997] Fam Law 237 63, 156
FZ v SZ and others [2010] EWHC 1630 59

G

G (A Minor) (Parental Responsibility Order), Re [1994] 1 FLR 504 168
G (Children), In re [2006] UKHL 43 184
G (Costs: Child Case), Re [1999] 2 FLR 250 194
G (Domestic Violence: Direct Contact), Re [2000] 2 FLR 865 216

G (Interim Care Order: Residential Assessment), Re [2005] UKHL 68 219
G (Minors) (Ex parte Interim Residence Order), Re [1993] 1 FLR 910 191
G (Minors) (Interim Care Order), Re [1993] 2 FLR 839 219
G (Residence: Same Sex Partners), Re [2005] EWCA Civ 462 171
G v G (Financial Provision: Separation Agreement) [2000] 2 FLR 18 52
Gillick v West Norfolk and Wisbech Area Health Authority [1986] AC 112 166
Gojkovic v Gojkovic [1990] 1 FLR 140 57
Grant v Edwards [1986] Ch 638 258
Greasley v Cooke [1980] 3 All ER 710 260
Grey v Grey [2009] EWCA Civ 1424 125, 156
GW v RE [2003] EWHC 611 (Fam) 87

H

H (A Child) (Interim Care Order), Re [2002] EWCA Civ 1932 219
H (A Minor) (Custody: Interim Care and Control), Re [1991] 2 FLR 109 184
H (A Minor) (Parental Responsibility), Re [1993] 1 FLR 484 167
H (A Minor), Re (1990) The Times, 20 June 184
H (Contact: Domestic Violence), Re [1998] 2 FLR 42 175
H (Minors) (Local Authority: Parental Rights) (No 3), Re [1991] 2 WLR 763 167
H (Parental Responsibility), Re [1998] 1 FLR 855 170
H (Prohibited Steps Order), Re [1995] 1 FLR 638 179
H (Residence Order: Child's Application For Leave), Re [2000] 1 FLR 781 188
H and R (Child Sexual Abuse: Standard of Proof), Re [1996] 1 FLR 80 212
H v H (Financial Relief: Attempted Murder as Conduct) [2005] EWHC 2911 58
H v M (Property: Beneficial Interest) [1992] 1 FLR 229 258
H v O (Contempt of Court: Sentencing) [2004] EWCA Civ 1691 250
Haghighat (A Bankrupt), Re [2009] EWHC 90 (Ch) 116
Hale v Tanner [2000] 2 FLR 879 250
Hamilton Jones v David & Snape (A Firm) [2003] EWHC 3147 (Ch) 198
Hammerton v Hammerton [2007] EWCA Civ 248 250
Hanlon v Law Society [1980] 2 All ER 199 15
Harvey v Harvey [1982] 3 FLR 141 106, 107
Hedges v Hedges [1991] 1 FLR 196 64
Hewett v First Plus Financial Group PLC [2010] EWCA Civ 312 108
Hill v Haines [2007] EWCA Civ 1284 116
Hopes v Hopes [1948] 2 All ER 920 26
Hope-Smith v Hope-Smith [1989] 2 FLR 56 104
Hoppe v Germany [2003] 1 FLR 384 182
Hvorostovsky v Hvorostovsky [2009] EWCA Civ 791 156

I

Imerman v Imerman [2010] EWCA Civ 908 123

J

J (Child's Religious Upbringing and Circumcision), Re [2000] 1 FLR 571 170
J (Specific Issue Order: Leave to Apply), Re [1995] 1 FLR 669 208
J and Another v C and Others [1969] 1 All ER 788 182
J v J (A Minor: Property Transfer) [1993] 2 FLR 56 202, 260
Johansen v Norway (1996) 23 EHRR 33 230
Johnston v Ireland (1987) 9 EHRR 203 19
Jones v Kernott [2011] UKSC 53 257, 258, 259
Judd v Brown [1998] 2 FLR 360 116
Julian v Julian (1973) 116 SJ 763 29

K

K (Care Proceedings: Notification of Father without Parental Responsibility), Re [1999] 2 FLR 408 226
K (Contact: Mother's Anxiety), Re [1999] Fam Law 527 175
K (Supervision Orders), Re [1999] 2 FLR 303 208
K v K (Ancillary Relief: Prenuptial Agreement) [2003] 1 FLR 120 60
K v K (Conduct) [1990] 2 FLR 225 58
K v K (Minors: Property Transfer) [1992] 2 FLR 220 201

K v L [2010] EWCA Civ 125 59
KD (A Minor) (Access: Principles) [1998] 2 FLR 139 231
Kehoe v United Kingdom [2008] All ER (D) 198 151
Kimber v Brookman Solicitors [2004] 2 FLR 221 123
Kingdon v Kingdon [2010] EWCA Civ 1251 153
Kokosinski v Kokosinski [1980] Fam 72 57
Krystman v Krystman [1973] 3 All ER 247 57
KSO v MJO and JMO (PSO intervening) [2008] EWHC 3031 (Fam) 128

L

L (a child) (internal relocation: shared residence order), Re [2009] EWCA Civ 20 174
L (Contact: Domestic Violence), Re [2000] 2 FLR 334 175, 176, 216
L (Police Investigation: Privilege), Re [1996] 1 FLR 731 229
L and H (Residential Assessment), Re [2007] EWCA Civ 213 219
L-A (Children), Re [2009] EWCA Civ 822 219
Lambert v Lambert [2002] EWCA Civ 1685, [2003] 1 FLR 139 58
Lancashire County Council v B [2000] 1 FLR 583 212
Langley v Liverpool City Council [2005] EWCA Civ 1173 222
Le Foe v Le Foe and Woolwich plc; Woolwich plc v Le Foe and Le Foe [2001] 2 FLR 970 258
Livesey (formerly Jenkins) v Jenkins [1985] AC 424, [1985] FLR 813 55, 123, 153
Lloyds Bank plc v Rosset [1990] 2 WLR 867, [1990] 1 All ER 1111 258
Lomas v Parle [2003] EWCA Civ 1804 250
Lord Lilford v Glynn [1979] 1 WLR 78 60
L-W (children) (contact order: committal), Re [2010] EWCA Civ 1253 178

M

M (A Minor) (Care Order: Threshold Conditions), Re [1994] 2 FLR 577 212
M (Care: Contact: Grandmother's Application for Leave), Re [1995] 2 FLR 86 216
M (Contact: Violent Parent), Re [1999] 2 FLR 321 175
M (Intractable Contact Dispute: Interim Care Order), Re [2003] EWHC 1024 (Fam), [2003] 2 FLR 636 177
M (Minors) (Sexual Abuse: Evidence), Re [1993] 1 FLR 822 226
M (Section 91(14) Order), Re [1999] 2 FLR 553 216
M v M [2009] EWHC 1941 (Fam) 129
M v M (Ancillary Relief: Division of Assets Accrued Post Separation) [2004] All ER (D) 83 62
M v M (Parental Responsibility) [1999] 2 FLR 737 168
M v M (Third Party Subpoena: Financial Conduct) [2006] 2 FLR 1253 125
M v M (Transfer of Custody: Appeal) [1987] 1 WLR 404 183
MacLeod v MacLeod [2008] UKPC 64 160, 162
Maharaj v Chand [1986] AC 898 260
Marinos v Marinos [2007] 2 FLR 1018 21
Martin v Martin [1976] 3 All ER 625 58
Martin v Martin [1978] Fam 12 106
Martin-Dye v Martin-Dye [2006] EWCA Civ 681 115
Maskell v Maskell [2001] EWCA Civ 858, [2001] 1 FLR 1138 115
McCartney v Mills McCartney [2008] EWHC 401 (Fam) 99
McFarlane v McFarlane [2009] EWHC 891 99, 156
McMichael v UK (1995) 20 EHRR 205 169, 262
Merritt v Merritt [1970] 1 WLR 1121 255
Mesher v Mesher and Hall [1980] 1 All ER 126 106
Michael v Michael [1986] 2 FLR 389 50, 54
Miller v Miller; McFarlane v McFarlane [2006] UKHL 24 53, 99, 156, 160
Miller-Smith v Miller-Smith (No 2) [2010] 2 FLR 351 42
Milne v Milne [1981] 2 FLR 286 64
Minwalla v Minwalla [2005] 1 FLR 771 18
MK v CK [2011] EWCA Civ 793 173
Morgan and Others v Legal Aid Board [2000] 3 All ER 974 16
Mossop v Mossop [1988] 2 All ER 20 256
Mountney v Treharne [2002] EWCA Civ 1174 116
Mubarak v Mubarak [2001] 1 FLR 698 149
Myerson v Myerson (No 2) [2009] EWCA Civ 282 154
Myerson v Myerson [2008] EWCA Civ 1376 127

N

N v N (Consent Order: Variation) [1993] 2 FLR 868 157
N v N (Financial Provision: Sale of Company) [2001] 2 FLR 69 113
Negus v Bahouse and Another [2007] EWHC 2628 (Ch) 264
Norris v Norris [2002] EWHC 2996 (Fam), [2003] 1 FLR 142 115
North v North [2008] 1 FLR 158 156
Nottinghamshire County Council v P [1993] 1 FLR 115 174, 211
Nunn (Bankruptcy: Divorce: Pension Rights), Re [2004] 1 FLR 1123 116
Nwogbe v Nwogbe [2000] 2 FLR 744 242
NXS v Camden London Borough Council [2009] EWHC 1786 (QB) 232

O

O (A Minor) (Care Order: Education: Procedure), Re [1992] 2 FLR 7 211
O (A Minor) (Contact: Imposition of Conditions), Re [1995] 2 FLR 124 175
O'Neill v O'Neill [1975] 1 WLR 1118 25

P

P (A Minor) (Adoption), Re [1990] 1 FLR 96 185
P (A Minor) (Education: Child's Views), Re [1992] 1 FLR 316 183
P (Child Financial Provision), Re [2003] EWCA Civ 837 202
P (Parental Responsibility), Re [1998] 2 FLR 96 168
P (Section 91(14) Guidelines) (Residence and Religious Heritage), Re [1999] 2 FLR 573 194
P (Terminating Parental Responsibility), Re [1995] 1 FLR 1048 169
P v P (Financial Relief: Non-Disclosure) [1994] 2 FLR 381 59, 123
P, C and S v United Kingdom [2002] 2 FLR 631 230
Parkes v Legal Aid Board [1997] 1 FLR 77 15
Pascoe v Turner [1979] 1 WLR 431 259
Payne v Payne [2001] EWCA Civ 166, [2001] 1 FLR 1052 173, 182
P-B (Children) (Contact: Committal), Re [2009] EWCA Civ 143 216
Pearce v Pearce [2003] 2 FLR 1144 155
Pettit v Pettit [1970] AC 777 254
Phillips v Peace [2004] EWHC 3180 (Fam) 201
Piglowska v Piglowski [1999] 2 FLR 763 103
Practice Direction (Ancillary Relief: Costs), 20 February 2006 129
Practice Direction (Applications: Liberty to Apply) [1980] 1 All ER 1008 156
Practice Direction (Divorce: Decree Absolute: Application to Expedite) [1977] 2 All ER 714 41
Practice Direction (Family Business: Transfer between High Court and County Court) [1992] 3 All ER 151 58
Practice Direction (Family Division: Disclosure of Addresses by Government Departments) [1989] 1 All ER 765 38
Practice Direction (Human Rights Act 1998) (24 July 2000) [2000] Fam Law 670 9
Practice Direction (Minor: Preventing Removal Abroad) [1986] 1 WLR 475, [1986] 1 All ER 983 198

R

R (A Minor) (Blood Transfusion), Re [1993] 2 FLR 757 179
R (A Minor) (Residence: Religion), Re [1993] 2 FLR 163 185
R (CD) v Isle of Anglesey County Council [2005] 1 FLR 59 209
R (on the application of Kehoe) v Secretary of State for Work and Pensions [2005] UKHL 48 151
R (Residence Order: Finance), Re [1995] 2 FLR 612 183
R v Cornwall County Council, ex p LH [2000] 1 FLR 234 210
R v London Borough of Barnet, ex p B [1994] 1 FLR 592 206, 209
R v London Borough of Brent, ex p S [1994] 1 FLR 203 209
R v R (Lump Sum Repayments) [2004] 1 FLR 928 114
Radmacher v Granatino [2009] EWCA Civ 649 160
Radmacher v Granatino [2010] UKSC 42 52, 159
Roberts v Roberts [1986] 2 FLR 152 50
Robinson v Murray [2005] EWCA Civ 935 250
Robson v Robson [2010] EWCA Civ 1771 53, 55
Rowley v Secretary of State for Work and Pensions [2007] EWCA Civ 598 151
Royal Bank of Scotland v Etridge (No 2) [2001] 4 All ER 449 108

S

S (A Minor) (Independent Representation), Re [1993] 3 All ER 36 188

S (Adoption Order or Special Guardianship Order), Re [2007] EWCA Civ 54 180
S (Care Proceedings: Split Hearing), Re [1996] 2 FLR 773 230
S (Child: Financial Provision), Re [2004] EWCA Civ 1685 201, 202
S (Children) and W (A Child), Re [2007] EWCA Civ 232 214
S (Contact: Children's Views), Re [2002] EWHC 540 (Fam), [2002] 1 FLR 1156 183
S (Minors: Access), Re [1990] 2 FLR 166 185
S (Minors) (Care Order: Implementation of Care Plan), Re; W (Minors) (Care Order: Adequacy of Care Plan), Re [2002] UKHL 10, [2002] 1 FLR 815 215
S (Removal from Jurisdiction), Re [1999] 1 FLR 850 173
S v P [2008] 2 FLR 2040 7
S v S (Child Abduction: Child's Views) [1992] 2 FLR 492 183
S v S (Financial Provision: Departing from Equality) [2001] 2 FLR 246 56
S v S [1977] 1 All ER 56 57
Santos v Santos [1975] 2 All ER 246 27
S-B (children) (non-accidental injury), Re [2009] UKSC 17 213
Sears Tooth (A Firm) v Payne Hicks Beach (A Firm) and Others [1997] 2 FLR 116 17
Slater v Slater and Another [1982] 3 FLR 364 55
Smallwood v UK (1999) 2 EHRLR 221 262
South Glamorgan County Council v W and B [1993] 1 FLR 574 217, 222
SRJ v DWJ (Financial Provision) [1999] 2 FLR 176 63
Stack v Dowden [2007] UKHL 17 256
Sutton v Mischon De Reya and Gower & Co [2003] EWHC 3166 (Ch), [2004] 1 FLR 837 255

T

T (A Child) (Order for Costs), Re [2005] EWCA Civ 311 194
T (A Minor) (Care or Supervision Order), Re [1994] 1 FLR 103 218
T (A Minor) (Parental Responsibility: Contact), Re [1993] 2 FLR 450 175
T (Accommodation by Local Authority), Re [1995] 1 FLR 159 209
T (Divorce: Interim Maintenance: Discovery), Re [1990] 1 FLR 1 128
T (Judicial Review: Local Authority Decisions Concerning Child in Need), Re [2003] EWHC 2515 (Admin) 209
T v T (Financial Relief: Pensions) [1998] 1 FLR 1072 65
T v T (Interception of Documents) [1994] 2 FLR 1083 59
Talbot v Talbot (1971) 115 SJ 870 28
Tanner v Tanner [1975] 3 All ER 776 259
Taylor v Warners (1988) 85(25) LSG 26 254
Thompson v Thompson [1986] Fam 38 156
TL v ML and Others [2006] 1 FLR 465 49
Treharne & Sand v Forrester [2004] 1 FLR 1173 116
Trowbridge v Trowbridge [2003] 2 FLR 231 112
Truex v Kitchin [2007] 2 FLR 1203 17

V

V v V (Contact: Implacable Hostility) [2004] 2 FLR 851 177
Vaughan v Vaughan [2007] EWCA Civ 1085 115
VB v JP [2008] 1 FLR 742 156

W

W (A Minor) (Consent to Medical Treatment), Re [1993] 1 FLR 1 183
W (A Minor) (Residence Order), Re [1992] 2 FLR 332 179, 184
W (Children), Re [2010] UKSC 12 193
W (Section 34(2) Orders), Re [2000] 1 FLR 502 216
W and B, Re; W (Care Plan), Re [2001] EWCA Civ 757, [2001] 2 FLR 582 214, 219
W v A (Child: Surname) [1981] 1 All ER 100 172
W v W (Ancillary Relief: Practice) [2000] Fam Law 473 127
W v W [2009] 1 FLR 92 156
W, Re [1997] 1 FLR 793 175
Walkden v Walkden [2009] EWCA Civ 627 154
Walker v Hall [1984] FLR 126 254
Waterman v Waterman [1989] 1 FLR 380 63
Westbury v Sampson [2001] EWCA Civ 407, [2002] 1 FLR 166 155
White v White [1998] 2 FLR 310; [2000] 2 FLR 981 53, 114, 125
Whitehouse-Piper v Stokes [2008] EWCA Civ 1049 121, 122

Williams v Lindley [2005] EWCA Civ 103 153

X

X (Emergency Protection Orders), Re [2006] EWHC 510 (Fam) 221
X (Parental Responsibility Agreement: Children in Care), Re [2000] 1 FLR 517 214
X & Y (Bundles) [2008] EWHC 2058 (Fam) 127
X Council v B (Emergency Protection Orders) [2004] EWHC 2015 (Fam) 220

Y

Yemshaw v London Borough of Hounslow [2011] UKSC 3 83

Z

Z v Z (Divorce: Jurisdiction) [2010] 1 FLR 694 21
Zamet and Others v Hyman and Another [1961] 3 All ER 933 255

Table of Statutes

Access to Justice Act 1999 11
s 10(7) 15
s 11 14
Adoption and Children Act 2002 215
s 46 169
Attachment of Earnings Act 1971 148, 242

Child Abduction Act 1984 173, 197, 198, 199, 203, 292–4
s 1 197, 198
s 2 198
Child Abduction and Custody Act 1985 199
Child Maintenance and Other Payments Act 2008 85, 88, 89, 92, 97, 150, 151
s 25 151
Child Support Act 1991 2, 47, 60, 61, 62, 68, 85, 86, 87, 88, 89, 90, 94, 97, 102, 105, 119, 132, 138, 150, 151, 161, 200, 201, 202, 256, 263, 348–58
s 3(1)–(3) 86
s 4 89
s 4(10) 89
s 8 86, 87, 147
s 8(1) 87
s 8(3) 49, 87, 88
s 8(3A) 87, 89
s 8(4) 87
s 8(5) 88, 89
s 8(6)–(7) 87
s 8(8) 87, 88
s 8(9) 88
s 9(2)–(4) 88
s 11 86
s 12 95
s 14A 146
s 15 146
s 26 86
s 28A 94
s 28G 94
s 28J 96
s 28J(4) 96
s 30(2) 150
ss 32A–32L 151
s 33 151
s 39 151
s 39A 151
s 40 151
s 44(2A) 86, 90
s 55 140
s 55(1) 86
Sch 1 90
para 6 92
para 7 92
Sch 4B 94
para 4 94–5
Child Support Act 1995 85
Child Support, Pensions and Social Security Act 2000 85, 94
Children Act 1989 29, 30, 39, 40, 41, 90, 161, 165, 166, 167, 173, 182, 187, 189, 198, 200, 201, 202, 203, 229, 256, 263, 264, 295–347
Part I 14
Part II 14
Part III 206, 208, 210
Part IV 211, 213, 223
Part V 220, 223
s 1 173, 213, 217, 218
s 1(1) 174, 181, 220, 223, 231
s 1(2) 184, 186
s 1(3) 174, 181, 182, 220, 223
s 1(3)(g) 213
s 1(5) 181, 186, 220, 223
s 2(2)(a) 261
s 2(5) 169
s 2(7) 170
s 2(9) 170
s 3(1) 166
s 3(5) 170
s 4 214
s 4(1)(a)–(c) 166
s 4A 169
s 4ZA 169
s 5 168
s 5(1)(a) 168
s 7 192, 193, 225
s 8 170, 179, 181, 182, 186, 189, 191, 194, 197, 199, 200, 202, 203, 213, 215, 216, 218, 224, 228, 233, 262
s 9(2) 207
s 9(5) 178
s 9(6) 195
s 10(5) 187
s 10(5)(b)–(c) 181
s 10(8) 188
s 10(9) 216
s 11(1) 184
s 11(4) 171
s 11(5)–(6) 195
s 11(7) 174
ss 11A–11H 176
ss 11I–11P 177
s 12(2) 171
s 13(1) 172, 197
s 14 197
s 14A 180, 232, 233
s 14A(7) 181
ss 14B–14F 180, 232
s 15 201, 259, 260, 263
s 16 179, 180, 213
s 16(6) 180
s 16A 165, 180, 191, 192
s 17 206, 207, 208

Children Act 1989 – *continued*
s 17(10) 206
s 20 83, 207, 209
s 20(11) 207
ss 22–24 217
s 24B 217
ss 25A–25C 230
s 26 208, 215
s 31 182, 211, 218
s 31(10) 211
s 31A 214
s 33(3) 169
s 34 215, 216, 224, 233, 262
s 34(1) 215, 216
s 34(11) 214
s 37 177, 181, 209, 218, 220, 223, 225
s 37(1) 186
s 38 210, 218, 228
s 38(6) 219
s 38A(2) 219
s 39 216, 224
s 41(3) 227
s 43 222
s 43(3) 223
s 44 220
s 44A(2) 220
s 46 222
s 47 210
s 47(6) 210
s 91(10) 170, 194
s 91(11) 195
s 91(14) 194, 216
s 92(2) 223
Sch 1 201, 239, 240, 259, 260, 263
Sch 2
para 9 207
Children and Adoption Act 2006 176, 177, 180
Children (Leaving Care) Act 2000 217
Civil Evidence Act 1968
ss 11–12 23
Civil Partnership Act 2004 23, 47, 253, 264
s 66 134
Sch 5
Part 5
para 22 61
Part 9 66
Cohabitation Bill 2008 254
County Courts Act 1984
s 38 152
Criminal Justice and Court Services Act 2000 165

Data Protection Act 1998 123
Debtors Act 1869 149, 242
Divorce (Religious Marriages) Act 2002 42
Domestic Proceedings and Magistrates' Courts Act 1978 66, 67, 68, 159, 187, 200, 201, 202, 290–1
s 1 67
s 2 20, 67
s 3 67
s 6 67
s 20 157
s 25(1) 67
Domicile and Matrimonial Proceedings Act 1973
s 5 20, 43

Family Law Act 1996 2, 22, 42, 43, 110, 117, 141, 197, 209, 236, 237, 243, 250, 251, 252, 260, 261, 264, 359–72
Part IV 16, 20, 236, 244, 259
Part IVA 251
s 29 119
s 30 111, 117, 237, 238, 241
s 30(3) 111, 240
s 30(4)–(6) 240
s 33 197, 237, 238, 239, 240, 241, 242, 243
s 33(5) 111
s 33(6)–(7) 238
s 34 177, 197
s 35 237, 239, 240, 241, 242, 243
s 35(6) 239
s 36 237, 239, 240, 241, 242, 243
s 36(6) 240
s 36(13) 240
s 37 237, 241, 243
s 38 237, 241, 243
s 40 242
s 42 237
s 42(5) 237
s 42(7) 237
s 42A 244, 248, 249
s 43 237
s 45 244
s 46 244
s 47 249
s 59 245
s 62 236
Sch 7 110, 261
Family Law Reform Act 1969
s 20(1) 167
Family Law (Scotland) Act 2006 253
Finance Act 1985
s 83 72
s 83(1) 257
Financial Services and Markets Act 2000 66
Forced Marriage (Civil Protection) Act 2007 251, 252
Fraud Act 2006 123

Homelessness Act 2002 82
Housing Act 1985 84
s 79 261
Housing Act 1988
Part VII 261
Housing Act 1996 82, 83, 260
Human Fertilisation and Embryology Act 2008 169, 262
Human Rights Act 1998 8, 17, 149, 169, 182, 216, 230, 231, 262
s 4 8, 9

Inheritance (Provision for Family and Dependants) Act 1975 60, 135, 263, 264, 287–9
s 2 64
s 3 264
s 15 64

Inheritance Tax Act 1984
ss 10–11 72
s 18 71

Law of Property Act 1925
s 30 261
s 53(1)(b) 254, 259
Law of Property (Miscellaneous Provisions) Act 1989
s 2 160
Law Reform (Succession) Act 1995 264
Legal Aid, Sentencing and Punishment of Offenders Bill 2011 11
Legitimacy Act 1976
s 1 31
Life Assurance Act 1774
s 1 254

Magistrates' Courts Act 1980
s 93(6) 149
Maintenance Enforcement Act 1991 147, 149
Married Women's Property Act 1882 256
s 17 134, 256
Matrimonial Causes Act 1973 7, 14, 23, 28, 29, 42, 43, 47, 51, 64, 85, 90, 102, 110, 112, 117, 162, 187, 200, 201, 202, 253, 267–86
s 1(1) 23
s 1(2) 23, 31, 34
s 1(2)(a) 23
s 1(2)(b) 25
s 1(2)(c) 26
s 1(2)(d) 27, 138
s 1(2)(e) 28
s 1(4) 23
s 2 31, 39
s 2(1)–(2) 24
s 2(3) 25
s 2(5) 26, 27
s 2(6) 27
s 3 20
s 4(1) 32
s 4(2) 23
s 5 28, 29
s 5(1) 28, 44
s 5(2)–(3) 28
s 9(2) 42
s 10 28
s 10(1) 27
s 10(2) 27, 28, 29, 42, 44
s 10(3)–(4) 28, 42
s 10A 42
s 11 30
s 13(1) 31
s 13(4) 31
s 17(2) 31
s 19 32
s 22 47, 48, 131
s 23 16, 47, 52, 67, 131
s 23(1)(a)–(b) 49, 62, 63, 137, 139, 140, 142
s 23(1)(c) 50, 62
s 23(1)(d)–(e) 49
s 23(1)(f) 50
s 23A 239

Matrimonial Causes Act 1973 – *continued*
s 24 16, 47, 50, 51, 52, 62, 110, 116, 131, 239
s 24(1)(b) 133
s 24A 51, 52, 62, 103, 116, 131, 148, 149, 155, 156, 157
s 24A(2) 104
s 24B 16, 47, 51, 65, 131
s 24B(3)–(4) 66
s 24C 131
s 24D 131
s 25 52, 53, 58, 59, 60, 65, 66, 68, 99, 102, 103, 105, 113, 114, 117, 124, 153, 159, 161, 162, 201, 254, 257
s 25(1) 52, 57, 60, 64, 67, 68, 87
s 25(2) 52, 59, 68
s 25(2)(a) 55, 57, 61, 64, 65
s 25(2)(b) 55, 81
s 25(2)(c) 56, 61
s 25(2)(d) 56, 57
s 25(2)(e) 61
s 25(2)(f) 57
s 25(2)(g) 58, 59, 60
s 25(2)(h) 60
s 25(3) 52, 60, 61, 68, 87
s 25(3)(e) 61
s 25(4) 52, 60, 61, 68, 87
s 25A 62, 68, 113, 134
s 25A(1) 62
s 25A(2) 49, 63
s 25A(3) 62
s 25B 52, 65
s 25B(4) 155
s 25C 65, 155
s 25D 65
s 27 20, 66, 67, 68, 201, 202
s 28 49
s 28(1A) 63, 140, 155
s 28(3) 48, 121, 122
s 29 49
s 29(3) 49, 67
s 31 63, 67
s 31(2) 154
s 31(2A) 155
s 31(7) 156
s 31(7A)–(7B) 16
s 34 162
s 34(2) 162
s 35 162, 163
s 35(2) 163
s 36 162, 163
s 37 112, 113, 117, 120, 151
s 37(2)(a)–(c) 112
s 41 29, 30, 35, 40, 41, 42, 44, 45
s 52(1) 29
Matrimonial and Family Proceedings Act 1984 62
s 33 7

Pensions Act 1995
s 166 65
Pensions Act 2008 51
Protection from Harassment Act 1997 236, 250, 251, 252

Protection from Harassment Act 1997 – *continued*
s 2 251
s 3 251
s 3(6) 251
s 3(9) 251
ss 4–5 251
s 5A 251
s 7 251
Public Bodies Bill 2010 86

Rent Act 1977 110, 261

Stamp Act 1891
s 57 257

Taxation of Chargeable Gains Act 1992
s 21 71
s 225 71
s 251 71
Trusts of Land and Appointment of Trustees Act 1996 260, 261, 373
s 14 256, 260, 261
s 15 260

Welfare Reform Act 2007 79
Welfare Reform Act 2009 74, 166
s.19 81
s 51 152
Welfare Reform and Pensions Act 1999 65
ss 11–12 116
Welfare Reform Bill 2011 96

International legislation

European Convention on Human Rights 8
Art 3 9
Art 5 9
Art 6 9, 17, 149, 151, 177, 186, 215, 219, 221, 231, 250, 262
Art 6(1) 188
Art 8 8, 116, 125, 177, 182, 215, 219, 221, 222, 230, 231, 232, 250, 262
Art 8(2) 231
Art 12 19
Art 13 232
Art 14 9, 262
Seventh Protocol
Art 5 60
European Convention on Recognition and Enforcement of Custody Decisions 199
Hague Convention on International Child Abduction 199

Table of Statutory Instruments and Codes of Practice

Access to Justice Act 1999 (Destination of Appeals) (Family Proceedings) Order 2011 (SI 2011/1044) 152
Allocation and Transfer of Proceedings Order 2008 (SI 2008/2836) 189, 194, 223, 245
art 15 189
art 16 189
Practice Direction 189, 194, 223

Child Maintenance (Written Agreements) Order 1993 (SI 1993/620) 88, 89
Child Support (Maintenance Calculation Procedure) Regulations 2000 (SI 2001/157)
reg 5 146
reg 7 95
Child Support (Maintenance Calculations and Special Cases) Regulations 2000 (SI 2001/155) 91
Child Support (Variations) Regulations 2000 (SI 2001/156) 94
reg 13 94
reg 15 94
regs 18-20 95
reg 23 94
Civil Procedure Rules 1998 (SI 1998/3132) 119, 124
r 44.13 129, 135
r 71 148
Community Legal Service (Cost Protection) Regulations 2000 (SI 2000/824)
reg 5 14
Community Legal Service (Financial) Regulations 2000 (SI 2000/516) 135, 141
Contracting Out (Functions Relating to Child Support) Order 2006 (SI 2006/1692) 151

Family Procedure Rules 2010 (SI 2010/2955) 6, 7, 8, 9, 19, 124, 228, 374–405
Part 1
r 1.1(1) 119
Part 3 6, 119
r 3 120
PD 3A 119, 120, 187
para 4.1 120
Annex C 120
Part 4 43
Part 5
r 5.1 33
PD 5 39
PD 5A 33
Part 6 38
r 6.2 38
r 6.5(3) 37
r 6.9 37
r 6.14 39

Family Procedure Rules 2010 – *continued*
r 6.15 37
r 6.16 37
r 6.19(2) 38
r 6.20 38
PD 6B 38
Part 7
r 7.6 36
r 7.8 36
r 7.12(1) 39, 43
r 7.12(8) 40, 43
r 7.12(12) 27
r 7.13 35
r 7.20 40
r 7.32 41
r 7.32(2) 42
r 7.33 42
PD 7A 24
para 2.1 24
Part 9 119
r 9.7 128
r 9.12(1) 122
r 9.13(3) 122
r 9.14(5) 124
r 9.17(3) 126
r 9.27 128
r 9.28 127
r 9.31 122
r 9.33 122
r 9.40 122
PD 9A 119, 124, 130
para 6.3 126
Part 12 187, 223, 225, 227
PD 12A 223, 225, 226, 227, 229
PD 12B 187, 190
PD 12C 190
PD 12J 191
Part 16 226
r 16.6 188
PD 16A 190, 226
Part 17
r 17.2 193
Part 21
r 21.2 125
r 21.2(3) 125
Part 25 125, 229
r 25.7 125
PD 25A 229
Part 27
PD 27A 127, 194
Part 28
r 28.3 128, 129
Part 30 152
Part 33
r 33.3(2) 148

Family Proceedings (Amendment) Rules 2003 (SI 2003/184) 149
Family Proceedings Rules 1991 (SI 1991/1247)
rr 7.4–7.6 149

Insolvency (Amendment) Rules 2005 (SI 2005/527) 116

Parental Responsibility Agreement Regulations 1991 (SI 1991/1478) 167

Stamp Duty (Exempt Instruments) Regulations 1987 (SI 1987/516) 72, 257

European secondary legislation

Regulation 2201/2003 (Brussels II Revised) 20, 22

Codes

Experts in Family Proceedings relating to Children Practice Direction 193
Funding Code 11, 12
Inland Revenue SP 27 April 1990 257
Law Society's Family Law Protocol 4, 35, 235
Part III, para 4.10 198
Part V, para 2.2 255
Mediation Code of Conduct 6
Public Law Outline 2008 223
Public Law Outline 2010 206, 223
Resolution Code of Practice 4, 407
SRA Code of Conduct 2011
Outcome 3.5 3
Outcome 4.1 3
Outcome 4.2 3
Outcome 5.3 199

Table of Abbreviations

AJA 1999	Access to Justice Act 1999
CA 1989	Children Act 1989
CAA 1984	Child Abduction Act 1984
CACA 1985	Child Abduction and Custody Act 1985
Cafcass	Children and Family Court Advisory and Support Service
CGT	capital gains tax
C-MEC	Child Maintenance and Enforcement Commission
CMOPA 2008	Child Maintenance and Other Payments Act 2008
CPA 2004	Civil Partnership Act 2004
CPR 1998	Civil Procedure Rules 1998
CSA 1991	Child Support Act 1991
CS(MCSC) Regs 2000	Child Support (Maintenance Calculations and Special Cases) Regulations 2000
CSPSSA 2000	Child Support, Pensions and Social Security Act 2000
DPMCA 1978	Domestic Proceedings and Magistrates' Courts Act 1978
DWP	Department for Work and Pensions
FDR	Financial Dispute Resolution
FHDRA	First Hearing Dispute Resolution Appointment
FLA 1996	Family Law Act 1996
FLBA	Family Law Bar Association
FPR 2010	Family Procedure Rules 2010
HMRC	HM Revenue and Customs
HRA 1998	Human Rights Act 1998
I(PFD)A 1975	Inheritance (Provision for Family and Dependants) Act 1975
MCA 1973	Matrimonial Causes Act 1973
MIAM	Mediator Information and Assessment Meeting
MWPA 1882	Married Women's Property Act 1882
PHA 1997	Protection from Harassment Act 1997
PPO	periodical payments order
SSCSAT	Social Security and Child Support Appeals Tribunal
TLATA	Trusts of Land and Appointment of Trustees Act 1996
WRPA 1999	Welfare Reform and Pensions Act 1999

Chapter 1
Introduction: The Family Practice

1.1	The family client	1
1.2	The family practitioner	3
1.3	Support for family clients	5
1.4	Alternative dispute resolution	6
1.5	The family courts	7
1.6	Human Rights Act 1998	8
1.7	Family law in the future	9
1.8	Conclusion	9
1.9	Chapter summary	9

1.1 The family client

There is a wide range of reasons why a client would wish to discuss family problems with a solicitor. The most common reason is that a relationship has permanently broken down. Some clients, however, may seek advice because they are encountering temporary difficulties and have no wish to terminate the relationship formally. Yet others may have some domestic problem which they need to resolve but are undecided and unclear as to the future of the relationship.

Whether or not a client has made a firm decision about the relationship, he will usually be reasonably clear about his more immediate problems which prompted him to seek legal advice. The three most common problem areas concern money and property (see **Chapters 4** to **11**), children (see **Chapters 13** and **14**) and protection from domestic abuse (see **Chapter 15**). How these problems are to be dealt with depends in the first place on whether the couple are married (or, in the case of a same-sex couple, whether they have registered a civil partnership) or living together. The problems and concerns of cohabiting couples are virtually indistinguishable from those of married couples or civil partners; the legal remedies, however, are by no means the same and are more limited for cohabitees. A large part of this book is devoted to married couples as these will form the vast majority of the clients for most family solicitors. However, the cohabiting family is considered in detail in **Chapter 16**, and comparisons between the positions of cohabitees, civil partners and spouses are made throughout this book.

In the case of married couples, there is a broad range of solutions to the key problems. The skill of the family lawyer is to match the appropriate solution to the needs of the individual client. Which measures are to be taken will depend on whether the client has made the decision to end the marriage, or whether a more temporary solution is favoured. The marriage may be terminated formally by divorce (or nullity), or the couple may separate formally by judicial separation (these options are considered in **Chapter 3**). Alternatively, the client may not wish to make any final decision about the relationship itself but merely wish to seek advice on a particular problem: for example, a wife may be anxious about her position in the matrimonial home, or a father may be being denied contact with his children.

It is worthwhile pausing to consider some of the likely issues and concerns facing a family client. Whilst there is no such thing as a 'typical' family client (and it would be a mistake to assume that there was), there are certain concerns which are common to many families.

Example

Beverley is a mother with two young children. She has been married to Colin for the last 10 years, but is seeking a divorce because Colin has recently begun to be violent towards her and on one occasion to her son. Beverley does not work and has no savings. She has fled the family home and her main worry is to be able to return to the home in safety.

One of the first issues for the solicitor to consider is how the client will pay for the legal advice. This will also be high on the client's list of concerns. The question of costs, including Legal Aid, is considered in context throughout this book and in **Chapter 2**. A private client should be advised about the costs policy of the firm and will usually be asked to make a payment on account. As with most contentious work, it is difficult to give an accurate prediction of costs in the initial interview as so much depends on the attitude of the other party, and indeed of the client himself. In this example, Beverley is likely to be eligible for public funding.

Beverley's primary need is to seek protection from the violence and to be able to return home. It will be necessary, therefore, to take instructions to prepare for proceedings for a non-molestation and occupation order under the Family Law Act 1996 (FLA 1996) (see **Chapter 15**). As Beverley wishes to obtain a divorce, the solicitor will also need to obtain the information and prepare the documentation required to institute divorce proceedings (see **Chapter 3**). Since the order under FLA 1996 will provide only a temporary solution to Beverley and the children's housing needs, the solicitor must also discuss the future arrangements in relation to the former matrimonial home (see **Chapter 9**). Although it will be some time before this can be dealt with, the solicitor needs to think ahead and obtain public funding in good time to commence financial proceedings. The solicitor should also be aware of the need to protect his client's interest in the matrimonial home. He will, therefore, need to establish how the property is held between the parties and make any necessary registrations against the title. In addition, Beverley should be advised to make (or alter) a will. Further, there may be a problem regarding the mortgage, as Colin may stop paying the mortgage if he is ordered to leave the home (although, if an occupation order is made, provision can be included instructing Colin to continue to pay the mortgage). It will probably be necessary, therefore, to advise Beverley regarding maintenance, and possibly to write to the lender to explain any short-term difficulties which there may be in relation to the mortgage. The procedure for obtaining financial orders is considered in **Chapter 10**, and their enforcement and variation is considered in **Chapter 11**.

As it will be some time before any application for maintenance for Beverley can be considered in detail, she should be advised of her entitlements to welfare benefits (see **Chapter 6**) and for maintenance for the children under the Child Support Act 1991 (see **Chapter 7**).

The other important consideration is, of course, the children (see **Chapters 13** and **14**). At an early stage, it is likely to be necessary to raise the question of the children's contact with their father. As with the other issues, this may be agreed upon between the parties (after negotiation), but in Beverley's case, in view of her husband's violence towards her son, she may well object to any contact, and this could involve further proceedings.

It will not always be appropriate to discuss all of these issues at the initial interview but the solicitor will need to be aware of the wider picture from the outset. He will need to raise the various issues at an appropriate stage and encourage his client to confront the future and make informed decisions. The topics covered in this book deal with all of the problems faced by Beverley in the example above. Of necessity, the book takes each issue in turn, but it is important to appreciate from the beginning that all the issues are strongly interrelated and that several disputes and difficulties can occur concurrently.

1.2 The family practitioner

1.2.1 Professional conduct

Family solicitors owe the same duties towards their clients as those of any other solicitor. The solicitor may not act for both parties, no matter how amicable their separation, as there is an inherent client conflict (see SRA Code of Conduct 2011, Outcome 3.5). Confidentiality towards clients' affairs must also be observed, for example a client's address cannot be disclosed without his consent. There are, however, particular professional conduct issues which may arise in the context of a family law case. The solicitor may, for example, have previously acted for the husband and wife jointly in a property or business matter during the marriage. On the breakdown of the marriage the husband may ask the solicitor to act for him in the divorce. The solicitor will need to consider whether he has relevant confidential information about the wife which will require the solicitor to decline to act for the husband (see SRA Code of Conduct 2011, Outcomes 4.1 and 4.2).

A solicitor acting in a children case may be given information by his client which the client does not wish to be disclosed, and yet which causes the solicitor to believe that the mental or physical safety of a child is at risk. The solicitor will need to consider whether it is an exceptional situation which would justify the solicitor breaching client confidentiality under SRA Code of Conduct, Outcome 4.1.

1.2.2 Adviser – not decision-maker

There are certain special considerations to be borne in mind when dealing with a family matter. Family clients are likely to be more vulnerable than other clients. They may have only recently (or are even yet to) come to terms with the breakdown of their relationship and the consequent breakup of their home and family. They will invariably face many problems, be presented with a bewildering array of options, and be called upon to make many important decisions. It is hardly surprising, therefore, that such clients may be tempted to pass the responsibility to make these decisions on to their solicitor. However, it is important that the family solicitor is able to distinguish between advising the client of his choices and influencing the client's decisions, or even assuming certain choices on the client's behalf. However much a client's marriage appears to the solicitor to be irredeemably lost, the solicitor must be careful to advise the client fully of all the options and not to push the client prematurely down the route to divorce. If the solicitor is in any doubt as to what the client really wants to do about his relationship, he should pause to allow the client time to make a free and firm decision. Many clients will find the initial interview an emotional and stressful experience and, bearing in mind that many important and complex matters will have been discussed in the interview, it is sensible to confirm advice given and to set out the options in a letter following the interview. This enables the client to absorb the advice and reflect upon it before embarking upon a particular course of action.

1.2.3 Objectives

A further important consideration for the family solicitor is to keep sight of the client's overall long-term objectives. If a relationship has finally broken down, it is fair to assume that a family client's ultimate objective is to be able to unravel the legal ties of that relationship and to begin life afresh with the minimum of pain and bitterness. This will apply particularly where children are involved. There will be times when a client may be so involved in the detail of a particular dispute that he loses sight of this wider aim. It is here that the good family practitioner can make a positive contribution; by maintaining a sufficiently detached viewpoint the professional may enable a client to refocus on his goal and to regard matters in the round.

In pursuing these long-term objectives the good family solicitor has a very positive role to play. The approach taken by the solicitor can significantly influence a client's response. If a solicitor takes an aggressive stance, advising in terms of 'winning' and 'losing' and 'fighting' and 'giving in', then this is likely to serve to stir up bitterness and lead a client to set his face against compromise. Conversely, the solicitor who attempts to defuse tensions, concentrating on important issues rather than petty matters, and who talks in terms of arriving at fair solutions and compromise is likely to find that his client is more willing to follow this lead. It is important to address the advantages of a negotiated settlement whilst at the same time assuring the client that, where appropriate, a firm stance will be taken to protect his interests. The people most likely to come through the trauma of a divorce or separation successfully are those who have been involved in reaching agreement about important issues. A party is also much more likely to abide by such an agreement than by an arrangement imposed by the court. Most important of all is the benefit of reducing the impact of the disputes on any children who are at risk of being caught in the cross-fire. The Resolution Code of Practice (set out in **Appendix 2**) advocates a constructive and non-confrontational approach in family matters. Resolution has a membership of over 6,000 family law solicitors and other legal justice professionals. Its Code of Practice is endorsed by The Law Society and supported by many senior members of the judiciary (see, for example, *Dutfield v Gilbert H Stephens & Sons* [1988] Fam Law 473). The Resolution Code of Practice should be read in conjunction with the Law Society's Family Law Protocol, which sets out guidelines for all solicitors for the conduct of proceedings which are designed to promote a constructive and conciliatory approach in family cases.

In order to achieve these objectives, the family practitioner must acquire negotiating skills; he must know when and how to achieve a settlement (see ***Skills for Lawyers***). Having successfully negotiated a settlement, the family solicitor must use his drafting skills to draw up a clear and enforceable agreement (see ***Skills for Lawyers***). This document may take the form of a consent order (see **Chapter 9**), or a separation agreement (see **Chapter 11**).

If a negotiated settlement cannot be achieved, the matter must be determined in court. Since most proceedings will be dealt with in chambers in the county court the family solicitor will have rights of audience. This will call for the use of advocacy skills (see ***Skills for Lawyers***).

1.2.4 Interviewing skills

The success of the solicitor–client relationship in family cases is to a large extent dependent upon the impression created in the first interview. The practitioner may be in the privileged position of being the first person with whom the client has discussed his relationship difficulties. The client will be sensitive to the atmosphere in that interview, and it is of crucial importance that the solicitor attempts to create the right environment and to adopt an appropriate tone for the interview.

Preparation for the interview is vital. Thought should be given to the length of the interview and its venue, as well as to the information which should be obtained from, and given to, the client. In family matters the interview could also be complicated by the fact that the client may bring his children with him, or have chosen to bring a friend for support. This field of interviewing is a hugely important subject in itself which cannot be considered in detail here, but reference should be made to the section on interviewing in ***Skills for Lawyers***). Use of a checklist or instruction sheet will ensure that the information required is obtained. However, care must be taken when using such aids to explain their use to the client and to ensure that the interview does not become too formal or narrow.

1.2.5 Awareness and balance

When a relationship is in crisis, each party may experience a wide range of feelings. These will inevitably vary between individuals, but may variously include disappointment, anger and blame, hurt, sadness, self-doubt, loss, guilt, uncertainty and anxiety. For some time, there may be a sense of relief that an unhappy situation is being addressed. Sometimes, there may be worry and concern for the other partner. It is not uncommon for people in this crisis situation to move inconsistently from one feeling to another. There is no standard reaction to relationship breakdown, and family solicitors need to be aware of the sensitivity of the situation in which they are intervening.

Most clients need, and are entitled to have, solicitors who will advise and support them in these difficult times. Their solicitors may have to act as their champions, protecting their rights and position. However, while maintaining awareness of these legitimate expectations, the family solicitor also needs to be aware that supporting the client can sometimes mean helping him to understand and come to terms with unpalatable consequences, or seeking compromises which the client may prefer not to make. Parents may be able to keep their children's best interests in mind, but in that situation those interests may sometimes blur with the client's own preferences, antagonisms or strength of feeling; and here again the solicitor may have a role in helping the client to be aware of the children's needs and interests as well as the client's.

The family solicitor accordingly has to maintain a balance between the supportive, partisan role and the need to confront the client's perceptions where appropriate. As previously stated, an objective view, sympathetically but not patronisingly expressed, may be necessary to help the client make necessary shifts. The solicitor must also appreciate the extent to which his actions and approach can have an effect, whether helping or damaging, on the client and on the relationship between the parties and their children. Communications with the other side can always be courteous and sensitive, even where tough positions are being stated. Opportunities for dialogue can be established early on and maintained even when confrontation is indicated. This is all consistent with having a sympathetic and effective relationship with the client. Resolution encourages the development of these skills in a number of ways, for example by issuing guides to good practice in various areas of family law (for example, correspondence, disclosure and working with the Bar in family cases) and by holding seminars and workshops on understanding the emotional aspects of family life and of the personal consequences which may follow any change, and increasing members' self-awareness, as well as training in 'black letter' family law.

1.3 Support for family clients

Family clients often need emotional support through the process of family breakdown. Whilst the family solicitor provides support in the form of guiding the client through the process, it is important to be able to recognise the boundaries of the solicitor's role and the limitations of his skills. There is a range of support services available to complement the work of the family practitioner. The family solicitor should be aware of the local agencies and services which are more suitable and capable of meeting the client's emotional needs and recommend them, as appropriate.

The client may, for example, benefit from counselling. Counselling takes different forms and may have different aims. It may involve working with an individual, the couple, members of the family or the whole family together. It may be relatively short-term, or may involve longer-term marital or family therapy; and there are different theoretical perspectives.

One of the aims of counselling may be to try to save the relationship where it is under stress, or to establish a reconciliation where it has already broken down. Another may be to explore whether there is any basis for continuing with the relationship and, if so, what has to happen to make this possible. Not uncommonly, a couple may disagree about the future of the relationship, one wishing to end it and the other to continue with it. Counselling may assist the couple to come to their own conclusion, whether this proves to be preserving the relationship or bringing it to an end. Counselling may therefore help a couple to accept the ending of their relationship, if that is appropriate.

Parents may benefit from guidance as to how best to support their children through the changes brought about by family breakdown. Parenting workshops, such as those run by various agencies under the umbrella of Resolution's *Parenting after Parting* programme, can help parents to understand how children react to parental separation, and how to 'manage' the process of family breakdown and its aftermath in such a way as to minimise the impact on their children.

1.4 Alternative dispute resolution

Alternative dispute resolution (ADR) exists across a range of legal disciplines. It is the generic term used to describe any process aimed at resolving disputes without going to court.

Following the implementation of the Family Procedure Rules (FPR) 2010 (SI 2010/2955), there is a much greater emphasis on ADR in family cases than in the past. Part 3 of the FPR 2010 focuses on the courts' powers to encourage and facilitate the use of ADR. The court is obliged to consider at every stage of family proceedings whether ADR is appropriate, and may adjourn the case for the purpose of obtaining information about ADR and, with agreement, for ADR to take place.

A variety of processes fall within the term 'ADR'. In family cases the most common ADR processes are mediation, collaborative law and arbitration (see further below). Direct negotiation through solicitors is not usually considered to be an ADR process. However, negotiation remains an essential part of the role of a family solicitor and the most common means of achieving a consensual resolution of family cases.

1.4.1 Mediation

In family mediation the couple engage the assistance of one or two impartial mediators, who have no authority to make any decisions for them but who use certain skills to help them to resolve their issues by negotiated agreement without adjudication. Mediation does not aim to save the relationship but to help parties deal, by agreement, with the consequences of its breakdown.

The mediator (or co-mediators) will usually meet the parties together (although, in some circumstances, may see them separately) and will try to help them to clarify and resolve their issues on a basis which they find mutually acceptable. Depending on the issues, this may involve obtaining all relevant facts, including, where appropriate, financial data, exploring alternative settlement options and their acceptability and viability, and generally helping the couple to communicate and make decisions. The mediator may give information, but will not advise the couple what terms they should agree, this being a matter for them; and may help them to examine different solutions but will not try to press the one which the mediator may prefer.

There are various facilitation, communication and management skills which mediators should have and which generally necessitate special training. Mediators should also work to a Code of Conduct which regulates the ethical and practical approach which they adopt. Many solicitors have undergone training to become accredited mediators. Family mediators are also drawn from other ranks, including social workers, probation officers, children and family reporters, psychotherapists, counsellors and mental health professionals.

A solicitor cannot act as a mediator for his own client and would need to refer to an outside organisation or individual mediator. The solicitor should take the earliest opportunity to assess the suitability of mediation as a means of attempting to resolve the client's case. If relevant, information should be given to the client about the availability of mediation and the nature of the process.

Following a change in procedure introduced by the FPR 2010, anyone now wishing to start court proceedings in most types of family cases (not including the divorce itself) is expected first to attend a Mediation Information and Assessment Meeting (see **10.4.1**). The purpose of the meeting is for a mediator to provide information about the process of mediation and to indicate whether the particular case is a suitable one in which to attempt mediation. Although there is no compulsion to proceed with mediation following the meeting, it remains to be seen whether there will in fact be a greater use of mediation as a way of resolving disputes as a result of this change.

1.4.2 Collaborative law

In England and Wales collaborative law is in its relative infancy, but is growing in importance as family solicitors begin to be trained as collaborative lawyers. Collaborative law operates as a series of meetings aimed at enabling the parties to resolve the issues resulting from the breakdown of a relationship. The process requires the parties and their solicitors to sign up to an agreement promising to try to reach an amicable consensus on all issues without recourse to court proceedings. If it transpires that a settlement cannot be reached then the parties cannot continue to instruct their collaborative lawyers and must instruct other solicitors to represent them in subsequent court proceedings. Therefore both the parties and their solicitors have an interest in making the process work.

Collaborative law views the breakdown of a relationship in the round, and enables the parties to explore the issues and find solutions outside the constraints of court proceedings. Mainstream legal issues such as the financial consequences of the ending of the relationship are explored and, if possible, agreed upon; but collaborative law also recognises that the concerns which a client has when a relationship ends may not be of a 'legal' nature and yet those concerns must be addressed if the parties are to be able to make sensible decisions about the future. Collaborative law also allows these issues to be looked at through the use of outside experts, as necessary.

Collaborative law has now received judicial approval. In *S v P* [2008] 2 FLR 2040, Coleridge J said, 'I think every conceivable encouragement should be given to parties to negotiate by this method.'

1.4.3 Arbitration

In arbitration an independent third party considers the dispute and makes a decision. Arbitration is widely used in other areas of law, but despite having being available in family cases for many years it remains relatively uncommon in this context. One of the main reasons for this is that in family cases, arbitration is not binding on the parties. At the date of writing a new scheme, administered by Resolution, is about to be launched.

1.5 The family courts

The family practitioner must not only be able to identify the client's needs and determine the correct approach to meet these, but must also decide in which court the remedies will be sought and, if a choice of venue exists, which will be the most appropriate. Often proceedings can be brought in the county court, or the High Court or the family proceedings court.

1.5.1 County court

All proceedings under the Matrimonial Causes Act 1973 (MCA 1973) (ie for divorce, judicial separation or nullity) begin in a divorce county court. This is a county court which has jurisdiction to deal with matrimonial causes (conferred by the Matrimonial and Family Proceedings Act 1984, s 33). In London, the Principal Registry acts also as a divorce county court. Most work is carried out by the district judge from whom appeal may be made to a county court judge. A judge is required to try most defended cases.

1.5.2 The High Court

Generally, proceedings are dealt with in the Family Division of the High Court only if the nature of the issues involves facts or arguments which are complex, difficult or grave. Cases may be transferred down to the county court, or referred up by the latter to the High Court. If, for example, a financial dispute involved substantial sums of money invested in complex assets, perhaps coupled with allegations of non-disclosure or misappropriation, the county court might prefer to decline jurisdiction and transfer the case to the High Court. Certain applications in relation to children (eg wardship) must be brought in the High Court, as must cases seeking a declaration of incompatibility under s 4 of the Human Rights Act 1998 (HRA 1998) (or where an issue in any case may lead to the court considering making such a declaration).

1.5.3 The family proceedings court

Magistrates, when dealing with domestic matters, sit as a family proceedings court. The magistrates (including at least one man and one woman) are selected from the family panel and receive special training to deal with family matters. The hearing is entirely different from criminal proceedings in magistrates' courts and there are restrictions on those who may be present.

Magistrates have no jurisdiction to deal with divorce, nullity or judicial separation proceedings. They can deal with orders for periodical payments and lump sums for married applicants during the marriage; they can also deal with protection orders and children orders.

1.5.4 Transparency in family cases

Historically, in contrast to, say, criminal court hearings which are generally open for public and press to attend, most family court hearings have been conducted in private. However, with effect from April 2009, representatives of the media have been able to attend family court hearings. This change was introduced with the aim of establishing greater transparency in the family justice system. The provisions cover most types of family hearings, with the exception of those specifically conducted for the purpose of conciliation or negotiation.

Although the press may attend the hearing, they do not have access to the documents relating to the case. The media are also restricted in the detail which they are able to report as it remains contempt of court to publish the specifics of many family cases. The court has the power to exclude the media if this is necessary to protect the interests of a child or the safety of a witness or to ensure the proper conduct of the proceedings.

1.5.5 A family court?

For many years now there have been calls to rationalise family litigation through a single, comprehensive family court. There can be no doubt that a unified family court would end the confusing disparity which currently exists in the plethora of family courts. The FPR 2010 have recently laid the foundation of unification by harmonising procedures across the current family court system.

1.6 Human Rights Act 1998

The HRA 1998 incorporates the European Convention for the Protection of Human Rights and Fundamental Freedoms into the law of England and Wales. It provides a scheme whereby domestic legislation must be read and given effect so as to be compatible with the rights and freedoms guaranteed by the Convention as far as is possible. If a Convention right is infringed then an application for judicial review, or proceedings against the appropriate public body for failure to act compatibly with the Convention, may be appropriate. The most relevant of the Convention rights for the purposes of family law is Article 8 (right to respect for family and private life), which provides:

1. Everyone has the right to respect for his private and family life, his home and his correspondence.
2. There shall be no interference by a public authority with the exercise of this right except such as is in accordance with the law and is necessary in a democratic society in the interests of national security, public safety or the economic well-being of the country, for the prevention of disorder or crime, for the protection of health or morals, or for the protection of the rights and freedoms of others.

Public law relating to children (see **Chapter 14**) is an obvious example of an area of UK law where this Article will need to be taken into account.

Other Convention rights which could give rise to litigation and, potentially, changes in UK law are Article 3 (prohibiting inhuman or degrading treatment); Article 5 (the right to liberty and security of person); Article 6 (right to a fair hearing); and Article 14 (prohibiting discrimination on any ground, including sex, birth or other status). The significance of these Articles will be considered in more detail in the relevant chapters of this book.

A case seeking a declaration of incompatability under s 4 of the HRA 1998 must be brought in the High Court, as must any case which raises an issue which may lead to the court considering making such a declaration (*Practice Direction (Human Rights Act 1998)* (24 July 2000) [2000] Fam Law 670).

1.7 Family law in the future

These are certainly changing times in family law. The FPR 2010, which were implemented in April 2011, have brought about significant procedural changes whilst at the same time introducing a different approach to family law cases, with a much greater emphasis being placed on ADR. At the time of writing the Government appears to be determined, at least for the time being, to pursue controversial changes to the public funding of family cases. Yet further changes may emerge in the family justice system once the Government-commissioned Family Justice Review produces its final report. The family solicitor will need to respond and adapt to these changes.

1.8 Conclusion

The problems facing a family client are as diverse as families themselves. The challenge facing the family practitioner is to steer a client through those problems on to a new life. This requires the practitioner to fit the appropriate solution from a diverse range of remedies to meet the specific needs of each individual client. To succeed in this, the family solicitor must acquire a firm grasp of a broad range of law and develop a variety of legal skills. A healthy measure of common sense and a sense of humour are also invaluable. Thus equipped, the family practitioner can look forward to a highly interesting and rewarding career.

1.9 Chapter summary

(1) The family client will usually want advice on money and property, children and protection from violence.

(2) The family practitioner will need to consider professional conduct, the need to advise but not take decisions for a client, and the need to keep in mind long-term objectives.

(3) Outside agencies can also help a client, for example counselling and mediation services.

(4) The courts that generally deal with family matters are the county court (all divorces start here), the High Court (which deals with complex matters) and the family proceedings court (which has no divorce jurisdiction but which deals with finance within marriage and other family matters).

Chapter 2
Funding

2.1	Introduction	11
2.2	Contracting	11
2.3	Levels of service and fees	12
2.4	Effect of public funding	14
2.5	The statutory charge	15
2.6	Human rights	17
2.7	Other methods of funding	17
2.8	Chapter summary	18

2.1 Introduction

At the first interview, one of the client's major concerns may be how he is going to pay for legal advice. A solicitor cannot enter a conditional fee agreement with a client in relation to family proceedings. However, where the client is of modest means, public funding or, as it is more commonly known, Legal Aid may be available. A Legal Aid scheme has been in existence for many years. However, the scheme's present form originates in the Access to Justice Act 1999 (AJA 1999). The 1999 Act radically reformed public funding for legal services. It introduced the Legal Services Commission to oversee and coordinate the provision of legal services and established the Funding Code, which sets down criteria for the funding of individual cases. In 2010 the Government announced its intention to abolish the Legal Services Commission in its present form and to replace it with an Executive Agency of the Ministry of Justice.

Since the AJA 1999, the Legal Aid scheme has been subject to seemingly constant review and reappraisal. However, the period from late 2007 to date has seen the most wide-ranging changes that the scheme has undergone for many years. The changes emanate from the recommendations made by Lord Carter of Coles in his Review of Legal Aid Procurement in 2005/6. A significant feature of these changes is the replacement of the long-established system whereby solicitors are paid an hourly charging rate for the work they undertake, by a new system of fixed fees in most family cases. Even more dramatic changes look set to be introduced. At the time of writing the Legal Aid, Sentencing and Punishment of Offenders Bill is going through Parliament. If implemented as currently envisaged, it will lead to the removal of most types of private family law cases from the ambit of public funding.

This chapter provides an outline of public funding in relation to family work. The AJA 1999, regulations made under it and the Funding Code (plus guidance on the Code) should be consulted if more detail is needed. The chapter concludes with a brief look at some other methods a family client may use to pay for legal advice.

2.2 Contracting

A family law solicitor may undertake publicly-funded work only if his firm has signed a Unified Contract with the Legal Services Commission specific to family law. Part of the Legal Services Commission's function is to ensure that the clients have access to competent, quality assured, best value legal services. Contracts are awarded only to those firms which both meet the Legal Services Commission's criteria and are judged to be best placed to meet the need for legal services in that area.

2.3 Levels of service and fees

The Funding Code sets down various levels of service. Broadly, the more litigious the case becomes, the higher the level of service that will be appropriate. The levels which are most relevant to the family practitioner are Level 1 – Legal Help, Level 2 – Family Help (Lower), Level 3 – Family Help (Higher) and Level 4 – Legal Representation. Not all levels of service will be relevant in every case and it is possible to move, say, from Level 1 to Level 3, without using Level 2. The levels of service operate slightly differently in public law cases such as care proceedings (see **14.11.4**), and some types of family case fall under different funding schemes (eg child abduction proceedings).

For most family cases the level of service corresponds with a level of standard fixed fee which the solicitor will receive for the work undertaken on the client's behalf at the relevant level.

Once beyond Level 1, the amount of the fixed fee depends on the type of case (financial cases receiving a higher fee than children cases, for example), the geographical location of the firm (higher fees being paid in London) and the level of court. If appropriate, the solicitor can claim one fixed fee for, say, the children case and a second fee for the financial case. Similarly, if the case progresses through all four levels then four separate fixed fees may be claimed.

The solicitor receives the same fee regardless of how much work he actually carries out, unless the case becomes 'exceptional'. Broadly speaking, a case becomes exceptional only when the solicitor's costs, if calculated on an hourly charging rate basis, would amount to three times the fixed fee. So, for example, the raising of difficult international issues in a complex divorce could result in the case becoming exceptional. If the case is exceptional the solicitor is paid on an hourly charging rate basis. Only certain types of cases are capable of qualifying as exceptional.

Once beyond Level 1, if the case ends in settlement the solicitor receives a fixed fee for the work carried out, plus an additional settlement fee. The Legal Services Commission takes the view that the provision of this extra settlement fee encourages a non-litigious approach.

2.3.1 Level 1 – Legal Help

This enables people who are eligibile financially and on merit to obtain initial advice from a solicitor on any question of English law or procedure, for example in relation to domestic abuse. It will usually extend to only very limited steps following on from that advice, such as writing a letter. However, when advising a petitioner in a divorce, Legal Help covers all the steps taken by the solicitor throughout the divorce process itself.

To be financially eligible a client must come within the financial limits for both capital and income. The capital limit is at present £8,000. If the client is in receipt of certain welfare benefits, such as income support, income-based jobseeker's allowance or guaranteed State pension credit, he will automatically qualify; otherwise the solicitor will need to calculate his disposable income and capital. If the client is eligible, he will not have to pay a contribution, although the statutory charge (see **2.5**) may be relevant.

The case itself must also merit Legal Help. Legal Help will be provided only where there is sufficient benefit to the client, having regard to the circumstances of the case, including the personal circumstances of the client, to justify work being carried out. Legal Help will not be provided, therefore, if the claim is clearly hopeless, vexatious or would be an abuse of the process, or if the client is seeking advice on non-legal matters.

Legal Help is Controlled Work, which means that it is carried out under the firm's contract and does not require separate applications to be made to the Legal Services Commission at the outset of each case. Instead, under the terms of its contract, each firm is given a maximum number of new cases (or 'new matter starts') to be undertaken during the period of the contract.

It is for the solicitor to ensure both that the client is financially eligible and that Legal Help is justified on merit.

2.3.2 Level 2 – Family Help (Lower)

This covers work done by the solicitor up to, but not including, the issue of proceedings (except proceedings to obtain a consent order in financial proceedings). The solicitor will be able to advise the client, draft documentation, write correspondence, negotiate and/or support the client through mediation. However, Family Help (Lower) is available only where the help required is more than simply taking instructions and providing follow-up written/telephone advice, the solicitor is involved in substantive negotiations with a third party and the case is a significant family dispute (ie the case must be one which, if unresolved, would result in family proceedings). Family Help (Lower) is not available for divorce, or those cases where the issues relate to child support and the Child Support Agency has jurisdiction, or where the client requires only general advice about the dispute and method of dispute resolution, such as mediation.

As with Legal Help (see **2.3.1**), if the client is in receipt of income support, income-based jobseeker's allowance or guaranteed State pension credit, he will qualify automatically on financial grounds. Otherwise the client must come within the capital and income limits.

Family Help (Lower) may be provided only where the benefits to be gained from the help justify the likely costs, such that a reasonable private paying client would be prepared to proceed in all the circumstances. The likely cost of achieving the benefit must be proportionate to the benefit sought. So, for example, where the solicitor receives an offer of settlement from the other party, he must carefully consider whether the additional costs of further negotiation to improve on that offer would be proportionate to any improvement likely to be gained.

As with Legal Help, Family Help (Lower) is Controlled Work granted under the firm's contract and does not require an application to be made to the Legal Services Commission.

2.3.3 Level 3 – Family Help (Higher)

Fees at Level 3 are covered by the Private Family Law Representation Scheme. In essence, Family Help (Higher) will be justified only where it is necessary to litigate or proceedings are already underway. Family Help (Higher) is available for financial and children cases, but not for domestic abuse cases. In financial cases, Family Help (Higher) covers all work from the issue of proceedings up to and including the Financial Dispute Resolution hearing. In children cases, all work undertaken from the issue of proceedings is covered save in relation to or at the final hearing.

If the client is in receipt of certain welfare benefits, such as income support, income-based jobseeker's allowance or guaranteed State pension credit, he will qualify automatically on financial grounds without having to pay a contribution. In other cases, both his capital and income must come within the current financial limits. A contribution may be payable from capital or income depending on resources. It is essential that the solicitor explains to the client the effect of the statutory charge (see **2.5**).

Family Help (Higher) may be provided only where the benefits to be gained for the client justify the likely cost, such that a reasonable private paying client would be prepared to proceed in all the circumstances.

Family Help (Higher) may be refused if alternative funding is available to the client. This might occur where the client could raise the money to pay his legal fees by selling assets or taking out a loan.

Family Help (Higher) will be refused unless the case is first referred to a mediator, who has determined whether mediation is suitable in the circumstances for the dispute and the parties. Certain cases are exempt from this requirement:

(a) urgent cases when the criteria for emergency representation are satisfied;

(b) where no recognised mediator is available;

(c) where the mediator is satisfied that mediation is not suitable because the other party is unwilling to attend an assessment meeting to consider mediation;

(d) where proceedings are already in existence and the client is the respondent who has been given a court hearing date within the next six weeks;

(e) where the applicant has a reasonable fear of violence or significant harm from his or her partner or former partner.

Family Help (Higher) requires an application to be made to or registered with the Legal Services Commission in every case. The Legal Services Commission will assess whether the client is eligible for funding. If a certificate is to be granted and the client has a contribution to pay, an offer of funding is sent out direct to the client, with a copy to the solicitor. If no contribution is payable, the certificate is sent out immediately.

2.3.4 Level 4 – Legal Representation

This covers preparation for and representation at the final hearing. In children and financial cases, all work which could be done at Level 3 must have been carried out before moving on to Legal Representation. In domestic abuse cases, Legal Representation will be the initial application. Legal Representation does not cover advocacy at the hearing. Advocacy is dealt with and paid separately under the Family Advocacy Scheme, irrespective of whether the advocate is a solicitor or counsel.

Eligibility for Legal Representation, the application process and the criteria by which it is granted are the same as for Family Help (Higher) (see **2.3.3**).

2.4 Effect of public funding

2.4.1 Duty to notify the court and other parties

Immediately upon receipt of the certificate, or if proceedings have not yet commenced, when they do, the solicitor must file the original public funding certificate at court and must inform all other parties of the fact that the client is publicly funded by serving upon them a notice of issue of funding.

2.4.2 Relationship between solicitor and client

The solicitor will continue to owe the normal solicitor–client duties to a publicly funded client. In addition, the solicitor will owe duties to the Legal Services Commission. If the client acts unreasonably (eg refuses a reasonable offer of settlement) or has given inaccurate, misleading or incomplete information, the solicitor must report this to the Legal Services Commission. This duty to the Legal Services Commission overrides the solicitor's usual duty of confidentiality to his client.

2.4.3 Costs

If a publicly-funded party loses, it is possible for him to be ordered to pay the winning party's costs. Section 11 of the AJA 1999 provides that such an order for costs is limited in that an unsuccessful publicly-funded party cannot be ordered to pay an amount which exceeds the amount (if any) which is a reasonable one for him to pay having regard to all the circumstances, including the means of the parties and their conduct in relation to the dispute. However, since 2005 this limitation has not been applicable to most family proceedings (including those under MCA 1973 and CA 1989, Pts I and II). This change was introduced with the intention of ensuring that funded litigants are subject to the same costs risks as privately paying litigants. If the winner is the respondent, he had no choice but to defend the proceedings. In this situation, the court has power under reg 5 of the Community Legal Service (Cost Protection) Regulations 2000 (SI 2000/824) to order that the respondent's costs be paid from the Community Legal Service Fund. Again, with effect from July 2005, this power no longer applies to most family proceedings.

2.5 The statutory charge

Legal Aid does not necessarily amount to free legal representation for the client. In broad terms, if the client benefits financially from the case, any property that he receives can be taken by the Legal Services Commission and applied in payment of his solicitor's fees. This is the so-called statutory charge. The underlying principle is to put the funded client as far as possible in the same position as the privately paying client.

The statutory charge is potentially relevant to all levels of public funding, and consequently the solicitor is obliged to explain the effect of the statutory charge to the client. Given its obvious financial implications, it is vital that client fully understands the charge, and he should be reminded of it throughout the proceedings. The client should also be advised periodically as to the approximate costs accumulated.

2.5.1 The operation of the charge

The Legal Services Commission will be responsible for paying the assisted party's legal fees. The Commission will attempt to recoup these fees where possible. In order to do so, it first claims any money paid pursuant to an order for costs made in favour of the assisted party. Secondly, if a shortfall remains, it will retain any contribution paid by the assisted party under the terms of the offer of public funding. Thirdly, if there is still a deficit to the fund, the statutory charge will apply (AJA 1999, s 10(7)). The effect of this is that any property (including money) 'recovered or preserved in the proceedings' may be applied to make up the shortfall.

It was said in the case of *Hanlon v Law Society* [1980] 2 All ER 199:

> ... property has been recovered or preserved if it has been in issue in the proceedings: recovered by the claimant if it has been the subject of a successful claim, preserved by the respondent if the claim fails ...

So, property is 'recovered' if the funded client successfully obtains that property – ie, he makes a net gain. Property is 'preserved' if the funded client successfully defends a claim – ie, he retains property which he regarded as his own. The Legal Services Commission will determine from the statements of case, correspondence and order what the issues of the case were.

To facilitate collection of the charge, the assisted party's solicitor is required to pass any money payable to the assisted party under an agreement or court order to the Legal Services Commission. In addition, the solicitor must notify the Legal Services Commission of any property recovered or preserved by his client. If a party receives a lump sum well in excess of the anticipated statutory charge, the solicitor may apply to the Legal Services Commission for authority to release some of the money to the client, provided sufficient sums are retained to cover the firm's costs. In all cases, once the solicitor's costs have been finally determined and the statutory charge has been satisfied, any balance is sent to the assisted party.

The statutory charge may even apply where the ownership of the property has not been in dispute but proceedings were brought to determine what should happen to the property, ie whether it is to be sold, transferred or retained (see *Curling v Law Society* [1985] 1 All ER 705 and, similarly, *Parkes v Legal Aid Board* [1997] 1 FLR 77).

The costs are not limited to property obtained as a result of contested proceedings. Whilst a settlement will reduce the overall costs of the case, s 10(7) of the AJA 1999 ensures that a settlement will not avoid the effect of the statutory charge unless the settlement occurs at an early stage (see **2.9.2**). Where there has been a compromise, the property itself does not need to have been in issue for the statutory charge to apply, provided that it has been recovered or preserved in substitution for property which was in issue. For example, if the parties were arguing over the matrimonial home and a compromise was reached which instead transferred a holiday home (which had not been in issue) from the husband's sole name to the wife, the statutory charge can apply to the holiday home (see *Morgan and Others v Legal Aid Board* [2000] 3 All ER 974).

2.5.2 Exemptions

Some cases are not subject to the statutory charge. Those cases which conclude at Level 1 (Legal Help) are exempt from the operation of the charge. Those cases which conclude at Level 2 (Family Help (Lower)) are also exempt provided only the standard fixed fee is claimed. If a case becomes exceptional at Level 2, the statutory charge applies only to those fees above the exceptional case threshold and the charge will not attach to the matrimonial home. If a case goes beyond Level 2 the statutory charge applies to all costs, including those incurred at Levels 1 and 2, and applies to the costs incurred in all proceedings, meaning the entire cause or matter and not just the financial proceedings.

Some types of property will be exempt from the charge, irrespective of the level of funding that led to their being recovered or preserved. The following are not subject to the statutory charge:

(a) periodical payments;

(b) payments on or after the making of an occupation order under Pt IV of the FLA 1996;

(c) lump sums or property adjustment orders made after divorce in substitution for spousal maintenance under s 31(7A) or (7B) of the MCA 1973; and

(d) pension attachments or pension sharing orders (other than lump sum pension attachments) under ss 23, 24 and 24B of the MCA 1973.

2.5.3 Postponing the charge

There is no discretion to waive the statutory charge, but the Legal Services Commission can agree to postpone enforcement of the charge where it is charged on either:

(a) property which is expressly stated (in the order or agreement) to be used as a home by the assisted person or his dependants; or

(b) a lump sum which is agreed or ordered with the express purpose of it being used to purchase a home (the purchase to be made within one year).

In both cases, before agreeing to postponement, the Commission will need to be satisfied that the property represents adequate security for the charge.

Historically, provided these conditions were met, the postponement of the statutory charge was virtually automatic. However, following the Carter Review, the Legal Services Commission emphasised the discretionary nature of its power to postpone. Postponement will therefore not be allowed if, for example, the client could pay the statutory charge immediately by increasing the mortgage on the property. Even where the Legal Services Commission has initially exercised its discretion to allow the statutory charge to be postponed, that postponement will be kept under review and repayment sought immediately in the event of an improvement in the client's financial circumstances.

The charge will be protected by registration against the title of the property and simple interest will accrue. The interest rate is currently 8%. This may influence a client's decision to pay or postpone the charge. In most cases, the charge and interest will be enforced when the home is sold. However, it is possible for the charge to be transferred to a substitute property, provided, first, that the consent of the Legal Services Commission is obtained before the charged property is sold and, secondly, that the substitute property represents adequate security.

Where an assisted party recovers both a lump sum and property, the Legal Services Commission will look to take its charge from the money first, attaching the charge to property only as a last resort.

2.6 Human rights

The Legal Services Commission is a public body, and therefore it cannot act in a way that is incompatible with Convention rights under the HRA 1998.

Article 6 of the European Convention on Human Rights provides that 'everyone is entitled to a fair and public hearing within a reasonable time by an independent and impartial tribunal established by law'. Article 6 thus focuses on effective access to the courts. In *Airey v Ireland* (1979) 2 EHRR 305, a wife wanted to bring proceedings for judicial separation. She could not afford legal representation and her application was complex but she was refused public funding. The European Court held that Article 6 might sometimes compel the State to provide legal assistance if such assistance was indispensable for effective access to court. The Court said that complexity of procedure, complicated points of law, the need to call expert witnesses or the emotional involvement of the parties might all result in a requirement that legal assistance be provided. In *Airey*, for access to be effective, the wife required legal representation which, in her case, meant granting Legal Aid.

Subsequently, the European Commission on Human Rights has attempted to confine the application of the *Airey* principles. It recognised that, due to limited resources, States might legitimately restrict the grant of public funding, provided the decision whether or not to grant such funding was not taken arbitrarily. However, under HRA 1998, the Legal Services Commission may potentially be liable to challenge if it fails to grant public funding in circumstances that result in a litigant being unable to have effective access to the court.

2.7 Other methods of funding

Where a solicitor is instructed by a client and takes the view that the client may be eligible for public funding, he must advise the client accordingly, even though the solicitor or his firm do not themselves undertake publicly funded work. This advice must be given promptly, before the client incurs significant costs on a privately paying basis. In the case of *Truex v Kitchin* [2007] 2 FLR 1203 a solicitor who did not give this advice was required to repay virtually the whole of the amount which the client had already paid towards the solicitor's fees.

However, there will be cases where a client is not eligible for public funding and yet does not have sufficient resources to continue to pay his solicitor's fees on a privately paying basis. It has already been noted that a solicitor cannot enter a conditional fee agreement with a client in relation to family proceedings (see **2.1**). In appropriate cases there are other possible ways in which this problem can be resolved.

2.7.1 A 'Sears Tooth agreement'

This type of agreement is named after the case of *Sears Tooth (A Firm) v Payne Hicks Beach (A Firm) and Others* [1997] 2 FLR 116, where its validity was discussed. In this case, Sears Tooth acted for a wife in financial proceedings. She agreed to assign any award for financial relief (other than for maintenance) or costs to them as far as was necessary to pay their fees. The court stated that this device was a valid contract to assign a future chose in action and was not contrary to public policy. Such agreements are, however, rare in practice.

2.7.2 Maintenance pending suit

In *A v A (Maintenance Pending Suit; Provision of Legal Fees)* [2001] 1 FLR 377, the judge awarded a sum of maintenance pending suit at such a level as to include money for the wife to pay her solicitor's fees on the basis that she had a pressing need for legal representation.

The ability to include an element for legal fees within an award of maintenance pending suit was endorsed in a number of subsequent cases. The most notable was *Currey v Currey* [2006] EWCA Civ 1338, where the Court of Appeal said that such an award would be appropriate in cases where the applicant was able to demonstrate that he could not reasonably obtain legal advice by any other means. However, the test is stringent since the 'other means' of funding which must be considered first include borrowing money, charging assets, public funding and '*Sears Tooth* agreements'.

2.7.3 Lump sum orders

In *Minwalla v Minwalla* [2005] 1 FLR 771, in making a lump sum order in favour of the wife, Singer J ordered a further £500,000 as a separate and additional instalment of the lump sum to provide the wife with a fund from which she would be able to pay her legal fees in future anticipated litigation between the parties. The use of such orders will, however, be limited given the restrictions placed on the court's ability to make lump sum orders (see **4.4.1**), but they could be appropriate if, say, at the conclusion of the ancillary relief case, further proceedings were anticipated in relation to the children.

2.7.4 Bank loans

In some instances the only practical solution may be for the client to borrow money in order to meet his legal fees. It is becomingly increasingly common for banks to lend money to fund matrimonial litigation. Across the leading banks the conditions attached to such loans differ and have become more stringent in the current economic climate. Some banks, for example, will lend only where the client can offer security for the borrowing; other banks require a favourable opinion from counsel on the outcome of the proposed litigation. Whilst perhaps something of a last resort, such loans may be appropriate for some clients. However, the family solicitor must be careful not to infringe any rules of professional conduct when informing a client of the availability of such loans.

2.8 Chapter summary

(1) Where a client is of modest means, public funding may be available to enable that client to pay for legal advice and representation.

(2) Family law solicitors can undertake publicly-funded work only if their firm has a specialist contract with the Legal Services Commission.

(3) There are various 'levels of service' which may need to be provided by the family law solicitor:

- (a) Legal Help;
- (b) Family Help (Lower);
- (c) Family Help (Higher);
- (d) Legal Representation.

(4) The client will usually need to satisfy both means and merits tests to be eligible for public funding.

(5) Public funding is not 'free' and will need to be repaid from any property 'recovered or preserved' (with some exceptions) – the statutory charge.

(6) Where public funding is not available, other methods of paying for legal fees could be considered:

- (a) a *Sears Tooth* agreement;
- (b) maintenance pending suit;
- (c) lump sum orders;
- (d) bank loans.

Chapter 3
Divorce Law and Procedure

3.1	Introduction	19
3.2	One-year rule	20
3.3	Jurisdiction of the English courts to hear suits for divorce	20
3.4	The ground for divorce	22
3.5	Protection of children: Matrimonial Causes Act 1973, s 41	29
3.6	Nullity	30
3.7	Judicial separation	31
3.8	Presumption of death and dissolution of marriage	32
3.9	Divorce procedure	32
3.10	Defended divorces	43
3.11	Costs	43
3.12	Divorce law and procedure in the future	43
3.13	Chapter summary	43

3.1 Introduction

3.1.1 Terminology

The language used in the FPR 2010 was intended to modernise legal terminology in family cases. However, funding issues with the court computer system meant that this modernisation could not be carried through to court documentation. The result is that for the time being there are inconsistencies between, for example, the FPR 2010 referring to 'an application for a matrimonial order' whilst the relevant court document itself is still styled a 'divorce petition'. This chapter will in the main retain traditional terminology, not least because this remains consistent with the underlying legislation. However, this is a period of transition, with the likelihood of modern and traditional terminology being used interchangeably in practice for some time to come.

3.1.2 General

Over 110,000 couples divorce each year in England and Wales. By comparison, relatively few proceedings for judicial separation and nullity are brought. This chapter therefore deals in detail with the law relating to divorce and contains an outline of the law relating to judicial separation and nullity. The same procedures are available to civil partners, although termed 'dissolution', 'separation' and 'nullity'.

The chapter also deals with the procedure for divorce. Since less than 1% of all divorces are defended, only the undefended procedure is dealt with in detail. A checklist summarising the undefended divorce procedure is given at **3.12.2**.

3.1.3 Human rights

Article 12 of the European Convention on Human Rights gives 'men and women of marriageable age the right to marry and found a family according to the national laws governing the exercise of that right'. Marriage is the only relationship that is given special treatment under the Convention. The protections of Article 12 are limited to unions between members of the opposite sex and Article 12 has no application to same-sex relationships.

By way of contrast, there is no similar right to divorce, whether this is to re-marry or for any other reason (*Johnston v Ireland* (1987) 9 EHRR 203).

3.2 One-year rule

A petition for divorce cannot be presented to the court before the end of a period of one year from the date of the marriage (MCA 1973, s 3). The reason for this restriction is to discourage over-hasty decisions to end such short marriages.

The rule cannot be waived in any circumstances. However, provided that grounds for divorce can be satisfied, a petition may be presented after one year based on matters which occurred during this time; for example, the respondent's adultery or other behaviour during the first year of marriage can form the basis of a petition as soon as the year has expired. A solicitor should also bear in mind the alternative solutions which exist to protect a client with matrimonial problems, even during the first year. A decree of nullity or judicial separation is not affected by the one-year rule (see **3.6** and **3.7**). Maintenance can be applied for in the divorce county court (MCA 1973, s 27), or in the family proceedings court (Domestic Proceedings and Magistrates' Courts Act 1978 (DPMCA 1978), s 2). A spouse could be protected from violence by using Pt IV of the FLA 1996 (see **Chapter 15**).

3.3 Jurisdiction of the English courts to hear suits for divorce

3.3.1 General

The English courts do not have the right to deal with a person's matrimonial affairs merely because that person is a British citizen or is present in this country. The position is governed by s 5 of the Domicile and Matrimonial Proceedings Act 1973, which itself incorporates Council Regulation (EC) No 2201/2003 known as Brussels II Revised. The English courts have jurisdiction to hear a divorce suit only where:

(a) both parties are habitually resident in England and Wales; or

(b) both parties were last habitually resident in England and Wales, and one of them still resides there; or

(c) the respondent is habitually resident in England and Wales; or

(d) the petitioner is habitually resident in England and Wales and has lived there for at least a year immediately before the petition is filed; or

(e) the petitioner is domiciled in England and Wales and has been residing in England and Wales for at least six months immediately before the petition is filed; or

(f) both parties are domiciled in England and Wales; or

(g) if none of (a)–(f) above applies and no court of another EU State has jurisdiction, either of the parties is domiciled in England and Wales on the date when the proceedings are begun.

These various bases of jurisdiction are not ranked in any order of precedence. More than one basis may apply on the individual facts of the case, but only one needs to be satisfied. In practice the easiest approach is for the family solicitor to work down the list and to rely upon the first basis that is applicable to the client's case.

Example

Sophie, who is French, marries Tim, who is English. The couple make their married home in England for 10 years. The marriage breaks down and Sophie returns home to France; Tim remains in England. Six months later Tim decides to seek a divorce through the English courts. On the facts, Tim has been habitually resident and domiciled in England throughout. Sophie has been habitually resident and in England during the marriage, but she is now both habitually resident and domiciled in France. The English courts have jurisdiction to deal with Tim's divorce on the basis of (b), (d) or (e) above. Tim needs to satisfy only one basis, and in practice the simplest approach is rely on the first, ie (b).

3.3.2 Habitual residence

Habitual residence is a term which can be found in a variety of statutory provisions, and its meaning differs according to the context in which it is used. In the specific context of Brussels II Revised, the first point to note is that a person can only be habitually resident in one place at any given time.

The essence of habitual residence lies in establishing the 'centre of interests' of a person's life. This is a question of fact to be decided in the individual circumstances of each case. To establish a person's place of habitual residence therefore requires a careful consideration of the facts of the case. In *Z v Z (Divorce: Jurisdiction)* [2010] 1 FLR 694 Ryder J offered some guidance and said:

> A centre of interests may be established quickly or slowly, depending on the circumstances. Habitual residence in one country may not be lost despite a lengthy period in another . . . There is no requirement that the centre of interests has to be permanent; it need only be habitual. But it must have a stable character.

On the unusual facts of *Marinos v Marinos* [2007] 2 FLR 1018, the wife had been resident in both England and Greece. However, in deciding where the wife was *habitually* resident, Munby J found that even if she had previously been habitually resident in Greece, she became habitually resident in England as soon as she executed her 'planned, permanent and purposeful relocation' to England. Consequently, she became habitually resident the moment her plane landed in England, thereby enabling her validly to petition the English court the following day.

3.3.3 Domicile

Domicile is a more universal concept. However, no simple definition of 'domicile' is possible and, if issues arise in this respect, reference should be made to textbooks on private international law.

Broadly, a person is said to be domiciled in a territory having a single legal system if he has his permanent home there.

Everyone has a domicile and can only have one operative domicile at any one time. However, a person's domicile may alter as his circumstances change throughout his life. A person may acquire, and lose, any of three types of domicile. Each is described in outline below.

3.3.3.1 Domicile of origin

A person acquires domicile of origin at birth. In the case of a child whose parents are married, it is the father's domicile. In the case of a child whose parents are not married, it is the mother's domicile. It is therefore irrelevant where the child was born.

A domicile of origin is never lost, and even though it may not be operative for any period during which the person acquires a domicile of choice, it will revive if the domicile of choice is lost until another domicile of choice is acquired.

Example

Maria's domicile of origin is Italy. She marries an Englishman, Nigel, and moves to London, intending that England will be her permanent home. Maria acquires a domicile of choice of England. The marriage breaks down and Maria permanently leaves England to take up temporary residence in Paris whilst she contemplates her future. Maria has lost her English domicile of choice. Her Italian domicile of origin is therefore revived until such time as she acquires a new domicile of choice.

3.3.3.2 Domicile of choice

Every person aged 16 or over may acquire a domicile of choice. This requires, first, residence in a country other than the domicile of origin and, secondly, an intention to remain there permanently or indefinitely. This intention may be shown by becoming a citizen of that country, by the purchase of a home or by the length of time spent in that country. No single factor will be decisive.

3.3.3.3 Domicile of dependence

A child can acquire an independent domicile only at 16 years of age, or on marriage under that age. If he is under 16 years old and unmarried, his domicile will follow his father's domicile if his parents are married, or his mother's if his parents are not married. If married parents separate, the child will acquire the domicile of the parent with whom he lives.

Example

Assume that Maria and Nigel, in the example at **3.3.3.1**, had a daughter, Olivia, who lives with Maria after the marriage breaks down. At birth Olivia acquired her domicile of dependence from Nigel, ie England. After the separation, Olivia's domicile follows that of her mother as a domicile of dependence. Olivia therefore has an Italian domicile of dependence.

3.3.4 Choice of forum

In many cases, it will be clear that the divorce will take place in England and Wales. In other cases, for example where one of the couple has been habitually resident in England for the past year but the other has not, it may be possible to choose whether to start proceedings in England and Wales or elsewhere. Such a choice will be governed by a number of factors, such as convenience and the law of the other jurisdiction(s) involved. Where the other jurisdiction is within the EU (apart from Denmark) then the situation will be governed by Brussels II Revised. This states that where a party commences proceedings for divorce, nullity or judicial separation in a jurisdiction of one of the Member States covered by Brussels II Revised, the court of the State which is first seized of the matter shall have exclusive jurisdiction. Any proceedings for divorce, etc subsequently commenced in another Member State must be stayed once the jurisdiction of the first State has been established. Where choice of forum is an issue, the solicitor must contact a lawyer in the other jurisdiction as soon as possible for advice on the legal position should a divorce be started there. Speed will normally be of the essence, since usually proceedings will continue in the jurisdiction where they were first started, any which commence later in an alternative jurisdiction being stayed (and if the other jurisdiction is an EU country covered by Brussels II Revised, this will *always* be the case).

3.3.5 Recognition of foreign decrees by the English courts

A relevant factor when dealing with foreign marriages is to check that the English courts recognise a foreign decree, for example, of divorce. If the English courts recognise the foreign decree then the parties are free to remarry in England and Wales, and no English divorce is necessary or, indeed, possible. However, in these circumstances, the English courts can make financial orders. If, on the other hand, the foreign decree is not recognised, the parties are still married and they will have to petition for a divorce through the English courts, in which case financial orders can be made in the normal way. The law is set out in the FLA 1986 and reference should be made to this, and to relevant textbooks, should an international aspect arise.

3.4 The ground for divorce

3.4.1 General

There is only one ground on which a petition for divorce may be presented to the court by either party to the marriage; that is, that the marriage has broken down irretrievably (MCA

1973, s 1(1)) (see **3.4.2** to **3.4.6** below). However, the court cannot hold that the marriage has broken down unless the petitioner satisfies the court of one or more of the five facts specified in s 1(2) of the MCA 1973. There is no need for there to be a causal relationship between the fact and the breakdown. Therefore, it is no defence to a divorce suit that, for example, the respondent committed adultery after having left the petitioner because the marriage had broken down; the fact does not have to precede and cause the breakdown, but can follow and merely evidence it.

If the court is satisfied that a fact is proved, it must grant the decree nisi unless it is satisfied that the marriage has not broken down (MCA 1973, s 1(4)). This could occur if the parties began living together again before the divorce was granted.

The equivalent process to end a civil partnership is dissolution. The statutory provisions are to be found in the Civil Partnership Act 2004, although they effectively mirror those of the MCA 1973.

3.4.2 Fact A: adultery and intolerability

> (a) That the respondent has committed adultery *and* the petitioner finds it intolerable to live with the respondent. (MCA 1973, s 1(2)(a), emphasis added)

There are two elements to this fact, which must both be proved to the court:

(a) adultery; and

(b) intolerability.

It should be noted that this fact is not available as the basis for a petition to dissolve a civil partnership.

3.4.2.1 Adultery

Case law defines adultery as voluntary sexual intercourse between two persons of the opposite sex, one or both of whom is or are married, but not to each other.

Adultery may be proved or inferred from the following:

(a) A confession of adultery by the respondent. This is the method often used in undefended divorces. Proof can either be by way of a separate confession statement signed by the respondent, or by the respondent answering 'yes' to a question in the Acknowledgement of Service form which is served on the respondent with the petition. If this method is to be used, the Acknowledgement must be returned to court signed by the respondent personally.

(b) Birth of a child to the wife on proof that the husband was not the father.

(c) Circumstantial evidence showing both guilty purpose and the opportunity to gratify it, for example, an enquiry agent's report which shows that the respondent and a member of the opposite sex are cohabiting.

(d) A finding of paternity against the respondent in Children Act proceedings (Civil Evidence Act 1968, s 12).

(e) Conviction of the respondent in a criminal court of an offence entailing sexual intercourse, for example, rape (Civil Evidence Act 1968, s 11). Although by definition the act of sexual intercourse is not voluntary on the part of the victim, a conviction for rape will be sufficient to satisfy the definition of adultery as against the perpetrator.

(f) A finding of adultery against the respondent in an earlier case in the High Court or county court (Civil Evidence Act 1968, s 12). If the petitioner had already been granted a decree of judicial separation on the grounds of adultery, the court can treat the judicial separation decree as sufficient proof of the adultery (MCA 1973, s 4(2)).

3.4.2.2 Intolerability

Intolerability must be proved as well as the adultery, but this element rarely causes any problem. In the first place, the petitioner does not have to show that it was in consequence of the adultery that he found it intolerable to live with the respondent. He could say, for example, that he found it intolerable to live with her because of her treatment of the children, or because of some behaviour of the respondent other than the adultery. Secondly, the test of intolerability is subjective. The petitioner has merely to convince the court that he finds it intolerable to live with the respondent.

The intolerability can be proved by an assertion of intolerability in an affidavit sent to the court as part of the divorce proceedings. In practice, in undefended cases, courts do not even require the petitioner to state the reason why he finds it intolerable to live with the respondent.

3.4.2.3 The co-respondent

The person with whom the respondent committed adultery can be made a party to the divorce proceedings and is called the co-respondent. However, even if the co-respondent is made a party, it is not necessary to obtain an admission of adultery from the co-respondent if the respondent admits the adultery, because the fact requires only evidence that the respondent has committed adultery.

For many years the rules have given a petitioner the option not to name the co-respondent in the petition, in which case it is not necessary to make the co-respondent a party to the divorce. It has become established good practice to refrain from naming a co-respondent so as to reduce animosity between the parties. The FPR 2010 Practice Direction 7A now goes a little further in saying, at para 2.1, that the co-respondent *should not* be named unless the petitioner believes that the respondent is likely to object to the divorce. So in the future naming a co-respondent should be reserved for those cases in which there is a genuine risk of the proceedings being defended.

3.4.2.4 Effect of cohabitation

Adultery

The petitioner is not entitled to rely on adultery committed by the respondent if the parties cohabit for a period, or periods together, exceeding six months after the petitioner has discovered the adultery (MCA 1973, s 2(1)).

The purpose behind this provision is to allow the parties a reasonable length of time in which to achieve a reconciliation without prejudicing their ground for divorce.

The time begins to run when the petitioner discovers the adultery. It is not relevant how long ago the adultery was actually committed. The six months can be made up of a number of periods of cohabitation, they need not constitute a continuous period. If the respondent has committed adultery on several occasions, time will not begin to run until after the petitioner learns of the last act of adultery.

Intolerability

Where the parties have lived together for a period or periods not exceeding six months in total after the petitioner knew of the adultery, the court must disregard the cohabitation when considering whether the petitioner finds it intolerable to live with the respondent (MCA 1973, s 2(2)).

This is another attempt to encourage the parties to attempt reconciliation. Without it, any cohabitation after discovery of the adultery could be used by the respondent as evidence that the petitioner did not in fact find it intolerable to live with the respondent.

> **Example**
>
> Abigail and Brian marry in 1995. In 1997 Brian has an affair which ends after one month. In December 2011 a friend tells Abigail about Brian's affair. Initially the couple stay together and try to make the marriage work. However, in February 2012, Abigail decides that she cannot forgive Brian for the affair and she decides to start divorce proceedings. The lengthy cohabitation since the affair took place is irrelevant. Time begins to run only when Abigail knew of the affair, ie December 2011. As fewer than six months have elapsed since that date, Abigail's petition can proceed based on the adultery in 1997.

3.4.3 Fact B: behaviour

(b) That the respondent has behaved in such a way that the petitioner cannot reasonably be expected to live with the respondent. (MCA 1973, s 1(2)(b))

3.4.3.1 The respondent's behaviour

The phrase 'cannot reasonably be expected to live with the respondent' lays down an objective test. The court must make a value judgement about the respondent's behaviour and its effect on the petitioner. In contrast to the test for intolerability (see **3.4.2.2**), the petitioner's word alone is not enough. However, the court must have regard to the history of the marriage as well as to the personalities of the individual spouses. In the case of *O'Neill v O'Neill* [1975] 1 WLR 1118, the respondent, after retiring, bought a flat for himself, his wife and teenage daughter. He then personally began extensive renovation, involving mixing cement in the living room and leaving the toilet without a door for eight months, embarrassing his wife and daughter. After two years of the upheaval the wife left, and was entitled to a decree using this fact.

In the case of *Birch v Birch* [1992] 1 FLR 564, the wife's main complaint against the husband was that he was dogmatic and dictatorial, with nationalistic, male chauvinistic characteristics which she had resented for many years. The court granted the divorce and acknowledged that the wife's sensitive nature made it unreasonable for her to go on living with him.

It is a question of fact in each case whether the behaviour is such as to entitle the petitioner to a decree; it does not have to be grave and weighty behaviour. There is also no need to prove that the respondent had any intention to inflict misery on the petitioner.

In practice, again, each case depends on its facts, but typically, in an undefended divorce the court will look for three to six examples of behaviour. A further guide to follow in drafting a behaviour petition is 'first, worst and last'. This will ensure that the length of time that the behaviour has been suffered will be established, the major incidents included and when the latest example occurred.

The type of conduct that can be included will always depend on the particular circumstances of the case, but relevant matters include physical violence, verbal abuse (which could include insults, threats, nagging), demanding sexual intercourse too often or not agreeing to intercourse at all, intimate relationships with people of the same or opposite sex (even if they fall short of sexual acts), cruelty, and failure to provide money or food as well as failure to provide affection or attention. However, the mere fact that the petitioner has become bored with the marriage, or that the parties are simply incompatible, will not be sufficient.

3.4.3.2 Effect of cohabitation on behaviour

The fact that the petitioner and respondent have lived with each other for a period or periods not exceeding six months in total after the last incident of behaviour relied on must be disregarded in deciding whether the petitioner can reasonably be expected to live with the respondent (MCA 1973, s 2(3)). This is to encourage the parties to consider reconciliation as cohabitation will not immediately prevent a divorce.

If the parties have lived together for longer than six months, this will not be an absolute bar to a petition being granted. However, the court will take the length of the cohabitation into account in determining whether the petitioner can reasonably be expected to live with the respondent. The longer the cohabitation, the less likely it will be that the court will grant the petition. It would always be open to the petitioner to show a good reason why the cohabitation continued. In *Bradley v Bradley* [1973] 1 WLR 1291, the wife had continued to cohabit, but proved to the court that she had no choice but to do so as she had seven children, nowhere else to go and was frightened that unless she went on sleeping with the husband and looking after the house he would seriously injure her.

3.4.4 Fact C: desertion

> (c) That the respondent has deserted the petitioner for a continuous period of at least two years immediately preceding the presentation of the petition. (MCA 1973, s 1(2)(c))

3.4.4.1 What constitutes desertion?

The elements needed to constitute the fact of desertion are as follows:

(a) There must be a separation. In calculating the period of separation, the date of separation itself will not be included. In most cases the parties are living apart, but people who are living under the same roof can be separated in law if the common home and the common life have ceased altogether. The petitioner must establish that there are, in fact, two separate households under the same roof (see *Hopes v Hopes* [1948] 2 All ER 920). The court will examine the extent to which the parties share domestic life; whether they cook for each other, eat together and sleep together will all be relevant considerations.

(b) There must be an intention to desert, ie to bring the matrimonial union permanently to an end.

(c) The petitioner must not consent or agree to the separation.

(d) The respondent must not have a just cause for leaving. This could apply if the respondent were away on business, or if his leaving was because of the wife's adultery.

(e) The desertion must be continuous. Normally, several periods of separation cannot be added together to form the two-year period.

(f) The desertion must immediately precede the presentation of the petition, ie the date when it is filed.

In practice, desertion is rarely cited in a petition because it is so technical and because other facts can usually be cited where the parties are living separately.

3.4.4.2 Effect of cohabitation on desertion

In considering whether a period of desertion has been continuous, no account is to be taken of a period or periods not exceeding six months in total during which the parties cohabited (MCA 1973, s 2(5)). However, any period of cohabitation cannot be counted as part of the period of desertion.

Example

Lisa deserted Martin on 31 January 2010. They make an attempt at reconciliation and live together for two months in 2011. The cohabitation will not prevent Martin from petitioning on the basis of desertion, but he cannot file the petition until a period of two years and two months has expired since Lisa first deserted. Martin will therefore be able to start divorce proceedings on 1 April 2012.

3.4.5 Fact D: two years' separation and consent

> (d) That the parties to the marriage have lived apart for a continuous period of at least two years immediately preceding the presentation of the petition ... *and* the respondent consents to a decree being granted. (MCA 1973, s 1(2)(d), emphasis added)

The elements which are necessary for this fact are, first, separation and, secondly, the respondent must consent to the decree.

3.4.5.1 Separation

Two years' separation is necessary. The spouses are treated as living apart unless they are living with each other in the same household (MCA 1973, s 2(6)). The test is similar to the test of separation in desertion cases (see **3.4.4.1**); accordingly, people can be living apart even though living under the same roof if they are living completely separate lives. The actual date of separation will not be included when calculating the period of separation.

A physical separation does not of itself constitute living apart. There must also be a mental element, ie one of the spouses must regard the marriage as a mere shell, never intending to live with the other spouse again (*Santos v Santos* [1975] 2 All ER 246). This intention does not necessarily have to be communicated to the other spouse and the petitioner could, in theory, rely on the respondent's intention. However, in practice, it is almost always the petitioner's intention that is relied on, and the standard-form divorce documents are drafted on this basis.

3.4.5.2 Consent

The respondent must consent to the divorce. This consent can be given any time after the service of the petition. Consent must be given in writing (FPR 2010, r 7.12(12). In practice, in an undefended divorce, this is given in the Acknowledgement of Service form returned by the respondent to the court following service of the petition on him. All a respondent has to do is answer 'yes' to one of the standard questions and sign the form personally.

The respondent may give notice to the court that he does not consent, or that he withdraws consent already given. No reason for this is needed (FPR 2010, r 7.12(12)).

Any attempt to withdraw consent once decree nisi has been obtained is likely to be ineffective. However, even after the decree nisi, the court has discretion to rescind the decree nisi on the respondent's application if satisfied that the petitioner misled the respondent (whether intentionally or unintentionally) about any matter which he took into account in deciding to give his consent (MCA 1973, s 10(1)). This could apply in a situation where the respondent was misled about a financial or property matter, but could also apply where the respondent was misled about the petitioner's intention to remarry. However, in many cases the court will use its discretion to grant the decree absolute even though the respondent has been misled by the petitioner, so long as this does not have serious consequences.

3.4.5.3 Effect of cohabitation on separation

Section 2(5) of the MCA 1973 applies to the continuity of separation in the same way as it does to desertion (see **3.4.4.2**). Therefore, in deciding whether the living apart has been continuous, a period not exceeding, or periods together not exceeding, six months will be ignored. However, they must be added to the total period of separation so that the time that the parties have actually lived apart is at least two years.

3.4.5.4 Financial position of the respondent (MCA 1973, s 10(2))

If the only fact found is Fact D (or Fact E, see **3.4.6**) the respondent may apply to the court for a consideration of his financial position following the divorce (MCA 1973, s 10(2)).

If such an application is made, the court must consider all the circumstances and will not make the decree absolute unless satisfied that:

(a) the petitioner should not be required to make any financial provision for the respondent; or

(b) the financial provision made is fair and reasonable, or the best that can be made in the circumstances (MCA 1973, s 10(3)).

The court may proceed without observing the above requirements if it is satisfied that the circumstances make it desirable that the decree should be made absolute without delay *and* that the court has obtained a satisfactory undertaking from the petitioner that he will make such financial provision for the respondent as the court may approve (MCA 1973, s 10(4)).

In practice, s 10 is rarely used, and is often treated as something of a negotiating mechanism. The court has no power under this section actually to make financial orders, so it will generally insist that a court order is obtained in financial proceedings under MCA 1973 before the decree absolute is granted.

If the court exercised its discretion under s 10(4) to enable the decree absolute to be granted without satisfactory provision being made (it might do so, eg, if the petitioner's new partner was about to have his child and he urgently wanted to marry her), it would still insist on detailed provisions being included in any undertaking given by the petitioner.

3.4.6 Fact E: five years' separation

> (e) That the parties to the marriage have lived apart for a continuous period of at least five years immediately preceding the petition. (MCA 1973, s 1(2)(e))

After five years' separation, there is no need for the petitioner to obtain the respondent's consent to the divorce and either party can petition. Living apart has the same meaning as in Fact D (see **3.4.5.1**).

There is no defence to a Fact E petition except to deny the separation, or to prove grave hardship under s 5 of the MCA 1973 (see **3.4.6.1**).

The decree may also be delayed by the respondent asking for his financial position to be considered under s 10(2) of the MCA 1973 (see **3.4.5.4**).

3.4.6.1 Grave hardship

It is a defence to proceedings for divorce, where the only fact found is Fact E, that the dissolution of the marriage would result in grave financial or other hardship to the respondent *and* in all the circumstances it would be wrong to dissolve the marriage (MCA 1973, s 5(1)).

In deciding whether s 5 applies, the court must take account of all the circumstances, including the parties' conduct, the interests of the parties, and the interests of any children or other persons concerned (MCA 1973, s 5(2)).

In *Talbot v Talbot* (1971) 115 SJ 870, the husband left his wife for another woman and ceased maintaining his wife and children. He obtained a divorce under Fact E. The court held that the s 5 defence did not apply as his wife's hardship arose from the breakdown of the marriage and not from the prospective divorce. Accordingly, granting the decree would not add to it. The court may also grant the decree even though grave hardship does result, provided it is satisfied that it is not wrong to grant it. In *Brickell v Brickell* [1973] 3 All ER 508, the Court of Appeal looked at the surrounding circumstances, including the conduct of the parties, and concluded that the husband was entitled to a decree, even though the wife would suffer grave financial hardship, because the wife had behaved so badly during the marriage.

The grave hardship most commonly pleaded is financial; this will include the loss of the chance of acquiring any benefit which the respondent might acquire if the marriage were not dissolved (MCA 1973, s 5(3)). If, for example, the husband was contributing to an occupational pension scheme, his wife could be faced with grave financial hardship if he obtained a divorce because she would then cease to be entitled to a widow's pension under his pension scheme (*Julian v Julian* (1973) 116 SJ 763). However, the defence would not succeed if the petitioner could show that the hardship was not grave because, for example, the wife was entitled to her own occupational pension, or the husband could compensate her for the loss with, say, a deferred annuity, or by 'earmarking' the pension or 'splitting' it (see **4.7**). In practice, this defence is usually used by the respondent to persuade the petitioner to make satisfactory financial provision.

Grave hardship may take other forms and may necessitate examination of hardship caused by religious censure or social ostracism. In practice, it is very difficult to establish that such other hardships are grave enough to warrant refusing a decree.

3.4.6.2 Distinction between MCA 1973, s 5 and s 10(2) of the MCA 1973

Section 5 is a complete defence, therefore, if the defence succeeds, the couple remain married. Section 10(2) merely delays the decree absolute. Section 5 requires the respondent to establish 'grave' financial or other hardship, whereas under s 10(2) the respondent must merely show that the provision is not fair and reasonable. It is easier to establish that s 10(2) applies, but its effect is less drastic.

3.4.6.3 Effect of cohabitation on separation

The effect of cohabitation on Fact E is the same as on Fact D (see **3.4.5.3**).

3.5 Protection of children: Matrimonial Causes Act 1973, s 41

Although children are not parties to the divorce, it is accepted that they often suffer most on a breakdown of marriage. Therefore, the welfare of the children must be considered before a divorce is finalised.

3.5.1 Child of the family

The MCA 1973 requires the court to consider the welfare of any child who is a 'child of the family'. A child of the family is a child who is either:

(a) a child of both parties to the marriage; or

(b) any other child (not having been placed with the parties as foster parents by the local authority or voluntary organisation) who has been treated by both parties as a child of the family (MCA 1973, s 52(1)).

The definition therefore applies to all natural children of both parties, but can apply to a wide variety of more distantly related or unrelated children, for example, step-children or adopted children.

3.5.2 Protection of children on divorce under MCA 1973, s 41

In any proceedings for a decree of divorce or judicial separation the court must consider:

(a) whether there are any children of the family to whom s 41 applies. The section will apply to any child of the family who, at the date when the court considers the case, is under 16, or any other child of the family of 16 and over to whom the court directs that s 41 shall apply. This could cover a child still in full-time education or who is suffering from a disability; and

(b) where there are any such children, whether in the light of the arrangements which have been, or are proposed to be, made for their upbringing or welfare it should exercise any of its powers under CA 1989 with respect to any of them (eg that the child resides with a particular parent, or that the child has contact with a parent).

This function will normally be carried out by the district judge. He will usually decide on the papers alone without any hearing. In such a case, the court is unlikely to wish to exercise any of its powers under the CA 1989 (for the detailed procedure, see **3.9.12**).

3.5.3 Power to delay decree absolute

The court is given the power to delay the grant of the decree absolute if:

(a) the circumstances of the case require it, or are likely to require it, to exercise any of its powers under the CA 1989 with respect to any such child; and

(b) it is not in a position to exercise that power without giving further consideration to the case; and

(c) there are exceptional circumstances which make it desirable in the interests of the child that the court should give a direction under s 41.

In reality, this power is rarely exercised. However, it could apply, for example, where the court considers that there is a problem with the arrangements for the children, it asks the parents to attend court to explain the circumstances but the parents fail to co-operate and do not attend the appointment. By delaying the decree the court might force the parents to address themselves to the problems and to work out satisfactory arrangements.

3.6 Nullity

This section gives an outline of the decree of nullity which can, in certain circumstances, be sought as an alternative to a decree of divorce. In comparison with divorce, relatively few decrees of nullity are sought.

3.6.1 General

A decree of nullity may declare that a marriage is either void from the outset, in which case it is treated as never having existed at all, or voidable, in which case it will be treated as being valid and subsisting until the decree is obtained.

3.6.2 Void marriages

A marriage will be void in situations which include the following:

(a) where the parties are too closely related to each other; or

(b) either party was under 16 years of age at the time of the ceremony; or

(c) either party was already lawfully married (MCA 1973, s 11).

If a marriage is void, it never existed. Therefore, a decree is not needed to end it. However, since a decree is needed if financial orders are required, a decree is usually obtained.

3.6.3 Voidable marriages

A marriage will be voidable in situations which include the following:

(a) non-consummation, either due to incapacity of one party or wilful refusal (non-consummation does not give rise to a voidable civil partnership as, in contrast to marriage, there is no requirement that the relationship between civil partners be of a sexual nature); or

(b) lack of consent, for example, due to duress; or

(c) one party was suffering from a mental disorder such as to make them unfit for marriage; or

(d) an interim gender recognition certificate was issued to the respondent after the marriage.

A voidable marriage exists until such time as a decree of nullity is obtained. A bar to obtaining a decree can exist if the respondent satisfies the court, first, that the petitioner, knowing that the marriage could be ended, behaved in such a way as to lead the respondent reasonably to believe that he would not seek to end it and, secondly, that it would be unjust to the respondent to grant the decree (MCA 1973, s 13(1)).

Generally, the petitioner must apply for the decree within three years of the date of the marriage. This does not apply to non-consummation cases nor to cases based on an interim gender recognition certificate, and, in any event, the court also has a discretion to extend the time limit (MCA 1973, s 13(4)).

3.6.4 Consequences of a decree of nullity

3.6.4.1 Ancillary orders

The parties to a suit for nullity are entitled to apply for all those orders in relation to children, property and finance as are available on divorce.

3.6.4.2 Children

Children born to parents who subsequently obtain a decree of nullity are automatically legitimate if the parents' marriage is voidable, because the marriage existed up to the time of the decree. If the marriage is void, the children will be legitimate if, at the time of conception (or the celebration of the marriage if this is later), both or either of the parents reasonably believed the marriage was valid and the father was domiciled in England and Wales at the time of the birth, or, if he died before the birth, was so domiciled immediately before his death (Legitimacy Act 1976, s 1).

3.6.4.3 Wills

A voidable marriage revokes a previous will, whereas a void marriage, as it never existed, does not have this effect.

When a decree of nullity is granted, whether in respect of a void or voidable marriage, it will have the same effect on a will as a decree of divorce. This means that the former spouse is to be treated as having died on the date of the decree.

Neither spouse will be able to claim in the event of the other's intestacy.

3.6.5 Divorce or nullity?

In some cases, there may be grounds for both divorce and nullity. It is then for the client to choose which to pursue. Influencing factors may be the fact that nullity can be obtained in the first year of marriage, or there may be religious reasons for wanting to have the marriage declared non-existent rather than dissolved, making nullity the preferred option.

3.7 Judicial separation

An alternative to a decree of divorce is a decree of judicial separation (or separation order for civil partners). It does not dissolve the marriage but can be used, for example, if religious beliefs forbid divorce.

3.7.1 Grounds for judicial separation

The grounds on which a decree of judicial separation may be obtained are the same as the facts that need to be proved to obtain a divorce (MCA 1973, s 1(2)) (see **3.4.2** to **3.4.6**). This means that s 2 of the MCA 1973 will apply regarding periods of reconciliation and cohabitation, and s 41 will apply in relation to any children of the family. However, the parties do not need to show irretrievable breakdown (MCA 1973, s 17(2)). The same procedure available in undefended divorces applies to undefended petitions for judicial separation although, in contrast to divorce, there is only one stage to the decree. The public funding position on judicial separation is the same as for divorce.

3.7.2 Effect of decree of judicial separation

When a decree of judicial separation has been obtained the parties are still married, as the decree does not dissolve the marriage but only releases the parties from the duty to live together.

3.7.3 Reasons for seeking judicial separation

Reasons for seeking judicial separation include the following:

(a) Judicial separation may be sought at any time after the marriage, so this could assist a spouse who separates within the first year who cannot start divorce proceedings.

(b) Broadly, the same financial and other ancillary orders can be obtained on judicial separation as on divorce.

(c) Some clients have religious or moral objections to divorce and so this decree offers an alternative.

(d) The fact used in the judicial separation proceedings can subsequently be used as proof of a fact in later divorce proceedings (MCA 1973, s 4(1)).

Note that judicial separation does not affect existing wills and advice should be given to clients recommending that they review their wills in the light of their separation. If, subsequently, a spouse dies intestate, his or her property will devolve as if the other spouse was already dead, so the surviving spouse will not benefit.

3.8 Presumption of death and dissolution of marriage

If the respondent has disappeared in circumstances where it is reasonable to suppose he is dead, the petitioner can apply under s 19 of the MCA 1973 for a presumption of death and dissolution of marriage. There is a presumption that, after seven years' continuous absence, during which time the petitioner has had no reason to believe that the respondent was alive, the respondent is dead.

3.9 Divorce procedure

3.9.1 Legal Help

On marriage breakdown, it is usual for both spouses to seek legal advice. A solicitor must be able to assess whether a client is eligible for public funding towards his legal costs and advise him accordingly.

An outline of public funding is provided in **Chapter 2**. This section highlights some points of particular relevance to the divorce suit itself.

Legal Help is available to advise and assist a client who qualifies on means and merits.

Where a solicitor advises under Legal Help, he is not treated by the court as 'acting' for the client and so the solicitor's name will not appear on the court record. The client is a litigant in person, which means that all procedural documents in the divorce must be signed by the client personally.

If Family Help (Higher) or Legal Representation is subsequently obtained (eg for an ancillary financial claim), the solicitor must place his name on the court record for that matter by filing a Notice of Acting with the court and serving any other party with a copy. However, the client will remain a litigant in person in the divorce.

3.9.2 The first interview

The first interview is of crucial importance. It is the first meeting with the client and gives the opportunity for the solicitor to obtain information needed from the client as well as to give advice and plan what is to be done (for general advice on interviewing, see **1.2.4**).

When a client seeks advice on his marriage, it is important to discover the client's intentions. The solicitor must not assume that the client wants a divorce. Instead the solicitor must establish whether the client regards the marriage as at an end, or whether he is still hopeful of a reconciliation.

Assuming that the client wants to obtain a divorce, the following areas will need to be covered in the interview. Appropriate use of a checklist or instruction sheet will help to obtain the information. For example:

(a) general advice on divorce and alternatives, for example, grounds, timing, mediation;

(b) information sufficient to complete the divorce petition and the supporting documents;

(c) advice on costs;

(d) financial matters, for example, property and maintenance principles and orders that could be made;

(e) children, for example, advice on general principles and orders available;

(f) welfare benefits;

(g) public funding: statutory charge. If the client is eligible for public funding for ancillary matters, advice must be given on the effect that the statutory charge will have on any order obtained (for a more detailed explanation, see **2.9**);

(h) injunction law and procedure. If the client has problems with domestic abuse, appropriate advice should be given (see **Chapter 14**).

A file note of the interview should be made as soon as possible after the interview. A letter should be written to the client reminding him of what happened at the interview and what advice was given, as well as reminding the client of any action he has asked for. Advice given on costs, including public funding, should be repeated.

3.9.3 The petition

3.9.3.1 The prescribed form

The FPR 2010, r 5.1 provides that every divorce must be begun using the form prescribed in Practice Direction 5A. The standard form petition is drafted (see **Appendix 3(A)**) to enable the solicitor to insert certain required information. This is as follows:

(a) Names of the parties and date and place of the marriage. This information should be copied exactly from the marriage certificate.

(b) The last address where the parties lived as husband and wife.

(c) The ground on which it is alleged that the court has jurisdiction.

(d) Present occupations and residences of the parties. There are provisions enabling the petitioner's address to be concealed if this is necessary for the protection of the petitioner, for example, where there is a fear of violence from the respondent.

(e) Information about the children of the family. The full names and dates of birth of all children of the family under 18 years must be given; and where there are children of the family of over 18 years, their names should be given together with the words 'over 18 years'.

(f) Information about any other living child born to either party who is not a child of the family. This could cover any children from an extramarital relationship. Details of their full names and dates of birth must be given as above.

(g) Information about any other court proceedings in England and Wales or elsewhere relating to the marriage or to any children of the family, or between the parties regarding any property of either or both. If there have been any earlier proceedings, full details must be given, including any order made and, if the proceedings related to the marriage, whether the parties have lived together since any order was made.

(h) Whether or not any agreement between the parties has been made or is proposed for the support of any party or any child of the family. This statement is needed only if the petition is based on five years' separation (Fact E). It is required in these cases because of the grave financial hardship defence (see **3.4.6.1**). The court therefore needs to know about any existing arrangements or proposals.

(i) Statement that the petitioner applies for a divorce on the ground that the marriage has irretrievably broken down.

(j) Statement of the Fact under s 1(2) of the MCA 1973 relied upon, together with Statement of Case giving details of the incidents relied on, but not the evidence by which these will be proved.

The wording used to describe the incidents relied upon is a drafting matter for the solicitor. However, examples of how the particulars may appear in the petition are as follows:

Fact A – 'In or about November 2011 in Barchester, Wessex the Respondent committed adultery with a person whom the Petitioner does not wish to name'

Fact D – 'The parties separated on 17 February 2010 and have not lived together since that time'

(k) The petition must end with a prayer for the following:

(i) dissolution of the marriage;

(ii) any claim for financial relief which is required. It is important that the petitioner makes an application for all forms of financial order which might be needed in the petition. If this is not done, leave of the court will be required for a later application. The petitioner could also be prejudiced as orders for periodical payments can only be backdated to the date of application, which will be the date of the petition unless leave of the court is needed for a later application when it will be the date of actual application. If the petitioner remarries, he will be prevented from making a claim for a lump sum or property adjustment order. If he had applied in the prayer, ie before remarriage, a hearing could take place after remarriage. There is provision on the standard form to claim financial orders for any children of the family. If a Child Support Agency application is to be made, the court will not usually have jurisdiction to grant periodical payments. However, other forms of financial order, for example a lump sum order, could be applied for;

(iii) a claim for costs if required. In a divorce under Legal Help, costs will only be those of a litigant in person, and therefore it is not usual to ask for costs, especially as there is a risk that if costs are sought the respondent might be sufficiently annoyed to defend the petition. When the petition is drafted, it is not certain whether the proceedings will be defended or not. It is possible to claim costs in the petition but abandon that claim if the divorce proceeds undefended. Where the petitioner is paying privately, costs may be claimed in relation to fault-based divorces. The costs being sought in the prayer will only cover costs incurred in dissolving the marriage. Costs for ancillary matters, for example financial orders, will be sought separately during the financial proceedings.

The prescribed form of divorce petition is signed by the petitioner and details are given of any solicitor acting. If the petitioner is simply receiving advice from a solicitor, for example because he is in receipt of Legal Help and therefore a litigant in person, this must be indicated on the form.

The remainder of the petition lists the names and addresses of persons to be served with the petition and the petitioner's address for service. If there is a co-respondent in a Fact A petition, the co-respondent must be served with the petition, and his address must be added.

The Family Law Protocol requires the petitioner's solicitor in most cases to give the respondent at least seven days' notice of the filing of the petition, and to give the Fact on which the petition will be based together with the Statement of Case. This is to avoid the potential acrimony which could result if the respondent simply received the petition without warning. In practice it is common for the parties' solicitors to agree the contents of the petition in advance with the intention of reducing animosity and ensuring from the outset that the divorce will proceed undefended.

3.9.3.2 Amendments

If an error or omission is discovered in a petition – for example, the prayer does not include an application for financial relief, or the petitioner's domicile is stated incorrectly – it will have to be amended. The petition can be amended without permission of the court, unless an answer has been filed in which case permission is required. After the application for decree nisi, permission of the court will generally be needed for amendments (FPR 2010, r 7.13).

Permission may be given without notice if the respondent agrees to the amendment. If the respondent does not agree, an on notice application to the district judge will have to be made. Whenever a petition is amended after service, the amended petition will have to be served on the respondent (and co-respondent, if any).

In practice, very minor amendments – for example, an incorrect date of birth of a child, or incorrect occupation of a party – can be corrected by referring to the error in the petitioner's affidavit (see **3.9.9**). The district judge can then give permission for the petition to stand as corrected without the need for re-service.

3.9.4 The supporting documents

The following additional documents must be prepared and filed with the petition.

3.9.4.1 Statement relating to the proposed arrangements for any children of the family

The Statement of Arrangements is a standard form which gives details of the children of the family. It provides the court with the information it needs in order to consider the arrangements for the children under s 41 of the MCA 1973. (See **Appendix 3(B)**.)

The Statement of Arrangements covers accommodation, education, child-care arrangements, health, maintenance and arrangements which have been made or which are proposed for contact with the parent with whom the child does not live full time. If the child is disabled or has a medical problem, details will have to be given and, where necessary, be supported by a medical report or doctor's letter confirming the nature of the problem and its likely effect on the child.

If practicable, the Statement of Arrangements should be agreed with the respondent. This should be attempted by sending the completed and signed form to the respondent before filing the petition. The respondent is able to add his agreement and signature before returning the Statement of Arrangements to the petitioner. If the respondent's agreement has not been, or cannot be, obtained then the petitioner can still file the petition. In these circumstances, it would be sensible to file with the Statement of Arrangements a letter explaining the situation to the court.

3.9.4.2 Marriage certificate

If the client cannot produce the original marriage certificate, a certified copy may be obtained on payment of a small fee either from the Superintendent Registrar of Marriages for the district where the marriage took place, or from the General Register Office. If the marriage certificate is in a foreign language, an authenticated translation must also be obtained and filed with the divorce documents.

3.9.4.3 Statement of reconciliation

Where a solicitor is acting for a client, there is an obligation to file a statement of reconciliation which states whether or not the solicitor has discussed with the petitioner the possibility of a reconciliation and has given him details of agencies which are qualified to help effect a reconciliation (FPR 2010, r 7.6).

There is no duty on a solicitor to discuss reconciliation in every case in which he acts, although it will usually be good practice to do so. If he decides not to discuss this matter, he will inform the court of this in the statement.

The obligation to file this statement does not arise if a client is receiving advice under Legal Help as the client is then acting in person. However, this does not prevent a solicitor from advising a client who is receiving advice under Legal Help on reconciliation if appropriate.

3.9.4.4 Service copies of the petition and Statement of Arrangements

It is necessary to file the original petition plus one copy for each party who is to be served. One copy will be sufficient unless a co-respondent is involved in a Fact A petition, in which case two service copies will be needed.

The Statement of Arrangements is served on the respondent even if he has already signed the form and agreed to the arrangements; therefore, the original plus one copy of this form should be filed. It is never served on a co-respondent.

3.9.4.5 Fee or application for exemption from fees

A fee is payable on filing the petition. The client will be exempt from paying the fee if he is in receipt of income support, guaranteed State pension credit or income-based jobseeker's allowance; or his income falls below a threshold and he is receiving working tax credit and child tax credit, or working tax credit with a disability element; or he is receiving Legal Help. If the client would suffer hardship through paying the fee (usually because his income is low), he can apply to the court to have all or part of the fee remitted. However, a form applying for exemption or remission must be completed and filed at court, and supported by financial documentation evidencing the client's means.

3.9.5 Filing

The petition and the appropriate additional documents and fee can be filed at any divorce county court (or the Divorce Registry in London).

3.9.6 Service of the petition

The petition and other appropriate documents must be served on the respondent and any co-respondent (FPR 2010, r 7.8).

3.9.6.1 Usual method of service

The court will usually serve the petition by sending it by first-class post to the address given in the petition.

The court attaches the following to each service copy of the petition:

(a) A Notice of Proceedings. This is a general explanation to the respondent of the divorce procedure with detailed instructions on completing and returning the Acknowledgement of Service.

(b) An Acknowledgement of Service. This is an important procedural document which could furnish proof of service of the petition or of the fact relied on as well as other useful information, for example, whether the respondent intends to defend (see **3.9.7**).

(c) A copy of the Statement of Arrangements for the children. This is attached only to the respondent's copy of the petition.

If the respondent then completes and returns the Acknowledgement of Service to the court, this is proof of service (FPR 2010, r 6.15). When the court receives the Acknowledgement from the respondent, it will send a copy to the petitioner's solicitors.

3.9.6.2 Alternative methods of service

If postal service by the court is unsuccessful or inappropriate, alternative methods of service are available, and proof of service will depend on which method is used.

Personal service

(a) *Service through the petitioner.* Service is carried out through the petitioner. A process server will be instructed, or the petitioner's solicitors will themselves serve the documents. The Rules prohibit the petitioner himself from serving the documents on the respondent (FPR 2010, r 6.5(3)). Proof of service in these cases will be by certificate of service by whoever served the documents.

(b) *By court bailiff.* The petitioner may request bailiff service by lodging the appropriate form (FPR 2010, r 6.9). A fee is payable unless the petitioner has filed an exemption form. A request for bailiff service must be accompanied by evidence that postal service has already failed or an explanation as to why postal service is not appropriate. A description of the respondent, normally a photograph, must also be lodged in order to enable the bailiff to identify the respondent. The bailiff will then serve the documents personally and file a certificate of service. If the Acknowledgement of Service is then returned by the respondent, this will be proof of service; if not, the bailiff 's certificate will be used. A request for bailiff service will rarely be granted where the petitioner is legally represented, as it is unlikely that the petitioner will be able to demonstrate the need to serve by bailiff rather than by process server.

Deemed service

If the respondent does not return the Acknowledgement of Service to the court, the petitioner can apply for deemed service if he can satisfy the court that the respondent has in fact received the petition (FPR 2010, r 6.16).

An application without notice should be made to the district judge supported by evidence showing why the petitioner is of the view that the respondent has received the petition. This can be done by using evidence from a third party, or, for example, even from the petitioner himself that the respondent read the petition and then threw it away, or an open letter from solicitors instructed by the respondent to act for him referring to the petition.

Service by alternative means

Service by alternative method or at an alternative place will be relevant when all the petitioner's efforts to serve by post and personal service have failed and there is insufficient evidence to apply for deemed service.

An application should be supported by evidence setting out the attempts made to serve personally/by post and the basis on which alternative means are thought likely to be successful (FPR 2010, Practice Direction 6A, para 6.2).

If the order is granted, it will specify the alternative method to be used. This could be by advertisement if there is a reasonable likelihood that it will come to the respondent's notice, for example by placing it in a newspaper which he is known to read regularly. Another method that could be specified is service on another person, for example a relative whom he visits regularly, or a person with whom he lives or works.

An application for service by alternative means may also be used retrospectively. If the respondent has in fact already received the papers by some alternative means, an application may be made for this to be accepted as good service (FPR 2010, r 6.19(2)).

Dispensing with service

Dispensing with service is used only as a last resort where all other methods have failed and the district judge is of the opinion that it is impracticable to serve the petition (FPR 2010, r 6.20). It is treated by the court very seriously as, by granting the order, the respondent can find that he is divorced without knowing that a divorce petition had been filed and having had no opportunity to defend. An application without notice should be made to the court setting out the grounds for the application (ie why there is a problem and what has been done to trace the respondent). The district judge can require the petitioner to attend to give evidence. Service will be dispensed with only where the petitioner can show that every effort has been made to trace the respondent.

3.9.6.3 Other problems with service

Finding the respondent

If the petitioner does not know the whereabouts of the respondent, enquiries must be made so that postal or personal service can be used. If particular difficulty is encountered, reference should be made to the *Practice Direction (Family Division: Disclosure of Addresses by Government Departments)* [1989] 1 All ER 765. This enables the court to request a search for the respondent's address in the records of the Department of Work and Pensions or the Passport Service. If the respondent is in the Armed Services, the relevant service department can be asked for the respondent's address.

Serving on the co-respondent

The petition must also be served on any co-respondent. The co-respondent is not served with a copy of the statement of arrangements for the children. The same methods of service are available as for the respondent.

Service of the petition must also be proved, and this will normally be done by the co-respondent returning the completed Acknowledgement of Service to the court. If this is not done, another method of proving service will have to be used, for example, a certificate of service following bailiff service or personal service. Otherwise an order for deemed service, service by alternative means or, as a last resort, an order dispensing with service will have to be obtained.

Service outside England and Wales

The divorce petition may be served outside England and Wales. Special rules apply and reference should be made to FPR 2010, Pt 6 and Practice Direction 6B.

Service on children and protected parties

The court cannot serve the petition if the respondent is a minor (under 18 years of age) or a protected party (eg someone who lacks capacity). Special rules apply and reference should be made to r 6.14 of the FPR 2010.

3.9.7 Return of the Acknowledgement of Service

The respondent is required to complete and return the Acknowledgement of Service to the court within seven days of service of the petition (FPR 2010, r 7.12(1)).

The respondent is given guidance as to how to complete this form in the Notice of Proceedings. He may also have instructed his own solicitors. When the court sends a copy of the Acknowledgement of Service to the petitioner, the replies to the straightforward questions it contains may reveal the following information:

(a) Proof of service (see **3.9.6**).

(b) Whether the respondent intends to defend the petition. Since the reply is not binding on the respondent, he can later change his mind.

(c) Whether the respondent is satisfied with the proposals in the Statement of Arrangements for the children. Again, he is not bound by his reply and can commence an application under CA 1989 even if he has not indicated this in his reply.

(d) Whether the respondent has admitted adultery or consented to the decree. If the petition is based on Fact A, the respondent can admit the adultery and, provided he has signed the form personally, this will be sufficient proof of his adultery. If the petition is based on Fact D and the respondent has given his consent in this form, this will be proof of his consent, provided he has signed the form personally.

3.9.8 Application for decree nisi

Provided the respondent has not given notice of intention to defend and a period of seven days after service of the petition has expired, the next step is for the petitioner's solicitors to file an application for decree nisi, together with an affidavit containing proof of the fact relied on and other essential matters. If the respondent has given a notice of intention to defend, the petitioner must wait 28 days from service of the petition to file an application for decree nisi.

3.9.9 Petitioner's affidavit in support of the petition

The petitioner's affidavit in support of the petition is filed with the application for decree nisi. The Rules provide standard form affidavits to suit each Fact (see FPR 2010, Practice Direction 5, Forms D80A–E). The affidavit is in question and answer form. The main matters which are dealt with are as follows:

(a) The petitioner must confirm that the contents of his petition are true and that no amendments or alterations are required.

(b) If the parties have cohabited since the date of the incidents relied on, the affidavit requires the petitioner to give details of the periods of cohabitation to ensure that the fact is not barred by s 2 of the MCA 1973.

(c) The Acknowledgement of Service will need to be attached if the petitioner is relying on it as proof of service, or if it has been signed by the respondent to admit adultery (Fact A), or to consent to the divorce (Fact D).

(d) The petitioner must confirm that the contents of the Statement of Arrangements for the children are still correct and identify the signature of the respondent on that form.

3.9.10 Directions for hearing

On receipt of the application for decree nisi the court will check the following:

(a) that the petition has been served. The district judge will check that proof of service is evident from the documents lodged. If the petitioner is relying on return of the Acknowledgement of Service and it is a case where this has been signed personally by the respondent, the court will check that the petitioner's affidavit identifies the respondent's signature;

(b) that the case is undefended. The case will be undefended if:

   (i) the respondent has told the court that he does not intend to defend (usually in the Acknowledgement of Service), or

   (ii) no notice of intention has been given and seven days have elapsed since service of the petition, or

   (iii) the respondent has filed a notice of intention to defend but the time limit for filing the answer has expired. Rule 7.12(8) of the FPR 2010 provides that this time limit is 28 days from the date of service of the petition;

(c) if the petition relies on Fact D, that the respondent's consent has been given. Consent may be given either in the Acknowledgement of Service, or in a separate document.

If all the above matters are satisfied, the court will consider the evidence of the petitioner on the court file and in particular the petition, Statement of Arrangements, the Acknowledgement of Service, the petitioner's affidavit and any exhibits. If the court is satisfied that the petitioner is entitled to a decree nisi it will do the following:

(a) direct that the application for the decree nisi be listed before a district judge for the making of the decree nisi on the next available date (FPR 2010, r 7.20);

(b) if there is a prayer for costs in the petition, make a direction for costs if it considers that the petitioner is entitled to them, or if not so satisfied, make no direction as to costs.

The court will then send a notice of the date on which the decree nisi will be granted, together with any direction as to costs, to both parties. If either party objects to the direction as to costs, he must give notice not less than two days before the decree nisi hearing of his wish to make representations at the hearing (FPR 2010, r 7.20).

If the court is not satisfied that the petitioner has proved his case, it may:

(a) ask for further evidence. This could clarify, for example, an uncertainty revealed in the petition relating to domicile or habitual residence, or an ambiguity in the petitioner's affidavit relating to any period during which the petitioner cohabited with the respondent;

(b) list the case for a case management hearing.

If there is a problem which cannot be resolved by supplying further information, eg a question of whether there was sufficient behaviour to amount to grounds for a Fact B divorce or a complex jurisdictional issue, the court will set a procedure and timetable as to how to progress the case. This could lead to a hearing to resolve the problem. If the problem is resolved and the ground for divorce is proved, the decree nisi will be made at the hearing. If not, the petition will be dismissed.

3.9.11 Section 41 certificate

Before the court can direct that the decree nisi be listed for hearing, it will consider the question of the arrangements for children to whom s 41 of the MCA 1973 applies (see **3.5**).

3.9.11.1 Where there is no pending application for an order under the Children Act 1989

If there has been no application under the CA 1989 made by either party, there being no dispute between the parties as to arrangements for the children, the district judge will examine the Statement of Arrangements and check that the arrangements proposed are acceptable. When he has done this, he can certify that either:

(a) there are no children of the family to whom s 41 applies; or

(b) there are such children, but that the court need not exercise its powers under the CA 1989.

If, having considered the Statement of Arrangements, he is not satisfied that the arrangements are satisfactory, he can give one of the following directions:

(a) that the parties file further evidence as to the arrangements for the children (eg a medical report);

(b) that a welfare report be prepared;

(c) that either party, or both parties, attend before him.

The evidence so obtained might satisfy the district judge that in fact the arrangements are satisfactory, in which case he can issue a certificate that there is no need for the court to exercise its powers under the CA 1989.

If, on his initial consideration, or having made directions and further investigations the district judge considers that:

(a) the exercise of his powers is, or is likely to be, necessary but the court is not in a position to exercise them without further consideration; and

(b) there are exceptional circumstances which make it desirable in the interests of the child to do so,

then he may direct that the decree nisi of divorce is not made absolute until the court directs.

This power will be used very rarely, and only if delaying the decree will actually be in the interests of the child. This might apply where both parents were happy to proceed with the divorce but had not attempted to make arrangements for the children; withholding the decree absolute could persuade them of the seriousness of their behaviour.

3.9.11.2 Where there are pending proceedings under the Children Act 1989

Where an application has already been made under the CA 1989, it is open to the district judge either to grant a certificate under s 41 of the MCA 1973 enabling the divorce to go ahead, or to delay the grant of the decree absolute by making a direction that there are exceptional circumstances making it desirable to delay the grant of the decree absolute.

3.9.12 Decree nisi

The decree nisi (or conditional order for civil partners) will be read out on the appointed day by the judge or district judge in open court. However, unless there is any dispute as to costs, neither party need attend. A copy of the decree nisi is sent to the parties. This decree does not dissolve the marriage.

3.9.13 Decree absolute

The final step in the undefended divorce procedure is to obtain the decree absolute (or dissolution order for civil partners) which will end the marriage.

3.9.13.1 Petitioner's notice

Once six weeks have elapsed since the grant of the decree nisi, the petitioner can give notice that he wishes the decree nisi to be made absolute (FPR 2010, r 7.32). In extremely rare cases, the court does have the power to reduce this six-week period (*Practice Direction (Divorce: Decree Absolute: Application to Expedite)* [1977] 2 All ER 714). However, when urgency is anticipated it is better to speed up the earlier part of the divorce proceedings rather than relying on this power.

The client may qualify for exemption or remission of the fee in the same circumstances as on the filing of the petition (see **3.9.4.5**).

The district judge will grant the decree absolute, provided that the matters set out in r 7.32(2) of the FPR 2010 are satisfied, for example:

(a) that there is no appeal relating to the decree nisi;

(b) that the provisions enabling the respondent's financial position to be considered under s 10(2)–(4) of the MCA 1973 do not apply or have been complied with;

(c) that the court has complied with s 41 of the MCA 1973 and there is no direction to delay the decree absolute;

(d) that any order under s 10A of the MCA 1973 has been complied with (see **3.9.14.3**).

In the case of *Miller-Smith* v *Miller-Smith (No 2)* [2010] 2 FLR 351 the court decided that, in addition to the statutory grounds for delaying the decree absolute to be found in the MCA 1973, the court also has a discretionary power under its inherent jurisdiction to stay or delay the decree absolute. However, the court emphasised that this is a power to be exercised in 'special and exceptional' circumstances.

The decree absolute certificate is sent to the petitioner and the respondent. The marriage is now dissolved.

It is important not to seek to obtain the decree absolute automatically after the six-week period as there could be good reasons to delay. For example, it might be important to preserve the petitioner's right of occupation under the FLA 1996 (see **9.6.2.1**), or to preserve pension rights until a pension sharing order becomes effective, or even at this late stage the petitioner might be considering a reconciliation.

If the petitioner delays obtaining the decree absolute for more than 12 months after the decree nisi, the notice must be accompanied by a written explanation for the delay. This is to ensure that there has not been an attempted reconciliation which may have prejudiced the grounds, and that no child has been born who should be considered under s 41 of the MCA 1973.

3.9.13.2 Respondent's application

The petitioner may choose not to obtain the decree absolute for the reasons mentioned above, or perhaps where the petitioner knows that the respondent is anxious to remarry and wishes to use the delay as a negotiating weapon in the financial proceedings. In this situation, the respondent can apply for the decree absolute once a period of some four and a half months has elapsed from the date of the decree nisi (ie three months after the earliest date (ie six weeks after decree nisi) on which the petitioner could have obtained the decree absolute) (MCA 1973, s 9(2)). The petitioner must be served with notice of the application. The court will then consider the respondent's application and any objections that the petitioner has made. The court can then decide to make the decree absolute, require further investigations or, if necessary, rescind the decree nisi (FPR 2010, r 7.33).

3.9.13.3 Religious marriages

Historically, some family clients have found themselves in the difficult position of being divorced in law and yet their marriage remains intact according to their own religious rules and customs, usually because the other party refuses to co-operate in ending the marriage according to religious practices. The Divorce (Religious Marriages) Act 2002 inserted provisions into the MCA 1973 designed to overcome this problem. Section 10A applies where the parties have been married according to particular religious usages and must co-operate if the marriage is to be dissolved according to those usages. The court may, on application by either party, order that the decree nisi is not to be made absolute until such time as the parties produce a declaration to the court confirming that they have taken such steps as are necessary to dissolve the marriage according to the appropriate religious usages.

3.10 Defended divorces

As defended divorces are so rare, the detail of defended procedure is outside the scope of this book and reference should be made to specialist textbooks.

If the respondent intends to defend, he will normally return the Acknowledgement of Service stating that he intends to defend the petition. He must give this notice within seven days from service of the petition (FPR 2010, r 7.12(1)).

If he does not file this notice, he can still file an answer. If he does give notice, he is under no obligation to file an answer if he changes his mind. The answer is the defence to the petition and must be filed within 28 days of service of the petition (FPR 2010, r 7.12(8)).

Where a divorce becomes defended, the court will fix a case management hearing for the purpose of deciding how to progress the case. The court will set a procedure and a timetable using its general case management powers in Pt 4 of the FPR 2010, ultimately leading to a hearing in open court.

3.11 Costs

On an application for costs, the decision is always in the discretion of the court, but the general principle is that an order for costs will be made in favour of the successful party. Sometimes such applications are not made, or are expressed as to be pursued only if the divorce is defended. This is particularly common where the divorce is not fault-based and it is thought that to pursue costs would introduce animosity into the proceedings, or where the petitioner is a litigant in person and it may be uneconomic to pursue costs of only a small amount.

3.12 Divorce law and procedure in the future

Some would argue that divorce law based on a statute enacted in 1973 is now hopelessly out of step with modern family life. Certainly, at various times over the last 35 years there have been numerous calls for, and even attempts at, reform. The FLA 1996, for example, as originally envisaged would have brought a radically different divorce regime into being. However, these changes were eventually abandoned, and those parts of the Act that would have introduced them were never implemented. Recently, calls for the reform of divorce law have been renewed with, for example, Resolution launching a campaign for the introduction of 'no fault' divorce. The Government is now considering divorce law and procedure as part of the Family Justice Review.

3.13 Chapter summary

3.13.1 Divorce law

(1) No divorce proceedings can begin until one year after the marriage. Decrees of nullity and judicial separation can be sought at any time after the marriage.

(2) The English courts will have jurisdiction to hear a divorce only if one of the grounds in s 5 of the Domicile and Matrimonial Proceedings Act 1973 is satisfied (these relate to the parties' habitual residence or domicile).

(3) The only ground for divorce is that the marriage has broken down irretrievably.

(4) One or more of 'the five facts' must be proved:

Fact A: Adultery and Intolerability (not applicable to civil partners)

Fact B: Behaviour

Fact C: Desertion

Fact D: Two Years' Separation and Consent

Fact E: Five Years' Separation.

(5) Section 10(2) of the MCA 1973 enables a respondent in a Fact D or Fact E divorce to ask the court to consider his financial position after the divorce.

(6) Section 5(1) of the MCA 1973 is a defence to a Fact E divorce. The respondent must prove that the divorce would result in grave financial or other hardship and it would be wrong to dissolve the marriage.

(7) Section 41 of the MCA 1973 imposes a duty in divorce proceedings to consider the welfare of any 'child of the family'.

(8) A decree of nullity can declare that a marriage either never existed at all (a void marriage), or that it did exist but, due to certain circumstances, it has been ended (a voidable marriage).

(9) A decree of judicial separation can be obtained by proving one of the five facts.

3.13.2 Divorce procedure

UNDEFENDED DIVORCE: PROCEDURE CHECKLIST

PETITIONER	RESPONDENT
(1) Files at court: (a) Marriage certificate; (b) Petition + copy(ies); (c) Statement of Arrangements + copy (this should be sent to respondent for signature before filing); (d) Statement of reconciliation (only if solicitor on court record); (e) Fee or application for exemption.	
(2) Receives from court notification of case number allocated.	
	(3) Receives from court: (a) Copy petition; (b) Copy Statement of Arrangements; (c) Notice of Proceedings; (d) Acknowledgement of Service.
	(4) Returns completed Acknowledgement of Service to court.
(5) Receives from court photocopy of completed Acknowledgement of Service.	
(6) Files at court: (a) Application for decree nisi; (b) Affidavit of Evidence + exhibits.	
	(7) *Both* parties receive from court: a copy of s 41 certificate and notice of the date fixed for pronouncement of decree nisi in open court by judge/district judge.
	(8) Decree nisi pronounced – parties need not attend unless directed.
	(9) *Both* parties would be notified of any directions made by court if district judge not satisfied with arrangements for children, eg further information or appointment at court.
	(10) *Both* parties receive from court copy of decree nisi.
(11) Petitioner files notice for decree nisi to be made absolute (after 6 weeks from grant of decree nisi) and the fee (if appropriate).	
	(12) *Both* parties receive from court copy decree absolute.

Chapter 4
Financial Orders: The Law

4.1	Introduction	47
4.2	The powers of the court	47
4.3	Income orders	48
4.4	Capital orders	50
4.5	Deciding what orders to make	52
4.6	The clean break	62
4.7	Pensions on divorce	64
4.8	Financial cases in the future	66
4.9	Financial provision during marriage	66
4.10	Chapter summary	68

4.1 Introduction

This chapter deals with the law relating to financial provision on marriage breakdown. It covers the range of financial orders available to spouses under the MCA 1973 and to civil partners under the CPA 2004, and the principles applied by the court when making those orders. This chapter also deals with the wide range of orders available for children under the MCA 1973. However, in the majority of cases, maintenance for children is now governed by the Child Support Act 1991 (CSA 1991) to the exclusion of the MCA 1973. The CSA 1991 will be considered in **Chapter 7**. However, as financial provision between spouses is closely linked with provision for any children, it is important to appreciate the impact of the CSA 1991 on orders made by the court under the MCA 1973.

A significant minority of maintenance applications for children will continue to be dealt with by the court, and the court also retains sole jurisdiction to make lump sum and property adjustment orders in favour of children.

It should also be borne in mind that the nature of the civil partnership family is such that it may not fall under the provisions of the CSA 1991, for example because the potential payer is not the child's parent. Therefore it is more likely to prove necessary for a civil partner to turn to the court for financial orders for children than is the case for a spouse.

4.2 The powers of the court

4.2.1 Orders available

The powers of the court to make financial orders are found in ss 22 to 24B of the MCA 1973 (see **Appendix 1(A)**). The orders fall into two main categories: income orders and capital orders. The *income orders* are:

(a) maintenance pending suit;

(b) periodical payments;

(c) secured periodical payments.

The *capital orders* are more diverse and include:

(a) lump sum orders;

(b) property adjustment orders (for property to be transferred or held on trust);

(c) orders for sale;

(d) pension sharing orders;

(e) pension sharing compensation orders.

4.2.2 When available

Spouses may apply for any of these orders, or indeed all of them, on or after the filing of the divorce petition. However, with the exception of maintenance pending suit (MPS), the application cannot be heard until decree nisi and no order will take effect until decree absolute. By contrast, most applications for provision for children may be made and heard at any time, and such orders take immediate effect.

AVAILABILITY OF FINANCIAL ORDERS

Petition	*Decree nisi*	*Decree absolute*
Application for financial provision can be made	Order for financial provision for spouse can be made	Order for financial provision can come into effect ——► (Periodical payments can be back-dated to the date of the application)
Order for MPS for spouse can be made and take effect	——►	MPS ends
Order for financial provision for child(ren) can be made and take effect	———	——►

In most cases, the arrangements for financial provision for a spouse are finalised after the divorce itself has gone through. However, parties should take care to apply for financial provision before remarrying, because after they have remarried they are no longer entitled to apply (see MCA 1973, s 28(3) in **Appendix 1(A)** and **10.5.2**).

4.3 Income orders

4.3.1 Maintenance pending suit

An order for periodical payments for a spouse cannot take effect until decree absolute. However, the client may be in urgent need of money before then. Such clients may wish to apply for MPS under s 22 of the the MCA 1973 (the equivalent for civil partners is maintenance pending the outcome of dissolution proceedings). As the name suggests, MPS is an order for regular payments designed to tide a spouse over until the divorce is determined. At that time, an order for full periodical payments may take effect. In practice, however, the court will often not hear a financial application until some time after decree absolute is granted. If this would cause hardship to the applicant, an application for an interim periodical payments order could be made.

The application for MPS may be made, heard and take effect at any time after the petition has been filed. Any order will terminate on the grant or dismissal of the divorce. MPS is not available for a child; neither is it necessary, because periodical payments may be obtained for a child of the family (if appropriate) as soon as the petition is filed, or alternatively an application may be made to the Child Support Agency for a maintenance assessment.

Such MPS applications are not frequently pursued, as potential applicants often prefer to rely on welfare benefits. There are a number of reasons for this:

(a) Most applicants will require Legal Aid in order to make an application. This inevitably causes delay, so that, in any event, the applicant has to resort to welfare benefits in the interim.

(b) In practice, the court generally orders only modest sums to be paid, because the purpose of MPS is to provide adequate temporary provision during the proceedings. However, in *TL v ML and Others* [2006] 1 FLR 465 it was stressed that 'reasonableness' (which the judge equated with fairness) was the approach to be adopted when quantifying MPS and that the marital standard of living was an important factor in achieving 'reasonableness'.

(c) If the maintenance is so small that it has to be supplemented by income support or jobseeker's allowance, there is no advantage to the applicant as her benefit will be reduced by the maintenance pound for pound (see **Chapter 6**).

(d) There may be enforcement problems, especially in the early stages of the divorce, if a reluctant respondent or an aggrieved petitioner is still struggling to come to terms with the divorce or his responsibility to maintain the other party (or both).

(e) There may be a risk that an application for MPS might jeopardise the prospects of an uncontested divorce, or negotiations over the final settlement.

Despite its drawbacks, MPS may be worth pursuing, particularly if a party with ample means leaves another with onerous responsibilities and no ability to meet them.

4.3.2 Periodical payments

Periodical payments usually take the form of weekly or monthly sums. Periodical payments may be paid to a spouse (MCA 1973, s 23(1)(a)), or, in exceptional cases, to a child of the family (see CSA 1991, s 8(3), discussed at **7.4**) or to the spouse caring for the child on that child's behalf (MCA 1973, s 23(1)(d)). Periodical payments may be ordered for children even if the divorce petition is dismissed, either at the time of dismissal or within a reasonable period after the dismissal.

All periodical payments to a party terminate on the death or remarriage of the recipient. Unsecured periodical payments terminate on the death of the paying spouse (MCA 1973, s 28). A periodical payments order (PPO) is unaffected by the remarriage of the payer, save that remarriage could prompt an application to discharge (or reduce) the order if the payer would then be supporting his new spouse.

The court may limit the term of the PPO to years or months if it considers that a party should be able to become independent after a period of adjustment, for example, to allow a wife to retrain and obtain employment. The court is under a duty to consider whether such a limitation on maintenance is feasible (see MCA 1973, s 25A(2) and **4.6.2.1**).

In the few cases where the court has jurisdiction to make a PPO in favour of a child, it will terminate on the child's 17th birthday unless it is in the child's interest for it to continue until he is 18 (see MCA 1973, s 29, in **Appendix 1(A)**). The usual reason for such an extension is that the child will be continuing with full-time education.

The maintenance may continue beyond a child's 18th birthday only if the circumstances in s 29(3) apply, ie:

(a) the child is (or intends to be) in further education, academic or vocational; or

(b) there are special circumstances, for example, the child has a mental disability.

4.3.3 Secured periodical payments (MCA 1973, s 23(1)(b) and (e))

A party may be ordered to secure periodical payments which are payable to the other party or a child of the family. This is a device to ensure that the recipient will continue to receive the periodical payments even if the payer's income fluctuates, or if problems of enforcement are anticipated. Secured PPOs work by charging an asset with a sum fixed by the court from which the periodical payments can be met. Typically, that asset will be income producing, for example, shares or rented property. The income yielded by the charged asset will be paid to the recipient up to the amount specified in the PPO. Alternatively, a non-income producing asset such as a valuable painting, could be secured. If the periodical payments were not made from other sources, the asset would be liable to be sold and the proceeds used to pay the sum secured.

Secured PPOs terminate in the same circumstances as unsecured PPOs, save for one exception: unlike ordinary PPOs, secured PPOs do not terminate on the death of the payer. However, his death would be taken into account on any application by his estate to vary or discharge the order.

4.4 Capital orders

The purpose of capital orders is to settle once and for all any disputes in respect of the couple's capital. For most couples the matrimonial home represents the main, if not the only, family capital. This is considered in detail in **Chapter 9**. Some couples will, of course, have considerable assets in addition to the home, including savings, securities, etc which may be the subject of a lump sum order, a property adjustment order, an order for sale or, in the case of pensions, a pension sharing order or pension sharing compensation order.

4.4.1 Lump sum orders

Under s 23(1)(c) and (f) of the MCA 1973, the court can order a party to pay to the other, or to a child of the family, a cash lump sum. There are two main reasons for making such an order:

(a) to adjust the final division of the parties' assets. The order is frequently used in conjunction with an order dealing with the matrimonial home;

(b) to recompense the applicant for expenses incurred prior to the application as a result of inadequate support from the respondent for the applicant or a child of the family.

A spouse is entitled to apply for one lump sum order only (although see **11.8.1**, which deals with the court's power to make a second lump sum or property adjustment order on an application for variation or discharge of a periodical payments or a secured periodical payments order). The lump sum order may specify payment by several instalments. In common with the other capital orders, a lump sum order cannot be varied. However, there is jurisdiction to deal with an application to vary, suspend and even to discharge instalments of a lump sum. Where the court orders payment of the lump sum to be by instalments or to be deferred, for example to allow the payer time to raise the money, it may order interest to be paid at a specified rate. There is also power to secure payment of the instalments in the same way as for periodical payments.

It is sometimes the case that although there may be no funds immediately available for the payment of a lump sum, it is anticipated that money will be forthcoming. Examples include an expected dissolution of a partnership, or maturity of an insurance policy releasing capital. In such a case, the court may adjourn an application, although it will do so only where there is a real likelihood of a change of circumstances within a relatively short period. The court has said that an application should not be adjourned for longer than about five years (see *Roberts v Roberts* [1986] 2 FLR 152). It has also refused applications for adjournment based on a party's hopes of inheritance on the grounds that it was too uncertain whether and when the inheritance would occur (see *Michael v Michael* [1986] 2 FLR 389 and **4.5.1.2**).

Lump sum orders are also available for children. Whilst they are not common, they may be appropriate in high income families or if a child has a special need, for example he is disabled or has special educational needs. Unlike for spouses, more than one lump sum order can be made for a child, so several orders could be made over a period of time. The Child Support Agency has no jurisdiction to make capital awards for children.

4.4.2 Property adjustment orders

Under s 24 of the MCA 1973, the court has wide powers to redistribute family property between the parties and the children of the family. It may do so by ordering that property be transferred, for example, from one party to the other, or held on trust. Such orders are intended to be final. Consequently, no application may be made (not even for a child) for further property adjustment, neither is it possible to vary these orders (but, again, see **11.8.1** on the court's powers to make a property adjustment order on a variation of a periodical payments order).

4.4.3 Orders for sale

The court has power under s 24A of the MCA 1973 to order a sale of any property in which either party is beneficially entitled. The court can make this order only once it has also made one of the following orders:

(a) a secured periodical payments order;

(b) a lump sum order;

(c) a property adjustment order.

The order for sale may be made at the same time as the above orders or later. The order cannot take effect until decree absolute. The court has power to order that the sale shall not take place until a specified event has taken place or period has expired. For example, it may order that the property in question is not to be sold until essential works on it have been completed. Alternatively, the court may defer the sale to enable a party wishing to avoid the sale and remain in the property (or keep the car/shares, etc) to raise a lump sum to 'buy out' the other party's interest.

Orders for sale may also be used as a method of enforcement by ordering the sale of an asset if the owner has defaulted on a lump sum order (see **Chapter 11**).

The order for sale may contain consequential and supplementary provisions, directing, for example, how the sale price is to be fixed, or who should have the conduct of the sale.

If a party owns property jointly with another person, for example where a husband and his new partner are co-owners of a flat, the court must give the third party, here the partner, the opportunity to make representations on the matter before it decides whether to order the sale of the property. Alternatively, it may be, say, that the partner is living in a property but has no interest in it. In such a case, the s 24A order may include a consequential direction that she is to be given first refusal on the property before it is placed on the open market.

Although ss 24 and 24A apply to all types of property, for most families the matrimonial home is the most significant asset and, therefore, the issue on which feelings often run high. There are various ways of resolving disputes over the home and these are considered in detail in **Chapter 9**.

4.4.4 Pension sharing orders and pension sharing compensation orders

The court can make pension sharing orders under s 24B of the MCA 1973. The benefits which have accrued to one party under a pension scheme can be a valuable asset and yet they are not realisable until the pension scheme member reaches retirement. A pension sharing order enables the court to divide the pension rights between the parties at the time of the divorce. Pension sharing orders are considered further at **4.7.3**.

The Pensions Act 2008 inserted further provisions into the MCA 1973 which enable the court to make pension compensation sharing orders. These orders enable the court to divide compensation payments made by the Pension Protection Fund. The Fund was set up by the Government to compensate members of pension schemes which have failed.

4.5 Deciding what orders to make

The court has a great deal of discretion and flexibility when deciding on the appropriate division of matrimonial assets on divorce.

When the court is considering provision, whether for the parties to the marriage or for a child of the family, it must begin by considering the statutory criteria laid down in s 25 of the MCA 1973 (in **Appendix 1(A)**).

Section 25(1) states:

> It shall be the duty of the court in deciding whether to exercise its powers under sections 23, 24 or 24A above and, if so, in what manner, to have regard to all the circumstances of the case, first consideration being given to the welfare while a minor of any child of the family who has not attained the age of eighteen.

The section goes on to list factors applicable to provision for spouses (s 25(2)), children of the family (s 25(3)) and further factors for children of the family who are not natural children of both parties (s 25(4)). Those factors are examined below.

Section 25 does not represent an exhaustive list of factors. Indeed, s 25(1) makes it plain that the court must take into account 'all the circumstances of the case'. Thus, the interests of third parties, for example a party's new partner and children, will also be taken into account. A separation agreement or pre-nuptial agreement previously entered into by the parties (see *G v G (Financial Provision: Separation Agreement)* [2000] 2 FLR 18 and *Radmacher v Granatino* [2010] UKSC 42) would also be considered as part of 'all the circumstances'.

Any significant feature of the case not covered elsewhere can be considered. For example, the case of *A v T (Ancillary Relief: Cultural Factors)* [2004] 1 FLR 977 was unusual on its facts. An Iranian national living in England married an Iranian woman under a marriage contract entered into in Iran. The marriage ended after seven weeks and divorce proceedings were brought in England. In deciding the financial application the court found the cultural background of the parties to be a dominant factor, justifying the court taking into account (and indeed largely following) the way in which the courts of Iran would have dealt with such a case.

4.5.1 Provision for a spouse

Section 25(2) of the MCA 1973 lists the following eight factors to be considered by the court when dealing with financial orders for a spouse:

> (a) the income, earning capacity, property and other financial resources which each of the parties to the marriage has or is likely to have in the foreseeable future [but see s 25B and **4.7.2.1**], including in the case of earning capacity any increase in that capacity which it would be in the opinion of the court reasonable to expect a party to the marriage to take steps to acquire;
>
> (b) the financial needs, obligations and responsibilities which each of the parties to the marriage has or is likely to have in the foreseeable future;
>
> (c) the standard of living enjoyed by the family before the breakdown of the marriage;
>
> (d) the age of each party to the marriage and the duration of the marriage;
>
> (e) any physical or mental disability of either of the parties to the marriage;
>
> (f) the contributions which each of the parties has made or is likely in the foreseeable future to make to the welfare of the family, including any contribution by looking after the home or caring for the family;
>
> (g) the conduct of each of the parties, if that conduct is such that it would in the opinion of the court be inequitable to disregard it;
>
> (h) in the case of proceedings for divorce or nullity of marriage any benefit which, by reason of the dissolution or annulment of the marriage, that party will lose the chance of acquiring.

4.5.1.1 The courts' approach

Over the last decade there has been something of a re-evaluation of the approach taken by the courts when exercising their powers under s 25. That process began in the landmark case of *White v White* [2000] 2 FLR 981. Until that point, in very broad terms, the courts' approach had been that on marriage breakdown the entitlement of the financially weaker party (usually the wife) was to have her reasonable needs or requirements met, and nothing further. That approach was abandoned in *White*, where the House of Lords said that the courts should not focus exclusively on one factor in this way. Lord Nichols of Birkenhead stated, 'the objective must be to achieve a fair outcome'. All the s 25 factors are ranked equally at the outset and just gain or lose importance in each case, according to the relevant facts of that particular case and what seems to be fair between the parties.

Although emphasising 'fairness', the House of Lords rejected the idea of a presumption, or starting point, of equal division, preferring to leave it to the judge in each particular case to go through the exercise of weighing up all the s 25 factors. Significantly, though, Lord Nichols did go on to say:

> Before reaching a firm conclusion and making an order along these lines, a judge would always be well advised to check his tentative views against the yardstick of equality of division. As a general rule, equality should be departed from only if, and to the extent that, there is a good reason for doing so.

Mrs White was eventually awarded approximately 40% of the total net assets. The 'good reason' to depart from equality in her case was that Mr White's father had loaned the couple some money when they started out, without which they would not have been able to buy the first farm.

The House of Lords expanded on this approach in *Miller v Miller*; *McFarlane v McFarlane* [2006] UKHL 24. The House of Lords said that the general principles to be applied when making financial awards were 'needs, compensation and sharing'. It was recognised that in many cases, of necessity, achieving fairness did not go beyond the stage of dividing the assets so as to try to meet the parties' housing and financial needs, and that often those assets were insufficient to provide adequately for the needs of two homes. However, in appropriate cases fairness demanded that the court should exercise its discretion so as to compensate one party and redress the economic disparity between the parties arising from the way in which they had conducted their marriage. The House of Lords went on to state that there was additionally an 'equal sharing' principle deriving from the basic concept of equality which underlies modern marriages. Echoing his words in *White*, Lord Nichols said that 'when their partnership ends each is entitled to receive an equal share of the assets of the partnership unless there is a good reason to the contrary'.

Subsequent cases have wrestled with these principles of 'needs, compensation and sharing'. There has been much comment and debate on the order in which they should be addressed, the balance to be struck between them and how they should be applied to particular assets. In *Robson v Robson* [2010] EWCA Civ 1771, the Court of Appeal took the opportunity to issue a timely reminder that the focus must be on s 25, where Parliament had set out the factors to be considered. The Court went on to say that the objective is to achieve a just result and that 'needs, compensation and sharing' would inform and usually guide that search for fairness.

White and *Miller and McFarlane* were 'big money' cases where resources exceeded the parties' needs. Whilst the principles expressed in these cases are of universal application, the reality in many cases will be that most of the resources are required to meet the parties' basic needs (eg, to house the children and the spouse primarily caring for them), and this will provide good reason to depart from equality. In the case of *B v B* [2008] 2 FLR 1627 the court said that fairness is not necessarily the same as equality. Fairness will always depend on the individual facts of the case.

4.5.1.2 Resources

Although the statute does not list the factors in any specific order of importance, it is clear that generally the determining factor will be the parties' resources, income and capital. This is as much the case for PPOs as for lump sums and property adjustment orders. Whilst it is convenient to consider the various orders for financial provision separately, in reality the orders interrelate. For example, a husband with a high income may be able to transfer the home to his wife because he is able to raise a mortgage to purchase a new home for himself, but this would be a sensible solution only if the wife has enough income to finance the costs of running her home.

The court will take into account the parties' income from all sources. Earnings are the starting point. Fringe benefits, such as a company car, free petrol, paid telephone bills, etc, will also be taken into account.

As well as looking at actual earnings, the court will also consider potential earnings. When assessing a party's earning capacity the court will take a realistic approach. If a wife has qualifications which are in demand and has recent work experience, the court will bear in mind her ability to earn a living taking into account her commitments to the children. Before deciding on a party's earning capacity, the court will carefully consider the person's skills, age and time out of work, the possibility and cost of retraining and the job market. If the court is of the view that a party is perversely refusing to work in order to frustrate a financial application against him, it could make an order by attributing a notional earning capacity to him.

Earning capacity may be significant in determining the duration of periodical payments or a party's occupation of the matrimonial home. If the court considers that a party could reasonably be expected to take steps to increase his earning capacity by, say, undertaking further training, this could prompt the court to limit the period for which maintenance is payable (see **4.6**). It might also result in a reduction of a party's share on sale of the home if a return to work or significant promotion is anticipated with reasonable certainty.

As a general rule, means-tested welfare benefits will not be regarded as a resource since the supporting spouse cannot free himself of his responsibilities to maintain his family by casting that burden onto the taxpayer (*Barnes v Barnes* [1972] 3 All ER 872). However, there will frequently be cases where there are insufficient resources to maintain two households. In such cases, it would be an affront to common sense to ignore the availability of state benefits. The non-means tested child benefit will always be treated as a resource of the party caring for the child. If both parties are claiming benefit, it would be rare for the court to make any order because, as a general principle, the court would not make an order reducing the payer's income below subsistence level.

The court will give a wide interpretation to 'property' and 'financial resources'. The court is not limited to considering assets acquired jointly or during the marriage, or even existing assets. As with income, the court may take into account a party's future prospects, for example, a terminal gratuity, or an interest under a settlement or inheritance (but generally only if the donor has already died). If it is uncertain whether or when a party might acquire the anticipated property, or how much that property will be worth, it might be appropriate for the court to adjourn the application. In such a case, no final decision will be made, leaving the parties to wait and see whether (and to what extent) the anticipated property materialises during the period of the adjournment. In the case of *Michael v Michael* [1986] 2 FLR 389, Nourse LJ said it would be wrong to take into account the possibility of a wife's inheritance from her mother who was in her sixties and suffered from high blood pressure, saying the world was full of women in their eighties who had high blood pressure in their sixties.

In recent years there have been a number of cases in which it was argued that some assets should be categorised as 'non-matrimonial' and therefore unavailable for the court to distribute on divorce. Such assets might include those which were inherited or owned by one party before the marriage, or which have been acquired by one party after separation. What has emerged from those cases is a reiteration that s 25(2)(a) is not confined to assets accumulated during the marriage, and the courts have the power to deal with the parties' resources whenever and however acquired. How inherited assets or those acquired pre-marriage or post-separation are dealt with depends on the facts of the case. The nature and source of the assets will be taken into account when determining the requirements of fairness. The facts may require such assets to be treated differently, and there may be justification to depart from equality (see, eg, *Robson v Robson* [2010] EWCA Civ 1771). The court will have regard to the circumstances of the acquisition of the assets and may conclude that such assets should be kept by the spouse who acquired or inherited them. However, this depends on the effect of the other s 25 factors, and a claim to keep such property will carry little weight if the other spouse's needs could not be satisfied without it.

Income from other members of the household, such as 'board' paid by a working child or lodger, will be taken into account as a resource. More problematic is the extent to which the means of a party's new partner are taken into account. The court cannot redistribute a third party's assets and, therefore, it cannot, for example, order a new wife to pay maintenance to the former wife. However, if a second wife was earning and contributing to the household expenses, it would be wrong if the court was unable to take that fact into account. The practice which has emerged, therefore, is that the court will assess the extent to which contributions made by the new partner reduce the party's outgoings, thereby increasing the money available for maintenance payments (see *Slater v Slater and Another* [1982] 3 FLR 364). The paying spouse would still be expected to share the living costs with his new partner and, therefore, even if that partner was very wealthy and meeting all the expenses, this would not result in the payer being liable to pay his entire income to his first family. If the applicant has a new partner the same principles apply: to the extent that he is supporting the applicant her needs will be reduced. Clearly, the court will have regard to the stability of that relationship and may decide to preserve the party's option to apply to vary an order should the relationship break down. If the recipient remarries, she will lose her entitlement to maintenance altogether.

If a party has not remarried, the court will not speculate on that party's prospects of improving his financial circumstances by finding a partner. Nevertheless, if a party does have a firm intention to remarry or cohabit at the time an order for provision is being sought (including an order by consent), this will amount to a material fact which should be disclosed to the other party and to the court. This information may affect the outcome of proceedings or negotiations, for example as periodical payments terminate on remarriage they may be more appropriate than a lump sum or property adjustment order if a party is soon to be amply supported and housed by his new spouse. If remarriage plans are not disclosed then any order made is liable to be set aside (see *Livesey (formerly Jenkins) v Jenkins* [1985] AC 424 and **11.7**).

4.5.1.3 Needs

Section 25(2)(b) of the MCA 1973 directs the court to consider the parties' needs, obligations and responsibilities: for most couples the primary task will be to assess each party's essential needs. The most basic of these needs is the provision of accommodation for both parties and any children. Also important will be the expenses connected with the accommodation and the costs of food and clothing.

These costs will vary from case to case, depending on the size of the home, the number of people living in it and the general cost of living in the particular locality. In addition to considering these basic needs, the court must also consider the parties' existing obligations, for example, hire-purchase, bank loans, school fees, insurance premiums, etc. The courts have tended to construe s 25(2)(b) as confining them to have regard only to such requirements as are reasonable – as Ward J stated in *Delaney v Delaney* [1990] 2 FLR 457:

> In all life, for those who are divorced as well as for those who are not divorced, indulging one's whims or even one's reasonable desires must be held in check by the constraints imposed by limited resources and compelling obligations.

However, there will usually be little to gain in increasing the legal costs burden by challenging a party's existing outgoings unless he is being excessively extravagant. If a party is already committed to make certain payments, the courts will be reluctant to disregard the impact of those liabilities on that party's disposable income.

One of the most controversial obligations is that of the respondent who has 'indulged' himself by forming a new relationship (and possibly by having further children). It was noted (at **4.5.1.2**) that the resources of a party's new partner would be borne in mind when assessing that party's disposable income. It is, therefore, only reasonable that if the new partner is financially dependent upon the party, this fact will be taken into account. The court will consider the extent to which the financially dominant party can meet the needs of the other party and the children of the family, bearing in mind his additional responsibilities towards his new partner (and family). The result may be that a substantially reduced order is made, in some cases leaving the applicant to look to the State to meet her needs. The point was made graphically in the case of *Delaney* (above):

> Whilst this court deprecates any notion that a former husband and extant father may slough off the tight skin of familial responsibility and may slither into and lose himself in the greener grass on the other side, nonetheless this court has proclaimed and will proclaim that it looks to the realities of the real world in which we live, and that among the realities of life is that there is a life after divorce. The respondent husband is entitled to order his life in such a way as will hold in reasonable balance the responsibilities to his existing family which he carries into his new life, as well as his proper aspirations for that new future.

In *S v S (Financial Provision: Departing from Equality)* [2001] 2 FLR 246, the good reason for the (in this case, small) departure from equality was that the husband needed more to meet his responsibilities towards his new family.

Similarly, if a respondent has obligations to wives and children of former marriages, these will also be taken into account when considering the application of any subsequent spouse.

Where the parties are well off, the court will look beyond their basic needs, and the other s 25 factors are likely to play a more significant role in determining the outcome.

4.5.1.4 Standard of living

In applying s 25(2)(c), the court will not attempt the impossible by seeking to preserve both parties' standard of living at the level prior to the breakdown of the marriage. On separation, there will be the increased costs of running two households, usually without any increase in either party's income. Instead, the court will endeavour to ensure that the inevitable reduction in the parties' standard of living is borne by them evenly.

Where a couple have lived frugally and enjoyed only a modest standard of living, perhaps preferring to invest their resources in their business or to save for their retirement, the court will look at the wider picture. An applicant would not be penalised for having lived carefully during the marriage by an order for humble provision. On the contrary, the order should reflect the contributions made by the thrifty housekeeper towards the family's prosperity.

4.5.1.5 Ages of the parties and the duration of the marriage

Taken in isolation, the importance of s 25(2)(d) is not immediately obvious. However, taken in conjunction with the other factors, its significance is more apparent: a young wife without children ending a short marriage is likely to have an earning and borrowing capacity, and therefore a package of orders to enable a couple to achieve financial independence (known as a clean break: see **4.6**) may be appropriate. On the other hand, an older spouse leaving a long marriage may have little or no earning capacity, but is likely to have made a greater contribution to the marriage, and there are usually more family assets to distribute. A middle-aged or elderly couple may not necessarily have enjoyed a long marriage. However, if a mature couple have had only a short marriage, the court will bear in mind the consequences of that marriage on the parties. In particular, it will have regard to any loss of prospects resulting from the marriage, for example, jobs or promotion sacrificed or tenancies surrendered on entering into the marriage (see *S v S* [1977] 1 All ER 56). A similar principle applies to young couples ending a short marriage but who have children. The needs of the children will outweigh the fact that the marriage was short, not least because children are likely to diminish the earning capacity of the parent raising them (see *C v C (Financial Relief: Short Marriage)* [1997] 2 FLR 26).

In *Miller and McFarlane* (see **4.5.1.1**), the House of Lords said that the general approach in short marriages was to consider whether and to what extent there was a good reason to depart from equality. Lord Nichols referred to the 'instinctive feeling' that parties would generally have less call upon each other following the breakdown of a short marriage. Nevertheless the House of Lords was at pains to emphasise that each case would turn upon its own facts. On the unusual facts of *Miller*, the high standard of living that the parties had enjoyed and the fact that Mr Miller's wealth had increased dramatically during the marriage justified Mrs Miller receiving £5 million after less than three years of marriage.

It is the cohabitation during the marriage which is relevant in s 25(2)(d): the Court of Appeal in *Krystman v Krystman* [1973] 3 All ER 247 refused to order financial provision where the couple lived together for only two weeks of their 26-year marriage. As for cohabitation prior to marriage, the court is not required to take this into account under s 25(2)(d); however, it may be taken into account when the court considers 'all the circumstances of the case' under s 25(1) (*Kokosinski v Kokosinski* [1980] Fam 72). In the case of *Gojkovic v Gojkovic* [1990] 1 FLR 140, the wife received a substantial award based on her contributions to the family fortune made largely during their pre-marital cohabitation.

4.5.1.6 Disability

If a party suffers from a physical or mental disability, this may affect that party's resources as he may have a reduced (or no) earning capacity. It will also affect the sufferer's needs if, for example, expensive care, treatment or equipment is required. The court will also bear in mind the effect of any future deterioration in the party's condition. It has been held that damages awarded to compensate a party for personal injury are rightly to be regarded as a resource for that party under s 25(2)(a), notwithstanding that they were assessed to compensate that party for his loss, pain and suffering.

4.5.1.7 Contributions to the family

The court is required by s 25(2)(f) to consider the parties' past and anticipated future contributions to the welfare of the family, both materially and otherwise. Where the wife has contributed in non-financial terms to the marriage, it is not necessary for her to show the extensive contributions in kind of the sort required to establish a proprietary interest under a constructive trust (see **Chapter 16**). The court is not deciding the ownership of the family assets, but rather how each party's assets should be shared.

It has been recognised for some time that a wife who cares for the home and the family contributes as much to the family as the wife who goes out to work. Indeed in *Miller and McFarlane* (see **4.5.1.1**) Lord Nichols described as 'a principle of universal application' the fact that in assessing the parties' contributions there should be no bias in favour of the money-earner and against the home-maker. The court will bear in mind the impact of that role on the carer's career. It will also take into account the continuing contributions that the parent will make as the children grow up.

In the case of *Cowan v Cowan* [2001] 2 FLR 192, the Court of Appeal recognised that one party may have made an exceptional contribution in some way. In this situation, the Court found that fairness permitted, and sometimes required, recognition of the product of the skill or genius with which only one of the spouses might be endowed. This decision led to a number of cases in which the husband argued that his special entrepreneurial skill constituted a justification to depart from equality. In *Lambert v Lambert* [2002] EWCA Civ 1685, [2003] 1 FLR 139, however, the Court of Appeal made it clear that such an approach would be followed only in a truly exceptional case. Thorpe LJ commented:

> If all that is regarded is the scale of the breadwinner's success then discrimination is almost bound to follow since there is no equal opportunity for the homemaker to demonstrate the scale of her comparable success.

However, even in those exceptional cases where a special contribution can be shown, it would seem that its effect on the division of assets will be limited. In *Charman v Charman* [2007] EWCA Civ 503, whilst emphasising that it was not issuing any guidelines, the Court said that special contributions operated within a narrow band and would result in the contributor's share increasing from 50% to no more than 55–66.6%.

Conversely, the court may also take into account any negative contribution made by a party: in the case of *E v E (Financial Provision)* [1990] 2 FLR 233, Mrs E, while having an adulterous affair, was said to have spent thousands of pounds on clothes and to have withdrawn from family life. The judge found that 'the wife's contribution to the welfare of the family was negative' and added: 'I do not find it necessary to consider conduct as a separate item. Such conduct as has been shown can properly be dealt with by considering the contribution the wife has made to the welfare of the family'. Whilst, then, it would be exceptional for adultery to be taken into account under s 25(2)(g) (see **4.5.1.8**), if affairs have resulted in a party failing to contribute to the family, this may be taken into account.

4.5.1.8 Conduct

Under s 25(2)(g), the court is required to have regard to conduct which it would be inequitable to disregard. However, either party to the divorce may apply for financial provision: it is not a case of the 'guilty respondent' maintaining the 'innocent petitioner'. Whether, and to what extent, one party will be required to support the other will depend on all the factors appearing in s 25, of which conduct is but one.

If substantial allegations of misconduct are made, the case may be transferred to the High Court (see *Practice Direction (Family Business: Transfer between High Court and County Court)* [1992] 3 All ER 151).

In practice, it will be unusual for a party's misconduct to be raised. Conduct may particularly be an issue, however, where it has a direct bearing on the parties' finances. Examples of cases where conduct was an issue include:

(a) *Martin v Martin* [1976] 3 All ER 625: the husband frittered away joint assets in recklessly hopeless business ventures.

(b) *K v K (Conduct)* [1990] 2 FLR 225: the husband had a serious drink problem which contributed to his refusal to obtain employment and his neglect of the house which ultimately forced its sale. Although the husband succeeded in obtaining a lump sum, his application for periodical payments was dismissed.

(c) *H v H (Financial Relief: Attempted Murder as Conduct)* [2005] EWHC 2911: the husband subjected the wife to a vicious knife attack and was subsequently convicted of attempted murder. As a result of the attack the wife could no longer continue with her career as a police officer. The court considered it fair in all the circumstances that the wife should receive the greater share of the matrimonial assets, including the entire sale proceeds from the former matrimonial home. The husband's conduct had had the effect of placing the wife's needs as a much higher priority than the husband's in the court's consideration of s 25 of the MCA 1973, because the situation in which the wife found herself was clearly the husband's fault.

(d) *Evans v Evans* [1989] 1 FLR 351: the court discharged a maintenance order made in favour of the wife after she was convicted (and imprisoned) for inciting others to murder the husband.

The conduct does not have to have a bearing on finances to be taken into account. Some conduct may be of such a nature in itself to make it inequitable to disregard. In *K v L* [2010] EWCA Civ 125, the husband was awarded a negligible sum despite the wife's wealth of £4.3 million and a 24-year marriage. The husband had been convicted of the sexual abuse of two of the wife's grandchildren. The Court decided that such conduct was the ultimately decisive factor which overrode all the other s 25(2) factors.

The fact that an applicant has committed adultery will not bar him from seeking financial provision. The adultery itself will not be relevant unless there are aggravating circumstances, as there were in *Bailey v Tolliday* [1983] 4 FLR 542 where the petitioner's father was the co-respondent.

Another possibility is that a party's misconduct may relate to the proceedings themselves, such as failure to make full and frank disclosure of means. In *Clark v Clark* [1999] 2 FLR 498, the court distinguished between marital misconduct, which may affect the quantification of orders made, as opposed to litigation misconduct, which generally should only be penalised in costs. Examples of cases involving litigation misconduct include the following:

(a) *T v T (Interception of Documents)* [1994] 2 FLR 1083: the wife intercepted the husband's mail and broke into his office in an attempt to ascertain his true financial position. The court's approach was that, whilst this misconduct would not be brought into the reckoning of the substantive award, it was relevant in respect of costs.

(b) *P v P (Financial Relief: Non-Disclosure)* [1994] 2 FLR 381: the court found the wife guilty of misconduct when she concealed a number of assets and the presence of a cohabitee. Again, although she was not penalised by a reduction in the overall provision, she was ordered to pay her own costs (estimated at £40,000).

The distinction between litigation misconduct and conduct relevant for the purposes of s 25(2)(g) may be blurred. In *FZ v SZ and others* [2010] EWHC 1630, the parties had incurred some £2 million in costs as a result of numerous applications involving various allegations of false disclosure and non-disclosure, and obtaining evidence by underhand means. Mostyn J described the conduct of the case as 'attritional warfare which has been both unedifying and shameful'. He went on to find that both the husband's actions in disclosing court documents to overseas tax authorities alleging tax irregularities on the part of the wife's parents, and the wife's actions in making false allegations of domestic violence against the husband amounted to conduct for the purposes of s 25(2)(g). However, as the judge considered that each side had behaved equally badly, it had no effect on the final award.

In any event, the court is not obliged to treat litigation misconduct as an entirely separate matter. In *F v F* [2008] Fam Law 182, the court found that the husband had engaged in a conspiracy intended to deceive both the wife and the court in the financial case. The result was that costs of some £4 million were incurred, which amounted to 40% of the parties' assets. Although noting that technically this was litigation misconduct, the court decided that the husband's actions had resulted in such a serious erosion of the parties' assets that they could not adequately be dealt with through the making of a costs order. Consequently the court decided that the husband's actions amounted to conduct which it would be inequitable to disregard and which was therefore reflected in the final award.

Whilst the majority of cases on s 25(2)(g) deal with misconduct by one party, it should be noted that the wording of the sub-section is not restricted to 'wrongdoing'. In *K v K (Ancillary Relief: Prenuptial Agreement)* [2003] 1 FLR 120 the court found that the fact that the parties had previously entered into a pre-nuptial agreement was conduct which it would be inequitable to disregard.

4.5.1.9 Potential financial loss

When dealing with applications ancillary to divorce or nullity (but not judicial separation), s 25(2)(h) requires the court to consider any potential benefits a party might lose as a result of the termination of the marriage. The loss of certain types of pension rights is an example. As a widow or widower the applicant may be entitled to the deceased spouse's pension: that right would be lost on the termination of the marriage. This can be a serious problem to, say, a financially dependent middle-aged wife of a long marriage. In such cases there may be an argument for giving that spouse a greater share of the other matrimonial assets to mitigate the problem, and perhaps also for preserving the wife's claim under the Inheritance (Provision for Family and Dependants) Act 1975 (I(PFD)A 1975).

Other contingent benefits which a party might lose include a share in life policies which are yet to mature. The lost opportunity to share in the other party's prospective inheritance will be taken into account only if it is sufficiently certain in time and amount (see **4.4.1**).

4.5.1.10 Human rights

Some legislative provisions, including s 25 of the MCA 1973, cannot be interpreted in accordance with the European Convention on Human Rights. Article 5 of the Seventh Protocol states that 'spouses shall enjoy equality of rights and responsibilities of a private law character between them, and in their relations with their children, as to marriage, and in the event of dissolution'. Yet, under s 25, the starting point in a financial application is not necessarily equality between the spouses. Because of the difficulty in interpretation of s 25 and other provisions, Article 5 was specifically excluded from being incorporated into the HRA 1998.

4.5.2 Provision for children

The interests of the children of the family are borne in mind when any financial order is made under the MCA 1973. Section 25(1) requires the court 'to give first consideration to the welfare while a minor of any child of the family' when making any financial order on divorce. Therefore, when considering its powers to provide for the parties, any order made will reflect not only the needs of those parties but also the needs of the children.

The court has wide powers to make capital orders in favour of the children of the family. However, it is not usual for the court to make capital orders in favour of children: in *Lord Lilford v Glynn* [1979] 1 WLR 78, Orr LJ stated that

> a father, even the richest father, ought not to be regarded as under financial obligations or responsibilities to provide funds for the purpose of such settlements that are envisaged in this case on children who are under no disability and whose maintenance and education are secure.

In contrast, provision will be required for children's maintenance. It has already been noted (at **4.1**) that applications for children's maintenance will usually be made under the CSA 1991 to the Child Support Agency rather than to the court. This is considered in detail in **Chapter 7**. However, the court will continue to have limited jurisdiction to deal with maintenance orders for certain children, and in such cases the factors in s 25 must be taken into account.

When considering what orders should be made for children, the court is guided by s 25(3) in all cases. Section 25(4) lists further factors to be taken into account where the payer is not the natural parent of the child.

4.5.2.1 Children of the family

Section 25(3) directs the court to consider the following factors when making orders for children of the family:

> (a) the financial needs of the child;
>
> (b) the income, earning capacity (if any), property and other financial resources of the child;
>
> (c) any physical or mental disability of the child;
>
> (d) the manner in which he was being and in which the parties to the marriage expected him to be educated or trained;
>
> (e) the considerations mentioned in relation to the parties to the marriage in section 25(2)(a), (b), (c) and (e).

The factors are generally self-explanatory, but one or two points are worth noting. Clearly, the needs of the child will increase with age: the section does not refer to the child's future needs as these are best dealt with by further applications for increased maintenance as and when required.

Most young children do not have any income or earning capacity. However, maintenance may be sought for children who are receiving wages, grants or scholarships whilst in education or training, and such sums would be taken into account. In wealthier families, children may have trust income to be borne in mind.

The court will wish to ensure that adequate provision is made for children with a disability. It might, in particular, consider making secure PPOs to provide for a stable income. It might also be appropriate to make lump sum orders to meet capital expenditure on, for example, special equipment adapted for the child's handicap. The disability may also affect the duration of the order, as special circumstances could lead to the provision continuing well into adulthood.

Section 25(3)(e) requires the court to look at the parties' resources, needs, standard of living and any disability. This is because the parties' ability to provide for their children is directly related to and dependent upon their own circumstances.

4.5.2.2 Step-children

Section 25(4) requires the following additional factors to be considered where the child in question, although a child of the family, is not the natural child of the party against whom an order is being sought:

> (a) whether that party assumed any responsibility for the child's maintenance, and, if so, to the extent to which, and the basis upon which, that party assumed such responsibility and to the length of time for which that party discharged such responsibility;
>
> (b) whether in assuming and discharging such responsibility that party did so knowing that the child was not his or her own;
>
> (c) the liability of any other person to maintain the child.

The section recognises that a child may be a child of more than one family and, as a consequence, several people may be liable to maintain that child. For example, a husband may have treated his wife's child from a previous relationship as his own: in such a case both the husband and the father could be looked to for support. Clearly, the factors in s 25(4) will be highly relevant in determining the extent of this support. If the child's father is meeting the child's maintenance requirement under the CSA 1991 (see **Chapter** 7), this may relieve the step-father from paying maintenance.

Again it should be noted that the nature of the civil partnership family is such that it will more frequently be the case than with a married couple that these additional factors (mirrored in CPA 2004, Sch 5, Pt 5, para 22) will have to be considered.

4.6 The clean break

4.6.1 The principle

The object of the clean break is to settle once and for all the parties' financial responsibility towards each other and to end their financial interdependence, to enable them to leave their past behind them and begin anew. The advantages of such an approach have long been recognised, but with the enactment of the Matrimonial and Family Proceedings Act 1984, which introduced s 25A into the MCA 1973, the concept of the clean break was given statutory backing. The court has a duty to consider whether a clean break should be achieved.

Section 25A(1) states:

> Where on or after the grant of a decree of divorce or nullity of marriage the court decides to exercise its powers under sections 23(1)(a), (b) or (c), 24 or 24A above in favour of a party to the marriage, it shall be the duty of the court to consider whether it would be appropriate so to exercise those powers that the financial obligations of each party towards the other will be terminated as soon after the grant of the decree as the court considers just and reasonable.

The wording of the section only imposes a duty to consider the appropriateness of a clean break, it does not oblige the court to make a clean break wherever possible. In practice the judiciary view a clean break as the preferred outcome. For example, in *M v M (Ancillary Relief: Division of Assets Accrued Post Separation)* [2004] All ER (D) 83, Baron J commented: 'If it can be attained, it is better for there to be a clean break'. But the clean break is not to be imposed at all cost. In reality the court must weigh all the statutory factors in deciding whether a clean break is appropriate on the facts of the particular case; as Lord Nichols said in *Miller and McFarlane* (see **4.5.1.1**):

> ... if the claimant is owed compensation and capital assets are not available, it is difficult to see why the social desirability of a clean break should be sufficient reason for depriving the claimant of that compensation.

It will never be appropriate to have a clean break between a parent and child, as a party can never sever his responsibility towards a child of the family. It is possible, however, to have a clean break between the parties even where there are children involved. In cases where the court has jurisdiction to make orders for children, it might award less than it would otherwise do because the parent with whom the children are residing has agreed a clean break settlement. For example, the father might be using a significant amount of his income to pay for a loan which was raised in order to make a generous lump sum payment for the mother who is caring for the children. The father would clearly have less income available to support the children directly, but they will be benefiting indirectly from the lump sum payment. However, should the mother subsequently apply for a maintenance assessment under the CSA 1991, the father might then find himself being required to pay substantially more maintenance than he had bargained for. This is because when calculating the non-resident parent's liability to pay maintenance under the 1991 Act, generally no account is taken of any clean break made on divorce. However, if the clean break settlement was made before April 1993 (ie before the CSA 1991 came into force) then some allowance can be made (see **7.6.4.2**).

4.6.2 The practice

4.6.2.1 Income orders

So far as periodical payments are concerned, the most extreme form of clean break is an order dismissing the application coupled with a bar against the making of any further applications. Section 25A(3) empowers the court to make such an order:

> Where on or after the grant of a decree of divorce or nullity of marriage an application is made by a party to the marriage for a periodical payments order in his or her favour, then, if the court considers that no continuing obligation should be imposed on either party to make or secure

> periodical payments in favour of the other, the court may dismiss the application with a direction that the applicant shall not be entitled to make any further application in relation to the marriage for an order under section 23(1)(a) or (b) above.

Less extreme than this immediate clean break is an order for 'term maintenance'. Such an order allows a party to receive maintenance for a limited period only in order to tide him over while he adapts to becoming financially self-sufficient. The clean break will be deferred to a future date. The term of the maintenance will vary from case to case: it may be for six months to enable the party to find a job, or for two or three years to allow for retraining. If there are children, it may be for a longer period until they are less dependent on the applicant.

It is also not usually considered appropriate to provide for the termination of periodical payments for a spouse in his or her late forties or fifties, unless he or she has substantial capital of his or her own and significant earning capacity (see *Flavell v Flavell* [1997] 1 FLR 353). The courts are much more likely to favour at least a nominal periodical payments order (eg 5p per year), thereby keeping the spouse's periodical payments claim 'alive' so that it can be varied, if necessary, in the future (see *SRJ v DWJ (Financial Provision)* [1999] 2 FLR 176).

The benefits of term maintenance have been given statutory support by s 25A(2), which states:

> Where the court decides in such a case to make a periodical payments or secured periodical payments order in favour of a party to the marriage, the court shall in particular consider whether it would be appropriate to require those payments to be made or secured only for such term as would in the opinion of the court be sufficient to enable the party in whose favour the order is made to adjust without undue hardship to the termination of his or her financial dependence on the other party.

If events do not work out according to plan and the applicant fails to achieve the anticipated financial independence, in most cases the applicant will be able to apply under s 31 of the MCA 1973 to extend the maintenance for a further period. It is essential that any such application is made before the expiry of the term as the order itself ceases at that point. In deciding whether to grant such a request, however, the court would enquire into the reason for the applicant's failure to become self-sufficient. If, for example, the availability of work decreases and the court is satisfied that the applicant has made genuine efforts to seek employment, it is likely to deal with the application sympathetically.

The court is empowered under s 28(1A) to direct that the applicant will not be entitled to make any application to extend the term regardless of any change of circumstances. Whilst this has the advantage for the payer of certainty, in that he will eventually be rid of the obligation to maintain his ex-spouse, the inflexibility can lead to hardship to the recipient (see *Waterman v Waterman* [1989] 1 FLR 380). If the children are very young, the court is unlikely to consider non-extendable term maintenance to be appropriate.

An alternative approach, mentioned above, is to order substantive maintenance for a fixed period, after which it will drop to a nominal sum of, say, 5p per year, so keeping alive the recipient's option of applying for an increase. Such an order is not a clean break at all as it affords no certainty to the payer. However, substantive maintenance would be revived beyond the original term only if the circumstances justified it.

4.6.2.2 Capital orders

A clean break is commonly achieved by means of a lump sum payment in return for a dismissal of all other claims. One party may prefer to pay a relatively substantial lump sum rather than have the burden of even modest maintenance hanging over him for an indefinite period. This is possible, though, only if there are sufficient capital assets available. A party may need to borrow in order to raise the necessary capital.

Particular problems arise if the main asset involved is a business. Selling the business to realise capital may be 'killing the goose that lays the golden egg'.

Lump sums are discussed further at **9.7**. It may be that there is no clean break initially between the parties, but that one occurs later on; see **11.8.1**, which deals with the court's power to impose a clean break at a later stage, by making lump sum adjustment orders, on an application for variation or discharge of an existing periodical payment or secured periodical payments order.

There are only two ways of dealing with the matrimonial home to achieve an immediate clean break: by immediate sale, or by a transfer into one party's sole name. These and other orders for the matrimonial home are considered in detail in **Chapter 9**.

As part of a clean break package a provision is often included under s 15 of the Inheritance (Provision for Family and Dependants) Act 1975. This enables the court to direct that neither party may apply under s 2 of the 1975 Act for financial provision out of the other's estate.

4.7 Pensions on divorce

A pension is often a person's most valuable asset, or it will be when it comes to being paid, so it is not surprising that dividing it should be a major consideration in settling the financial aspects of divorce, particularly for older couples. Since its original enactment, the MCA 1973 has been the subject of significant amendments which have radically altered the treatment of pensions on divorce. As a result of these amendments, there are three possible ways of dealing with pension rights on divorce. These are:

(a) the traditional approach of adjusting the other matrimonial assets to take account of pension rights ('off-setting');

(b) an order which allows for all or part of any pension or lump sum arising at retirement to be 'earmarked' for the other spouse ('pension attachment');

(c) splitting the pension so that the pension benefits are physically subdivided at the time of the divorce; the parties will then have two entirely separate pensions which they can contribute to in the future in the normal way ('pension sharing').

4.7.1 The traditional approach – 'off-setting'

As originally enacted, the MCA 1973 was limited both in terms of taking pension rights into account and the orders that could be made regarding those rights. Section 25(2)(a) says that when the courts consider the 'financial resources' of the parties this can include those which will be available 'in the foreseeable future'. However, this phrase is not defined and the courts have sometimes interpreted it as meaning not more than 10 years away (*Milne v Milne* [1981] 2 FLR 286 and *Hedges v Hedges* [1991] 1 FLR 196). Historically this often meant that at best, pension rights were afforded a passing acknowledgement as one of 'all the circumstances of the case' in s 25(1), or at worst completely ignored despite their potential value.

Added to this, the courts, in the past, did not have any powers to make orders specifically dealing with the parties' pension arrangements. Historically, the best that the courts could do in making appropriate settlements on divorce was to allocate to one spouse (normally the wife) a proportion of the matrimonial assets equivalent to the approximate value of the pension benefits lost. This meant that a trade-off was being made between the pension rights and other matrimonial assets. However, this is not always an entirely appropriate solution: there are problems of valuation, and there is the fact that the trade-off must be made immediately at the time of the divorce, yet the pension benefits themselves will be in the future and are contingent on certain events (eg retirement, death) and possibly may never materialise. Despite subsequent amendments to the MCA 1973, off-setting is still available to the courts, and may remain the appropriate approach on the individual facts of the case.

4.7.2 'Pension attachments'

The obvious limitations to off-setting prompted the Government of the day to introduce reforms. The first step was taken in s 166 of the Pensions Act 1995, which inserted three new sections into the MCA 1973, namely ss 25B, 25C and 25D (see **Appendix 1(A)**). These sections allow the court to make pension attachment orders so that certain payments under a pension are to be paid not to the member of the pension scheme but to his former spouse. The amendments addressed the issue of the court being able to take pension rights into account.

Section 25B provides that, in relation to benefits under a pension scheme, the words 'in the foreseeable future' in s 25(2)(a) shall not apply. This means that the court can take into account any future pension benefits.

In terms of the orders that the court can make, s 25B gives the court the power, when making a financial provision order, to direct the trustees or managers of a pension scheme to pay some (or even all) of the pension to the spouse without the pension rights. If the pension is not yet payable (ie the member-spouse has not yet retired) the court may make a deferred order. Such orders are effectively deferred periodical payment orders.

Most pension schemes include a lump sum benefit payable on retirement, or on the death of the member before retirement. Section 25C gives the court the power to make a lump sum order which directs the trustees or managers of the pension scheme to pay the whole or part of that lump sum, when it becomes due, to the other spouse.

Although these amendments gave the courts more possibilities for redressing the harsh effects of loss of pension rights on divorce, there were still problems.

Pension attachments will usually be deferred until the member-spouse retires or dies. This means that the other spouse has no control over the money until that time and, for example, the member-spouse could decide to retire early or late. Also, such orders are contrary to the clean break principle. As a result of these problems, few pension attachments have been made in practice.

There have only been a few reported cases involving pension attachments (eg *T v T (Financial Relief: Pensions)* [1998] 1 FLR 1072, and *Burrow v Burrow* [1999] 1 FLR 508). In both these cases, the courts confirmed that the court, in determining whether to make a pension attachment and the amount, if any, should exercise its discretion under the established s 25 criteria.

4.7.3 'Pension sharing'

The final step in reform came with the Welfare Reform and Pensions Act 1999, which inserted s 24B into the MCA 1973, creating a new type of financial order – a pension sharing order (now further extended by the addition of a pension sharing compensation order). This additional power enables the courts to split pension rights at the time of divorce. This is done by directing a transfer payment equal in value to a proportion of the member-spouse's pension rights to be made to a pension arrangement which could then provide retirement benefits for the other spouse. In this way, both parties would have immediate control over their own pension provisions. Pension sharing orders can be made on divorce (or nullity) but not on judicial separation.

A pension sharing order may be made against an occupational pension scheme or personal pension scheme. Pension sharing also applies to most public service pensions and the State Earnings Related Pension Schemes (SERPS), but not to the basic State retirement pension.

The effect of a pension sharing order, is that the transferor loses the percentage required to be transferred which reduces the value of his fund – 'the pension debit'. The transferee acquires the right to be credited with that amount – 'the pension credit'. The transferee thus gains an amount which will fund a quite separate pension of her own, which is not in any way contingent on the transferor taking his own pension. The order cannot take effect until decree absolute.

Depending on the type of pension scheme involved, the transferee may have a choice as to whether to become a member of the transferor's pension scheme, but in her own right (known as an 'internal transfer'), or to transfer to a different pension scheme (an 'external transfer').

Pension rights will be valued using the method already in use for valuing the rights of 'early leavers' from occupational pension schemes, or of members of personal pension schemes who wish to transfer their accrued rights to another pension scheme. This is known as the Cash Equivalent Transfer Value.

Any solicitor advising a client about pension sharing must be careful not to infringe the provisions of the Financial Services and Markets Act 2000. For advice on, for example, whether to opt for an internal or external transfer, the client needs to be referred to an independent financial adviser.

4.7.3.1 Pension sharing and the other options

There is no obligation on the court to make a pension sharing order, and 'offsetting' or pension attachment orders remain alternatives. The court must, as always in financial matters, consider each case on its facts by applying the principles and factors set out in s 25 of the MCA 1973 (see **4.5**).

One restriction on the options available to the court is that it is not possible to make both a pension sharing order and a pension attachment in relation to the same pension arrangement. Therefore, the court could not, for example, make a pension attachment in relation to the lump sum death benefit and share the member's other rights. Also, a pension sharing order may not be made in relation to a pension arrangement which is already subject to such an order in respect of that marriage (MCA 1973, s 24B(3) and (4)). However, the fact that a pension is already subject to a sharing order made in respect of a previous marriage would not prevent a further order being made as a result of a second divorce.

4.8 Financial cases in the future

Calls for a review of the law on financial relief have been growing louder in recent years. The legislation remains in substantially the same form as when originally enacted over 30 years ago. Financial relief has always been an area dominated by judicial discretion. Yet the flurry of litigation which followed *White* and more recently *Miller and McFarlane* has arguably only served to add to the law's uncertainty. In *Charman v Charman* [2007] EWCA Civ 503 the President of the Family Division commented:

> Arguably . . . [the MCA] is . . . in need of modernisation in the light of social and other changes as well as in the light of experience.

Whether the calls for reform will be heeded by the Government will emerge when the outcomes of the Family Justice Review are revealed.

4.9 Financial provision during marriage

It may be that a spouse is in need of financial provision during a marriage and yet is not ready to make a decision regarding divorce or judicial separation. In such circumstances, a spouse may bring proceedings under s 27 of the MCA 1973 in a divorce county court (under CPA 2004, Sch 5, Pt 9 for civil partners), or under the Domestic Proceedings and Magistrates' Courts Act 1978 (DPMCA 1978) in the family proceedings court (see **Appendix 1(C)**).

4.9.1 Matrimonial Causes Act 1973, s 27

Section 27 of the MCA 1973 allows either party to a marriage to apply for financial provision on the ground that the respondent has failed to provide reasonable maintenance for the applicant, or has failed to provide or make a proper contribution towards the reasonable maintenance of any child of the family. The court can make orders for periodical payments (including secured provision) and lump sums. In contrast to the DPMCA 1978, there is no ceiling on the amount of any lump sum, although as with the 1978 Act there is no power to make property adjustment orders. In determining whether to make provision, the court will have regard to all the circumstances of the case, including many of the factors set out in s 25 (see **4.5.1**).

The duration of periodical payments orders made under s 27 is precisely the same as for ordinary periodical payments made on divorce (see **4.3.2**). The court also has power to make interim orders, and orders for periodical payments may be varied under s 31 of the MCA 1973 in the usual way (see **11.8**).

Applications under s 27 of the MCA 1973 have never been common. The need for such applications is now diminished since, where a married couple are separated and have natural children, the appropriate application for maintenance for the children will be to the Child Support Agency rather than under s 27 of the MCA 1973.

4.9.2 Financial provision in the family proceedings court

The DPMCA 1978 enables a party to a marriage to seek financial provision in the family proceedings court during the subsistence of the marriage. The court may make orders for periodical payments for a spouse as well as for a child of the family, and it may make lump sum orders. There are two main types of application under the DPMCA 1978: contested applications under s 2; and applications by consent under s 6.

4.9.2.1 Contested applications

In order to bring an application under s 2 of the DPMCA 1978, the applicant must establish one of the grounds in s 1, ie that the respondent has not sufficiently provided for the applicant or a child of the family, or the respondent's behaviour has been unreasonable, or the respondent has deserted the applicant. The court will have regard to the factors listed in s 3, which are broadly similar to s 25 of the MCA 1973.

Any lump sum order made on a contested application is limited to £1,000, although, unlike s 23 of the MCA 1973, there is no bar against making further applications.

4.9.2.2 Agreed applications

If the parties agree financial provision, either may apply for an order under s 6 of the DPMCA 1978 to endorse their agreement.

The court is also able to approve agreements to pay a lump sum of any amount.

4.9.2.3 Duration of periodical payments

Whether the order is made pursuant to s 2 or s 6, it may be backdated to the date of application. The order will cease on the death of either party, or on the remarriage of the recipient. It is unaffected by the termination of the marriage, although it will usually be discharged and replaced by any order made under s 23 of the MCA 1973 by the divorce county court. Periodical payments to a spouse for himself or for the benefit of a child will cease if the parties resume cohabitation for a continuous period of more than six months (DPMCA 1978, s 25(1)). Payments ordered to be payable direct to a child will be unaffected by cohabitation. The child's maintenance will terminate in the same circumstances as under s 29(3) of the MCA 1973 (see **4.3.2**).

Use of the DPMCA 1978 is less common following the enactment of the CSA 1991 (considered in detail in **Chapter** 7). If a couple separate, the parent with care may seek provision through the Child Support Agency unless the child does not qualify (eg a step-child). If a maintenance calculation could be made under the CSA 1991, it must be pursued through the Agency rather than the family proceedings court. However, the DPMCA 1978 may be invoked by children who are in higher education (and therefore no longer liable to be maintained under the CSA 1991) and for lump sum orders.

4.10 Chapter summary

(1) On divorce, a divorce county court (or the High Court) can make one or more of the following financial orders in favour of a spouse:

- (a) maintenance pending suit;
- (b) periodical payments;
- (c) secured periodical payments;
- (d) lump sum order;
- (e) property adjustment order;
- (f) order for sale;
- (g) pension sharing order;
- (h) pension sharing compensation order.

(2) The court can also make any of these orders (except for maintenance pending suit and pension sharing orders) in favour of a child. However, in most cases, periodical payments for a child are now dealt with by the Child Support Agency, and it is unusual to obtain the other types of order, such as a lump sum order, for a child.

(3) Whenever the court considers making a financial order on divorce, it must consider:

- (a) the general principle in s 25(1), ie all the circumstances of the case, with first consideration given to the welfare of any child of the family under 18 years; and
- (b) the factors in s 25(2):
  - (i) income, earning capacity and other resources;
  - (ii) needs and responsibilities;
  - (iii) standard of living;
  - (iv) age of the parties and duration of the marriage;
  - (v) disability;
  - (vi) contributions to the family;
  - (vii) conduct;
  - (viii) potential financial loss.

The House of Lords in *White* and *Miller and McFarlane* has reaffirmed that no one s 25 factor is more important than the others. The objective for the court is to achieve fairness.

There are other factors for the court to refer to when considering making financial orders for a child or step-child (s 25(3) and (4)).

(4) Under s 25A, the court always has a duty to consider whether a clean break should be achieved.

(5) It is important to be aware of the significance of pensions on divorce and the ways in which the court can try to adjust the financial position of the parties on retirement.

(6) A spouse who is not divorcing can still apply to the court for financial provision, either:

- (a) to the divorce county court, under s 27 of the MCA 1973, for periodical payments and/or a lump sum order; or
- (b) to the family proceedings court, under the DPMCA 1978, for periodical payments and/or a maximum £1,000 lump sum order.

Chapter 5
Tax on Marriage Breakdown

5.1	Introduction	69
5.2	Tax on marriage breakdown	69
5.3	Chapter summary	72

5.1 Introduction

This chapter deals with the effect of marriage breakdown on the tax position of the couple.

5.2 Tax on marriage breakdown

Where the assets owned by the divorcing couple are numerous and complicated, it may be wise to enlist the help of an accountant when considering tax planning. Nonetheless, the solicitor should be aware of the major tax effects of marriage breakdown and some basic tax planning points. For a reminder of the basic principles of income tax, capital gains tax and inheritance tax, see ***Legal Foundations***.

5.2.1 Income tax

Changes to the income tax regime which came into effect in April 2000 effectively removed the scope for tax planning. There is:

(a) no tax relief on maintenance payments, whether for a spouse or a child (maintenance is tax free in the hands of the recipient);

(b) no married couple's or single parent allowance;

(c) no tax relief on mortgage interest payments.

Consequently, how maintenance payments are arranged are not influenced by fiscal considerations.

There are four ways in which maintenance may be paid:

(a) purely voluntary payment;

(b) under a written agreement;

(c) by court order (whether made by consent or after a contested hearing);

(d) in compliance with a maintenance assessment by the Child Support Agency.

Voluntary payments are normally only a short-term arrangement. As between a written agreement and a court order, it is a question of balancing the potential advantages of speed, lower costs and flexibility of an agreement against the better provisions for disclosure and enforcement with a court order (see **12.3.3** and **12.3.4** for a more detailed comparison).

5.2.2 Capital gains tax

Capital gains tax (CGT) is charged on the chargeable gains made by a person on the disposal of chargeable assets. On marriage breakdown, capital assets commonly have to be sold or divided between the spouses, and this may give rise to a chargeable gain. Ordinarily transfers of assets between spouses are deemed to have occurred at a consideration which gives rise to neither a gain nor a loss. However, the benefit of this rule is lost at the end of the tax year of separation. The impact of CGT cannot be ignored as it may alter the effect of any negotiated settlement or court order.

5.2.2.1 Capital gains tax and the home

The home is often the largest capital asset and any transfer of it, or of a share in it, could potentially give rise to CGT. However, liability may be avoided due to two important exemptions:

(a) The private residence exemption: to qualify for full exemption, an individual must have occupied the home as his only or main residence throughout the period of his ownership. If he has occupied during part only of his ownership then the relief will be proportionately reduced, except that he is deemed to have occupied during the last three years of ownership whether or not this is in fact so (further details of this exemption can be found in ***Property Law and Practice***).

(b) Extra-statutory concession D6: this will apply where:
   (i) a husband and wife separate or divorce and one of them moves out of the home whilst the other continues to live there;
   (ii) under the subsequent financial settlement the non-occupying spouse transfers the home or an interest in it to the occupying spouse; and
   (iii) the non-occupying spouse has not elected to treat another property as his only or main residence.

If these conditions are fulfilled, the non-occupying spouse will be treated as having continued to occupy so that his gain will be exempt.

How do these exemptions work in practice?

Sale of the home to a third party

If the sale is within three years of the separation, any gain is exempt, being covered by the private residence exemption. If the sale is later, the proportion of the non-occupying spouse's gain not covered by the exemption may be taxable. The annual exemption, if available, can be applied to reduce the gain. (The spouse who has continued to occupy will, of course, be covered by the private residence exemption.)

Transfer of the home between spouses

This will be necessary where the court orders an outright transfer, or deferred trust of land or deferred charge where this requires a transfer, ie disposal of some interest in the home. The transferor's gain may be exempted under the following rules:

(a) where the transfer takes place in the tax year of separation, the rule relating to inter-spouse disposals; or

(b) where the transfer takes place within three years of separation, the deemed occupation rule; or

(c) extra-statutory concession D6 if later.

Where none of the above applies, probably because the transferor has made an election in respect of another home and the separation exceeds three years, the gain will be taxable in the same way as above. A proportion of the gain will thus be exempt due to the private residence exemption. The annual exemption, may help to reduce the remainder.

Future sale of home subject to a deferred trust of land or deferred charge

When the deferred trust of land or deferred charge is set up, one spouse may be required to transfer some, or all, of their interest in the home to the other. The CGT consequences of this have been dealt with above. However, when the house eventually comes to be sold, possibly many years into the future, a further CGT liability may arise.

The occupying spouse's gain will be exempt under the private residence exemption. The position of the non-occupying spouse will depend on whether the home was subject to a deferred trust of land, or a deferred charge:

(a) *Deferred trust of land.* As the court order created a settlement, it would appear that the non-occupying spouse will avoid CGT liability completely because of rules exempting gains on property occupied by a beneficiary entitled to do so under a settlement (Taxation of Chargeable Gains Act 1992, s 225).

(b) *Deferred charge.* Where the charge is expressed as a proportion of the proceeds, for example, one-third, the value of that share may have increased by the time the property is sold. In this situation, the non-occupier is likely to be liable to CGT, the redemption monies being a capital sum derived from an asset, ie the charge (Taxation of Chargeable Gains Act 1992, s 21). The annual exemption, may help to reduce the bill. However, if the deferred charge is for a fixed sum (rather than a proportion of the proceeds), there is no charge to CGT when the debt is paid (Taxation of Chargeable Gains Act 1992, s 251).

5.2.2.2 Other assets

Disposals giving rise to liability to CGT are most likely to arise, for example, on sale of an asset (say a valuable painting) to raise a lump sum, or on the transfer of property (say shares) between the parties.

> **Example**
>
> Jim and Kate bought a painting jointly seven years ago for £10,000. They separated two years ago. The financial order is made today, when the painting is worth £16,000. Under the order Jim must transfer his share in the painting to Kate. Jim has made a gain of £3,000 (£16,000 – £10,000 = £6,000, Jim's gain is half of this).

The gain on many disposals of matrimonial property may, however, be eliminated or reduced by an exemption or relief. The following should be considered:

(a) wasting assets, for example, the family car or electrical items;

(b) tangible moveable property disposed of for a consideration of less than £6,000;

(c) the annual exemption;

(d) the rule relating to inter-spouse transfers.

But these exemptions and reliefs will not eliminate CGT in every case. Consequently, the family solicitor must always have the impact of CGT in mind and ensure that settlements and orders are framed in a tax-efficient manner where possible. There may, for example, be merit in arranging a financial settlement so as to enable assets to be transferred between spouses before the tax year of separation expires. Similarly, the family solicitor may need to structure a financial settlement so as to stagger the disposal of assets across two tax years so that the transferor can take advantage of two annual exemptions.

5.2.3 Inheritance tax

Inheritance tax (IHT) is charged on the value transferred by a chargeable transfer. Transfers of assets or money between spouses on marriage breakdown have the potential to give rise to a charge to IHT as lifetime transfers. However, in reality there is rarely any liability to IHT on marriage breakdown. This is due to a number of exemptions and reliefs.

5.2.3.1 The spouse exemption (Inheritance Tax Act 1984, s 18)

The spouse exemption exempts transfers between the parties before decree absolute, even if separated. However, this exemption will rarely apply since lump sum and property adjustment orders are not effective until decree absolute (see **4.4.1** and **4.4.2**).

5.2.3.2 Dispositions for family maintenance (Inheritance Tax Act 1984, s 11)

This relief provides that a disposition is not a transfer of value if made by one spouse for the maintenance of the other spouse or of a child of either spouse, and applies both before and after divorce. The term 'maintenance' is not defined in the Act but clearly covers periodical payments. There is, however, doubt as to whether it is wide enough to cover capital provision, such as lump sum or property adjustment orders. However, capital orders should be covered by the following relief.

5.2.3.3 Dispositions without donative intent (Inheritance Tax Act 1984, s 10)

This provides that a disposition is not a transfer of value if it was not intended to confer a gratuitous benefit and that either:

(a) it was made in a transaction at arm's length between unconnected persons; or

(b) it was such as might be expected to be made in such a transaction.

To avoid any doubt about the application of this exemption to transfers on marriage breakdown, the Senior Registrar of the Family Division, with the agreement of the then Revenue, issued the following statement:

> Transfers of money or property pursuant to an order of the court in consequence of a decree of divorce or nullity will, in general, be regarded as exempt from [IHT] as transactions at arm's length which are not intended to confer any gratuitous benefit. ((1975) 119 SJ 596)

Care must be taken if the disposition concerned is a payment into or creation of a trust. Although at the time of the disposition there will be no IHT consequences by virtue of s 10, there may be anniversary charges during the lifetime of the trust and exit charges to be paid when the trust comes to an end.

5.2.4 Stamp duty land tax

Where property is transferred under a separation agreement or court order on divorce, the instrument effecting the conveyance is exempt from stamp duty land tax (Finance Act 1985, s 83 and Stamp Duty (Exempt Instruments) Regulations 1987 (SI 1987/516)).

5.3 Chapter summary

(1) The payment of maintenance, whether to a spouse or child, does not give rise to any income tax consequences.

(2) CGT may have to be paid when the matrimonial assets are divided on divorce.

(3) Where the asset is the home and it is transferred from one spouse to the other, CGT will not usually be payable. However, if the home is sold to a third party, some CGT may have to be paid by the non-occupying spouse.

Chapter 6
Welfare and Local Authority Housing

6.1	Introduction	73
6.2	Child benefit	73
6.3	Income support	73
6.4	Jobseeker's allowance	76
6.5	Working tax credit and child tax credit	76
6.6	Housing benefit	79
6.7	Council tax benefit	79
6.8	Discretionary housing payments	80
6.9	The social fund	80
6.10	Welfare benefits and marriage breakdown	81
6.11	Local authority housing	82
6.12	Chapter summary	84

6.1 Introduction

When a married couple or civil partners separate and the main earner leaves the home, the other spouse may be left with little or no money. Although this may be only a temporary situation and it is possible to apply for maintenance (see **4.3.1** and **4.9**), it may be preferable for that spouse to apply for welfare benefits (for reasons explained at **4.3.1**). In addition, since it is more expensive to run two households than one, many people, particularly if they are lone parents, find themselves reliant on welfare benefits on a more permanent basis after marriage breakdown.

In terms of eligibility for welfare benefits, cohabiting couples (ie those who are 'living together as husband and wife' or 'living together as civil partners') are treated in the same way as married couples and so, for example, their income will be aggregated.

The matrimonial solicitor thus needs to have a working knowledge of the main benefits available and how they may be affected by any financial settlement which the couple later reach.

The following is an outline of the most important current benefits for the family client. Further detail on these and other benefits can be found in specialist publications, such as *Welfare Benefits and Tax Credits Handbook* (Child Poverty Action Group, 2011–12).

Where examples are given, for the sake of simplicity, notional figures are used for the amount of benefit payable.

6.2 Child benefit

Child benefit is payable irrespective of the claimant's income (ie it is not means-tested) and is non-taxable. It is a weekly sum payable in respect of each child or qualifying young person to the person responsible for maintaining that child or qualifying young person. A 'child' is defined as being someone aged under 16. A 'qualifying young person' is defined as being someone who is under 20 and still in full-time secondary education. A higher amount of benefit is paid for the eldest child.

6.3 Income support

Income support has now largely been replaced by the jobseeker's allowance. However, income support is still available for, amongst others, lone parents who are looking after a child or children under 7. This age is to be reduced to 5 from early 2012. Claimants with children above that age will be expected to apply instead for jobseeker's allowance and look for work. Lone parents with a child or children of 12 years old or under may restrict their availability for work to school hours. The Welfare Reform Act 2009 abolishes income support altogether, moving all claimants physically able to work on to jobseeker's allowance. At the time of writing this section is not in force.

6.3.1 Eligibility

The claimant must:

(a) have a right to reside and be habitually resident in Great Britain;

(b) be aged between 16 and 60;

(c) not be in full-time work or full-time non-advanced education (most students will also be ineligible to claim). 'Full-time work' means working for at least 16 hours per week;

(d) not have income which exceeds his family's 'applicable amount' (see **6.3.2**);

(e) not have capital exceeding £16,000. Some capital will be ignored, eg the value of the home;

(f) usually attend work-focused interviews every six months.

6.3.2 Applicable amount

The maximum amount of benefit payable is called the applicable amount. The applicable amount will be made up of the following:

(a) Personal allowance: the amount of this will depend upon the age of the claimant.

(b) Various premiums, for example, for pensioners and those with disabilities.

(c) Mortgage interest (rent is covered by housing benefit, see **6.6**): interest at a standard rate will generally be paid on mortgages of up to £200,000 direct to the lender. Mortgages above the £200,000 limit still qualify, but claimants will have to pay any interest for the amount above £200,000 themselves. Mortgage interest only is paid and not other housing costs, eg repayments of capital, insurance premiums payable on an endowment policy, or payments for the insurance of the building or contents. There is a 'waiting period' of 13 weeks, so that claimants will not have their mortgage interest included in their applicable amount for the first 13 weeks of their claim. The £200,000 limit (and 13-week waiting period – previously it was longer) was introduced as part of a temporary package of measures during the economic downturn and only applies to those with a claim made on or after 6 January 2009. For claimants already in receipt of income support at that date, the limit is £100,000. This temporary package is due to expire in January 2012, but may be extended.

6.3.3 Income

Any income the claimant may have will reduce the amount of benefit payable pound for pound. The claimant's income will include:

(a) any earnings of the claimant net of tax, national insurance contributions and half of pension contributions. It is possible for a claimant to work for less than 16 hours per week and still claim income support. Earnings of dependent children, for example from a paper round, will not be included. There is an earnings disregard of £20. Thus, for example, if Sally is a lone parent who earns £50 per week net from a part-time cleaning job, only £30 will count as income for income support purposes;

(b) any maintenance payments paid to the claimant for his or her own benefit. Any child maintenance, for example under a child maintenance calculation, will not be included as income;

(c) income from capital. If the claimant has capital of more than £16,000, she will be ineligible for income support (see **6.3.1**). Any interest actually earned on capital of less than that amount will be ignored. However, capital of over £6,000 will be deemed to produce income at the rate of £1 per week for every £250 of capital over the £6,000 limit. So, for example, capital of £8,000 will be deemed to produce income of £8 per week (£8,000 – £6,000 = £2,000/250 = £8).

Note that child benefit and child tax credit are not included as income for income support purposes.

Any income will be deducted from the applicable amount to determine the amount of income support payable.

6.3.4 Passport benefits

Income support is a 'passport' to certain other benefits, ie where the claimant is claiming income support he will automatically be entitled to these other benefits as well. These passport benefits include:

(a) free school meals;

(b) exemption from NHS charges for prescriptions, dental treatment and eye-tests, and vouchers to help with the cost of glasses;

(c) Healthy Start food vouchers and Healthy Start vitamins for expectant and nursing mothers and pre-school children. Healthy Start food vouchers can be exchanged for cows' milk, cows' milk formula, fruit or vegetables;

(d) full housing and council tax benefits;

(e) the opportunity to apply for interest-free loans from the social fund (see **6.9**).

In addition, a claimant who is in receipt of maintenance may be able to make use of the diversion procedure (see **6.10.1**).

These passport benefits can be quite valuable. Thus it may be worth making a claim for income support even where the amount of income support paid will be small in order to take advantage of them. It is also important to consider the passport benefits when negotiating maintenance payments. It is often unwise to accept an offer of maintenance which is just sufficient to take the client off income support, as the value of these benefits will be lost (see also **8.4**).

6.3.5 Moving into work

A lone parent who obtains employment may be entitled to either or both of a job grant and in-work credit. Neither counts as income for the purpose of other benefits.

6.3.5.1 Job grant

A lone parent who loses income support because she starts full-time work (or increases her working hours to at least 16 hours a week) will be entitled to a job grant of £250 if she has been claiming income support for at least 26 weeks and expects to be in full-time work for at least five weeks. In these circumstances, she will also be entitled to extended payments of housing benefit and council tax benefit at the rate she received them before obtaining the job (or increasing her hours) for up to four weeks.

6.3.5.2 In-work credit

Where a lone parent, who has been in receipt of income support or jobseeker's allowance for 12 months or more, starts full-time work (or increases her working hours to at least 16 a week), she will also be entitled to a tax-free payment of £40 per week (£60 in London) for a year.

6.4 Jobseeker's allowance

Jobseeker's allowance will be the appropriate benefit for the client to claim if he is not in full-time work and either has no children living with him, or lives with a new partner who is also not in full-time work or (after early 2012) any children who live with him are at least 5 years old.

6.4.1 Eligibility

Eligibility is similar to that for income support (see **6.3.1**), but there is also a requirement that the claimant signs on as available for and actively seeking work.

In addition, the claimant's partner (if any) must not work for more than 24 hours per week.

Any capital of a partner will be added to the claimant's own when assessing eligibility.

6.4.2 Applicable amount

This is generally the same as for income support (see **6.3.2**). However, the personal allowance will be higher where the claimant is part of a couple. Also, mortgage interest will be included in the applicable amount for only two years for new claimants. This limitation does not apply if the claimant or partner was claiming income support and then moved on to jobseeker's allowance.

6.4.3 Income

This is similar to income support (see **6.3.3**). The income of any partner must be included. The earnings disregard is £5 if the claimant is single, or £10 if part of a couple.

6.4.4 Passport benefits

These are the same as for income support (see **6.3.4**).

6.4.5 In-work credit

This may be available in the same circumstances as for income support (see 6.3.5.2).

6.5 Working tax credit and child tax credit

Note that although these credits are administered and generally paid by HM Revenue and Customs (HMRC), they are not credits against tax and are payable whether or not the claimant has taxable income.

6.5.1 Working tax credit

6.5.1.1 Eligibility

The claimant must:

(a) be present and ordinarily resident in Great Britain;

(b) not be subject to immigration control;

(c) work (and/or partner must work) 16 or more hours a week and be responsible for a child or children, or be disabled; *or*

(d) work 30 or more hours a week and be over 25; *or*

(e) work 16 or more hours a week and qualify for a disability element; *or*

(f) work (and/or partner must work) 16 or more hours per week and qualify for a 50-plus element.

6.5.1.2 Amount

Working tax credit consists of a number of elements. The relevant ones for the family course are:

(a) basic element: payable to all qualifying claimants;

(b) couple and lone parent element: payable to qualifying claimants who are members of a couple, or who are lone parents;

(c) 30-hour element: payable to qualifying claimants who work 30 or more hours per week;

(d) childcare costs: for one child 70% of the weekly cost of childcare up to £175; for two or more children 70% of the weekly cost of childcare up to £300.

6.5.2 Child tax credit

6.5.2.1 Eligibility

The claimant must:

(a) be present and ordinarily resident in Great Britain with a right to reside here;

(b) be aged 16 or over;

(c) have a child or children under 16, or under 20 and in full-time secondary education, for whom he is responsible;

(d) not be subject to immigration control.

6.5.2.2 Amount

Child tax credit consists of a number of elements. The relevant ones for the family course are:

(a) family element: payable to all qualifying claimants;

(b) child element: one child element is payable per child.

6.5.3 Income

For both child tax credit and working tax credit any gross income will usually be taken into account. Capital is ignored, although income from capital (save the first £300 pa) will be taken into account. The following are *not* taken into account as income: maintenance payments, child benefit, housing or council tax benefit, student loans.

Awards will be made at the beginning of the tax year based on income from the last tax year. Where a couple have split up, only the income of the claimant will be taken into account. Should the claimant's income change during the year an adjustment can be made, but the first £10,000 rise in income will be ignored. The claimant has a choice whether to advise HMRC immediately of any change in income, or whether to wait until the end of the tax year. However, if HMRC is not informed immediately of any significant increase in income, this is likely to result in an overpayment which HMRC will recoup in subsequent years.

At present, any decrease in income will result in an increase in tax credit paid. However, the Government has proposed that, from April 2012, falls of up to £2,500 will not effect a claimant's entitlement.

6.5.4 Means testing

There are two lower income thresholds. These are currently:

(a) £6,420 pa (£123.46 per week) for people claiming working tax credit, or working tax credit and child tax credit;

(b) £15,860 pa (£305 per week) for people claiming child tax credit only (eg because they are not working, or working fewer than 16 hours a week).

If a person's gross income is over the threshold, his tax credits are reduced at the rate of 41p for every pound that his income exceeds the threshold. Working tax credit is reduced first then, once that has been reduced to nil, child tax credit is reduced.

There is also a higher income threshold of (at present) £40,000 for the family element of child tax credit. All families will receive the family element (£545 pa or £10.45 per week) unless their income exceeds £40,000. If it does exceed £40,000 then the family element is reduced by 41p for every £1 over the threshold. The Government has announced that it intends to reduce this higher income threshold to £30,000 from April 2012, and those earning over £25,000 a year will receive a reduced family element.

Example

Bethan is a lone parent with two children under 16, Caspar and Milo. She works 35 hours per week and earns £600 per week (£31,200 pa). She pays £350 per week in childcare.

Bethan's maximum tax credit entitlements (*using notional figures*) are:

Child tax credit	
Family element	£10.50
Element for Caspar	£50.00
Element for Milo	£50.00
Total	£110.50
Working tax credit	
Basic element	£37.00
Lone parent element	£37.50
30 hour element	£15.00
Childcare element*	£210.00
Total	£299.50

*Bethan pays £350 per week childcare. However, only £300 of this is eligible. She is entitled to 70% of that, ie 70% x £300 = £210 pw.

However, as Bethan's income exceeds the £123.46 threshold, credit will taper. She earns £600. This exceeds the threshold by £600 – £123.46 = £476.54.

She will lose credit at the rate of 41p in the £, ie £476.54 × 41% = £195.38. Thus she will get £299.50 – £195.38 = £104.12 working tax credit.

As her working tax credit has not been tapered to nil, Bethan will retain the full amount of child tax credit.

6.5.5 Passport benefits

6.5.5.1 Exemption from NHS charges etc

Where a claimant has gross income of £15,276 or less and is claiming:

(a) child tax credit alone; or

(b) both child tax credit and working tax credit; or

(c) working tax credit alone, but only if she gets a disability element;

she will be entitled to exemption from NHS charges for prescriptions, dental treatment and eye-tests, and to vouchers to help with the cost of glasses. An Exemption Certificate will automatically be sent to the claimant by the Prescription Pricing Authority if she fulfils these criteria.

6.5.5.2 Free school meals etc

Where a claimant has gross income of £16,190 or less and is claiming child tax credit alone (ie must not also be claiming working tax credit), she can claim free school meals for any of her children who are at a State school. In these circumstances she is also entitled to Healthy Start vouchers and Healthy Start vitamins for herself, if she is pregnant or nursing, and for her pre-school children.

6.6 Housing benefit

6.6.1 Eligibility

The claimant:

(a) must have a right to reside in and be habitually resident in Great Britain;

(b) must be liable to make payments of rent in respect of his home. Where a spouse is not technically liable to make such payments but is liable in practice, housing benefit will be available. For example, if the husband, who is the tenant of a council flat which is used as the family home, leaves home, the wife will be able to claim housing benefit;

(c) need not be in receipt of income support, jobseeker's allowance or working tax credit;

(d) must not have capital exceeding £16,000. Capital of over £6,000 will reduce the amount of housing benefit payable.

6.6.2 Amount

Under the Welfare Reform Act 2007, the amount of housing benefit paid to those who are not local authority tenants is called the local housing allowance. At present, the maximum rent payable is calculated by working out the median rent for the relevant size of property for the claimant in the relevant area up to a maximum of four bedrooms. This will generally be the amount paid regardless of how much rent is actually paid. From October 2011, the maximum rent will be set at the 30th percentile of rents rather than the median. The local housing allowance rates are capped at different amounts depending on the size of property (eg, £290 per week for a two-bedroom property and £400 for a four-bedroom or larger property).

Where the claimant is on income support or jobseeker's allowance, the maximum benefit will be paid. For local authority tenants, the amount will generally be 100% of the rent payable (subject to any reductions mentioned below).

Housing benefit will be reduced by approximately 65 pence for each pound by which the claimant's income exceeds the income support level.

Income is calculated in much the same way as for income support (see **6.3.3**). However, there are some disregards, for example for maintenance received, child care bills and earnings. Working tax credit and child tax credit count as income for housing benefit purposes.

The amount of benefit will be reduced if one or more non-dependants (who are not on income support or jobseeker's allowance) share the property.

Where the claimant is a council tenant, housing benefit will reduce the amount of rent payable so that no money will pass through his hands. Where the claimant is a private tenant, benefit will usually be paid to the tenant to pass on to the landlord.

6.7 Council tax benefit

6.7.1 Eligibility

The claimant:

(a) must be liable to pay council tax. Couples (whether married or cohabiting) will be jointly responsible for their council tax bill. Each of them can claim council tax benefit;

(b) need not be in receipt of any other benefits;

(c) must not have capital exceeding £16,000. Capital over £6,000 will reduce the amount of any council tax benefit payable.

6.7.2 Amount

(a) For claimants on income support (or whose income does not exceed the income support level), the amount is usually 100% of the council tax payable.

(b) Council tax benefit will be reduced by approximately 20 pence for each pound by which the claimant's income exceeds the income support level.

(c) Income is calculated in much the same way as for housing benefit.

(d) Council tax benefit may also be reduced where there are one or more non-dependants (who are not on income support) living with the claimant.

Council tax benefit is given by a reduction in the council tax bill.

6.8 Discretionary housing payments

Discretionary housing payments can be paid by the local authority to anyone entitled to housing benefit or council tax benefit who appears to require additional financial assistance to meet their housing costs (which include council tax). They are paid by the local authority from a cash-limited fund.

6.9 The social fund

The social fund is a fund operated by the Department of Work and Pensions out of which loans and grants may be paid to those in need. The first part of the fund, which is known as the 'regulated social fund', makes payments which are mandatory where the claimant meets all the qualifying conditions. The second part of the fund is known as the 'discretionary social fund'.

6.9.1 The regulated social fund

There are four types of payment which are made from the regulated social fund:

(a) Sure Start maternity grants to those on income support, jobseeker's allowance or child tax credit (provided this is paid at a rate which exceeds the family element). The maternity grant is paid at a flat rate, currently £500 for each child. The grant is available only if there are no other children aged under 16 in the claimant's household.

(b) Funeral grants paid to those in receipt of income support, jobseeker's allowance, housing benefit or child tax credit (provided this is paid at a rate which exceeds the family element) who were the partner or close relative of the deceased and are therefore responsible for making arrangements for the funeral. There is a ceiling on the amount which can be claimed. Wherever possible, the Department of Work and Pensions will recover these costs from the deceased person's estate.

(c) Cold weather payments to those on income support or jobseeker's allowance where this includes one of the pensioner or disability premiums, or the family includes a child under 5 years of age. Payments will be made automatically whenever the average temperature for seven days in a row is, or is forecast to be, freezing point or below.

(d) Winter fuel payments to certain people aged 60 or over.

6.9.2 The discretionary social fund

Payments from the discretionary social fund may be by way of grant or loan. There are three types of payment which may be made:

(a) Community care grants to those on income support or jobseeker's allowance. Such grants can be made in a number of situations, for example, to help elderly or disabled people to lead independent lives in the community when they leave hospital or residential care. Community care grants may also be made, for example, to ease exceptional pressures on families, and are subject to a wide discretion on the part of officers administering the fund. There is no maximum amount laid down for a community care grant, but claimants will have to use any savings they have in excess of £500 before a grant is payable. Section 19 of the Welfare Reform Act 2009 changes the way that community care grants are awarded so that claimants may receive goods or services instead of money. At the time of writing this section was not in force.

(b) Crisis loans to meet expenses which arise as the result of some disaster such as flood or fire. A crisis loan could, for example, cover living expenses for a short period (usually 14 days), or such items as essential household equipment. The loan is interest-free. The rate and period of repayment are based on the claimant's income and circumstances. To be eligible for a crisis loan, the claimant does not have to be in receipt of any other welfare benefit, but he must be without sufficient resources to meet the immediate short-term needs of himself and/or his family.

(c) Budgeting loans to those who have been on income support or jobseeker's allowance for at least 26 weeks to meet large, one-off expenses, for example, a replacement cooker or furniture. Claimants will be expected to use any savings they have in excess of £1,000 before a loan will be made. The social fund officer has a wide discretion as to the amount and purpose of these loans. However, there is a minimum of £100 and a maximum of £1,500. The loans are interest-free and repaid by deductions from benefit, the amount of the deduction depending on the claimant's individual circumstances.

6.10 Welfare benefits and marriage breakdown

6.10.1 Maintenance and income support/jobseeker's allowance

Any maintenance paid to the claimant for herself will count as income and will reduce income support or jobseeker's allowance paid pound for pound. Thus, where the maintenance is not sufficient to take the claimant above the income support/jobseeker's allowance level, she will receive her income partly from maintenance payments and partly from income support/ jobseeker's allowance. If the payer is erratic in his payments, the claimant will be forced to apply for further income support/jobseeker's allowance to top up her income whenever payments are not made.

To avoid this problem and to ensure that the claimant receives a regular income, it may be possible to assign the benefit of any maintenance order in her favour to the Department of Work and Pensions. The Department will then collect payments due under the order and pay the claimant her full benefit entitlement. The Department will also be responsible for enforcing any arrears. Before the Department accepts an assignment under this 'diversion procedure', any county court maintenance order must be registered in the family proceedings court. In addition, it will usually allow the diversion procedure to be used only where the payer has defaulted on past payments (practice differs from area to area, but usually the payer must have missed at least two monthly payments out of the last 12 payments).

If the maintenance eliminates the income support/jobseeker's allowance claim altogether, the claimant will also lose her passport benefits (see **6.3.4**).

6.10.2 Maintenance and working tax credit/ child tax credit

Any maintenance paid will not affect the amount of working tax credit or child tax credit received.

6.10.3 Maintenance and housing benefit/council tax benefit

Unless the claimant is on income support, spousal maintenance can reduce her entitlement to housing benefit and council tax benefit, or even eliminate it. However, any child maintenance will be disregarded in full.

6.10.4 Lump sum payments

Where a lump sum payment brings the claimant's capital above the relevant capital limits, entitlement to the appropriate benefit will be eliminated.

Where a lump sum payment brings the claimant's capital to over £6,000 but under the relevant capital limits, the capital will be deemed to produce income (see **6.3.3**).

Special rules apply to lump sum payments where the claimant is on income support or jobseeker's allowance. These rules are meant to ensure that the claimant cannot avoid losing income support or jobseeker's allowance by accepting a lump sum payment rather than maintenance. Thus, when a lump sum payment is intended as a form of maintenance, it will be treated as income and may debar the claimant from income support or jobseeker's allowance for a period of time while the lump sum is used up. The formula applied when decapitalising lump sums is:

$$\frac{\text{Lump sum}}{\text{Weekly income support} + 2} = \begin{array}{l}\text{Number of weeks income support or}\\ \text{jobseeker's allowance is eliminated}\end{array}$$

Example

Willa receives £48 income support per week. She receives no maintenance from Den, her ex-husband, but one day Den offers her a lump sum of £500, which she accepts. Willa will be denied income support for:

$$\frac{500}{48 + 2} = 10 \text{ weeks}$$

During this time, Willa must live off the lump sum at the rate of £50 per week.

None of the above rules will apply where the lump sum payment represents the claimant's share in the home and it is used to buy another home within six months, when the payment will be ignored.

6.10.5 Property adjustment

The value of the claimant's home is generally ignored in assessing benefits.

6.11 Local authority housing

The family solicitor must be able to give immediate advice to a client who finds herself in a situation where she is, or might be, without a roof over her head. The two most common situations where this might occur are where the client has been subjected to domestic abuse (see **Chapter 15**), or when she cannot stay in the former matrimonial home for financial reasons (eg because there are large mortgage arrears and the home must be sold).

Local authorities are under certain duties to provide help (including, in some cases, accommodation) to people who are homeless or threatened with homelessness. These duties are set out in the Housing Act 1996, as amended by the Homelessness Act 2002. The duty owed will depend upon whether the person applying is homeless or threatened with homelessness, whether that homelessness is intentional and whether the applicant has a priority need.

6.11.1 Homelessness

A person is homeless if:

(a) there is no reasonable accommodation which he and his family are entitled to occupy; or

(b) he has such accommodation but he cannot secure entry.

A person may also be entitled to local authority help if he is 'threatened' with homelessness, which means that he is likely to become homeless in the next 28 days.

6.11.2 Intentional homelessness

A person is intentionally homeless if he deliberately does or fails to do anything in consequence of which he ceases to occupy accommodation which was available for occupation by him and his family and which it would have been reasonable for him to continue to occupy.

It is not reasonable for a person to continue to occupy accommodation if it is probable that this will lead to domestic violence or other violence against him or other members of his household. In *Yemshaw v London Borough of Hounslow* [2011] UKSC 3, the Supreme Court held that 'domestic violence' in the Housing Act 1996 includes physical violence, threatening or intimidating behaviour and any other form of abuse which, directly or indirectly, may give rise to the risk of harm.

6.11.3 Priority need

The applicant will be treated as having a priority need if:

(a) he has dependent children who are living with him or might reasonably be expected to live with him; or

(b) his homelessness resulted from flood, fire or other disaster; or

(c) he (or a member of his household) is vulnerable through old age, mental illness or handicap, physical disability or other special reasons; or

(d) she (or a member of the household) is pregnant; or

(e) he is aged 16 or 17, has not been in care and no duty to accommodate is owed to him under s 20 of the CA 1989; or

(f) he is aged under 21 and was in care whilst aged 16–18, but has now left care; or

(g) he is 'vulnerable' as a result of having been in care, having served in the armed forces, or having been in prison, custody or detention; or

(h) he has ceased to occupy accommodation as a result of violence or threats of violence.

6.11.4 Local authority duties

The local authority has the following duties:

(a) to rehouse a homeless person with a priority need who did not become homeless intentionally;

(b) to provide temporary housing for a homeless person with a priority need who did become homeless intentionally. This accommodation must be provided for such period as the authority considers will give the homeless person a reasonable opportunity of finding his own accommodation. The authority is under a further duty to give advice and assistance to help him find such accommodation;

(c) to advise and assist a homeless person without a priority need to help him find his own accommodation. In addition, if satisfied that he did not become homeless intentionally, the authority *may* secure that accommodation is available for his occupation.

6.11.5 Local connection provisions

Generally, the local authority to which the applicant applies will be the one under the duty mentioned at **6.12.4**. However, that local authority may not be under such a duty if the applicant has no local connection with its area. This is so that local authorities in, for example, seaside areas do not become overwhelmed with applications. In this case, the local authority can refer the applicant to a local authority with which he does have a local connection (provided that the applicant is not at risk of domestic abuse in that authority's area).

The applicant will have a local connection with the area in which he is normally resident, or where he is employed, or where he has family associations.

6.11.6 Local authority tenancies

A local authority tenancy is classed as a secure tenancy under the Housing Act 1985. This means that a council tenant has a great deal of security of tenure. In particular, he cannot be evicted without an order for possession from the court, and such an order is available only on specified grounds, for example, non-payment of rent. This security depends partly on the tenant (or one of them where the property is on a joint tenancy) remaining in occupation.

On divorce, the court can order the tenant spouse to transfer the tenancy to the other spouse, and when this is done security of tenure is not lost (see further **9.5**).

6.12 Chapter summary

(1) On marriage breakdown one or both of the parties may need to claim welfare benefits. The following may be available:

- (a) child benefit;
- (b) income support or jobseeker's allowance or working tax credit;
- (c) child tax credit;
- (d) housing benefit;
- (e) council tax benefit;
- (f) loans or grants from the social fund.

(2) Local authorities have duties towards homeless people. Where a person is homeless unintentionally and has a priority need (eg if she has a child with her), the local authority must generally rehouse her.

Chapter 7
Calculating Child Maintenance

7.1	Introduction	85
7.2	The Child Support Agency and the Child Maintenance and Enforcement Commission	85
7.3	When does the CSA 1991 apply?	86
7.4	The jurisdiction of the court	86
7.5	Maintenance agreements and consent orders	88
7.6	Calculating the child maintenance	90
7.7	Further reforms	96
7.8	Chapter summary	97

7.1 Introduction

This chapter covers the Child Support Act 1991 (CSA 1991), which deals with maintenance for most children. In response to some of the criticisms raised against the Child Support Agency ('the Agency'), the CSA 1991 was amended by the Child Support Act 1995, the Child Support, Pensions and Social Security Act 2000 (CSPSSA 2000) and the Child Maintenance and Other Payments Act 2008 (CMOPA 2008). Throughout this book, any reference to the CSA 1991 includes the 1995, 2000 and 2008 Acts.

Chapter 4 dealt with the statutory criteria used by the court when considering applications for child maintenance under the MCA 1973 on marriage breakdown. These factors are of a general nature and do not assist the court in arriving at specific figures for maintenance. Accordingly, the orders for children's maintenance could vary enormously from one court to another.

However, the approach under the CSA 1991 is entirely different. This legislation introduced a precise method of assessing maintenance using a formula. The CSA 1991, as it was originally enacted, used a detailed and complex formula. This led to long delays in assessing liability and enforcement. The Act has now been amended by the CSPSSA 2000, which replaced the detailed formula with a calculation based on a simple percentage of the non-resident parent's net income. This will be discussed in detail at **7.6.2**. The CSPSSA 2000 came into effect on 3 March 2003 for new cases. Further amendments to the formula have been made under the CMOPA 2008. These are expected to come into force in 2012 and are discussed at **7.6.1.5**.

7.2 The Child Support Agency and the Child Maintenance and Enforcement Commission

The original idea behind the CSA 1991 was that the Child Support Agency ('the Agency') would deal almost exclusively with child maintenance. However, the Agency was beset with problems from the beginning, and the CMOPA 2008 has established the Child Maintenance and Enforcement Commission (C-MEC) which has now assumed responsibility for the Agency. The Child Support Agency will continue to administer the current scheme on behalf of C-MEC until all cases have been transferred to the new gross income scheme (see **7.6.1.5**) when it will be disbanded.

The main objective of C-MEC is to maximise the number of children for whom effective maintenance arrangements are in place. To achieve this, C-MEC has the further objectives of, first, encouraging and supporting parents to make voluntary maintenance arrangements and, secondly, supporting any applications to the Agency. Thus the preferred route is now private maintenance arrangements with resort to the Agency only when these would not be appropriate. To help accomplish these objectives, C-MEC has set up an information and support service for parents called Child Maintenance Options. This service aims to help parents understand the options available for child maintenance and choose the one which is most suitable for them.

The Government announced in October 2010 that, using powers to be granted to it under the Public Bodies Bill, it intended to abolish C-MEC and move its functions to the Department of Work and Pensions.

7.3 When does the CSA 1991 apply?

Section 11 of the CSA 1991 provides:

> For the purposes of this Act, each parent of a qualifying child is responsible for maintaining him.

This calls for a number of definitions to be considered.

Section 55(1) defines 'a child' as an unmarried person under 16, or a person under 19 receiving full-time education which is not advanced education.

Section 3(1) defines the 'qualifying child' as such if:

> (a) one of his parents is in relation to him a non-resident parent; or
>
> (b) both of his parents are, in relation to him, non-resident parents.

As the name suggests, a non-resident parent is one who is not living in the same household as the child (s 3(2)). The term 'parent' takes its usual meaning of being a person who is in law the mother or father of the child, ie the natural parent or adoptive parent of the child. Where the child has been born through artificial insemination, the non-biological parent will also be treated as a 'parent' under the CSA 1991 if he or she is a spouse or civil partner. If the non-biological parent is not married or a civil partner, he or she can choose to become a 'parent' with the mother's consent. Clearly, the definition includes unmarried as well as married parents, and it is immaterial whether or not the non-resident parent knows that the child is his. The definition does not extend to a step-parent. In cases of disputes over parentage, C-MEC (through the Child Support Agency) may make a maintenance calculation only in certain cases, for example, where the alleged father was married to the mother throughout the period of conception to birth, where the alleged father has been registered as the father of the child or where the alleged father has refused to take a scientific paternity test (CSA 1991, s 26). In other cases the Agency may not make a maintenance calculation until the court has determined parentage.

The CSA 1991 also refers to the person with care. Section 3(3) defines this person as one with whom the child lives and who usually provides the child's day-to-day care (this may not necessarily be the child's parent). It will generally be the person with care who will apply for the maintenance calculation, although the non-resident parent may choose to apply for a calculation against himself.

The child support officer has jurisdiction to make a maintenance calculation only if the qualifying child, the person with care and the non-resident parent are all habitually resident in the UK. This is subject to exceptions under s 44(2A) of the CSA 1991, relating to certain non-resident parents who are not habitually resident in the UK. These include civil servants and members of the armed forces working abroad, and employees of UK companies who are working abroad but whose employer calculates and arranges payment within the UK.

7.4 The jurisdiction of the court

By virtue of s 8 of the CSA 1991, C-MEC, rather than the court, has almost exclusive jurisdiction to deal with child maintenance.

Section 8(3) states:

> Except as provided in subsection (3A), in any case where subsection (1) applies, no court shall exercise any power which it would otherwise have to make, vary or revise any maintenance order in relation to the child and non-resident parent concerned.

The cases covered by s 8(1) are those where C-MEC would have jurisdiction to make a maintenance calculation with respect to a qualifying child and his non-resident parent. In other words, if an application could be dealt with by C-MEC (using the Child Support Agency), it must be pursued there. However, the court retains jurisdiction to deal with those cases in which C-MEC has no jurisdiction. The court, therefore, continues to deal with maintenance for step-children who are children of the family, and for those natural children who are too old to be qualifying children, for example, those aged 19 or over who are in education or training. If either the child, or the non-resident parent or the person with care is not habitually resident in the UK, C-MEC will have no jurisdiction, but the court would have jurisdiction. The court also retains jurisdiction to make capital orders on behalf of children, ie a lump sum or property adjustment order. The court has power to vary or revoke existing maintenance orders in all cases (CSA 1991, s 8(3A) and (4)).

In the limited cases where the court retains jurisdiction, it will have the widest discretion to determine the amount of a child's periodical payments. It will consider the factors listed in s 25(3) and (4) of the MCA 1973, giving first consideration to the child's welfare as directed in s 25(1) (discussed in **Chapter 4**). In practice, the court is likely to take as the appropriate starting point for a child maintenance order the figure produced by a maintenance calculation under the CSA 1991 (*GW v RE* [2003] EWHC 611 (Fam)). It will, therefore, be worthwhile calculating what a parent would be ordered to pay for a child were an application to the Agency possible. Indeed, in ancillary relief proceedings the parties must generally include the figure a maintenance calculation would produce in Form E (see **10.7.2** and **Appendix 3(E)**). If the child is a step-child, regard must be had to the liability of the child's natural parents to maintain the child. Consequently, the step-parent may be ordered to pay an amount significantly less than a natural parent would be required to pay under the CSA 1991 formula, particularly if the parent with care could claim against the natural parent through the Agency.

In cases where a maintenance calculation has been (or is about to be) made, this must be taken into account in proceedings by the carer for maintenance for herself, as it will have a direct bearing on both parties' means (see **8.3**).

As well as dealing with those cases which cannot be dealt with by C-MEC, the court retains jurisdiction to make maintenance orders for children in the three circumstances specified in s 8. These are discussed in **7.4.1** to **7.4.3** below.

7.4.1 Supplementary maintenance

Under s 8(6), the court will have jurisdiction if it is of the view that maintenance should be paid in addition to that assessed by the Agency. This will apply to wealthy families only as it is a prerequisite that the Agency has already made a calculation up to the maximum level and therefore that the non-resident parent has a net income of over £2,000 per week (see **7.6.2**).

There are not very many applications under this subsection as the courts will rarely be persuaded that further sums should be paid. The circumstances when a child might require further assistance, for example, because he needs school fees or because of a disability, are in any event separately provided for in s 8(7) and (8).

7.4.2 Educational expenses

Section 8(7) provides that the court may continue to exercise its jurisdiction if the child is in education and provision is required to meet some or all of the expenses connected with it.

Typically, applications under this section will be made to cover the cost of school fees which are not fully met from the maintenance calculation. They may also be made to cover the payment of school uniforms, sports equipment, books, etc.

7.4.3 Children with a disability

If a child has a disability, this is not taken into account by the Agency when making the maintenance calculation. Such children, however, will frequently have additional expenses to meet their needs. Section 8(8) enables the court to make an order to supplement the maintenance calculation to meet expenses attributable to that disability.

Section 8(9) defines a child as disabled if he is blind, deaf or dumb, or is substantially and permanently handicapped by illness, injury, mental disorder or congenital deformity, or such other disability as may be prescribed.

7.5 Maintenance agreements and consent orders

Section 8(3) restricts the jurisdiction of the court to determine maintenance for children. However, it is still open to parents to arrange maintenance for children without going to the Agency. The principle underlying the CMOPA 2008 is that it is preferable for parents to come to an agreement between themselves over child maintenance, only involving the state where this is not possible or the non-resident parent is trying to evade his or her responsibilities. Thus, in practice, many couples are making an effort to avoid the involvement of the Agency in the following ways.

7.5.1 Maintenance agreements

Maintenance agreements represent an alternative method of finalising family finances on the breakdown of the relationship. They are frequently used by those who are unable or do not wish to obtain a court order, and who have agreed their own arrangements and wish to put their agreements in writing. A maintenance agreement is not a court order but is enforceable in the same way as any other binding contract (see **12.3.4.1**).

Following the CSA 1991, parents may still make maintenance agreements, and s 9(2) specifically preserves this right. However, just as in the past such agreements could not oust the jurisdiction of the court to determine maintenance, neither can the jurisdiction of C-MEC be ousted. Section 9(3) and (4) rule out any attempts to undermine C-MEC's jurisdiction by prohibiting applications to the Agency. As a result, any carer who enters into a separation agreement (even one which expressly purports to restrict the parties' rights to make any further claims) will, nevertheless, be able to apply to the Agency for a maintenance calculation.

7.5.2 Consent orders

Some couples may want to do more than just put their agreement in writing; they may want their agreement embodied in a court order. If so, they can apply for a consent order.

In spite of the clear wording of s 8(3), which prohibits the court from making (varying or reviving) maintenance orders where C-MEC would have jurisdiction, s 8(5) preserves the power of the court to make an order if:

(a) a written agreement (whether or not enforceable) provides for the making or securing by a non-resident parent of the child of periodical payments to or for the benefit of the child; and

(b) the maintenance order which the court makes is, in all material respects, in the same terms as that agreement.

This provision was implemented by the Child Maintenance (Written Agreements) Order 1993 (SI 1993/620). Therefore, a separation agreement may be converted into a court order in the same terms. All that is required is for there to be a written agreement (this can be evidenced in a separate agreement, or incorporated in the recitals to the consent order). As a result of s 8(5) and the Regulations, parents may continue to side-step the Agency and embody a clean break agreement in a consent order.

Where a consent order was made before 3 March 2003, no application can be made to the Agency under s 4 whilst that order is in force. If a consent order is made after 3 March 2003, no application can be made to the Agency under s 4 for one year (CSA 1991, s 4(10)). Thus consent orders made after 3 March 2003 will be binding as to child maintenance for only one year, after which the parent with care can apply for a maintenance calculation. The Family Law Committee of The Law Society recommended in its 2003 report, *Financial Provision on Divorce: Clarity and Fairness – Proposals for Reform*, that this provision be scrapped and that couples should still be able to agree consent orders in relation to child maintenance which will bind until the child(ren)'s majority. Unfortunately, the CMOPA 2008 has not introduced this reform. Thus family law practitioners are having to use various devices to try to mitigate the effect of s 4(10) of the CSA 1991. One way is to enter a contract ancillary to the consent order whereby the parties agree to pay (or repay) any difference between the agreed maintenance order and a maintenance calculation subsequently made by the Child Support Agency. Another is to agree to an annual child periodical payments order (or 'Christmas order'). Such an order lasts for a day short of a year and is then replaced by an order in identical terms the following day. However, there is some criticism of such Christmas orders as contrary to public policy (see, for example, Nicholas Mostyn QC in *Child's Pay*, a computer package by Class Publishing). Lastly, '*Segal* orders' are global orders combining maintenance to both spouse and child. The amount to be paid is reduced by the amount of any subsequent maintenance calculation by the Child Support Agency. Such orders are possible only if there is a substantial element within them for the financial support of the parent with care. However, although it appears that some courts are prepared to endorse each of these mechanisms, there is no guarantee that they will be upheld by a higher court.

Irrespective of s 4(10) of the CSA 1991, if the order or agreement is revoked an application may be made to the Agency immediately. The decision whether or not to revoke an existing order rests with the court. It may not be prepared to revoke its original order, which would in effect block an early application to the Agency. In the case of *B v M (Child Support: Revocation of Order)* [1994] Fam Law 370, an order was made for the maintenance of three children in 1986. The mother wanted to apply under CSA 1991 for an assessment in respect of the two younger children, and applied for the original maintenance order to be revoked to enable her to do so. The father successfully appealed against the district judge's revocation. The court stated that the proper course would be to vary the original order, and that it was inappropriate to exercise its discretion to revoke the order purely because the mother wished to apply to the Agency. However, the court made it clear that each case must be considered on its merits.

Where a court order has been made, the court will retain its power to vary the order (CSA 1991, s 8(3A)).

7.5.3 Child maintenance flowchart

In practical terms, parents with care will have three choices when it comes to obtaining child maintenance: entering an agreement with the non-resident parent (which should be in writing for clarity and certainty); applying to the court; and applying to the Child Support Agency. The following flowchart may help to clarify when each of these options is appropriate.

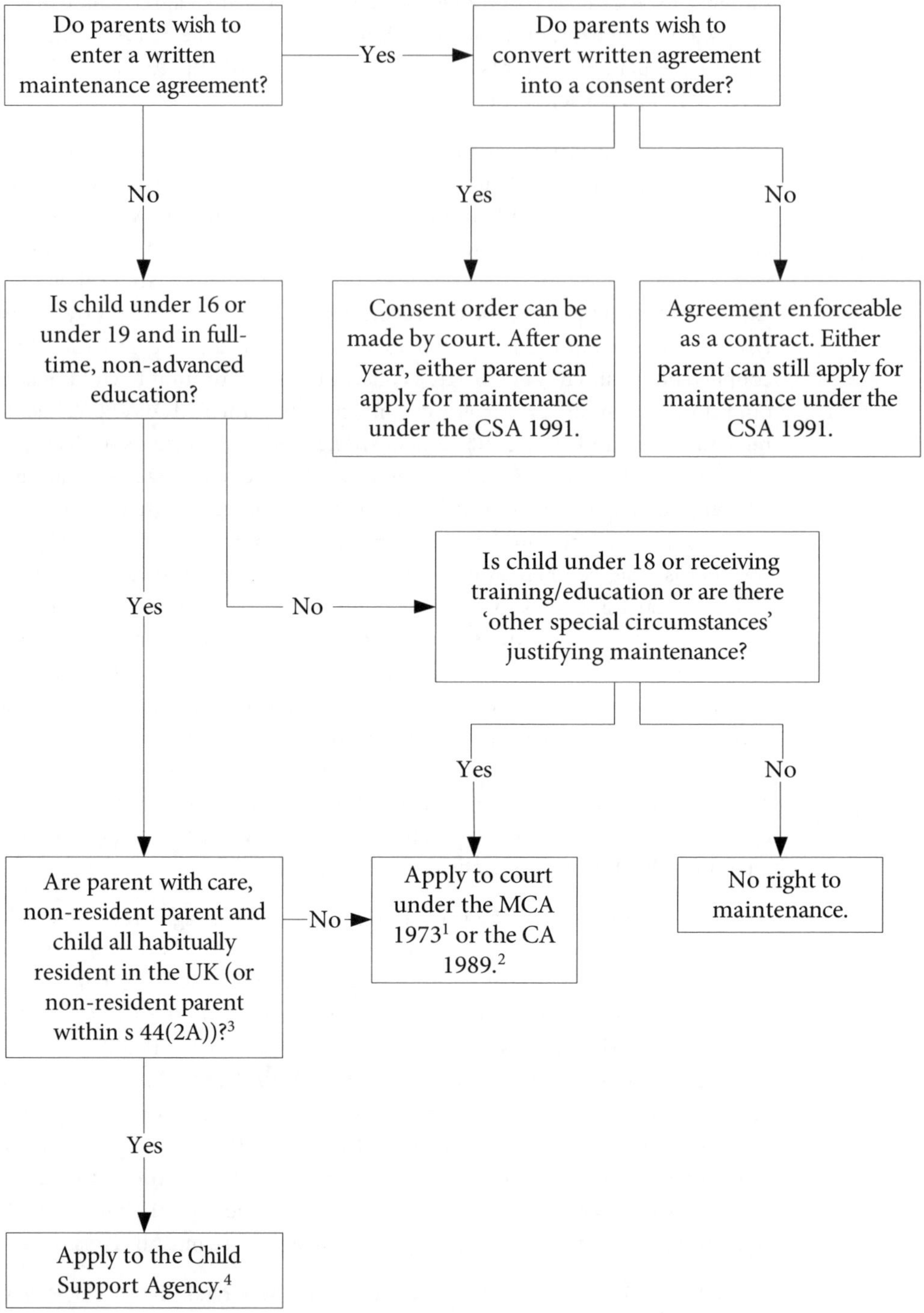

1 For MCA, see **4.3.2** and **Appendix 1(A)**.
2 For CA, see **13.10.4** and **Appendix 1(E)**.
3 See **7.3**.
4 Court may order additional maintenance if child is disabled, to cover educational expenses or where the family is very wealthy – see **7.4.1–7.4.3**.

7.6 Calculating the child maintenance

When an application is made to the Child Support Agency, a formula is applied in order to calculate the maintenance payable in respect of a child by the non-resident parent. The key elements of the formula are set out in Sch 1 to the Act (see **Appendix 1(F)**).

7.6.1 The formula

This is based solely on the non-resident parent's net earned income (ie income net of tax, national insurance and pension payments) and the number of children for whom that parent is responsible. The maintenance calculation is at one of four rates: the basic rate, the reduced rate, the flat rate or the nil rate.

7.6.1.1 The basic rate

This will be the usual rate. It provides that the non-resident parent should pay a proportion of his net income as follows:

Number of children	*Proportion of net income*
One	15%
Two	20%
Three or more	25%

Thus a non-resident parent with two children and a net weekly income of £500 will pay £100 per week. There is a cap on the amount of net income which will be taken into account, so that net weekly income of over £2,000 will be ignored.

If the non-resident parent has other children living with him, for whom either he or any partner he is living with receives child benefit, his net income is reduced by the following amount before the basic rate is applied:

Number of other children	*Proportion net income is reduced*
One	15%
Two	20%
Three or more	25%

Example

George is living with Linda and her two children, Doug (9) and Chloe (4). His ex-wife lives with their only child, Patricia (7). George has net income of £500. The maintenance calculation for Patricia will be:

£500 × 20% = £100

£500 – £100 = £400

£400 × 15% = £60

7.6.1.2 The reduced rate

This will apply where the non-resident parent's net weekly income is more than £100 but less than £200. The amount payable increases in proportion to the amount by which the non-resident parent's income exceeds £100. The exact method of calculation is contained in the Child Support (Maintenance Calculations and Special Cases) Regulations 2000 (SI 2001/155) (CS(MCSC) Regs 2000).

7.6.1.3 The flat rate

This will apply if the non-resident parent's net weekly income is £100 or less; he is in receipt of certain benefits, pensions or allowances (including income support, jobseeker's allowance and incapacity benefit), or his partner is in receipt of income support or income-based jobseeker's allowance. The flat rate is currently £5 per week (CS(MCSC) Regs 2000).

7.6.1.4 The nil rate

This applies where the non-resident parent has net income of below £5 or comes within a prescribed category (including full-time students in advanced education and prisoners).

7.6.1.5 The formula under the CMOPA 2008

Under the CMOPA 2008, gross weekly income will be used instead of net weekly income when calculating the amount of child maintenance to be paid. When calculating gross income, the latest available information from HMRC will be used. Once made, the maintenance award will be fixed for a year unless the payer's income varies by more than 25%. The percentages to be applied for the basic rate will be as follows:

Number of children	Proportion of gross income up to £800 per week	Proportion of gross income between £800 and £3,000 per week
One	12%	9%
Two	16%	12%
Three or more	19%	15%

C-MEC anticipates that this formula will begin to be used early in 2012, although its Chair has stated that this will not be done until IT systems are up and running properly, which may mean that this date will be put back. At this time, parents on the existing schemes will be invited either to apply for the new scheme or to make a private maintenance agreement. That process is expected to take around three years, after which the existing schemes will close.

7.6.2 Special cases

7.6.2.1 Apportionment

The position where a non-resident parent has more than one qualifying child and those children are looked after by more than one person with care is covered by Sch 1, para 6 to the CSA 1991. In such a case, the maintenance calculation is divided by the number of qualifying children and then shared between the parents with care in proportion to the number of qualifying children in each family.

Example

Jon has four qualifying children, one being cared for by Lisa and three by Anita. His net income is £800. The maintenance calculation is therefore 25% × £800 = £200. Lisa will receive £50 maintenance (one quarter) and Anita the remaining £150 (three quarters).

7.6.2.2 Existing court order

Where there is an existing court order in respect of one or more of the non-resident parent's qualifying children, the maintenance calculation will be similarly apportioned, although the actual amount paid to any children in respect of whom there is a court order will be the amount under that order.

Example

Red has four children. His eldest, from a previous marriage, is now living with her mother, Maria, in Spain. He pays maintenance of £75 for her under a court order. Emily, from whom he has recently separated, applies for a maintenance calculation for his other three children. Red has a net income of £1,000. The maintenance calculation is therefore 25% x £1,000 = £250. Emily will receive £187.50 (three quarters). Red will continue to pay £75 under the court order to Maria.

7.6.2.3 Shared care

Where both parents share care, the maintenance calculation will be reduced. The amount of this reduction will depend on the number of qualifying children and the amount of time they spend in the care of each parent (CSA 1991, Sch 1, para 7).

Shared care – basic and reduced rates

The amount of reduction for one child is:

No of nights per year	*Fraction to subtract*
52–103	one-seventh
104–155	two-sevenths
156–174	three-sevenths
175 or more	one half

Where the parent with care is looking after more than one qualifying child of the same non-resident parent the reduction will be the sum of the relevant fractions divided by the number of children. Put simply, this means that where the children stay the same number of nights each with the non-resident parent then, generally, the maintenance calculation will be reduced by one-seventh for each night of the week that they stay.

Example

Nick and Maria have three children. They all stay with Nick on Friday and Saturday night each week. The initial maintenance calculation is £210. This will be reduced by $\frac{2}{7}$ (ie $\frac{2}{7}+\frac{2}{7}+\frac{2}{7} \div 3$). $\frac{2}{7} \times$ £210 = £60. So the final maintenance calculation will be £210 – £60 = £150.

However, note that there is a further reduction of a flat rate of £7 per child where that child is looked after by the non-resident parent for 175 nights or more. Care must also be taken in the calculation where the children stay for a different number of nights with the non-resident parent.

Example

Duncan and Nicola have two children, Jack and Georgia. Jack stays with Duncan for 180 nights a year, Georgia for 156. Duncan's maintenance calculation will be reduced by $\frac{13}{28}$ ($[\frac{7}{14}+\frac{6}{14}] \div 2$), and then by a further £7.

Shared care – flat rate

Where:

(a) child support maintenance would be payable at the flat rate because the non-resident parent is in receipt of prescribed benefits, pensions or allowances, or his partner is in receipt of prescribed benefits; and

(b) the non-resident parent cares for one or more qualifying children for at least 52 nights a year

then the maintenance calculation will be nil.

There is some criticism of the shared care provisions on the basis that they can encourage arguments about the amount of staying contact for the non-resident parent as this will affect the amount of child support he must pay. In *Re B (A Child)* [2006] EWCA Civ 1574 the court made it clear that when deciding the level of staying contact or whether a joint residence order was appropriate, any impact this would have on the amount of child support being paid should be ignored. The father argued that an increase in child support payable would impact on the welfare of the child, since it would reduce his disposable income and thus the child's enjoyment of contact. This argument was dismissed as being wrong in principle and impractical.

7.6.3 Variations

The application of a rigid formula may inevitably lead to harsh results in certain cases. For this reason, the CSA 1991 (as amended) allows for applications for variation. Any such application can be made either before a final maintenance calculation has been made (CSA 1991, s 28A), or after (CSA 1991, s 28G). However, variations will be allowed only in certain tightly defined circumstances as set out in Sch 4B to the CSA 1991 and the Child Support (Variations) Regulations 2000 (SI 2001/156) (see below). In addition, the Agency must be of the opinion that, in all the circumstances of the case, it would be just and equitable to agree to a variation.

7.6.3.1 Special expenses

These are:

(a) costs incurred by the non-resident parent maintaining contact with a qualifying child;

(b) costs attributable to a long-term illness or disability of another relevant child;

(c) certain debts incurred before the parent became a non-resident parent (generally only if these debts were incurred for the benefit of both parents or the child);

(d) the maintenance element of boarding school fees for the child in relation to whom the application for a maintenance calculation is made; and

(e) mortgage payments on the home the non-resident parent and parent with care shared, provided the non-resident parent no longer has an interest in the property and the parent with care and child still live there.

These expenses must be of at least a 'threshold' amount to be taken into account (unless the expense relates to ground (b) when there is no threshold). Where the non-resident parent has a net weekly income of £200 or more these expenses must total in aggregate £15 or more a week. Where the non-resident parent has a net weekly income of less than £200 the expenses must in aggregate total £10 or more a week. If the Agency considers any of these special expenses to be unreasonably high or to have been unreasonably incurred, it may substitute such lower amount as it considers reasonable (Child Support (Variations) Regulations 2000, reg 15).

Generally speaking, if allowable, these expenses will be deducted from the net weekly income of the non-resident parent before making the maintenance calculation (Child Support (Variations) Regulations 2000, reg 23). However, any reduction for boarding school fees are not to reduce the net weekly income by more than 50% (Child Support (Variations) Regulations 2000, reg 13).

7.6.3.2 Property or capital transfers

One of the main criticisms of the original formula was that it failed to take into account any capital transfers made by the non-resident parent to the parent with care. For example, one parent may have transferred the matrimonial home to the other parent, in return for which that parent agreed to forgo maintenance (entirely or in part) for herself and the children. A non-resident parent who, having entered into such a clean break agreement prior to the CSA 1991, subsequently faces a maintenance calculation, is likely to feel very aggrieved as this strikes at the very basis of the original settlement.

In response to these criticisms, the formula was revised in April 1995 to take such disposals broadly into account, and this has been kept (in a slightly amended form) by the CSPSSA 2000. However, this applies only to capital transfers made before the CSA 1991 came into force (ie before April 1993). On this basis, no further details of this variation will be considered here.

7.6.3.3 Additional cases

Non-resident parents may apply for a downwards variation of any maintenance calculation on the basis of special expenses, or property or capital transfers as set out above. However, Sch 4B, para 4 to the CSA 1991 and the Child Support (Variations) Regulations 2000, regs 18–20 allow for variations to be made in other cases which may result in an increase in the amount of child maintenance payable. These are:

(a) The non-resident parent has assets, such as cash, shares or land but excluding, amongst other things, his home and business assets, with a net value exceeding £65,000. The value of these is calculated by applying the statutory rate of interest (currently 8% pa) and dividing by 52. This amount is then added to the non-resident parent's net income. For example, if the non-resident parent owned shares worth £80,000, these would be taken to produce income of (£80,000 × 8%) ÷ 52 = £123.08 per week.

(b) The maintenance calculation is at the nil rate due to the non-resident parent coming within a prescribed category, or at the flat rate due to the non-resident parent being in receipt of a prescribed benefit, pension or allowance, but the Agency is satisfied that the non-resident parent is in receipt of net income of over £100 which would otherwise be taken into account. This would cover, for example, the earnings of a non-resident parent who was a student. The whole of this income will be taken into account as net income.

(c) The non-resident parent has the ability to control the amount of income he receives from a company or business, including earnings from employment or self-employment. The net weekly income so assessed must exceed £100. This would cover, for example, income received by way of dividends.

(d) The Agency is satisfied that the non-resident parent has unreasonably reduced the amount of his net income in order to reduce his liability to pay child support maintenance, eg where a non-resident parent reduces the amount of his net income by making excessive payments into a pension scheme.

(e) The non-resident parent's lifestyle is inconsistent with the amount of his declared income. In such a case a variation can be made on the basis that the non-resident parent is in fact in receipt of the amount of income required to support his lifestyle.

7.6.4 Default and interim maintenance decisions (CSA 1991, s 12)

In certain circumstances, it will not be possible to make a final maintenance calculation straightaway. If this is because there is insufficient information to complete the calculation, the Agency may make a default maintenance decision. If it is because an application for variation is outstanding, the Agency may make an interim maintenance decision.

7.6.4.1 Default maintenance decision

Where there is insufficient information to make a final maintenance calculation, maintenance can be calculated at the default rate. This is £30 per week if one qualifying child, £40 per week if two qualifying children and £50 per week if there are three or more qualifying children (Child Support (Maintenance Calculation Procedure) Regulations 2000 (SI 2001/157), reg 7). When the relevant information is provided, a new maintenance calculation will be made. If non-provision of information by the non-resident parent led to the making of the default maintenance decision, her maintenance liability for the period that the default rate was in place will be recalculated only if the full rate is higher than the default rate. The Government hopes that this will provide an incentive for non-resident parents to provide information quickly. It will also avoid the situation where overpayments need to be recovered from the parent with care.

7.6.4.2 Interim maintenance decision

Where there is an application for a variation outstanding, maintenance may be calculated as normal, ignoring the variation application. If the variation application is successful, this interim rate will be replaced with the new level of maintenance calculated taking into account the variation. The maintenance calculation at this new level will have retrospective effect.

7.6.5 Voluntary payments

A non-resident parent may wish to ensure that he is given credit for any payments of child support maintenance that he makes whilst a maintenance calculation is being made. Section 28J of the CSA 1991 provides that voluntary payments can be set off against any child support maintenance liability under a maintenance calculation, but, by s 28J(4), such a voluntary payment must be made to the Agency unless agreed otherwise.

Another possible device was discussed in *Dorney-Kingdom v Dorney-Kingdom* [2000] 2 FLR 855. The court stated that a provision in an order for spouse maintenance which incorporated some of the costs of caring for the children and which was reduced once the Agency had assessed child support was legitimate provided it included a substantial amount of spousal support. Such orders ('*Segal* orders') are useful since the ancillary relief proceedings are often heard before the child maintenance has been calculated and such an order will ensure that the parent with care has sufficient money to support the children in the interim.

7.7 Further reforms

To give further effect to its policy of encouraging parents to make voluntary maintenance arrangements, the Government published a Consultation Paper, 'Strengthening families, promoting parental responsibility: the future of child maintenance'. The consultation period ended in April 2011 and the Government produced its response on 12 July 2011. Legislation implementing some of the proposals is now before Parliament as the Welfare Reform Bill. The Government intends to bring in other proposals using regulations.

Under the Welfare Reform Bill, parents wishing to use the statutory scheme will need to pass through a 'gateway'. This requires them to have taken 'reasonable steps' to establish whether it is possible or appropriate to make a private maintenance agreement. A private agreement may not be appropriate, for example, where the separation is due to violence or risk of abuse. In order to help parents agree on the amount of maintenance, the Welfare Reform Bill contains a provision allowing parents to apply to C-MEC for a 'indicative maintenance calculation', which will tell the parents what the maintenance calculation would be if an application were made under the statutory scheme but will not create any liability to pay.

Once the gateway is passed through, an applicant will need to pay an application fee. This will be £100, unless the applicant is on benefit, when it will be £50, with £20 being payable initially and the rest in instalments (which may be waived if the applicant opts to use the 'maintenance direct' option (see below)). Victims of domestic violence will be exempt from the fee.

Should C-MEC collect the child maintenance from the non-resident parent, further charges will be payable. This 'collection fee' has not been finalised but is anticipated to be between 7% and 12% of the maintenance to be paid. Thus the parent with care will receive the maintenance with this fee deducted. In addition, the non-resident parent will need to pay a surcharge of between 15% and 20% on top of the maintenance paid. These collection fees can be avoided if the non-resident parent pays the maintenance directly to the parent with care rather than through C-MEC.

Under the Welfare Reform Bill, the parent with care may utilise the collection service only either if the non-resident parent agrees, or if C-MEC is satisfied that the non-resident parent is unlikely to make payments.

The Government is also considering whether it should change the one-year rule in relation to consent orders (see **7.5.2**). It has stated that it will consider these arrangements in the light of the ongoing Family Justice Review.

7.8 Chapter summary

(1) The Child Support Agency will deal with maintenance for a child where the child is:

(a) under 16;

(b) under 19 and in full-time, non-advanced education.

(2) The courts will deal with maintenance for a child in the following circumstances:

(a) where the child is a step-child;

(b) where the child is aged 16–19 and in advanced education or is aged over 19;

(c) where either parent or the child is not habitually resident in the UK;

(d) to provide top-up maintenance;

(e) to cover education expenses;

(f) to cover disability expenses; or

(g) by making a consent order.

(3) A simple formula is applied to calculate maintenance for a child under CSA 1991, based on a flat-rate percentage of the non-resident parent's net income. This will change once the CMOPA 2008 comes fully into force, to a two-tiered percentage of gross income.

(4) Variations from the simple formula are possible in certain tightly defined cases.

Chapter 8
Maintenance for a Spouse

8.1	Introduction	99
8.2	High income families	99
8.3	Middle income families	100
8.4	Low income families	101
8.5	Chapter summary	102

8.1 Introduction

The amount of maintenance to be paid by one spouse to the other will depend on numerous variables, and a case-by-case approach will be taken by the solicitor and the court. Figures cited in reported decisions are of little assistance as there are rarely two cases with identical facts. However, one variable will always be significant and that is the presence or otherwise of dependent children. If there are children to provide for, this will have a significant impact on each party's needs and resources. The maintenance being paid and received for children must be taken into account when calculating maintenance for a spouse. In many instances, there will be insufficient resources remaining for maintenance to be paid to a spouse after paying maintenance for children. It is especially so in low income families. In middle and higher income families, spouses may wish to pursue claims for their own provision in addition to maintenance for their children.

8.2 High income families

In high income families, the courts will be less concerned about meeting an applicant's basic needs than ensuring a fair apportionment of the family's wealth. In doing so, they will bear in mind the standard of living enjoyed prior to the breakdown of the marriage, as well as all the other relevant factors in the s 25 of the MCA 1973 (see **4.5.1**). Commonly, where significant capital is available, it will not be appropriate for there to be any maintenance payable between spouses. In such cases, a clean break will be favoured instead (see **4.6**).

A clean break will not always be appropriate in wealthy families as there may be insufficient liquid capital. Assets may be tied up in land or in a business. It will frequently be counter-productive to realise such assets, as their loss could have a disproportionately adverse effect on the income generated by the assets as a whole. In such cases, it would be more sensible and profitable for the assets to be retained and for a maintenance order to be made instead.

In certain cases there may be insufficient capital for an immediate clean break but a very large amount of income (perhaps, for example, a young person 'up and coming' in the City). In *Miller v Miller; McFarlane v McFarlane* [2006] UKHL 24, the House of Lords upheld an award of £250,000 per annum to Mrs McFarlane and extended its duration for her lifetime. The size of the award was partly to compensate her for the couple's joint decision that she should give up her successful career to care for the children. The House of Lords made it clear that it was in fact unlikely to be appropriate for maintenance to continue at this level indefinitely. However, their Lordships took the view that the onus should be on the husband to seek a variation once Mrs McFarlane had revived her earning capacity and he had reduced his outgoings, by which time a clean break might be possible. Subsequently, Mrs McFarlane successfully applied for an increase in her periodical payments to enable a clean break to occur on or before the husband's retirement (see *McFarlane v McFarlane* [2009] EWHC 891). In cases where the compensation principle does not apply, the court is likely to use the applicant's needs (generously interpreted) as a guiding principle (see eg *McCartney v Mills McCartney* [2008] EWHC 401 (Fam)).

8.3 Middle income families

The approach taken by the courts to the large group of people who are neither wealthy nor on or near subsistence level has varied over the years. The current guiding principle would appear to be needs, which may be generously interpreted where funds allow. In cases where there are minor children and a maintenance calculation has been or is to be made by the Child Support Agency, the court is likely to calculate whether the non-resident parent can afford to make any additional periodical payment to the parent with care of the children.

In order to decide what figure (if any) is appropriate for spouse maintenance, or to decide on whether a figure proposed by the other party is reasonable, the solicitor must make a calculation.

It is important to consider the reality behind a particular figure to ensure that the payer can afford to make any payment proposed and that the recipient can manage to live off her income (which will of course include the proposed maintenance). It is important to compare the size of their respective households and the extent of their liabilities. If maintenance is also being paid for children, this must also be borne in mind, as it represents an additional obligation for the payer and an additional resource for the parent to whom it is being paid.

The solicitor should calculate the parties' net income, taking into account any income tax, national insurance and pension contributions. The figure for any child support maintenance must be added to the recipient's income and correspondingly deducted as an expense from the payer's income. A budget will need to be drawn up for each household, which should be compared against the available income. Clearly, there is scope for argument about what represents a reasonable budget, and the solicitor will need to look at the figures carefully. However, care must be taken not to waste costs in a disproportionate manner.

Example

This simple example uses *notional figures* to establish whether maintenance should be paid to a wife in addition to child support. In reality, a budget is likely to include a number of other expenses, for example, holidays, etc.

Fergus and Rose have two children, aged 8 and 10. Fergus earns £35,000 annually (gross) and Rose earns £7,000 annually (gross). Fergus has been assessed to pay £100.00 per week by the Child Support Agency. Rose has remained in the family home with the children and Fergus is in rented accommodation.

Stage 1: Calculate each spouse's net income:

	Fergus	Rose
	£	£
Earnings	675.00	135.00
Less tax	105.00	14.00
National Insurance	55.00	12.00
Pension	30.00	5.00
	485.00	104.00
Child benefit	–	30.00
Child tax credit		10.00
	485.00	144.00

Stage 2: Take child maintenance of £100.00 into account:

	Fergus		Rose
	£		£
Net income	485.00	Net income	144.00
less	100.00	plus	100.00
	385.00		244.00

Stage 3: Deduct each spouse's budgeted expenses:

	Fergus			Rose
	£	£	£	£
Net income		385.00		244.00
Less expenses:				
Gas and electricity	10.00		15.00	
Council tax	25.00		30.00	
Mortgage	–		135.00	
Rent	115.00		–	
Car insurance, tax and petrol	35.00		–	
TV licence	3.00		3.00	
Bus fares	–		10.00	
Childcare	–		20.00	
Clothing	40.00		20.00	
Food, etc	50.00		75.00	
Total		278.00		308.00
Balance available		107.00		- 64.00

Thus it would appear that Fergus would need to pay maintenance of over half his available income to enable the books to balance. Even so, clearly money is very tight, as there are no allowances for entertainment or holidays in the figures. However, it can be seen that Fergus claims he needs £40 per week for clothes, whereas Rose is claiming she needs only £20 for herself and the two children. Thus it would be sensible to query Fergus's budgeted figure for clothes.

It is likely that for any family, a number of such budget calculations will need to be made before an appropriate settlement is reached. An online tool which can help with this is the divorce and separation budget calculator on the Money Advice Service's website.

8.4 Low income families

If there are clearly insufficient resources for both parties to be independent of welfare benefits, the court and practitioners take a pragmatic approach. Although generally a spouse cannot cast his or her responsibility to maintain the other and their children onto the State, common sense dictates that in low income cases the availability of welfare benefits must be taken into account. The calculation of maintenance in such cases will often be a relatively straightforward process, as it will be a matter of identifying how much the recipient needs to live on and how much the payer can spare. The court will never order a party to pay a sum which would place him below a notional subsistence level. This means the payer would be allowed to keep sufficient money to pay his housing costs, as well as the sum he would be entitled to were he to claim income support or jobseeker's allowance. The reason for this is plain: there would be little incentive for such a person to earn a living or to pay the maintenance if he would be worse off than if he were unemployed.

The court is even reluctant to make an order which would reduce the payer to this subsistence level. It is more common for the payer to be able to retain a percentage (say 15%) of his net earnings above his subsistence level.

If the recipient is receiving income support or jobseeker's allowance and will continue to do so when maintenance is paid, she will not be any better off as a result. This is because any maintenance she receives forms part of her income when calculating her benefit entitlement and reduces her entitlement pound for pound. Her income will, therefore, remain at the level of her applicable amount.

> **Example**
>
> Lucy is 45, unemployed and has no dependent children. Her applicable amount for jobseeker's allowance is £45. She has no income of her own and, therefore, receives £45 jobseeker's allowance. Her husband Bill is ordered to pay her £10 per week maintenance. Thereafter, she will receive only £35 jobseeker's allowance, but when this is added to her maintenance her income remains at £45 per week.

In such circumstances, clients may be unenthusiastic about claiming maintenance. However, if the client has any prospects of finding employment, even modest maintenance when combined with wages may, in time, assist her to become independent of State benefits altogether.

Careful calculation must be made in the case of low income families to ensure that the recipient is not worse off with maintenance than without it. This can arise if the maintenance raises the recipient's income to, or only slightly above, her applicable amount. If this occurs, she will lose her right to income support (or jobseeker's allowance), but more particularly to the passport benefits to which a claimant is automatically entitled. She will lose the right to free prescriptions and school meals for her children, and as a result would be worse off. She would also lose the right to full housing benefit and full council tax benefit, although she would be able to make a means-tested claim. It will often be appropriate to accept a reduced sum of maintenance to ensure that the recipient is still eligible for income support (or jobseeker's allowance), thereby enabling her to continue to qualify for these other benefits. This is discussed further in **Chapter 6**.

Where both parties are in receipt of income support or jobseeker's allowance, it will not usually be appropriate to apply for maintenance for a spouse. If a spouse is earning and receiving working tax credit, it may be possible (although uncommon) for very modest maintenance to be paid to the other spouse. The position is different, however, with children's maintenance. Even parents on income support or jobseeker's allowance may be expected to pay maintenance for their children under the CSA 1991 (see **Chapter 7**). In low income families in particular, if maintenance is payable for children, it is likely that the non-resident parent will have insufficient resources to pay maintenance for the parent with care as well. If, after paying the child maintenance, the payer's income is close to his subsistence level, no spouse maintenance will be paid.

8.5 Chapter summary

(1) In practice, it is not possible to isolate issues of maintenance from other issues, such as where the children are going to live and what is going to happen to the matrimonial home and other property.

(2) Maintenance for a spouse is dealt with by the courts under the MCA 1973. The court will consider what the Child Support Agency assessment will be for any relevant children and then decide whether any payment in addition for the spouse can be afforded and is appropriate, bearing in mind the s 25 factors. The court will consider the effect of any proposed order on both household's budgets.

(3) In higher income cases the courts will use a guideline of needs (generously interpreted) when calculating the amount of maintenance to be paid. If significant capital is available, maintenance is likely to be capitalised to effect a clean break.

Chapter 9
Dealing with the Capital Assets

9.1	Introduction	103
9.2	Selling the home	103
9.3	Retaining the home	105
9.4	The interests of third parties	108
9.5	The rented home	110
9.6	Protecting the capital assets	110
9.7	Lump sums	113
9.8	Pensions	115
9.9	Bankruptcy	115
9.10	Chapter summary	116

9.1 Introduction

The matrimonial home is generally the most important property owned by the family. As well as providing a home for the parties and their children, it is an important capital asset. The court must decide whether it is appropriate to retain the property so that it will continue to provide a home, or whether to sell it and thereby realise the capital. The home also represents a liability, as it must be maintained and in most cases it will be subject to a mortgage. In deciding what should be done with the home, the court is required to have regard to the factors in s 25 of the MCA 1973, considered in **Chapter 4**. These factors assist the court in deciding which type of order to make and what size each party's respective share in the home should be. Although the court will take into account the financial contributions made by the parties to the purchase of the home, it is not fettered by proprietary interests, and such contributions will frequently be outweighed by other factors. The court has a wide discretion to determine how the property should be held and in what shares. It will take into account the parties' past and future non-financial contributions, as well as the other factors referred to in s 25, in an attempt to reach a fair outcome. The House of Lords has made it clear that there is no presumption that both spouses invariably have a right to be able to buy a new home from the assets available to the family. Instead, the court will exercise its discretion in each and every case, in the light of the relevant s 25 factors as applied to that case (*Piglowska v Piglowski* [1999] 2 FLR 763).

Although this chapter is confined to considering the matrimonial home, lump sum orders and pensions, it is important to bear in mind that the court will not look at the capital assets in isolation. It will decide upon a package of complementary orders dealing with income and capital. Any agreement will require careful drafting. In **Chapter 10**, consideration is given to drafting the various orders examined in this chapter.

The following property adjustment orders may be made and are considered below:

(a) Immediate sale.

(b) Outright transfer.

(c) Deferred trust of land.

(d) Deferred charge.

9.2 Selling the home

There is a variety of reasons why the court might exercise its powers under s 24A of the MCA 1973 to order the immediate sale of the matrimonial home and the division of the proceeds between the parties. Typically, an immediate sale of the house will be appropriate where the court is effecting an immediate clean break. Each party will be able to use his or her share of the equity towards purchasing separate homes. They will first redeem the existing mortgage from the proceeds of sale, which benefits the parties by releasing them from a significant debt which bound them together. For the sake of clarity, any order for sale should deal with the liabilities to be met out of the proceeds of sale, such as the existing mortgage, estate agent's commission and solicitor's conveyancing fees. When calculating the value of the equity, the costs of purchase and removal should also be borne in mind. For a publicly funded client the statutory charge will also be paid out of the proceeds of sale. However, it may be possible for the payment of the charge to be postponed by registering it against the assisted party's new home (see **2.9**).

When making an order that the home be sold (whether immediately or on the triggering of a deferred trust of land or deferred charge – see **9.3.2** and **9.3.3** below), it is generally preferable to specify that the parties should receive a set percentage of the proceeds of sale rather than a set sum (*Browne (formerly Pritchard) v Pritchard* [1975] 1 WLR 1366 and *Hope-Smith v Hope-Smith* [1989] 2 FLR 56). This is fairer, since both parties will be equally at risk in a fluctuating property market.

Section 24A(2) (see **Appendix 1(A)**) provides that the order may contain such consequential or supplementary provisions as the court thinks fit. This therefore gives the court the widest discretion to make directions about the sale, for example, which party's solicitors should have the conduct of the sale, how the price is to be determined and what payments should be made out of the proceeds, etc.

There will not usually be sufficient equity for both parties to be able to purchase alternative homes outright. However, if the couple are both earning, they may be able to do so with the aid of a new mortgage. If one party has only low earnings (or low earning capacity), that party may receive a greater proportion of the equity to enable him to reaccommodate himself. A party may be willing to forgo some of his share of the equity in order to achieve a clean break. This may be regarded as the lesser of two evils if the only other viable alternative is for the other party to remain in the property for many years. If the parties are relatively young and without children, the house is likely to be sold even if the equity is very small, as there is a strong presumption in favour of a clean break in these circumstances. If there are minor children, the court must give first consideration to their welfare when determining what should happen to the matrimonial home, and will thus wish to be satisfied that they will be suitably accommodated. The court will also have regard to the disruption which a move might cause to the children and to the adverse effect this could have on their stability and security. If a move to a cheaper area would involve a change in the children's schooling, the court may be hesitant to order this. However, children frequently adapt well to change and if the home (or the school) has been unhappy, a move might benefit them. If the house is larger than needed and has a substantial equity, it may well be unduly harsh on the non-resident parent to deny him the opportunity to realise some of his capital. In such a case, the court may order sale and perhaps give a weighted share of the equity to the parent caring for the children, as she will require a larger property than the non-resident parent and will frequently have a smaller income.

An immediate sale may be ordered out of necessity if there are insufficient resources to retain and maintain the house. If the couple's finances were already stretched before the marriage breakdown, then plainly it would not be possible for one party to remain in the home and for the other party to accommodate himself as well. It may be that both parties will have to rent properties. Typically, the couple may have purchased the property relatively recently with the aid of a large mortgage, and consequently there may be little or (in times of falling house values) no equity.

If one party wishes to sell the home while the other wishes to remain in it, the former could transfer his interest in the home to the latter in return for a lump sum. Whether or not such a 'buy out' can be achieved depends upon whether the spouse who wishes to stay has the means to make the lump sum payment. He may have savings, or sufficient income to raise the sum by borrowing. Provided the equity is sufficient, the sum may be raised by increasing the mortgage. The spouse who wishes to sell may agree to a smaller lump sum rather than have the delay and inconvenience of sale on the open market.

9.3 Retaining the home

The matrimonial home may be retained for the occupation of one party and the children of the family. This occupation may be permanent in the case of an outright transfer, or in the medium to long term in the case of a deferred trust of land or deferred charge.

9.3.1 Outright transfer

Outright transfer is another method of achieving a clean break between the parties as it determines immediately and finally the ownership of the home. The court is unlikely to order an immediate outright transfer unless the transferee spouse has the means to pay the outgoings on the house, including the mortgage. It will also wish to ensure that the transferor spouse has suitable alternative accommodation. He need not necessarily own this accommodation: he may, for example, be provided with accommodation through his employment, or he may be living in his new partner's home.

If the transferor is giving up a significant amount of capital, the court will seek to compensate him for this loss. An order for the transfer of a property may be coupled with a lump sum payment from the transferee to the transferor (see the example of Shah at **10.13.13**). The extent to which the transferor spouse will be compensated depends on the value of the equity and on s 25 of the MCA 1973 factors in general. If the equity is small, the transferor may not receive anything in return. In a sluggish market, a party may be glad to be relieved of responsibility for the property.

Another means of compensating a transferor is by releasing him from paying maintenance to the transferee. However, a spouse cannot generally be compensated by being released from his obligations to pay maintenance for his children. This is because, in many cases, the transferor will be bound to pay maintenance for the children under the CSA 1991. When assessing the amount payable, the Child Support Agency will not generally take into account any disposals of capital made by the non-resident parent on divorce (see **7.6.3**). Similarly, any agreement by the transferee to forgo any claim under the CSA 1991 will be unenforceable (see **7.5**). In the less common cases, where the court, rather than the Agency, has jurisdiction to make periodical payment orders for children, it will take into account all the circumstances of the case, including a sacrifice by the transferor of his interest in the matrimonial home. As a result, the court may take the view that the transferor should pay only modest maintenance for the children.

Faced with the prospect of forgoing capital in the matrimonial home and paying substantial income in the form of CSA 1991 maintenance, outright transfers of the matrimonial home are used less frequently than in the past. If the transferee spouse is unable to pay a lump sum to the transferor by way of compensation, the transferor may prefer to preserve his interest in the matrimonial home by means of a deferred charge or trust of land.

9.3.2 Deferred trust of land

The deferred trust of land is a compromise solution to the problem of the matrimonial home. Where the court is of the view that an immediate sale is inappropriate and an outright transfer too harsh on the transferring spouse, it can order the house to be held in the parties' joint names on trust of land. It will specify which spouse is to occupy the home pending sale. The sale of the property is postponed until the first of a number of specified triggering events occurs. The order will also settle how the net proceeds of sale are to be shared between the parties. The main advantage of the trust of land is that it allows a party and the children to remain in the home after the divorce, and it enables the non-occupying spouse to retain an interest in the home which may be realised at a later date.

There are several variations on the trust of land; the differences lie in the events which trigger sale. The main variations are known as the *'Mesher'* order (see *Mesher v Mesher and Hall* [1980] 1 All ER 126), the *'Martin'* order (see *Martin v Martin* [1978] Fam 12) and the *'Harvey'* order (see *Harvey v Harvey* [1982] 3 FLR 141), named after the cases in which they were considered.

9.3.2.1 *Mesher* order

Triggering events

Typically, the events which will trigger the sale in a *Mesher* order will be the first of the following to occur:

(a) the occupying spouse dies, remarries or voluntarily leaves the property; or

(b) the youngest child reaches a specified age (usually 17 or 18 years), or ceases full-time education (if this happens earlier/later).

For an example of a *Mesher* order, see Levy at **10.13.13**.

The advantage of this order is that it provides a secure home for the children of the family and offers medium-term security to the occupying spouse. In addition, each party will know fairly clearly when the sale will take place and can plan accordingly. The non-occupying spouse can be confident that the day will come when he will realise his capital and be released from making any contributions towards the outgoings on the former matrimonial home.

The court's attitude towards the sale of the home on the occupying spouse's remarriage varies. Given that the court's primary consideration is the welfare of the minor children, there is some force to the argument that the children's home should not be jeopardised by the remarriage of their parent. Their step-parent may have little or no resources of his own. On the other hand, the non-occupying spouse will feel aggrieved to watch another person living in his property with his ex-spouse and children. Consequently, most judges are prepared to order that the sale is triggered by the occupying spouse's remarriage. A more controversial trigger for sale is cohabitation by the occupying spouse with a new partner. Such orders require careful drafting, as cohabitation is by no means as clearly definable as marriage. Further, a cohabitee would be under no obligation to maintain his partner or her family. It is also arguable that such a trigger would be unduly restrictive on the occupying spouse's personal freedom.

If the occupying spouse gives up occupation of the home, this would trigger sale. The order may, however, provide for the occupying spouse to move to an alternative property without having to settle the non-occupying party's share. Care must be taken when drafting such a clause; the non-occupying spouse will wish to ensure that the substitute property will adequately protect his interest by being marketable and of sound construction, etc. The substitute property may also be cheaper or more expensive than the original property, which requires further consideration.

Reference to the youngest child may be drafted so that the sale is triggered on the child reaching the specified age whether or not he or she remains in education. Alternatively, it may be worded so that the sale is postponed while the child is in full-time secondary (or even higher) education on the basis that the adult child will still require a home.

Use

As we have seen, the *Mesher* order is a compromise solution; it does not resolve all the difficulties with the matrimonial home. Its main shortcoming is that it is only a medium-term solution. The widespread use of *Mesher* orders has been criticised for simply postponing the 'evil day' so as to avoid facing the harsh reality of the present (*Harvey v Harvey* [1982] 3 FLR 141). Sooner or later the occupying spouse will have to leave the home and then start from scratch to find new accommodation. A wife may have to take that step at a vulnerable time in her life when she has a diminishing earning capacity. The court cannot predict with any accuracy how much time the occupying spouse will need to reaccommodate herself, or what the housing and job market will be many years ahead. The court has no discretion to postpone the sale beyond the triggering events and it may not interfere with the apportionment once it has been settled in the original order. On the other hand, the very fact that the sale is postponed will enable the wife to look to the future and make efforts to become financially independent. Her position may be eased to a certain extent by giving her a greater share of the net proceeds of sale on the assumption that the non-resident parent will have been able to establish himself and secure accommodation in the years which have elapsed since divorce.

9.3.2.2 *Martin* order

The *Martin* order operates in a similar way to the *Mesher* order, save that the triggers for sale make no reference to the children of the family. The result is that the house need be sold only if the occupying spouse so chooses by leaving or remarrying, or, ultimately, when she dies. Thus, she has the right to remain in the home for life. The *Martin* order will be most appropriate where one spouse is in a significantly weaker financial position than the other. For example, a middle-aged wife may not have worked for many years having cared for the home and family, whereas the husband may be living with a new partner and have reasonable earnings. In such a case, the capital realised by the sale would be a bonus to the husband, whereas the wife would have to apply her money towards a new property. The court is likely to order that the house should be retained to be used as a home for the wife for life. However, it would not make such an order if the matrimonial home were manifestly surplus to her needs. In such a case, an order for sale and division of the proceeds would be more appropriate.

The obvious advantage of this variation on the trust of land is that it avoids the 'evil day' encountered with the *Mesher* order. Provided the occupying spouse remains in the home and unmarried, she will not be faced with the prospect of a forced sale. The disadvantages of this type of order are equally apparent: the non-occupying spouse has an indefinite wait to realise his capital. Indeed, he may predecease his wife, in which case only his estate would benefit. As the occupying spouse has a secure home for life with this type of order, she will not have the same need for capital when the house is sold. The non-occupying spouse may therefore acquire a greater share of the equity than is usually the case with a *Mesher* order. This may go some way to compensate him for the indefinite wait to realise his capital. The court would be unlikely to make a *Martin* order if the occupying spouse could not afford to pay the outgoings on the property, as this would be unduly harsh on the non-occupying spouse. If, exceptionally, the non-occupying spouse is required to pay maintenance to the occupying spouse, he could expect that fact to be reflected by an order giving him an even larger share of the equity upon sale.

9.3.2.3 *Harvey* order

In *Harvey v Harvey* [1982] 3 FLR 141, the court sought to mitigate the hardship which a *Martin* order causes to the non-occupying spouse. A *Harvey* order has triggers similar to the *Martin* order, but in addition it provides for the payment of an 'occupation rent' by the occupying spouse. The obligation to pay the 'rent' is itself triggered by the children growing up or the mortgage being paid off, whichever first occurs. Although the order attempts to do justice between the parties, it is not without its difficulties and is not commonly made.

Consideration would have to be given as to how the 'rent' is to be assessed and paid. The rent is taxable in the hands of the recipient spouse.

9.3.3 Deferred charge

A deferred charge is a further method of retaining a home for a spouse and the children. Although similar to the trust of land, the property remains (or is transferred) into the sole name of the occupying spouse. The non-occupying spouse's interest in the home is represented by a charge over the property. This charge cannot be enforced until one of the triggering events discussed in **9.3.2.1** and **9.3.2.2** occurs (*Mesher* or *Martin* triggers). If the occupying spouse cannot pay the charge, at this point the property must be sold. The charge will usually be expressed as a proportion of the net proceeds of sale, thereby allowing the charge holder to benefit from any increase in the value of the property (as in the Brown example at **10.13.13**). Less commonly, the charge may be expressed as a fixed sum, but this has the obvious disadvantage of its value being eroded by the effects of inflation. The charge will be registered against the title and will take priority over any subsequent liabilities incurred by the owner.

In practical terms, there is very little difference between the deferred charge and the trust of land, although the former is less advantageous from a CGT point of view (see **5.2.2**). If the property is already in the parties' joint names, a trust of land will be the preferred method as it avoids interfering with the legal estate. On the other hand, if the property is already in the name of the occupying spouse, the deferred charge may be the preferred method.

9.4 The interests of third parties

9.4.1 Co-owners

If a party owns property with a third party the court may make an order only with respect to the spouse's share of the asset. It cannot interfere with the third party's interest. A third party who is not a legal owner but claims to be beneficially entitled to a property may intervene in proceedings for sale and make representations. So, for example, a parent of one of the parties who has been living in the matrimonial home, having contributed towards the deposit or mortgage, may apply to have the extent of his beneficial interest determined by the court. If the court decided that the property should be sold in such a case, it would probably direct that the parent should be offered the right of first refusal.

9.4.2 Lenders

9.4.2.1 Undue influence

Where both husband and wife are parties to a mortgage, they will both be bound by the mortgage. This is true unless one of them can argue that the mortgage should not be enforced against them because their consent to the mortgage was obtained by undue influence. For example, a wife may argue that the mortgage should be set aside as against the husband because she was induced to enter into the mortgage as a result of his undue influence. In *Royal Bank of Scotland v Etridge (No 2)* [2001] 4 All ER 449, the House of Lords reviewed the law on undue influence, and it is now the leading case in this area. The wife may either prove actual undue influence (ie overt act(s) of the husband actually putting unfair pressure on her or making misrepresentations), or raise a 'rebuttable evidential presumption' of undue influence.

This 'rebuttable evidential presumption' arises where the wife shows that her relationship with her husband is one of trust and confidence in such matters and that the transaction 'calls for explanation' (ie if it is explicable only on the basis of undue influence). This may rarely be the case since such transactions will generally be likely to benefit the family as a whole, although there will be cases where the remortgage is to finance the husband's debts, for example *Hewett v First Plus Financial Group PLC* [2010] EWCA Civ 312.

If there is such undue influence, the wife can have the mortgage set aside as against the lender (ie the lender will not be able to enforce the mortgage against her) only if the lender had actual or constructive notice of the risk of this. The lender will now be 'put on inquiry' (ie fixed with constructive notice) whenever the relationship between debtor and guarantor is non-commercial (eg spouses). However, this will not apply where the money is being advanced jointly, as opposed to the wife acting as guarantor, unless the lender is aware that the loan is being made for the husband's purposes.

Where the lender has notice, either actual or constructive, it must take reasonable steps to satisfy itself that the transaction was properly entered into. In order to do this, the lender must comply with the requirements now laid down in *Royal Bank of Scotland v Etridge* regarding explanations and warnings. The lender may either do this itself, or send the necessary information to the wife's solicitor and obtain confirmation from the solicitor that the transaction and its practical implications have been fully explained. If the lender fails to comply with the requirements it may not be able to enforce the mortgage against the wife, who will be entitled to take her share of the house free from the mortgage. As these requirements are quite stringent, it is likely that, in future, most lenders will rely on the wife's solicitor, rather than attempting to comply with them themselves.

As a result of the House of Lords decision in *Royal Bank of Scotland v Etridge*, in future it will be more difficult for wives to argue undue influence; lenders are less likely to be 'put on inquiry' where the money is advanced jointly. Even where they are, the insistence on confirmation from solicitors is likely to mean that most transactions have been properly entered into and are therefore enforceable.

9.4.2.2 Property adjustment orders on divorce

Leaving aside the cases of possible undue influence and returning to more usual circumstances, what is the position of a lender when a court is considering making a property adjustment order with respect to a matrimonial home on divorce?

If a property is ordered to be sold immediately, there will be no problem with the lender: on completion the mortgage (including any arrears which may have built up) must be paid. It may be necessary to obtain the lender's agreement to postpone any possession proceedings to allow a private sale if substantial arrears have built up. The lender may agree to extend the mortgage term, or perhaps to accept only interest payments in the short term. Mortgage interest at a standard only rate may be paid through income support (and full mortgage interest will not be immediately included in a claim, see **6.3.2**).

If the property is to continue in the parties' joint names under a trust of land, this should not cause any difficulties with the lender. The parties may agree between themselves how the mortgage is to be paid. The occupying spouse may undertake to indemnify the non-occupying spouse for his liability under the mortgage. However, as joint owners and joint borrowers, the lenders have the right to look to both spouses to make the repayments. The lender's rights are unaffected by the terms of the trust. However, if the court alters the legal estate by transferring the property into a party's sole name, the lender is entitled to object. Invariably, the lender will be asked to release the transferor spouse from his liability under the mortgage and thereby relinquish the right to pursue the transferor for payment of the debt. Before agreeing to do so, the lender will need to be satisfied that the transferee spouse will be able to meet the payments. If the lender is not confident that this will be the case, it may refuse to release the transferor. This condition may defeat the object of the transaction, ie of achieving a clean break. Full disclosure of the transferee's resources should be made to the lender in advance of any hearing or agreement to avoid such an objection.

9.5 The rented home

If the former matrimonial home is a rented property, the court will have to consider whether the tenancy can and should be transferred into the sole name of one party. Section 24 of the MCA 1973 allows the court to transfer 'property': most tenancies will be regarded as 'property' for this purpose. If the tenancy contains a prohibition against assignment, the court cannot order the transfer under this provision unless the landlord consents. As with lenders, the landlord should be contacted at an early stage in the proceedings.

Statutory tenancies which arose under the Rent Act 1977 on the termination of a protected tenancy do not amount to 'property' for the purposes of s 24 of the MCA 1973, and cannot therefore be transferred under this section. However, under Sch 7 to the FLA 1996, a statutory tenancy can be vested in the name of one spouse. Strictly speaking this is not a transfer of the tenancy and so may be ordered notwithstanding a prohibition in the tenancy against assignment. However, the landlord would be entitled to make representations before the court, and if his objections were reasonable they would be unlikely to be overridden. Protected, assured and secured tenancies may be transferred under s 24 of the MCA 1973. Protected, assured and secured tenancies may also be transferred under FLA 1996. There will, therefore, be a choice (in most cases) of whether to deal with the tenancy under the MCA 1973, or under the FLA 1996. Any public funding for ancillary relief will normally specify that orders may be made only under the MCA 1973, and as proceedings will already have been brought under that Act, it will normally be convenient to use this jurisdiction.

9.6 Protecting the capital assets

The matrimonial home is almost invariably the most important (and valuable) family asset. It is also true to say that the issue of what to do with the home is among the most contentious on marriage breakdown. It is a subject on which emotions frequently run high. One fear which a party may have is that the other party will seek to avoid his responsibilities by disposing of the property. Such a suspicion may be well founded. There is a variety of measures available to prevent a party from disposing of (or charging) the matrimonial home, or any other property, and to reverse any attempt by a party to do so.

Whether or not any action need be taken will depend upon how the property is held.

9.6.1 Property in joint names

If the parties hold the property in joint names, neither party can deal with it unilaterally. Any sale or mortgage will require the consent and signature of both parties; therefore, no steps need be taken to guard against this other than advising the client not to sign anything without legal advice (see also **9.4.2** and the possible problem of undue influence).

However, consideration should be given to the question of the parties' beneficial interests in the property. If the parties hold the property jointly in law and equity then their interests will automatically pass to the survivor on death. Given the breakdown of the relationship, the parties are likely to want their shares in the property to form part of their own estates. If this is the case, the joint tenancy must be severed to allow the parties to become beneficial tenants in common. This may be achieved by giving written notice of severance to the other party. The severance should be recorded on the title of the property, by a restriction on the proprietorship register (if the property is registered) or by a memorandum of severance on the conveyance to the parties (if the title is unregistered).

Even if this step is taken, if a party dies intestate prior to decree absolute, the spouse is liable to inherit by default through the rules on intestacy. Clearly, the client should be advised to make a will, or any existing will may need to be reviewed.

9.6.2 Property in a party's sole name

9.6.2.1 Matrimonial home rights: FLA 1996, s 30

If a spouse is not a legal owner of the property, she may feel in a vulnerable position. In such a case, the spouse should be advised of her matrimonial home rights with respect to the matrimonial home by virtue of s 30 of the FLA 1996 (see **Appendix 1(G)**). These rights protect a non-owning spouse (husband, wife or civil partner) against eviction from the matrimonial home without the leave of the court. A spouse will be non-owning for these purposes even if she owns an equitable interest. The rights exist in respect of only one property at a time and it must have been the matrimonial home at some stage.

The rights under s 30 of the FLA 1996 terminate on the death of the owning spouse or on the grant of a decree absolute or dissolution order, although the court has power under s 33(5) of the FLA 1996 to direct that the rights should continue beyond these events.

The matrimonial home rights should be registered so that they bind any subsequent buyers and lenders. As always, the rights will not take priority over any pre-existing interests, such as a prior mortgage.

In order to ascertain where the registration should be made, it may be necessary to carry out an Index Map Search at Land Registry. This will indicate whether or not the property is registered and, if it is, its title number. If it is registered, an agreed notice should be placed on the register (despite the fact that this is an 'agreed notice', it does not need the owning spouse's consent to be registered). If the title is unregistered, a Class F land charge should be registered against the name of the owning spouse. If a spouse fails to register the rights, she will be unable to assert her rights against any third party.

In practice, Land Registry automatically notifies the registered proprietor that an entry relating to the matrimonial home has been made. It will also hold any application made for a period of one week to give the applicant the opportunity to consider fully the effect of her application.

A non-owning spouse may also have concerns about the payment of the original mortgage. Whether or not a spouse has registered her rights, s 30(3) of the FLA 1996 obliges a lender to accept payments from a non-owning spouse (a similar principle applies to payments of rent by a non-tenant spouse). If possession proceedings are brought, the non-owning spouse must be notified (if she has registered her rights) and she may apply to be made a party to the proceedings. If the court is persuaded that the non-owning spouse is able to pay the mortgage and the arrears within a reasonable time, it will usually refuse an order for possession.

A non-owning spouse may also feel vulnerable if the owning spouse faces bankruptcy, because bankruptcy vests the owning spouse's property in his trustee in bankruptcy. Once registered, the matrimonial home rights are binding on the trustee and on the creditors. However, the trustee may apply to the court to terminate the rights. If the application to terminate is made more than a year after the bankruptcy, the court is bound to grant it unless the circumstances are exceptional. The client should be advised of this and warned that having no alternative accommodation for herself and her children will not amount to exceptional circumstances.

9.6.2.2 Pending land action

The limitations of the matrimonial home rights may leave a spouse with inadequate protection. For this reason the registration of a pending land action should be considered. This can be done once proceedings have commenced in relation to property. A request for a property adjustment order in the prayer of the petition or Form A suffices. The registration is not confined to the matrimonial home and it is effective beyond the termination of the marriage. If the property in question is registered land, a unilateral notice should be lodged in the proprietorship register. If the land is unregistered, registration is by way of a pending action against the name of the owning spouse. This prevents any new dealing with the property taking place without first being brought to the attention of the non-owning spouse.

9.6.2.3 Injunctions: MCA 1973, s 37

Preventing disposals

It is possible to seek an injunction from the court under s 37(2)(a) of the MCA 1973 (see **Appendix 1(A)**) to prevent a party from disposing of property. This can be done in relation to any type of property, but if the property is land in England or Wales, it is usually easier to protect it by registering a matrimonial home right or pending land action (as explained at **9.6.2.1** and **9.6.2.2**).

If a client wishes to make use of s 37, he must first have made an application for financial relief under the MCA 1973 (eg for a lump sum or property adjustment order). An injunction may then be granted where the court is satisfied that the other party is about to make a disposition of property with the intention of defeating the claim for financial relief, or with the intention of frustrating or impeding its enforcement. The court has power to make whatever order it thinks fit to restrain the party from making the disposition. The applicant must have placed evidence before the court that the disposition is likely and the application is not simply being taken as a precautionary measure. There is a (rebuttable) presumption that the respondent to the injunction application intends to make the disposition in order to jeopardise the applicant's claim, if it would have that consequence.

> **Example**
>
> Mrs Edwards learns that her husband is about to transfer the funds in his savings account to his girlfriend's account. Mrs Edwards can apply for an injunction to freeze the savings account. A copy of the injunction should be served on the bank.

Setting aside

If the spouse does not learn of the disposition until after it has taken place, all is not lost. Section 37(2)(b) empowers the court to grant an injunction setting aside a reviewable disposition made with the intention of defeating a claim for ancillary relief, if financial provision or different financial provision would be made to the applicant as a result.

A disposition will be reviewable unless it was made for valuable consideration to a bona fide purchaser without notice of the respondent's intention. A transaction at an undervalue, provided it was not purely nominal, would constitute 'valuable consideration' (*Trowbridge v Trowbridge* [2003] 2 FLR 231). If the disposition took place less than three years before the application, the malevolent intention will be presumed.

> **Example**
>
> Mr Philips gave his valuable yacht to his brother 18 months ago. Regardless of whether the brother was aware of Mr Philips' purpose, the disposition may be set aside as it was not made for valuable consideration.

Avoiding enforcement

If a reviewable disposition is made after financial proceedings have been determined, with the object of avoiding enforcement of an order for financial relief, it may be set aside under s 37(2)(c) of the MCA 1973.

> **Example**
>
> Mr Clark is ordered to pay a lump sum of £10,000 to his wife. In order to frustrate this, he transfers his entire investments to his mother. Mrs Clark can seek an injunction to reverse this disposition and enforce the lump sum by means of an order for sale against the investments.

Dispositions

A disposition includes any disposal of property except one contained in a will.

Other options

The procedure above under the MCA 1973, s 37 is by far that most commonly used. However, it may instead be possible to obtain an injunction in the High Court using the court's inherent jurisdiction, or to obtain a *Mareva* injunction. Neither of these options will be considered in any further detail here.

9.7 Lump sums

9.7.1 Lump sums generally

The power of the court to make lump sum orders is discussed at **4.4.1**. Lump sums have also been examined throughout this chapter in the context of a division of the net sale proceeds of the matrimonial home. The assessment of the amount of a lump sum remains to be considered here.

Generally, no lump sum would be awarded where the family assets are modest, otherwise than in relation to a division of the net proceeds of the matrimonial home. However, if following the breakdown of the marriage the applicant spouse has incurred debts due to the failure of the respondent to maintain her, the court may remedy the problem by ordering a lump sum. Careful thought should be given to the impact of any lump sum on the recipient's eligibility for welfare benefits (see **Chapter 6**).

The impact of the statutory charge could also seriously erode the net value of any lump sum awarded (see **2.9**).

9.7.2 Lump sums in 'big money' cases

If the family assets are substantial, the court will usually consider making a lump sum order in addition to making an order regarding the matrimonial home. The reason for this can be traced to s 25A of the MCA 1973, which requires the court to facilitate a clean break wherever appropriate. If the family assets are substantial, there will be ample opportunity to achieve a clean break by making a lump sum order and dismissing any claim for spousal periodical payments.

In determining how much the lump sum should be, the court will have regard to the s 25 factors and the cases of *White* and *Miller v Miller; McFarlane v McFarlane* (examined in detail in **Chapter 4**). Any contributions made by a spouse towards the family prosperity or to the welfare of the family generally will be particularly influential.

It seems likely that, as a result of the case of *White* and the 'yardstick of equality', lump sum awards in 'big money' cases will be more substantial. A difficulty that may arise is one of liquidity, as one spouse may not have sufficient available resources to pay the other such significant sums of money. This may mean that a clean break may be more difficult to achieve in certain cases. It is particularly problematic if the main asset is a business (or various businesses). In the past, the courts tended to be very reluctant to break up such a business in order to give the other spouse their due. However, the case of *N v N (Financial Provision: Sale of Company)* [2001] 2 FLR 69 suggests that this attitude may be changing. As Coleridge J graphically explained:

> There is no doubt that had this case been heard before the *White* decision last year the court would have strained to prevent a disruption of the husband's business and professional activities except to the minimum extent necessary to meet the wife's needs.
>
> However, I think that it must now be taken that those old taboos against selling the goose that lays the golden egg have largely been laid to rest; some would say not before time. Nowadays the goose may well have to go to market for sale, but if it is necessary to sell her it is essential that her condition be such that her egg laying abilities are damaged as little as possible in the process. Otherwise there is a danger that the full value of the goose will not be achieved and the underlying basis of any order will turn out to be flawed.

So, whilst the business may have to be sold, it is important to consider how and when and to give the husband every opportunity to raise funds to buy out the wife's share if at all possible as an alternative.

However, as was emphasised in *D v D and B Ltd* [2007] EWHC 278 (Fam), despite the desirability of achieving a clean break, there will be some cases, especially those involving private companies, where the commercial reality was that a fairer result would be achieved by not selling the business. Thus it will not always be practical or desirable to value and sell the business and then divide the proceeds. The courts have used a variety of different devices where it is either not practical or not desirable to sell the business. For example, in *F v F (Clean Break: Balance of Fairness)* [2003] 1 FLR 847, the court ordered substantial periodical payments to the wife instead of imposing a clean break. In *R v R (Lump Sum Repayments)* [2004] 1 FLR 928, the court made a 'frankly unusual order for a lump sum payment'. This order provided that the husband would pay an initial lump sum instalment of £30,000, followed by 240 further monthly instalments of the amount needed to repay the wife's mortgage liability under a mortgage of £225,000. The judge explained that the reason that these payments were to be made by lump sum rather than periodical payments was that 'it will endure beyond remarriage, ie will in that regard equate to conventional capital provision, and will bind the husband's estate in the unlikely event of his death within the 20-year period'. The lump sum order was secured by giving the wife a first charge over the husband's shares in the company. In *C v C (Variation of Post-Nuptial Settlement: Company Shares)* [2003] 2 FLR 493, the court varied a post-nuptial settlement to give the wife a shareholding in the company.

In cases where a lump sum is used to capitalise maintenance, the courts have in the past based awards on actual assessments of the capital sum required to produce a given income for the remainder of the wife's life (see *Duxbury v Duxbury* [1987] 1 FLR 7). Computer programs have been devised by accountants and lawyers which can calculate the lump sum which, if invested, will produce enough to meet the recipient's requirements for the rest of her life. The calculations are based on certain assumptions, such as to life expectancy and rates of inflation, etc. This complicated method is designed to produce an index-linked net income where both the capital and income are used with the result that the fund would be exhausted, in the main, on the recipient's death. This method cannot, however, protect a spouse against unforeseen future adversity: it may be appropriate to increase the lump sum to provide additional resources to cushion a spouse against such unfortunate eventualities. Whichever method of assessment is used, such calculations can only ever be a guide to the court. The court will keep sight of its wide discretion and its obligation to consider all relevant factors in s 25. In various recent cases, the court has stressed that '*Duxbury* is a tool and not a rule' (as observed by Thorpe LJ in *White v White* [1998] 2 FLR 310 in the Court of Appeal).

Indeed, it has been recognised for some time that *Duxbury* calculations result in the paradox that the longer the marriage, and hence the older the wife, the less the capital sum required for a *Duxbury*-type fund. The case of *White* brought about the demise of the reliance on 'reasonable requirements' and emphasised the importance of considering all the relevant s 25 factors, including contributions. Since, after a long marriage, a spouse will almost certainly have made substantial contributions, whether financial or not, to the welfare of the family, this will have to be reflected in the award made.

9.8 Pensions

In many cases the pensions of either or both of the spouses will be a most valuable asset, and in some cases, *the* most valuable. There are three possible ways of dealing with pension rights on divorce: off-setting; pension attachment; and pension sharing (see **4.7**). One potential problem to be resolved in deciding which option to choose is how to value the pension rights. This problem arises since a pension is not realisable as a capital sum and, unless the pension is already in payment, represents money which may not become payable until far into the future. The problem is particularly acute when off-setting is being considered, since it is almost impossible to decide what amount of non-pension assets represents the equivalent of the pension value. For this reason, it may be preferable to opt for pension attachment or pension sharing.

9.8.1 Valuation of the pension

The starting point is the Cash Equivalent Transfer Value ('CETV'), but it would often be inappropriate simply to include this sum as if it were extra capital. This problem was raised in two cases: *Maskell v Maskell* [2001] EWCA Civ 858, [2001] 1 FLR 1138 and *Norris v Norris* [2002] EWHC 2996 (Fam), [2003] 1 FLR 142. In *Maskell,* the Court of Appeal took the view that the pension should be valued at the amount of capital which could be taken on retirement, the rest providing an income stream. This amounted to only 25% of the CETV. However, in different circumstances in *Norris,* the court held that it would not be unfair to include the full CETV as part of the assets. The case of *Martin-Dye v Martin-Dye* [2006] EWCA Civ 681 may provide a solution. In this case the Court of Appeal took the view that the best way to achieve fairness was to exclude the pensions from the capital assets altogether and instead make a pension-sharing order in the same percentages as the capital had been divided. Thus, as the capital assets had been divided 57:43 in favour of the wife, there should also be an order sharing the pensions 57:43 in favour of the wife. This case involved a pension in payment, but could equally apply when the respondent has not retired. However, it would not necessarily be fair in all cases. Cases will inevitably turn on their own facts, and in a case where pension rights are substantial, expert advice should be sought as to their valuation.

9.8.2 A practical approach

In *Vaughan v Vaughan* [2007] EWCA Civ 1085, Wilson LJ suggested that when setting out the parties' capital assets, first the capital other than the pensions should be totalled. Then the CETV of the pensions should be set out underneath, leading to a grand total. It is then possible to apply the 'yardstick of equality' to the resultant figures.

9.9 Bankruptcy

9.9.1 Bankruptcy and the matrimonial home

When a spouse becomes bankrupt, his property will vest in the trustee in bankruptcy. The making of a bankruptcy order will sever any joint tenancy. Where the matrimonial home is in the sole name of the bankrupt spouse, the non-owning spouse's matrimonial home rights bind the trustee and creditors (see **9.6.2.1**). However, the trustee in bankruptcy can apply to the court for the sale of the matrimonial home to satisfy the creditors, whether the home is in the sole name of the bankrupt or in the joint names of the bankrupt and spouse. In deciding whether to order a sale the court must take into account the following factors:

(a) the interests of the bankrupt's creditors;

(b) the conduct of the spouse or former spouse, so far as contributing to the bankruptcy;
(c) the needs and financial resources of the spouse or former spouse;
(d) the needs of the children; and
(e) all the circumstances of the case other than the needs of the bankrupt.

However, if the trustee applies more than one year after the bankruptcy, the court must assume that the interests of the creditors outweigh all other considerations unless the circumstances are exceptional. There is no definition of what amounts to 'exceptional' circumstances and cases coming within this are likely to be rare. Two examples are *Judd v Brown* [1998] 2 FLR 360, where the wife was suffering from cancer and needed to undergo a course of chemotherapy, and *Re Haghighat (A Bankrupt)* [2009] EWHC 90 (Ch), where there was a seriously disabled adult child who needed constant care. However, the fact that the wife and children will be rendered homeless is unlikely to be regarded as exceptional circumstances (*Re Citro* [1991] 1 FLR 71). In *Donohoe v Ingram (Trustee in Bankruptcy of Kirkup)* [2006] EWHC 292, the court held that such an interpretation of 'exceptional circumstances' did not breach Article 8 of the European Convention of Human Rights. Thus, generally, the non-bankrupt spouse and any children will have a one-year 'breathing space' in which to find themselves alternative accommodation.

9.9.2 Bankruptcy and ancillary relief orders

If the court has made a property adjustment order in favour of the spouse of a bankrupt, it would seem that the trustee will take subject to that spouse's interest, provided that the property adjustment order has become effective (ie, decree absolute has been pronounced) at the date of presentation of the bankruptcy petition (*Mountney v Treharne* [2002] EWCA Civ 1174). The only exceptions to this would be if there was evidence of fraud (eg collusion between the spouses designed adversely to affect the creditors) or some other vitiating factor, such as a failure to make full and frank disclosure (*Hill v Haines* [2007] EWCA Civ 1284). If the property adjustment order has not been made and become effective by the date of the presentation of the bankruptcy petition, any property adjustment order made will be void (*Treharne & Sand v Forrester* [2004] 1 FLR 1173).

In *Re Nunn (Bankruptcy: Divorce: Pension Rights)* [2004] 1 FLR 1123, the court held that a pension attachment order made in 1994 was not enforceable against the trustee in bankruptcy as the order did not give the wife an equitable interest in the proceeds of the pension lump sum. However, since May 2000 pension rights under an approved pension scheme are excluded from the bankruptcy estate, and they may be excluded where the scheme is unapproved (see Welfare Reform and Pensions Act 1999, ss 11 and 12).

Under the Insolvency (Amendment) Rules 2005 (SI 2005/527), where the bankruptcy order was made on or after 1 April 2005, lump sum orders and costs orders made in family proceedings are provable in bankruptcy. Thus, where a lump sum order has been made and the payer then becomes bankrupt, the recipient spouse will be in the same position as the bankrupt's other creditors. Arrears of periodical payments and child support maintenance arrears are not provable.

9.10 Chapter summary

(1) Under ss 24 and 24A of the MCA 1973, the court may make the following orders with respect to the matrimonial home:
   (a) immediate sale (and division of the proceeds, if any);
   (b) outright transfer to one spouse;
   (c) home retained under a deferred trust of land (eg a *Mesher* order) or subject to a deferred charge.

When deciding what order to make, the court will consider the factors in s 25 of the MCA 1973. It must also take into account the interests of any third party, such as a lender.

(2) If the matrimonial home is rented, the court has powers under the MCA 1973 and FLA 1996 to order the transfer of the tenancy to one spouse.

(3) Several measures are available (eg an injunction under MCA 1973, s 37) to protect against one party disposing of property in order to thwart the other party's financial claim. In particular, a non-owning spouse's matrimonial home rights, under s 30 of the FLA 1996, should be registered to prevent the owning spouse selling the matrimonial home.

(4) Lump sums are most commonly ordered either in the context of a division of the net sale proceeds of the home (or other property), or as a form of capitalised maintenance, particularly in cases of substantial assets.

(5) Where one spouse becomes bankrupt, the non-bankrupt spouse and any children will generally have one year in which to find alternative accommodation.

Chapter 10
Procedure for Obtaining a Financial Order

10.1	Introduction	119
10.2	Public funding	119
10.3	Overview of the procedure	119
10.4	The pre-application protocols	120
10.5	The application	121
10.6	Filing and service	122
10.7	Obtaining the evidence	123
10.8	Court hearings	125
10.9	Interim orders	128
10.10	Costs	128
10.11	Negotiations	129
10.12	Consent orders	130
10.13	Drafting financial orders	130
10.14	Summary of court procedure	143
10.15	Maintenance calculations	146

10.1 Introduction

This chapter deals first with how to obtain a court order in divorce proceedings providing for the distribution of the matrimonial assets. The order may follow a court hearing or agreement between the parties. Throughout this chapter, the spouse who is applying for the order is called the applicant and the other spouse is called the respondent (regardless of who was the petitioner or respondent in the divorce itself).

The drafting of an order to record any agreement between the parties or order of the court will then be considered. Lastly, the chapter briefly examines the procedure to be followed to obtain a maintenance calculation under the CSA 1991.

10.2 Public funding

Initial advice and negotiations can be carried out using Legal Help and Family Help (Lower). Once proceedings are about to be issued, the solicitor will need to apply for Family Help (Higher). However, before he does so, unless the client is exempt, the solicitor will first need to make a referral appointment for mediation (see FLA 1996, s 29 and **2.6.5**). If it transpires that mediation is unsuitable, then the solicitor can apply for funding in the usual way.

10.3 Overview of the procedure

The rules relating to financial procedure are set out in Pt 9 of the FPR 2010 (see **Appendix 1(I)**) which came into force on 6 April 2011. There is an accompanying Practice Direction 9A which has a pre-application protocol annexed to it. Also relevant are Pt 3 of the FPR 2010 (alternative dispute resolution) and protocol Practice Direction 3A which accompanies it (see **10.4.1**). This requires a potential applicant for a financial order to consider with a mediator whether the dispute may be capable of being resolved through mediation before commencing proceedings (see further **10.4** below).

The FPR 2010 contain an overriding objective 'of enabling the court to deal with cases justly, having regard to any welfare issues involved' (FPR 2010, r 1.1(1)). Dealing with a case justly includes dealing with it expeditiously and proportionately. To this end, similar to the CPR, the court is given a duty to manage cases actively and a number of general case-management powers.

Once proceedings for a financial order have commenced, the procedure falls into three phases, each of which ends with a court hearing:

Phase 1: Filing of the application until the end of the First Appointment.

Phase 2: End of the First Appointment until the end of the Financial Dispute Resolution (FDR) hearing.

Phase 3: End of FDR until the Final Hearing.

In many cases, only the first two phases will be needed to achieve a final consent order.

10.4 The pre-application protocols

10.4.1 Pre-application protocol for mediation information and assessment (PD3A)

Under this protocol, before making an application to court in relevant family proceedings, all applicants will be expected (unless an exemption applies) to attend an information meeting about family mediation and other forms of ADR (a 'Mediation Information and Assessment Meeting' or 'MIAM'). Relevant family proceedings for this purpose are all proceedings for a financial remedy (apart from under s 37 of the MCA 1973) and private law proceedings relating to children. Exemptions include where the mediator is satisfied that the case is not suitable for mediation; where there is an allegation of domestic abuse against a party; where the application is urgent; and where the applicant (or his legal representative) has contacted three mediators within 15 miles of the applicant's home and none is able to conduct a MIAM within 15 working days of the date of contact (see FPR 2010, Practice Direction 3A, Annex C; and **Appendix 1(I)**).

Thus, unless the applicant comes within an exemption, before making any application to court he (or his solicitor) should contact a family mediator to arrange for the applicant to attend a MIAM. The mediator should be provided with contact details for the respondent so that he can contact the respondent to discuss her willingness and availability to attend a MIAM.

The applicant should then attend the MIAM arranged by the mediator. If the parties are willing to attend the MIAM together the meeting may be conducted jointly, but where necessary, separate meetings may be held. At the MIAM the mediator should consider with the parties whether public funding may be available to meet the cost of the meeting and any subsequent mediation. Unless the parties attending the MIAM are publicly funded, they will need to pay the mediator's fees.

If the applicant then makes an application to court in respect of the dispute, he should file a completed Form FM1 (see **Appendix 3(C)**) confirming attendance at a MIAM or giving the reasons for not attending. Note that the FPR 2010, r 3 and Practice Direction 3A do not require a client to undertake mediation, only to obtain information and advice.

The court will expect all applicants to have complied with the protocol before commencing proceedings, and will also expect respondents to have attended a MIAM if invited to do so. In considering the conduct of any relevant family proceedings, the court will take into account any failure to comply with the protocol and may refer the parties to a meeting with a mediator before the proceedings continue further (Practice Direction 3A, para 4.1).

10.4.2 Pre-application protocol for applications for a financial remedy

This protocol states that pre-application disclosure should be encouraged only where both parties agree to it and disclosure is not likely to be an issue. Where pre-application disclosure and negotiation are appropriate, they must be carried out in accordance with the overriding objective and be proportionate. Solicitors should bear in mind the advantage of a court timetable and a court-managed process. Thus, making an application to court should not be regarded as a hostile step or as a last resort, but rather as a way of starting the court timetable, controlling disclosure and endeavouring to avoid the costly final hearing and the preparation for it. In addition, solicitors should consider at an early stage and keep under review whether it would be appropriate to suggest mediation and/or collaborative law to the clients as an alternative to solicitor negotiation or court-based litigation.

10.5 The application

10.5.1 Making the application for a financial order

The method of application will depend upon whether the applicant is the petitioner or the respondent in the divorce.

The petitioner-applicant makes the formal application in the prayer to the petition. Therefore, the applicant should tick all the boxes relating to applications for financial orders which appear in the petition.

The petitioner-applicant must follow up the formal application in the petition by filing a notice of intention to proceed in Form A (see **Appendix 3(D)**). A respondent-applicant merely has to file Form A.

Form A is a straightforward form in tick-box format. Where Form A includes an application for a property adjustment order, the address will need to be given. It is also good practice to state the title number if it is registered land, and give details of any mortgage.

It is good practice to apply for all available types of financial order (see **Chapter 4**). This not only prevents the client falling into the remarriage trap (see **10.5.2**), but also allows for a change in circumstances or for a clean break to be effected (see **4.6**).

10.5.2 Potential danger areas

Generally, the application should be made at an early stage. There are several reasons for this:

(a) If the petitioner-applicant omits to apply in the petition then he may apply later using Form A, but only if either the respondent has agreed to the terms of the proposed order or the petitioner obtains the leave of the court. Although leave will usually be given where the applicant has a seriously arguable case and a reasonable prospect of obtaining the relief sought, it will not be given if there has been an unjustifiable delay. Clearly, it is not worth taking the risk of leave being refused, and so the application should be submitted as soon as possible.

(b) The remarriage trap: this is caused by s 28(3) of the MCA 1973, which states: 'If after the grant of a decree . . . either party remarries . . . that party shall not be entitled to apply . . . for a financial provision order in his or her favour, or for a property adjustment order'. Thus the court cannot make an order in such circumstances, even by consent; see *E v E (Premature Remarriage)* [2008] 1 FLR 220).

> **Example**
>
> Henry has petitioned for divorce. His wife Eileen is very pleased since she wishes to marry her new partner. The decree absolute is granted and Eileen remarries. Only at this stage does she consult her solicitor about obtaining a lump sum order. It is too late – she has fallen into the remarriage trap.

A potential solution to this problem was found in the case of *Whitehouse-Piper v Stokes* [2008] EWCA Civ 1049. Here, the husband had remarried and thus could not apply for ancillary relief himself. However, his wife applied for a property adjustment order against herself which would transfer the former matrimonial home to her husband with a balancing lump sum for herself. The court made the property adjustment order in favour of the husband but declined to make the lump sum order for the wife. The Court of Appeal made it clear that a party is entitled to make a claim against him or herself.

Note that, in the above example, if Eileen had applied for a lump sum order at any time before remarrying, that application could be heard after her remarriage, as s 28(3) of the MCA 1973 prevents only the *making* of an application after remarriage (*Whitehouse-Piper v Stokes*).

(c) A lengthy delay in making or proceeding with the application may result in a less advantageous order being made if, for example, the delay has prejudiced the respondent.

(d) The court has power to backdate a periodical payments order to the date of the application (provided it believes the respondent has the means to pay). Therefore, the earlier the application, the further it can be backdated.

It is particularly important to remember to apply where the applicant is the respondent in the divorce, as the solicitor must file Form A without the benefit of any reminders. In contrast, the petitioner's solicitor is reminded by the petition itself.

Although the application should be made as soon as possible, the court has no power to make the order before decree nisi (and if it purports to do so, any order it makes is void). Also, most orders will not take effect until decree absolute (see **4.2**).

10.6 Filing and service

10.6.1 Filing

The applicant needs to file at court:

(a) Form A in duplicate;

(b) Form FM1;

(c) Public Funding certificate and notice of issue (if relevant);

(d) application fee;

(e) notice of acting where the client received Legal Help in the divorce and now has Family Help/Legal Representation. This is because the client will have been acting in person in the divorce. Now a solicitor is acting, he will need to ensure that his firm appears on the court file.

Upon filing the Form A, the court will at once (on Form C) fix the date for the First Appointment between 12 and 16 weeks ahead. The timing of this First Appointment cannot be altered without permission from the court. Within this period, much, if not most, of the important financial information-gathering and appraisal of the case will take place.

10.6.2 Service

The court must serve on the respondent a copy of Forms A and C within four days of filing (FPR 2010, r 9.12(1)).

The applicant must serve on the respondent:

(a) notice of issue of public funding (if relevant);

(b) copy of notice of acting (Legal Help divorce case only).

The Form A must also be served on any lender or person responsible for a pension arrangement mentioned in the application (FPR 2010, rr 9.13(3), 9.31, 9.33 and 9.40). Although the applicant is required to confirm to the court prior to the First Appointment (see **10.8.1**) that this step has been taken, if it is overlooked and the lender or person responsible for a pension arrangement is not served with a copy of the application, the hearing may have to be adjourned while the mistake is rectified, with a consequent costs penalty.

Once served, the mortgagee can apply for a copy of the financial statement within 14 days and the pension provider can apply for a copy of section 2.13 of the financial statement within 21 days. Either may then file a statement in answer if they wish.

10.6.3 Pensions

Unless the party with pension rights has a valuation less than 12 months old at the date of the first appointment, he must, within seven days of receiving notification of the date of the first appointment, request one from the pension arrangement. The pension arrangement must provide a valuation within six weeks. When the party with pension rights receives the valuation, he must send it to the applicant within seven days of receipt. Where the Pension Protection Fund has become involved with the pension scheme, the party with pension rights must also send to the applicant a copy of any notification received from the Pension Protection Fund.

10.7 Obtaining the evidence

10.7.1 Duty of disclosure

Each party is under a duty of full and frank disclosure. This duty is underlined in the pre-application protocol for applications for financial relief. This duty of disclosure is ongoing and includes the duty to disclose any material changes after initial disclosure has been given. Should the parties not give full disclosure, this may result in a reduced order (if the party is the applicant); a penalty in costs (see, eg, *P v P (Financial Relief: Non-Disclosure)* [1994] 2 FLR 381); the forfeiture of legal professional privilege protection (see *Kimber v Brookman Solicitors* [2004] 2 FLR 221); the final order being set aside at a later date (see *Livesey (formerly Jenkins) v Jenkins* [1985] AC 424 and **11.7**); or even criminal sanctions under the Fraud Act 2006 (see para 7 of the protocol). The bulk of the information needed should be contained in each party's Form E (see **10.7.2**).

The case of *Bokor-Ingram v Bokor-Ingram* [2009] EWCA 412 makes clear that the duty of disclosure not only applies to current resources but extends to facts relevant to resources that parties may have in the foreseeable future. In that case the husband omitted to disclose job negotiations with new employers which had reached a very advanced stage. The consent order reached was set aside.

In many cases, the applicant may believe that the respondent is concealing, or will conceal, assets to avoid his financial responsibilities. In such a situation the so-called Hildebrand rules have enabled the applicant to take and copy documents belonging to the respondent provided that no force is used, the originals are returned and the existence of copies is disclosed. However, the recent case of *Imerman v Imerman* [2010] EWCA Civ 908 makes it clear that there is no legal basis for the Hildebrand rules and that such 'self help disclosure' was an actionable breach of confidence. It may also amount to a criminal offence, such as theft or burglary or under, for example, the Data Protection Act 1998. In such a situation the correct approach is for the applicant to apply for an injunction preserving assets, a freezing (Mareva) order, a disclosure order (under the *Norwich Phamacal* principle) or even a search (Anton Pillar) order.

10.7.2 The evidence

Both parties must complete and swear a financial statement (Form E) (see **Appendix 3(E)**). This form is quite lengthy and gives details of: the parties and any children; means (including pension); capital and income needs; standard of living; contributions made to the family; conduct (in exceptional cases only); and any other relevant circumstances. Thus, all the essential information required by s 25 of the MCA 1973 should be included in Form E. Each party should also set out any order sought in Form E.

Certain essential documents must be filed and served with Form E:

(a) last three payslips and last P60 or, if self-employed or in partnership, a copy of the latest tax assessment;
(b) bank/building society statements for the last 12 months for all accounts;
(c) any property valuation obtained during the last six months;
(d) most recent mortgage statement(s);
(e) the last two years' accounts for any business, and any documentation relating to a valuation of the business;
(f) valuation of any pension;
(g) surrender value quotations for any life insurance policies; and
(h) the latest statement or dividend counterfoil for any investments.

Any necessary explanatory documents must also be annexed.

Various computer packages have been developed to help the solicitor complete Form E, for example *Quantum* (Class Legal). Both Form Es should be filed and simultaneously exchanged at least 35 days before the First Appointment. What if one party's solicitor is ready to exchange Form E but the other side is refusing to? In such a situation, the solicitor who is ready to exchange should send a copy of Form E to the court (but not to the other side) to prove compliance with the FPR 2010. Additionally, the solicitor could apply for a without notice order that the defaulting party should comply, although it is probably better to wait until the First Appointment to ask for such an order.

Both parties should then draft the following documents:

(a) A concise statement of the issues. This will require the parties to focus on the real issues in the application.
(b) A chronology.
(c) A questionnaire of further information and documents requested from the other party. This must be drafted with reference to the issues raised in the statement of issues. In many cases it may be that Form E and the attachments leave no matters outstanding and, in these cases, the parties will file a statement that no further information and documents are required.
(d) A notice stating whether that party will be in a position at the First Appointment to proceed on that occasion to an FDR appointment. This will be the case where both parties feel that they have all the disclosure they need, and it allows a form of 'fast tracking' in these cases.

These four documents must be filed and served by both parties at least 14 days before the First Appointment (FPR 2010, r 9.14(5)).

As well as the documents required by r 9.14(5), Practice Direction 9A states that the parties should, if possible, exchange and file with the court:

(a) a summary of the case agreed between the parties;
(b) a schedule of assets agreed between the parties; and
(c) details of any directions they seek, including, where appropriate, the name of any expert they wish to be appointed.

In addition, immediately before the First Appointment, the solicitors for both parties must produce a written estimate of the costs incurred so far in Form H. Note that this is something separate from the statement of costs required by the CPR 1998 (see **10.10.2**). Thus, if the solicitor wishes to claim the costs of the First Appointment, he must complete and serve a statement of costs at least 24 hours before the hearing.

10.8 Court hearings

10.8.1 The First Appointment

The court will fix a date for this when the applicant files Form A (see **10.6.1**). The short timetable is to allow the court to monitor the application and its progress from an early stage, with a view to limiting the issues and saving costs. Both parties and all legal representatives must attend. At this appointment, the district judge will give directions and decide how the application should proceed from then on.

The directions will deal with:

(a) the extent to which the questionnaires need to be answered;

(b) documents to be produced;

(c) valuations or other expert evidence (joint independent experts should be instructed where practicable). Part 25 of the FPR 2010 deals with experts, and under r 25.7, the court can direct evidence to be given by a single joint expert;

(d) the production of other evidence, such as schedules of assets or, in some cases, affidavits.

Particular considerations which may arise at this stage include the following:

(a) *Valuation of the home.* Directions will usually require that the parties agree a valuation, and if they are unable to agree, that they appoint a joint expert valuer. If they cannot agree on a valuer then the court will appoint one.

(b) *Valuation of the family business.* There may be a family business which the client wants to be valued. The court will not generally order a sale of the family business, nor make an order which would mean in effect that the owner was forced to sell to comply with the order or where such an order would prejudice third party investors (see **9.7**). The court will also be anxious to ensure that the family assets are not needlessly wasted on expensive valuations of the business (*Evans v Evans* [1990] 1 FLR 319). Therefore, usually, an approximate valuation is all that is needed. However, since *White v White* [2000] 2 FLR 981, a more exact valuation may be required in big money cases. Again, the court is likely to restrict the use of experts by giving a direction for joint appointment or, in default, only allowing one per party.

(c) *New partners.* One party may claim that the other party has a new partner who is working, and who therefore is able to contribute to the outgoings, thus freeing more cash for the former family or reducing the new family's needs. Say, for example, that the wife had a new partner. The husband might want to know what that partner's assets were. Rule 21.2 of the FPR 2010 allows a party to apply to court for an order that a non-party disclose relevant documents. However, case law states that the court will not order disclosure unless the non-party is to attend the final hearing as a witness. Thus it would appear that the correct procedure in such a situation is to apply for a subpoena for the new party to attend the final hearing. In deciding whether to grant such a subpoena, the court will take into account that any requirement for a third party to disclose financial information is potentially a breach of that party's right to respect for his private life under Article 8 of the European Convention on Human Rights. Thus ordering disclosure must be necessary and proportionate (*M v M (Third Party Subpoena: Financial Conduct)* [2006] 2 FLR 1253; FPR 2010, r 21.2(3)).

Alternatively, a practical answer to any potential difficulties was set out in *Grey v Grey* [2009] EWCA Civ 1424. The judge can require the party to proceedings to produce evidence of the new partner's means and, in default, the court could draw adverse inferences.

(d) *Pensions.* Where a pension sharing or pension attachment order is sought, the court is likely to direct the completion of all or part of a Pension Inquiry Form (Form P) within a set time limit before the FDR. When a pension compensation sharing order or a pension compensation attachment order is sought, the court is likely to direct the completion of all or part of a Pension Protection Fund Inquiry Form (Form PPF1 or PPF2) within a set time before the FDR.

The district judge will then usually give a date for an FDR appointment unless, exceptionally, he decides that this is not appropriate. In these exceptional cases (which are likely to be those which are very complicated), the district judge must give one of the following directions:

(a) that a further directions appointment be fixed;
(b) that an appointment be fixed for an interim order;
(c) that the case be fixed for a final hearing; or
(d) that the case be adjourned for mediation or negotiation.

Alternatively, unless there are considerable assets involved or the assets require further investigation, the district judge will treat the First Appointment as an FDR appointment.

Both parties' representatives will produce their written costs estimates. The district judge must consider whether he should make a costs order at this stage, having regard to the general rule on costs and the extent to which the parties have adhered to the rules (see **10.10.2**). Thus if, for example, one party fails to provide the relevant documentation with Form E, and this wastes the opportunity of having an FDR, he is likely to have a costs order made against him.

10.8.2 From First Appointment to FDR

Both parties should comply with all directions made at the First Appointment before the FDR. Neither party can insist on any further disclosure without leave of the court.

The applicant must inform the court of all offers or proposals and responses made to him at least seven days before the FDR (FPR 2010, r 9.17(3)). This should give the lawyers sufficient time to consider any proposals and ensure that their clients are not surprised by them at the hearing. The court will expect the parties to make offers and proposals, to give them proper consideration and not to attempt to exclude their consideration at the FDR (Practice Direction 9A, para 6.3).

Immediately before the FDR, both parties must produce a second written costs estimate in Form H.

10.8.3 The FDR appointment

The aim of the FDR is to produce a settlement. Both parties and all legal representatives must attend. The FDR will be conducted by a district judge who will then have nothing more to do with the case. The district judge will attempt to help the parties towards settlement by exploring common ground. Any offer made so far can be referred to at the FDR, even 'without prejudice' offers. All discussions at the FDR will be completely privileged. Documents referring to prior offers must be returned to the party who filed them at their request and not kept on the court file.

Where a settlement is reached at the FDR, the district judge may make a consent order reflecting the agreement. The district judge may also adjourn the FDR to allow one or both parties time to consider their position. Where no agreement is reached, the judge must make further directions, including, where appropriate, setting a hearing date. In cases involving large sums of money, the district judge may make a direction that narrative affidavits be filed by the parties at this stage to give a broader presentation of the historical background of the application than that allowed for in Form E. These might cover, for example, the respective contributions of the parties, the genesis of current resources and the standard of living during the marriage (*W v W (Ancillary Relief: Practice)* [2000] Fam Law 473).

Where heads of agreement reached at the FDR need to be converted into a court order, the FDR judge can be consulted about the necessary wording. However, if the agreement leaves some peripheral issues outstanding, to be later agreed by the parties or, if they cannot agree, the court, any subsequent dispute about these terms must be dealt with by a different judge (*Myerson v Myerson* [2008] EWCA Civ 1376).

10.8.4 From FDR to hearing

Any directions made at the FDR should be complied with. Either party can apply for further directions, and the court may direct a further FDR.

Before the hearing, both parties must draft a statement of proposed orders, file this at court and serve it on the other party. The applicant must do this at least 14 days before the hearing, and the respondent within seven days of being served with the applicant's proposals (FPR 2010, r 9.28). These statements are open and no privilege will attach to them. However, this rule has no effect on without prejudice offers and such offers may continue to be made at any time.

At least 14 days before the final hearing both parties must file and serve on the other party a statement of costs in Form H1. This requires full details of all costs incurred to date in the proceedings and an estimate of those to be incurred (including the estimated costs of implementation of the order).

The applicant's solicitor should ensure that the relevant bundle of documents is prepared and lodged with the court at least two working days before the hearing, in accordance with FPR 2010, Practice Direction 27A. Failure to comply with this Practice Direction may result in costs orders, the case being moved to the end of the list or being adjourned altogether, or the naming and shaming of offenders – *X & Y (Bundles)* [2008] EWHC 2058 (Fam).

10.8.5 The Final Hearing

The hearing is usually before a district judge, in chambers and in private.

In theory, the hearing should follow the same course as ordinary civil proceedings. However, such hearings are often much more informal. Having read the papers, the district judge may open by letting the parties know what he has in mind and inviting them to discuss and negotiate around this for a while.

If this does not succeed, or if the district judge wishes the proceedings to follow a more formal course, then the applicant's solicitor (or counsel) will open. He will outline the case and then call his evidence. The evidence will often consist only of that of the applicant, but other witnesses, for example a new partner or valuer, may be called. Generally, a party's witness statement will be his evidence in chief. He may amplify his witness statement or give evidence of new matters which have arisen since the statement was served only with permission from the court. The witnesses will then be cross-examined by the respondent's solicitor. He will then present his own client's case. Once all the evidence has been given, the district judge will make the order (or may reserve his judgment until a later date). A careful note should be taken of exactly what is said in case it should be necessary to appeal.

In the case of *Behzadi v Behzadi* [2008] EWCA Civ 1070, the Court of Appeal stated that the court should produce a balance sheet of the parties' assets and the effect of the order, and distribute this to the parties to enable them to see how the sharing principle has been applied in their case.

It is possible that the district judge will not feel able to make a final order at this time, for example, because it appears that the respondent is about to obtain (or lose) a job, or because the respondent has not turned up to the hearing. In such a situation, the district judge could make an interim order on such terms as he considers just.

Copies of any order made are sent to both parties by the court. In addition, where a pension sharing, pension attachment, pension compensation sharing or pension compensation attachment order is made, within seven days of the making of the order or of the decree absolute (whichever is the later) the court must send, or direct one of the parties to send, a copy of the decree nisi, a copy of the decree absolute and a copy of the relevant pension order and annex to the pension sharing arrangement or Pension Protection Fund Board, as appropriate.

10.9 Interim orders

Despite the fact that one of the aims of the procedure is to save time, it may still be many months before a final order is made. Thus, FPR 2010, r 9.7 allows a party to apply at any stage of the proceedings for an order for maintenance pending suit (see **4.3.1**), interim periodical payments or an interim variation order. The application will be made by application notice. The notice must state what order is being sought and why the order is required. It should be verified by a statement of truth. Where the application is made before filing a financial statement, up-to-date information about the applicant's financial circumstances must be given. On filing the application notice, the court will give a hearing date which must be at least 14 days later. The applicant must then immediately serve the respondent with a copy of the application notice (and accompanying documents where relevant). Where the respondent has not already filed Form E, he must file and serve a short sworn statement setting out his means at least seven days before the hearing.

10.10 Costs

10.10.1 Costs generally

The importance of costs in ancillary proceedings cannot be over-emphasised. It is essential that the question of costs is kept in sight and in proportion to the overall assets in dispute. In the case of *Re T (Divorce: Interim Maintenance: Discovery)* [1990] 1 FLR 1, the entire litigation costs were said to exceed £1.2 million, and in *KSO v MJO and JMO (PSO intervening)* [2008] EWHC 3031 (Fam) the costs amounted to over 70% of the total matrimonial assets, leaving insufficient funds to both house the children and pay their school fees. The impact of costs on the family finances is so significant that, under r 9.27 of the FPR 2010, each party must produce to the court, at each court appointment, a written estimate of costs and, before the Final Hearing, a written statement of costs (see **10.8.4**). In addition, adherence to the overriding objective and active case management by the courts under the new financial order procedure should help to ensure that costs are kept in proportion to the overall assets.

10.10.2 The costs rules

The costs rules are set out in r 28.3 of the FPR 2010 (see **Appendix 1(I)**). The general rule is that the court will not make a costs order in financial order proceedings unless such an order is justified by the litigation conduct of one of the parties. Costs will normally be treated as a liability of the relevant party and be taken into account when making the substantive order. To enable the court to have an accurate picture of the costs incurred, each party must file a statement of costs in Form H1 at least 14 days before the final hearing (see **10.8.4**).

In deciding whether to make a costs order on the basis of a party's litigation conduct the court must take into account the following factors:

(a) any failure to comply with the rules, any court order or any practice direction which the court considers relevant. Thus, for example, where a party does not make any proposals for settlement before the FDR and in consequence the FDR is adjourned, he is likely to be ordered to pay the costs of the wasted hearing;

(b) any open offer to settle made by a party;

(c) whether it was reasonable for a party to raise, pursue or contest a particular allegation or issue. Thus, for example, the wife was ordered to make a contribution towards the husband's costs where she had made a wholly misconceived application to transfer the husband's shares to her weeks before the final hearing and this had vastly increased the costs (*M v M* [2009] EWHC 1941 (Fam));

(d) the manner in which a party has pursued or responded to the application or a particular allegation or issue. This would cover, for example, the situation where an allegation of non-disclosure of assets was pursued too far;

(e) any other aspect of a party's conduct in relation to the proceedings which the court considers relevant. This is a general sweeping-up factor which could cover, for example, where one party instructed a sole expert after a joint expert report had been prepared;

(f) the financial effect on the parties of any costs order.

A party who intends to seek a costs order at a hearing must give advance notice of that fact in open correspondence or in his skeleton arguments (*Practice Direction (Ancillary Relief: Costs)*, 20 February 2006). If a summary assessment of costs is likely, the claiming party must also file a statement of costs in CPR Form N260, as Form H1 is insufficiently detailed for such an assessment.

Note that the costs rules in r 28.3 of the FPR 2010 do not apply to proceedings for maintenance pending suit or for an interim order. In these cases CPR r 44.3 will apply, giving the court discretion as to whether or not to order costs.

10.11 Negotiations

One of the key features of the financial order procedure is the promotion and facilitation of settlements. Most cases do, in fact, settle by agreement, often during informal discussions following the FDR. However, negotiations are an on-going process and may well commence at a very early stage. This is generally to be encouraged as it will probably be quicker and will cost the parties less, so leaving more of the assets available to be divided between them. Further, it may help to lessen any ill-feeling caused by the breakdown of the marriage and, therefore, aid the parties' future relations, in particular with the children. In addition, the respondent is more likely to comply with an order to which he has agreed, thus avoiding the need for enforcement proceedings.

However, the client must beware of settling at any price. Any agreement represents a compromise, but the solicitor must ensure that negotiations are carried out with full knowledge of all material facts. Both parties are under a duty of full and frank disclosure (see **10.7.1**). Do not be afraid to ask the other party for the same level of disclosure as he would give if the matter was to proceed to a hearing.

In addition, the solicitor should be aware of the type of order which the court might be expected to make, thus ensuring that he does not allow his client to accept too little or offer too much. Take care to check that the client is not willing to accept a very low offer simply because he is in an emotionally vulnerable state following the breakdown of the marriage.

If a settlement is reached, heads of agreement should be drawn up and signed by the parties and their legal representatives to evidence the necessary consensus.

10.12 Consent orders

Once the parties have reached agreement, the applicant's solicitor should draw up a draft consent order and send it to the respondent's solicitor. To enable the court to investigate the parties' means, a statement of information must also be completed (Form D81 – see **Appendix 3(F)**). This statement sets out information such as an estimate of the approximate value of the capital resources and net income of each party and of any minor child of the family; what arrangements are intended for the accommodation of the parties and any minor child of the family; and whether either party has remarried, or has any present intention to remarry or to cohabit with another person.

Both applicant and respondent may complete the relevant information on one statement of information, or each may each complete his own. A party must sign a statement of truth on any statement of information he completes. Each party must also certify that he has read the contents set out by the other party.

The applicant must then file the statement(s) of information together with two copies of the draft order sought, one of which must be endorsed by the respondent to signify his agreement. Practice Direction 9A states that this rule is complied with if the endorsed statement is signed by solicitors on the record as acting for the respondent, with the important proviso that, if the consent order includes undertakings, it must be signed by the party giving the undertaking as well as by that party's solicitor. The applicant must also file Form A if agreement was reached at such an early stage that this has not yet been done.

The district judge will then peruse the filed documents and, if satisfied, can make an order in the agreed terms. In the rare event that he is not satisfied, he can order the parties to attend a hearing.

If agreement is reached at a hearing, the district judge can dispense with the need for filing a statement of information.

The consent order is then drafted immediately by both parties' solicitors, and approved and made by the district judge.

10.13 Drafting financial orders

It is very important for a family solicitor to be able to draft orders which give effect to any financial agreement between husband and wife (or order of the court) in the way intended. It is equally important for the solicitor to be able to spot any errors in a draft order that is sent to him for his approval. At **10.13.13**, there are three specimen orders: Shah, Levy and Brown. These should be read carefully, as they will be referred to throughout **10.13** to illustrate a variety of drafting points.

10.13.1 Form of order

The order should be set out in three parts as follows:

(a) Title of suit.

(b) Preamble. This can deal with matters the court has no power to order, for example, mortgage payments, paying for outgoings on the house (but see **10.13.5.3** – deferred trusts of land). It:

   (i) states whether the order is made by consent (as in Shah and Levy) or (in a contested case) after hearing representations from the parties (and their solicitors/counsel) (see Brown);

   (ii) may indicate the basis on which the order is made, for example, on the basis that the applicant pays the mortgage instalments out of her maintenance payments (see Levy);

(iii) recites any undertakings given by either party, for example, to discharge outgoings on the property (see Brown).

(c) Operative part of order. This is prefaced by the words 'It is ordered'. It must be couched in clear and unambiguous terms so that each party can see, for example, what he or she is required to do, by when and/or until when. It must also reflect what the court's powers under ss 22–24D of the MCA 1973 actually are. Even by consent, the court cannot order a party to do something which it has no power to do (eg order the husband to pay the premiums on an insurance policy).

Note that third parties cannot be ordered to do anything, for example, a building society cannot be ordered to grant or transfer a mortgage.

10.13.2 Undertakings

The court may accept undertakings to do things which it cannot itself expressly order. The terms of an undertaking will be set out in the preamble to the order. Common examples would include provisions for one party:

(a) to make payments to a third party, for example, the husband to pay mortgage instalments to the building society direct in addition to, or instead of, periodical payments, or to pay debts;

(b) to take out a life insurance policy for the benefit of the other;

(c) to seek the release of the other party from mortgage or leasehold covenants, or to indemnify him/her in respect of them;

(d) to guarantee a mortgage;

(e) to purchase property.

Failure to comply with an undertaking to do or abstain from doing any act other than the payment of money may be punished by imprisonment for contempt of court. The undertaking must be endorsed with a notice setting out the consequences of disobedience, as follows:

> You may be sent to prison for contempt of court if you break the promises you have given to the court.

The person giving the undertaking must also sign a statement that he understands the terms of the undertaking being given and the consequences of failing to comply with it, as follows:

> I understand the undertaking that I have given, and that if I break any of my promises to the court I may be sent to prison for contempt of court.

An undertaking for the payment of money can be enforced like an order, for example by attachment of earnings or third party debt order (see **11.2.2**). It will also be contempt of court to fail to comply with such an undertaking. An undertaking for the payment of money must be endorsed with a notice setting out the consequences of disobedience, as follows:

> If you fail to pay any sum of money which you have promised the court that you would pay, a person entitled to enforce the undertaking may apply to the court for an order. If it is proved that you have had the means to pay the sum but you have refused or neglected to pay that sum, you may be sent to prison.

The person giving the undertaking must also sign a statement that he understands the terms of the undertaking being given and the consequences of failing to comply with it, as follows:

> I understand the undertaking that I have given, and that if I break my promise to the court to pay any sum of money, I may be sent to prison.

See, for example, the specimen order in Shah at **10.13.13** below.

10.13.3 Periodical payments

The order must indicate in relation to the payments:

(a) by whom they are payable;
(b) to whom they are payable;
(c) period by reference to when calculated, eg £2,000 per annum;
(d) period by reference to which payable, eg monthly in advance;
(e) from what date or event payments are to commence; and
(f) until what date or event they are to continue (remember the age limits for children (see **4.3.2**)).

> **Example**
>
> The Respondent shall pay periodical payments to the Petitioner. Payments shall be at the rate of £5,000 per annum payable monthly in advance. Payments shall commence on 1 April 2012. They will end on the first to occur of:
>
> (a) the death of the Respondent or the Petitioner; or
> (b) the Petitioner's remarriage; or
> (c) further order of the court.

Spouse and child provision (if any) should appear in separate clauses. In cases where maintenance for a child is not covered by the CSA 1991, child provision should clearly indicate whether the payer is to:

(a) pay direct to the child; or
(b) pay to a third party (usually the other parent) for the child's benefit.

Where (as is usual) the order provides for payment to continue until the child reaches 17 (or 18) or ceases full-time education, the words 'whichever is the later' should be added.

Note that, where the Child Support Agency makes a calculation, this will not appear in the operative part of the order.

10.13.4 Lump sums

Remember that an order may provide that payment be deferred until a later date or an event and/or be by instalments (see **4.4.1**). The order must indicate in respect of each sum:

(a) by whom it is payable;
(b) to whom it is payable;
(c) by what date or contingency it is to be paid;

For example, 'on or before the 30th day of June 2012'.

10.13.5 Property adjustment orders (not requiring an immediate sale)

Remember that although such orders usually affect only the home, any property may be covered, such as furnishings, stocks and shares, other land, cars (see Shah). The following points primarily relate to land, including the home.

10.13.5.1 Preliminary considerations

The order must make sense from a conveyancing and property law point of view. The solicitor will need to ascertain the following:

(a) Where is the legal estate now? Is it in joint names, or his or hers alone?

(b) Where is the legal estate going? Is it to stay in joint names, or to be put into joint names for the purposes of a deferred trust of land? Or is it to be transferred into the sole name of one? This will be so for an outright transfer (with or without a lump sum in return), or a deferred charge.

(c) What are the equities now, and what are they going to be? This is relevant in two main cases:

   (i) where the house is in one spouse's sole name but the other spouse may have an equitable interest from contributions to purchase or improvement. If the owning spouse is to keep the home outright, perhaps paying the other a lump sum, the non-owner should agree she has no interest in the property in the preamble;

   (ii) a *Mesher*- or *Martin*-type order creating a deferred trust of land, where the new equities will be set out in the order.

10.13.5.2 Outright transfers (with or without lump sums in return)

The legal estate and/or equitable interests must be ordered to be transferred to one party as appropriate (see, eg, Shah, clause 2) and a date or event for compliance must be inserted. This date/event must be after the decree absolute (see **4.2**).

10.13.5.3 Deferred trusts of land

The legal estate must be vested in trustees (usually but not necessarily the parties) and ordered to be transferred if need be, with a date for compliance if that is so. The terms of the trust must be set out, including:

(a) a statement of who has the right to occupy until sale;

(b) the determining (or 'triggering') event(s) for sale to take place, for example, the occupying spouse's remarriage;

(c) the proportions of the sale proceeds to which the parties will be entitled on sale.

Other provisions may be included, for example, detailed provisions to enable the original property to be sold and another bought on the same trusts if the occupier wishes to move, or as to who should have responsibility for repairs.

Contrary to the usual position, where there is a deferred trust the wording of s 24(1)(b) of the MCA 1973: 'an order that a settlement of such property ... be made to the satisfaction of the court ...', is wide enough to allow the court actually to order a party to pay the mortgage or insurance on the property, for example, rather than having to deal with it by way of undertaking (see, eg, Levy, clause 2.3).

10.13.5.4 Deferred charge

If necessary, the legal estate must be ordered to be transferred into the sole name of the intended occupier with a date for compliance. She will then be ordered to execute a legal charge (within a specified time) to secure payment to the non-occupier of a sum representing a proportion of the value of the property as defined in the order, or a fixed sum (as agreed). (See Brown in **10.13.13**.)

The order will require the charge deed to specify the events which will make the statutory power of sale arise and become exercisable, and may provide for matters such as removal and repairs to be covered by covenants to be set out in the deed.

10.13.5.5 Transfer of tenancies

The court also has power to order the transfer of most types of tenancy (see **9.5**). The wording of an order to effect this is relatively straightforward, for example, 'The Respondent do transfer his tenancy in Flat 2, The Broadway, Guildshire, to the Petitioner within one month of decree absolute'. Remember that the landlord should be contacted at an early stage so that his consent can be obtained.

10.13.5.6 Further points

The orders do not operate to vest or transfer legal estates, nor to create legal charges. Conveyancing documents will be required to do this.

10.13.6 Orders for sale

In some cases, property may need to be sold in order to realise and divide the cash value. Remember that orders for sale cannot be made on their own, and the court must also have made an order for secured periodical payments, a lump sum order or a property adjustment order (see **4.4.3**). Where the home is in the sole name of one party this will most commonly be achieved by ordering the property owner to pay a lump sum to the other party equivalent to the desired share. The owner may raise the sum either by borrowing against the property, or by selling it, at his option. The non-owner is unaffected either way so long as the cash is paid.

Where property is in joint names, the court has power under s 17 of the the Married Women's Property Act 1882 (MWPA 1882) to order simply that the trust of land be executed and the proceeds divided. On divorce, the court may exercise its powers under s 17 of the MWPA 1882 without a separate formal application. A similar power exists in relation to civil partnerships under s 66 of the Civil Partnership Act 2004. This means that, where the property is in joint names, no lump sum, etc order needs to be made.

10.13.7 Pensions

The order must state that there is to be a provision by way of pension attachment, pension sharing, pension compensation sharing order or pension compensation attachment order in accordance with an annex in Form P1 (pension sharing), Form P2 (pension attachment), Form PPF1 (pension compensation sharing order) or Form PPF2 (pension compensation attachment order).

10.13.8 Dismissals

Just as an application for a particular type of order may be granted by the making of an order, for example for the payment of a lump sum, so an application may be dismissed. Any application by either party which is not granted by the making of an order should be dismissed to prevent that party from reactivating his or her claim in the future. The dismissal may be of an individual application, or the order may provide for the dismissal of all outstanding applications (see, eg, Levy, clause 7).

However, an application can be dismissed only if it has been made. If the husband is the respondent in the divorce, he may not have made any applications. Some courts will require that he files Form A so that his applications can be dismissed. However, no fee will be required if Form A is marked 'for dismissal purposes only'.

10.13.9 Clean break orders

Remember that such orders involve either an immediate dismissal of all maintenance claims, or an order that maintenance should be paid for a finite term only (see **4.6.2**).

Where an application for periodical payments for a spouse is dismissed to effect a clean break, the order should go on (under MCA 1973, s 25A) to direct that she 'shall not be entitled to make a further application in relation to the marriage' for a secured or unsecured periodical payments order (as in Shah, clause 4).

Where the order is for term maintenance, to effect a clean break it should direct that the applicant 'shall not be entitled to apply for an order to extend this deadline' (see Levy, clause 4).

The order should normally state that neither party, on the death of the other, shall be entitled to apply for an order under the I(PFD)A 1975 (see Shah, clause 5).

10.13.10 'Liberty to apply'

The words 'Liberty to apply' are conventionally included in an order. They simply envisage that the parties may need to come back to the court to resolve any difficulties over the interpretation of the order in the light of circumstances which may occur on putting it into effect, for example if, when the house is sold, there is a dispute over which/how many estate agents to use. They do not in any way affect the court's power to vary an order and the restrictions on that power (see **11.8**).

10.13.11 Costs

The costs of each ancillary matter is a separate matter distinct from the main suit and any other application. When considering the costs of the financial order proceedings, remember that the general rule is that the court will not make a costs order unless it is appropriate to do so because of the litigation conduct of one of the parties. On an earlier hearing, there may already have been a summary assessment of costs. Alternatively, if the order was silent as to costs, no party is entitled to costs in relation to that order (CPR 1998, r 44.13).

Where the court orders one party to pay the costs of the other party, it may either make a summary assessment, or order a detailed assessment of the costs (for further details, see ***Civil Litigation***).

Where the general rule applies, the order will say that there be 'no order as to costs'. Where it is an application for a consent order (see **10.12**), the parties should agree a figure for costs to be inserted in the order, or agree there should be no order as to costs, as otherwise it will be necessary for attendance at the hearing.

If the receiving party is publicly funded:

(a) there must be a detailed assessment of costs, if not agreed (see, eg, Brown, clause 9); and
(b) where property or cash 'recovered or preserved' is intended to provide a house, a statement to that effect must be included in the body of the order to enable the Legal Services Commission to exercise its discretion to postpone the enforcement of the statutory charge. The Lord Chancellor has prescribed the following clause:

> And it is certified for the purpose of the Community Legal Service (Financial) Regulations 2000 [that the lump sum of £X has been ordered to be paid to enable the applicant/respondent to purchase a home for himself/herself (or his/her dependants)] [that the property (address) has been preserved for/recovered by the applicant/respondent for use as a home for himself/herself (or his/her dependants)].

See Brown, clause 1.

Lastly, remember to deal with the costs of implementing the order, for example conveyancing costs.

10.13.12 Side-letters

In some cases, it may be useful to record in a side-letter the background to the order and the result that it is trying to achieve. This can aid the court if at a later date one of the parties seeks to vary the order (see **11.8.3**).

10.13.13 Specimen orders

There follow three specimen orders: Shah, Levy and Brown. These should be read carefully as they are referred to throughout **10.13** to illustrate a variety of drafting points.

SHAH v SHAH

[Order for transfer of property with lump sum back or sale in default.]

There follows an outline of the facts of the case which resulted in the order below (note that these facts are *not* part of the order):

Mr and Mrs Shah are both working and self-supporting. There are no children. The matrimonial home is owned in joint names and is subject to a mortgage to the Halnat Building Society. It has been agreed that Mrs Shah (respondent) will transfer to Mr Shah her half share in the property in return for £15,000, being approximately half the net equity. Mr Shah will finance this by a second mortgage. Should it not be possible for him to raise the money within three months of decree absolute the house will be sold and the proceeds divided as to £15,000 to Mrs Shah and the balance to Mr Shah. Each party is to pay their own costs.

IN THE HULLPOOL COUNTY COURT		2012	No ....
BETWEEN	RAJ SHAH		Petitioner
	AND		
	GITA SHAH		Respondent
	ORDER		

UPON the Petitioner and Respondent agreeing that the terms of this order are accepted in full and final satisfaction of all claims for income, capital and pension sharing orders which either may be entitled to bring against the other in relation to the marriage

UPON the Petitioner UNDERTAKING to the court to indemnify the Respondent against any future liability under the mortgage dated ... in favour of the Halnat Building Society ('the Mortgage') secured on the property at 93 Brook Court Hullpool ('the Home') and to use his best endeavours to obtain her release from her covenants under the Mortgage and to pay for the costs of transfer of the Home as set out in clause 2

BY CONSENT IT IS ORDERED THAT:

1. The Petitioner shall within 3 months of decree absolute in this cause ('the Payment Date') pay or cause to be paid to the Respondent the sum of £15,000 (the 'Lump Sum').
2. On payment of the Lump Sum on or before the Payment Date the Respondent shall transfer to the Petitioner;
   (i) all her legal estate and beneficial interest in the Home
   (ii) all fixtures and chattels now in the Home which belong to her alone and her interest in any such items which are jointly owned.
3. If the Lump Sum is not paid by the Payment Date then the Home shall be sold on the open market and the following consequential provisions shall apply:

3.1 the Home shall be sold for such price as may be agreed by the parties or in default of agreement determined by the court;

3.2 both parties shall have the conduct of the sale;

3.3 the Petitioner's solicitors shall have the conduct of the conveyancing work relating to the sale;

3.4 the Home shall be offered for sale by such estate agents as may be agreed by the parties or in default of such agreement nominated by the court.

3.5 The proceeds of sale of the Home shall be applied as follows:

(i) to discharge the Mortgage

(ii) in payment of the Petitioner's solicitors' conveyancing costs and disbursements in connection with the sale;

(iii) in payment of the charges of the estate agents;

(iv) in payment to the Respondent of the Lump Sum of £15,000 referred to in Clause 1 of this order;

(v) in payment of the balance to the Petitioner.

4. Upon compliance with clauses (1)–(3) and the Petitioner's undertakings to the court, the Petitioner's and the Respondent's claims for financial provision, property adjustment and pension sharing orders do stand dismissed and neither the Petitioner nor the Respondent shall be entitled to make any further application in relation to their marriage for an order under s 23(1)(a) or (b) of the Matrimonial Causes Act 1973.

5. Neither the Petitioner nor the Respondent shall be entitled on the death of the other to apply for an order for provision out of the other's estate.

6. There be liberty to apply as to the implementation and timing of the terms of this order.

7. It is ordered that the Petitioner and Respondent shall each bear their own costs of this application and the ancillary negotiations.

Dated the day of 2012.

Signed	Signed ....
Petitioner	Respondent

You may be sent to prison for contempt of court if you break the promises you have given to the court

I understand the undertaking that I have given, and that if I break any of my promises to the court I may be sent to prison for contempt of court.

Signed ....

Petitioner

We request that the court make an order as set out above to which our clients respectively consent.

Signed	Signed ....
Solicitors for the Petitioner	Solicitors for the Respondent

LEVY v LEVY

[*Mesher* order: periodical payments to wife (linked to payment of mortgage) and step-child; dismissal of prayer for lump sum and respondent's application.]

Background information (note that this is *not* part of the order): Michelle Levy has recently obtained a decree absolute against Michael Levy under s 1(2)(d) of the MCA 1973. The parties have agreed that the three children of the family, Anthony (7) (who is Mrs Levy's child by her first husband who is now dead), Robert (5) and Peter (3), will remain with Mrs Levy. Mr Levy will pay maintenance for all three children (for his natural children via the Child Support Agency). The parties are in their mid-thirties. Mr Levy is a partner in a firm of surveyors. Mrs Levy has not been in paid employment since the birth of their first child. The former matrimonial home is in joint names and subject to a mortgage. Mr Levy has agreed that Mrs Levy and the children will remain in the home while the children are being educated. Mr Levy now lives in a flat. A consent order has been negotiated. Neither is publicly funded. Mr Levy had agreed to pay Mrs Levy's costs, the sum has already been agreed.

IN THE HIGHBRIDGE COUNTY COURT 2012 No ....

BETWEEN MICHELLE ANN LEVY Petitioner

AND

MICHAEL JAMES LEVY Respondent

ORDER

UPON the Petitioner and Respondent agreeing that the terms of this order are accepted in full and final satisfaction of all claims for income, capital and pension sharing orders which either may be entitled to bring against the other in relation to the marriage.

AND UPON the Petitioner and the Respondent agreeing that the contents of the Property (described below) and their personal belongings are to be divided in accordance with the schedules attached to this order

This order is on the basis that:

(a) a Child Support Act calculation has been made in relation to Robert Levy and Peter Levy in the sum of £ to be paid each month from the 1st April 2012 and that it will continue at approximately this level for the foreseeable future AND

(b) the Petitioner will use the periodical payments made to her by clause 4 of this order to discharge the mortgage with Barcloyds Bank on the Property (described below)

BY CONSENT IT IS ORDERED:

1. With effect from the making of this order the property known as Twintrees, Hill Road, Highbridge ('the Property') shall be held by the Petitioner and Respondent upon a trust of land for themselves as beneficial tenants in common.

2. That the trust be subject to the following terms and conditions:

   2.1 The Petitioner shall be entitled to occupy the Property to the exclusion of the Respondent until sale

   2.2 The Property shall not be sold without the prior written consent of both parties or further order until the first to happen of the following events ('the Determining Events'), namely:

   2.2.1 the Petitioner remarries; or

   2.2.2 the Petitioner dies; or

2.2.3 all the children of the family reach the age of 18 or finish full-time undergraduate education if later.

2.3 The Petitioner shall with effect from the date of this order be solely responsible for all payments of capital and interest on the mortgage in favour of Barcloyds Bank

2.4 The Petitioner shall be responsible for all routine maintenance and decorative repairs to the Property

2.5 The cost of insuring the Property and of any structural repairs shall be shared equally between the Petitioner and the Respondent provided that no works of structural repair shall be carried out to the Property save by agreement between the parties or by further order of the court

2.6 In the event of the Petitioner wishing to move to another house with the agreement of the Respondent (such agreement not to be unreasonably withheld) during the subsistence of this trust:

(i) the trustees shall, if requested by the Petitioner, sell the Property and re-invest the proceeds in the purchase of such other dwelling ('the Substitute Property') as she shall direct for her occupation

(ii) the Petitioner shall pay the costs of and incidental to such sale and purchase

(iii) the Substitute Property shall be held on the same trusts terms and conditions as the Property and the trustees shall have full power as if they were beneficial owners to execute such mortgage deed as may be necessary to enable the purchase to be completed

(iv) if the purchase price excluding stamp duty land tax, Land Registry fees and conveyancing costs of the Substitute Property shall be less than the net proceeds of the Property the difference shall be divided as to 75% to the Petitioner and 25% to the Respondent

2.7 On or before the Determining Event the Petitioner shall have the right to purchase the Respondent's interest in the Property at an open market valuation to be agreed, or in default of agreement, to be determined by a valuer nominated by the court

2.8 If either the Petitioner or the Respondent shall die during the currency of the trust, the power of appointing a substitute trustee shall be exercised by his or her personal representatives.

3. That upon sale (except in accordance with clause 2.6), the proceeds shall be applied in redeeming the mortgage, and paying the costs of the sale. The balance remaining shall be divided in the proportion of 75% to the Petitioner and 25% to the Respondent.

4. The Respondent shall pay periodical payments to the Petitioner.

Payments shall be at the rate of £X per annum payable monthly in advance.

Payments shall commence on .

They will end on the first to occur of:

(a) the death of either the Petitioner or the Respondent; or

(b) the Petitioner's remarriage; or

(c) (subject to clause 2.6) the Petitioner voluntarily vacating the Property for a period in excess of 3 months in any 12 month period; or

(d) all the children of the family reaching the age of 18 or finishing full-time undergraduate education if later; or

(e) further order of the court

after which the Petitioner will not be entitled to make any further application in relation to the marriage for an order under the Matrimonial Causes Act 1973, s 23(1)(a) or (b) for periodical payments or secured periodical payments. Furthermore, pursuant to the

Matrimonial Causes Act 1973, s 28(1A), the Petitioner may not apply for an order to extend this deadline.

5. The Respondent shall make periodical payments to the Petitioner for the benefit of Anthony Levy at the rate of £X per month.
   (a) Payments shall be made monthly in advance on the 1st of each month
   (b) They shall commence on 1st April 2012
   (c) They shall end on the later of the child
      (i) reaching the age of 18; or
      (ii) ceasing full-time secondary education unless the court makes an order for the payments to continue to a later date.

6. From the date when the Child Support Agency ceases to have jurisdiction for Robert Levy and Peter Levy because they are no longer in full-time, non-advanced education as set out in the Child Support Act 1991, s 55, the Respondent shall pay periodical payments to the Petitioner for the benefit of Robert Levy at the rate of £X per month and for the benefit of Peter Levy at the rate of £X per month.

   Payments shall be made monthly in advance on the 1st day of each month.

   They shall commence on the date on which the Child Support Agency ceases to have jurisdiction for the child.

   They shall end on the later of the children respectively:
   (a) reaching the age of 18; or
   (b) (if later) ceasing full-time secondary education unless the court makes an order for the payments to continue to a later date.

7. Save as aforesaid, the applications by the Petitioner and the Respondent for financial provision, property adjustment and pension sharing orders do stand dismissed and the Respondent shall not be entitled to make any further application in relation to their marriage under the Matrimonial Causes Act 1973, s 23(1)(a) or (b).

8. Liberty to each party to apply as to the implementation and timing of the terms of the order.

9. That the Respondent shall pay the Petitioner's costs of this application in the sum of £ .

Dated the day of 2012.

Signed	Signed ....
Petitioner	Respondent

We request that the court make an order as set out above to which our clients respectively consent.

Signed	Signed ....
Solicitors for the Petitioner	Solicitors for the Respondent

BROWN v BROWN

[Deferred charge on *Martin* contingencies; order for nominal maintenance.]

Background information (note that this is *not* part of the order): Eileen and Arthur Brown are in their fifties, and were married for 35 years. Mr Brown is an office manager and Mrs Brown is a typist. The children of the family are married and self-supporting. Mrs Brown has obtained a decree absolute based on Mr Brown's adultery with a woman with whom he now lives permanently. Mrs Brown continues to live at the former matrimonial home, a small three bedroomed terraced house which is in Mr Brown's sole name. The mortgage was paid off two years ago, and Mrs Brown can afford to pay the outgoings from her earnings. Mrs Brown has arthritis and has been advised that she will probably have to stop work in about three years' time. Mr Brown wants the house sold, and has offered Mrs Brown one-third of the net proceeds. Mrs Brown, who has registered an agreed notice under the Family Law Act 1996, has rejected the offer, saying this will be insufficient to rehouse her. She wishes to remain in the house. Mrs Brown obtains public funding and applies to the court. The district judge makes the following order.

IN THE LOKE COUNTY COURT 2012 No ....

BETWEEN EILEEN AUDREY BROWN Petitioner

AND

ARTHUR GEORGE BROWN Respondent

ORDER

UPON the basis that the Property (described below) be used as a home for the Wife AND UPON the Petitioner UNDERTAKING to the court to discharge all outgoings and expenses on the Property

AND UPON the Respondent UNDERTAKING not to change employment and not to retire until the pension sharing provision in clause 6 of this order is implemented

IT IS ORDERED:

1. That the Respondent shall on or before the day of transfer all his legal and beneficial interest in the property at 34, Lower Lane, Loke ('the Property') into the name of the Petitioner AND it is hereby certified for the purpose of the Community Legal Service (Financial) Regulations 2000 that the Property has been preserved for the Petitioner for use as a home for herself.
2. The Petitioner shall within one month of the transfer of the Property execute a legal charge ('the Charge') to secure the payment to the Respondent of a sum equivalent to one half of the actual proceeds of sale.
3. The Charge shall not become exercisable until:–
   (a) the death or remarriage of the Petitioner; or
   (b) voluntary vacation of the Property by the Petitioner for a period in excess of 4 months in any 12 month period; or
   (c) sale of the Property by the Petitioner; or
   (d) upon such earlier date as a further order of the court may provide

   whichever occurs first.
4. The Respondent shall pay periodical payments to the Petitioner.

   Payments shall be at the rate of 5 pence per annum payable in advance.

   Payments shall commence on the day of 2012.

   They will end on the first to occur of:

(a) the death of either the Respondent or the Petitioner; or
(b) the Petitioner's remarriage; or
(c) further order of the court.

5. There is to be provision by way of pension sharing in favour of the Wife in respect of the Husband's rights under his pension arrangement with [ ] in accordance with the annex to this order it being agreed between the parties that in the event of the Respondent predeceasing the Petitioner after this order has taken effect but before implementation the Petitioner shall have the Respondent's personal representative's consent to an application for leave to appeal out of time against the terms of this order.
6. Save as aforesaid, the applications by the Petitioner and the Respondent for financial provision, pension sharing and property adjustment orders do stand dismissed and the Respondent shall not be entitled to make any further application in relation to their marriage under the Matrimonial Causes Act 1973, s 23(1)(a) or (b).
7. That there be liberty to both parties to apply as to the implementation and timing of the terms of the order.
8. The Respondent shall pay the costs of implementation of this order. Detailed assessment of the Petitioner's costs.

Dated the day of 2012.

Signed:

District Judge

10.14 Summary of court procedure

Financial order procedure can effectively be illustrated by way of checklists. Two such checklists follow. One shows the contested procedure and the other the procedure to be followed where the parties have reached agreement.

10.14.1 Application to the court for a financial order

	Applicant (A)		*Court*		*Respondent (R)*
(1)	Files at court: — Form A — court fee — public funding certificate (where appropriate) — notice of issue of public funding (where appropriate) — notice of acting (Legal Help divorce cases only) — Form FM1	(2)	Fixes First Appointment (FA) 12–16 weeks ahead (Form C)		
		(3)	Serves on Respondent within 4 days copy Forms A and C		
(4)	Serves on Respondent — notice of public funding, (where appropriate) — copy notice of acting (Legal Help divorce cases only) Serves on lender and person responsible for any pension arrangement copy Form A			(4)	Requests information from pension arrangement. Serves information on Applicant within 7 days of receipt.
(5)	Completes, files and exchanges Form E at least 35 days before FA			(5)	Completes, files and exchanges Form E at least 35 days before FA

Applicant (A)	*Court*	*Respondent (R)*
(6) Drafts, files and serves: (a) statement of issues; (b) chronology; (c) questionnaire and documents requested; (d) notice whether ready to proceed to FDR at least 14 days before FA		(6) Drafts, files and serves: (a) statement of issues; (b) chronology; (c) questionnaire and documents requested; (d) notice whether ready to proceed to FDR at least 14 days before FA
(7) Produces costs estimate immediately before FA in Form H		(7) Produces costs estimate immediately before FA in Form H
(8) Attends FA with client		(8) Attends FA with client
	(9) Makes directions; usually fixes FDR	
(10) Complies with directions		(10) Complies with directions
(11) Gives notice to court of all offers and responses 7 days before FDR		
(12) Produces costs estimate immediately before FDR		(12) Produces costs estimate immediately before FDR
(13) Attends FDR with client		(13) Attends FDR with client
	(14) May: (a) make consent order; (b) give directions; (c) fix final hearing; (d) adjourn for ADR	
(15) Drafts, files and serves on R statements of open proposals 14 days before hearing		
		(16) Drafts, files and serves on A statement of open proposals 7 days after receipt of A's proposals

Applicant (A)		Court		Respondent (R)	
(17)	Produces costs statement (H1) immediately before hearing			(17)	Produces costs statement (H1) immediately before hearing
(18)	Attends hearing with client			(18)	Attends hearing with client
		(19)	Makes order		

10.14.2 Consent orders

There are two possible procedures. Which is appropriate depends on how far (if at all) the application has progressed on a contested basis when the parties reach agreement. Whichever is used, Form A must be filed before an order can be made. This will either have taken place before the steps described below, or (if not) can be incorporated into para 3 (see note (ii) below).

10.14.2.1 Normal consent procedure (no court attendance)

Applicant (A)		Court		Respondent (R)	
(1)	Completes Statement of Information Prepares draft order and submits it to R for approval/ amendment				
				(2)	Completes Statement of Information. Endorses consent on draft order. Returns both documents to A
(3)	Files at court: (a) Draft order, endorsed with R's (and A's) consent, plus (b) 2 copies; (c) Statement of Information signed by both parties				
		(4)	If satisfied, makes order. Sends copy to A and R. If not satisfied, may require parties to attend		

Notes

(i) Where appropriate, public funding certificate, notice of issue of certificate and notice of acting should be filed and/or served.

(ii) If A has not yet filed Form A, the draft order can conveniently be incorporated into that application which will be endorsed with R's consent.

10.14.2.2 Where attendance at court

The normal contested procedure will be followed up to the date of the hearing.

Once agreement has been reached, provided the district judge has the prescribed information as to parties' resources etc, an order may be made despite the lack of a draft order and written statement of information.

10.15 Maintenance calculations

The parent with care applies for a maintenance calculation using a standard form available from the Child Support Agency. Alternatively, the form can be completed on-line at the Child Support Agency website (www.csa.gov.uk).

The Child Support Agency must then notify the non-resident parent as soon as reasonably practicable, requesting such information as it may require to make the maintenance calculation (Child Support (Maintenance Calculation Procedure) Regulations 2000 (SI 2001/157), reg 5). This is usually done by telephone, with the Child Support Agency filling in the information on a Maintenance Enquiry Form. This form is then sent to the non-resident parent for his signature. At this time, the Child Support Agency will also inform the non-resident parent of the effective date of the maintenance calculation. Provided that the non-resident parent returns the form within 28 days, this will be eight weeks after the Maintenance Enquiry Form was sent. If he does not do so, the effective date will be the date that the form was sent out.

If the non-resident parent does not respond, or responds without having given all the information required, the Agency has a number of powers under the Act to enable it to obtain the information. For example, the Child Support Agency may approach other bodies, such as the local authority or HMRC, for information. In addition, the Secretary of State may appoint inspectors with power to enter premises where the non-resident parent is or has been employed, or where he carries out his trade, profession, vocation or business, to acquire information (CSA 1991, s 15). Lastly, s 14A of the CSA 1991 makes it a criminal offence for the non-resident parent to fail to supply information, or to supply false information. If after using these powers the Agency still does not have the information, it has the power to make a default maintenance decision (see **7.6.4.1**).

Chapter 11
Enforcement, Appeals, Setting Aside and Variation

11.1	Introduction	147
11.2	Financial orders in the county court	147
11.3	Enforcement in the family proceedings court	149
11.4	Collection and enforcement by the Child Maintenance and Enforcement Commission	150
11.5	Property adjustment orders	152
11.6	Appeals	152
11.7	Setting aside	153
11.8	Variation	154
11.9	Chapter summary	157

11.1 Introduction

Frequently, the respondent to an order for financial relief will fail to comply with some, or all, of the provisions of that order. It is essential, therefore, that the solicitor should be aware not only of the methods of enforcement which are available, but also which of those methods is most appropriate in the circumstances.

A client may wish to appeal against an order which he thinks is unfair. In certain situations an order may even be set aside. If the circumstances have changed since the order was made, the client may wish to have that order varied. This chapter deals with what action the solicitor can take on these occasions.

11.2 Financial orders in the county court

Financial orders in the county court comprise all orders apart from property adjustment orders (which are considered at **11.5**), but most commonly will be spouse periodical payments orders or lump sum orders. Enforcement of child maintenance calculations will be effected by the Child Maintenance and Enforcement Commission (C-MEC) (see **11.4**), but where a child maintenance order has been made by the court, enforcement will generally be through the court in the usual way. However, C-MEC can collect and enforce 'top-up' child maintenance orders made by the court under s 8 of the CSA 1991.

Payments of money orders made by the county court are made direct between the parties. This can sometimes lead to problems since not only may the parties have to remain in direct contact (which could result in continued acrimony), but, as there is no independent record of payments, proof of payment (or non-payment) may be difficult. These problems can be mitigated by use of the Maintenance Enforcement Act 1991. This Act provides that, when granting or varying a periodical payments order, or at any time after doing so, the High Court or county court can order:

(a) payment by standing order;

(b) the payer to open a bank account;

(c) attachment of the payer's earnings (see **11.2.2**).

11.2.1 Preliminary steps

When the order is first obtained the solicitor should tell his client to contact him immediately if the respondent defaults. This is particularly important in the case of periodical payments, because leave will be required to enforce arrears that are more than 12 months old. The court may refuse leave, remit the arrears and give the respondent a fresh start.

If the client was in receipt of public funding for the financial orders proceedings and the certificate has not been discharged, the solicitor will need to extend the certificate to cover enforcement proceedings. If the certificate has been discharged then the solicitor must apply for a new certificate.

The method of enforcement used will depend upon the decision as to which method would be most effective. This in turn will usually depend upon the assets the respondent owns. The applicant will already have this information where the respondent has defaulted shortly after the order was made. However, in other cases, the applicant can apply to the district judge for an order to have the respondent attend court for questioning under CPR, r 71. If the district judge agrees to the application, the respondent will be ordered to attend court and asked to bring relevant documents with him. He will then be thoroughly examined by a court officer (or exceptionally by a judge) as to his means. Failure to attend is contempt of court.

Under r 33.3(2) of the FPR 2010, when applying for enforcement an applicant may either specify the method of enforcement, or apply for an order for such method of enforcement as the court may consider appropriate. Should the applicant chose the latter option then an order for the respondent to attend court will be made and he will be questioned as to his assets so that the court can decide on the appropriate method of enforcement.

11.2.2 Methods of enforcement

11.2.2.1 Attachment of earnings

Under an attachment of earnings order (made under the Attachment of Earnings Act 1971) the respondent's employer will deduct a specified sum from his earnings. This sum will represent the amount of the maintenance order plus, possibly, a proportion of the arrears. The order must also specify a minimum amount, known as the 'protected earnings rate', below which the respondent's wages cannot fall. This rate is generally the amount that the respondent would be entitled to if he was reliant on welfare benefits. The employer will forward the money deducted from the respondent's wages to the court.

An attachment of earnings order is probably the best method of enforcement for a periodical payments order. It can be applied for either when the order is first made, or later when the respondent defaults. Fear of embarrassment with his employer may prompt the debtor to pay. However, the drawback of this method of enforcement is that the respondent must be in employment. It cannot be used if the respondent is self-employed or unemployed, and can be administratively difficult if the respondent frequently changes jobs.

11.2.2.2 Warrant of execution

A warrant of execution enables the county court bailiff to seize and sell assets belonging to the respondent sufficient to meet the outstanding amount. The solicitor applies to the court for a warrant, no hearing is needed. This method is most useful for unpaid lump sums, but could also be used for substantial arrears of maintenance.

11.2.2.3 Third party debt order

A third party debt order enables the applicant to receive payment direct from a third party who owes the respondent money, for example, a bank or building society. Third party debt order proceedings involve two stages. At first, an interim third party debt order (obtained without notice) will freeze the account. At the subsequent 'on notice' hearing the district judge can make a final third party debt order, which will require the bank or building society to pay the applicant the amount outstanding. This method is most useful for unpaid lump sums.

11.2.2.4 MCA 1973, s 24A

Under s 24A of the MCA 1973, the court can make an order for sale to enforce, for example, a lump sum or secured periodical payments order (see **4.4.3**). The s 24A order for sale can be made at the same time as the original order as a type of precaution. Thus, for example, an order could provide that the respondent is to pay the applicant a lump sum of £30,000 (representing her share in the home) and that, if that sum is not paid within three months of decree absolute, the home is to be sold and the £30,000 paid to the applicant out of the proceeds of sale. Alternatively, the order for sale can be made later, if the respondent defaults.

11.2.2.5 Charging order

The applicant can apply to charge land (and/or certain securities) which the respondent owns, or in which he has an interest, with the amount outstanding. However, the procedure involved is protracted. The applicant needs to apply for an interim charging order which can be made final at the subsequent hearing. This will give the applicant security for the debt, but a further hearing is needed to obtain an order for sale. At that further hearing, the court will have total discretion as to whether to order sale and it may decide not to, for example, if the charging order is over the respondent's home and the amount owed is relatively small. It is usually far better to use s 24A (see **11.2.2.4**).

11.2.2.6 Judgment summons

Under the Debtors Act 1869, the court has power to commit to prison a respondent who has not paid a periodical payments order or a lump sum order. This can be done provided:

(a) the respondent has defaulted; and

(b) the respondent has the means to pay but is neglecting or refusing to do so.

Until recently, the judgment summons procedure provided that the respondent must attend before the judge and be examined as to his means. However, in *Mubarak v Mubarak* [2001] 1 FLR 698, the Court of Appeal held that this procedure was in breach of the European Convention on Human Rights, Article 6 in particular, since it breached the respondent's right not to incriminate himself. As a result of *Mubarak*, it is now necessary for the applicant to produce evidence to show beyond reasonable doubt that the respondent has the means to pay. This may be very difficult for the applicant to do. The Family Proceedings (Amendment) Rules 2003 (SI 2003/184) subsequently amended the relevant procedure (under FPR 1991, rr 7.4–7.6) to make it compliant with the HRA 1998. The judgment summons procedure was already rarely used, partly because public funding is not available in the county court. A consequence of *Mubarak v Mubarak* and the amendments to the procedure mean that it is likely to be used even more rarely in the future and only as a last resort.

11.3 Enforcement in the family proceedings court

Where orders for maintenance have been made in the family proceedings court, the respondent must usually make payments to the clerk to the justices (although under the Maintenance Enforcement Act 1991 the family proceedings court can direct payments to be made in other ways, for example, by standing order between the parties). The court clerk will then forward the payments to the applicant. Thus, the court will have a complete record of all payments made and the parties need not be in contact with each other.

Before enforcement proceedings are commenced, and if the client is eligible, the solicitor should apply for public funding.

11.3.1 Methods of enforcement

If it becomes necessary to enforce the order, four methods are available:

(a) An attachment of earnings order. This has already been considered (see **11.2.2.1**).

(b) Committal to prison. This is very much a last resort. Three conditions must be fulfilled (Magistrates' Courts Act 1980, s 93(6)). These are:

(i) the court must inquire, in the respondent's presence, whether the default was due to his wilful refusal or culpable neglect, and impose imprisonment only if satisfied that either was the case; and

(ii) the court must be satisfied that an attachment of earnings order is either not possible or not appropriate; and

(iii) the respondent must be present when committal is ordered.

The arrears will not continue to accrue while the respondent is in prison (unless the court directs that they should), although imprisonment does not discharge the arrears. The respondent can obtain his release if he pays the whole amount due, or reduce the length of detention if he makes part-payment. Imprisonment lasts for a maximum of six weeks. The committal can be suspended on condition that the respondent pays the order in future together with gradual repayment of the arrears.

(c) A warrant of distress. This is similar to a warrant of execution (see **11.2.2.2**). It is an order to the police to seize and sell goods belonging to the respondent, using the proceeds of sale to repay the arrears. It is not an appropriate method for enforcing maintenance and is rarely used.

(d) The order can be registered in the High Court or county court so that the methods of enforcement available in that court can be used. However, the arrears will rarely be substantial enough to make this course of action appropriate.

As in the county court, the family proceedings court has power to remit all or part of the arrears and will generally not enforce arrears which are more than 12 months old.

11.3.2 Registration of county court maintenance orders

Once a periodical payments order has been made in the county court, it can be registered in the family proceedings court. To do this, the solicitor lodges a standard form in duplicate plus a copy of the maintenance order at the court which made the order. Some district judges will not agree to the order being registered unless there are arrears of maintenance.

Once the order has been registered, payments under the order will be made to the clerk to the justices, so there will be a full record of all payments. The family proceedings court will enforce the order on the applicant's behalf. Another consequence of registration is that if the applicant is on welfare benefits and the respondent is a persistently poor payer, the applicant may be able to take advantage of the diversion procedure (see **6.11.1**).

Lastly, once the order has been registered, the family proceedings court has power to vary the order, thus possibly making subsequent variation quicker and cheaper than in the county court.

11.4 Collection and enforcement by the Child Maintenance and Enforcement Commission

Where child maintenance is calculated by the Child Support Agency (acting on behalf of C-MEC), the parents can agree either for the non-resident parent to pay the parent with care direct or for the non-resident parent to make his payments to the Agency. If the parents agree that the non-resident parent will pay direct to the parent with care, this is likely to be done by standing order. If payment is through the Agency, this is likely to be by direct debit or deduction from earnings request. This works in the same way as an attachment of earnings order but there is no court involvement (see **11.2.2.1**).

Should the non-resident parent not pay child maintenance, the Agency can serve a deduction from earnings order on the non-resident parent's employer by way of enforcement (CSA 1991, s 30(2)). The CMOPA 2008 has amended the CSA 1991 so that now, where the non-resident parent is self employed, the Agency can make an order requiring the non-resident parent's bank or building society to make regular deductions from his account and pay the money to the Agency (CSA 1991, ss 32A–32D). Alternatively, the Agency can make a lump sum deduction order, which is a two-part process similar to a third party debt order (CSA 1991, ss 32E–32K).

Where one or more payments remain unpaid and the above methods of enforcement are inappropriate or have proved ineffective, the Agency can apply to the family proceedings court for a liability order (CSA 1991, s 33). Section 25 of the CMOPA 2008 amends the CSA 1991 to allow the Agency to make a liability order of its own accord without going to court. At the time of writing this section was not in force. Once a liability order has been obtained, the debt can be recovered by distress. If this proves ineffective, the Agency can apply to the county court for a third party debt order or charging order. In the last resort, the Agency can apply to the family proceedings court to have the absent parent committed for up to six weeks or disqualified from driving for up to two years (CSA 1991, ss 39, 39A and 40).

Anti-avoidance provisions have been introduced and are contained in s 32L of the CSA 1991. These provisions are very similar to s 37 of the MCA 1973 (see **9.6.2.3**) and allow the court to prevent a non-resident parent from disposing of property. The non-resident parent must have failed to pay child support maintenance and must be disposing of the property with the intention of avoiding payment of child support maintenance. However, if the disposition would have the effect of frustrating the enforcement of the unpaid child support maintenance, the intention will be presumed. Alternatively, where the property has already been disposed of, the court can set aside the disposition, unless it was made for valuable consideration to a person who was acting in good faith and without notice of an intention to avoid payment of child support maintenance.

In *R (on the application of Kehoe) v Secretary of State for Work and Pensions* [2005] UKHL 48, Mrs Kehoe sought a declaration that her inability personally to enforce arrears of child maintenance under a maintenance calculation by the Agency breached her rights of access to the court under Article 6 of the European Convention on Human Rights. The House of Lords held that Mrs Kehoe had no right under the CSA 1991 which she could exercise against Mr Kehoe entitling her to play any part in the assessment or enforcement process. Thus her 'civil rights' had not been engaged for the purposes of Article 6 and her claim failed. Mrs Kehoe then appealed to the European Court of Human Rights. Her appeal failed, the Court stating that her ability to apply for a court order via judicial review directing the Agency to take appropriate enforcement action meant that there was no breach of Article 6 (*Kehoe v United Kingdom* [2008] All ER (D) 198).

One of the major criticisms of the Agency has been its failure to enforce payments rigorously. In order to mitigate this, the Government has decided to contract out debt recovery work (the Contracting Out (Functions Relating to Child Support) Order 2006 (SI 2006/1692)). However, the private debt collectors have succeeded in getting payment in only a very small percentage of cases. In *Rowley v Secretary of State for Work and Pensions* [2007] EWCA Civ 598, Mrs Rowley and her three children brought proceedings against the Secretary of State on the basis that he was negligent in carrying out his functions under the Child Support Act 1991, with the consequence that maintenance totalling £53,000 due to them remained unpaid. The Court of Appeal held that it was not just to impose a common law duty of care on the Secretary of State as such a duty would be inconsistent with the statutory scheme.

Despite the fact that, generally, C-MEC is overseeing a continued improvement in the performance of the Child Support Agency, the issue of arrears and enforcement still causes problems. As stated above, the Child Maintenance and Other Payments Act 2008 gives C-MEC further powers, for example to make regular deductions of money directly from an absent parent's bank account, or to deduct a lump sum from such an account. Other enforcement powers have been included in the CMOPA 2008 so that once a liability order has been made and other methods of enforcement have proved ineffective, C-MEC can apply to court to have the absent parent's passport confiscated for up to two years, or to impose a curfew of between two and 12 hours a day on the absent parent for up to six months. At the time of writing, these powers are not yet in force. Section 51 of the Welfare Reform Act 2009 further amends these enforcement powers to enable C-MEC to make orders disqualifying a parent from holding or obtaining a driving licence and/or passport without the need to apply to court.

11.5 Property adjustment orders

If the respondent fails to execute the documents required to effect a property adjustment order, then the court has power to order the document to be executed by another person, usually the district judge, on his behalf (County Courts Act 1984, s 38). Should there be a problem with drafting the documents, the court can refer the matter to conveyancing counsel. In such a case, the court can direct that the granting of any decree be deferred until the documents have been executed.

11.6 Appeals

11.6.1 Financial orders

The Access to Justice Act 1999 (Destination of Appeals) (Family Proceedings) Order 2011 (SI 2011/1044) provides that appeals from decisions of a district judge of the county court will lie to a circuit judge of the county court. Appeals from decisions of a district judge of the Principal Registry of the Family Division, a district judge of the High Court or a costs judge will lie to a judge of the High Court. Under Pt 30 of the FPR 2010, permission to appeal must first be obtained. Permission may be sought from the lower court at the hearing at which the decision to be appealed was made, or to the appeal court in an appeal notice. The appeal notice must be filed at the appeal court within 21 days unless the lower court specifies a different period. Permission to appeal will be given only where the court considers that the appeal would have a real prospect of success, or where there is some other compelling reason why the appeal should be heard.

Generally an appeal will be limited to a review of the decision of the district judge, unless the appeal court considers that in the circumstances it would be in the interests of justice to hold a rehearing.

Further appeal to the Court of Appeal will be available only where the Court of Appeal considers that the appeal would raise an important point of principle or practice, or there is some other compelling reason for it to be heard.

11.6.2 Maintenance assessments

Where the non-resident parent or the person with care is unhappy with the amount awarded, he can ask for a review of the maintenance calculation within one month of the date of the decision. If still dissatisfied, he can usually appeal to the First-tier Tribunal (Social Security and Child Support) (SSCS), again within one month of the decision. A decision of that tribunal can be appealed on a point of law to the Upper Tribunal. There is a further right of appeal on a point of law to the Court of Appeal.

Where a person is dissatisfied with the actions (or inactions) of the Child Support Agency, he can make use of the internal review procedure. If still dissatisfied, he can apply to the Independent Case Examiner within six months of the final decision of the internal review. Compensation may be available for any maladministration.

11.6.3 Welfare benefits

Generally, most decisions relating to welfare benefits will be reviewed internally on request. An appeal on fact or law can then be made to the SSCS, provided that the appeal is lodged within one month from the decision. Further appeal on a point of law then lies to the Upper Tribunal.

11.7 Setting aside

One of the parties may attempt to have the order set aside. Generally, the court is reluctant to set aside orders for reasons of certainty – divorcing couples should be able to organise their future lives without fear of their divorce settlement being reopened. An application to set aside therefore can be made only on narrow grounds, the scope of which are not totally clear. These grounds include:

(a) Non-disclosure of material evidence. In the case of *Livesey (formerly Jenkins) v Jenkins* [1985] AC 424 (see **10.7.1**) the House of Lords stated that each party owed to the other a duty of full and frank disclosure. Where this duty is breached the order may be set aside. It must be emphasised, however, that not every non-disclosure will justify setting an order aside. The non-disclosure must have resulted in the court granting an order substantially different from that which it would have granted had the true facts been known or the court will not agree to set the original order aside.

The court in *Kingdon v Kingdon* [2010] EWCA Civ 1251 made it clear that in cases of non-disclosure it would not always be necessary to set aside the whole order and conduct the entire s 25 exercise again. The final order should reflect the order the court would have made had there been no material non-disclosure. It may be possible, as in this case, to achieve this simply by adding further provision to the order already made rather than starting from scratch.

(b) Fraud. For example, if one party deliberately misrepresents the size of his assets.

(c) Events occurring after the order is made. The House of Lords in *Barder v Barder* [1988] AC 20 laid down four conditions which must be fulfilled before the order will be set aside:

(i) the subsequent events must have invalidated the basis upon which the order was made; and

(ii) these events must have occurred within a relatively short time of the original order; and

(iii) the application to set aside must be made promptly; and

(iv) the granting of the application must not prejudice the rights of a bona fide purchaser for value of any property in question.

The facts of *Barder v Barder* provide a useful example of the extreme circumstances which are necessary for the court to set aside an order on this ground. As part of a consent order, Mr Barder agreed to transfer the home to his ex-wife within 28 days so that she could live in it with their children. Before he had done so, Mrs Barder killed both children and committed suicide. Under her will, all her property would go to her mother. The House of Lords agreed to set the order aside. In *Williams v Lindley* [2005] EWCA Civ 103, the Court of Appeal set aside a consent order where the wife became engaged to (and subsequently married) a wealthy man within one month of the making of the order. This event invalidated the basis of the original order which had been to provide the wife and children with a home. In other cases, where the basis of the original order is not invalidated, remarriage will not lead to the order being set aside (*Dixon v Marchant* [2008] 1 FLR 665).

What if the order involves assets which change dramatically in value a short time after the order is made? In the case of *Cornick v Cornick* [1994] 2 FLR 530, Hale J (as she then was) set out three possible causes of the change in value of the assets:

(i) An asset which was taken into account and correctly valued at the date of the hearing changes value within a relatively short time owing to natural processes of price fluctuation. This would not justify setting aside the order as it would amount to varying a capital order which the court has no power to do (see **11.8.2**).

(ii) A wrong value was put upon that asset at the hearing, which had it been known about at the time would have led to a different order. Provided that it is not the fault of the person alleging the mistake, it is open to the court to give leave for the matter to be reopened.

(iii) Something unforeseen and unforeseeable has happened since the date of the hearing which has altered the value of the assets so dramatically as to bring about a substantial change in the balance of assets brought about by the order. Then, provided that the other three conditions are fulfilled, the *Barder* principles may apply. However, Hale J went on to state that the circumstances in which this can happen are very few and far between.

In the case of *Myerson v Myerson (No 2)* [2009] EWCA Civ 282, the parties had reached an agreement at an FDR that the wife was to receive 43% of the assets and the husband 57%. The husband's share consisted of shares in his business, the value of which over the following year fell dramatically such that his share now represented, at best, only 14% of the assets. The Court of Appeal held that this case fell within the first of Hale J's categories and that 'the natural processes of price fluctuation, whether in houses, shares or any other property, and however dramatic, do not satisfy the *Barder* test'. Similarly, where a shareholding dramatically increased in value, the Court of Appeal held that this fell within the first of Hale J's categories (*Walkden* v *Walkden* [2009] EWCA Civ 627).

A subsequent maintenance calculation by the Child Support Agency will not be sufficient grounds for setting aside a clean break order (see *Crozier v Crozier* [1994] 1 FLR 126).

There are two routes by which an order may be set aside:

(a) an application for permission to appeal out of time made to the relevant appeal court; or

(b) an application to set aside made to the court which originally made the order.

It is not entirely clear when each route is appropriate and in most cases either procedure may be used. However, it would seem that where the applicant is arguing fraud or non-disclosure, set aside is the appropriate method; and where supervening events are argued, leave to appeal out of time is to be preferred. In either case it is essential that the application is made promptly (see, eg, *Burns v Burns* [2004] EWCA Civ 1258, where Mrs Burns's claim failed due to undue delay).

11.8 Variation

11.8.1 Types of county court order which can be varied

It is possible to apply to the court to vary an order not only where that order was made after a contested hearing, but also where the order was made by consent. However, it will not be possible to vary an order which effected a clean break.

Orders which can be varied are set out in s 31(2) of the MCA 1973 (see **Appendix 1(A)**), and include orders for:

(a) maintenance pending suit and interim maintenance;

(b) periodical payments and secured periodical payments. Periodical payments orders are the type of order most commonly varied. Applications are made either by the recipient to increase the amount being paid, or by the payer to reduce or extinguish the payments. Several points should be noted:

(i) Where the court makes an order for fixed-term maintenance, the term can usually be extended, provided that the application for an extension is made before the original order has expired (although the actual hearing may take place after expiry). However, this can be prevented by the court including a direction in the original order that no application for an extension may be made (see MCA 1973, s 28(1A) and **4.6**).

(ii) The court may impose a 'deferred clean break'. To achieve this, the court has power when discharging a periodical payments order or varying it to last for a further limited time only, also to make a lump sum order, or one or more property adjustment orders, or one or more pension-sharing orders. It may also include a direction that no application for an extension of a limited-term periodical payments order can be made. Whether a deferred clean break is appropriate will depend on much the same factors as those taken into account when deciding whether a clean break is appropriate (see **4.6**). In particular, the payer should consider whether the recipient is likely to remarry in the near future, since the court is unlikely to set aside the order if he does (*Dixon v Marchant* [2008] 1 FLR 665). If publicly funded, the recipient should be reminded that a lump sum payment will attract immediate enforcement of the statutory charge, unless the money is to be used to purchase a home and the order includes the necessary clause to enable the Legal Services Commission to postpone the charge (see **2.9**). In *Pearce v Pearce* [2003] 2 FLR 1144, the Court of Appeal made it clear that when making such a deferred clean break the court was only entitled to capitalise the remaining periodical payments and could not reopen capital claims and further redistribute the capital assets. The court also stated that, in deciding what substitute order to make, a pension sharing order should be the first choice if it were available. This is because no capital would have to be raised or paid by the payer, and the recipient would continue to get regular income.

(iii) When varying a periodical payments order the court has power to remit any arrears due under the order (MCA 1973, s 31(2A)). This power could be used, for example, where the payer had become unemployed and arrears had built up before he had a chance to apply for a downward variation;

(c) payment of a lump sum by instalments. Generally, this power will only enable the court to vary the number and amount of the instalments so that the amount payable overall will remain the same. However, the Court of Appeal stated in *Westbury v Sampson* [2001] EWCA Civ 407, [2002] 1 FLR 166 that the power to vary included varying the overall sum. Nevertheless, the court made clear that, in order to achieve finality, this would be done only in exceptional cases where the anticipated circumstances had changed significantly, making it unjust to hold the payer to the original quantum agreed;

(d) payment of a lump sum ordered in relation to pensions under s 25B(4) or s 25C of the MCA 1973;

(e) the sale of property under s 24A of the MCA 1973. This could be used, for example, where the order for sale was made as a way of enforcing a lump sum order. If the payer could find some other means to pay, he could then apply to have the order for sale discharged.

11.8.2 Types of county court order which cannot be varied

Orders for capital provision usually cannot be varied. This is to avoid uncertainty and so that the parties can make plans for the future on the basis that the distribution of capital is permanent.

(a) Lump sum orders cannot be varied unless they are payable by instalments, or ordered in relation to a pension (see **11.8.1**).

(b) Transfer of property and settlement of property orders cannot be varied. So, for example, if the court orders a deferred trust of land on *Mesher* contingencies, the occupier will not be able successfully to apply to court at a later date to have the sale further postponed. However, it may sometimes be possible to obtain a sale at a date earlier than that set out in the original order by applying for an order for sale under s 24A of the MCA 1973. The court can make an order for sale either at the same time as making the original order, or at a later date (see **4.4.3**). It is totally in the court's discretion whether to make such an order, but it may do so if, for example, it is the spouse in occupation who is seeking the sale against the wishes of the non-occupying spouse. On the other hand, an application by the non-occupying spouse is likely to be rejected if the home is still needed for the children (see, eg, *Thompson v Thompson* [1986] Fam 38).

(c) Pension sharing orders cannot generally be varied. The only exception to this is when the variation takes place before the order comes into effect and before the decree absolute. Once the decree has been made absolute, or if the order is in effect, it cannot be varied.

Many orders contain a clause which gives the parties 'liberty to apply'. This does not allow the parties to return to court to vary the order. Instead, it gives the parties the opportunity to return to court if they experience trouble implementing the order, for example, due to conveyancing difficulties or misunderstanding of minor terms where property is settled (see *Practice Direction (Applications: Liberty to Apply)* [1980] 1 All ER 1008). In *W v W* [2009] 1 FLR 92 the court differentiated a 'working out' of an order under a liberty to apply clause and a variation by considering the end result. Under a 'liberty to apply' clause, the court could select a different method of achieving the stated objective provided that the end result was, as far as practicable, the same as the original order. If the end result was more favourable to one of the parties, then this was a variation and not permitted.

11.8.3 Factors to be considered on a variation

The factors to be considered on a variation are set out in s 31(7) of the MCA 1973 (see **Appendix 1(A)**), which requires the court to have regard to all circumstances of the case, giving first consideration to the welfare of any child of the family who is not yet 18. This subsection also states that 'all the circumstances of the case' includes any change in the matters which the court was required to consider when making the original order, ie any change in the s 25 factors. However, case law makes clear (see, eg, *Flavell v Flavell* [1997] Fam Law 237) that the court is not restricted to considering changes in the matters which were taken into account when making the original order, but can consider the case afresh.

The principles set out in *Miller and McFarlane* (see **4.5.1.1**) apply equally on a variation application (*VB v JP* [2008] 1 FLR 742). Needs are likely to be the dominant factor. However, where those needs have been created by the recipient's own financial mismanagement or extravagance, the payer will not be expected to meet them (*North v North* [2008] 1 FLR 158 and *McFarlane v McFarlane* [2009] EWHC 891). Conversely, needs are not a limiting factor, so that the principles of compensation and sharing can lead to an increase in maintenance where the payer's income has increased (see, for example, *McFarlane v McFarlane* [2009] EWHC 891 and *Hvorostovsky v Hvorostovsky* [2009] EWCA Civ 791).

Unlike remarriage, the payee's cohabitation with another partner will not automatically terminate periodical payments. However, it will be one of the 'circumstances of the case' and will be taken into account. The effect such cohabitation will have on the award will depend on the facts of the case. The court will take into account the financial resources of the new partner and will ask what that partner *ought* to contribute to the household (*Grey v Grey* [2009] EWCA Civ 1424).

Where the party against whom the order was made has died, 'all the circumstances of the case' include the change in circumstances as a result of his death. This will generally be relevant only in the case of secured periodical payments orders.

The court must also consider on a variation application (even if it decides not to vary the amount of the order) whether the term of any payments ordered could be limited without causing undue hardship to the payee.

The court will need to take into account the 'package' made by the original order for financial relief. For example, perhaps the wife received less maintenance than she otherwise would have done in return for a greater share in the home. This must be taken into consideration on the variation application in order to maintain the balance achieved by the original order.

Lastly, remember that it is possible to record in a side-letter the reasons why a particular order has been made (see **10.13.12**). Any side-letter should be drawn to the court's attention on a later variation application and, although it will not bind the court, it is likely that the court will uphold its terms (see *N v N (Consent Order: Variation)* [1993] 2 FLR 868).

11.8.4 Procedure

The procedure to be followed is very similar to that used for the original order (see **Chapter 10**). Where appropriate, an application for public funding should be made. If both parties agree to the variation sought, then the normal consent procedure must be followed (see **10.12**).

11.8.5 Variation in the family proceedings court

Either party can apply to vary or revoke a periodical payments order made in a family proceedings court. Either party can also apply for a lump sum order, or further lump sum order. In deciding whether or not to grant the application, the court will have regard to any change in the circumstances since the original order was made (DPMCA 1978, s 20).

11.9 Chapter summary

(1) Financial orders can be enforced by the county court, or by the family proceedings court.

(2) The order will usually be enforced in the court that made it; however, sometimes it may be advantageous to register an order obtained in the county court with the family proceedings court and then enforce it in the family proceedings court.

(3) The following methods of enforcement are available in the county court:
- (a) attachment of earnings;
- (b) warrant of execution;
- (c) third party debt order proceedings;
- (d) s 24A of the MCA 1973;
- (e) charging order;
- (f) judgment summons.

(4) The following methods of enforcement are available in the family proceedings court:
- (a) attachment of earnings;
- (b) committal to prison;
- (c) warrant of distress.

(5) The Child Support Agency will enforce payments of child maintenance where a maintenance assessment has been made.

(6) The county court can execute documents to transfer property where the respondent fails to do so.

(7) It may be possible to appeal an order for ancillary relief, but this must be done without delay.

(8) In exceptional circumstances the court may set aside an order. This may happen if, for example, the respondent did not disclose the existence of certain of his assets and this led to a substantially different order being made.

(9) Orders for maintenance can be varied, as can instalments of a lump sum and lump sum orders made in relation to a pension.

(10) Other lump sum orders, pension sharing orders and property adjustment orders cannot be varied.

Chapter 12

Pre-marital Agreements and Separation Agreements

12.1	Introduction	159
12.2	Pre-marital agreements	159
12.3	Post-nuptial and separation agreements	160
12.4	Reform	163
12.5	Chapter summary	163

12.1 Introduction

This chapter looks at the ways in which married couples can achieve a binding agreement to cover maintenance and other matters without starting court proceedings. It looks at the validity of agreements entered into before marriage. It then examines how a spouse can enter into a maintenance or separation agreement as an alternative to starting divorce proceedings or obtaining an order under the DPMCA 1978.

12.2 Pre-marital agreements

12.2.1 General

An increasing number of cohabiting couples are entering into 'cohabitation agreements' governing the ownership of property and chattels (see **Chapter 16**). The general consensus is that, subject to general contractual principles, cohabitation agreements are binding.

What if a couple wish to enter a pre-marital agreement? The Supreme Court in *Radmacher v Granatino* [2010] UKSC 42 stated that the old rule that post and pre-marital agreements were contrary to public policy was obsolete and should be swept away. If parties who have made such an agreement should then decide to live apart they should be entitled to enforce their agreement. However, such an agreement would not oust the jurisdiction of the court and would not prevent one party from arguing in financial order proceedings that he or she should not be held to the terms of the agreement.

In financial order proceedings, the court may take pre-marital agreements into account as 'one of the circumstances of the case', or as 'conduct which it would be inequitable to disregard' under s 25 of the MCA 1973.

In recent years the courts have been willing to place an increasing amount of weight on such agreements, provided certain safeguards are met. In *Radmacher v Granatino* (above) the court held that if a pre-nuptial (or indeed post-nuptial) agreement is to carry full weight, both the husband and the wife must enter into it of their own free will, without undue influence or pressure, and informed of its implications. Each party would need to have all the information that is material to his or her decision and each party should intend that the agreement should govern the financial consequences of the marriage coming to an end.

The principle for the court to apply in deciding whether to uphold the agreement is that '[t]he court should give effect to a nuptial agreement that is freely entered into by each party with a full appreciation of its implications unless in the circumstances prevailing it would not be fair to hold the parties to their agreement' (para 75). The reason for this is that there should be respect for individual autonomy. An agreement is likely to be upheld where it is motivated by a wish to make provision for existing property owned by one of the parties, or anticipated to be received.

However, a pre-marital agreement would not be upheld if this would prejudice the reasonable requirements of any child of the family. It would also be unfair to hold the parties to their agreement where circumstances had changed in a way that was not envisaged when the agreement was entered. It may well be unfair to hold the parties to their pre-marital agreement where the needs of one of the parties would not be met by doing so, or he or she would not be compensated under the second strand indentified in *Miller v Miller; McFarlane v McFarlane* [2006] UKHL 24.

In *Crossley v Crossley* [2007] EWCA Civ 1491, which followed a short, childless marriage of wealthy parties in their 50s and 60s who had entered into a pre-nuptial agreement, the Court of Appeal decided that the judge had a discretionary power to require a party to show cause why the pre-nuptial agreement should not rule the outcome of a claim for financial orders. The Court stated that if ever there was to be a paradigm case in which the court would look to the pre-nuptial agreement not simply as one of the peripheral factors in the case but as a factor of magnetic importance, the instant case was such. In *Radmacher v Granatino* (above), the Supreme Court gave decisive weight to the pre-marital contract which had been entered into by the parties.

In these circumstances, an increasing number of couples do choose to use pre-marital agreements, and there are precedents available to use (see, for example, *Precedents for separation, pre-marriage and pre-civil partnership* (Resolution) and *Consensus* (Class Legal)). Such an agreement would assist in resolving matters if the breakdown was amicable.

A pre-marital agreement will need to comply with general contract principles. There will need to be offer and acceptance, intention to create legal relations, certainty and consideration. In *Radmacher v Granatino* (above), the court held that it should no longer be a problem to prove intention to create legal relations which would be presumed. Unless the contract is by deed there could be a problem in establishing consideration. The agreement would also be set aside if a party could show that undue influence was exerted over him or her when the agreement was entered into.

12.2.2 Law of Property (Miscellaneous Provisions) Act 1989, s 2

Section 2 of the Law of Property (Miscellaneous Provisions) Act 1989 provides that all the terms of any contract for the disposition of any interest in land must be in writing and signed by all the parties. This means that any informal agreement between spouses relating to ownership of the home will not be enforceable unless it is properly recorded.

12.3 Post-nuptial and separation agreements

12.3.1 General

Once the couple are married, it is open to them to enter into a post-nuptial agreement to regulate their financial arrangements, both during the marriage and after separation, and such agreements will be valid and enforceable, subject to the court's power of variation (see **12.3.5**) (*MacLeod v MacLeod* [2008] UKPC 64, endorsed in *Radmacher v Granatino* (above)).

If spouses separate, they can, as an alternative to divorce or other court proceedings, enter into an agreement which provides for maintenance, care of the children and division of any property (for precedents, see *Precedents for separation, pre-marriage and pre-civil partnership* (Resolution)). These agreements are known as either separation agreements or maintenance agreements. The only distinction is that a separation agreement will always include a clause in which the parties agree to an immediate separation. If one party has deserted the other, it is important that, if the parties have agreed on financial matters, a maintenance agreement is used. This will ensure that there is no suggestion that the other spouse is agreeing to the separation, which would end the desertion and the possibility of obtaining a divorce using Fact C (see **3.4.4**).

A separation agreement, like any other contract, must be formed in accordance with contract principles. A vital element is an intention to create legal relations. The agreement can be challenged by a party on the grounds of fraud, mistake, duress or undue influence. It is therefore important that both parties have independent legal advice before entering into this type of agreement.

12.3.2 Contents

The matters that typically are covered by a post-nuptial or separation agreement are as follows.

12.3.2.1 Agreement to separate

In a separation agreement the parties can state that they are going to live apart. Their agreement effectively prevents either party being in desertion and is evidence that the parties are treating the marriage as at an end, so that a period of separation can begin to run for the purposes of divorce on the grounds of two or five years' separation (Facts D or E: see **3.4.5** and **3.4.6**).

12.3.2.2 Periodical payments

The agreement can contain provision, on separation, for the payment of maintenance to the parties and any children. In relation to children, any agreement to pay money will be binding. However, a separation agreement cannot oust the jurisdiction of the Child Support Agency under the CSA 1991, so either party can at any later time apply to the Agency to determine the amount of maintenance payable. Any agreement to pay maintenance to a spouse cannot prevent either party applying to the court for financial orders as part of divorce, nullity or judicial separation proceedings. However, were this to happen, the separation agreement would be one of the factors that the court would consider under s 25 of the MCA 1973 in the financial order proceedings and may well carry significant weight. Care must also be taken to draft maintenance provisions for spouse and child clearly, making provision for how long the maintenance is to last and what will happen if the parties resume cohabitation.

12.3.2.3 Property

If appropriate, an agreement about the home and/or other property can be included.

12.3.2.4 Children

There is no need for any arrangements to be included relating to the children. Both parents still share parental responsibility and can make decisions jointly or alone relating to the children. However, if the parents wish, any agreement about where the children should live and how much contact is to be given to the parent with whom they do not live can be included. This would not prevent either parent from making an application under the CA 1989 at any later date.

12.3.3 Advantages of a post-nuptial or separation agreement

The parties' decision to enter into a post-nuptial or separation agreement will usually be based largely on a desire to avoid court proceedings, including applying to court for a consent order. They should also take into account the following factors.

12.3.3.1 Speed

A post-nuptial or separation agreement may be entered into quickly; a contested court order may not be made for a considerable time. A post-nuptial or separation agreement is, therefore, cheaper. It may also assist the parties by avoiding the confrontation and bitterness that is often caused by protracted court proceedings.

12.3.3.2 Flexibility

Anything can be agreed and included in a post-nuptial or separation agreement. So, for example, a husband could agree to pay the outgoings and repairs on the home in which the wife and family remained living, or to pay off outstanding hire-purchase debts. Neither of these matters can be ordered by the divorce courts under the MCA 1973, even if the parties apply for a consent order.

12.3.4 Disadvantages of a post-nuptial or separation agreement

12.3.4.1 Enforceability

A post-nuptial or separation agreement is enforced in the same way as any other contract. The usual remedies for breach of contract must, therefore, be sought, ie damages to cover any loss from arrears of maintenance payments and the equitable remedies of specific performance or an injunction to force the other party to carry it out. This means that in comparison with a court order (see **Chapter 11**), a post-nuptial or separation agreement is much more difficult to enforce.

12.3.4.2 Finality

A court order for a 'clean break' can prevent either party from applying to court again and achieves a once-and-for-all settlement. A post-nuptial or separation agreement can never be a guaranteed final solution. A party to a post-nuptial or separation agreement can always apply at a later date, for example on divorce, for further provision from the court. However, on a later application the post-nuptial or separation agreement will be taken into account under s 25 of the MCA 1973, and may be followed. In *Edgar v Edgar* [1980] 3 All ER 887, the court laid down the principle that formal agreements properly and fairly arrived at, with competent advice, should not be displaced unless there are good and substantial grounds for concluding that an injustice will be done by holding the parties to the terms of their agreement. In *MacLeod v MacLeod* [2008] UKPC 64 the Privy Council stated that when deciding what weight to give such an agreement in financial order proceedings, the court should, by analogy, start with the statutory provisions relating to whether such an agreement should be varied. Thus, the agreement should be upheld unless there had been a change of circumstances that would make the arrangements manifestly unjust or a failure to make proper provision for a child of the family. However, whilst the Supreme Court in *Radmacher v Granatino* (above) stated that the tests in *Edgar v Edgar* (above) and *MacLeod v MacLeod* (above) were appropriate for separation agreements and may be appropriate for post-nuptial agreements entered well into a marriage, they were not appropriate for all post-nuptial agreements. They gave as an example of a time when they would not be appropriate that of a young couple entering a post-nuptial agreement shortly after marriage. In such circumstances the effect to be given to the post-nuptial agreement would depend on wider considerations.

12.3.4.3 Variation

A court order for periodical payments can always be varied by the court by an application by either party at a later date. All written separation agreements can also be varied by the court (see **12.3.5**). However, if the agreement is not in writing it can be varied only by agreement between the parties.

12.3.5 MCA 1973, ss 34–36

Despite the fact that separation agreements are made between the parties and do not involve the court, the MCA 1973 does contain provisions giving the court power to vary them.

The court will have jurisdiction if the agreement comes within the wide definition of 'maintenance agreement' under s 34(2) of the MCA 1973. This will include any written agreement containing financial arrangements, or any written agreement to separate which does not contain any financial arrangements (where no other document exists which does contain such arrangements).

12.3.5.1 The court's jurisdiction

Any provision in a maintenance agreement which restricts the right of either party to apply to court for financial provision is void. However, any other provision in the agreement will still be binding.

12.3.5.2 Variation

If the parties can agree a variation, the original separation agreement can be varied by them without application to the court. If they cannot agree, either party can apply to court and the court has jurisdiction to vary or to insert financial arrangements in a written maintenance agreement during the lives of the parties under s 35 of the MCA 1973. It will vary the agreement only if there has been a change in circumstances justifying this or the agreement did not make proper financial arrangements for any child of the family (MCA 1973, s 35(2); **Appendix 1(A)**). The court can then make such order as it thinks just having regard to all the circumstances.

The court can also in certain circumstances vary a written maintenance agreement after the death of one of the parties (MCA 1973, s 36).

12.4 Reform

The Law Commission published a Consultation Paper, 'Marital Property Agreements', on 11 January 2011, which examined the status and enforceability of agreements made between spouses or civil partners either before or after the marriage or civil partnership. The Paper asked whether such agreements should be enforceable and, if so, whether they should apply to all property, or only to wealth acquired before the marriage or civil partnership. The Commission went on to make provisional proposals should it be decided that such agreements would be enforceable. These included that such agreements would be enforceable only if they satisfied certain criteria, such as being contractually valid, were entered into only after material disclosure of each party's assets and where each party had received legal advice. The Commission also proposed that agreements might be varied or set aside by the court if they made insufficient provision for children of the family or left either party reliant on State benefits. The consultation period ended on 11 April 2011. The Law Commission is currently analysing the responses and aims to produce its final report in 2012.

12.5 Chapter summary

(1) Pre-marital agreements (ie agreements made *before* marriage dealing with what will happen on divorce) are not necessarily binding, although they may carry significant weight depending on the circumstances of the case.

(2) Post-nuptial and separation agreements (ie agreements made when a couple *actually* separate) *can* be binding contracts.

(3) A separation agreement may be made as an alternative to a court order.

(4) The advantages of a separation agreement are:
   (a) speed;
   (b) flexibility.

(5) The disadvantages of a separation agreement: are
   (a) difficult to enforce;
   (b) not final;
   (c) variation by court.

Chapter 13
Children

13.1	Introduction	165
13.2	Parental responsibility	166
13.3	Section 8 orders	170
13.4	Welfare principle	181
13.5	Checklist of factors to be taken into account in applying welfare principle	182
13.6	The 'no order' presumption	186
13.7	Avoiding delay	186
13.8	Procedure for s 8 orders	187
13.9	Protection of children	197
13.10	Financial provision and property orders for children	200
13.11	Chapter summary	202

13.1 Introduction

The Children Act 1989 (CA 1989), which came into force in 1991, has been described as 'the most comprehensive and far reaching reform of child law … in living memory' (Lord Mackay, *Hansard*, House of Lords, 6 December 1988). The aim of the Act was to simplify the law relating to children, making it more consistent and more flexible, and to make the law more appropriate to the needs of children by making it more child-centred. The 1989 Act deals with both pubic and private law.

Children are sometimes described as a solicitor's invisible clients in divorce proceedings. The client is usually the parent, not the child, but a solicitor must consider the effect of his client's actions on the child involved. A solicitor may often feel that the client would be helped by mediation in relation to decisions about the children, and should recommend that an appropriate agency is consulted (see **1.3.2**).

The CA 1989 enables a child to apply for an order himself. The requirements involved are considered in this chapter. Provisions dealing with financial orders for children are summarised at **13.10**.

13.1.1 Cafcass

The Children and Family Court Advisory and Support Service (Cafcass) was established by the Criminal Justice and Court Services Act 2000. Cafcass is a non-departmental body, accountable to the Department for Children, Schools and Families (DCSF). In respect of family proceedings in which the welfare of children is in question, the Service has the principal function of safeguarding and promoting the welfare of the children, giving advice to any court about any application made to it in such proceedings, making provision for the children to be represented in such proceedings, and providing information, advice and other support for the children and their families. Cafcass 'case workers' now fulfil the roles of children and family reporters (in private law proceedings: see **13.3.5** and **13.8.5.6**) and children's guardians (in public law proceedings: see **14.11.6.1**).

Since its inception Cafcass has experienced serious problems with shortages of staff and a lack of experienced guardians, resulting in a delay in the allocation of cases. Since October 2007, the requirement in s 16A of the CA 1989 for Cafcass to carry out a risk assessment in respect of any child whom it is given cause to suspect is at risk of harm and to provide that risk assessment to the court, and more recently the requirement for Cafcass to carry out safeguarding screening enquiries of every application and the surge of public law cases following the death of Baby P, have led to overwhelming delays in the allocation of cases and preparation of reports in some parts of the country.

In July 2009 the President of the Family Division announced Interim Guidance setting out short-term measures to be adopted between judges and Cafcass to reduce the backlogs and delays. This Guidance was extended for a further year until September 2011, when it was decided that it had been successful in achieving its aims and no longer needed to continue.

13.2 Parental responsibility

13.2.1 What is parental responsibility?

The CA 1989 introduced the concept of parental responsibility, which was a deliberate shift away from the idea that parents have 'rights' over their child towards the idea that they have 'responsibilities' towards their child. Parental power to control a child is not for the benefit of the parents but for that of the child. The Act defines this term as 'all the rights, duties, powers, responsibilities and authority which by law a parent of a child has in relation to the child and his property' (CA 1989, s 3(1) – see **Appendix 1(E)**). In reality, it gives the parent responsibility for taking all the important decisions in the child's life, for example, education, religion and medical care. It also enables a parent to take day-to-day decisions, for example, in relation to nutrition, recreation and outings. The duties involved in parental responsibility will change from time to time with differing needs and circumstances, and vary with the age and maturity of the child. It is important to bear in mind that a child will gradually become mature enough to take decisions himself. The House of Lords, in *Gillick v West Norfolk and Wisbech Area Health Authority* [1986] AC 112, said that 'parental authority ceases in respect of any aspect of a child's upbringing about which the child himself is sufficiently mature to make decisions for himself'.

13.2.2 Who has parental responsibility?

Married parents have joint parental responsibility; if parents are not married, only the mother has parental responsibility.

13.2.3 How can you acquire parental responsibility?

13.2.3.1 Unmarried fathers

An unmarried father can acquire parental responsibility in any one of six ways:

(a) by being registered as the father on the child's birth certificate with the consent of the mother (after 1 December 2003) (CA 1989, s 4(1)(a)) (the Welfare Reform Act 2009, which at the time of writing is not yet in force, will provide a requirement for births to be registered jointly by both parties);

(b) by entering into a 'parental responsibility agreement' with the mother (CA 1989, s 4(1)(b)): this must be on a prescribed printed form (see below);

(c) by applying to the court for a parental responsibility order (CA 1989, s 4(1)(c)) (see below for the courts' approach on such applications);

(d) by being appointed a guardian either by the mother or by the court, although in these cases he will assume parental responsibility only on the mother's death (see below);

(e) by obtaining a residence order from the court (see **13.3.1**);

(f) by marrying the mother.

Parental responsibility agreement

Many unmarried parents will be living together and will be happy to acknowledge their shared responsibility for their children. In this case, they are able to enter into an agreement which will give the father joint parental responsibility with the mother. It will put them into the same position as if a parental responsibility order had been made.

Regulations provide that the agreement must be in a prescribed form, signatures of the parents must be witnessed by a Justice of the Peace, a justices' clerk or a county court officer (not by a solicitor), and the agreement must be recorded by sending it together with two copies to the Principal Registry of the Family Division. No fee is payable. The Registry will seal the copies and send one to the mother and one to the father. Agreements are open to public inspection (Parental Responsibility Agreement Regulations 1991 (SI 1991/1478)).

Even though a parental responsibility agreement was entered into with the agreement of the parents, it cannot be ended by agreement. It will end only when the child reaches 18 years of age, unless a court order has been obtained either on the application of anyone with parental responsibility or on the application of the child (with leave).

Previous available figures show that, in a typical year, only about 3,700 agreements were being registered, which represents a tiny proportion of children born outside marriage. It appears that either lack of information about these agreements, or the formalities involved or the reluctance of mothers to sign them is discouraging parents from entering into parental responsibility agreements. These agreements are likely to be even less common now that parental responsibility can be obtained by registration on the birth certificate.

Parental responsibility order

If the father wants to share parental responsibility with the mother and she is not willing to agree to this, the father can apply to court for a parental responsibility order. Such an order will give him joint parental responsibility with the mother and place him in virtually the same position legally as if he were married. Since the parents may not be living with each other when this order is made, the father may wish to apply at the same time for a contact order (*Re H (A Minor) (Parental Responsibility)* [1993] 1 FLR 484).

If there is a dispute about paternity, s 20(1) of the Family Law Reform Act 1969 can be used to obtain a court direction for blood tests. The court has a discretion to give such a direction (*Re F (A Minor) (Blood Tests)* [1993] 1 FLR 598). In deciding whether to grant the parental responsibility order, the court will use the welfare principle (but not, specifically, the statutory checklist). The court will also have regard to the non-intervention principle, although it will generally be necessary to intervene when this order is sought as the parents will be in dispute.

In *Re H (Minors) (Local Authority: Parental Rights) (No 3)* [1991] 2 WLR 763, the court looked at which factors would be important in this situation and concluded that it was important to look at:

(a) the father's degree of commitment to the child;
(b) the state of the father's current relationship with the child; and
(c) his reasons for making the application.

The court will not automatically refuse an order just because at the present time there is no likelihood of the order resulting in the father being able to exercise any of his responsibilities. A committed father could be granted the order if it would ultimately be in the welfare of the child to make it (*Re C (Minors) (Parental Rights)* [1992] 1 FLR 1). In *Re A (Minors) (Parental Responsibility)* [1993] Fam Law 464, the father, who had lived with the mother, was present at the child's birth and whose name was entered on the birth certificate (this case predated the changes to the CA 1989 which would mean this automatically gave him parental responsibility), was granted a parental responsibility order (despite the mother's resistance and the fact that he had not seen the child for one year) as he had shown considerable commitment.

A series of more recent cases has shown that the court is willing to make a parental responsibility order to give a father a recognised legal status, and objections, such as a mother's hostility to a father's involvement in the child's life, or that the court refuses to grant the father a contact order, do not necessarily prevent the parental responsibility order being made (*Re G (A Minor) (Parental Responsibility Order)* [1994] 1 FLR 504) (and see *Re D (Contact and Parental Responsibility: Lesbian Mothers and Known Father)* [2006] EWHC 2 (Fam), where unusually the court made a parental responsibility order in favour of the father on the basis that the father would not contact the child's school or any health care professional involved in her care without the consent of the child's mother or her female partner, who had a shared residence order in respect of the child).

However, the court may still refuse a parental responsibility order where the father has shown a high degree of commitment if it is clear that the father may abuse his parental responsibility. Thus in *Re P (Parental Responsibility)* [1998] 2 FLR 96, the Court of Appeal refused to grant a parental responsibility order where the father had been very critical of the mother's care and made it clear that he would use his parental responsibility order as an excuse to monitor the arrangements for the child's care. In another case, *M v M (Parental Responsibility)* [1999] 2 FLR 737, the court declined to make a parental responsibility order where the unmarried father had been involved in an accident, resulting in serious, permanent brain injuries. Although there had been a significant degree of commitment and attachment to the child, the father was incapable of exercising parental responsibility (and, in fact, required something akin to parental responsibility to be exercised by others over him).

A parental responsibility order, once made, will end automatically on the following events:

(a) the majority of the child;

(b) the marriage of the father to the mother during the minority of the child. The marriage will give the father parental responsibility for his child;

(c) a court order discharging the parental responsibility order. An application to discharge the original order can be made by anyone who has parental responsibility for the child, for example the mother, or by the child himself provided the court is satisfied that the child has sufficient understanding to make the application.

The application for a parental responsibility order can be made in the family proceedings court, High Court or county court. There is a standard application form which sets out details of the child and the applicant, including his reasons for applying. Figures available show that, in a typical year, about 5,500 parental responsibility orders are made, the majority in the family proceedings court.

Guardianship (CA 1989, s 5)

A mother with sole parental responsibility could appoint the father as a guardian in her will. On her death, the father would then acquire parental responsibility because he is a guardian, even if he had never obtained parental responsibility during the mother's lifetime. If the mother had not appointed a guardian on her death, the court has the power to appoint a guardian and it could decide to appoint the father. Alternatively, in these circumstances the father could apply to the court to be appointed guardian (CA 1989, s 5(1)(a); see **Appendix 1(E)**).

If a mother with sole parental responsibility has appointed someone other than the child's father as guardian, this appointment will take effect on her death and give the guardian sole parental responsibility, which the father could challenge only by applying for a residence order and/or a parental responsibility order.

If the father has acquired parental responsibility during the mother's lifetime, any appointment by her of a guardian will be postponed while the surviving parent has parental responsibility. The only way a mother in this situation could ensure that the appointment of a guardian had immediate effect would be for her to seek a residence order in her own favour. In this case, on her death, the guardian and the father would share parental responsibility. This could be of great importance to a mother who is no longer cohabiting with the father of her child and who is anxious to safeguard a child after her death by making, for example, her mother a joint guardian with the father.

13.2.3.2 Step-parents and civil partners

Section 4A of the CA 1989 allows step-parents and civil partners to obtain parental responsibility agreements with the consent of all parents with parental responsibility, or to apply to the court for a parental responsibility order.

13.2.3.3 Others

Various other people may also acquire parental responsibility towards the child. A local authority will acquire parental responsibility if a care order is made in relation to the child, or anyone who is granted a residence order in relation to the child, or even the court if the child is made a ward of court. Also anyone obtaining a new special guardianship order will acquire parental responsibility (see **13.3.6**).

The Human Fertilisation and Embryology Act 2008, which came into force in April 2009, allows, in the case of female same-sex couples who have not entered into a civil partnership and who are having a child conceived at a licensed clinic by IVF or artificial insemination, for the natural mother to nominate her same-sex partner as the 'parent' of the child. Under s 4ZA of the CA 1989, the parent will then be able to apply for parental responsibility by being registered as a parent on the register of births, by making a parental responsibility agreement with the mother or by obtaining a parental responsibility order from the court.

13.2.4 How can you lose parental responsibility?

There is no limit to the number of people who can have parental responsibility at any one time, and no one will lose parental responsibility just because another person acquires it (CA 1989, s 2(5)). If, on divorce, a residence order is made in favour of a grandparent, this will mean that the child's mother, father and grandparent will all have parental responsibility. The parents 'lose' the responsibility of having the child living with either of them because of the residence order but retain all other responsibilities. If a care order is made, the local authority acquires parental responsibility but the parents still, in theory, retain parental responsibility. However, in practice the local authority is given the discretion to determine the extent to which a parent may meet his or her parental responsibility (CA 1989, s 33(3)).

Two situations in which parents will lose parental responsibility are:

(a) the parent's death; and

(b) the child's adoption. Section 46 of the Adoption and Children Act 2002 provides that an adoption order will automatically extinguish the parental responsibility which any person had before the making of the order.

An unmarried father who has acquired parental responsibility by a parental responsibility order or parental responsibility agreement, or by registration on the birth certificate, can lose it if the court makes a further order ending it. (See *Re P (Terminating Parental Responsibility)* [1995] 1 FLR 1048, where an unmarried father who had acquired parental responsibility then lost it under a court order, having inflicted serious injury on the child.) Similarly, a step-parent or civil partner who acquires parental responsibility under s 4A of the 1989 Act (see **13.2.2** above) can have it removed by the court.

Anyone other than an unmarried father, who has acquired parental responsibility by being granted a residence order, will lose it automatically when the residence order terminates.

The acquisition and loss of parental responsibility in the case of unmarried fathers raises potential issues of discrimination under the HRA 1998. However, in *McMichael v UK* (1995) 20 EHRR 205, the European Court of Human Rights accepted that discrimination between married and unmarried fathers could be justified as identifying 'meritorious' fathers who might be accorded parental rights, thereby protecting the interests of the child and the mother.

13.2.5 Exercising parental responsibility

Even though several people may have parental responsibility for a child, in theory it is possible for each to act alone with no duty to consult anyone else (CA 1989, s 2(7)). However, in *Re C (Change of Surname)* [1998] 1 FLR 549, the court held that when there was joint parental responsibility, this did not confer the right unilaterally to change the child's surname, and suggested that good practice is to refer to the court all disputed issues regarding change of surname regardless of who has parental responsibility. Also, in *Re J (Child's Religious Upbringing and Circumcision)* [2000] 1 FLR 571, the court held that there is a small group of important decisions made on behalf of a child which, in the absence of agreement by all those with parental responsibility, ought not to be carried out or arranged by the one-parent carer, notwithstanding s 2(7). Instead, they should be referred to the court for the court's determination, on the facts of the case each time, by way of a specific issue order. As well as change of a child's surname, the court gave sterilisation and circumcision as examples of such decisions. In *Re H (Parental Responsibility)* [1998] 1 FLR 855, the court also said that a parent with parental responsibility would have the right to be consulted on schooling.

In *B v A and others (Parental Responsibility)* [2006] EWHC 2 (Fam), the father had responded to an advertisement by the mother and her lesbian partner, to father a child. The court made a parental responsibility order in favour of the father on the basis the father would not contact the child's school or any health care professional involved in her care without the consent of the child's mother or her female partner, who had a shared residence order in respect of the child.

Subject to these exceptions, one parent can determine questions such as medical treatment and religion without consulting the other. The only way to challenge a decision is to make an application to court, for example, for a specific issue order or a prohibited steps order (see **13.3.3** and **13.3.4**). If a child is being adopted, or taken out of the UK, there are specific provisions requiring both parents' consent, or the consent of the court.

It is not possible to transfer or surrender parental responsibility (CA 1989, s 2(9)). However, parents can delegate responsibility for a child on a temporary basis, for example, to a school for a school trip, or to a nanny or childminder. Temporary carers do not acquire parental responsibility but 'may do what is reasonable in all the circumstances of the case for the purpose of safeguarding or promoting the child's welfare' (CA 1989, s 3(5)). This could cover emergency medical treatment for the child if needed when the parent is absent, for example during a school trip, or when the parent is at work during the day and a nanny is in charge.

13.3 Section 8 orders

Under s 8 of the CA 1989 (see **Appendix 1(E)**), four different types of orders can be made in relation to children:

(a) residence orders;

(b) contact orders;

(c) prohibited steps orders;

(d) specific issue orders.

Each of these orders will determine a particular matter relating to the child's upbringing. A s 8 order lasts until the child reaches the age of 16 (or 18, in exceptional circumstances) (CA 1989, s 91(10)).

13.3.1 Residence order

A residence order is an order settling the arrangements to be made as to the person with whom the child is to live.

Following a divorce, parents will share parental responsibility and, therefore, the making of a residence order will only decide where a child will live.

A residence order can be made in favour of non-parents and, if this is done, the non-parent will automatically have parental responsibility as well, but only for so long as the residence order is in force (CA 1989, s 12(2)). The parental responsibility acquired in this way also has two limitations as, first, no agreement or refusal to an adoption order or freeing for adoption can be given and, secondly, no guardian can be appointed by the non-parent.

When deciding an application for a residence order, the child's welfare is the paramount concern. In *Re B (a child) (residence order)* [2009] UKSC 5 the court awarded residence of a four-year-old child to the child's grandmother with whom he had lived all his life, rather than to his father. The Court said that:

> All consideration of the importance of parenthood in private law disputes about residence must be firmly rooted in an examination of what is in the child's best interests. This is the paramount consideration. It is only as a contributor to the child's welfare that parenthood assumes any significance.

A shared residence order can be made in favour of two or more persons who do not all live together. The order can specify the periods during which the child is to live in the different households involved (CA 1989, s 11(4)). This means that a court could order that a child lives alternate weeks with each parent, or lives during term-time with one parent and during the holidays with the other, or spends a fixed period (say, the summer holidays) with one parent. A residence order is therefore a flexible power which can be adapted to the needs of a particular family. Obviously, the court will make a shared residence order only if it feels that it is in the welfare of the child to do so. It is not the case that shared residence orders can be made only in exceptional circumstances (as was once thought) (*Re D (Children) (Shared Residence Orders)* [2001] 1 FLR 495), and in recent years shared residence orders have been increasingly used. In *Re K (A Child) (Shared Residence Order)* [2008] EWCA Civ 526 it was stated that the approach when deciding whether to make a shared residence order is to decide first how the children are to divide their time and then to decide if it should be expressed as a shared residence order or a contact order.

In *Re G (Residence: Same Sex Partners)* [2005] EWCA Civ 462, the biological mother of two children conceived by artificial insemination by donor and her same-sex partner separated, leaving the children with the biological mother. The mother tried to marginalise the applicant's contact with the children. The applicant was granted a shared residence order as the only way to obtain parental responsibility and prevent such marginalisation.

In *Re A (a child) (joint residence: parental responsibility)* [2008] EWCA Civ 867 the Court upheld a shared residence order in favour of a man who discovered during contact proceedings that he was not the father of the child concerned. The man had believed himself to be the child's father, and the Court said that by reason of the role he had played and should continue to play in the child's life he was entitled to an order conferring parental responsibility on him. As he was neither the child's father nor stepfather, he could only obtain parental responsibility through a residence order.

The court is given wide powers to attach directions, conditions, and incidental and supplementary provisions to the residence order. These could, for example, direct where the child is to be educated, or impose a ban on removing the child from the country; or could direct that the non-resident parent be informed if the child requires medical treatment in circumstances where the parent with whom the child is living has religious objections to blood transfusions.

When a residence order has been made, two aspects of parental responsibility are automatically affected, as follows.

13.3.1.1 Change of surname

Where a residence order is in force, the order will provide that no person can cause the child to be known by a new surname without either:

(a) the written consent of every person who has parental responsibility; or

(b) the leave of the court (CA 1989, s 13(1)).

However, following *Re C* (see **13.2.5**), it seems that where there is joint parental responsibility, regardless of whether there is a residence order, the same conditions will apply and the consent of the other person with personal responsibility should be sought. In *Re C* it was further suggested this would be good practice even if the father did not have parental responsibility.

If a mother wants to change her child's surname, perhaps following remarriage or reverting to a maiden surname herself, she will have to obtain the permission of the child's father; and if this is not given, she will have to apply to court. The court will base any decision on the welfare principle (see **13.4**). The court is generally reluctant to authorise a change of surname unless it is in the interests of the child to do so. Factors to weigh up include embarrassment to the child and parent of having different surnames, the child's wishes and the extent to which the child's original surname is important to maintain links with the parent and other relations with whom he does not live. In *W v A (Child: Surname)* [1981] 1 All ER 100, both parents had remarried. The mother wanted to emigrate to Australia with her second husband who was Australian, and take the two children (aged 12 and 14) from her first marriage with her. The mother wanted to change the children's surnames to the new husband's surname. The children, who were interviewed by the judge, also wanted to change their surname. The judge decided that the children should keep their natural father's name. He stressed that change of name was a serious issue and, in this case, it had not been shown that it was in the children's best interests to change their name. He did not place great weight on the children's wishes in this case as he felt that they had been influenced by their mother and were merely reflecting her view.

This case was followed in *Re F (Child: Surname)* [1993] 2 FLR 837, where it was stated that allowing a child to be known by a different surname is an important matter which is not to be undertaken lightly. In *Dawson v Wearmouth* [1999] 1 FLR 1167, the majority of the House of Lords considered that there had to be particular circumstances to justify a change of name; effectively, there is a presumption in favour of the status quo.

13.3.1.2 Leaving the UK

Residence order in force

Where a residence order is in force, no person may remove the child from the UK without either:

(a) the written consent of every person who has parental responsibility; or

(b) leave of the court (CA 1989, s 13(1)).

The Act does allow the person in whose favour the residence order is made to take the child out of the UK for periods of less than one month without such consent.

Thus, the parent with whom the child lives can take the child abroad as many times as he or she likes, provided each individual trip does not last more than one month. The parent without the residence order needs to seek consent every time he or she wants to take the child abroad for whatever period. However, at the time that the residence order is granted, the court can add a direction authorising removal to avoid repeated applications to court. This would be sensible in a situation where the non-residential parent lives abroad, so that regular trips to stay with the parent will be permitted without consent being needed.

No residence order in force

If no residence order is in force, either parent can (in theory) take the child abroad without any restriction or need for consent under the CA 1989. However, the parent proposing the trip could be prevented from going by the other parent obtaining a prohibited steps or specific issue order forbidding the child being taken abroad. Additionally, a criminal offence under the Child Abduction Act 1984 will be committed by the parent taking the child if permission of the other parent, or the court, is not obtained (see **13.9.1.3**).

Application to court to remove

If a parent needs to apply to court to seek permission to take the child abroad, the court will again base its decision on the welfare principle. It will therefore seldom be difficult to persuade the court that a holiday abroad is in the best interests of the child, unless, for example, it is a cover for an abduction.

Where emigration is intended, in *Payne v Payne* [2001] EWCA Civ 166, [2001] 1 FLR 1052, the Court of Appeal stressed that there is no presumption in law in favour of the applicant parent wishing to move the child abroad. The welfare of the child is the paramount consideration, and the court must apply the principles and factors set out in s 1 of the CA 1989 (see **13.5**). The President of the Family Division also set out the following specific considerations which 'should be in the forefront of the mind of a judge' in these difficult cases:

(a) the reasonable proposals of the parent with a residence order wishing to live abroad carry great weight;
(b) consequently, those proposals need to be scrutinised with care to ensure that there was a genuine motivation for the move;
(c) the effect on the applicant parent and any new family of the child of a refusal to grant leave had to be considered;
(d) the effect on the child of the potential denial of contact with the other parent and, in some cases, with their family was very important; and
(e) the opportunity for continuing contact between the child and the parent left behind might be very significant.

Following a series of cases which appeared to criticise *Payne v Payne*, the recent case of *MK v CK* [2011] EWCA Civ 793 affirmed that the only principle arising out of *Payne and Payne* was the welfare principle and that all the rest was guidance. The guidance helped judges identify the likely most important factors to consider and the weight to attach to them, but the circumstances in which decisions had to be made varied infinitely and judges had to be free to weigh up the individual factors and make whatever decision they felt to be in the best interests of the child.

In *Re B (Removal from Jurisdiction); Re S (Removal from Jurisdiction)* [2003] EWCA Civ 1149, [2003] 2 FLR 1043, Thorpe LJ in the Court of Appeal extended the list in *Payne*, so that where the mother cares for a child within a new family, the impact of refusal on the new family and the stepfather or prospective stepfather must also be carefully evaluated.

Where there is concern over future contact arrangements, the court could impose conditions. For example, in *Re S (Removal from Jurisdiction)* [1999] 1 FLR 850, prior to authorising removal, the court required the resident parent to deposit a large sum of money pending authentication of the English contact order by the Chilean Supreme Court.

Relocation within the UK

Relocation within the UK does not require the consent of the court. However, if a resident parent's plans to relocate are opposed by the non-resident parent, an application may be made to the court. The resident parent would apply for a specific issue order (see **13.3.4**) and a non-resident parent would apply for a prohibited steps order (see **13.3.3**) or a residence order in his favour (rather than applying for conditions to be attached under s 11(7) to an existing residence order in favour of the resident parent; *Re F (children) (internal relocation)* [2010] EWCA Civ 1348). The case of *Re E (Residence: Imposition of Conditions)* [1997] 2 FLR 638 stated that it would be possible in 'exceptional cases' to attach conditions to a residence order preventing relocation, but that that did not sit easily with the general understanding of a residence order and had not been what Parliament had intended. Instead the court should consider where the children will live as one of the relevant factors in cross-applications for residence. The use of the term 'exceptional' in the above case had led courts to apply a test of 'exceptionality' when refusing a request to relocate, ie it would be refused only where there are 'exceptional' circumstances. In *Re F (children) (internal relocation)*, the court suggested that this was 'an impermissible gloss' on the application of s 1(1) and s 1(3). Therefore, in internal relocation cases, the proposals of the relocating parent are not subject to the same degree of scrutiny as in external relocation cases. However, if the case is finely balanced, they will be of increased importance.

In the recent case of *Re L (a child) (internal relocation: shared residence order)* [2009] EWCA Civ 20, the Court said that there should not be a difference of approach when considering internal relocation cases simply because a shared residence order existed. The court needed to look at the underlying factual situation in welfare terms, bearing in mind the tension which may well exist between the freedom to relocate which any parent must enjoy against the welfare of the child which may militate against relocation.

13.3.2 Contact order

A contact order is an order requiring the person with whom the child lives, or is to live, to allow the child to visit or stay with the person named in the order, or for that person and the child otherwise to have contact with each other.

A contact order can authorise physical contact but can also cover contact by letter, e-mail or by telephone (or even by video). The amount of contact can either be specified in the order, to cover weekend visits or holidays, or the order could be for 'reasonable contact', in which case the arrangements can be made by the parents. The latter is obviously preferable as the parents can make and alter arrangements to suit the circumstances. A contact order can also be made preventing contact with someone (*Nottinghamshire County Council v P* [1993] 1 FLR 115). The alternative way to achieve this is by a prohibited steps order (see **13.3.3**).

Since the order can be made in favour of a parent or any other person, it could enable contact to be maintained with more distant relatives or other friends of the child.

A contact order can contain conditions and directions. These could be used to build up contact gradually between a young child and a parent who had not seen the child for a while, or to ensure supervised contact to protect the child. This could take place at a local Child Contact Centre. These centres have been set up across the country to provide an opportunity and setting for contact to take place in circumstances where arranging contact might otherwise be difficult. Only some centres can offer fully supervised contact, but most can provide 'supported' contact, whereby contact can take place in the centre or children can be handed from one parent to another.

The court's approach is that the child has a right to know both parents, and therefore the starting point is that a child should have contact with the non-resident parent (*Re D (A Minor) (Contact)* [1993] 1 FCR 9). However, the court will always consider all the circumstances and may decide that because of factors such as the parent's conduct, the emotional welfare and stability of the child, or even the attitude and behaviour of a step-parent, it is in the best interests of the child not to grant a contact order (*Re T (A Minor) (Parental Responsibility: Contact)* [1993] 2 FLR 450).

Although there is a presumption that a child should have contact with both parents (unless there are cogent reasons to the contrary), that is not necessarily the approach towards any other member of the family, such as a grandparent. In *Re A (Section 8 Order: Grandparent Application)* [1995] 2 FLR 153, the Court of Appeal stressed that just because the grandmother had succeeded in obtaining leave to apply for a contact order, that did not mean that there was a presumption that she should actually be granted a contact order; the court had to consider what was in the child's best interests (although see also the case of *Re W* [1997] 1 FLR 793).

In *Re O (A Minor) (Contact: Imposition of Conditions)* [1995] 2 FLR 124, the Court of Appeal confirmed that the court had a wide and comprehensive jurisdiction to make contact orders, including for indirect contact, such as the non-resident parent being sent school progress reports and any cards or letters sent by him being read to the child. The court rejected the mother's argument that it was wrong in principle to compel her to read the father's communications when she was unwilling and hostile to such contact, saying that would mean that the mother was being given a power of veto. She was subject to an enforceable duty to promote contact if the court considered that that promoted the child's welfare: that was a decision for the court, not for the mother.

Domestic violence

A distinction must be made between cases where a parent is opposed to contact for no good reason, when the court will be very slow to conclude contact would harm the child, and those where there are genuine and rational reasons for opposing contact. A particular difficulty arises where, during the relationship, the resident parent has been subjected to violence by the other parent. In *Re H (Contact: Domestic Violence)* [1998] 2 FLR 42, the Court of Appeal stated that domestic violence was not, of itself, a bar to contact but one factor in a very complex equation. While the courts have re-emphasised the presumption in favour of contact, some cases have shown a willingness to hold that the presumption is rebutted on the facts. See, for example, *Re M (Contact: Violent Parent)* [1999] 2 FLR 321, where Wall J stated:

> Too often, notwithstanding that domestic violence had been found, the mother was none the less ordered to arrange for contact with the father, the courts neglecting the other side of the equation which was that such a father should first demonstrate by changing his behaviour, that he was a fit person to have contact and would not destabilise or upset the children.

See also *Re K (Contact: Mother's Anxiety)* [1999] Fam Law 527, where the court found that the mother had been so traumatised by the father's behaviour that direct contact would bring about a state of heightened anxiety and fear which would inevitably be conveyed to the boy, causing him significant emotional harm.

The issue came before the Court of Appeal in four cases, heard together, where, in each case, the father's application for direct contact was refused because of a background of domestic abuse between the parents (*Re L (Contact: Domestic Violence)* [2000] 2 FLR 334). The Court of Appeal eschewed any presumption either for or against direct contact in cases involving domestic abuse. The balancing exercise required to determine what was best for a child's welfare had to be carried out in the usual way. However, the court should particularly consider the following points:

(a) the past and present conduct of both parties;

(b) the effect of the violence on the child and the residential parent;

(c) the motivation of the parent seeking contact; and

(d) in cases of serious domestic violence, the ability of the offending parent to recognise his past conduct, be aware of the need to change and to make genuine efforts to do so .

The Court of Appeal also pointed out the need for family judges and magistrates to have a heightened awareness of the effects on children of being exposed to domestic abuse by one parent against the other.

Practice Direction 12J, '*Residence and Contact Orders: Domestic Violence and Harm*', is a detailed Practice Direction (formerly issued in 2008 and 2009) which requires the court to consider at all stages of the proceedings whether domestic violence is raised as an issue and, if so, what those issues are and whether they may affect the decision to make a residence or contact order, and the court should give directions to determine these issues quickly and efficiently.

The Practice Direction requires extensive steps to be taken, including, upon issue, the prompt sending of the documents to Cafcass for their initial screening and any ensuing risk assessment, consideration of the need for an initial fact-finding hearing to determine the issue of violence, and the consideration of separate representation for the children. Where a welfare report is ordered, the court order should contain specific directions to the reporter to address the issue of domestic violence.

When considering making a residence or contact order in cases where domestic violence has occurred, the court is to have regard to a list of factors similar to those in *Re L (Contact: Domestic Violence)*, above. On the making of a contact order where domestic violence has been proved, the court should consider what directions or conditions should be attached, such as whether the contact should be supervised and whether the order should be reviewed by the court at a later date. In its reasons the court should also make clear how its findings have influenced its decision on the issue of residence or contact, and why it considers the order made is in the best interests of the child.

13.3.2.1 Contact activity directions and conditions

Sections 11A–11H of the CA 1989 (inserted by the Children and Adoption Act 2006), which came into force on 8 December 2008, give the court powers to make contact activity directions and conditions with the aim of promoting and facilitating contact as follows:

Directions

Contact activity directions can only be made when the court is *considering* making, varying or discharging a contact order (within the proceedings rather on final disposal). A contact activity direction is a direction to a party to the proceedings to take part in a specified activity which promotes contact with the child.

Conditions

Contact activity conditions can be attached to a final contact order, or a contact order can be varied to impose conditions that an individual take part in an activity that promotes contact with the child concerned.

Activities

The activities that can be made the subject of directions and conditions include: programmes, classes, counselling or guidance sessions to establish, maintain or promote contact, or to address violent behaviour to enable or facilitate contact and information meetings regarding the making of arrangements for contact including making arrangements by mediation. At the time of writing, Cafcass offers the following contact activities: one-off mediation assessment meetings; parenting courses consisting of two, two-hour sessions; and domestic violence perpetrator programmes lasting over 60 hours.

Before making contact activity directions or conditions, the court must be satisfied that the activity proposed is appropriate in the circumstances of the case, that the specified provider of the activity is suitable to provide it and that it is provided at a place where the individual can reasonably be expected to travel.

Monitoring

When making the contact activity direction or condition, the court can require a Cafcass officer to monitor compliance with the direction or condition and report to the court on any failure to comply. The court can also ask Cafcass to monitor compliance with the contact order itself by the individual having contact or being asked to allow contact and to report to the court on the individual's compliance.

13.3.2.2 Enforcement of contact orders

A practical problem with contact orders is how to enforce them if the parent with day-to-day care is determined that contact will not occur. The court has power to enforce contact orders (FLA 1986, s 34). In practice, though, this is often ineffective in contact disputes.

The court can penalise in costs the party who is breaching the contact order (*Re B (Contact Application: Costs)* [1995] Fam Law 650). Ultimately, contempt proceedings may be used, or at least threatened, as a measure of last resort, when a parent with whom the child lives consistently and unreasonably refuses contact. However, these proceedings are often inappropriate and could cause the child added trauma, especially if the unfortunate result is the imprisonment of the parent with whom the child lives. Nevertheless, in *A v N (Committal: Refusal of Contact)* [1997] 1 FLR 533 the Court of Appeal upheld a decision to commit to prison a mother who had breached a suspended order for imprisonment.

The court is also able to transfer residence of the child from the parent with care who is obstructing contact to the other parent (*V v V (Contact: Implacable Hostility)* [2004] 2 FLR 851). This is, however, a judicial weapon of last resort (*Re A* [2009] EWCA Civ 1141).

In *Re M (Intractable Contact Dispute: Interim Care Order)* [2003] EWHC 1024 (Fam), [2003] 2 FLR 636, Wall J directed the local authority to investigate the case under s 37 of the CA 1989 (see **13.3.7**) with a view to taking care proceedings when faced with a mother who repeatedly frustrated contact. This resulted in the children being removed from the care of their mother under an interim care order, followed by a residence order in favour of the father.

This and a series of other recent cases have highlighted the difficulties in enforcement of contact orders. In *Re D (Intractable Contact Dispute: Publicity)* [2004] EWHC 727, [2004] 1 FLR 1226, Munby J listed a catalogue of failings in the court system in dealing with problems in contact, and said it could no longer be assumed that our approach to enforcement of contact orders meets the standards required by Article 6 and Article 8 of the European Convention on Human Rights.

New provisions for the enforcement of contact

As a result of concerns raised in the above cases, the Children and Adoption Act 2006 also inserted new ss 11I–11P in the CA 1989, which came into force on 8 December 2008 and gave the court additional powers to deal with breaches of contact orders as follows:

(a) *Warning notices.* Where the court makes or varies a contact order, it is to attach to the order a notice warning of the consequences of failing to comply with the contact order. The warning notice warns that non-compliance with the contact order may result in the individual being held in contempt of court and imprisoned or fined, and/or an order requiring him to undertake unpaid work (an enforcement order) or pay financial compensation.

For contact orders made before 8 December 2008, an application can be made on Form C78 to the court for a warning notice to be attached to the contact order.

(b) *Enforcement orders.* Where the court is satisfied beyond reasonable doubt that a person has failed to comply with a contact order, it may make an enforcement order imposing an unpaid work requirement of up to 200 hours. The court may not make an enforcement order if it is satisfied that the person had reasonable excuse for failing to comply with the order.

The court must be satisfied that making the enforcement order is necessary to ensure compliance with the contact order, and that the effect of the enforcement order is proportionate to the seriousness of the breach of the contact order. The court must also be satisfied that the work can be done in the area where the person lives, and must obtain and consider information about the person and the likely effect of the enforcement on him, including as to any conflict with his religious beliefs and interference with his work or study times.

The court must take into account the welfare of the child who is the subject of the contact order when making an enforcement order.

When making an enforcement order, the court must attach a notice warning of the consequence of failure to comply. When making the enforcement order, the court may also ask Cafcass to monitor compliance with the order and report to the court as required.

(c) *Compensation for financial loss.* If the court is satisfied that a person has breached a contact order without reasonable excuse and this has caused financial loss then the court may order that person to pay compensation in respect of the financial loss (which may not exceed the amount of the applicant's financial loss). So, for example, if a father booked a holiday for himself and his child to take during a contact visit, and the mother refused to allow the child to go without reasonable excuse, then the mother could be ordered to pay the father compensation.

The recent case of *Re L-W (children) (contact order: committal)* [2010] EWCA Civ 1253 dealt with an appeal against the making of enforcement and compensation orders and of a committal order for several breaches by a father of contact orders. The court overturned the majority of the orders on the basis that that whilst the father had not encouraged the child to go on the visits, he was required by the orders only to 'allow' contact and to 'make (the child) available' for contact, and this was not an obligation to 'make sure' that the child went and that contact took place if the child himself refused to attend contact.

13.3.3 Prohibited steps order

A prohibited steps order is an order that no step that could be taken by a parent in meeting his or her parental responsibilities for a child and which is of a kind specified in the order, shall be taken by any person without the consent of the court. This order deals with a specific problem which has arisen. However, it cannot overlap with a residence or contact order. Section 9(5) of the CA 1989 provides that the court cannot make a prohibited steps order or a specific issue order with a view to achieving a result that could be achieved by a residence or contact order. For example, the court could not grant an order prohibiting the child living with anyone other than the applicant as this would in effect be a residence order. It can be used to restrict anyone, not just a parent. So, it could be used to prevent a grandparent with whom the child lived from removing the child from the jurisdiction.

Another situation in which the overlap between the various s 8 orders must be considered is child abduction. If, in an abduction case, the result that is required is for the abducted child to be returned to live with the non-abducting parent, the correct order for this parent to seek is a residence order (with appropriate conditions and directions) and not a specific issue order ordering return of the child coupled with a prohibited steps order to prevent further removal

(*Re W (A Minor) (Residence Order)* [1992] 2 FLR 332). If the required result is to obtain the return of the child to the UK and prevent further removal, but the child is to remain living with the abducting parent, then a prohibited steps order is the correct order to obtain (*Re D (A Minor) (Child: Removal from Jurisdiction)* [1992] 1 FLR 637).

If no residence order were in force, a prohibited steps order could be used to prohibit the removal of the child from the country, or to prevent a change of surname.

If it is desired to prevent someone having contact with the child, it is possible to make a contact order providing for no contact. Therefore, the person with whom a child lives could be prevented from allowing contact with an abusing parent or anyone else who the court considered was harming the child in any way. However, in *Re H (Prohibited Steps Order)* [1995] 1 FLR 638, where the mother's cohabitee had abused the children, the court decided that a 'negative' contact order preventing the mother from allowing contact would afford only partial protection. Instead, the court made a prohibited steps order against the cohabitee, even though he was not a party to the proceedings and had not been given notice.

An important restriction on a prohibited steps order is that it can relate only to matters which are included within parental responsibility. If an order is needed to restrict publicity, for example, the wider powers of wardship are needed as this is not one of the matters included within parental responsibility.

13.3.4 Specific issue order

A specific issue order is an order giving directions for the purpose of determining a specific question which has arisen or which may arise in connection with any aspect of parental responsibility for a child.

It does not give a parent a general power, it just makes a decision on one issue over which there is a disagreement which cannot be resolved. It could be used to decide which school a child should attend, whether a child should have a particular operation (including, for example, sterilisation or circumcision) or course of treatment or immunisation (such as the MMR vaccination), or the religion a child should adopt.

It can be used by non-parents, for example the local authority, or doctor or relation, to resolve issues involving the child, for example, over abortion or life-saving medical decisions. In *Re R (A Minor) (Blood Transfusion)* [1993] 2 FLR 757, a specific issue order was used to deal with a situation where a child needed a blood transfusion and his parents refused to give consent due to their religious beliefs.

Again, it cannot be used to achieve a 'back-door' residence or contact order, for example by ordering a child to attend a particular school thereby necessitating a change of residence (see **13.3.3**).

13.3.5 Family assistance order

A family assistance order is not a s 8 order at all, although it is closely connected. Section 16 of the CA 1989 allows the court, in any family proceedings where it has power to make a s 8 order, to make an order requiring, for example, a Cafcass officer or local authority officer to be made available to advise, assist and befriend any person named in the order. The aim of the family assistance order is to support the family in the immediate aftermath of a family breakdown and to help everyone to adjust to the changed circumstances. The order can only be made by the court of its own motion and is likely to be made in conjunction with one or more s 8 orders. It can last for a maximum of 12 months.

Before making a family assistance order, the court must obtain the opinion of the appropriate officer, as to whether it will be in the best interests of the child to have such an order and how the order might operate.

Until recently, it could be made only in exceptional circumstances and only if everyone named in the order, excluding the child, consented. The Children and Adoption Act 2006, which came into force on 1 October 2007, amends s 16 of the CA 1989 and removes the requirement that the order be made only in exceptional circumstances and also provides, where a contact order is in force, that the officer give advice and assistance to establish, improve and maintain contact. It also amends s 16(6) of the 1989 Act, to provide that where a family assistance order is in force at the same time as a s 8 order, the family assistance order may direct the officer to report to the court on matters relating to the s 8 order, as the court requires, including whether to vary or discharge the s 8 order. Also, the new duty under s 16A of the CA 1989, to carry out a risk assessment and report to the court where the officer has cause to suspect the child is at risk of harm, applies for the duration of any family assistance order.

Family assistance orders had not been widely used, and it was hoped that the recent changes outlined above would increase their effectiveness. Initial data seems to indicate that more of these orders are being made since 2007.

13.3.6 Special guardianship order

Sections 14A to 14F of the CA 1989 provide for special guardianship orders, a type of order which appoints one or more individuals to be a child's special guardian or special guardians.

13.3.6.1 Effect of order

The special guardianship order gives the holder parental responsibility, which he is entitled to exercise to the exclusion of any other person with parental responsibility. However, it does not extinguish the parents' parental responsibility.

Where a special guardianship order is in force, no one can cause the child to be known by a new surname or remove him from the UK (except for the special guardian who can remove the child for a period of less than three months) without the written consent of everyone with parental responsibility or permission of the court.

It is a private law order, but it may be useful in cases where the local authority is or has been involved. It provides permanence without the legal separation involved in adoption. For example, it may be used in the case of an older child in long-term foster care, or for a child being looked after permanently by a member of his extended family.

In *A Local Authority v YZ and Others* [2006] 2 FLR 41, on the local authority's application for care orders in respect of five children, the court made special guardianship orders in respect of the three eldest of five children. The two eldest had lived with an aunt and uncle for two years and the third child, aged five, had lived with another aunt and her partner for almost two years. The two youngest were made subject to care orders with a care plan for adoption.

In *Re S (Adoption Order or Special Guardianship Order)* [2007] EWCA Civ 54 the court gave examples of some circumstances in which a special guardianship order may be appropriate:

(a) older children who do not wish to be legally separated from their birth families;

(b) children being cared for on a permanent basis by members of their wider birth family;

(c) children in some minority ethnic communities, who have religious and cultural difficulties with adoption as it is set out in law;

(d) unaccompanied asylum-seeking children who need secure, permanent homes, but have strong attachments to their families.

13.3.6.2 Who can apply?

A special guardian must be 18 or over and must not be a parent of the child.

Those able to apply for the order are:

(a) any guardian of the child;
(b) any holder of a residence order or anyone listed within s 10(5)(b) or (c) of the CA 1989;
(c) a relative or local authority foster carer with whom the child has lived for one year preceding the application; and
(d) anyone who has obtained leave of the court to make the application.

The court can also make a special guardianship order of its own motion, even if no application has been made.

13.3.6.3 Procedure

Before applying, the applicant must give the local authority three months' written notice of his intention to apply (s 14A(7)). On receipt of the notice, the local authority must investigate and prepare a report for the court dealing with matters such as the suitability of the applicant to be a special guardian. The court cannot make a special guardianship order unless this report has been received.

The court must consider the welfare principle (s 1(1)), the welfare checklist (s 1(3)) and the no order principle (s 1(5)) when deciding whether to make a special guardianship order. In *Re S* (**13.3.6.1** above) the court said that a special guardianship order was only appropriate if, in the particular circumstances of the particular case, it was best fitted to meet the needs of the child concerned, and that each case would be decided on its facts.

Before making the order, the court must also consider whether to make a contact order, whether any s 8 order in force with respect to the child should be varied or discharged, and whether to discharge any enforcement orders or contact activity directions in force.

On making a special guardianship order, the court may also:

(a) give leave for the child to be known by a new surname;
(b) grant leave for the child to be removed from the UK either generally or for specified purposes.

13.3.6.4 Special guardian support services

The local authority must provide special guardian support services, including counselling, advice and financial support. Financial support can be used to facilitate a person becoming a special guardian, or to facilitate the continuation of the special guardianship order. Examples of financial assistance provided are payment of the prospective special guardian's legal fees to apply for the order, payment for the provision of furniture or equipment, and for adaptation of the home or the additional cost of buying a larger home.

13.3.7 Local authority investigation

If exceptional circumstances are revealed in family proceedings, for example on an application for a s 8 order serious neglect is discovered which makes it unlikely that either parent should look after the children, the court may not be prepared to grant either parent a s 8 order. The court does not have the power to make a care order relating to a child without an application from the local authority, and what it will have to do is to make an order under s 37 of the CA 1989 to direct the local authority to investigate the child's circumstances. It is then for the local authority to decide whether or not to bring care or supervision proceedings, depending on the outcome of its inquiries. The court can, when making a s 37 order, make an interim care order to protect a child pending the investigation (see **14.9.1**).

13.4 Welfare principle

Section 1(1) of CA 1989 states:

> When a court determines any question with respect to—

> (a) the upbringing of a child; or
>
> (b) the administration of the child's property or the application of any income arising from it,
>
> the child's welfare shall be the court's paramount consideration.

The welfare principle will determine any contested proceedings under s 8 of the CA 1989, and it will also extend to care proceedings (CA 1989, s 31) and related public law orders.

It is a concept that has been used for many years in cases concerning children, and is summarised by the words of Lord MacDermott in *J and Another v C and Others* [1969] 1 All ER 788:

> More than that the child's welfare is to be treated as the top item in a list of items relevant to the matter in question, [the words] connote a process whereby, when all the relevant facts, relationships, claims and wishes of parents, risks, choices and their circumstances are taken into account and weighed, the course to be followed will be that which is most in the interest of the child's welfare as that term has now to be understood ... [It is] the paramount consideration because it rules upon or determines the course to be followed.

13.4.1 Human Rights Act 1998

Article 8 of the European Convention on Human Rights provides that 'everyone has the right to respect for his private and family life, his home and his correspondence'. Although the welfare of the child is paramount under CA 1989, under Article 8 the starting point is that each family member is on an equal footing.

There has been debate as to whether the welfare principle is incompatible with Article 8 and an individual's right to respect for family life. In other words, placing the child's welfare as paramount does not involve balancing the family rights of the other relevant individuals. In the past, the European Court has tended to adopt more of a straightforward balancing exercise and the idea of paramountcy has not been supported.

Any inconsistency between the approach of the English courts and the minimum standards required by the Convention needed to be reconciled. For example, in contact applications, it could be argued that the court must consider the right of the parent and other family members to contact, as opposed to this being the right of the child.

Similarly, where an application is made to remove a child from the jurisdiction, the welfare of the child is paramount. If this means that the resident parent is allowed to leave with the child, the other parent's right to family life has been infringed. On the other hand, if the resident parent's application is refused, this inhibits his right to a private life. Nevertheless, in *Payne v Payne* [2001] EWCA Civ 166, [2001] 1 FLR 1052, the Court of Appeal held that the Convention had not affected the longstanding underlying principles (focusing on the welfare of the child) to be applied when dealing with such applications .

The position was confirmed by the case of *Hoppe v Germany* [2003] 1 FLR 384, where the European Court of Human Rights finally made plain its acceptance of the primacy of the interests of the child where a balance was required to be struck between competing Convention rights.

13.5 Checklist of factors to be taken into account in applying welfare principle

Section 1(3) of CA 1989 (see **Appendix 1(E)**) directs the court to pay particular attention to seven factors when it is applying the welfare principle in contested s 8 proceedings and any proceedings for care and supervision orders.

The aim of the checklist is to promote a consistent approach by providing a framework to use when solicitors are preparing evidence and when courts are making decisions. It could sometimes be a very useful tool to use to explain to clients the approach that they should, and that the court certainly will, take in making a decision.

It provides a minimum that must be considered in every case. Thpermissionpermissione Act gives no indication of the relative importance of the factors, so the court is left to assess the relative importance of each factor in the circumstances of each case. The checklist is not exhaustive and the court can also take any other relevant factors into account. For example, in *Re R (Residence Order: Finance)* [1995] 2 FLR 612 it was confirmed that a judge was entitled to look at the case in the round, which could include taking into account financial considerations, such as a possible assessment by the Child Support Agency.

13.5.1 The ascertainable wishes and feelings of the child concerned (considered in the light of his age and understanding)

This factor reflects the importance of allowing the child's wishes to be given a place in deciding what is in his or her welfare (see the *Gillick* case at **13.2.1**). Lord Justice Butler-Sloss (as she was then) in the Cleveland Report made the point that 'a child is a person, not an object of concern'.

There are a number of cases where, on the particular facts, the court not only considered but also followed the wishes of children. In *M v M (Transfer of Custody: Appeal)* [1987] 1 WLR 404, the trial judge said that it was wrong to order that a 12-year-old girl should live with her father instead of her mother without taking proper account of her adamant and strong opposition to this. In another case, the wishes of a 'sensible and mature' boy aged 14 years were the deciding factor in ordering that he should go to a local day school, enabling him to live with his father rather than go away to a boarding school. The boy was very anxious to build a relationship with his father with whom he had not lived for five years (see *Re P (A Minor) (Education: Child's Views)* [1992] 1 FLR 316). In *S v S (Child Abduction: Child's Views)* [1992] 2 FLR 492, the Court of Appeal said that there was no age below which a child was to be considered as not having attained sufficient maturity for his views to be taken automatically into account.

A child's wishes do not necessarily always take precedence and the court may sometimes feel that the children's wishes are not in their best interests (*Re DW (A Minor)* [1984] Fam Law 17).

However, in *Re S (Contact: Children's Views)* [2002] EWHC 540 (Fam), [2002] 1 FLR 1156, the court expressed the view that if young people (here a 14- and a 16-year-old) are to respect the law, the law has to respect them and their wishes, even to the extent of allowing them, as occasionally they may do, to make mistakes.

There are a number of ways in which the child's wishes and feelings can be made known. The court will place great importance on the welfare report prepared by the children and family reporter, which will consider the child's wishes as well as the maturity of the child and the extent to which the parents may have exerted influence over the child in forming any views. In some cases, a judge may interview a child privately during the case to form his own opinion, but this is not common. However, in April 2010 the Family Justice Council produced 'Guidelines for meeting children who are subject to family proceedings', the purpose of which is to encourage children to feel more involved and connected with proceedings, and to give them the opportunity to satisfy themselves that the judge has understood their wishes and feelings and to understand the nature of the judge's task.

Alternatively, the child may need separate legal representation. This may happen in difficult cases, with disputed facts, and where the child's views are perhaps not sufficiently dealt with in the welfare report (see *Re A (Contact: Separate Representation)* [2001] 1 FLR 715, CA and **13.8.3**).

A wider issue involving a child's wishes is the extent to which a child can consent to or refuse medical treatment (see *Re W (A Minor) (Consent to Medical Treatment)* [1993] 1 FLR 1). If a child is sufficiently mature, he can consent to treatment and only the court can override his consent. If such a child refuses consent to treatment then either the court or anyone with parental responsibility can give consent.

13.5.2 The child's physical, emotional and educational needs

This factor focuses on the child and will look at accommodation, medical needs and education, as well as how close the child is to brothers and sisters and others with whom he may lose touch if a particular order is made.

When the court has to decide between placing a child with a parent or another carer, there is a strong supposition that, other things being equal, it is in the interests of the child that it shall remain with its natural parents (*Re H (A Minor) (Custody: Interim Care and Control)* [1991] 2 FLR 109). In *In re G (Children)* [2006] UKHL 43, Baroness Hale identified three ways in which a person may be or may become the natural parent of a child: the genetic parent; the gestational parent; or the social and psychological parent. In most cases, the natural mother combines all three. This was a case which involved former lesbian partners. One of the partners (CG) had had two children by artificial insemination, which both partners raised. The court said that the fact that CG was the natural mother in every sense of the term, whilst raising no presumption in her favour, was undoubtedly an important and significant factor in determining what was best for the children.

The court will not equate welfare with material advantages and the fact that one parent can offer more is of little weight, particularly because the court could compensate for this when making financial orders.

The court will consider the circumstances very carefully before splitting brothers and sisters (*C v C (Minors: Custody)* [1988] 2 FLR 291). This will mean that it will be unusual to separate siblings, especially when they are close in age, although the larger the age gap, especially if linked with the fact that one child is at boarding school, could mean that children might be happier separated with generous contact during holidays.

13.5.3 The likely effect on the child of any change in circumstances

If the current arrangements for a child are working satisfactorily the court will be very unlikely to change them. This attitude, which is often referred to as maintaining the status quo, was explained in *Allington v Allington* [1985] FLR 586:

> It is generally accepted by those who are professionally concerned with children that particularly in the early years, continuity of care is a most important part of a child's sense of security and that disruption of established bonds is to be avoided whenever it is possible to do so.

A result of this attitude is that the person with whom the child is living is at a considerable advantage, and it may encourage them to increase this advantage by delaying the proceedings. This problem is tackled by the Act, where it provides that any delay is 'likely to prejudice the welfare of the child' (CA 1989, s 1(2)), and it further discourages delay by its imposition of a litigation timetable (CA 1989, s 11(1) and see **13.8.5.6**).

13.5.4 The child's age, sex, background and any characteristics of the child which the court considers relevant

Age may be important as very young babies tend to need to live with their mothers, whereas a 15-year-old child can generally cope with living with either parent. Also, age has a decisive influence on the importance a court will attach to a child's wishes, but there is no presumption of law that a child of any age should be with one parent or the other (*Re W (A Minor) (Residence Order)* [1992] 2 FLR 332).

The sex of the child can be taken into account. In *Re H (A Minor)* (1990) *The Times,* 20 June, the court agreed that a 2-year-old girl should live with her father and stated that 'It may be natural for young children to be with their mothers but this is merely one consideration not a presumption'. Obviously, the needs of a teenager might best be met by living with a parent of the same sex. The factor also refers to the background of the child. This can cover race, culture and religion. The needs of a mixed-race child are of particular difficulty when deciding where a child should live. The court will look at how the child has been brought up and the influence of each culture, and make appropriate residence and contact arrangements (see *Re P (A Minor) (Adoption)* [1990] 1 FLR 96).

13.5.5 Any harm that the child has suffered or is at risk of suffering

This factor will cover any past or future harm to the child. Harm is a very broad term and will cover both physical and psychological injury.

The court will also consider the harm caused to a child by not seeing both parents. In the case of *Re S (Minors: Access)* [1990] 2 FLR 166, the court said that contact 'is the right of the child not of the parent … The child has a right to know his other parent'.

13.5.6 How capable each of the child's parents and any other person in relation to whom the court considers the question relevant is of meeting the child's needs

This factor involves the court looking at the parents or other proposed carers to assess their ability to care for the child. The parents' conduct will be relevant to the extent that it may affect their suitability as a parent. Any criminal record, say, for violence or dishonesty, will be relevant.

In disputes between a natural parent and another, for example a grandparent, the courts tend to presume that, unless there is positive evidence to the contrary, it is in the child's interests to live with his natural parent. The question was not which household would provide the best home (*Re D (Care: Natural Parent Presumption)* [1999] 1 FLR 134).

Whether a parent works will influence the care of the child. A parent's lifestyle and sexual orientation may also be relevant. Issues of homosexuality and lesbianism can affect the child, especially if this causes problems, for example teasing or bullying, at school. However, the courts' attitudes to homosexual parenting are now very different to what they were several years ago and these issues are now likely to carry less weight.

A parent who suffers from a mental or physical illness which could mean sudden or long-term stays in hospital might also be less suitable as a full-time carer. Religion, too, may have an influence on a court's decision, especially if it may adversely affect a child's health, or have a harmful influence on the child's development. In *Re R (A Minor) (Residence: Religion)* [1993] 2 FLR 163, the court said that there was no rule of law or legal principle that it could never be right to force a child to abandon his religious beliefs. The court made a residence order that a child of nine years of age live with his father, even though the child had been brought up in a strict religious sect from which the father had been excluded. The court took the religious issue into account but felt that it was in the child's best interests to be with his father.

If a parent is proposing to share care with someone else, that person's capabilities will also be considered. This means that new partners or spouses, relatives and friends may be relevant, as well as nannies and childminders.

13.5.7 The range of powers available to the court under this Act in the proceedings in question

This factor encourages the court to think laterally and consider every option open to it, including that of not making an order at all (see **13.6**).

The court has the power to make any order in favour of any person, irrespective of who has applied and for what. Thus, in the course of an application for a residence order by a parent, the court may decide that the child would be better off living with a grandparent. It can make this order even though the grandparents were not parties to the application. The deciding factor is the welfare of the child.

The court could also adjourn s 8 proceedings brought by a parent if it felt that a care or supervision order would be the best thing for the child (CA 1989, s 37(1)). This section enables the court to direct the local authority to investigate the circumstances of the child and, following this, the local authority could start care proceedings. The divorce courts do not have the power to make a care or supervision order themselves.

13.6 The 'no order' presumption

Section 1(5) of the CA 1989 states:

> Where a court is considering whether or not to make one or more orders under this Act with respect to a child, it shall not make the order or any of the orders unless it considers that doing so would be better for the child than making no order at all.

This means that there is a policy that the court will not intervene and make an order unless it can be shown that there is a positive need and benefit to the child in doing so.

On divorce, the court should not make an order automatically for the children as part of the 'divorce package'. If the parties agree on where a child is to live after the divorce and when the other parent should see him, no court will make an order.

The aim of this presumption is to try to reduce the bitterness felt by a parent who may feel that he has 'lost' if a court order is imposed ordering the child to live with the other parent, or allowing him contact only at defined times. The long-term damage to a child following divorce is greatly reduced if bitterness can be minimised, and the absence of unnecessary court intervention will help this. If parents are in dispute from the outset, or if agreed arrangements break down, the court can always be asked to make appropriate orders.

Other circumstances when the court will be likely to consider that an order is necessary include where there is a real danger that one parent may abduct the child and it is, therefore, an advantage to have in operation the restrictions on removal from the UK contained in a residence order, or, perhaps, where both parents agree that an order is preferable. Another situation where the court made an order despite the fact that all parties were in agreement was where parents agreed with the maternal grandmother that the child should live with her. The court said that there was a reason to grant a residence order to the grandmother as it would give her parental responsibility for the child and give her important rights, for example, it would enable her to give consent to medical treatment and authorise school trips. The granting of a residence order also gave the arrangement more stability, as the parents could not change their minds without going back to court (*B v B (A Minor) (Residence Order)* [1992] 2 FLR 327).

13.7 Avoiding delay

Section 1(2) of the CA 1989 states:

> In any proceedings in which any question with respect to the upbringing of a child arises, the court shall have regard to the general principle that any delay in determining the question is likely to prejudice the welfare of the child.

Delay can be particularly damaging in children cases, as a child's timescale is different from that of an adult. Six months is half a lifetime to a one-year-old child. The object is to avoid drift or delay for no reason, which can be very damaging to a child. Note, though, that sometimes delay can be positively beneficial, for example an adjournment to see how the child is settling down to new arrangements.

Inappropriate delay may also now be a breach of Article 6 of the European Convention on Human Rights (the right to a hearing within a reasonable time).

13.8 Procedure for s 8 orders

The procedure for making s 8 applications is governed by the FPR 2010. The rules are largely contained in Pt 12, which is supplemented by Practice Direction 12B.

The pre-application protocol for mediation information and assessment in Practice Direction 3A also applies (as for applications for financial orders) (see **10.4.1**) and requires the parties to attend a MIAM before issuing an application, unless one of the exceptions applies.

13.8.1 Public funding

Public funding is available for Children Act proceedings. The client will need to apply for Level 3 funding if he or she is to issue proceedings, and this will cover work up to but not including preparation for and attendance at the Final Hearing. If the matter proceeds to a Final Hearing, the client will need to apply for Level 4 Legal Representation. If an application is made, both the means and merits tests must be satisfied (see **Chapter 2**). If a certificate for Family Help (Higher) or for Legal Representation has already been issued, for example for financial proceedings in a divorce, the Legal Representation certificate issued in these proceedings will need to be amended. In urgent cases, emergency Legal Representation can be used.

13.8.2 Jurisdiction

Applications for s 8 orders can be made within any family proceedings; in fact the court can make an order of its own motion in such proceedings. Family proceedings are defined in the Act and cover divorce, nullity or judicial separation, financial orders applications (MCA 1973 and DPMCA 1978) and domestic abuse applications under the FLA 1996. Alternatively, 'freestanding' applications can be made where no order other than under the CA 1989 is needed.

13.8.3 Is leave of the court needed?

13.8.3.1 Who can apply for a s 8 order?

The following may apply for *any* s 8 order without permission of the court:

(a) a parent (which includes an unmarried father, whether or not he has parental responsibility);

(b) a step-parent or civil partner who has parental responsibility for the child;

(c) a guardian or special guardian; or

(d) any person with a residence order in his or her favour (CA 1989, s 10(5): see **Appendix 1(E)**).

The following may apply for a residence or contact order *only* without permission:

(a) a step-parent or civil partner who has treated the child as a child of the family; or

(b) any person with whom the child has lived for at least three years out of the last five years (but the period must not have ended more than three months before the application is made); or

(c) any person who has obtained the consent of all those people whose legal position would be affected, ie anyone with parental responsibility, or anyone with a residence order or the local authority if the child is in care.

Since 1 September 2009 a relative or foster parent of a child can apply for a residence order if the child has been living with that person for at least one year immediately preceding the application.

All other people not within the above require permission.

Therefore, for example, grandparents will require permission unless the child has been living with them for one year or they have the necessary consents. An application for permission must be made in writing.

It is unlikely that the requirement for certain categories of parties to apply for permission violates Article 6(1) of the European Convention on Human Rights, as it is not a blanket denial of access to the court but rather a hurdle to overcome.

13.8.3.2 Application by the child

A child can apply on his own behalf for a s 8 order, but permission of the court is required (see CA 1989, s 10). There have been several cases where teenage children have been granted permission to apply and have gone on to obtain s 8 orders (see *Re AD (A Minor) (Child's Wishes)* [1993] 1 FCR 573). Even if a child obtains a residence order allowing him to live apart from his parents, his parents will still retain parental responsibility. Orders have been sought to enable a child to live with grandparents or the parents of the child's boyfriend, and could also be used where a pregnant teenager did not want an abortion which her parents were forcing her to undergo.

If a child wants to obtain a s 8 order, there are four hurdles to overcome:

(a) *To obtain a solicitor to act for him.* A minor can start proceedings without a litigation friend provided the court gives permission to proceed without a litigation friend *or* a solicitor considers that the child has sufficient understanding to give instructions in relation to proceedings (FPR 2010, r 16.6). If the permission of the court is sought, it will base its decision on whether the child is mature enough to exercise a wise choice in his own interests in the circumstances that exist (*Re S (A Minor) (Independent Representation)* [1993] 3 All ER 36). In complex cases, the court is likely to recommend that a third party, such as an officer of Cafcass Legal (in a role formerly carried out by the Official Solicitor) or a children's guardian, acts for the child.

    If a child approaches a solicitor direct, that solicitor can take the decision whether to act for the child. The Resolution guidelines (Section F: Assessing Understanding) point out that initially it is the solicitor's duty to assess the child's understanding. (See *Re CT (A Minor) (Wardship: Representation)* [1993] 2 FLR 278.) The solicitor must also be sensitive to his duty of confidentiality to the child.

(b) *To obtain public funding.* A child will usually need public funding and will have to convince the Legal Services Commission that his application has merit. The means test will usually not be a problem, as it is the child's resources that are relevant when assessing financial eligibility. Legal Help is also available to a child to cover the cost of the initial interview.

(c) *To obtain the court's permission.* The child will need to obtain permission of the court to start s 8 proceedings (CA 1989, s 10(8)). Permission will be given only if the court is satisfied that the child has sufficient understanding to make the application.

    In *Re H (Residence Order: Child's Application For Leave)* [2000] 1 FLR 781, a 12-year-old boy was refused leave to apply for a residence order in the course of his parents' divorce proceedings. The boy wished to live with his father and was worried that the court would not attach enough weight to his wishes unless he made his own application. The court decided that, although he had sufficient understanding to instruct a solicitor independently, the boy did not have a separate argument to make that would not be made on the father's behalf. The judge also said that the boy must be assured that experienced judges would take full account of his wishes and are conscious that it is not usually a good idea to impose a result contrary to a child's wishes, even though those wishes are not decisive.

(d) *To show that the merits of the case justify the order sought.* At the eventual hearing the court will consider the child's welfare and the statutory checklist (see **13.5**) when deciding whether to grant the order sought.

13.8.4 Which court?

The CA 1989 also introduced a concurrent jurisdiction of family proceedings court, county court and High Court, with specially trained officials and judiciary available at each level to deal with CA 1989 matters. The Allocation and Transfer of Proceedings Order 2008 (SI 2008/2836) and accompanying Practice Direction of 3 November 2008 set out the criteria for deciding which court is the most appropriate and are designed to ensure that cases are dealt with at the lowest appropriate level commensurate with their complexity.

13.8.4.1 The family proceedings court

The family proceedings court can deal with private law applications for s 8 orders but it does not deal with divorce cases. In practice, many s 8 applications will be linked to divorce proceedings and are still being issued in the county court, but they are likely to be transferred down to the family proceedings court if they do not come within the criteria set out in art 15 of the Allocation and Transfer of Proceedings Order 2008 (see **13.8.4.4**).

A straightforward freestanding s 8 application is likely to be suitable for the family proceedings court.

Most public law cases, for example for care or supervision orders, will start in the family proceedings court (see **14.11.2**).

The work is mainly dealt with by lay magistrates, who have had special training to deal with family cases and are therefore on a Family Panel.

13.8.4.2 County court

As well as dealing with CA 1989 cases linked to divorce, the county court is suitable for more complex s 8 applications. However, not all county courts have jurisdiction to hear cases under the CA 1989.

13.8.4.3 High Court

The High Court can hear all types of CA 1989 cases, as well as appeals in CA 1989 cases from the family proceedings court. In practice, it will generally deal with exceptionally complex cases, which either could be started there or which are transferred from other courts.

13.8.4.4 Transfer of cases

Irrespective of where a case started, it may be transferred to another, more appropriate court. This is generally governed by the general principle that any delay is likely to prejudice the child's welfare, but art 15 of the Allocation and Transfer of Proceedings Order 2008 sets out a list of criteria which would be necessary to transfer a case from the family proceedings court to the county court. Article 16 states that if those criteria are not present in a case issued in or transferred to the county court, it should be transferred down to the family proceedings court. Examples of these criteria include possibility of conflict between expert witnesses, existence of a novel or difficult point of law and international law issues. This should result in a significant increase in the number of cases transferred from the county court to the family proceedings court.

It is possible for cases to be transferred either vertically or horizontally. Thus, a difficult case could be transferred from the family proceedings court up to the county court, or, if a family proceedings court is too busy, it could transfer the case to another family proceedings court. It is also possible for a case to be transferred down from the High Court to a county court.

13.8.5 The Revised Private Law Programme – FPR 2010, Practice Direction 12B

Practice Direction 12B incorporates the Private Law Programme which was in effect before the FPR 2010 came into force, and contains much of the procedure for application issue, service and listing, and conduct of the first hearing.

13.8.5.1 The application

The applicant must file Form C100 (see **Appendix 3(J)**) (or Form C2 if there are already existing family proceedings), together with sufficient copies for service (and a fee). If the applicant alleges that the child has suffered or is at risk of suffering harm, he must also file a completed Form C1A (see **Appendix 3(K)**) and completed Form FM1 (see **Appendix 3(C)**). Form C100 requires the applicant to give details of his address and that of the respondent during the previous five years to enable Cafcass to carry out safeguarding checks. The form also enables the applicant to include the details of the order needed and the reasons for applying. Form C100 (and all other documents used in the proceedings) should be simply worded using non-inflammatory language. Form C100 also refers parents to a Parenting Plan booklet, which offers guidance to parents on making arrangements for their children on relationsip breakdown and asks about the parties' attempts to mediate.

Under the Revised Private Law Programme, the court must issue the application on the day of receipt, and within 24 hours of issue (48 hours in courts where applications are first considered on paper) the court must send (or hand) to the applicant and Cafcass:

(a) a copy of Application Form C100 (together with Supplemental Information Form C1A if provided) and Form FM1;

(b) the Notice of Hearing;

(c) the Acknowledgment Form C7;

(d) a blank Form C1A;

(e) the Certificate of Service Form C9; and

(f) information leaflets for the parties.

The court will list the case for a First Hearing Dispute Resolution Appointment (FHDRA) to take place within four weeks of the application and no later than six weeks from the date of the application.

The applicant must join as a party every person whom he believes to have parental responsibility for the child. This would not cover a step-parent or putative father. However, any person may apply to be joined, and the court has power to direct that anyone else be joined as a party. Therefore, all people with a genuine interest and active role in the child's upbringing can be involved in court proceedings.

The court may make a child a party to proceedings if it is in the best interests of the child to do so. Practice Direction 16A sets out guidance on what the court should consider before making a child a party and states that it will happen only in cases that involve an issue of significant difficulty, and consequently will occur only in a minority of cases.

13.8.5.2 Service

Copies of the application must be served on all parties at least 14 days before the hearing, together with a Notice of Proceedings (Form C6) showing the date for the directions appointment, and blank Acknowledgement (Form C7). The applicant must then file a Statement of Service (Form C9) at court, setting out how service was effected.

The FPR 2010, Practice Direction 12C also provides that notice of the application must be given to a number of other interested people, so that they are given the chance to decide whether they want to be joined as a party. This will include anyone caring for the child, anyone who is a party to other proceedings which affect the child or anyone with whom the child has lived for at least three years prior to the application.

13.8.5.3 Without notice applications

All s 8 orders can be made without notice. However, without notice interim orders should be made only in exceptional circumstances where it is necessary to protect the child. For example, a without notice application would be justified in a 'snatch' situation, where no order was made at the time of the divorce but a crisis arose when the parent failed to return the child to the other parent following a day's contact, or where an urgent medical problem arose and the parents were in dispute over a life-threatening decision. In *Re G (Minors) (Ex parte Interim Residence Order)* [1993] 1 FLR 910, the Court of Appeal granted an interim residence order to a father because of evidence that the mother was taking drugs and that the children needed to be removed from her care immediately.

When a without notice application is made, the full application should be filed either at the same time, or on the next business day if the order is obtained by telephone. The application and order must be served on the respondent within 48 hours after the making of the without notice order.

13.8.5.4 Acknowledgement

Within 14 days of the FHDRA, the respondent must complete the Acknowledgement (Form C7), file it at court and serve a copy on the other party. If the applicant has filed Form C1A then the respondent may make comments on the form in response to the information given on Form C1A by the applicant.

13.8.5.5 Cafcass, safety checks and risk assessments

The Revised Private Law Programme (and in line with Practice Direction 12J, 'Residence and Contact Orders: Domestic Violence and Harm' (see **13.3.2**)) requires the court to send the documents listed at **13.8.5.1** to Cafcass to enable Cafcass to carry out its initial safeguarding checks. Cafcass is required by the Revised Private Law Programme and in accordance with its safeguarding framework to make enquiries of local authorities and the police and to carry out risk identification interviews by telephone with the parties. The purpose of these checks is to identify any issues of domestic violence, social services involvement or other issues which might pose a risk of harm to the child. Cafcass must report to the court at least three days before the FHDRA the outcome of risk identification by completing and filing a Sch 2 Form.

Section 16A of the CA 1989 requires Cafcass to carry out a risk assessment in relation to any child whom it is given cause to suspect is at risk of harm and to provide the risk assessment to the court. The above initial safeguarding checks will enable Cafcass and the court to identify cases where a s 16A risk assessment is required.

13.8.5.6 First Hearing Dispute Resolution Appointment (FHDRA)

The Revised Private Law Programme sets out the procedure at the FHDRA. The parties and a Cafcass officer are required to attend the hearing, and a mediator may attend where available. The Cafcass officer will speak to each party at court individually before the hearing.

Conciliation will take place in court with a Cafcass officer and with a mediator, if available, to assist the parties in conciliation and resolution of the issues between them. The Revised Private Law Programme provides for the attendance of mediators but leaves the detailed arrangements to be decided at a local level by courts, which means that different courts may have different coverage.

The Revised Private Law Programme provides that at the FHDRA the following matters will be considered.

Safeguarding

The court will inform the parties of the outcome of the safeguarding enquiries carried out by Cafcass and decide whether a risk assessment should be carried out. The court should also decide whether a fact finding hearing is needed to determine allegations which are likely to affect the decision of the court, for example to determine if there has been domestic violence within the family where this is being denied.

Dispute resolution

The court will, with the assistance of the Cafcass officer and any mediator present, seek to conciliate and to resolve all or some of the issues between the parties. The court will identify any remaining issues and consider what other options are available to resolve them, for example further intervention by Cafcass; mediation; collaborative law; use of a parenting plan or attendance at a Parenting Information Programme.

Consent orders

Where agreement is reached at the hearing or submitted in writing to the court, no order shall be made without scrutiny by the court So if safeguarding checks or risk assessment work remain outstanding, the making of the order will be deferred until completion of such work.

Reports

The court shall decide if a report is necessary under s 7 of the CA 1989 to address any welfare issues or other specific considerations. Before ordering a report, the court should consider alternative ways of working with the parties as stated above. If a report is ordered, it should be directed specifically towards and limited to those issues, and the court should state in the order the specific factual and other issues which are to be addressed in a focused report. The s 7 report is usually prepared by a Cafcass officer but can be prepared by a local authority if it has had involvement with the family. The court will consider the evidence Cafcass provides about the extent and nature of the local authority's recent involvement with the family before deciding who should prepare the report. The reporter will have access to the court file and, depending on the nature of the report ordered, will interview the parties and/or the child, may visit the parties' homes and interview anyone else who appears relevant, such as a grandparent or a school teacher. A written report will be prepared which will often include conclusions and recommendations, for example as to what order should be made. The report should be filed with the court at least 14 days before the final hearing and should be made available to the parties.

The President's Interim Guidance (see **13.1.1**) set out, amongst other points, a timeframe for the expected delivery of s 7 reports:

(a) 6 weeks for a wishes and feelings report;

(b) 6 weeks for a single issue report;

(c) 6–12 weeks for a report dealing with more than one issue; and

(d) 6–8 weeks for a s 16A risk assessment.

It was recognised that these timeframes were rarely being met in practice, but the Guidance required Cafcass to work to eliminate backlogs and to reduce delays so that delivery came within the expected timeframe.

Expert evidence

The court is also required to consider if any expert evidence is required and to make directions accordingly. The court must give leave before any medical or psychiatric examination or other assessment of the child takes place for the purpose of preparation of expert evidence in proceedings, to protect the child from unnecessary and repeated assessment. In practice, the court tends to prefer to rely on the s 7 report.

If it is necessary to instruct an expert, the court must comply with the Practice Direction, 'Experts in Family Proceedings Relating to Children', 1 April 2008, which applies to all family proceedings relating to children. The aim of the guidance is to provide the court with early information to decide if expert evidence will assist the court to:

(a) identify, narrow and, where possible, agree the issues between the parties;
(b) provide an opinion about a question that is not within the skill and experience of the court;
(c) encourage the early identification of questions that need to be answered by an expert; and
(d) encourage disclosure of full and frank information between the parties, the court and any expert instructed.

The Practice Direction gives very detailed guidance on the duties of experts and of the parties proposing to instruct the expert.

Wishes and feelings of the child

The court is to consider how the wishes and feelings of the child are to be ascertained (if at all) and how the child is to be involved in the proceedings (if at all). This may involve consideration of joining the child as a party.

Case management

The court is to establish what issues are agreed and what issues remain to be determined.

The court must also consider making any interim orders which may be useful, such as indirect or supervised contact.

Witness statements

The court must make directions to actively case manage the application and to ensure it is ready for final hearing. This will include directing the preparation and filing of witness statements. It is usual for the parties to file witness statements and, as no document can be filed or served without the court's leave, the court will have to make directions for this.

A witness statement must be signed and dated, and include a statement of truth (FPR 2010, r 17.2).

Hearsay evidence may be included (as in other civil proceedings). So, for example, a children and family reporter can include in his report a remark made in a conversation with the child's schoolteacher that 'the child was always upset on the Mondays following a visit to his father'. The court can decide what weight to give to such evidence.

It is not usual for a child to be called to give evidence, but in *Re W (Children)* [2010] UKSC 12, which was a public law application, it was held that the existing presumption against a child giving evidence, which needed to be rebutted by anyone seeking to put questions to the child, could not be reconciled with the approach of the European Court of Human Rights and that, in deciding to call a child to give evidence, the court would have to carry out a balancing exercise between the advantages that that would bring to the determination of the truth and the damage it could do to the welfare of that child or any other child.

Timetabling further hearings

In accordance with the 'no delay' principle, the court will need to list the next hearing date. The court must also list the case for final hearing. Usually, a Final Directions Appointment will also be timetabled to take place when all the evidence and any welfare report has been filed. This will consider what evidence can be agreed and what is in dispute, together with final arrangements for the hearing.

Transfer to the family proceedings court

The case should be transferred to the family proceedings court in accordance with the Allocation and Transfer of Proceedings Order 2008 unless one of the specified exceptions applies (see **13.8.4.4**).

The order

The Revised Private Law Programme specifies what matters should be set out in the order made at the FHDRA and suggests use of Form PLP10 as a template.

13.8.6 Judgment

The Final Hearing will be held in chambers before the appropriate judge. The applicant's solicitor should ensure that the relevant bundle of documents is prepared and lodged with the court at least two working days before the hearing, in accordance with FPR 2010, Practice Direction 27A. Sanctions are available for failure to comply with this Practice Direction, such as costs orders or removing the case from the list.

Judgment must be delivered as soon as possible after the Final Hearing. Orders must be in writing and a record of any finding of fact and the reasons for the decision will be kept on the file. A copy of the order must be served on each party and on any person with whom the child is living.

13.8.6.1 Section 91(14) order

In addition to deciding on the s 8 application, the court also can order that no further application is made without leave of the court (see also **14.5.4**). This can be ordered, for example, when there have been repeated and protracted Children Act proceedings, and the court feels it is in the best interests of the child to have a break from them. In the case of *Re P (Section 91(14) Guidelines) (Residence and Religious Heritage)* [1999] 2 FLR 573, the Court of Appeal set out guidelines extracted from earlier cases on the making of orders under s 91(14). These guidelines include that on the making of such an order, the child's welfare is the paramount consideration and that the power should be used sparingly and be the exception, not the rule.

13.8.6.2 Costs

It is general practice not to order costs in children cases, although it may be appropriate to do so if the parent goes beyond what is reasonable. This means unreasonableness in relation to the conduct of the litigation, rather than unreasonableness in relation to the child. In *Re G (Costs: Child Case)* [1999] 2 FLR 250, the court drew a distinction between 'hopeless' and 'unreasonable' applications. In that case, although the court considered the father's application for a residence order was hopeless, it was not in itself unreasonable. However, it is possible that the stage will be reached where the pursuit of a hopeless application becomes, in itself, unreasonable. In *Re T (A Child) (Order for Costs)* [2005] EWCA Civ 311 the court made an order for costs against a mother who, it found, was behaving unreasonably in obstructing contact, and in *Re J (Costs of Fact Finding Hearing)* [2009] EWCA Civ 1350 a father was ordered to pay two-thirds of the mother's costs of a fact finding hearing where many of the allegations of domestic violence which were denied by the father were proved.

13.8.7 Duration of s 8 orders

Section 8 orders, except for residence orders, will normally be expressed to cease to have effect when the child reaches 16 years of age (CA 1989, s 91(10)). The court has power in exceptional circumstances to make or extend a specific issue, contact or prohibited steps order beyond the child's 16th birthday (CA 1989, s 9(6)). In any event, all s 8 orders will end when the child reaches 18 years of age (CA 1989, s 91(11)).

If a residence or contact order is made in favour of a parent, these orders will automatically end if the child's parents live together for a continuous period of more than six months (CA 1989, s 11(5) and (6)). The only difference between the two types of orders is that a residence order will automatically end in the circumstances only if both parents have parental responsibility.

CHECKLIST FOR THE PROCEDURE FOR A CONTESTED S 8 APPLICATION IN THE COUNTY COURT

OBTAIN LEGAL REPRESENTATION IF RELEVANT

↓

OBTAIN LEAVE OF THE COURT IF NECESSARY

↓

A FILES AT COURT:
(i) Application: Form C100 or Form C2 (existing family proceedings), Form C1A (if harm alleged) and Form FM1 and copies for Cafcass and every respondent
(ii) Fee [Legal Representation (LR) Certificate]
[(iii) Notice of Acting (if necessary)]

↓

A SERVES ON R:
(i) Copy Application (and Form C1A if filed)
(ii) Notice of Proceedings (Form C6)
(iii) Blank Acknowledgement (Form C7)
[(iv) Notice of Issue of LR Certificate]
[(v) Copy Notice of Acting (if necessary)]
[Give at least 14 days' notice of first hearing]

↓

A FILES AT COURT:
Statement of Service (Form C9)

↓

R FILES AND SERVES:
Completed Acknowledgement [within 14 days] and Form C1A (if necessary)

↓

ATTEND FHDRA:
Conciliation and directions
[Court fixes next hearing date]

↓

PREPARE FOR HEARING
(i) Witness statements filed and exchanged
(ii) Welfare report filed at least 14 days before hearing
(iii) Bundle lodged and written estimate of length of hearing if necessary

↓

FINAL DIRECTIONS APPOINTMENT

↓

ATTEND HEARING:
Before a judge in chambers

↓

ORDER MADE:
Served on each party

Note: The procedure followed in the High Court or family proceedings court is broadly similar.

13.9 Protection of children

This section deals with emergency situations concerning children. It covers the threatened abduction of the child, recovering a child already removed from the UK, general emergency protection of a child by a parent or other interested person and, lastly, an outline of how a local authority may protect children.

13.9.1 Abduction of children

If a child is not returned to the parent with whom he lives following an agreed visit to the other parent and abduction is suspected, a legal adviser needs to assess the situation quickly and obtain such protection as the law offers to try to ensure that the child is returned as soon as possible. A list of relevant considerations is set out at **13.9.1.1** to **13.9.1.7** below.

13.9.1.1 Has a s 8 order already been made?

If the parent with whom the child normally lives already has a residence order in his or her favour, this will contain a provision preventing the other parent removing the child from the UK without consent of the parent with the residence order or consent of the court (CA 1989, s 13(1) and see **13.3.1**). This provision can be enforced by the court by an order that the child be produced to the parent with the residence order (CA 1989, s 14; FLA 1986, s 34).

If there is no s 8 order in force, a without notice application for a residence order or prohibited steps order could be applied for and then enforced by the court.

A court has the power, in proceedings for or relating to an order under s 8, to order any person who may have information as to the child's whereabouts to disclose it to the court (FLA 1986, s 33). This could be used to force relations or friends of the abductor to disclose addresses or likely destinations.

13.9.1.2 Family Law Act 1986

If a child has been removed from the jurisdiction of the English courts to another part of the UK, for example to Scotland or Northern Ireland, this Act enables a s 8 order to be recognised and enforced by the local court. In order for this to be done, the s 8 order must first be registered with the appropriate court in the other part of the UK.

13.9.1.3 Child Abduction Act 1984

The Child Abduction Act 1984 (CAA 1984) (see **Appendix 1(D)**) contains criminal offences which will be committed if a child is removed without the appropriate consents, irrespective of whether any residence order is in force:

(a) It is an offence for a parent of a child, or any person with parental responsibility for a child, to take or send that child out of the UK without either the consent of all persons with parental responsibility, or the leave of the court (CAA 1984, s 1).

However, no offence is committed by a person in whose favour a residence order is in force who takes or sends the child out of the UK for a period of less than a month. There are also provisions in the Act, which apply where no residence order has been made, which provide a defence if the person who removes the child either reasonably believes that he has consent, or has taken all reasonable steps to obtain it.

If, following divorce, no s 8 order has been made, neither parent will be in contempt of court if they remove the child without the consent of the other under the CA 1989 as each has parental responsibility. However, neither can take the child out of the UK for any time whatsoever without committing a criminal offence under the CAA 1984, unless they obtain the appropriate consents.

(b) It is also an offence for any person, except a person with parental responsibility for a child, to take that child from any other person who has lawful control of the child without lawful authority or reasonable excuse (CAA 1984, s 2).

This will not affect married parents. However, a putative father who has not obtained parental responsibility will commit the s 2 offence, but has a defence if he can show that he had reasonable grounds for believing that he was the child's father. He will nevertheless be liable under s 1 (above) if he takes the child abroad, unless he has the mother's consent.

Difficult ethical problems can arise for a solicitor if a client informs him that he intends to abduct his child from the mother. There is a duty of confidentiality towards a client, but a solicitor cannot ignore the interests of the child and must decide which duty prevails. A solicitor in this situation should discuss the issue with the Solicitors Regulation Authority's Professional Ethics Department (see the Law Society's Family Law Protocol, para 3.4.10). It is important that a solicitor ensures that a client is made fully aware of the consequences of the crime he is proposing to commit and that the solicitor does not assist him to commit it.

13.9.1.4 'Port alert' procedure

The provisions in both the CA 1989 and the CAA 1984 may deter a potential abductor but do not contain any practical safeguards actually to prevent a determined abductor from removing the child. The 'port alert' procedure is designed physically to prevent a child from being taken abroad. The detail of this procedure is set out in *Practice Direction (Minor: Preventing Removal Abroad)* [1986] 1 WLR 475.

It is operated by the police on a 24-hour basis. If instituted, the police will liaise with immigration or security officials at ports and airports to try to find and stop the child from being taken abroad. The police have the power to arrest without warrant. There is no need for a s 8 order to have been obtained if the child is under 16, although if there is an order it should be produced to the police. The system is available for children over 16 only if, unusually, a s 8 order exists. The police will operate the port alert procedure only if they are satisfied that there is a real and imminent risk that a child will be taken out of the UK. 'Imminent' is taken to mean within 24 to 48 hours, and 'real' means that the system is not being used just as insurance.

Application should be made to a police station (preferably the applicant's local station) with full details of the grounds for applying, the child, the person likely to remove the child, the applicant, the likely destination, and the likely time of travel and port of embarcation. Any other helpful information should also be given, as well as recent photographs of the child and the abductor. If the police feel that the requirements are satisfied, they will put the child's name on a stop list which is circulated to all ports and airports. The child will remain on this list for four weeks, and will then be removed unless a further application is made.

13.9.1.5 Passports

Preventing issue of a passport

If the child does not have a passport already, it is possible for an interested party to give written notice to the Identity and Passport Service that a passport should not be issued to a child without the consent of the court, or of both parents or others (*Practice Direction (Minor: Preventing Removal Abroad)* [1986] 1 All ER 983). In *Hamilton Jones v David & Snape (A Firm)* [2003] EWHC 3147 (Ch), solicitors were found negligent in failing to re-register children with the passport agency or advising the mother to do so.

Surrender of passports

If the above provision is not applicable as the child already has a passport, an order can be obtained for the surrender of the relevant passport. This can be done only if there is in existence an order prohibiting or restricting the removal of the child from the UK. A without notice application for a residence order or a prohibited steps order may therefore need to be made. If a residence order or other s 8 order (eg a prohibited steps order) has been obtained, the court that made the order can order any person to surrender the child's passport, or any other passport which includes details of the child.

If a contact order has been made, it is possible to include a direction that the parent exercising contact must lodge his passport with his solicitor during contact visits. Care must be taken by a solicitor acting for the parent with contact in these circumstances, as if this involves giving an undertaking to the court, there will be a conflict of interest if the client subsequently requests the return of the passport in breach of any undertaking given. If the solicitor returns the passport to his client, this will be a matter of professional misconduct, as well as a contempt of court which could lead to a fine or imprisonment. If the client has given an undertaking to the court to lodge his passport with his solicitor, again the solicitor should not aid or abet his client to disobey a lawful court order (see Outcome 5.3 of the SRA Code of Conduct 2011).

13.9.1.6 Recovering a child abducted abroad

If the child has been removed from the UK, the abductor will have committed a criminal offence under the CAA 1984, but this by itself will not bring about the return of the child. Provisions do exist to obtain an order from the country to which the child has been taken to return the child. The Child Abduction and Custody Act 1985 (CACA 1985) brought the provisions of the Hague Convention on International Child Abduction into force in this country. If a child is taken to a country which is a party to this Convention, it is possible to request the return of the child. This will usually be ordered if less than one year has elapsed since the removal. After this time the child will still be returned, unless settled in his new environment. The CACA 1985 also brought the provisions of the European Convention on Recognition and Enforcement of Custody Decisions into force. This should also mean that provided the country to which the child has been taken is a party to the Convention, an order can be obtained for the return of the child, although there are certain grounds on which the court in the country to which the child has been taken can decide that it is in the child's best interests to remain there.

Reference should be made to the CACA 1985 and specialist textbooks for the detail of this area.

International child abduction is a specialist area and solicitors should take specialist advice. Solicitors should discuss all such cases with the Department of Constitutional Affairs' Child Abduction Unit. A source of general advice and support for clients with problems in this area is an organisation called Reunite, the International Child Abduction Centre.

13.9.1.7 Practical advice

In considering the legal steps which can be taken in this area, the solicitor must remind the client of the practical steps that can be taken to prevent an abduction occurring. These could include notifying the child's school to ensure that the child will not be collected by the potential abductor, in serious cases refusing to allow unsupervised contact, ensuring that the child's passport is kept safe and ensuring that the telephone number of the local police station is kept to hand.

13.9.2 General protection of children

The protection a child needs may relate to a wide range of issues. It might concern a medical issue, an abortion, a proposed marriage, a change of name or religion, or protection from a violent parent. Those with parental responsibility may not be prepared to make a decision, or may have made a decision with which another interested party disagrees. In this situation, a s 8 order may be used by parents and others to obtain a court decision. In urgent cases, all s 8 orders can be obtained without notice.

The availability and flexibility of s 8 orders means that there is less need to resort to the High Court's wardship jurisdiction. However, there is no restriction on anyone (other than a local authority) making a child a ward of court. If this is done, parental responsibility will vest in the High Court. The High Court will also have the power to make any s 8 order, unless the child is also subject to a care order.

13.9.3 Protection of a child by the local authority

The CA 1989 introduced a new legal framework for care and supervision orders (see **Chapter 14**).

A care or supervision order can be applied for only by the local authority, or by the NSPCC. The effect of a care order will be to vest parental responsibility in the local authority, who will then take over responsibility for the child from his parents or other carers, including deciding where he lives. A supervision order gives someone, usually a social worker, the duty to oversee the child, who will generally remain living in his home.

The 1989 Act also introduced new orders for the emergency protection of children. These are:

(a) emergency protection orders: these are usually obtained by the local authority to protect the child in an urgent case where, because of some neglect or abuse, it is essential to remove the child from his home immediately;

(b) child assessment orders: these can be used by the local authority to ensure that an essential examination or other assessment of the child, for example a medical examination, can be undertaken in circumstances where the parents are unco-operative and where the local authority suspects some harm is occurring but does not have enough evidence to bring care proceedings.

13.10 Financial provision and property orders for children

The law relating to financial provision and property orders for children is complex and is scattered throughout a number of statutes. This section summarises and cross-refers the main provisions, as well as dealing with the financial provisions contained in the CA 1989.

The following jurisdictions are relevant:

(a) maintenance under the CSA 1991;

(b) maintenance and property orders in matrimonial proceedings under the MCA 1973;

(c) maintenance and lump sums during marriage under the DPMCA 1978;

(d) financial relief under the CA 1989.

13.10.1 Maintenance under the Child Support Act 1991

The maintenance of most children is currently dealt with by the Child Support Agency using the statutory formula. The CSA 1991 has ousted the court's jurisdiction to make maintenance orders in the majority of cases (see **Chapter 7**).

The Agency will have jurisdiction whether the parents are married or unmarried, but can make an order only if the parents are no longer living together. Orders can be made in favour of children under 16 years of age, and those under 19 years of age who are in full-time education. The Agency does not have jurisdiction to deal with step-children or children over 19 years still in full-time education, and in these cases application will have to be made to the courts to determine maintenance. Other situations where the courts can still be used include payment of school fees and, in wealthy families, when an amount exceeding the maximum figure payable by the Agency's calculation is sought, and also where the child lives abroad.

13.10.2 Maintenance and property orders in matrimonial proceedings

If a parent is involved in divorce, judicial separation or nullity proceedings, he could apply for a lump sum or property adjustment order for a child of the family as part of these proceedings (see **Chapter 4**). However, in practice, unless the family is wealthy, relatively few orders of this type are made in favour of children.

Apart from the situations mentioned above (see **13.10.1**), maintenance will generally be dealt with by the Child Support Agency.

13.10.3 Maintenance and lump sums during marriage

A married parent can apply during marriage for a maintenance order and a lump sum order of up to £1,000 for a child of the family from the other parent. This can be done using the DPMCA 1978 in the family proceedings court (see **4.9.2**), or s 27 of the MCA 1973 in the county court (see **4.9.1**). However, in most cases, maintenance will be dealt with by the Child Support Agency under the CSA 1991 as the courts will have no jurisdiction.

13.10.4 Financial relief under the Children Act 1989

Section 15 of and Sch 1 to the CA 1989 enable a parent (for these purposes, 'parent' includes an unmarried parent, a parent with whom the child does not reside (*Re S (Child: Financial Provision)* [2004] EWCA Civ 1685), a step-parent and a civil partner), guardian, anyone with a residence order in their favour or a child to apply for the following orders against one or both parents of a child:

(a) periodical payments to the applicant for the benefit of the child, or to the child direct;

(b) lump sum to the applicant for the benefit of the child, or to the child direct;

(c) settlement of property for the benefit of the child;

(d) transfer of property to the applicant for the benefit of the child or to the child direct.

Application can be made to the High Court or county court for any of the orders. An application to the family proceedings court can be made only for periodical payments and/or a lump sum up to £1,000.

If the child lives abroad with one parent and the other parent lives in the UK, the court can make orders for periodical payments only.

There is no limit to the amount of orders for periodical payments or lump sum orders, but the court can make only one order for either a settlement of property or a transfer of property for the child. In *Phillips v Peace* [2004] EWHC 3180 (Fam), where a settlement of property order had already been made for the child, the mother, who wanted capital to buy a larger home, was precluded from applying for a further settlement of property or property adjustment order. She therefore applied for a lump sum to fund the rehousing, on conditions including that it was to be repaid to the father when the child was older. The court stated that a lump sum was not intended to revert to the payer and that the proposals would produce an effect so close to a settlement that it would be tantamount to varying the settlement or ordering a second settlement, which it could not do.

The principles which the court must use in deciding whether to make an order are broadly similar to s 25 of the MCA 1973. This means that the child's welfare is not paramount when deciding financial provision (*K v K (Minors: Property Transfer)* [1992] 2 FLR 220). In very wealthy families, standard of living is to be considered as part of all the circumstances even though it is not included specifically in the checklist in Sch 1 (*F v G (Child: Financial Provision)* [2005] 1 FLR 261).

The provisions in the CA 1989 are rarely needed by married parents as they will normally apply only on marriage breakdown, when the MCA 1973 can be used for lump sums and property adjustment orders, and the CSA 1991 will be used for maintenance. However, the CA 1989 can be very important to an unmarried parent as it can be used to obtain property orders for the benefit of the child, which could secure the right for the child and the caring parent to occupy the home (*J v J (A Minor: Property Transfer)* [1993] 2 FLR 56). In *Re P (Child Financial Provision)* [2003] EWCA Civ 837, which involved a very wealthy father, the Court of Appeal gave guidance on how applications involving very wealthy parents should be dealt with. The Court said that the starting point should be to determine the home that needed to be provided, and then to decide the lump sum needed, usually to furnish the home and to provide a car. Then the court should determine what budget the carer required and, in assessing this, should recognise the responsibility and often the sacrifice of the carer. The Court of Appeal said that the budget should reflect the social and financial position of the carer and the absent parent.

The order must be for the benefit of the child and can include money to pay a parent's legtal costs. See *Re S (Child: Financial Provision)* [2004] EWCA Civ 1685, where the court was asked to make financial orders in favour of a mother whose child had been wrongfully retained by the father in Sudan after a contact visit. The money was to be used by the mother to travel to the Sudan to have contact with the child and to enforce the child's return through the Sudanese courts. The Court of Appeal did not finally decide the matter, but indicated that the courts should give the term 'for the benefit of the child' a wide construction.

The court can make any s 8 order it considers necessary in the financial proceedings.

13.10.5 Summary of financial orders for children

13.10.5.1 Parties divorcing

(a) CSA 1991 for maintenance;

(b) MCA 1973 for lump sum/property adjustment order.

13.10.5.2 Parties staying married

(a) CSA 1991 for maintenance;

(b) DPMCA 1978 for £1,000 maximum lump sum;

(c) MCA 1973, s 27 for lump sum;

(d) CA 1989 for lump sum/property adjustment order.

13.10.5.3 Parties never married

(a) CSA 1991 for maintenance;

(b) CA 1989 for lump sum/property adjustment order.

13.11 Chapter summary

(1) Issues concerning children are dealt with under the CA 1989.

(2) Married parents have joint parental responsibility for their child. An unmarried mother has parental responsibility but an unmarried father does not, although he can acquire it by:

    (a) registration on the child's birth certificate;

    (b) court order;

    (c) residence order;

    (d) parental responsibility agreement;

    (e) guardianship;

    (f) marriage to mother.

    Step-parents and civil partners can also acquire parental responsibility.

(3) The court can make s 8 orders. These are:

    (a) residence orders;

- (b) contact orders;
- (c) prohibited steps orders; and
- (d) specific issue orders.

(4) When making any order, the court must consider:

- (a) the welfare principle;
- (b) the 'no order' presumption; and
- (c) the principle of avoiding delay.

(5) When applying the welfare principle, the court must pay attention to the factors in s 1(3):

- (a) the ascertainable wishes and feelings of the child;
- (b) the child's physical, emotional and educational needs;
- (c) the likely effect on the child of any change in circumstances;
- (d) the child's age, sex, background, etc;
- (e) any harm the child has suffered/may suffer;
- (f) the capability of the parents (and other relevant people) to care for the child; and
- (g) the range of powers available to the court.

(6) A checklist for the procedure for a contested s 8 application is set out below.

(7) There are various procedures available to try to prevent the abduction of a child. The CAA 1984 is also relevant.

(8) Financial provision for children can be obtained under several different jurisdictions, including the CA 1989.

Chapter 14
Children: Public Law

14.1	Introduction	205
14.2	Local authority support for children and families (CA 1989, Pt III)	206
14.3	Preventing neglect or abuse	209
14.4	Care and supervision orders (CA 1989, Pt IV)	211
14.5	Contact (s 34)	215
14.6	Discharge of care orders (s 39)	216
14.7	Effect of a supervision order	217
14.8	Care or supervision order	218
14.9	Interim orders (s 38)	218
14.10	Emergency protection and assessment (CA 1989, Pt V)	220
14.11	Procedure for care and supervision orders	223
14.12	Human rights implications	230
14.13	Compensation for local authority failings	232
14.14	Special guardianship order	232
14.15	Chapter summary	232

14.1 Introduction

The CA 1989 introduced fundamental changes to child law, and this chapter considers those changes in relation to public law proceedings. The Act followed a number of reviews and reports, notably the *Cleveland Report*, which expressed concern that the local authority had acted too precipitately in removing children from their parents. Paradoxically, in other cases, the concern was that the authority had not acted promptly enough. One of the aims of the Act was to have a more balanced approach to the protection of children. Central to this is the concept of partnership: partnership between the local authority and parents, and co-operation between all the agencies relevant to the child's well-being. To this end, the Act is supplemented by guidance in a document called 'Working Together to Safeguard Children: A guide to inter-agency working to safeguard and promote the welfare of children' (TSO, 2010) (together with various regulations). Although 'Working Together to Safeguard Children' does not have the force of statute, the guidance must be complied with and can be departed from only if good reasons can be shown.

Recent tragic cases have highlighted, however, that there is still much progress to be made in the area of child protection. Following the death of Victoria Climbie at the hands of her great aunt and the man they lived with in 2001, Lord Laming, who chaired the inquiry into her death, made specific recommendations to improve the implementation of the child protection system which had failed to adequately protect her. The Government responded by issuing a green paper, *Every Child Matters*, in 2003 and *Every Child Matters: Next Steps* in 2004, and enacting the resulting Children Act 2004.

Sadly, the death of Baby Peter in 2007 revealed continuing inadequacies in the implementation of the child protection system, and in 2008 the Government asked Lord Laming to undertake an independent progress report on child protection in England following that tragic death. Lord Laming's report, *The Protection of Children in England: A Progress Report*, was published in March 2009 and made many recommendations. The Government accepted all his recommendations and published its response in May 2009. One of its responses was to revise *Working Together* (republished in March 2010) to take account of Lord Laming's recommendations to strengthen policy and practice, and to place a stronger focus on the perspective of the child. Also, the Ministry of Justice issued a *Best Practice Guide: Preparing for*

Care and Supervision Proceedings in August 2009 to complement the statutory guidance and the Public Law Outline (the Practice Direction which governed procedure in applications for care and supervision orders).

On 17 March 2010 the Government published 'Establishment of a system-wide target for reducing delays in care and supervision proceedings', an inter-agency approach to reducing unnecessary delay in care and supervision proceedings, which came into force on 1 April 2010.

14.2 Local authority support for children and families (CA 1989, Pt III)

14.2.1 Introduction

The Act imposes responsibilities on local authorities to provide certain services, in particular for 'children in need' (see **14.2.3**). The local authority has to make an initial assessment as to whether a child is a 'child in need'. The local authority then has to decide how to discharge its responsibilities to that child, either by providing services directly or by facilitating their provision by, for example, voluntary organisations.

14.2.2 Prevention of harm

Every local authority must take reasonable steps through the provision of services to prevent children in its area suffering ill-treatment or neglect. There is also a related duty to take reasonable steps to reduce the need to bring care or supervision proceedings.

14.2.3 Children in need

14.2.3.1 Definition of a child 'in need'

A child is to be taken to be 'in need' if:

(a) he is unlikely to achieve or maintain, or to have the opportunity of achieving or maintaining, a reasonable standard of health or development without the provision for him of services by a local authority; or

(b) his health or development is likely to be significantly impaired, or further impaired, without the provision for him of such services; or

(c) he is disabled (s 17(10)).

The definition therefore includes not just those children who are suffering, but also those who may be prejudiced in the future, if assistance is not provided for them.

'Development' is defined as physical, intellectual, emotional, social or behavioural development; 'health' as meaning physical or mental health; and 'disabled' as blind, deaf, dumb, suffering from mental disorder, or substantially and permanently handicapped by illness, injury or congenital deformity.

The definition of 'in need' is therefore very wide and reflects the Act's emphasis on local authorities taking preventative action through the provision of support services to families and commencing court proceedings only where absolutely necessary to protect the child.

The linking of 'need' to the provision of 'services' means that an authority could not identify a child as 'in need' and at the same time refuse to provide any service to meet that need. However, although the authority is obliged to provide some service to meet the child's needs, it has a discretion in deciding which service and at what level. In *R v London Borough of Barnet, ex p B* [1994] 1 FLR 592, the court held that the obligations placed on a local authority to provide services must be subject to the ability to do so within its own budget restraints.

14.2.3.2 Duty to children in need (s 17)

It is the duty of every local authority:

(a) to safeguard and promote the welfare of children within its area who are in need; and

(b) so far as is consistent with that duty, to promote the upbringing of such children by their families,

by providing a range and level of services appropriate to those children's needs.

Any service provided by the authority to the child can also be provided to the child's family or any member of the family, if it is provided with a view to safeguarding or promoting the child's welfare. 'Family' is widely defined to include any person with parental responsibility and any other person with whom the child is living.

A local authority could provide a range of services to help the parents cope with a child with disabilities, for example: a home help, day-care provision (whether for the disabled child or another child in the household) and a short-term placement for the child to relieve the carers.

In support of the general duty under s 17 to provide services, local authorities are given a number of specific duties, such as to provide day-care services for pre-school children in need and to provide family centres. The definition of a family centre in Sch 2, para 9 is a centre where family members may attend for, among other things, advice, guidance or counselling and may be provided with accommodation while receiving advice, guidance or counselling.

14.2.4 Provision of accommodation (s 20)

A local authority must provide accommodation for any child in need within its area if there is no person who has parental responsibility for him, he is lost or abandoned, or the person who has been caring for him is prevented (whether or not permanently and for whatever reason) from providing him with suitable accommodation or care.

14.2.4.1 Limits on providing accommodation

A local authority may not provide accommodation if anyone with parental responsibility, who is willing and able to provide accommodation, objects. This means that if both parents have parental responsibility and one places the child in accommodation, the other parent can remove him.

The right of a person with parental responsibility to object does not apply if a person or persons with a residence order in their favour agree to the child being accommodated.

Also, the right of a person with parental responsibility to remove a child in these circumstances does not apply where the child is aged 16 or over and the child agrees to being accommodated by the local authority (s 20(11)). This is a reflection of the principle of allowing the mature child more say in important decisions, such as where he or she should live.

14.2.4.2 Preventing removal from accommodation

The local authority should ensure that all those with parental responsibility are involved in the initial negotiations and agree on the provision of accommodation to avoid any subsequent problems. However, it is always open to a person with parental responsibility to remove the child at any time without notice.

If there is a risk that one parent may seek to remove the child, the authority may suggest that the other seeks a residence order (which may be granted without notice) to prevent the removal (a local authority cannot itself apply for a residence order (s 9(2)).

If that is not appropriate, or if both parents are seeking the child's return which the authority does not consider to be in the child's best interests, it could apply for an emergency protection order or interim care order.

14.2.5 Children 'looked after' by a local authority

Children who are in care (pursuant to a care order) or provided with accommodation (for a continuous period of more than 24 hours) are 'looked after' by the authority. This also includes children accommodated by a local authority under an emergency protection order, or in police protection (see **14.10**).

When an authority is 'looking after' a child, it is acting in a parental role. It is under a duty to safeguard and promote the child's welfare and to make use of services available for children (ie under Pt III).

It is central to the philosophy of the Act that an authority should seek to act in consultation (and, it is hoped, agreement) with all interested parties. Before making any decision with regard to the child it must find out, if reasonably practicable, the wishes and feelings of the child, parents and other relevant persons. Any decision should give due consideration to those wishes and to the child's religious persuasion, racial origin, and cultural and linguistic background.

Where the child is accommodated is of crucial importance. To foster the prospect of rehabilitation, the authority should first consider whether it is practicable for the child to live with a member of his family or other persons connected with him. If it is not practicable, consideration should be given to placing the child near to the family home.

14.2.6 Significance of the provision of services

As already seen, so far as it is consistent with the child's welfare, the local authority's duty under s 17 is to promote the upbringing of the child by his family through the provision of services. The authority should not initiate care proceedings unless there is clear evidence that the provision of services has failed to meet the child's needs, or is unlikely to be successful in meeting them.

In most cases, it is better to advise the parents to co-operate and throw the onus onto the local authority to show it has done everything reasonable to assist the child and his parents.

Accordingly, in appropriate circumstances, a local authority should be required to explain:

(a) what steps it took to identify the child as being in need;

(b) what its plans are if a care order is made; in particular, what services it would then provide which it could not provide without a court order;

(c) what evidence there is that what the authority is seeking to achieve by means of a court order could not be more satisfactorily achieved by the provision of appropriate services, with the child remaining at home.

In *Re K (Supervision Orders)* [1999] 2 FLR 303, the court said it was wrong to make a supervision order where the duties imposed on the local authority (under Pt III) would sufficiently meet the child's needs.

14.2.7 Challenging the local authority

There is no provision in Pt III for compelling a local authority to provide services. Neither can a specific issue order be used for that purpose. The courts have said that a local authority's powers and duties under Pt III should not be subject to judicial scrutiny except by way of judicial review (*Re J (Specific Issue Order: Leave to Apply)* [1995] 1 FLR 669).

14.2.7.1 Complaints procedure (s 26)

Every local authority must establish a procedure for considering representations about the discharge of any of its functions under Pt III.

If dissatisfied with the local authority's response, the complainant can require that the matter is referred to a review panel which must then make a recommendation. Although the ultimate decision remains with the local authority, if it ignores the panel's findings, or fails to give satisfactory reasons for not implementing the recommendation, its actions may be subject to judicial review. In *Re T (Accommodation by Local Authority)* [1995] 1 FLR 159, the court quashed the refusal of the authority to ratify the recommendation of the panel on the basis that it had failed to take into account the correct considerations in deciding that the child's welfare would not be seriously prejudiced by not being accommodated.

14.2.7.2 Judicial review

Only in exceptional circumstances will the court consider an application for judicial review where the statutory right of appeal under the complaints procedure has not been exhausted (*R v London Borough of Brent, ex p S* [1994] 1 FLR 203). Even if the statutory procedures have been exhausted, judicial review is unlikely to be successful if there has been a genuine and fair consultation. In *R v London Borough of Barnet, ex p B* [1994] 1 FLR 592, the court said that it is essentially a matter for the local authority, not the court, to decide what consideration and what weight should be given to the circumstances of any given child. In *Re T (Judicial Review: Local Authority Decisions Concerning Child in Need)* [2003] EWHC 2515 (Admin), the court confirmed it could only direct the local authority to reconsider the services it should provide by quashing the local authority's decision and directing reconsideration, it could not direct the local authority to take a particular course.

In *R (CD) v Isle of Anglesey County Council* [2005] 1 FLR 59, the court found that the local authority's care plan for a 15-year-old girl with cerebral palsy, who was being accommodated under s 20 of the CA 1989, was unlawful, as it failed to provide services appropriate to her needs and did not give due consideration to her wishes.

14.3 Preventing neglect or abuse

A central feature of the provisions for the protection of children is that this should be done in partnership with the family and in full consultation with other relevant agencies and professionals. Any assessment of the child should, wherever possible, be done following consultation and with the family's co-operation. The authority should seek to agree any protection plan for the child with the parents.

14.3.1 Court-directed investigation (s 37)

The court has no power to direct a local authority to commence proceedings for a care or supervision order. However, if in any 'family proceedings' where the court is considering the child's welfare, it appears to the court that it may be appropriate for a care or supervision order to be made, the court may direct the authority to investigate the child's circumstances. In deciding whether to make a direction under s 37 (see **Appendix 1(E)**), the child's welfare must be the court's paramount consideration.

'Family proceedings' include divorce, judicial separation, financial relief applications, domestic abuse applications under FLA 1996 and all Children Act proceedings other than emergency provisions (see **14.11.1**).

When undertaking the investigation, the local authority must consider whether it should apply for a care or supervision order, provide services or assistance for the child or his family, or whether to take any other action with respect to the child. If the authority decides not to apply for a care or supervision order it must inform the court within eight weeks (unless otherwise directed) of its reasons and other action, if any, it intends to take.

When directing an investigation, as an exception to the general rule, the court may make an interim care or supervision order without a formal application if satisfied as to the criteria in s 38 (see **14.9**). It would be usual in such circumstances for a children's guardian to be appointed for the child.

14.3.2 Local authority investigation (s 47)

When a child is subject to an emergency protection order, in police protection or where the authority suspects the child is suffering or likely to suffer significant harm, it must investigate the child's circumstances. (See **Appendix 1(E)**.)

The enquiries should involve a detailed assessment of the needs of the child and his family, and may lead to the provision of services under Pt III, including an offer of accommodation. Alternatively, the authority may decide it is necessary to commence proceedings for a care or supervision order (or an emergency protection order if the child's immediate protection is in issue).

As part of its investigation, the authority should normally see the child. If access is refused, or it is denied information as to the child's whereabouts, the authority *must* make an application to the court unless satisfied that his welfare can be safeguarded without such an order (s 47(6)).

14.3.3 Child protection conferences

Where, following an investigation, the local authority considers that there might be a risk of significant harm to the child, the local authority will consider convening a child protection conference.

This is a formal meeting attended by representatives from all the agencies concerned with the child's welfare, ie social services, police, health and education, and often the child's parents. Its purpose is to gather together and evaluate all the relevant information about the child and plan any immediate action which may be necessary to protect the child.

Parents should be encouraged to attend and may bring a solicitor or other person to support them. Certainly, in the case of *R v Cornwall County Council, ex p LH* [2000] 1 FLR 234, the court made it clear that it would be unlawful for a local authority to have a policy of a blanket refusal of attendance of solicitors.

The conference has to decide whether the child should be the subject of a child protection plan. It must do this if it decides that the child is at continuing risk of significant harm under the category of either physical, emotional or sexual abuse, or neglect. If the conference decides that a child protection plan is necessary, it must also formulate an outline child protection plan.

If a child becomes the subject of a child protection plan, this must be reviewed after three months and thereafter at no more than six-monthly intervals at child protection review conferences.

Even if the decision is that the child does not require a child protection plan, the conference may decide what further support and services may be offered to the family.

14.3.4 Recording that a child is the subject of a child protection plan

All local authorities should record that a child is the subject of a child protection plan. Local authorities are required to record this information electronically on a nationally integrated register, the Integrated Children's System (ICS). This register makes agencies and professionals aware of children judged to be at risk of significant harm and enables legitimate enquirers such as police and health professionals to obtain information about children they have concerns about.

The act of registration itself provides no protection and must always be supported by a child protection plan.

14.4 Care and supervision orders (CA 1989, Pt IV)

A care order is an order placing the child in the care of a designated local authority.

A supervision order is an order putting the child under the supervision of a designated local authority, or of a probation officer.

14.4.1 Application

An application for a care order or supervision order can be made only by a local authority (or NSPCC). The court has no power to require a local authority to commence proceedings, nor can it make an order unless there has been an application (*Nottinghamshire County Council v P* [1993] 1 FLR 115).

14.4.2 Grounds for a care or supervision order (s 31)

A court may make a care order or supervision order in respect of a child under 17 only if it is satisfied that:

(a) the child concerned is suffering, or is likely to suffer, significant harm; and

(b) the harm or likelihood of harm is attributable to –

   (i) the care given to the child, or likely to be given to him if the order were not made, not being what it would be reasonable to expect a parent to give to him; or

   (ii) the child's being beyond parental control.

These conditions have become known as the 'threshold criteria', because they are not in themselves grounds for making a care or supervision order but the minimum circumstances which must be found before the court could be justified in making such an order.

Accordingly, in considering an application, the court must approach the matter in two distinct stages. First, it must establish whether the threshold criteria are satisfied and, secondly, if the criteria are satisfied, whether an order should be made and, if so, what type of order, bearing in mind the welfare principle (see **13.4**). Note, however, that the court has power to make a s 8 order (eg a residence order) whether or not the threshold criteria are satisfied (see **13.3**).

14.4.3 Interpreting the criteria

14.4.3.1 Significant harm

The central concept is whether there is harm which is significant. 'Harm' is defined as ill-treatment, or the impairment of health or development, including, for example, impairment suffered from seeing or hearing the ill-treatment of another. These terms are further defined:

(a) 'ill-treatment' includes sexual abuse and forms of ill-treatment which are not physical;

(b) 'health' means physical or mental health;

(c) 'development' covers physical, intellectual, emotional, social or behavioural development.

Where the question of whether the harm suffered by a child is significant turns on the child's health or development, it is necessary to compare his health or development with what could reasonably be expected of a similar child (s 31(10)). In *Re O (A Minor) (Care Order: Education: Procedure)* [1992] 2 FLR 7, it was held that, in relation to a truant child, the comparison should be made with a child attending school rather than one who was not. Where the child has learning difficulties or medical problems it would seem appropriate to compare with a child suffering similar difficulties.

The court must be satisfied that the child is suffering, or is likely to suffer harm.

14.4.3.2 'Is suffering'

In *Re M (A Minor) (Care Order: Threshold Conditions)* [1994] 2 FLR 577, the House of Lords held that the relevant date for ascertaining whether the child is suffering significant harm is either at the hearing of the application for a care or supervision order, or the date on which the local authority initiated 'protective arrangements' for the child, provided there has been no lapse in those arrangements before the hearing of the application. Protective arrangements could, for example, be an emergency protection order, an interim care order or being 'looked after' by the local authority. Accordingly, the court can find that the child is suffering significant harm at the date of the hearing, or alternatively, looking backwards, was so suffering when steps were taken to protect the child, provided these steps have continued in place until the hearing.

14.4.3.3 'Is likely to suffer'

This allows the court to consider whether a child is likely to suffer significant harm in the future, and would enable the court to protect a child where, for example, an acknowledged abuser returns to the household, or where another child has suffered in the same family.

If the facts which form the basis for concern over likely harm in the future are disputed (eg the alleged abuser disputes having previously abused another child), the court will have to make a finding as to whether the facts took place. The standard of proof when assessing the evidence is the balance of probabilities.

In *Re H and R (Child Sexual Abuse: Standard of Proof)* [1996] 1 FLR 80, the court held that 'likely to suffer' meant 'a real possibility, a possibility that cannot sensibly be ignored having regard to the nature and gravity of the feared harm in the particular case'.

The approach which should therefore be adopted is that, first, the local authority must prove the disputed facts on the balance of probabilities. Secondly, on the strength of such facts as are proved, the authority must ask: is there a real possibility that future significant harm will occur?

In *CL v East Riding Yorkshire Council and Others* [2006] EWCA Civ 49, injuries were caused to a child whilst in the care of both parents, which could not be proved to be non-accidental. The Court of Appeal said that if non-accidental injury cannot be proved then the court should not use that injury as a basis for submitting that the threshold criteria are established in relation to that injury and that one or both of the parents are responsible. But the court is allowed to use the parents' behaviour in failing to ensure the child received immediate medical treatment and lying over how the injury occurred, as a basis for reaching the conclusion that a child is likely to suffer significant harm.

14.4.3.4 Causation of the harm

A finding of significant harm or its likelihood is not sufficient. There must be a link between that finding and either the standard of parental care, or the child being beyond parental control.

The standard of care against which parental care is judged is not what it would be reasonable to expect *this* parent to give, but what a hypothetical reasonable parent would give to meet the child's needs. Accordingly, the fact that the parents have their own particular problems (eg low intelligence, addiction, mental or physical disability) does not justify them in providing a lower standard of care.

Where the care of the child is shared between a number of individuals and the child has suffered serious harm through lack of proper care, there is no need to prove that it was due to a failure by one or more indentified individuals before the court can make a care order. See *Lancashire County Council v B* [2000] 1 FLR 583, where a baby had suffered non-accidental head injuries. The House of Lords held that the threshold criteria were met (and a care order was made) even though it was not possible to make a definitive finding of fact on whether the injuries were caused by the parents or the child minder. The court acknowledged that this might mean that innocent parents might face the possibility of losing their child, but held that the factor which outweighed all others was the prospect that any unidentified, and unidentifiable, carers might inflict further damage on the child.

In *Re D (Care Proceedings: Preliminary Hearing)* [2009] EWCA Civ 472 the Court said that if identification of a perpetrator, for example between one of two parents, was not possible, it was a judge's duty to state that as his conclusion and not strain to identify the perpetrator of non-accidental injuries to children. If an individual perpetrator could be properly identified on the balance of probabilities, it was a judge's duty to identify him, but a judge should not start from the premise that it would only be in an exceptional case that it would not be possible to make such an identification. If the judge is not able to identify the perpetrator or perpetrators on the balance of probabilities, it is still important to identify the pool of possible perpetrators (*Re S-B (children) (non-accidental injury)* [2009] UKSC 17).

14.4.3.5 Concurrent applications

Where there has been an application for a care order, the court may be faced with a competing application for a residence order. Before considering the merits of making a residence order, the court should decide whether the criteria for a care order are satisfied, and therefore whether the full range of orders is available to the court (see **14.4.5** and *Re M* (at **14.4.3.2**)).

14.4.4 Welfare principle (s 1)

If the court is satisfied that the threshold criteria are met, it must then decide what order, if any, to make. In doing so, it must apply the principle contained in s 1 (that the welfare of the child is the paramount consideration and that delaying a decision is likely to prejudice the child: see **13.4**), consider the checklist (see **13.5**) and not make an order unless it considers that doing so would be better for the child than making no order at all (see **13.6**).

14.4.5 Orders available to the court

Even if the threshold criteria are satisfied and the court considers that it is in the child's interests to make an order, as applications under Pt IV are 'family proceedings' it is not merely a question of whether to make a care or supervision order.

Under s 1(3)(g), the court is required to have regard to the range of orders available to it. On hearing an application for a care or supervision order, the court may make, amongst others:

(a) a care order *or* supervision order if the threshold criteria are satisfied;

(b) a residence or other s 8 order, whether or not the criteria are satisfied, (however, a residence or contact order cannot be made in favour of a local authority);

(c) a s 8 order in combination with a supervision order if the criteria are satisfied;

(d) a special guardianship order;

(e) a family assistance order under s 16, with the agreement of all the persons (other than the child) named in the order, whether or not the criteria are satisfied.

14.4.6 Care plans

In the application for a care order, the authority should outline what plans it has if a care order is made.

Guidelines on the structure, content and format of care plans for use in court proceedings are set out in Local Authority Circular LAC (99) 29 (12 August 1999) 'Care Plans and Care Proceedings under the Children Act 1989'.

Examples of some of the typical matters to be covered in the care plan are:

(a) the child's identified needs (including needs arising from race, culture, religion or language, special education or health needs) and how those needs might be met;

(b) the aim of the plan and the time-scale;

(c) the proposed placement (type and details) and a contingency plan if the placement breaks down;

(d) other services to be provided to the child and/or the family;

(e) arrangements for contact and reunification; and

(f) the extent to which the wishes of the child, his or her parents and anyone else relevant have been obtained and acted upon, or the reasons why such wishes have been discounted.

Section 31A of the CA 1989 requires the local authority to prepare a care plan in every case in which it seeks a care order. The court will not be able to make a care order until it has considered such a 's 31A care plan'.

Any care plan is carefully scrutinised by the court. If it is not satisfied about material aspects of the care plan (eg where it is proposed to place the child with identified foster-parents, failure to give details as to the foster-parents and the proposed placement) it may refuse to make a care order, or adjourn and invite the local authority to reconsider its care plan (*Re S (Children) and W (A Child)* [2007] EWCA Civ 232). Alternatively, it seems that the court may choose to make an interim order instead, until satisfied about the details of the care plan (*Re W and B, Re W (Care Plan)* [2001] EWCA Civ 757, [2001] 2 FLR 582).

Before making a care order the court must also consider the authority's arrangements for contact and invite the parties to comment (s 34(11)).

14.4.7 Effect of a care order

The order remains in force until the child reaches 18, unless it is brought to an end earlier.

The local authority must receive the child into its care and provide accommodation and maintain the child for the duration of the order.

The care order gives the local authority parental responsibility jointly with any other holder. However, it is not an equal partnership. The authority has the power to determine the extent to which a parent may exercise parental responsibility, provided it is necessary to do so in the child's welfare. However, before making any decision, the authority should take into account the wishes and feelings of the child and parents.

While a care order is in force, as with a residence order, no person may change the child's surname without the written consent of every person with parental responsibility, or leave of the court. In addition, the child may not be removed from the UK without similar consent or leave. This does not prevent the authority arranging for the child's temporary removal for a period of less than one month.

Most other court orders are incompatible with a care order and, accordingly, the making of a care order automatically discharges any s 8 order (but not a s 4 parental responsibility order). Interestingly, however, the fact that the local authority has a care order in relation to a child does not mean that it can prevent the mother from entering into a parental responsibility agreement with the father (*Re X (Parental Responsibility Agreement: Children in Care)* [2000] 1 FLR 517).

On the making of a final care order, the court is effectively handing over responsibility for the child to the local authority. The court cannot impose any conditions on the local authority, nor seek to keep the implementation of the care plan by the local authority under review. This has meant that the local authority can either change the care plan, or simply fail to deliver aspects of the plan without being challenged. There was a significant, but ultimately unsuccessful, challenge to this position using Articles 6 and 8 of the European Convention on Human Rights in *Re S (Minors) (Care Order: Implementation of Care Plan); Re W (Minors) (Care Order: Adequacy of Care Plan)* [2002] UKHL 10, [2002] 1 FLR 815, where the local authority had promised support and therapy for the mother, leading to rehabilitation with the children. This support was not provided, mostly due to a funding crisis at the local authority. The House of Lords stressed the pressing need for the Government to consider whether some court supervision might improve the quality of child care provided by local authorities.

Following this, the Adoption and Children Act 2002 amended s 26 of the CA 1989 and, since 2004, local authorities are required to appoint an Independent Reviewing Officer (IRO) in connection with each child subject to a care order. The care plans for these children must be kept under review, and the IRO must monitor the local authority's performance, make sure the child's views are understood and taken into account, ensure that any matters of concern are brought to the attention of an appropriately senior member of the local authority and, in necessary cases, refer the matter to Cafcass, who will have the power to bring the case back to court for directions. So far, IROs have not made any significant use of this referral system.

14.5 Contact (s 34)

Regular contact with parents and other relatives can be important in enabling the child to adjust to his new environment, and is essential if there is to be a successful rehabilitation with the family.

Section 34 (see **Appendix 1(E)**) is a self-contained section and provides a completely different structure from private law proceedings. Any s 8 contact order is discharged upon the making of a care order.

14.5.1 Initial considerations

Before making a care order, including an interim order, the court must consider the local authority's arrangements for contact and invite the parties to comment.

As contact is so important for a child, the local authority should, if possible, place the child with a member of his family or, if that is not appropriate, in accommodation near to the child's home. The local authority may also give assistance in travel and other expenses incurred in visiting the child to any person to whom there is a duty to promote contact.

14.5.2 Local authority duties

There is a general duty to promote contact between a child 'looked after' and his parents, others with parental responsibility and relatives, friends and other persons connected with him, unless it is not reasonably practicable or consistent with the child's welfare.

By s 34(1), the authority is also under a *positive* duty to allow a child in care reasonable contact with his parents (including a father without parental responsibility) and any person with whom the child previously lived by virtue of a court order, for example a residence order. The courts have said that reasonable contact is not the same as contact at the discretion of the local authority. 'Reasonable' means contact which is agreed, or, in the absence of agreement, contact which the authority can demonstrate is objectively reasonable.

14.5.3 Application to the court

Any person mentioned in s 34(1), for example parents, can apply as of right to be allowed contact with the child. As there is a presumption of reasonable contact in this case, usually contact will be by agreement. It would be necessary for the parents to apply only if they were dissatisfied with the level of contact offered.

In *Re G (Domestic Violence: Direct Contact)* [2000] 2 FLR 865 the court stated that *Re L (Contact: Domestic Violence)* [2000] 2 FLR 334 (see **13.3.2**) applied equally in public law cases when parents were applying for contact with their child, and made an order allowing the local authority to terminate direct contact.

Any other person, for example grandparents, can apply with permission. On an application for permission the court should apply the criteria set out in s 10(9) (*Re M (Care: Contact: Grandmother's Application for Leave)* [1995] 2 FLR 86). In particular, it should consider the nature of the contact sought, the connection of the applicant to the child, the risk of harm to the child and the wishes of the local authority and the parents.

A child in care has a right to apply for contact under s 34 with any named person. However, where contact is sought in relation to another child then, unless the local authority is opposing contact, the application should be under s 8 (requiring permission) rather than s 34, and it is the respondent child's welfare which is paramount (*Re F (Contact: Child in Care)* [1995] 1 FLR 510).

In *Re P-B (Children) (Contact: Committal)* [2009] EWCA Civ 143 it was held that a contact order under s 34 of the CA 1989 was capable of being enforced by committal.

14.5.4 Refusal of contact

Where an application for a contact order under s 34 is refused, no further application can be made by the applicant for six months, without permission. Furthermore, on disposing of *any* application for an order, the court may direct that no application for any specified order may be made by a person without permission (s 91(14)) (see also **13.8.6.1**). Such a direction would be made only in exceptional circumstances (*F v Kent County Council and Others* [1993] 1 FLR 432). Although the most likely reason for granting a restriction is where the applicant has made repeated and unreasonable applications with no hope of success, the court could make such an order, in the absence of repeated applications, if the welfare of the child requires it. In *Re M (Section 91(14) Order)* [1999] 2 FLR 553, the court imposed a restriction because it considered that the children urgently needed to settle down and make a permanent home away from their mother, and that a premature application by her could disrupt them and hinder their permanent placement. Such a restriction is unlikely to infringe the Human Rights Act 1998, as it does not restrict access to the courts but just imposes a requirement for leave.

The local authority cannot refuse contact with persons to whom the presumption of reasonable contact applies. However, the authority can apply to the court for an order authorising it to refuse contact between the child and any person mentioned in s 34(1). In an emergency, the local authority can temporarily suspend contact without an order, for a period of not more than seven days.

Although the court can authorise the refusal of contact by a local authority, it cannot, on the other hand, use its jurisdiction under s 34 to prohibit the local authority from allowing parental contact which the local authority considers to be advantageous to a child's welfare (*Re W (Section 34(2) Orders)* [2000] 1 FLR 502).

A contact order may be varied or discharged on the application of the child, local authority or the person named in the order. If the order is discharged, the presumption of reasonable contact with persons mentioned in s 34(1) still applies.

14.6 Discharge of care orders (s 39)

A care order remains in force until the child reaches 18, unless it is brought to an end earlier. The order may be brought to an end by the making of a residence order (the only s 8 order which can be applied for), the substitution of a supervision order, or by the making of an adoption order or a discharge order.

The application for a discharge can be made by any person with parental responsibility, the child or the local authority. There is no requirement for a child to seek leave before making an application.

On hearing an application to discharge the care order, the court may substitute a supervision order. The court must apply the welfare principle in s 1, but there is no requirement to find that the threshold criteria are still satisfied.

Where there has been a previous application to discharge a care order (other than an interim order) or to substitute a supervision order, no further application can be made for six months without leave.

If the care order is discharged without any other order being made, care of the child reverts to those having parental responsibility. A pre-care residence order will not be revived, although on discharge the court has power to make any s 8 order.

There has been an increasing trend for children in the care of local authorities (either under care orders, or being accommodated by voluntary agreement) to leave care early (ie between the ages of 16 and 18) with very little support provided for them. Research carried out by the Department of Health showed that the future for these children is often bleak. As a result, the Government introduced the Children (Leaving Care) Act 2000. It amended ss 22–24 of the CA 1989 to provide that it is the duty of the local authority looking after children to advise, assist and befriend them with a view to promoting their welfare when it has ceased to look after them. Each child must have a 'pathway plan' to cover the period from 16 to independence (whether they remain in care until then or not) and to look beyond the age of 18 to 21. The plan will be reviewed at least every six months. The local authority must also arrange for each child to have a personal adviser (who does not necessarily have to be a social worker). With regard to education and training, the local authority has a power, but not a duty, to assist with the cost of this up to the age of 24 (CA 1989, s 24B).

14.7 Effect of a supervision order

Although the criteria are the same as for a care order (see **14.4.2**), the effect of a supervision order is very different. The order places the child under the supervision of a local authority, but the supervisor does not acquire parental responsibility.

The basic duties of the supervisor are to advise, assist and befriend the child, and to take steps to give effect to the order. Other powers of the supervisor depend on the order.

The order could include:

(a) a requirement for the child to live at a specified place, or participate in specified activities;

(b) with the consent of any 'responsible person' (any person with parental responsibility and any other person with whom the child lives), a requirement for that person to take all reasonable steps to ensure the child complies with any direction and also to comply with any directions to take part in specified activities. This has been used to require the responsible person to undergo treatment, for example in relation to sexual offences;

(c) a requirement that the child submits to specified medical or psychiatric examination or treatment. Where the child has sufficient understanding to make an informed decision, he may refuse to submit to the examination or assessment. However, it has been held that under its inherent jurisdiction, the High Court has power to override a child's refusal (*South Glamorgan County Council v W and B* [1993] 1 FLR 574).

The court decides on the broad structure of the supervision to take place, but the detailed implementation of any requirement in the order is left to the supervisor (ie the local authority). If the supervisor's directions are not complied with, the supervisor can only seek a variation or discharge of the order. The directions cannot be directly enforced either by the supervisor, or by the court.

A supervision order is normally made for up to one year, but it can be extended for a further period of up to three years from the date of the original order. An application to extend the supervision order is governed by the principles in s 1, but there is no need to consider whether the threshold criteria are satisfied.

14.8 Care or supervision order

The protection of the child is the decisive factor when the court is deciding whether to make a care or supervision order. The court must weigh the likelihood of future harm to the child against the potential harm of removing the child from his parents under a care order. Note, however, that a care order may still be justified where the local authority intends for the child to remain at home (*Re T (A Minor) (Care or Supervision Order)* [1994] 1 FLR 103).

With a care order, the authority acquires parental responsibility and has an obligation to safeguard the child's welfare. In an emergency it can remove the child without recourse to a court.

In contrast, a supervision order is made to help and assist the child; responsibility for safeguarding the child's welfare rests with his parents. In an emergency, the local authority would have to apply to the court to remove the child. However, a supervision order does give the court a degree of control over the upbringing of the child.

In recent cases, the courts have emphasised that, when deciding whether to make a care order or a supervision order, the order that represented the most proportionate response to the risks involved should be made. When the balance between the two orders is equal, the court should adopt the least interventionist approach (see *Re C and B (Care Order: Future Harm)* [2001] 1 FLR 611 and *Re C (Care Order or Supervision Order)* [2001] 2 FLR 466).

14.9 Interim orders (s 38)

14.9.1 The court's powers to make interim orders

Once care proceedings have been instituted, the court has the power to make:

(a) an interim care order;

(b) an interim supervision order;

(c) a residence or other s 8 order for a limited period.

See **Appendix 1(E)**.

Where care or supervision proceedings are adjourned, or the court in any proceedings (eg divorce proceedings) gives a direction to a local authority under s 37 to investigate the child's circumstances (see **14.3.1**), the court may make an interim care or supervision order.

It may not make the order unless satisfied that there are reasonable grounds for believing that the threshold criteria (s 31: see **14.4.2**) are satisfied. At this stage, 'reasonable grounds' means that the court is likely to be relying to a large extent on the child's version of events, or on medical evidence that certain symptoms are consistent with abuse. The fact that belief suffices at the interim stage should be contrasted with the position at the Final Hearing, where the court must be satisfied by proof that the threshold criteria are met.

Alternatively, if the court makes a residence order pending the outcome of the care/supervision application, it must also make an interim supervision order (unless satisfied that the child's welfare will be satisfactorily safeguarded without it).

An interim order has the same effect as a final care or supervision order, except that the order can include directions as to the examination or assessment of the child and will be of limited duration.

It is common for a number of interim orders to be made pending a Final Hearing, although on each renewal the court must be satisfied that the criteria are still met.

In *Re G (Minors) (Interim Care Order)* [1993] 2 FLR 839, the court stated that an interim care order was an impartial step to preserve the status quo pending the Final Hearing and did not give a tactical advantage to the local authority. However, in *Re H (A Child) (Interim Care Order)* [2002] EWCA Civ 1932 the Court held that the rights of parents protected by Articles 6 and 8 of the European Convention on Human Rights required the judge in the instant case to abstain from premature determination of the case unless the welfare of the child demanded it. Where the effect of an interim care order would result in separation from a child's lifelong parents, it was only to be contemplated if the child's safety demanded immediate separation. This was recently confirmed by the Court of Appeal in *Re L-A (Children)* [2009] EWCA Civ 822.

It may be appropriate to delay making a final decision pending the outcome of an assessment of the child or a parent, or until the court is in possession of all material facts. The court must also be satisfied the local authority care plan is in the child's best interest. In *Re W and B, Re W (Care Plan)* [2001] EWCA Civ 757, [2001] 2 FLR 582, the Court of Appeal held that trial judges should have a wide discretion to make use of interim care orders where the proposed care plan seems uncertain or incomplete, or could be clarified after a relative brief adjournment.

When the court makes an interim care or supervision order, it may direct a medical, or psychiatric or other assessment of the child, under s 38(6) of CA 1989. This can include a residential assessment of the child with his family. These assessments are often very expensive, and in the past the LSC funded a significant proportion of these costs. Since 2007 it will no longer do so, and so the cost of these assessments will now fall on the local authority.

The case of *Re C (A Minor) (Interim Care Order: Residential Assessment)* [1996] 4 All ER 871, established that it was for the court to determine whether an assessment under s 38(6) would provide the court with the relevant material it required to make a decision at the Final Hearing. In *Re G (Interim Care Order: Residential Assessment)* [2005] UKHL 68, the House of Lords held that, to come within s 38(6), the assessment must be of 'the child' and the main focus must be on the child. It may include an assessment of the child's relationship with his or her parents, the risk the parents may present to him or her, and ways in which those risks may be avoided or managed, all with a view to enabling the court to make decisions under the Act. Any services which are provided for the child and his family must be ancillary to that end; they must not be an end in themselves.

Recent cases have given further guidance on the ordering of residential assessments under s 38(6). In *Re L and H (Residential Assessment)* [2007] EWCA Civ 213, the Court of Appeal stated that where there was some evidence that a residential assessment would be useful, the court should give serious consideration on an application for a s 38(6) assessment, in the interests of fairness, to the importance of having before it all the relevant evidence to make a decision at the Final Hearing.

14.9.2 Exclusion requirements

If the court makes an interim care order, it may include an 'exclusion requirement', provided there is reasonable cause to believe that if a person is excluded from the house where the child lives, the child will no longer suffer, or be likely to suffer, significant harm (s 38A(2)).

Before including such a requirement, another person (whether or not a parent) living in the house with the child must be able to look after the child and consent to the requirement being made. The 'exclusion requirement' may require the person to leave the dwelling house, or not to enter the dwelling house. It can also require the person not to enter an area surrounding the house. A power of arrest can be attached to the exclusion requirement. The requirement will cease to have effect if the local authority removes the child to other accommodation for a continuous period of more than 24 hours.

14.9.3 Contact

The provisions regarding contact with a child in care (see **14.5**) apply equally on the making of an interim care order. However, as the issue is only being considered pending a Final Hearing, contact between a parent and child should be maintained unless there are exceptional circumstances.

14.10 Emergency protection and assessment (CA 1989, Pt V)

14.10.1 Emergency protection order (s 44)

An emergency protection order (EPO) is an order, initially limited to eight days, to protect a child in an emergency where he is otherwise likely to suffer significant harm (see **Appendix 1(E)**). Recent cases have emphasised that the draconian nature of an EPO removing a child from his parent requires exceptional circumstances and proof of imminent danger (*X Council v B (Emergency Protection Orders)* [2004] EWHC 2015 (Fam)).

14.10.2 Grounds

The court may make an EPO on the application of any person, if it is satisfied that there is reasonable cause to believe that the child is likely to suffer significant harm if he:

(a) is not removed to accommodation provided by or on behalf of the applicant; or

(b) does not remain in the place where he is being accommodated.

The application will usually be made by a local authority, but anyone (such as a police officer or a relative) can apply. If the local authority is not the applicant, it has power to take over the order.

A local authority can also apply for an order where it is making enquiries because, for example, it suspects the child may be suffering significant harm and believes access is required as a matter of urgency, which is being unreasonably refused.

If the court finds that either condition applies, before making an order it must consider the welfare principle (s 1(1): see **14.4.4**) and the no order presumption (s 1(5): see **13.6**), although there is no requirement to apply the checklist under s 1(3) (see **13.5**).

If the court makes an order under s 44, it may include an 'exclusion requirement' if there is reasonable cause to believe that if a person is excluded from the dwelling house in which the child lives, the child is unlikely to suffer significant harm (s 44A(2)). The exclusion requirements and conditions are the same as when made in conjunction with an interim care order (see **14.9.2**).

14.10.3 Application

The application must be made to a family proceedings court unless it arises out of a direction under s 37 to the local authority to investigate, when it should be made to the court which gave that direction. The application may not be transferred to a higher court and there is no appeal against the making or refusal of an order.

The application can be made on one day's notice. The application may also be made without notice with the consent of the justices' clerk and may be heard by a single justice. However, due consideration must be given to parents' rights under Articles 6 and 8 of the European Convention on Human Rights, and notice of the hearing should generally be given, unless it is genuinely an emergency or a case of great urgency. A copy of the application and order must be served on each party (every person with parental responsibility and the child) within 48 hours of the order.

In *X Council v B* (see **14.10.1**) the court gave detailed guidance on emergency protection orders generally and also on the use of without notice applications, stating that, save in wholly exceptional cases, parents must be given notice. The case also stated the need for courts hearing without notice applications to keep a note of the evidence received, of its reasons and any findings of fact. This guidance was endorsed in *Re X (Emergency Protection Orders)* [2006] EWHC 510 (Fam) which said it is the duty of an applicant in an emergency protection order to ensure that the guidance in *X Council v B* is brought to the court's attention, ie, following a without notice hearing, the parents should be given a copy of the clerk's notes, a copy of any material submitted to the court and a copy of the justices' reasons. *Re X (Emergency Protection Orders)* also stated that, on a without notice application, the court needed to determine whether or not the hearing should proceed on a without notice basis and to give reasons for that decision.

The court will normally appoint a children's guardian for the child (see **14.11.6.1**). The court may take account of any statement contained in any report made to the court, or any evidence given during the hearing which is relevant to the application.

14.10.4 Effect of the order

The order operates as a direction to any person who is in a position to do so to comply with any request to produce the child to the applicant, and authorises the removal or prevention of removal of the child from his present accommodation. The order may authorise the applicant to enter specified premises and search for the child. If the applicant is likely to be refused entry, the court can issue a warrant authorising the police to assist, using reasonable force if necessary.

The order also gives the applicant parental responsibility for the child, but this is limited to doing what is necessary to safeguard and promote the child's welfare.

The local authority should return the child to his parents as soon as it appears safe to do so, thus it should review the case regularly to ensure that the parents and child are separated for no longer than is necessary.

14.10.5 Contact

During the currency of the order, the applicant must, subject to any direction of the court, allow the child reasonable contact with his parents, any other person with parental responsibility, any person with whom he was living prior to the order and any person in whose favour there is an existing contact order.

The court can give such directions and impose such conditions as it considers appropriate in relation to contact. However, where the applicant is a local authority, the court will usually leave contact to be negotiated between the parties unless the issue is clearly disputed. In *X Council v B (Emergency Protection Orders)* (see **14.10.1**), Mumby J emphasised that arrangements for contact must be driven by the needs of the family, not stunted by lack of resources.

14.10.6 Examination or assessment

The court may give directions as to a medical, or psychiatric examination or other assessment of the child, or may alternatively direct that there be no such examination or assessment. However, in an emergency, where the examination is required for medical reasons, this could be undertaken without the need for a court order under the applicant's parental responsibility.

A child of sufficient understanding to make an informed decision may refuse to submit to an examination or assessment, but it has been held that the High Court may overrule the child and give consent under its inherent jurisdiction (*South Glamorgan County Council v W and B* [1993] 1 FLR 574).

14.10.7 Duration

An EPO order may be granted for up to eight days, although it should not be granted for any longer than is necessary to protect the child. The court can grant one extension for up to seven days on the application of the local authority, if it has reasonable cause to believe the child is likely to suffer significant harm if the order is not extended.

An application to discharge the order can be made on one day's notice. The application can be made by the child, a parent, any other person with parental responsibility or any person with whom the child was living prior to the order, unless that person was present at the hearing. As an application to extend the duration must be on notice, no one can apply for a discharge once the order has been extended.

14.10.8 Police protection (s 46)

A child may be taken into 'police protection' for up to 72 hours if a constable has reasonable cause to believe that the child is likely to suffer significant harm if he does not remove the child to suitable accommodation, or take steps to prevent removal from his present accommodation (these are the same criteria on which the *court* must be satisfied to make an EPO: see **14.10.2**). This power could be used, for example, where a child has run away, been abandoned or is found in unsuitable home circumstances, or alternatively to prevent his removal from, say, a hospital. (See **Appendix 1(E)**.)

The police do not acquire parental responsibility but must do what is reasonable in the circumstances to safeguard or promote the child's welfare. They must inform the local authority who, if requested, must provide accommodation for the child. Following investigation, the police or local authority could, if appropriate, apply for an emergency protection order.

In *Langley v Liverpool City Council* [2005] EWCA Civ 1173 the Court of Appeal held that, where an EPO is in force, the police can remove a child under s 46 only if there are 'compelling reasons' to do so. If the police, knowing that an EPO was in force, removed a child under s 46 without compelling reasons, the police would be acting unlawfully and in breach of the family's rights under Article 8 of the European Convention on Human Rights.

14.10.9 Child assessment order (s 43)

This is an order for the assessment of the child's health or development, or of the way in which he has been treated. It is intended to deal with the situation where there is a suspicion that the child is suffering and there has been a denial of co-operation on the part of the child's carers. It is part of the 'planned responses' by a local authority rather than a device to provide emergency protection.

The grounds for the order are very specific. Essentially, the local authority must have reasonable cause to suspect the child is suffering, or is likely to suffer, significant harm. The court must be satisfied that an assessment is necessary to confirm or dismiss those suspicions and that the child's carers are unlikely to co-operate with such an assessment. Although the checklist in s 1(3) need not be applied, the court must have regard to the welfare principle (s 1(1)) and no order presumption (s 1(5)).

Under s 43(3), the court may make an EPO on an application for a child assessment order.

14.11 Procedure for care and supervision orders

The procedure for making applications is mostly contained in the FPR 2010, Pt 12 and supporting practice directions. The Public Law Outline (PLO) was a Practice Direction which governed the procedure on applications for care and supervision orders before implementation of the FPR 2010. The PLO has been incorporated into the new rules at Practice Direction 12A. It divides the procedure into four stages around four hearings (see **14.11.6**).

14.11.1 Jurisdiction

Proceedings under Pt IV of the CA 1989 (care and supervision orders, contact orders) are classified as 'family proceedings', allowing the court to make any of the orders under the Act, including s 8 orders. Proceedings under Pt V (emergency protection orders, child assessment orders) are not included in the definition, but, by virtue of s 92(2), all Children Act proceedings in the family proceedings court are to be treated as 'family proceedings'.

14.11.2 Which court?

The jurisdiction of a particular tier of court to entertain an application is governed by the Allocation and Transfer of Proceedings Order 2008 and accompanying Practice Direction. This aims to ensure that cases are heard at the lowest most appropriate level commensurate with their complexity, to ease pressure on the High Court and county court, and to make the best use of under-utilised family proceedings courts as well as reducing delays.

An application for a care or supervision order (or for an emergency protection or child assessment order) must normally be made to a family proceedings court. However, the general rule is subject to two provisos. First, if the application arose in consequence of a direction under s 37 (eg during divorce proceedings) for the local authority to investigate, the application should be made to the court which gave the direction. Secondly, any application to extend, vary or discharge an order under the Act, or where the outcome of the proceedings may have that effect, should be made to the court which made the original order.

14.11.3 Transfer of cases

Irrespective of where a case started, it can be transferred to another, more appropriate court. It is possible for cases to be transferred either horizontally or vertically. The exception is an application for an EPO, which cannot be transferred from the family proceedings court to a higher court (see **14.10.3**).

Transfers between the same tier of court are essentially governed by the need to avoid delay in the proceedings. Accordingly, if, for example, a particular family proceedings court is too busy to deal with the application, or it is desirable to consolidate with other pending proceedings, the application could be transferred to another family proceedings court.

Applications commenced in the family proceedings court can be transferred to the county court, and the county court can transfer a case to the High Court if 'appropriate' and 'in the interests of the child'.

14.11.4 Public funding

Legal Representation is available for public law proceedings under the Children Act, but is based on a special regime which depends on the nature of the proceedings and the status of the party.

14.11.4.1 Family Help (Lower)

Family Help (Lower) is available only to parents and those with parental responsibility, and only once the local authority has given written notification of its intention to issue proceedings (see **14.11.5.2**). It is non means-tested and has a low merits test, which is likely to be met if the local authority intends to take proceedings. It will cover liaison and negotiations with the local authority before proceedings are issued.

14.11.4.2 Legal Representation

Family Help (Higher) is not available in public law family proceedings. Legal Representation is available to the child, his parents and those with parental responsibility once the local authority has issued its application. For these parties it is non means-tested and subject only to a merits test in respect of the need for parents to be separately represented.

Any other person who applies to be joined as a party can apply for Legal Representation but it will be means- and merits-tested.

14.11.4.3 Other applications

Applications by anyone for s 34 contact orders, s 39 discharge orders or any s 8 order are subject to the usual means and merits test.

14.11.4.4 Related proceedings

In those cases where Legal Representation can be granted automatically, the certificate can cover proceedings relating to the application in question. A related matter is one where an order is sought at the same time as, and as an alternative to, the main proceedings. So, for example, applying for a s 8 residence order in the context of care or supervision proceedings would be covered by the Legal Representation certificate (although it may need to be formally amended).

Legal Representation is not available to a children's guardian, but Cafcass is responsible for paying for the services of the guardian.

14.11.5 Pre-proceedings action

The revised *Children Act 1989 Guidance and Regulations*, Vol 1, requires local authorities to carry out certain steps before issuing proceedings in all but extremely urgent cases. This statutory guidance is supplemented by the *Best Practice Guide: Preparing for Care and Supervision Proceedings*, August 2009.

14.11.5.1 Kinship assessments

Before deciding to issue proceedings, the local authority should have explored, possibly through a family group conference or other family meeting, whether the child could safely be cared for by a relative or friend, and should have assessed the suitability of such arrangements and considered the appropriate legal status of such arrangements.

14.11.5.2 Letter before proceedings

When the local authority decides it is going to issue proceedings, it must immediately notify the parents orally and in writing. This written notification is known as the 'letter before proceedings'. The letter before proceedings should set out a summary of the local authority's concerns, the steps the local authority has taken, what needs to be addressed by the parents and what support will be provided to them, as well as what will happen if the problems are not addressed. It should invite the parents to a meeting to discuss these concerns and invite them to bring a solicitor. Details of how to obtain free legal advice and details of local solicitors should also be given.

The letter before proceedings should entitle the parents to Family Help (Lower) (see **14.11.4.1**).

14.11.5.3 Meeting with parents

The meeting which takes place as a result of the letter before proceedings should be followed by a letter and written revised plan for the child, setting out what the parents and local authority are to do to safeguard the child and what steps will be taken if this action is not effective. If the local authority continues to be concerned, following the meeting, that the child is suffering or is likely to suffer significant harm, it remains responsible for issuing an application to the court for a care or supervision order.

14.11.6 The FPR 2010, Pt 12

The FPR 2010, Pt 12 reinforces and incorporates the PLO in Practice Direction 12A.

This divides the procedure into four stages around four hearings.

14.11.6.1 Stage 1: Issue and the First Appointment

Practice Direction 12A envisages that Stage 1 will take six days from issue to the First Appointment.

On Day 1, when the local authority issues the application, it files an application form. This is currently Form C110, which was introduced on 1 April 2010 (see **Appendix 3(L)**).

Form C110 contains an annex with a list of six documents which need to be filed with the application at the time of issue. These are known as the annex documents and are:

(a) social work chronology;
(b) initial social work statement;
(c) initial and core assessments;
(d) letters before proceedings;
(e) schedule of proposed findings; and
(f) care plan.

It is accepted that in some urgent cases the local authority will not have all the documents. If any document is not filed with the application, the reason why and the expected date of filing must be stated on Form C100.

The local authority will also need to pay a fee.

Practice Direction 12A provides for other documents, known as other checklist documents, to be disclosed to the parties, usually before the First Appointment, but not filed at court. These checklist documents include: previous court orders, s 7 and s 37 reports, records of discussions with the family, and pre-existing care plans (eg child protection plan).

On issue the court will, amongst other steps, decide the appropriate level of court, nominate one and not more than two case managers, list the First Appointment to take place by Day 6, appoint a children's guardian and solicitor for the child, and give any other directions, known as standard directions on issue, such as for the filing of checklist documents which have not been filed, and appointment of the children's guardian and solicitor for the child.

The applicant must join as a party the child and every person whom he believes to have parental responsibility. In public law proceedings, unlike private law proceedings, the child is automatically a party. This is because public law proceedings are based on the concept of significant harm attributable to the standard of parental care. This can create a conflict of interest between the child and his parents and between the child and the local authority, and therefore requires the child to be separately represented. In the case of parents, consideration should always be given as to whether separate representation is appropriate because of a potential conflict of interest.

In addition, any person who is not automatically a respondent may apply to be joined. A distinction is drawn between a putative father and other applicants. In the case of a putative father, his application should be granted unless there is some justifiable reason for not doing so (see *Re K (Care Proceedings: Notification of Father without Parental Responsibility)* [1999] 2 FLR 408). In the case of other applicants, the court will not join someone (other than a parent) where their interests and views are the same as an existing party. In *Re M (Minors) (Sexual Abuse: Evidence)* [1993] 1 FLR 822, the court held that, where the grandparents were offering a 'fall back' position to that of the mother, and were presenting the same case as her, there was no purpose in their separate representation and they should not have been made parties unless they had a separate point to advance.

Service

By Day 3, copies of the application, supplementary forms and checklist documents must be served on all respondents, together with a Notice of Proceedings (C6) giving the date of the hearing. The applicant must file a Statement of Service (C9).

Within the same time period, the applicant must also give notice of the proceedings (C6A) to anyone caring for the child, an unmarried father who does not have parental responsibility and anyone who is a party to other relevant proceedings, so that they can consider whether to apply to be joined as a party.

In relation to a child, service must be on the solicitor acting for the child, or, if none, on the children's guardian. The court has power to direct that a requirement as to service on anyone shall not apply, or shall be effected in such manner as the court directs.

Appointment of a children's guardian

On the day the application is issued, the court must appoint a children's guardian for the child, unless the court considers it is not necessary to safeguard the child's interests.

Children's guardians are usually experienced social workers who are contracted to Cafcass as officers of the service. They operate through regional offices around the country. Practice Direction 12A provides that a guardian must be allocated by Cafcass by Day 3.

It is important to appreciate that the guardian is 'for the child', rather than to 'represent' the child. Accordingly, the guardian's role is to put forward what he considers to be in the best interests of the child, even though that may not coincide with the child's views. The problems of delay and backlogs in Cafcass (see **13.1.1**) apply equally to public law proceedings, and in many parts of the country there is substantial delay in the appointment of a children's guardian. The President's Interim Guidance and Agreement with Cafcass of 1 October 2010 seek to alleviate the situation.

Duties of the children's guardian

The duties of the children's guardian are contained in the FPR 2010, Chapter 16 and Practice Direction 16A. If the court has not already appointed a solicitor to represent the child (see below), the guardian will need to appoint one.

The guardian must give instructions to the solicitor representing the child, give the child appropriate advice, investigate the case and file a written report at least 14 days before the Final Hearing.

In addition, the guardian must attend all directions appointments and hearings (unless excused) and advise the court, amongst other things, on:

(a) whether the child is of sufficient understanding for any purpose;

(b) the wishes of the child in respect of any relevant matter;

(c) the appropriate timing of the proceedings;

(d) the options available to the court in respect of the child;

(e) any other appropriate matter.

Under r 12 and Practice Direction 12A, the children's guardian is also required to prepare an initial case analysis document for the First Appointment. This document will set out a summary of the alleged harm, of the proposed solutions, and any further assessments, investigations and directions the guardian feels are appropriate. It will include details of the parties' views on the key issues, including those of the child. Therefore the guardian will need to have read the local authority evidence, carry out his own further enquiries and have ascertained the views of the child by the First Appointment. Thereafter the guardian is required to file an interim case analysis for each of the hearings, and a final case analyses in advance of the Final Hearing.

Appointment of solicitor for the child

Under the FPR 2010, r 12 and Practice Direction 12A, and pursuant to s 41(3) of the CA 1989, the court can appoint a solicitor for the child on issue of the application.

Duties of the solicitor

Where a children's guardian has been appointed, the solicitor must follow the instructions given by the guardian. However, in some cases it becomes apparent that the views of the child do not coincide with what the guardian considers to be in his best interests. In circumstances where the child wishes to give instructions which conflict with those of the guardian and the solicitor considers that the child is able, having regard to his understanding, to give such instructions, the solicitor must follow the child's instructions. Where this happens, the guardian must notify the court and may seek leave to have separate legal representation.

Cafcass is currently experiencing lengthy delays in the allocation of children's guardians (see **13.1.1**). The delays have led to solicitors being appointed to act for the child where a guardian is not immediately available. The Law Society issued a detailed practice note in the summer of 2009, *Acting in the absence of a children's guardian*, clarifying what a solicitor should do in this situation. In the absence of a guardian to give instructions, the solicitor should take instructions from the child where the child is able to understand the situation and give such instructions, and in default of instructions the solicitor should represent the child 'in furtherance of the best interests of the child'.

The First Appointment

On the filing of the application, the court must fix a date for a preliminary hearing and appoint a children's guardian and solicitor to represent the child. According to Practice Direction 12A, this First Appointment should take place within six days of the issuing of the application. By Day 6 the court should have been notified of the need for any contested hearing (for example for an interim care order) and should have made arrangements for the hearing to take place.

At the First Appointment the main objectives are, in line with the strong emphasis of the FPR 2010 on robust case management by the court, to confirm the case has been allocated to the right level of court and to give initial case management directions having regard to the PLO.

The court will:

(a) confirm the Timetable for the Child. The Timetable for the Child is the timetable for the proceedings set by the court and shall take into account dates of the significant steps (including legal, social, care, health and education steps) in the life of the child and shall be appropriate for the child. This timetable should be considered at every stage of the proceedings and reviewed regularly;

(b) confirm allocation or transfer;

(c) identify additional parties and representation, including allocation of a children's guardian;

(d) give standard directions including ordering:
   (i) further case analyses,
   (ii) case summaries by the local authority and other parties,
   (iii) parties' initial witness statements,
   (iv) listing of the case management conference.

The court can make an interim care or supervision order if the conditions in s 38 are met, or a s 8 residence order together with a supervision order, or list the application for an urgent contested interim hearing.

Attendance

The parties must attend any court appointments unless otherwise directed.

The court has power to direct that a child does not, or need not, attend. The general tendency is to allow the child's attendance only if satisfied that it would clearly be in his interests, and in practice the courts tend to assume that the child will not attend without the need to make a formal direction.

Evidence

Admissibility

As in private law children proceedings, the general rules as to the admissibility of evidence are relaxed.

Of particular relevance is that any statement contained in a children's guardian's report, and any evidence given in respect of matters referred to in it, is admissible. This provision is very wide in that 'any statement' is not restricted to one made by the guardian himself and could include a statement made by, for example, a home help or a school teacher. Further, the court may allow 'any evidence' from any witness to be admitted if it relates to a matter referred to in the report.

A children's guardian has the right to examine and take copies of records held by a local authority. However, the local authority may claim, for example in relation to social work records, that public interest requires that the evidence should be excluded. In that case, the guardian would have to apply to the court for a direction as to its admissibility.

Witness statements

Each party must file and serve on the other parties and on the children's guardian written statements of the oral evidence it intends to use, together with copies of any documents, including expert reports, which will be relied on, at or by such time as the court directs. Failure to do so means the evidence can be admitted only with leave.

Expert evidence

Expert witnesses such as doctors or psychologists are often used in CA 1989 cases to assist the court in its decision-making. However, in family proceedings relating to children, the court's permission is required to instruct an expert. These proceedings are confidential and disclosure of information and documents to an expert may only be permitted to an expert whose instruction has been permitted by the court. Further, the court's leave is needed for any medical or psychiatric examination, or other assessment of the child, for the purpose of preparing expert evidence and, where leave has not been given, no evidence arising from the examination or assessment of the child can be produced without the court's leave.

The FPR 2010, Pt 25 and Practice Direction 25A govern the instruction of expert evidence. The Practice Direction sets out the timing for obtaining the court's permission, which should be sought before or at the case management conference in public law proceedings. It sets out the duties of the party proposing to instruct an expert, including guidance on the letter of instruction, which must be agreed between the parties. It also sets out duties of the expert and guidance on the report to be prepared by the expert. In addition, it provides guidance on the purpose and arrangements of experts' discussions and meetings and on the attendance of experts at court.

Disclosure

Although privilege from disclosure applies to solicitor/client communications, it does not apply in children cases to reports and other documents prepared for the purpose of the proceedings. Accordingly, where a party obtains an expert report, with or without the court's leave, no privilege will attach to the report and it must be disclosed to the court and to the other parties (*Re L (Police Investigation: Privilege)* [1996] 1 FLR 731).

14.11.6.2 Stage 2: Case management conference

The case management conference should take place no later than 45 days from issue. Practice Direction 12A requires an advocates' meeting to take place not less than two days before the case management conference. At the advocates' meeting the main objective is to prepare the Draft Case Management Order, and to identify any experts required and to draft questions for them. The Draft Case Management Order, which is to be filed at court no later than 11am on the day before the case management conference, is a lengthy pro forma document setting out the matters the court will deal with at the case management conference, that is, further evidence and documents to be filed, and details of experts sought and details of their instruction, and any other case management issues.

The case management conference is the main hearing at which the court manages the case. The main objectives are to identify key issues and give full case management directions, which will be given effect by the final approved Draft Case Management Order.

The court will also set a date for the Issues Resolution Hearing, which should be between 16 and 25 weeks from the date of issue and in line with the timetable for the child.

14.11.6.3 Stage 3: Issues Resolution Hearing

The Issues Resolution Hearing is likely to be the hearing before the Final Hearing. Again, Practice Direction 12A requires the advocates to meet between two and seven days before the Issues Resolution Hearing to consider the evidence and any further case management issues, and to draft the Case Management Order, which must be filed with the court by 11am one working day before the Issues Resolution Hearing.

The purpose of the Issues Resolution Hearing is to resolve and narrow issues and identify any remaining key issues, as well as final case management by the court. The court will issue a Case Management Order.

14.11.6.4 Stage 4: The Final Hearing

In advance of the Final Hearing all case management documents and bundles must be filed and served, and Draft Final Orders prepared.

Where all the parties are agreed that a care order should be made, the court's consideration may be limited to a perusal of the documentation and approval of the agreed order. On the other hand, where there are unresolved issues, for example as to physical or sexual abuse, the court may order a split hearing (*Re S (Care Proceedings: Split Hearing)* [1996] 2 FLR 773) – the first hearing to resolve these issues; the second, substantive hearing to concentrate on what is in the child's best interests.

14.11.7 Judgment

Judgment must be given as soon as practicable after the hearing. The court must state any findings of fact and the reasons for its decision.

The order must be in writing (on Form C32) and a copy served on each party and on any person with whom the child is living.

14.11.8 After a care order is made

Once a final care order has been made, the local authority has control over decisions relating to the child's welfare. The local authority should review its care plan on a regular basis and, before conducting such reviews, it should seek and take into account the wishes and views of the child and his parents.

The court has no future role in monitoring the local authority or the execution of its care plan unless some substantive issue comes before the court, such as an application for contact or discharge of the care order. This is a situation which has caused increasing judicial concern over the years, especially since enactment of the Human Rights Act 1998. As a result, s 25A–25C of the CA 1989 now require local authorities to appoint a named Independent Reviewing Officer (IRO) in connection with each looked-after child. The care plan for any such child must be kept under review, and the IRO must monitor the local authority's performance, make sure the child's views are understood and taken into account, ensure that any matters of concern are brought to the attention of an appropriately senior member of the local authority and, in necessary cases, refer the matter to Cafcass, who may seek to resolve issues by mediation or by issuing proceedings such as judicial review or under the Human Rights Act 1998.

14.12 Human rights implications

Taking a child into care clearly constitutes an interference with family life under Article 8 of the European Convention on Human Rights. The local authority, as a public body, must act in a way that is compatible with Convention rights. Taking a child into care will not breach Article 8 provided the interference is in accordance with the law, it pursues a legitimate aim (namely, the protection of children) and is necessary.

In the context of public law proceedings, the European Court of Human Rights has repeatedly emphasised that interference in the right to family life by taking a child into care should be regarded as a temporary measure to be discontinued as soon as circumstances permit (*Johansen v Norway* (1996) 23 EHRR 33).

The manner in which a child is taken into care may also be open to challenge. The European Court of Human Rights has emphasised that it is important to involve parents in the decision-making process leading to care proceedings. This would include being involved in child protection conferences. In addition, in *P, C and S v United Kingdom* [2002] 2 FLR 631, the European Court of Human Rights stated that it is essential that parents involved in care proceedings have effective and competent legal representation. If they do not, Article 6 and the procedural guarantees inherent in Article 8 of the Convention are breached.

14.12.1 The welfare principle

As mentioned in **Chapter 13**, there is a debate as to whether the welfare principle in s 1(1) of the CA 1989 is incompatible with Article 8 of the European Convention on Human Rights and an individual's right to respect for family life. In other words, placing the child's welfare as paramount does not involve balancing the family rights of the other relevant individuals. But the decisions of the European Court of Human Rights make it clear that the rights of the parent may have to defer to the interests of the child. In *Johansen v Norway* (see **14.12** above), the Court said that 'the parent cannot be entitled under Article 8 ... to have such measures taken as would harm the child's health and development'.

In the domestic case of *Dawson v Wearmouth* [1999] 1 FLR 1167 the court said:

> It is submitted that the father's rights under Article 8 are infringed. There is no basis for this submission. The present case is concerned with the welfare of the child, not with the rights of the father. There is nothing in the Convention which requires the courts of this country to act otherwise than in the interests of the child.

Also, in *KD (A Minor) (Access: Principles)* [1998] 2 FLR 139, there was an argument between the local authority and the parent as to contact. The mother relied on Article 8 of the Convention and submitted that contact was a parental right and not a child's right. Lord Oliver said it would not be inappropriate to describe a parent's claim to contact as a 'right' It was also a normal assumption that a child will benefit from continuing contact with his natural parents:

> But both the 'right' and the assumption will always be displaced if the interests of the child dictate otherwise.

These cases suggest that there is no conflict between s 1(1) and Article 8, because Article 8(2) contains the important qualification of the right to respect for family life that 'there shall be no interference except such as in accordance with the law and is necessary in a democratic society for the protection of health or morals or for the protection of the rights and freedoms of others' (ie the child involved).

14.12.2 The care plan

One significant impact of the Human Rights Act 1998 in public law cases is how it has been used to highlight the courts' inability to maintain some judicial control over the implementation of a care plan by the local authority.

If the court makes a care order, it then has no further control over the care plan for the child and the local authority can change that plan at any time. If the parents are unhappy about the care plan, all they can do is apply to discharge the care order, or apply for contact if the arrangements are unreasonable.

This position has been criticised by many for some time as conflicting with the principle that the interests of the parent and of the child in the decision-making process should be given sufficient procedural protection. It has also been argued that the inability of the parents to question or call for any review of the care plan can lead to breaches of Articles 6 and 8 of the Convention and is incompatible with the 1998 Act.

As a result, the Government introduced the role of Independent Reviewing Officer (see **14.11.8**), who will review the care plan and, if necessary, refer the matter to Cafcass, which can seek to resolve problems through mediation or by issuing proceedings.

14.13 Compensation for local authority failings

In *D v East Berkshire Community Health NHS Trust, K and Another v Dewsbury Healthcare NHS Trust and Another, K and Another v Oldham NHS Trust and Another* [2005] UKHL 23, the House of Lords held that the local authority owes a duty of care to a child in relation to investigating abuse and commencing care proceedings, but not to the parent who is suspected of abusing the child.

An example of this is *NXS v Camden London Borough Council* [2009] EWHC 1786 (QB) where the court awarded the claimant £60,000 damages for the local authority's failure to properly investigate and monitor allegations of violence by the mother towards the claimant as a baby and young child, as a result of which the abuse continued until she was 14 years old.

Compensation can also be awarded to children and parents where breaches of the Convention are found. In *AD and OD v UK* [2010] ECHR 340 the European Court of Human Rights awarded €15,000 damages and €10,000 costs to a child and his mother for breaches of Articles 8 and 13.

14.14 Special guardianship order

Sections 14A to 14F of the CA 1989 provide for special guardianship orders, a type of order (see **13.3.6**) which gives the holder parental responsibility, which he is entitled to exercise to the exclusion of any other person with parental responsibility. However, it does not extinguish the parents' parental responsibility. The local authority must provide special guardian support services, including counselling, advice and financial support.

It is a private law order, but it may be useful in cases where the local authority is or has been involved. It provides permanence without the legal separation involved in adoption.

In *Re A-J (Adoption Order or Special Guardianship Order)* [2007] EWCA Civ 55, the Court of Appeal attached a schedule of the main differences between special guardianship orders and adoption, prepared by counsel in the case.

14.15 Chapter summary

(1) There is a duty on local authorities to take reasonable steps through the provision of services to avoid the need for court proceedings.

(2) A care or supervision order can be made only on application by a local authority (or NSPCC).

(3) In contrast to private law proceedings, the child is always a party.

(4) Before making a care or supervision order, the court must be satisfied both that the threshold criteria are met and that such an order is in the child's best interests.

(5) Legal Representation for the main respondents is automatic.

(6) There is a presumption of reasonable contact for parents.

(7) In an emergency, anyone can apply for an emergency protection order.

(8) Checklists detailing grounds for a care or supervision order and the procedure are set out below.

GROUNDS FOR A CARE OR SUPERVISION ORDER – CHECKLIST

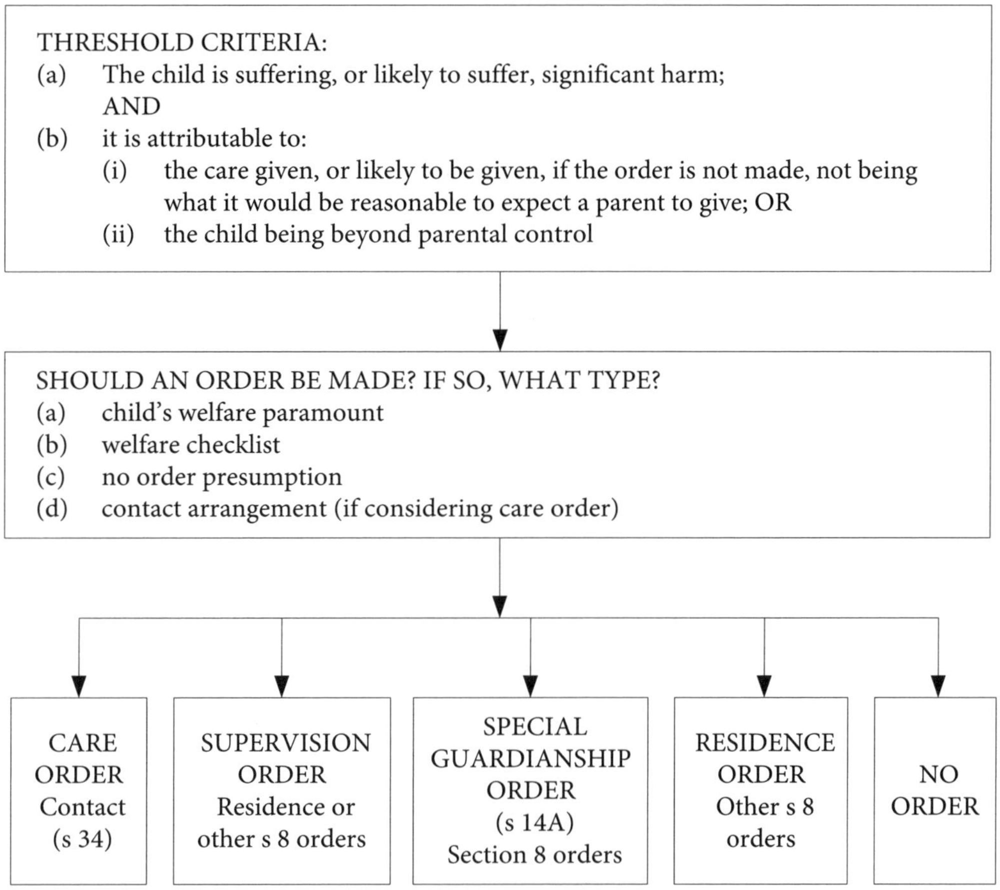

PROCEDURAL CHECKLIST FOR A CARE ORDER

1.	Applicant	Local authority (or NSPCC)
2.	Which court?	Family proceedings court (unless s 37 direction or effect existing order)
3.	Application	Form C110
4.	Children's guardian	Appointed by the court. Court appoints solicitor for child
5.	Respondents	Every person with parental responsibility and the child
6.	Notice	Parent without parental responsibility Person with whom child living
7.	Legal Representation	As of right for child, parents and others with parental responsibility
8.	Service	Three days' notice
9.	First Appointment	Initial case management directions
10.	Interim order	Care/supervision orders if criteria satisfied or s 8 residence order with supervision order
11.	Case management conference	Case management directions
12.	Issues Resolution Hearing	To narrow remaining issues and final case management
13.	Final Hearing	Findings of fact/reasons

Chapter 15
Domestic Abuse

15.1	Introduction	235
15.2	Protection under Pt IV of the Family Law Act 1996	236
15.3	Human rights implications	250
15.4	Protection from Harassment Act 1997	251
15.5	The Forced Marriage (Civil Protection) Act 2007	251
15.6	Chapter summary	252

15.1 Introduction

The term 'domestic abuse' is adopted by the Law Society's Family Law Protocol to cover cases involving personal violence, threats, intimidation and harassment. Particular sensitivity needs to be employed by the solicitor in such cases, as the client is likely to be distressed and may be reluctant to talk about the abuse.

This chapter is written on the basis that it is the wife or female partner who is seeking protection since this is the most common situation. However, men can be the victims of abuse too and are entitled to the same legal remedies. Any children who are with the victim can usually be protected at the same time as their carer. However, if protection is needed specifically for the children alone, this should generally be dealt with by using the procedures outlined in **Chapters 13** or **14**.

Although there is a variety of potential remedies available in situations of domestic abuse, the solicitor must be careful not to raise the client's expectations too high. A court order may give limited protection, but much will depend on the personality of the respondent. When the respondent is served with a court order, or arrested by the police (and later released), further violence may result. It is therefore crucial for the solicitor to adapt his advice to the particular circumstances of the applicant, taking into account the personalities of the parties, and to avoid giving the applicant a false sense of security.

The main emphasis here is on how to proceed in the civil courts, but the solicitor should be aware that court action is not the only possible remedy, and may not be the most appropriate one. For example, a solicitor's letter warning the perpetrator to desist from his behaviour or face court action may act as a deterrent. However, this would not be appropriate in cases of serious violence. In these cases the victim may consider going to the police. Police forces are now becoming more involved in cases of domestic violence and many have their own domestic violence unit.

As part of the Government's drive to tackle domestic abuse, specialist domestic violence courts have been opened across England and Wales to deal with criminal cases which bring together prosecutors, police and court staff with specially trained magistrates, and where victims receive support and advice.

The most recent measure by the Government is the introduction of 12-month pilot schemes from Summer 2011, operated by the Greater Manchester, Wiltshire and West Mercia police forces. Police officers will have the power to issue Domestic Violence Protection Notices (DVPN), which require someone to leave the home immediately for up to 48 hours or until an application for a Domestic Violence Protection Order (DVPO) is heard at a magistrates' court. The police may issue a DVPN if they consider that there are reasonable grounds for believing the alleged abuser has used or threatened violence and the notice is necessary to protect the victim. The police will then need to apply to the magistrates' court for a DVPO, which will last for between 14 to 21 days.

If the client is in such fear that she does not want to return home, the solicitor should consider the possibility of finding a place for her in a women's refuge or in temporary local authority housing (see **6.11**).

If the appropriate course of action is to apply to the court for an order or orders to protect your client, the application will in most cases be made under Pt IV of the FLA 1996, which codified the law in this area, making the same remedies available in any level of court and extending protection to a wider group of people than before.

Another relevant statute in this area is the Protection from Harassment Act 1997 (PHA 1997). This Act will be considered briefly, later in the chapter.

15.2 Protection under Pt IV of the Family Law Act 1996

The FLA 1996 is likely to provide the remedies which will be most frequently utilised by the family law practitioner. Its provisions are therefore dealt with in some detail.

15.2.1 Types of order available

The types of order available fall into two main categories:

(a) 'Non-molestation orders' for the protection of parties and any children. These can be applied for by a wide range of 'associated persons'.

(b) 'Occupation orders' which exclude the other party from occupation of the home. They can extend to excluding that party from a specified area around the home if necessary. Occupation orders can be applied for by spouses and cohabitants. Other 'associated persons' can apply only in specified circumstances.

15.2.2 Who can apply?

One of the most important changes brought about by FLA 1996 was the extension of the right to apply for non-molestation and (sometimes) occupation orders to a wide group of associated persons. Section 62 states that a person is associated with another if:

(a) they are or have been married to each other, or they are or have been civil partners of each other;

(b) they are cohabitants or former cohabitants (ie they are or have been living together as husband and wife) (this includes same-sex couples);

(c) they live or have lived in the same household, otherwise than by reason of one of them being the other's employee, tenant, lodger or boarder;

(d) they are relatives (this term includes immediate relations and other close relations such as grandparents, grandchildren, aunts, uncles, nieces, nephews, cousins, step-parents and step-children);

(e) they have agreed to marry or enter into a civil partnership with one another (whether or not that agreement has been terminated – however, where the agreement has been terminated, any application must be made within three years of the termination date), or, since 1 July 2007, they have or have had an intimate personal relationship with each other which was of significant duration;

(f) in relation to a child, they are both parents or have, or have had, parental responsibility (where a child has been adopted or freed for adoption, two people will be associated if one is the natural parent and the other is the child or adoptive parent of the child);

(g) they are parties to the same family proceedings (other than proceedings under Pt IV of the FLA 1996 itself).

In addition, children (ie those under 18) can apply for non-molestation and/or occupation orders in their own right. However, if they are under 16 they will require leave of the court, which will be given only if the court is satisfied that the child has sufficient understanding to make the application (s 43).

15.2.3 Non-molestation orders (s 42)

The court can grant an order prohibiting the respondent from molesting the applicant or a child. The word 'molestation' covers not only violence and threats of violence, but also pestering. Thus, such an order could be granted against a respondent who sends abusive letters to his wife, or who persistently telephones his former partner in the middle of the night.

The court can grant a non-molestation order on the application of any associated person within any family proceedings, or the applicant may make a 'free standing' application under the FLA 1996. The court can also make such an order of its own motion in family proceedings. Since 1 July 2007, the court is required, when considering making an occupation order, also to consider making a non-molestation order.

15.2.3.1 Factors that the court must consider

Section 42(5) specifies that the court must have regard to all circumstances, including the need to secure the health, safety and well-being of the applicant and any child. Thus, provided the applicant can show a genuine need for protection, a non-molestation order will be granted.

15.2.3.2 Duration

Section 42(7) states that the order may be made for a specified period or until further order. Thus, such an order may be made for an indefinite period (*Re B-J (Power of Arrest)* [2000] 2 FLR 443).

15.2.4 Occupation orders (ss 33 and 35–38)

The provisions relating to occupation orders are quite detailed and complex. The status of the applicant (ie whether she has a right to occupy the home, or is a former spouse, cohabitant or former cohabitant) will determine:

(a) whether the proposed applicant can apply for an order;

(b) the provisions of any order granted;

(c) the factors that the court will take into account in deciding whether to grant any order; and

(d) the duration of any occupation order.

An application for an occupation order can be made in the course of other family proceedings, or the applicant can make a 'free standing' application under FLA 1996.

15.2.4.1 Applicant has an existing right to occupy the home (s 33)

An applicant will have a right to occupy the home for the purposes of this section if she is entitled to occupy by virtue of a beneficial estate, or interest, or contract or statutory entitlement (eg under s 30 of the FLA 1996). The home in question must be, have been or have been intended to be the home of the applicant and the person with whom she is associated (the respondent). Thus *any* associated person can apply under s 33 where she has an existing legal right to occupy the home.

Where the above conditions are satisfied, the applicant can apply for an occupation order which may:

(a) require the respondent to permit the applicant to enter and remain in the home or part of the home;

(b) regulate the occupation of the home by either or both parties;

(c) prohibit, suspend or restrict the respondent's exercise of his right to occupy the home;

(d) require the respondent to leave the home; or

(e) exclude the respondent from a defined area in which the home is situated.

Where the applicant has a right of occupation under s 30 of the FLA 1996 and the respondent is the other spouse, the occupation order may further provide that those rights will not be brought to an end by the death of the other spouse or dissolution of the marriage. Unless such a provision is included in the order, it will cease to have effect on the death of either party or dissolution of the marriage.

Factors that the court must consider

Section 33(6) provides that in deciding whether to grant the order sought, the court must take into account all circumstances, including:

(a) the respective housing needs and housing resources of the parties and any child;

(b) the respective financial resources of the parties;

(c) the likely effect of any order, or of any decision by the court not to make such an order, on the health, safety or well-being of the parties and any relevant child; and

(d) the conduct of the parties in relation to each other and otherwise.

However, s 33(6) is subject to the 'balance of harm' test contained in s 33(7). This provides that if it appears to the court that the applicant or any child is likely to suffer significant harm attributable to the conduct of the respondent if an occupation order is not made, then the court *shall* make such an order unless it appears to the court that:

(a) the respondent or any child is likely to suffer significant harm if the order is made; and

(b) the harm likely to be suffered by the respondent or child is as great as or greater than the harm attributable to the conduct of the respondent which is likely to be suffered by the applicant or child if the order is not made.

The case of *Chalmers v Johns* [1999] 1 FLR 392 makes it clear that the applicant must show that she would suffer significant harm attributable to the respondent's conduct before the court applies the balance of harm test. Where such harm was not shown, the case would be determined on the basis of the factors in s 33(6) alone. Therefore, if the balance of harm test is made out in the applicant's favour, the court must make the order. If the test is not made out then the court has a discretion to make the order by applying the factors in s 33(6).

The case of *B v B (Occupation Order)* [1999] 1 FLR 715 illustrates the interrelationship of s 33(6) and s 33(7) and the balance of harm test. The wife moved out of the matrimonial home with the couple's 2-year-old daughter due to the husband's violence. They were then temporarily rehoused by the local authority. The husband remained in the matrimonial home with his son (aged 6) from a previous relationship. Should the wife be granted an occupation order under FLA 1996, s 33? The Court of Appeal held that she should not. Although the wife and child would suffer significant harm attributable to the husband's conduct if an order were not made, the harm which the husband's child would be likely to suffer if an order were made was greater. This was on the basis of the housing needs of both parties and children. Whereas the wife was entitled to be rehoused by the local authority as she was not intentionally homeless, the husband would not be so entitled since he would be considered to be intentionally homeless on account of his violence. If the husband were forced to move out, his son would also need to change schools.

Duration

An occupation order made under s 33 may be for a specified period, until the occurrence of a specified event or until further order. Thus, such an order can be for an indefinite period. In practice it is likely, at least initially, to be for a specified period, probably six months.

15.2.4.2 Applicant has no existing right to occupy the home and respondent has such a right (s 35 and s 36)

Applicant is former spouse or former civil partner (s 35)

An applicant under s 35 must be the former spouse of the respondent. The respondent must be entitled to occupy the home (by virtue of a beneficial estate, or interest, or contract or by statute). The home must be, or have been or have been intended to be, the matrimonial home.

Where these conditions are satisfied, the applicant can apply for an occupation order. Any order granted under s 35 *must* contain a provision (an 'occupation provision') stating:

(a) if the applicant is in occupation, that the applicant has a right not to be excluded from the home or part of it by the respondent for a specified period and prohibiting the respondent from excluding the applicant during that period;

(b) if the applicant is not in occupation, that the applicant be given a right to enter and occupy the home for a specified period and requiring the respondent to permit the exercise of that right.

In addition, the order *may* contain one or more provisions ('exclusion provisions'):

(a) regulating the occupation of the home by either party;

(b) prohibiting, suspending or restricting the respondent's right to occupy;

(c) requiring the respondent to leave the home or part of it;

(d) excluding the respondent from a defined area in which the home is situated.

Factors that the court must consider

Note that the factors are slightly different for occupation provisions and exclusion provisions.

In deciding whether to make an *occupation provision*, the court must take into account all circumstances, including:

(a) the respective housing needs and housing resources of the parties and any child;

(b) the respective financial resources of the parties;

(c) the likely effect of any order, or of any decision by the court not to make such an order, on the health, safety or well-being of the parties and any relevant child;

(d) the conduct of the parties in relation to each other and otherwise;

(e) the length of time that has elapsed since the parties ceased to live together;

(f) the length of time that has elapsed since the marriage ended; and

(g) the existence of any pending proceedings between the parties under s 23A or s 24 of the MCA 1973 and Sch 1 to the CA 1989 (financial orders relating to children), or relating to the legal or beneficial ownership of the home (s 35(6)).

The factors the court must take into account when making an *exclusion provision* are the same as (a)–(e) above for an occupation provision. However, for an exclusion provision, the balance of harm test mentioned in **15.2.4.1** in relation to s 33 applies.

Duration

An occupation order made under s 35 must be made for a specified period not exceeding six months. The order can be extended any number of times, but any extension must be for a further specified period not exceeding six months. In addition, any order shall cease to have effect on the death of either party.

Applicant is cohabitant or former cohabitant (s 36)

An applicant under s 36 must be the cohabitant or former cohabitant of the respondent. Thus, other associated persons may not apply under this section. For example, a niece may not apply for an occupation order against her uncle under s 36. The respondent must be entitled to occupy the home (by virtue of a beneficial estate, or interest, or contract or by statute). The home must be, or have been or have been intended to be, the couple's home.

Where these conditions are satisfied, the applicant can apply for an occupation order. Any order granted *must* contain the same occupation provision as an order under s 35. In addition, it *may* contain any of the same exclusion provisions as an order under s 35.

Factors that the court must consider

In deciding whether to make an *occupation provision*, the relevant factors are in many ways similar to those under s 35. The court must take into account all circumstances, including:

(a) the respective housing needs and housing resources of the parties and any child;

(b) the respective financial resources of the parties;

(c) the likely effect of any order, or of any decision by the court not to make such an order, on the health, safety or well-being of the parties and any relevant child;

(d) the conduct of the parties in relation to each other and otherwise;

(e) the nature of the parties' relationship, and in particular the level of commitment involved in it;

(f) the length of time that they have lived together as husband and wife;

(g) whether there are or have been any children who are children of both parties, or for whom both parties have or have had parental responsibility;

(h) the length of time that has elapsed since the parties ceased to live together; and

(i) the existence of any pending proceedings between the parties under Sch 1 to CA 1989 (financial orders relating to children), or relating to the legal or beneficial ownership of the home (s 36(6)).

In deciding whether to make an *exclusion provision*, the court must take into account all circumstances, including the factors (a)–(d) above in relation to an occupation provision. In addition, the court must consider the following balance of harm questions:

(a) whether the applicant or any relevant child is likely to suffer significant harm attributable to the conduct of the respondent if the exclusion provision is not made; and

(b) whether the harm likely to be suffered by the respondent or child if the provision is included is as great or greater than the harm attributable to the conduct of the respondent which is likely to be suffered by the applicant or child if the provision is not included.

This is similar to the balance of harm test in ss 33 and 35. However, there is no duty on the court to make an order where the greater harm to the applicant or child is established, it is just one question to be considered.

Once an order has been made and for so long as it is in force, s 36(13) provides that the applicant will be afforded the same protection as a spouse under s 30(3)–(6). This means that a mortgagee or landlord must accept payments towards the mortgage or rent made by the applicant.

Duration

An occupation order made under s 36 must be for a specified period not exceeding six months. The order can be extended only once, for a further specified period not exceeding six months. Thus the longest period for which a cohabitant or former cohabitant can obtain an occupation order is one year. In addition, any order shall cease to have effect on the death of either party.

15.2.4.3 Neither party has a right to occupy the home (ss 37 and 38)

These sections enable one spouse or civil partner, a former spouse or former civil partner, cohabitant or former cohabitant to obtain an occupation order against the other in relation to a home in which they both live or lived together but which neither of them has a right to occupy. These sections could be used, for example, to give the applicant a licence to occupy a home which is owned by the respondent's parents. Section 37 applies to spouses or former spouses; s 38 to cohabitants or former cohabitants.

As with ss 33, 35 and 36, such an order may, amongst other things, exclude the respondent from the home or an area in which the home is situated.

Factors that the court must consider

In deciding whether to grant an order under this section, the court must take into account similar factors to those under s 33 (where a spouse or former spouse is applying) or s 36 (where a cohabitant or former cohabitant is applying).

Duration

Any order granted will last for a specified period not exceeding six months. Where the applicant is a spouse or former spouse, the order can be extended on one or more occasions, each time for a specified period not exceeding six months. Where the applicant is a cohabitant or former cohabitant, the order can be extended once only for a further specified period not exceeding six months.

15.2.4.4 Examples

The following examples illustrate the above provisions. You may also find the flowchart at **15.2.4.6** helpful.

(a) Eric and Nicola are married. They live in a house left to Eric by his parents. Eric has begun drinking heavily recently and been very violent towards Nicola.

Nicola would apply under s 33. As she is married, she would have a right to occupy the matrimonial home under s 30 of the FLA 1996 as Eric owns it.

(b) Lillian and John cohabit in John's flat which he bought years ago. John has told Lillian the relationship is over and that she must leave. She is unable to do so, as she is totally financially dependent on him and is not well at the moment. This has made John very angry and he has used violence against Lillian to try to make her leave.

Lillian would apply under s 36 as she is a cohabitant and she has no right to occupy the home, but John does.

(c) Jenny and Agnes live in flat which is a tenancy in their joint names. Agnes, who is suffering from depression, has been using violence against Jenny, who is now frightened to return home.

Jenny will apply under s 33 as she is entitled to occupy the home by virtue of her tenancy.

(d) Katie and Steve live in Steve's parents' holiday home as they cannot afford to live elsewhere. They are not married. Katie has recently become pregnant and Steve is furious as he does not want the baby; he has been violent towards Katie almost every day since he found out.

Katie will apply under s 38, as neither of them has a right to occupy the home and they are cohabitants.

15.2.4.5 Additional provisions in occupation orders made under s 33, s 35 or s 36 (s 40)

Section 40 enables the court, when making an occupation order under s 33, s 35 or s 36, to make an ancillary order dealing with such matters as the payment of the mortgage or other outgoings, and payment for repair and maintenance of the home. The court can also order the occupying party to pay the excluded party rent where the excluded party would (but for the occupation order) have a right to occupy the home. In addition, the court can grant either party use of the furniture or other contents of the home and order either party to take reasonable care of the furniture or other contents. In deciding whether to make such an ancillary order and in what terms, the court shall have regard to all circumstances of the case, including the financial needs, resources and obligations of the parties. Any ancillary order made will last for the same length of time as the occupation order itself.

There is, however, a problem of enforcement of any order for payments made under s 40. In *Nwogbe v Nwogbe* [2000] 2 FLR 744, the husband was ordered to pay rent, council tax and water rates but did not do so. The Court of Appeal held that it had no power to commit him. The payments did not fall within any of the exceptions to the Debtors Act 1869 (which abolished imprisonment for debt), neither did they come within the Attachment of Earnings Act 1971. Since payments were made to a third party, the wife did not become a judgment creditor and so none of the usual methods of enforcement were available to her. The court accepted that there was a clear lacuna in the law which would need to be filled by Parliament.

15.2.4.6 Flowchart

The flowchart set out below explains who can apply for occupation orders and the appropriate section of the FLA 1996 to use.

OCCUPATION ORDERS – WHO CAN APPLY?

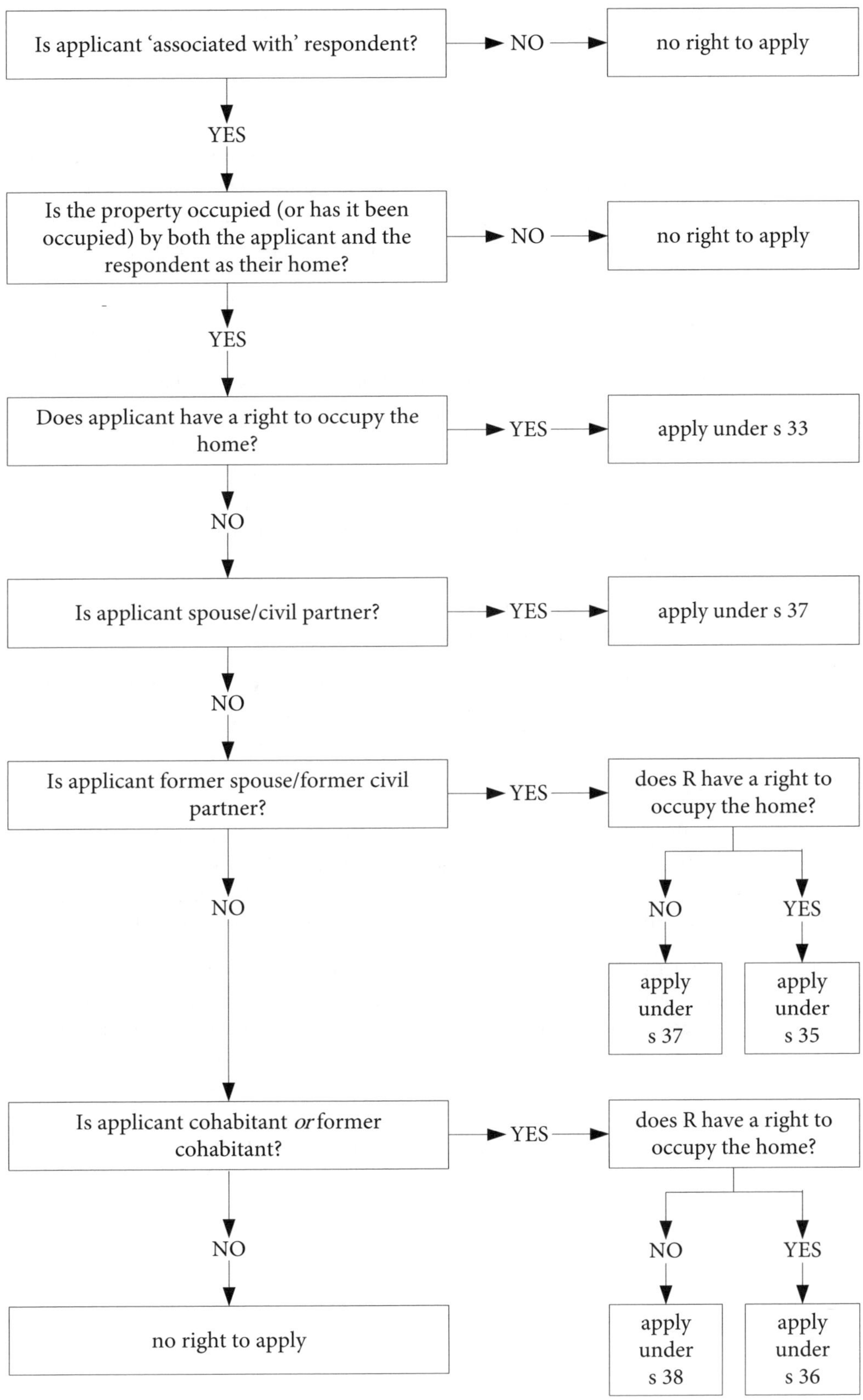

15.2.5 Emergency applications (s 45)

In urgent cases, it may be possible for the solicitor to protect an applicant or child on the same day that she comes to see him, or at least on the next day. Under s 45 of the FLA 1996, the court can make both non-molestation and occupation orders without notice to the respondent (or 'ex parte') where it considers that it is 'just and convenient' to do so. In deciding whether to allow an application to proceed without notice, the court will take into account all circumstances, including:

(a) any risk of significant harm to the applicant or child if the order is not made immediately;

(b) whether it is likely that the applicant will be deterred or prevented from pursuing the application if the order is not made immediately; and

(c) whether there is reason to believe that the respondent is evading service and delay in effecting service will seriously prejudice the applicant or child.

However, the courts are generally reluctant to grant orders where the respondent has been given no notice. Therefore, where it is not possible to give the respondent the full two clear days' notice required, the applicant's solicitor should consider whether to apply to abridge the notice period instead of applying without notice. Where the respondent has been given some notice (however short), he may be able to attend court to give his version of events. This will mean that the court will be in a better position to assess the situation and may therefore be persuaded to grant more wide-ranging relief than where the respondent has been given no notice at all. However, if the respondent has not had an opportunity to instruct a solicitor then the court is likely to make an interim (rather than final) order to allow the respondent time to seek legal advice before the final hearing.

Occupation orders are more rarely granted without notice, especially where they would involve ousting the respondent from his home.

It must be stressed that any order obtained without notice will be temporary only (an interim order). During the few days that the interim order is in force, the solicitor must obtain a hearing date for the final hearing and give the respondent the required notice.

15.2.6 Undertakings (s 46)

In the past, the necessity for a full hearing was often avoided by the respondent offering to give an undertaking, ie a promise to the court on similar terms to the proposed order. This avoided a court order being made against the respondent. The applicant was often prepared to accept the undertaking since, as it was made voluntarily, it was more likely to be complied with.

Under s 46 of the FLA 1996, the court may still accept an undertaking in any case where it has power to make an occupation or non-molestation order. However, no power of arrest can be attached to an undertaking, and the court will not accept an undertaking in a case where it would otherwise attach a power of arrest to an occupation order. The court will not accept an undertaking on an application for a non-molestation order where the respondent has used or threatened violence or a non-molestation order is necessary so that any breach can be punishable under s 42A as a criminal offence (see **15.2.9.1**)).

15.2.7 Procedure

15.2.7.1 Which court?

One of the innovations of Pt IV of the FLA 1996 was to introduce a unified system of courts to deal with domestic abuse applications. This means that the applicant's solicitor generally has a free choice whether to make the application in the county court, or in the family proceedings court.

The family proceedings court has no power to deal with disputes between the applicant and the respondent over the applicant's right to occupy the home (FLA 1996, s 59). A family proceedings court can make an order in such a case only where it is unnecessary to determine the ownership dispute in order to do so. Thus, any proceedings involving such a dispute should sensibly be commenced in the county court. However, where such proceedings are commenced in the family proceedings court and the court decides that it cannot deal with the application, it has the power to transfer the application to a county court.

Applications in the county court can be made only in divorce county courts or family hearing centres. Where proceedings are already pending in a particular court (eg divorce proceedings), the application should generally be made in those proceedings. Any application to extend, vary or discharge an order should be made to the court which originally made the order.

15.2.7.2 Transfer of cases

Irrespective of where a case started, it can be transferred to a more appropriate court. This will depend, amongst other things, upon whether the case raises a difficult point of law or a question of general public interest, and the need to consolidate it with proceedings which may have been started in another court (see Family Law Act 1996 (Part IV) (Allocation and Transfer of Proceedings) Order 2008).

Cases can be transferred either vertically or horizontally and between any level of court. Thus it would be possible, for example, for the High Court to transfer proceedings to a family proceedings court.

15.2.7.3 Public funding

Provided that the client is eligible, initial advice and assistance will be covered by Legal Help.

Once the decision has been taken to bring proceedings for a non-molestation order and/or an occupation order, Legal Representation should be applied for immediately. If the situation is urgent, there is no need to apply for Level 2 or 3 funding first. If there is an existing certificate for Family Help (Higher) or Legal Representation in force in matrimonial proceedings, the solicitor should apply to amend this rather than obtain a new certificate. Note that where the Legal Services Commission considers that it would be appropriate to write a warning letter to the respondent and/or to try to enlist the assistance of the police, it will not grant funding until these steps have been taken and proved ineffective. In addition, funding is likely to be refused unless the conduct complained of took place within the last two to three weeks, or if the conduct complained of is not likely to be repeated or is of a 'trivial nature'.

In most cases, it will also be necessary to apply for Emergency Legal Representation. Family solicitors can themselves grant Emergency Legal Representation under the terms of their contract if they have devolved powers. If they do not have devolved powers, they will need to apply to the Legal Services Commission by telephone or fax if it is an emergency.

The procedure set out below assumes that the applicant is entitled to public funding. For a privately paying client, simply omit all steps relating to public funding and remember that a court fee must be paid.

15.2.7.4 Obtaining a non-molestation or an occupation order without notice (ex parte)

(a) Grant Emergency Legal Representation. Emergency cover should only be granted for without notice proceedings where the applicant or child is in imminent danger of significant harm (ie there is a real risk that it will occur before a substantive application can be processed and brought before the court).

(b) Telephone the court to make an appointment before the judge or magistrate if necessary. In the family proceedings court, the clerk or the court must give leave to make an application without notice.

(c) Telephone a process server so that he can be at court at the end of the hearing to collect the without notice order to serve it on the respondent. The order must be served personally, and it is not usually thought wise for the solicitor to do this.

(d) Draft the following:

   (i) application in Form FL401 (see **Appendix 3(M)**);

   (ii) statement in support. This must give details of the respondent's behaviour and both parties' housing needs and financial resources. It should also explain why the application is made without notice. The statement must be signed by the applicant and sworn to be true in the county court, or declared to be true in the family proceedings court (which may also give leave to allow oral evidence instead of a written statement);

   (iii) notice of issue of Emergency Legal Representation;

   (iv) where the application is ancillary to a divorce under Legal Help, a notice of acting (for the reasons mentioned at **10.6.1**).

(e) It is not essential to draft the order sought. Generally, however, the court would find it helpful to have a draft and so, if time permits, draft the without notice order(s) on Form FL404 (occupation order) or Form FL404a (non-molestation order).

(f) File at court notice of issue of Emergency Legal Representation, the application in duplicate and the statement in support in duplicate, and notice of acting (if appropriate). A fee must be paid.

(g) Attend the hearing before the judge, district judge or magistrate (in the family proceedings court an application without notice can be heard by a single magistrate, on-notice applications must be heard by a panel – see **15.2.7.5**). The magistrate, judge or district judge will read the statement in support and listen to the applicant's oral evidence. Hand any draft order to the magistrate, judge or district judge.

(h) Any occupation order made will be issued in Form FL404 and any non-molestation order in Form FL404a. Where a power of arrest is attached to any of the provisions of an occupation order, those provisions shall be set out in Form FL406. A record of the hearing will be made on Form FL405. On filing, the court fixes a date for the on notice hearing, which will be inserted in a notice of proceedings (Form FL402). The respondent must be given two clear days' notice of this date.

(i) Hand the process server the without notice order(s), sealed copy application, copy statement in support, notice of proceedings and notice of issue of Emergency Legal Representation. Ask the process server to serve these documents on the respondent personally and then to swear an affidavit of service.

(j) If the court has made an occupation order, serve a copy of the application and the order on any mortgagee or landlord, together with a notice in Form FL416 informing him that he has a right to make representations in writing or at any hearing. These documents should be served by first-class post.

(k) If the court has made a non-molestation order or attached a power of arrest to an occupation order (see **15.2.9**), take a copy of Form FL404a or Form FL406 to the police station nearest to where the applicant lives and a statement showing that the respondent has been served with the order or informed of its terms. The police will not be prepared to exercise any power of arrest unless they have notice of it. Many breaches of orders occur shortly after they are made, so it is important to give the police notice of the order or the power of arrest as soon as possible.

Remember that any hearing without notice must be followed by a hearing on notice so that the respondent has an opportunity to put his side of the story.

15.2.7.5 Obtaining a non-molestation or an occupation order on notice

If a without notice order has been obtained, many of these steps may already have been completed:

(a) Grant Emergency Legal Representation.

(b) Draft the following:

  (i) application in Form FL401;

  (ii) statement in support. It must give details of the respondent's behaviour and both parties' housing needs and financial resources. The statement must be signed by the applicant and sworn to be true in the county court, or declared to be true in the family proceedings court (which may also give leave to allow oral evidence instead of a written statement). Where a without notice order has been obtained, the statement will probably already have been drafted. The same statement is generally used for both without notice and on notice hearings. However, where further instances of violence have occurred, or the initial statement has been hurriedly drafted, a further statement should be drafted;

  (iii) notice of issue of Legal Representation;

  (iv) where the application is ancillary to a divorce under Legal Help, a notice of acting (for the reasons mentioned at **10.6.1**).

(c) File the application in duplicate, statement in duplicate, notice of issue of Legal Representation, notice of acting (where appropriate) and Emergency Legal Representation certificate (where appropriate). A fee must be paid.

(d) On filing, the court fixes a hearing date which will be inserted in a notice of proceedings (Form FL402). The respondent must be given two clear days' notice of this date. Hand to a process server sealed copy application, copy statement in support, notice of hearing, notice of issue of Emergency Legal Representation and notice of acting (where appropriate). Ask him to serve these documents on the respondent personally and to swear an affidavit to confirm service.

(e) If the FL401 includes an application for an occupation order, serve any mortgagee or landlord with a copy of the application and a notice in Form FL416 informing him that he has a right to make representations in writing or at the hearing. These documents should be served by first-class post.

(f) Once the respondent (and mortgagee/landlord) has been served, file a statement confirming that this has been done in Form FL415.

(g) Prepare the draft order(s) required on Form FL404 or Form FL404a. This is not essential, but the court will find it useful.

(h) Attend the hearing before the judge or the district judge in chambers, or a panel of magistrates. In the family proceedings court, the hearing will take place before the domestic panel. This is a panel of magistrates who have received special training in family proceedings. The panel should consist of at least two magistrates, and should preferably include one man and one woman. The hearing will be in private. If the respondent fails to attend, service can be proved using the affidavit. The court can then make an order in the absence of the respondent.

   Hand any order(s) drafted to the judge, district judge or magistrates. The judge, district judge or magistrates will read any statements filed by the parties and may hear oral evidence from the applicant and respondent. If either of the parties has witnesses (eg a neighbour or relative) they may then give evidence. Any occupation order made will be issued on Form FL404 and any non-molestation order on Form FL404a. Where a power of arrest is attached to any of the provisions of an occupation order, those provisions will be set out on Form FL406. A record of the hearing will be made on Form FL405. The court may direct a further hearing to hear representations from any mortgagee or landlord.

(i) The respondent must be served personally with the order (even if he was present when it was made). Again, this is usually done by a process server who should swear an affidavit of service.

(j) If the court has made a non-molestation order or attached a power of arrest to an occupation order (see **15.2.9**), take a copy of Form FL404a or Form FL406 to the police station nearest to where the applicant lives.

15.2.8 Procedural checklist

A checklist of the appropriate procedure may be helpful. One is set out below.

ON NOTICE PROCEDURE CHECKLIST

OBTAIN LEGAL REPRESENTATION IF RELEVANT

FILE:
(i) Application (Form FL 401) in duplicate
(ii) Statement in support in duplicate
(iii) Legal Representation Certificate and Notice of Issue
(iv) Fee
(v) Notice of Acting (if client in divorce under Legal Help)

SERVE ON R:
(i) Copy Application
(ii) Copy Statement
[(iii) Notice of Issue of LR Certificate]
(iv) Notice of Hearing (Form FL 402)
[(v) Copy Notice of Acting]
[Give two clear days' notice]

SERVE ON MORTGAGEE/LANDLORD:
Notice in Form FL 416

FILE:
Statement of Service

ATTEND FIRST HEARING:
Present case
Produce draft order (if drafted)

SERVE order on R and mortgagee/landlord
LODGE copy at police station of Form FL404a or Form FL406

15.2.9 Enforcement

Since 1 July 2007 breach of a non-molestation order is a criminal offence (FLA 1996, s 42A). Before 1 July 2007 the basic method of enforcement where a respondent had breached a non-molestation order or an occupation order was committal for contempt of court. How the respondent came before the court depended generally on whether or not the order had a power of arrest attached to it. This position remains the same for breaches of an occupation order, but for non-molestation orders made after 1 July 2007 breach will be a criminal offence and dealt with differently.

15.2.9.1 Breach of a non-molestation order

Section 42A of the FLA 1996 makes breach of a non-molestation order a criminal offence punishable by up to five years' imprisonment on indictment and 12 months' imprisonment on conviction in the magistrates' court. Where a respondent breaches a non-molestation order, he will be arrested for the crime of breaching the order and can be charged and brought before a criminal court. The prosecution will be handled by the CPS and the solicitors for the complainant will not play any role.

A respondent cannot, however, be punished for the same offence twice, so if he is convicted of an offence under s 42A he cannot be punished for contempt of court for the same conduct.

15.2.9.2 Breach of an occupation order

Power of arrest

Under s 47 of the FLA 1996, where the court makes an occupation order (or, before 1 July 2007, where it made a non-molestation order) and it appears to the court that the respondent has used or threatened violence against the applicant (ie any associated person) or a child, then it *shall* attach a power of arrest to one or more provisions of the order. The only exception to this is where the court is satisfied that the applicant or child will be adequately protected without such a power of arrest.

The court can attach a power of arrest to one or more provisions of the order. Any power of arrest will be drafted on Form FL406, which will set out which provisions the power of arrest will apply to.

A power of arrest can also be attached to one or more provisions of a without notice order, but only where it appears to the court that the respondent has used or threatened violence against the applicant or child and that there is a risk of significant harm to the applicant or child if the power of arrest is not attached immediately.

Any power of arrest granted will usually be expressed to last for the same period as the provisions of the order to which it is attached (although this will not always be the case). This period can be extended any number of times.

A police officer will have the power to arrest the respondent without warrant if he has reasonable cause to suspect the respondent of being in breach of any of the terms of the order set out in the power of arrest. Once arrested, the respondent must be brought before a judge, district judge or magistrate within 24 hours.

Warrant of arrest

Where the court has not attached a power of arrest, or the respondent's breach is not covered by the power of arrest, or an undertaking is breached, the applicant may apply for a warrant of arrest. The applicant will need to give evidence on oath to satisfy the judge, district judge or magistrate that there are reasonable grounds for believing that the respondent has breached the order. The judge, district judge or magistrate can then issue a warrant of arrest.

Penalty

The penalty available will depend upon whether the respondent is brought before a judge in the county court, or a magistrate in the family proceedings court. In the county court, the judge can commit the respondent for up to two years (and/or impose an unlimited fine). In the family proceedings court, the respondent can be fined up to £5,000 or committed for up to two months.

In the case of *Hammerton v Hammerton* [2007] EWCA Civ 248, the Court of Appeal said proceedings for committal were a criminal charge for the purposes of Article 6 of the European Convention on Human Rights, so a defendant had the right to representation. Where a defendant to committal proceedings was unrepresented, the judge should enquire as to the circumstances in which he was unrepresented and consider, at the outset of the hearing, whether there should be an adjournment to enable the defendant to be represented.

In both the county court and the family proceedings court, immediate committal was a remedy of last resort and was unlikely to be ordered save in exceptional situations. General guidelines on committal were given by the Court of Appeal in *Hale v Tanner* [2000] 2 FLR 879. These include:

(a) that imprisonment is not the automatic consequence of the breach of an order but there was no principle that imprisonment should not be imposed on a first breach;

(b) that the court should bear in mind the context – there could be aggravating or mitigating factors;

(c) that the length of committal had to bear some reasonable relationship to the maximum available;

(d) that suspension was available in a much wider range of circumstances than in a criminal case and should usually be used initially where committal is contemplated to try to secure compliance with the order.

Since the Protection from Harassment Act 1997 (see **15.4** below), which provides greater sentencing powers, recent cases have seemed to indicate that courts are willing to impose longer custodial sentences for breaches of FLA 1996 orders than in the past. In *Lomas v Parle* [2003] EWCA Civ 1804, the Court of Appeal increased a sentence of imprisonment from four months to eight months, and said care must be taken that sentences for breach of FLA 1996 orders are not manifestly discrepant with those under the Protection from Harassment Act 1997. In *H v O (Contempt of Court: Sentencing)* [2004] EWCA Civ 1691, the Court of Appeal, whilst reducing a sentence of imprisonment from 12 months to nine months, stated that it felt that Parliament and society now demanded more deterrent punishment than in the past for domestic violence. In *Robinson v Murray* [2005] EWCA Civ 935, where the Court of Appeal upheld a sentence of eight months' imprisonment, it suggested if a case warranted a sentence near the top of the range, the appropriate course is to bring proceedings under the Protection from Harassment Act 1997 so that the greater powers of punishment are available to the court.

Finally, if the order had no power of arrest attached, the judge or magistrate may attach a power of arrest.

15.3 Human rights implications

Non-molestation or occupation orders may raise issues under Article 6 of the European Convention on Human Rights. Public funding is often denied to respondents to such orders, who may be advised to give undertakings on the basis of no admissions. Consideration may have to be given as to whether public funding should be provided, given that undertakings can be the first step in committal proceedings which may result in imprisonment or a fine. One of the Article 6 guarantees is that the proceedings are fair and that each party has 'equality of arms' with the other. Yet if a respondent is not represented on an application, can he be said to have 'equality of arms'?

Occupation orders may also raise issues under Article 8 (the right to respect for family life and home). Interference with this right must be necessary and proportionate. Courts must therefore give careful consideration to the duration and scope of such orders.

15.4 Protection from Harassment Act 1997

In the past, when an applicant did not come within the ambit of the relevant domestic abuse legislation, for example if she was the partner of the abuser but they had not cohabited, she would have to bring an action for an appropriate tort, for example, assault. However, until quite recently, there was no tort of harassment, so protection could be obtained only where the conduct complained of amounted to an established tort (see, eg, *Burris v Azadani* [1995] 4 All ER 802).

The PHA 1997 plugged this gap in the law. Section 3 of the PHA 1997 created a statutory tort where a person pursues a course of conduct which amounts to harassment of another and which he knows or ought to know amounts to harassment of the other. There is no definition of harassment, save that the PHA 1997 states that this includes 'alarming the person or causing them distress' (s 7). A 'course of conduct' must include conduct on at least two occasions.

Section 3 provides that where the statutory tort has been committed or is apprehended, the victim may claim damages and/or an injunction. Should the injunction be breached, then the victim may apply for a warrant of arrest in the same way as under the FLA 1996. Also, breach of the injunction may be a criminal offence, punishable by up to five years' imprisonment on conviction on indictment (s 3(6) and (9)).

The PHA 1997 also created two new criminal offences, criminal harassment and the more serious offence of putting someone in fear of violence (ss 2 and 4 respectively). In addition, s 5 gives the criminal courts power to make restraining orders prohibiting the perpetrator from engaging in further harassment on conviction (since 30 September 2009 this has been widened to include conviction of any offence, not just offences under the PHA 1997). From 30 September 2009, the new s 5A allows the criminal courts to make restraining orders on the acquittal of a defendant if they consider it necessary to protect a person from harassment by the defendant.

15.5 The Forced Marriage (Civil Protection) Act 2007

The Forced Marriage (Civil Protection) Act 2007, which came into force in November 2008, inserted a new Pt IVA into the FLA 1996, which allows the court to make a forced marriage protection order to protect a person from being forced into marriage, or an attempt being made to force a person into marriage, or to protect a person who has been forced into marriage. The order can contain such prohibitions, restrictions or requirements and other terms as the court considers appropriate for the purposes of the order, and it may cover conduct outside England and Wales.

An application may be made by the victim or, from 1 November 2009, by a relevant third party (the local authority) or by another person with leave of the court (this envisages including friends, boyfriends and girlfriends, or teachers of the victim). An order may alternatively be made without application in existing family proceedings. The respondent need not be the other party to the forced marriage and can include additional third parties beyond those who are forcing the victim to marry, such as those who are, amongst other behaviour, aiding and abetting or encouraging or assisting those who are forcing or attempting to force the victim to marry.

In deciding whether to exercise its powers under this section and, if so, in what manner, the court must have regard to all the circumstances, including the need to secure the health, safety and well-being of the person to be protected. In ascertaining that person's well-being, the court must, in particular, have such regard to the person's wishes and feelings (so far as they are reasonably ascertainable) as the court considers appropriate in the light of the person's age and understanding.

Orders can be made without notice where it is 'just and convenient' to do so, and a power of arrest can be attached to an order. If the respondent breaches the order it is contempt of court, which is punishable by a maximum of two years' imprisonment.

15.6 Chapter summary

(1) In cases of domestic abuse, a solicitor will have to decide whether to take action in the civil courts, or whether other remedies, for example writing a warning letter, involving the police or removing the victim to a safe environment, may be more appropriate.

(2) The FLA 1996 allows applicants to apply for two main types of relief:

  (a) non-molestation orders;

  (b) occupation orders.

(3) Non-molestation orders can be obtained by a wide range of 'associated persons'.

(4) Occupation orders can be applied for by a more limited range of people. Whether a person has a right to occupy the home, or is a former spouse, cohabitant or former cohabitant will determine whether they can apply at all and the relief they can obtain.

(5) In urgent cases, it may be possible to obtain orders under the FLA 1996 without notice.

(6) The respondent may give an undertaking instead of having an order made against him.

(7) A power of arrest must generally be attached to an occupation order unless the court is satisfied that the applicant will be adequately protected without it.

(8) Where a non-molestation order is breached it is a criminal offence.

(9) Where an occupation order is breached it can be enforced by applying for committal of the respondent for contempt of court.

(10) The PHA 1997 created a new statutory tort of harassment which may be used where the applicant does not fall within the provisions of the FLA 1996.

(11) The Forced Marriage (Civil Protection) Act 2007 protects a person being forced into marriage or who has been forced into marriage.

Chapter 16
The Cohabiting Family

16.1	Introduction	253
16.2	Setting up home together	254
16.3	Breaking up	256
16.4	Children	261
16.5	Bankruptcy	263
16.6	Death	263
16.7	Chapter summary	264

16.1 Introduction

In this chapter the terms 'cohabiting family' and 'cohabiting couples' are used to refer to couples who live together without marrying (or entering into a civil partnership).

The number of couples who are living together has dramatically increased in recent years and over 40% of births are outside marriage. Family lawyers have traditionally been consulted by such couples when their relationship breaks down; but increasingly nowadays, they are being instructed by couples who want advice on setting up home together.

In July 2004 the (then) Department for Constitutional Affairs launched a public information campaign, 'Living Together'. This had the aim of making cohabiting couples more aware of their legal status and providing them with practical advice on how they could protect themselves and their families, as survey results had shown there was a common public misconception that cohabiting couples enjoy similar rights to married couples. Unfortunately, research published in 2008 showed that 51% of people still believe that there is a status of 'common law marriage' which gives cohabitants the same rights as married couples.

The financial orders available under the MCA 1973 do not apply to cohabiting couples, and to date English law has developed piecemeal to deal with the problems of such couples.

The Civil Partnership Act 2004 arose as a result of pressure for reform in this area. However, this deals with the position of same-sex couples only. The Government's reason for not extending it to heterosexual couples was that they already have the option of marriage available to them.

During the passage of the Civil Partnership Act through Parliament, concerns were expressed about the lack of a coherent scheme of remedies to relieve the potential financial hardship of cohabiting couples on relationship breakdown. As a result of this the Law Commission was asked to review the law in this area and to suggest possible reforms. In July 2007 the Law Commission published its report, *Cohabitation: The Financial Consequences of Relationship Breakdown*, which proposed a scheme to provide remedies for eligible applicants (such as those with children or who have lived together for a specified time), so long as they had not agreed to disapply the scheme and only if the applicant had made qualifying contributions to the relationship giving rise to enduring consequences at the point of separation (such as giving up a career to care for the couple's children). In March 2008 the Government announced that it would delay acting on the Law Commission's proposals, as it wanted to examine research on the Family Law (Scotland) Act 2006, which came into force in Scotland in 2007 and contains provisions similar to those recommended by the Law Commission. The Government announced in September 2011, following the results of the research on the Family Law (Scotland) Act 2006, that it did not intend to take forward the Law Commission's recommendations in this parliamentary term.

For several years Resolution has been actively considering the question of comprehensive reform in this area, and in 2008 a Cohabitation Bill was introduced into Parliament which did not succeed.

This chapter summarises the current legal position both during the time when the couple are living together, including advice on how to avoid problems in the first place, and when the relationship breaks down.

16.2 Setting up home together

16.2.1 Ownership of the home

16.2.1.1 Duty of the buyers' solicitor

When a solicitor acts for joint buyers, he has a duty to advise on the relative merits of owning as joint tenants and tenants in common, and may be sued in negligence if he fails to do this (see *Walker v Hall* [1984] FLR 126, *Taylor v Warners* (1988) 85(25) LSG 26).

It is also important to consider when advising joint buyers whether there is any conflict, or potential conflict, of interest between them, in which case a solicitor should not act for both of them.

16.2.1.2 Declaration as to beneficial interests

An effective way to clarify beneficial interests in a jointly-owned property is by using a declaration of trust. Section 53(1)(b) of the Law of Property Act 1925 requires that a declaration must be in writing signed by the buyers. This will generally be conclusive evidence as to the ownership (*Pettit v Pettit* [1970] AC 777). Since there is no equivalent to s 25 of the MCA 1973 (see **4.5**) for an unmarried couple, the arrangement cannot be undone by the court at a later stage. Therefore, the buyers must both understand the position and be in agreement as to their respective shares at the time of purchase.

The declaration can either be included in the purchase deed, or be contained in a separate deed. On balance, it is preferable to prepare a separate document, especially if the property is registered, because Land Registry will not return the transfer after registration.

A further advantage is that some other important matters can be dealt with in a separate document, for example division of outgoings such as repairs, insurance and the mortgage repayments; circumstances in which a sale may take place or be postponed; and, if necessary, provisions giving one party an option to buy the other's share.

16.2.2 Life insurance

It is important that couples living together make provision for life insurance to cover each of them against the financial consequences of the death of the other.

There is a legal requirement that provides that the person for whom the benefit of a life assurance policy is made must have an insurable interest in the life of the assured, otherwise the policy will be void and illegal (Life Assurance Act 1774, s 1). This interest must be of a financial nature. This can be a problem because, whilst marriage is recognised as giving the parties an insurable interest in each others' lives without the need to prove financial loss, cohabitation is not so recognised. It is therefore essential that where couples are living together, mutual financial support can be shown.

Most couples are concerned with life insurance in relation to an endowment or repayment mortgage upon their home. Clear advice must be given to them on the validity of the policy and the consequences if they split up. Insurance is also relevant in the guise of death benefit paid as part of an employment contract. Often the employee can nominate to whom the money should be paid by giving instructions to the trustees of the scheme.

16.2.3 Wills

The vast majority of people die intestate. This is not advisable, especially for a cohabiting couple (see **16.6.2**). When a couple decide to live together, they should discuss whether provisions should be made for the survivor if one of them should die. Wills that contain complementary provisions could then be made. A solicitor acting on a house purchase can explain the problems and encourage the buyers to make a will. A will might appoint a guardian for any children and deal with the division of assets.

16.2.4 Cohabitation agreements

A cohabiting couple can enter into an agreement setting out arrangements which will apply while they are living together, as well as establishing rights on the breakdown of the relationship. This is a developing area of the law and as yet there is no modern decision on the validity of such agreements. However, in *Sutton v Mischon De Reya and Gower & Co* [2003] EWHC 3166 (Ch), [2004] 1 FLR 837, the court gave the strongest indication yet that there was nothing contrary to public policy in a cohabitation agreement. It is clear that solicitors are increasingly being asked to advise on and draft agreements in this field. The Law Commission, in its report (see **16.1**), recommends legislation to make clear that cohabitation agreements are not contrary to public policy.

16.2.4.1 Validity of cohabitation agreements

In the absence of modern authority, cohabitation agreements are governed by general principles of the law of contract. The following issues could therefore be relevant.

Illegality on grounds of public policy

To avoid challenge on the ground of illegality on grounds of public policy an agreement must avoid any implication that cohabitation is part of the obligations of the agreement. It is, therefore, safer to enter into the agreement after, rather than before, the couple have started living together.

Undue influence

Undue influence may arise if the agreement is unduly favourable to one party and that party cannot show that it was entered into freely or following independent advice (see *Zamet and Others v Hyman and Another* [1961] 3 All ER 933).

A related issue for a solicitor is to bear in mind that it is likely to be impossible to act for both parties due to the potential conflict of interest. For example, one party may be contributing all the finance for a house purchase, which would mean that the other party, in agreeing to this in a cohabitation agreement, would give up any chance of obtaining a share if the relationship broke down. As a general principle, The Law Society's Family Law Protocol (Part V, para 2.2) says that solicitors should advise clients that they can only act for one party in drawing up such an agreement and that the other party should be separately represented.

Intention to create legal relations

In domestic circumstances there is a rebuttable presumption that the parties did not intend to enter into a contract. Where the couple have a written agreement, especially if they received separate legal advice upon it, it should not be difficult to rebut the presumption (see *Balfour v Balfour* [1919] 2 KB 571 and *Merritt v Merritt* [1970] 1 WLR 1121).

Certainty

Any arrangements proposed must be set out clearly, otherwise the agreement may fail through lack of certainty.

Consideration

Any potential problem arising from a failure of consideration can be avoided by making the agreement a deed.

16.2.4.2 Matters to be covered in a cohabitation agreement

The main issues which could usefully be covered in a cohabitation agreement are as follows:

(a) ownership of real and personal property (see **16.2.1**);

(b) finances, for example, how to divide bills and resolve ownership of joint accounts;

(c) children, for example, their maintenance and surnames. Any agreement made in relation to children will be limited by the CA 1989 and the CSA 1991 and will be open to review by the court (see **16.4**);

(d) other matters: here it is important not to include matters which are too trivial, or personal matters, for example housework or division of chores, because this could make it more likely that a court would hold that the parties did not intend to create legal relations.

16.2.4.3 Enforcement of cohabitation agreements

The general rules of contract will apply to the enforcement of cohabitation agreements. It might also be advisable to include an arbitration clause in the agreement for dealing with disputes between the parties. The Family Law Bar Association Conciliation Board's conciliation procedure is available to unmarried couples who have lived together.

16.3 Breaking up

When cohabiting couples split up, neither party has any right to claim maintenance from the other. Maintenance can nevertheless be claimed for children of the relationship (see **16.4.2**). Major disputes are therefore likely to centre around the ownership or occupation of their home. It is possible to bring the dispute before the court by seeking a declaration of ownership of the home under s 14 of the Trusts of Land and Appointment of Trustees Act 1996 (TLATA 1996) (see **Appendix 1(H)**).

If the couple were engaged within three years before the dispute, it might be possible to use s 17 of the Married Women's Property Act 1882. This Act enables property disputes to be determined summarily by the county court; generally it is used only by married couples. The Act confers no jurisdiction to vary property rights and so the court's powers are purely declaratory (*Mossop v Mossop* [1988] 2 All ER 20).

16.3.1 Ownership of the home

16.3.1.1 Jointly-owned property

If the correct procedure was adopted when the property was purchased, the couple's intentions as to ownership should be clear from the purchase deed or declaration of trust. If the couple purchased as joint tenants, either could apply to the court for an order of sale under s 14 of the TLATA 1996 and the proceeds would then be divided equally. If the couple purchased as tenants in common, or if the joint tenancy was severed, only a declaration of trust made by them will be decisive (see **16.2.1.2**).

If they own as tenants in common and there is no declaration of trust, it will be presumed they own in equal shares unless the contrary can be proved (*Stack v Dowden* [2007] UKHL 17). The onus is on the party who wishes to show that the beneficial interest is divided other than equally. In *Stack v Dowden*, the House of Lords said it would look at many factors as well as the financial contributions the parties made, such as how the parties conducted their finances and why the house was acquired, to determine whether they intended to own it in unequal shares.

It also said that cases where the joint legal owners were to be taken to have intended that their beneficial interests should be different from their legal interests would be very unusual.

In *Stack v Dowden*, the House of Lords said that when determining the size of a claimant's share, where there had been no express agreement, the court had to determine what the parties' intentions had been, actual or inferred, with respect to the property in the light of their whole course of conduct in relation to it.

This was further clarified and expanded on in *Jones v Kernott* [2011] UKSC 53 where the following principles were set out:

(a) the starting point is that they are joint tenants in law and equity;

(b) that presumption can be displaced by showing that they had a different common intention when they acquired the home or they later formed the common intention that their shares would change;

(c) their common intention is to be inferred or deduced objectively from their conduct;

(d) where it is clear the parties did not intend a joint tenancy at the outset or had changed their original intention, but it is not possible to ascertain by direct evidence or inference what they intended their shares to be, each party will be entitled to the share the court considers fair having regard to the whole course of dealing between them in relation to the property. Thus the court will impute an intention to the parties.

It is open to one partner to buy out the other's interest. If this is done, the prior permission of any lender must be sought. In contrast to divorcing couples, any transfer will be liable to stamp duty land tax on the consideration paid plus the amount of any mortgage debt assumed (see Stamp Act 1891, s 57, Inland Revenue SP 27 April 1990, Finance Act 1985, s 83(1), and Stamp Duty (Exempt Instruments) Regulations 1987 (SI 1987/516), Category H).

16.3.1.2 Legal estate in one name only

If a property is in the sole legal ownership of one party, the presumption is that that party also owns all the beneficial interest. In this situation the other party will have to establish a claim in equity. This will involve establishing a resulting or constructive trust, or proprietary estoppel. The court cannot alter an unmarried partner's share to reflect MCA 1973, s 25 principles as it is able to do with a married couple.

If a claim is successful and a trust is established, the non-legal owner will be entitled to a share in the property equal to his beneficial interest as determined by the court in accordance with land law principles. If proprietary estoppel is established then one of the remedies available is to give the claimant an interest in the property.

Until recently, interests based on direct contributions, for example, to the purchase price of a property have been dealt with under resulting trusts; interests founded on wider equitable principles, for example on the basis that it is just and equitable, are clearly constructive trusts or proprietary estoppel.

Resulting trusts

Resulting trusts can be established only by a direct contribution to the purchase price by the partner who is not the legal owner. *Curley v Parkes* [2004] EWCA Civ 1515 suggested that the contribution must be made at the time of purchase and that subsequent payments, such as mortgage payments, would not suffice. However, a direct contribution to the purchase price will not establish a trust if given by way of gift or loan. The successful claimant will be awarded a share to reflect the initial contribution made (contrast this with the position under constructive trusts (below) where, in the absence of any express agreement as to the size of the share, the court will decide what shares the parties intended by looking at the their whole course of conduct in relation to the property). *Stack v Dowden* suggests that, in domestic cases of cohabitants, resulting trusts are no longer the appropriate approach, and that these cases should be decided under the principle of constructive trusts (see below). This was continued more recently in *Jones v Kernott* [2011] UKSC 53.

Constructive trusts

In *Lloyds Bank plc v Rosset* [1990] 2 WLR 867, [1990] 1 All ER 1111, the House of Lords considered the law in this area in detail, and the case contains a clear analysis of the circumstances where equity will impose a trust on the legal owner.

For a constructive trust to arise the claimant must show there was a common intention to share ownership and that the claimant acted in reliance on this to his detriment.

The common intention can be established by an express agreement. In *H v M (Property: Beneficial Interest)* [1992] 1 FLR 229, the parties lived together for 11 years, had two children, but never married. The assets included two bungalows in Essex and a property in Spain, all in the legal ownership of the man. The woman claimed a beneficial interest in the property. The court looked very closely at exactly what had been said by the parties as to how any assets would be divided. The man had said to the woman, 'Don't worry about the future because when we are married it will be half yours anyway and I'll always look after you and the boy'. The man also made an excuse that the property was in his name alone for 'tax reasons'. As on the facts there was an express common intention (his statements to her), the woman had to show only that she had acted on this to her detriment. The court accepted that her detrimental action was the execution of a mortgage deed by her 'as occupier' postponing any rights she might have to the lender, thus prejudicing her domestic security. On this basis, the court awarded her an equal share in the English property, but dismissed her claim for a share of the Spanish house as no similar conversation had taken place.

The court will generally find a trust from discussions in the course of which the legal owner gives an excuse why legal ownership is not to be shared. In *Eves v Eves* [1975] 1 WLR 1338, a man told the woman that the property was only in his name as she was under 21 years of age. Subsequently, she worked on various structural alterations to it. She was held to be entitled to a 25% share (see also *Grant v Edwards* [1986] Ch 638).

If there is no evidence of an express agreement, a common intention to share the property can be inferred from the parties' conduct. Conduct such as payment of mortgage instalments and financial contributions to improvements to the property can be used to infer the common intention to share the property.

Contributions by labour may also count. In *Cooke v Head* [1972] 1 WLR 518, the woman non-legal owner made a small contribution to the mortgage payments as well as contributions by manual labour in helping to build a bungalow on land owned by the man. She was entitled to a one-third share for their 'joint efforts'. However, in the *Lloyds Bank* case (above) it was pointed out that a common intention by the parties to renovate a house as a joint venture did not throw any light on their intentions with respect to the beneficial ownership of the property. The work done by the wife in supervising and helping with work and decorating was not enough on its own in this case to justify the inference of a common intention to share.

Generally, contributions to household expenses other than the mortgage are much less likely to establish a trust. In *Burns v Burns* [1984] Ch 317, an unmarried couple with two children occupied for 17 years a house bought in the man's name. The woman made no contribution towards deposit or mortgage repayments, but fully performed the tasks expected of a wife and mother and, when able to return to work, was content to meet the household expenses out of her earnings. At no time did the man depend on her financial help. In that case, it was held that the necessary common intention could not be inferred from her natural concern with the well-being of the household. More recently, however, in *Le Foe v Le Foe and Woolwich plc; Woolwich plc v Le Foe and Le Foe* [2001] 2 FLR 970, the court decided that it was entitled to infer that the parties commonly intended that the wife should have a beneficial interest as a result of her indirect contributions to the mortgage.

However, in addition there must be detrimental reliance. The court appears to take a wide view of this, as illustrated above in *H v M*. Nevertheless, in *Midland Bank v Dobson and Dobson* [1986] 1 FLR 171, the performance by the woman of normal household duties and the purchase by her of household items were 'quite consistent with the man's absolute ownership of the house'. Unless followed by conduct of a sacrificial nature, the expression of intention was at best an unenforceable declaration of trust lacking the written evidence required by Law of Property Act 1925, s 53(1)(b).

Determining the size of the share

In *Jones v Kernott* [2011] UKSC 53, which was a case of jointly owned property, the Court said that in situations where the property is in the sole name of one party, the first issue is to determine whether the other party has any beneficial interest in the property at all. If that is established then the court has to decide what that interest is. There is no presumption of joint beneficial ownership. The parties' common intention had to be deduced objectively from their conduct, but if this is not possible then the parties will receive a share the court considers fair having regard to the whole course of dealing between them in relation to the property.

Proprietary estoppel

The doctrine of estoppel has been used to give rights of ownership: see *Pascoe v Turner* [1979] 1 WLR 431 (although remedies also include granting a licence to occupy (see **16.3.2**) or payment of money to the claimant). Three elements are required:

(a) an assurance of an interest in the property;

(b) reliance on that assurance;

(c) detriment suffered as a result.

Proprietary estoppel is wider and more flexible than a constructive trust, which requires common intention to be shown rather than just an assurance.

16.3.2 Occupation of home

If a non-legal owner does not have any beneficial interest in the property under the principles discussed above, he or she will have no right to remain there and may be excluded by the owner at any time on giving reasonable notice. However, in these circumstances the following ways of protecting the non-legal owner must be considered:

(a) contractual licence;

(b) licence by estoppel;

(c) FLA 1996, Pt IV;

(d) CA 1989, s 15 and Sch 1.

16.3.2.1 Contractual licence

It is necessary to establish the existence of a contract creating a licence. This means that a party will have to show that there was an intention to create legal relations, offer and acceptance, and consideration.

In *Tanner v Tanner* [1975] 3 All ER 776, a woman gave up a rent-controlled flat to occupy a house bought by the man, in which she brought up their children. The court found a licence for her to occupy the property did exist which would last until the children grew up.

Each case must depend on the particular circumstances and often the necessary elements for a contract will not be established (see *Coombes v Smith* [1986] 1 WLR 808).

16.3.2.2 Licence by estoppel

If there is insufficient evidence to establish a contract, the doctrine of estoppel has sometimes been invoked to give rise to rights of occupation rather than ownership.

Three elements are required:

(a) assurance of the right to occupy;

(b) reliance on that assurance;

(c) detriment suffered as a result.

In *Greasley v Cooke* [1980] 3 All ER 710, the woman was engaged initially as a maid, but subsequently cohabited with the son of the family for 30 years. The woman looked after the children and was led to believe she could remain in the property for as long as she wished. The court held that an equity had been raised that could only be satisfied by allowing her to remain in the house for as long as she wished (see also *Maharaj v Chand* [1986] AC 898).

16.3.2.3 Family Law Act 1996

Provided the man and woman are cohabitants or former cohabitants, an unmarried partner may obtain an order under the FLA 1996 either to protect her and any children living with her from further violence from her partner, or, in certain circumstances, an order to remove her partner from the home (see **Chapter 15**).

Even if the FLA 1996 is used, it will provide only short-term protection as the order will give no long-term right to remain in the home.

Reference should be made to the Housing Act 1996 (see **6.10**) to establish whether the local authority has any duty to provide alternative housing.

16.3.2.4 Children Act 1989, s 15 and Sch 1

An unmarried parent could apply on behalf of a child for financial orders from the other parent (see **13.10.4**). The orders that can be obtained include a property adjustment order or a settlement. It would be possible for a child to be granted a transfer of property order (which will include a tenancy), or a *Mesher* order to provide the child with a home until he is no longer dependent. The non-owning partner looking after the child would, therefore, be able to occupy the property as he would be looking after the child (see *J v J (A Minor: Property Transfer)* [1993] 2 FLR 56).

16.3.3 Sale of the property

If the property is jointly owned, or if it is established that a trust of land does exist by virtue of a resulting or constructive trust, one partner can apply to the court for an order to deal with any dispute. The most likely dispute is that one partner will want to sell the house and the other will wish to remain living there. The application will now be made under the TLATA 1996 (see **Appendix 1(H)**).

Sections 14 and 15 of the TLATA 1996 give the court wide powers to deal with any disputes concerning land subject to a trust. Section 14 gives the court power to make an order that reflects the underlying nature and purpose of the trust. Section 15 sets out the matters to which the court must have regard in determining any application for an order under s 14. They include:

(a) the intention of the person or persons who created the trust;

(b) the purpose for which the property subject to the trust is held;

(c) the welfare of any minor who occupies, or might reasonably be expected to occupy any trust property as his home; and

(d) the interests of any secured creditor (eg a mortgagee) of any beneficiary.

If the court finds that the home is still needed as a family home it will delay a sale. This could be until the children grow up. Even where there are no children, the court could postpone the sale of the house for a specified period, for example to give the occupier time to buy out the non-occupier, or until the occupier finds alternative accommodation. This will only be a postponement for a few months at the most.

The effect of the TLATA 1996 is to combine the old legal provisions in the Law of Property Act 1925, s 30 and the existing case law under that section (*Re Ever's Trust* [1980] 1 WLR 1327; *Bernard v Josephs* [1983] 4 FLR 178) to ensure that the court has broad and flexible powers.

If the client is publicly funded, the statutory charge will apply to proceedings under s 14 of the TLATA 1996 (see **2.9**). However, the Legal Services Commission has power, at its discretion, to postpone enforcement of the statutory charge in any case where the home is recovered or preserved under s 14 proceedings, or the proceedings result in the payment of a lump sum to the applicant which is to be used to purchase a home.

16.3.4 Tenancies

The FLA 1996 has altered the position of cohabitants in relation to certain tenancies. The basic position before the Act (which will still be the position if the FLA 1996 does not apply) is that if a tenancy is in the name of one partner, the other has no protection and will be a bare licensee who can be evicted on 'reasonable notice'. An occupation order may give protection under the FLA 1996 for a limited period (see **Chapter 15**). If the couple are joint tenants, both will be entitled to occupy the property. If one gives up occupation, the other's continued occupation ensures the continuance of the tenancy.

Sch 7 to the FLA 1996 introduced for the first time the right, in some circumstances, for a cohabitant to obtain a tenancy transfer order in relation to certain tenancies. The right to apply for a transfer order will apply irrespective of whether the tenancy is held jointly by the couple or by one of them alone, and will only be available on separation where the tenancy was of a dwelling house the couple occupied together as husband and wife. The court's powers are available only in relation to tenancies specified in the Act, including protected and statutory tenancies within the Rent Act 1977, some agricultural tenancies, a secure tenancy (Housing Act 1985, s 79) and an assured tenancy (Housing Act 1988, Pt VII).

When deciding whether to make a tenancy transfer order the court must have regard to all the circumstances of the case, including the circumstances in which the tenancy was granted or in which either party became the tenant, similar factors to those relevant when granting occupation orders (see **Chapter 15**) and the suitability of the parties as tenants. Schedule 7 contains detailed provisions specifying the transfer orders that can be made, and also gives the court a discretion to award compensation to the transferor. Orders under Sch 7 take effect without the need for any further document transferring the tenancy. The power to transfer tenancies could, therefore, be used as an alternative to an occupation order.

16.4 Children

There is an increasing number of children born each year to parents who are not married to each other. This makes no difference to the day-to-day care of the child while they are cohabiting, but there are legal differences which will alter the legal position if the parents separate. This section looks at the differences in the legal position where a child's parents are not married.

16.4.1 Parental responsibility

Where the parents of a child are not married at the time of the child's birth, the mother will have sole parental responsibility for the child (CA 1989, s 2(2)(a) (see **Appendix 1(E)**)). The father will not have parental responsibility unless he acquires it in accordance with the provisions of the Act (see **13.2.2**). Strictly, only the mother will have the right to sign a form of consent to an operation, decide where the child should be educated, or appoint a guardian for the child if the father does not have parental responsibility.

Not having parental responsibility does not cut the father off completely, because the Act allows even a father without parental responsibility to apply for any s 8 order without leave as he will come within the definition of 'parent' for the purposes of the Act. So, if he is unhappy about any aspect of the child's upbringing, he could apply for a specific issue order to determine the dispute with the mother. He could also apply for a residence order, so the child could live with him. If his child is in care, he can apply for contact with the child (CA 1989, s 34). However, in any event he may still prefer formally to share parental responsibility. This could be reassuring for him if, for example, the child's mother has religious objections to blood transfusions, and parental responsibility will give him more rights if the child is taken into care or put up for adoption.

The ways in which an unmarried father can acquire parental responsibility for his child are examined in detail at **13.2.2**.

Also, in the case of children born to female same-sex couples and conceived by IVF or artificial insemination at a licensed clinic, the Human Fertilisation and Embryology Act 2008 allows a mother to nominate her female partner as the 'parent' of the child in certain circumstances (see **13.2.3.3** above), which will enable the female 'parent' to obtain parental responsibility in similar ways to an unmarried father.

16.4.1.1 Human Rights Act 1998

The fact that some unmarried fathers (currently) have to apply for parental responsibility, unlike all mothers and married fathers, has not been found to violate their rights under the HRA 1998. In the Scottish case of *McMichael v UK* (1995) 20 EHRR 205, the child of unmarried parents was placed in care and then freed for adoption. The parents were denied access to essential documents and the mother brought a successful complaint under Article 6 of the European Convention on Human Rights. The father complained that, as an unmarried father without parental rights, he was discriminated against as he had no right to the legal custody of his son or to participate in the care proceedings. The European Court of Human Rights held that the relevant legislation, which distinguished between married and unmarried fathers, had the legitimate aim of providing a mechanism for identifying meritorious fathers. The conditions imposed on natural fathers for obtaining recognition of their parental rights were proportionate to that aim.

What is of perhaps greater concern is the fact that the court can remove parental responsibility from unmarried fathers but not from mothers or married fathers. In *Smallwood v UK* (1999) 2 EHRLR 221, a father whose contact order had been revoked then lost parental responsibility after the court considered that he would use it to disrupt the children. The father's application to the Commission was declared inadmissible on the basis that differences in treatment between married and unmarried men had an objective and reasonable justification. The Commission also said it was compatible with the Convention to have a system whereby the rights of unmarried fathers concerning care or custody over their children were more limited than those of the mother.

Removal of parental responsibility is clearly a serious interference with a father's right to family life under Article 8. Yet, on the basis of Convention cases, it seems likely that applications under the HRA 1998 may similarly fail on the basis that interference with this particular Convention right is justifiable and necessary.

In addition, there are other areas of potential disadvantage to unmarried fathers without parental responsibility where they may be able to argue a breach of Article 8 and Article 14 (the right not to be discriminated against in the delivery of Convention rights). For example, a child may not be removed from the jurisdiction without either the consent of everyone with parental responsibility or the leave of the court, which means that an unmarried father without parental responsibility has no right to object.

16.4.2 Financial provision and property orders

The ways of applying for maintenance and property orders for the benefit of children of unmarried parents are much more limited than those available for children of married parents (see **Chapter 13**). The two methods available are, first, to apply for maintenance using the CSA 1991 (this Act applies to all absent parents irrespective of their marital status) and, secondly, to apply under the CA 1989.

The CA 1989 expressly provides that a father's obligation to maintain his children does not depend on his having parental responsibility. The financial provisions contained in s 15 of and Sch 1 to the CA 1989 apply to both married and unmarried parents. The most useful provisions for an unmarried parent are those enabling lump sum orders and property transfer and settlement orders (see **13.10.4** and **16.3.2.4**).

16.5 Bankruptcy

A bankrupt's property vests in the trustee in bankruptcy. A partner remaining in the home may be a joint owner or have a beneficial interest. The trustee in bankruptcy can apply for an order for sale of the home and is likely to be successful. If the application for sale is made more than one year after the bankruptcy, the court must assume that the interests of the creditors outweigh all other considerations unless the circumstances of the case are exceptional (see **9.9.1**).

16.6 Death

16.6.1 Ownership rights

If the home was jointly owned as beneficial joint tenants, on the death of one party the survivor will become the sole owner. If the home was jointly owned as beneficial tenants in common, the deceased's share will pass in accordance with his will, or under the intestacy rules. In both cases there are inheritance tax problems because, as the parties were not married, the spouse exemption does not apply.

The sole legal owner of the home may die without leaving it by will to the other partner. If the survivor wishes to obtain a share, he will have to establish, either that he had a beneficial interest in the property, or successfully bring a claim under the I(PFD)A 1975 (see **16.6.3).** If the survivor is not successful, he will be a bare licensee. The licence can be terminated by the deceased's personal representatives on giving notice to the surviving partner.

If the survivor was the sole legal owner, there could still be complications if the deceased had a beneficial interest in the property which has passed by his will or intestacy to someone other than the survivor.

16.6.2 Intestacy

The intestacy rules do not make any provision for an unmarried partner. However, any children of the couple will have rights on their parents' intestacy. It is, therefore, essential that an unmarried couple make wills.

16.6.3 Family provision

If the survivor can establish that, before the deceased's death, he was being maintained by the deceased, he is likely to be able to bring a claim under the I(PFD)A 1975 (see **Appendix 1(B)**). Periodical payments, lump sum and transfer or settlement of property orders can be made by the court.

A change to the I(PFD)A 1975 introduced by the Law Reform (Succession) Act 1995 extended the circumstances in which a claim can be made. It is possible for an unmarried cohabitee to claim financial provision out of the deceased partner's estate if he or she lived with the deceased as husband and wife throughout a period of two years prior to the death, irrespective of whether he or she was financially dependent upon the deceased. The Civil Partnership Act 2004 has extended this provision to include same-sex partners. In addition to the common guidelines (I(PFD)A 1975, s 3) there are special guidelines for the court to consider in an application by an unmarried partner. The court must have regard to the age of the applicant, the length of the cohabitation with the deceased and the contributions made by the applicant to the welfare of the family of the deceased, including contributions made by looking after the home or caring for the family.

Despite these changes, an unmarried partner is still not treated as generously as a surviving spouse. First, the court can award an unmarried partner only such financial provision as it would be reasonable to receive for maintenance. A surviving spouse can be awarded such financial provision as it would be reasonable to receive whether or not the provision is required for maintenance. However, in the case of *Negus v Bahouse and Another* [2007] EWHC 2628 (Ch), the court awarded Ms Negus the transfer of a flat free of mortgage, plus a sum of £200,000 in addition to the £459,000 she had received from her former cohabitant's (the deceased's) pension policy and the half share of a flat in Spain he had left her. The court said that 'maintenance' did not mean just enough to enable a person to get by; lifestyle or 'tone' should be taken into account. Secondly, on an application by a spouse, the court will have regard to the provision that would have been awarded had the marriage ended with a divorce rather than with death. There is no similar provision for unmarried partners.

16.7 Chapter summary

(1) When couples decide to cohabit the following issues should be clarified:
- (a) how any property (especially the home) is owned as between the couple;
- (b) life insurance cover;
- (c) wills.

The couple should be advised to enter into a cohabitation agreement.

(2) When a cohabiting couple split up:
- (a) neither party can claim maintenance from the other;
- (b) maintenance for any children of the relationship can usually be claimed from the Child Support Agency;
- (c) ownership of the home will be determined by land law principles and an order for sale may be obtained;
- (d) occupation of the home may be obtained by establishing a contractual licence, or by obtaining a property order in favour of a child under the CA 1989 or, temporarily, by obtaining an occupation order under the FLA 1996;
- (e) transfer of tenancy orders can be made in some circumstances under the FLA 1996;
- (f) as regards children of an unmarried couple:
  - (i) mother has sole parental responsibility,
  - (ii) father can obtain parental responsibility;
- (g) if partner is bankrupt, sale of home can be delayed only if there are dependent children, and then only for 12 months;
- (h) if a cohabiting partner dies intestate there is no provision under the intestacy rules for the other partner to obtain any part of the estate. Any children of the couple will have a claim;
- (i) the I(PFD)A 1975 may be available to a cohabiting partner.

(3) There are various proposals for reform of the law relating to cohabiting couples.

APPENDICES

		Page
Appendix 1	**Legislation**	267
(A)	Matrimonial Causes Act 1973	267
(B)	Inheritance (Provision for Family and Dependants) Act 1975	287
(C)	Domestic Proceedings and Magistrates' Courts Act 1978	290
(D)	Child Abduction Act 1984	292
(E)	Children Act 1989	295
(F)	Child Support Act 1991	348
(G)	Family Law Act 1996	359
(H)	Trusts of Land and Appointment of Trustees Act 1996	373
(I)	Family Procedure Rules 2010	374
Appendix 2	**Code of Practice for Resolution Members**	407
Appendix 3	**Court Forms**	409
(A)	Divorce petition	409
(B)	Statement of arrangements for children	417
(C)	Form FM1 (Family mediation information and assessment)	423
(D)	Form A (Application for a financial order)	425
(E)	Form E (Statement for a financial order)	427
(F)	Form D81 (Statement of information for a consent order)	455
(G)	Parental responsibility agreement (1)	461
(H)	Parental responsibility agreement (2)	463
(I)	Form C1 (Children Act application)	465
(J)	Form C100 (Application for a s 8 order)	471
(K)	Form C1A (Supplemental information)	485
(L)	Form C110 (Application for a care or supervision order)	491
(M)	Form FL401 (Family Law Act application)	509

Appendix 1 – Legislation

(A) Matrimonial Causes Act 1973

1 Divorce on breakdown of marriage

(1) Subject to section 3 below, a petition for divorce may be presented to the court by either party to a marriage on the ground that the marriage has broken down irretrievably.

(2) The court hearing a petition for divorce shall not hold the marriage to have broken down irretrievably unless the petitioner satisfies the court of one or more of the following facts, that is to say—

- (a) that the respondent has committed adultery and the petitioner finds it intolerable to live with the respondent;
- (b) that the respondent has behaved in such a way that the petitioner cannot reasonably be expected to live with the respondent;
- (c) that the respondent has deserted the petitioner for a continuous period of at least two years immediately preceding the presentation of the petition;
- (d) that the parties of the marriage have lived apart for a continuous period of at least two years immediately preceding the presentation of the petition (hereafter in this Act referred to as 'two years' separation') and the respondent consents to a decree being granted;
- (e) that the parties to the marriage have lived apart for a continuous period of at least five years immediately preceding the presentation of the petition (hereafter in this Act referred to as 'five years' separation').

(3) On a petition for divorce it shall be the duty of the court to inquire, so far as it reasonably can, into the facts alleged by the petitioner and into any facts alleged by the respondent.

(4) If the court is satisfied on the evidence of any such fact as is mentioned in subsection (2) above, then, unless it is satisfied on all the evidence that the marriage has not broken down irretrievably, it shall, subject to section 5 below, grant a decree of divorce.

(5) Every decree of divorce shall in the first instance be a decree nisi and shall not be made absolute before the expiration of six months from its grant unless the High Court by general order from time to time fixes a shorter period, or unless in any particular case the court in which the proceedings are for the time being pending from time to time by special order fixes a shorter period than the period otherwise applicable for the time being by virtue of this subsection.

2 Supplemental provisions as to facts raising presumption of breakdown

(1) One party to a marriage shall not be entitled to rely for the purposes of section 1(2)(a) above on adultery committed by the other if, after it became known to him that the other had committed that adultery, the parties have lived with each other for a period exceeding, or periods together exceeding, six months.

(2) Where the parties to a marriage have lived with each other after it became known to one party that the other had committed adultery, but subsection (1) above does not apply, in any proceedings for divorce in which the petitioner relies on that adultery the fact that the parties have lived with each other after that time shall be disregarded in determining for the purposes of section 1(2)(a) above whether the petitioner finds it intolerable to live with the respondent.

(3) Where in any proceedings for divorce the petitioner alleges that the respondent has behaved in such a way that the petitioner cannot reasonably be expected to live with

him, but the parties to the marriage have lived with each other for a period or periods after the date of the occurrence of the final incident relied on by the petitioner and held by the court to support his allegation, that fact shall be disregarded in determining for the purposes of section 1(2)(b) above whether the petitioner cannot reasonably be expected to live with the respondent if the length of that period or of those periods together was six months or less.

(4) For the purposes of section 1(2)(c) above the court may treat a period of desertion as having continued at a time when the deserting party was incapable of continuing the necessary intention if the evidence before the court is such that, had that party not been so incapable, the court would have inferred that his desertion continued at that time.

(5) In considering for the purposes of section 1(2) above whether the period for which the respondent has deserted the petitioner or the period for which the parties to a marriage have lived apart has been continuous, no account shall be taken of any one period (not exceeding six months) or of any two or more periods (not exceeding six months in all) during which the parties resumed living with each other, but no period during which the parties lived with each other shall count as part of the period of desertion or of the period for which the parties to the marriage lived apart, as the case may be.

(6) For the purposes of section 1(2)(d) and (e) above and this section a husband and wife shall be treated as living apart unless they are living with each other in the same household, and references in this section to the parties to a marriage living with each other shall be construed as references to their living with each other in the same household.

(7) Provision shall be made by rules of court for the purpose of ensuring that where in pursuance of section 1(2)(d) above the petitioner alleges that the respondent consents to a decree being granted the respondent has been given such information as will enable him to understand the consequences to him of his consenting to a decree being granted and the steps which he must take to indicate that he consents to the grant of a decree.

3 Bar on petitions for divorce within one year of marriage

(1) No petition for divorce shall be presented to the court before the expiration of the period of one year from the date of the marriage.

(2) Nothing in this section shall prohibit the presentation of a petition based on matters which occurred before the expiration of that period.

5 Refusal of decree in five year separation cases on grounds of grave hardship to respondent

(1) The respondent to a petition for divorce in which the petitioner alleges five years' separation may oppose the grant of a decree on the ground that the dissolution of the marriage will result in grave financial or other hardship to him and that it would in all the circumstances be wrong to dissolve the marriage.

(2) Where the grant of a decree is opposed by virtue of this section, then—

(a) if the court finds that the petitioner is entitled to rely in support of his petition on the fact of five years' separation and makes no such finding as to any other fact mentioned in section 1(2) above, and

(b) if apart from this section the court would grant a decree on the petition,

the court shall consider all the circumstances, including the conduct of the parties to the marriage and the interests of those parties and of any children or other persons concerned, and if of opinion that the dissolution of the marriage will result in grave financial or other hardship to the respondent and that it would in all the circumstances be wrong to dissolve the marriage it shall dismiss the petition.

(3) For the purposes of this section hardship shall include the loss of the chance of acquiring any benefit which the respondent might acquire if the marriage were not dissolved.

6 Attempts at reconciliation of parties to marriage

(1) Provision shall be made by rules of court for requiring the legal representative acting for a petitioner for divorce to certify whether he has discussed with the petitioner the possibility of a reconciliation and given him the names and addresses of persons qualified to help effect a reconciliation between parties to a marriage who have become estranged.

(2) If at any stage of proceedings for divorce it appears to the court that there is a reasonable possibility of a reconciliation between the parties to the marriage, the court may adjourn the proceedings for such period as it thinks fit to enable attempts to be made to effect such a reconciliation.

The power conferred by the foregoing provision is additional to any other power of the court to adjourn proceedings.

10 Proceedings after decree nisi: special protection for respondent in separation cases

(1) Where in any case the court has granted a decree of divorce on the basis of a finding that the petitioner was entitled to rely in support of his petition on the fact of two years' separation coupled with the respondent's consent to a decree being granted and has made no such finding as to any other fact mentioned in section 1(2) above, the court may, on an application made by the respondent at any time before the decree is made absolute, rescind the decree if it is satisfied that the petitioner misled the respondent (whether intentionally or unintentionally) about any matter which the respondent took into account in deciding to give his consent.

(2) The following provisions of this section apply where—

(a) the respondent to a petition for divorce in which the petitioner alleged two years' or five years' separation coupled, in the former case, with the respondent's consent to a decree being granted, has applied to the court for consideration under subsection (3) below of his financial position after the divorce; and

(b) the court has granted a decree on the petition on the basis of a finding that the petitioner was entitled to rely in support of his petition on the fact of two years' or five years' separation (as the case may be) and has made no such finding as to any other fact mentioned in section 1(2) above.

(3) The court hearing an application by the respondent under subsection (2) above shall consider all the circumstances, including the age, health, conduct, earning capacity, financial resources and financial obligations of each of the parties, and the financial position of the respondent as, having regard to the divorce, it is likely to be after the death of the petitioner should the petitioner die first; and, subject to subsection (4) below, the court shall not make the decree absolute unless it is satisfied—

(a) that the petitioner should not be required to make any financial provision for the respondent, or

(b) that the financial provision made by the petitioner for the respondent is reasonable and fair or the best that can be made in the circumstances.

(4) The court may if it thinks fit make the decree absolute notwithstanding the requirements of subsection (3) above if—

(a) it appears that there are circumstances making it desirable that the decree should be made absolute without delay, and

(b) the court has obtained a satisfactory undertaking from the petitioner that he will make such financial provision for the respondent as the court may approve.

10A Proceedings after decree nisi: religious marriage

(1) This section applies if a decree of divorce has been granted but not made absolute and the parties to the marriage concerned -

(a) were married in accordance with—

(i) the usages of the Jews, or

(ii) any other prescribed religious usages; and

(b) must co-operate if the marriage is to be dissolved in accordance with those usages.

(2) On the application of either party, the court may order that a decree of divorce is not to be made absolute until a declaration made by both parties that they have taken such steps as are required to dissolve the marriage in accordance with those usages is produced to the court.

(3) An order under subsection (2)—

(a) may be made only if the court is satisfied that in all the circumstances of the case it is just and reasonable to do so; and

(b) may be revoked at any time.

(4) A declaration of a kind mentioned in subsection (2)—

(a) must be in a specified form;

(b) must, in specified cases, be accompanied by such documents as may be specified; and

(c) must, in specified cases, satisfy such other requirements as may be specified.

(5) The validity of a decree of divorce made by reference to such a declaration is not to be affected by any inaccuracy in that declaration.

(6) 'Prescribed' means prescribed in an order made by the Lord Chancellor after consulting the Lord Chief Justice and such an order—

(a) must be made by statutory instrument;

(b) shall be subject to annulment in pursuance of a resolution of either House of Parliament.

(7) 'Specified' means specified in rules of court.

(8) The Lord Chief Justice may nominate a judicial office holder (as defined in section 109(4) of the Constitutional Reform Act 2005) to exercise his functions under this section.

17 Judicial separation

(1) A petition for judicial separation may be presented to the court by either party to a marriage on the ground that any such fact as is mentioned in section 1(2) above exists, and the provisions of section 2 above shall apply accordingly for the purposes of a petition for judicial separation alleging any such fact, as they apply in relation to a petition for divorce alleging that fact.

(2) On a petition for judicial separation it shall be the duty of the court to inquire, so far as it reasonably can, into the facts alleged by the petitioner and into any facts alleged by the respondent, but the court shall not be concerned to consider whether the marriage has broken down irretrievably, and if it is satisfied on the evidence of any such fact as is mentioned in section 1(2) above it shall, subject to section 41 below, grant a decree of judicial separation.

(3) Sections 6 and 7 above shall apply for the purpose of encouraging the reconciliation of parties to proceedings for judicial separation and of enabling the parties to a marriage to refer to the court for its opinion an agreement or arrangement relevant to actual or contemplated proceedings for judicial separation, as they apply in relation to proceedings for divorce.

18 Effects of judicial separation

(1) Where the court grants a decree of judicial separation it shall no longer be obligatory for the petitioner to cohabit with the respondent.

(2) If while a decree of judicial separation is in force and the separation is continuing either of the parties to the marriage dies intestate as respects all or any of his or her real or personal property, the property as respects which he or she died intestate shall devolve as if the other party to the marriage had then been dead.

(3) (Not reproduced)

22 Maintenance pending suit

On a petition for divorce, nullity of marriage or judicial separation, the court may make an order for maintenance pending suit, that is to say, an order requiring either party to the marriage to make to the other such periodical payments for his or her maintenance and for such term, being a term beginning not earlier than the date of the presentation of the petition and ending with the date of the determination of the suit, as the court thinks reasonable.

23 Financial provision orders in connection with divorce proceedings etc

(1) On granting a decree of divorce, a decree of nullity of marriage or a decree of judicial separation or at any time thereafter (whether, in the case of a decree of divorce or of nullity of marriage, before or after the decree is made absolute), the court may make any one or more of the following orders, that is to say—

(a) an order that either party to the marriage shall make to the other such periodical payments, for such term, as may be specified in the order;

(b) an order that either party to the marriage shall secure to the other to the satisfaction of the court such periodical payments, for such term, as may be so specified;

(c) an order that either party to the marriage shall pay to the other such lump sum or sums as may be so specified;

(d) an order that a party to the marriage shall make to such person as may be specified in the order for the benefit of a child of the family, or to such a child, such periodical payments, for such term, as may be so specified;

(e) an order that a party to the marriage shall secure to such person as may be so specified for the benefit of such a child, or to such a child, to the satisfaction of the court, such periodical payments, for such term, as may be so specified;

(f) an order that a party to the marriage shall pay to such person as may be so specified for the benefit of such a child, or to such a child, such lump sum as may be so specified;

subject, however, in the case of an order under paragraph (d), (e) or (f) above, to the restrictions imposed by section 29(1) and (3) below on the making of financial provision orders in favour of children who have attained the age of eighteen.

(2) The court may also, subject to those restrictions, make any one or more of the orders mentioned in subsection (1)(d), (e) and (f) above—

(a) in any proceedings for divorce, nullity of marriage or judicial separation, before granting a decree; and

(b) where any such proceedings are dismissed after the beginning of the trial, either forthwith or within a reasonable period after the dismissal.

(3) Without prejudice to the generality of subsection (1)(c) or (f) above—

(a) an order under this section that a party to a marriage shall pay a lump sum to the other party may be made for the purpose of enabling that other party to meet any liabilities or expenses reasonably incurred by him or her in maintaining himself or herself or any child of the family before making an application for an order under this section in his or her favour;

(b) an order under this section for the payment of a lump sum to or for the benefit of a child of the family may be made for the purpose of enabling any liabilities or expenses reasonably incurred by or for the benefit of that child before the making of an application for an order under this section in his favour to be met; and

(c) an order under this section for the payment of a lump sum may provide for the payment of that sum by instalments of such amount as may be specified in the order and may require the payment of the instalments to be secured to the satisfaction of the court.

(4) The power of the court under subsection (1) or (2)(a) above to make an order in favour of a child of the family shall be exercisable from time to time; and where the court makes an order in favour of a child under subsection (2)(b) above, it may from time to time, subject to the restrictions mentioned in subsection (1) above, make a further order in his favour of any of the kinds mentioned in subsection (1)(d), (e) or (f) above.

(5) Without prejudice to the power to give a direction under section 30 below for the settlement of an instrument by conveyancing counsel, where an order is made under subsection (1)(a), (b) or (c) above on or after granting a decree of divorce or nullity of marriage, neither the order nor any settlement made in pursuance of the order shall take effect unless the decree has been made absolute.

(6) Where the court—

(a) makes an order under this section for the payment of a lump sum; and

(b) directs—

(i) that payment of that sum or any part of it shall be deferred; or

(ii) that the sum or any part of it shall be paid by instalments,

the court may order that the amount deferred or the instalments shall carry interest at such rate as may be specified by the order from such date, not earlier than the date of the order, as may be so specified, until the date when payment of it is due.

24 Property adjustment orders in connection with divorce proceedings etc

(1) On granting a decree of divorce, a decree of nullity of marriage or a decree of judicial separation or at any time thereafter (whether, in the case of a decree of divorce or of nullity of marriage, before or after the decree is made absolute), the court may make any one or more of the following orders, that is to say—

(a) an order that a party to the marriage shall transfer to the other party, to any child of the family or to such person as may be specified in the order for the benefit of such a child such property as may be so specified, being property to which the first-mentioned party is entitled, either in possession or reversion;

(b) an order that a settlement of such property as may be so specified, being property to which a party to the marriage is so entitled, be made to the satisfaction of the court for the benefit of the other party to the marriage and of the children of the family or either or any of them;

(c) an order varying for the benefit of the parties to the marriage and of the children of the family or either or any of them any ante-nuptial or post-nuptial settlement (including such a settlement made by will or codicil) made on the parties to the marriage, other than one in the form of a pension arrangement (within the meaning of section 25D below);

(d) an order extinguishing or reducing the interest of either of the parties to the marriage under any such settlement, other than one in the form of a pension arrangement (within the meaning of section 25D below);

subject, however, in the case of an order under paragraph (a) above, to the restrictions imposed by section 29(1) and (3) below on the making of orders for a transfer of property in favour of children who have attained the age of eighteen.

(2) The court may make an order under subsection (1)(c) above notwithstanding that there are no children of the family.

(3) Without prejudice to the power to give a direction under section 30 below for the settlement of an instrument by conveyancing counsel, where an order is made under this section on or after granting a decree of divorce or nullity of marriage, neither the order nor any settlement made in pursuance of the order shall take effect unless the decree has been made absolute.

24A Orders for sale of property

(1) Where the court makes under section 23 or 24 of this Act a secured periodical payments order, an order for the payment of a lump sum or a property adjustment order, then, on making that order or at any time thereafter, the court may make a further order for the sale of such property as may be specified in the order, being property in which or in the proceeds of sale of which either or both of the parties to the marriage has or have a beneficial interest, either in possession or reversion.

(2) Any order made under subsection (1) above may contain such consequential or supplementary provisions as the court thinks fit and, without prejudice to the generality of the foregoing provision, may include—

- (a) provision requiring the making of a payment out of the proceeds of sale of the property to which the order relates, and
- (b) provision requiring any such property to be offered for sale to a person, or class of persons, specified in the order.

(3) Where an order is made under subsection (1) above on or after the grant of a decree of divorce or nullity of marriage, the order shall not take effect unless the decree has been made absolute.

(4) Where an order is made under subsection (1) above, the court may direct that the order, or such provision thereof as the court may specify, shall not take effect until the occurrence of an event specified by the court or the expiration of a period so specified.

(5) Where an order under subsection (1) above contains a provision requiring the proceeds of sale of the property to which the order relates to be used to secure periodical payments to a party to the marriage, the order shall cease to have effect on the death or re-marriage of, or formation of a civil partnership by, that person.

(6) Where a party to a marriage has a beneficial interest in any property, or in the proceeds of sale thereof, and some other person who is not a party to the marriage also has a beneficial interest in that property or in the proceeds of sale thereof, then, before deciding whether to make an order under this section in relation to that property, it shall be the duty of the court to give that other person an opportunity to make representations with respect to the order; and any representations made by that other person shall be included among the circumstances to which the court is required to have regard under section 25(1) below.

24B Pension sharing orders in connection with divorce proceedings etc

(1) On granting a decree of divorce or a decree of nullity of marriage or at any time thereafter (whether before or after the decree is made absolute), the court may, on an application made under this section, make one or more pension sharing orders in relation to the marriage.

(2) A pension sharing order under this section is not to take effect unless the decree on or after which it is made has been made absolute.

(3) A pension sharing order under this section may not be made in relation to a pension arrangement which—

(a) is the subject of a pension sharing order in relation to the marriage, or

(b) has been the subject of pension sharing between the parties to the marriage.

(4) A pension sharing order under this section may not be made in relation to shareable state scheme rights if—

(a) such rights are the subject of a pension sharing order in relation to the marriage, or

(b) such rights have been the subject of pension sharing between the parties to the marriage.

(5) A pension sharing order under this section may not be made in relation to the rights of a person under a pension arrangement if there is in force a requirement imposed by virtue of section 25B or 25C below which relates to benefits or future benefits to which he is entitled under the pension arrangement.

24C Pension sharing orders: duty to stay

(1) No pension sharing order may be made so as to take effect before the end of such period after the making of the order as may be prescribed by regulations made by the Lord Chancellor.

(2) The power to make regulations under this section shall be exercisable by statutory instrument which shall be subject to annulment in pursuance of a resolution of either House of Parliament.

24D Pension sharing orders: apportionment of charges

If a pension sharing order relates to rights under a pension arrangement, the court may include in the order provision about the apportionment between the parties of any charge under section 41 of the Welfare Reform and Pensions Act 1999 (charges in respect of pension sharing costs), or under corresponding Northern Ireland legislation.

25 Matters to which court is to have regard in deciding how to exercise its powers under ss 23, 24, 24A, 24B and 24E

(1) It shall be the duty of the court in deciding whether to exercise its powers under section 23, 24, 24A, 24B or 24E above and, if so, in what manner, to have regard to all the circumstances of the case, first consideration being given to the welfare while a minor of any child of the family who has not attained the age of eighteen.

(2) As regards the exercise of the powers of the court under section 23(1)(a), (b) or (c), 24, 24A, 24B or 24E above in relation to a party to the marriage, the court shall in particular have regard to the following matters—

(a) the income, earning capacity, property and other financial resources which each of the parties to the marriage has or is likely to have in the foreseeable future, including in the case of earning capacity any increase in that capacity which it would in the opinion of the court be reasonable to expect a party to the marriage to take steps to acquire;

(b) the financial needs, obligations and responsibilities which each of the parties to the marriage has or is likely to have in the foreseeable future;

(c) the standard of living enjoyed by the family before the breakdown of the marriage;

(d) the age of each party to the marriage and the duration of the marriage;

(e) any physical or mental disability of either of the parties to the marriage;

(f) the contributions which each of the parties has made or is likely in the foreseeable future to make to the welfare of the family, including any contribution by looking after the home or caring for the family;

(g) the conduct of each of the parties, if that conduct is such that it would in the opinion of the court be inequitable to disregard it;

(h) in the case of proceedings for divorce or nullity of marriage, the value to each of the parties to the marriage of any benefit ... which, by reason of the dissolution or annulment of the marriage, that party will lose the chance of acquiring.

(3) As regards the exercise of the powers of the court under section 23(1)(d), (e) or (f), (2) or (4), 24 or 24A above in relation to a child of the family, the court shall in particular have regard to the following matters—

(a) the financial needs of the child;

(b) the income, earning capacity (if any), property and other financial resources of the child;

(c) any physical or mental disability of the child;

(d) the manner in which he was being and in which the parties to the marriage expected him to be educated or trained;

(e) the considerations mentioned in relation to the parties to the marriage in paragraphs (a), (b), (c) and (e) of subsection (2) above.

(4) As regards the exercise of the powers of the court under section 23(1)(d), (e) or (f), (2) or (4), 24 or 24A above against a party to a marriage in favour of a child of the family who is not the child of that party, the court shall also have regard—

(a) to whether that party assumed any responsibility for the child's maintenance, and, if so, to the extent to which, and the basis upon which, that party assumed such responsibility and to the length of time for which that party discharged such responsibility;

(b) to whether in assuming and discharging such responsibility that party did so knowing that the child was not his or her own;

(c) to the liability of any other person to maintain the child.

25A Exercise of court's powers in favour of party to marriage on decree of divorce or nullity of marriage

(1) Where on or after the grant of a decree of divorce or nullity of marriage the court decides to exercise its powers under section 23(1)(a), (b) or (c), 24, 24A, 24B or 24E above in favour of a party to the marriage, it shall be the duty of the court to consider whether it would be appropriate so to exercise those powers that the financial obligations of each party towards the other will be terminated as soon after the grant of the decree as the court considers just and reasonable.

(2) Where the court decides in such a case to make a periodical payments or secured periodical payments order in favour of a party to the marriage, the court shall in particular consider whether it would be appropriate to require those payments to be made or secured only for such term as would in the opinion of the court be sufficient to enable the party in whose favour the order is made to adjust without undue hardship to the termination of his or her financial dependence on the other party.

(3) Where on or after the grant of a decree of divorce or nullity of marriage an application is made by a party to the marriage for a periodical payments or secured periodical payments order in his or her favour, then, if the court considers that no continuing obligation should be imposed on either party to make or secure periodical payments in favour of the other, the court may dismiss the application with a direction that the applicant shall not be entitled to make any future application in relation to that marriage for an order under section 23(1)(a) or (b) above.

25B Pensions

(1) The matters to which the court is to have regard under section 25(2) above include—

(a) in the case of paragraph (a), any benefits under a pension arrangement which a party to the marriage has or is likely to have, and

(b) in the case of paragraph (h), any benefits under a pension arrangement which, by reason of the dissolution or annulment of the marriage, a party to the marriage will lose the chance of acquiring,

and, accordingly, in relation to benefits under a pension arrangement, section 25(2)(a) above shall have effect as if 'in the foreseeable future' were omitted.

(2) ...

(3) The following provisions apply where, having regard to any benefits under a pension arrangement, the court determines to make an order under section 23 above.

(4) To the extent to which the order is made having regard to any benefits under a pension arrangement, the order may require the person responsible for the pension arrangement in question, if at any time any payment in respect of any benefits under the arrangement becomes due to the party with pension rights, to make a payment for the benefit of the other party.

(5) The order must express the amount of any payment required to be made by virtue of subsection (4) above as a percentage of the payment which becomes due to the party with pension rights.

(6) Any such payment by the person responsible for the arrangement—

(a) shall discharge so much of his liability to the party with pension rights as corresponds to the amount of the payment, and

(b) shall be treated for all purposes as a payment made by the party with pension rights in or towards the discharge of his liability under the order.

(7) Where the party with pension rights has a right of commutation under the arrangement, the order may require him to exercise it to any extent; and this section applies to any payment due in consequence of commutation in pursuance of the order as it applies to other payments in respect of benefits under the arrangement.

(7A) The power conferred by subsection (7) above may not be exercised for the purpose of commuting a benefit payable to the party with pension rights to a benefit payable to the other party.

(7B) The power conferred by subsection (4) or (7) above may not be exercised in relation to a pension arrangement which—

(a) is the subject of a pension sharing order in relation to the marriage, or

(b) has been the subject of pension sharing between the parties to the marriage.

(7C) In subsection (1) above, references to benefits under a pension arrangement include any benefits by way of pension, whether under a pension arrangement or not.

25C Pensions: lump sums

(1) The power of the court under section 23 above to order a party to a marriage to pay a lump sum to the other party includes, where the benefits which the party with pension rights has or is likely to have under a pension arrangement include any lump sum payable in respect of his death, power to make any of the following provision by the order.

(2) The court may—

(a) if the person responsible for the pension arrangement in question has power to determine the person to whom the sum, or any part of it, is to be paid, require him to pay the whole or part of that sum, when it becomes due, to the other party,

(b) if the party with pension rights has power to nominate the person to whom the sum, or any part of it, is to be paid, require the party with pension rights to nominate the other party in respect of the whole or part of that sum,

(c) in any other case, require the person responsible for the pension arrangement in question to pay the whole or part of that sum, when it becomes due, for the benefit of the other party instead of to the person to whom, apart from the order, it would be paid.

(3) Any payment by the person responsible for the arrangement under an order made under section 23 above by virtue of this section shall discharge so much of his liability in respect of the party with pension rights as corresponds to the amount of the payment.

(4) The powers conferred by this section may not be exercised in relation to a pension arrangement which—

(a) is the subject of a pension sharing order in relation to the marriage, or

(b) has been the subject of pension sharing between the parties to the marriage.

27 Financial provision orders etc in case of neglect by party to marriage to maintain other party or child of the family

(1) Either party to a marriage may apply to the court for an order under this section on the ground that the other party to the marriage (in this section referred to as the respondent)—

(a) has failed to provide reasonable maintenance for the applicant, or

(b) has failed to provide, or to make a proper contribution towards, reasonable maintenance for any child of the family.

(2) The court may not entertain an application under this section unless it has jurisdiction to do so by virtue of the Maintenance Regulation and Schedule 6 to the Civil Jurisdiction and Judgments (Maintenance) Regulations 2011.

(3) Where an application under this section is made on the ground mentioned in subsection (1)(a) above then, in deciding—

(a) whether the respondent has failed to provide reasonable maintenance for the applicant, and

(b) what order, if any, to make under this section in favour of the applicant,

the court shall have regard to all the circumstances of the case including the matters mentioned in section 25(2) above, and where an application is also made under this section in respect of a child of the family who has not attained the age of eighteen, first consideration shall be given to the welfare of the child while a minor.

(3A) Where an application under this section is made on the ground mentioned in subsection (1)(b) above then, in deciding—

(a) whether the respondent has failed to provide, or to make a proper contribution towards, reasonable maintenance for the child of the family to whom the application relates, and

(b) what order, if any, to make under this section in favour of the child,

the court shall have regard to all the circumstances of the case including the matters mentioned in section 25(3)(a) to (e) above, and where the child of the family to whom the application relates is not the child of the respondent, including also the matters mentioned in section 25(4) above.

(3B) In relation to an application under this section on the ground mentioned in subsection (1)(a) above, section 25(2)(c) above shall have effect as if for the reference therein to the breakdown of the marriage there were substituted a reference to the failure to provide reasonable maintenance for the applicant, and in relation to an application under this section on the ground mentioned in subsection (1)(b) above, section 25(2)(c) above (as it applies by virtue of section 25(3)(e) above) shall have effect as if for the reference therein to the breakdown of the marriage there were substituted a reference to the failure to provide, or to make a proper contribution towards, reasonable maintenance for the child of the family to whom the application relates.

(4) ...

(5) Where on an application under this section it appears to the court that the applicant or any child of the family to whom the application relates is in immediate need of financial assistance, but it is not yet possible to determine what order, if any, should be made on the application, the court may make an interim order for maintenance, that is to say, an order requiring the respondent to make to the applicant until the determination of the application such periodical payments as the court thinks reasonable.

(6) Where on an application under this section the applicant satisfies the court of any ground mentioned in subsection (1) above, the court may make any one or more of the following orders, that is to say—

(a) an order that the respondent shall make to the applicant such periodical payments, for such term, as may be specified in the order;

(b) an order that the respondent shall secure to the applicant, to the satisfaction of the court, such periodical payments, for such term, as may be so specified;

(c) an order that the respondent shall pay to the applicant such lump sum as may be so specified;

(d) an order that the respondent shall make to such person as may be specified in the order for the benefit of the child to whom the application relates, or to that child, such periodical payments, for such term, as may be so specified;

(e) an order that the respondent shall secure to such person as may be so specified for the benefit of that child, or to that child, to the satisfaction of the court, such periodical payments, for such term, as may be so specified;

(f) an order that the respondent shall pay to such person as may be so specified for the benefit of that child, or to that child, such lump sum as may be so specified;

subject, however, in the case of an order under paragraph (d), (e) or (f) above, to the restrictions imposed by section 29(1) and (3) below on the making of financial provision orders in favour of children who have attained the age of eighteen.

(6A) An application for the variation under section 31 of this Act of a periodical payments order or secured periodical payments order made under this section in favour of a child may, if the child has attained the age of sixteen, be made by the child himself.

(6B) Where a periodical payments order made in favour of a child under this section ceases to have effect on the date on which the child attains the age of sixteen or at any time after that date but before or on the date on which he attains the age of eighteen, then, if, on an application made to the court for an order under this subsection, it appears to the court that—

(a) the child is, will be or (if an order were made under this subsection) would be receiving instruction at an educational establishment or undergoing training for a trade, profession or vocation, whether or not he also is, will be or would be in gainful employment; or

(b) there are special circumstances which justify the making of an order under this subsection,

the court shall have power by order to revive the first-mentioned order from such date as the court may specify, not being earlier than the date of the making of the application, and to exercise its powers under section 31 of this Act in relation to any order so revived.

(7) Without prejudice to the generality of subsection (6)(c) or (f) above, an order under this section for the payment of a lump sum—

(a) may be made for the purpose of enabling any liabilities or expenses reasonably incurred in maintaining the applicant or any child of the family to whom the application relates before the making of the application to be met;

(b) may provide for the payment of that sum by instalments of such amount as may be specified in the order and may require the payment of the instalments to be secured to the satisfaction of the court.

(8) ...

28 Duration of continuing financial provision orders in favour of party to marriage, and effect of remarriage or formation of civil partnership

(1) Subject in the case of an order made on or after the grant of a decree of a divorce or nullity of marriage to the provisions of sections 25A(2) above and 31(7) below, the term to be specified in a periodical payments or secured periodical payments order in favour of a party to a marriage shall be such term as the court thinks fit, except that the term shall not begin before or extend beyond the following limits, that is to say—

(a) in the case of a periodical payments order, the term shall begin not earlier than the date of the making of an application for the order, and shall be so defined as not to extend beyond the death of either of the parties to the marriage or, where the order is made on or after the grant of a decree of divorce or nullity of marriage, the remarriage of, or formation of a civil partnership by, the party in whose favour the order is made; and

(b) in the case of a secured periodical payments order, the term shall begin not earlier than the date of the making of an application for the order, and shall be so defined as not to extend beyond the death or, where the order is made on or after the grant of such a decree, the remarriage of the party, or formation of a civil partnership by, in whose favour the order is made.

(1A) Where a periodical payments or secured periodical payments order in favour of a party to a marriage is made on or after the grant of a decree of divorce or nullity of marriage, the court may direct that that party shall not be entitled to apply under section 31 below for the extension of the term specified in the order.

(2) Where a periodical payments or secured periodical payments order in favour of a party to a marriage is made otherwise than on or after the grant of a decree of divorce or nullity of marriage, and the marriage in question is subsequently dissolved or annulled but the order continues in force, the order shall, notwithstanding anything in it, cease to have effect on the remarriage of, or formation of the civil partnership by, that party, except in relation to any arrears due under it on the date of the remarriage or formation of the civil partnership.

(3) If after the grant of a decree dissolving or annulling a marriage either party to that marriage remarries whether at any time before or after the commencement of this Act or forms a civil partnership, that party shall not be entitled to apply, by reference to the grant of that decree, for a financial provision order in his or her favour, or for a property adjustment order, against the other party to that marriage.

29 Duration of continuing financial provision orders in favour of children, and age limit on making certain orders in their favour

(1) Subject to subsection (3) below, no financial provision order and no order for a transfer of property under section 24(1)(a) above shall be made in favour of a child who has attained the age of eighteen.

(2) The term to be specified in a periodical payments or secured periodical payments order in favour of a child may begin with the date of the making of an application for the order in question or any later date or a date ascertained in accordance with subsection (5) or (6) below but—

(a) shall not in the first instance extend beyond the date of the birthday of the child next following his attaining the upper limit of the compulsory school age (construed in accordance with section 8 of the Education Act 1996) unless the court considers that in the circumstances of the case the welfare of the child requires that it should extend to a later date; and

(b) shall not in any event, subject to subsection (3) below, extend beyond the date of the child's eighteenth birthday.

(3) Subsection (1) above, and paragraph (b) of subsection (2), shall not apply in the case of a child, if it appears to the court that—

(a) the child is, or will be, or if an order were made without complying with either or both of those provisions would be, receiving instruction at an educational establishment or undergoing training for a trade, profession or vocation, whether or not he is also, or will also be, in gainful employment; or

(b) there are special circumstances which justify the making of an order without complying with either or both of those provisions.

(4) Any periodical payments order in favour of a child shall, notwithstanding anything in the order, cease to have effect on the death of the person liable to make payments under the order, except in relation to any arrears due under the order on the date of the death.

(5) Where—

(a) a maintenance calculation ('the current calculation') is in force with respect to a child; and

(b) an application is made under Part II of this Act for a periodical payments or secured periodical payments order in favour of that child—

(i) in accordance with section 8 of the Child Support Act 1991, and

(ii) before the end of the period of 6 months beginning with the making of the current calculation,

the term to be specified in any such order made on that application may be expressed to begin on, or at any time after, the earliest permitted date.

(6) For the purposes of subsection (5) above, 'the earliest permitted date' is whichever is the later of—

(a) the date 6 months before the application is made; or

(b) the date on which the current calculation took effect or, where successive maintenance calculations have been continuously in force with respect to a child, on which the first of those calculations took effect.

(7) Where—

(a) a maintenance calculation ceases to have effect ... by or under any provision of the Child Support Act 1991; and

(b) an application is made, before the end of the period of 6 months beginning with the relevant date, for a periodical payments or secured periodical payments order in favour of a child with respect to whom that maintenance calculation was in force immediately before it ceased to have effect,

the term to be specified in any such order made on that application may begin with the date on which that maintenance calculation ceased to have effect, ... or any later date.

(8) In subsection (7)(b) above—

(a) where the maintenance calculation ceased to have effect, the relevant date is the date on which it so ceased;

(b) ...

30 Direction for settlement of instrument for securing payments or effecting property adjustment

Where the court decides to make a financial provision order requiring any payments to be secured or a property adjustment order—

(a) it may direct that the matter be referred to one of the conveyancing counsel of the court for him to settle a proper instrument to be executed by all necessary parties; and

(b) where the order is to be made in proceedings for divorce, nullity of marriage or judicial separation it may, if it thinks fit, defer the grant of the decree in question until the instrument has been duly executed.

31 Variation, discharge etc of certain orders for financial relief

(1) Where the court has made an order to which this section applies, then, subject to the provisions of this section and of section 28(1A) above, the court shall have power to vary or discharge the order or to suspend any provision thereof temporarily and to revive the operation of any provision so suspended.

(2) This section applies to the following orders, that is to say—

(a) any order for maintenance pending suit and any interim order for maintenance;

(b) any periodical payments order;

(c) any secured periodical payments order;

(d) any order made by virtue of section 23(3)(c) or 27(7)(b) above (provision for payment of a lump sum by instalments);

(dd) any deferred order made by virtue of section 23(1)(c) (lump sums) which includes provision made by virtue of—

(i) section 25B(4), or

(ii) section 25C,

(provision in respect of pension rights);

(e) any order for a settlement of property under section 24(1)(b) or for a variation of settlement under section 24(1)(c) or (d) above, being an order made on or after the grant of a decree of judicial separation;

(f) any order made under section 24A(1) above for the sale of property.

(g) a pension sharing order under section 24B above which is made at a time before the decree has been made absolute.

(2A) Where the court has made an order referred to in subsection (2)(a), (b) or (c) above, then, subject to the provisions of this section, the court shall have power to remit the payment of any arrears due under the order or of any part thereof.

(2B) Where the court has made an order referred to in subsection (2)(dd)(ii) above, this section shall cease to apply to the order on the death of either of the parties to the marriage.

(3) The powers exercisable by the court under this section in relation to an order shall be exercisable also in relation to any instrument executed in pursuance of the order.

(4) The court shall not exercise the powers conferred by this section in relation to an order for a settlement under section 24(1)(b) or for a variation of settlement under section 24(1)(c) or (d) above except on an application made in proceedings—

(a) for the rescission of the decree of judicial separation by reference to which the order was made, or

(b) for the dissolution of the marriage in question.

(4A) In relation to an order which falls within paragraph (g) of subsection (2) above ('the subsection (2) order')—

(a) the powers conferred by this section may be exercised—

(i) only on an application made before the subsection (2) order has or, but for paragraph (b) below, would have taken effect; and

(ii) only if, at the time when the application is made, the decree has not been made absolute; and

(b) an application made in accordance with paragraph (a) above prevents the subsection (2) order from taking effect before the application has been dealt with.

(4B) No variation of a pension sharing order shall be made so as to take effect before the decree is made absolute.

(4C) The variation of a pension sharing order prevents the order taking effect before the end of such period after the making of the variation as may be prescribed by regulations made by the Lord Chancellor.

(5) Subject to subsections (7A) to (7G) below and without prejudice to any power exercisable by virtue of subsection (2)(d), (dd), (e) or (g) above or otherwise than by virtue of this section, no property adjustment order or pension sharing order shall be made on an application for the variation of a periodical payments or secured periodical payments order made (whether in favour of a party to a marriage or in favour of a child of the family) under section 23 above, and no order for the payment of a lump sum shall be made on an application for the variation of a periodical payments or secured periodical payments order in favour of a party to a marriage (whether made under section 23 or under section 27 above).

(6) Where the person liable to make payments under a secured periodical payments order has died, an application under this section relating to that order (and to any order made under section 24A(1) above which requires the proceeds of sale of property to be used for securing those payments) may be made by the person entitled to payments under the periodical payments order or by the personal representatives of the deceased person, but no such application shall, except with the permission of the court, be made after the end of the period of six months from the date on which representation in regard to the estate of that person is first taken out.

(7) In exercising the powers conferred by this section the court shall have regard to all the circumstances of the case, first consideration being given to the welfare while a minor of any child of the family who has not attained the age of eighteen, and the circumstances of the case shall include any change in any of the matters to which the court was required to have regard when making the order to which the application relates, and—

(a) in the case of a periodical payments or secured periodical payments order made on or after the grant of a decree of divorce or nullity of marriage, the court shall consider whether in all the circumstances and after having regard to any such change it would be appropriate to vary the order so that payments under the order are required to be made or secured only for such further period as will in the opinion of the court be sufficient (in the light of any proposed exercise by the court, where the marriage has been dissolved, of its powers under subsection (7B) below) to enable the party in whose favour the order was made to adjust without undue hardship to the termination of those payments;

(b) in a case where the party against whom the order was made has died, the circumstances of the case shall also include the changed circumstances resulting from his or her death.

(7A) Subsection (7B) below applies where, after the dissolution of a marriage, the court—

(a) discharges a periodical payments order or secured periodical payments order made in favour of a party to the marriage; or

(b) varies such an order so that payments under the order are required to be made or secured only for such further period as is determined by the court.

(7B) The court has power, in addition to any power it has apart from this subsection, to make supplemental provision consisting of any of—

(a) an order for the payment of a lump sum in favour of a party to the marriage;

(b) one or more property adjustment orders in favour of a party to the marriage;

(ba) one or more pension sharing orders;

(c) a direction that the party in whose favour the original order discharged or varied was made is not entitled to make any further application for—

(i) a periodical payments or secured periodical payments order, or

(ii) an extension of the period to which the original order is limited by any variation made by the court.

(7C) An order for the payment of a lump sum made under subsection (7B) above may—

(a) provide for the payment of that sum by instalments of such amount as may be specified in the order; and

(b) require the payment of the instalments to be secured to the satisfaction of the court.

(7D) Section 23(6) above applies where the court makes an order for the payment of a lump sum under subsection (7B) above as it applies where the court makes such an order under section 23 above.

(7E) If under subsection (7B) above the court makes more than one property adjustment order in favour of the same party to the marriage, each of those orders must fall within a different paragraph of section 21(2) above.

(7F) Sections 24A and 30 above apply where the court makes a property adjustment order under subsection (7B) above as they apply where it makes such an order under section 24 above.

(7G) Subsections (3) to (5) of section 24B above apply in relation to a pension sharing order under subsection (7B) above as they apply in relation to a pension sharing order under that section.

(8) The personal representatives of a deceased person against whom a secured periodical payments order was made shall not be liable for having distributed any part of the estate of the deceased after the expiration of the period of six months referred to in subsection (6) above on the ground that they ought to have taken into account the possibility that the court might permit an application under this section to be made after that period by the person entitled to payments under the order; but this subsection shall not prejudice any power to recover any part of the estate so distributed arising by virtue of the making of an order in pursuance of this section.

(9) In considering for the purposes of subsection (6) above the question when representation was first taken out, a grant limited to settled land or to trust property shall be left out of account and a grant limited to real estate or to personal estate shall be left out of account unless a grant limited to the remainder of the estate has previously been made or is made at the same time.

(10) Where the court, in exercise of its powers under this section, decides to vary or discharge a periodical payments or secured periodical payments order, then, subject to section 28(1) and (2) above, the court shall have power to direct that the variation or discharge shall not take effect until the expiration of such period as may be specified in the order.

(11) Where—

(a) a periodical payments or secured periodical payments order in favour of more than one child ('the order') is in force;

(b) the order requires payments specified in it to be made to or for the benefit of more than one child without apportioning those payments between them;

(c) a maintenance calculation ('the calculation') is made with respect to one or more, but not all, of the children with respect to whom those payments are to be made; and

(d) an application is made, before the end of the period of 6 months beginning with the date on which the calculation was made, for the variation or discharge of the order,

the court may, in exercise of its powers under this section to vary or discharge the order, direct that the variation or discharge shall take effect from the date on which the calculation took effect or any later date.

(12) Where—

(a) an order ('the child order') of a kind prescribed for the purposes of section 10(1) of the Child Support Act 1991 is affected by a maintenance calculation;

(b) on the date on which the child order became so affected there was in force a periodical payments or secured periodical payments order ('the spousal order') in favour of a party to a marriage having the care of the child in whose favour the child order was made; and

(c) an application is made, before the end of the period of 6 months beginning with the date on which the maintenance calculation was made, for the spousal order to be varied or discharged,

the court may, in exercise of its powers under this section to vary or discharge the spousal order, direct that the variation or discharge shall take effect from the date on which the child order became so affected or any later date.

(13) For the purposes of subsection (12) above, an order is affected if it ceases to have effect or is modified by or under section 10 of the Child Support Act 1991.

(14) Subsections (11) and (12) above are without prejudice to any other power of the court to direct that the variation of discharge of an order under this section shall take effect from a date earlier than that on which the order for variation or discharge was made.

(15) The power to make regulations under subsection (4C) above shall be exercisable by statutory instrument which shall be subject to annulment in pursuance of a resolution of either House of Parliament.

35 Alteration of agreements by court during lives of parties

(1) Where a maintenance agreement is for the time being subsisting and each of the parties to the agreement is for the time being either domiciled or resident in England and Wales, then, subject to subsections (1A) and (3) below, either party may apply to the court or to a magistrates' court for an order under this section.

(1A) If an application or part of an application relates to a matter where jurisdiction falls to be determined by reference to the jurisdictional requirements of the Maintenance Regulation and Schedule 6 to the Civil Jurisdiction and Judgments (Maintenance) Regulations 2011—

(a) the requirement as to domicile or residence in subsection (1) does not apply to the application or that part of it, but

(b) the court may not entertain the application or that part of it unless it has jurisdiction to do so by virtue of that Regulation and that Schedule.

(2) If the court to which the application is made is satisfied either—

(a) that by reason of a change in the circumstances in the light of which any financial arrangements contained in the agreement were made or, as the case may be, financial arrangements were omitted from it (including a change foreseen by the parties when making the agreement), the agreement should be altered so as to make different, or, as the case may be, so as to contain, financial arrangements, or

(b) that the agreement does not contain proper financial arrangements with respect to any child of the family,

then subject to subsections (3), (4) and (5) below, that court may by order make such alterations in the agreement—

(i) by varying or revoking any financial arrangements contained in it, or

(ii) by inserting in it financial arrangements for the benefit of one of the parties to the agreement or of a child of the family,

as may appear to that court to be just having regard to all the circumstances, including, if relevant, the matters mentioned in section 25(4) above; and the agreement shall have effect thereafter as if any alteration made by the order had been made by agreement between the parties and for valuable consideration.

37 Avoidance of transactions intended to prevent or reduce financial relief

(1) For the purposes of this section 'financial relief' means relief under any of the provisions of sections 22, 23, 24, 24B, 27, 31 (except subsection (6)) and 35 above, and any reference in this section to defeating a person's claim for financial relief is a reference to preventing financial relief from being granted to that person, or to that person for the benefit of a child of the family, or reducing the amount of any financial relief which might be so granted, or frustrating or impeding the enforcement of any order which might be or has been made at his instance under any of those provisions.

(2) Where proceedings for financial relief are brought by one person against another, the court may, on the application of the first-mentioned person—

(a) if it is satisfied that the other party to the proceedings is, with the intention of defeating the claim for financial relief, about to make any disposition or to transfer out of the jurisdiction or otherwise deal with any property, make such order as it thinks fit for restraining the other party from so doing or otherwise for protecting the claim;

(b) if it is satisfied that the other party has, with that intention, made a reviewable disposition and that if the disposition were set aside financial relief or different financial relief would be granted to the applicant, make an order setting aside the disposition;

(c) if it is satisfied, in a case where an order has been obtained under any of the provisions mentioned in subsection (1) above by the applicant against the other party, that the other party has, with that intention, made a reviewable disposition, make an order setting aside the disposition;

and an application for the purposes of paragraph (b) above shall be made in the proceedings for the financial relief in question.

(3) Where the court makes an order under subsection (2)(b) or (c) above setting aside a disposition it shall give such consequential directions as it thinks fit for giving effect to the order (including directions requiring the making of any payments or the disposal of any property).

(4) Any disposition made by the other party to the proceedings for financial relief in question (whether before or after the commencement of those proceedings) is a reviewable disposition for the purposes of subsection (2)(b) and (c) above unless it was made for valuable consideration (other than marriage) to a person who, at the time of the disposition, acted in relation to it in good faith and without notice of any intention on the part of the other party to defeat the applicant's claim for financial relief.

(5) Where an application is made under this section with respect to a disposition which took place less than three years before the date of the application or with respect to a disposition or other dealing with property which is about to take place and the court is satisfied—

(a) in a case falling within subsection (2)(a) or (b) above, that the disposition or other dealing would (apart from this section) have the consequence, or

(b) in a case falling within subsection (2)(c) above, that the disposition has had the consequence,

of defeating the applicant's claim for financial relief, it shall be presumed, unless the contrary is shown, that the person who disposed of or is about to dispose of or deal with the property did so or, as the case may be, is about to do so, with the intention of defeating the applicant's claim for financial relief.

(6) In this section 'disposition' does not include any provision contained in a will or codicil but, with that exception, includes any conveyance, assurance or gift of property of any description, whether made by an instrument or otherwise.

(7) This section does not apply to a disposition made before 1st January 1968.

41 Restrictions on decrees for dissolution, annulment or separation affecting children

(1) In any proceedings for a decree of divorce or nullity of marriage, or a decree of judicial separation, the court shall consider—

(a) whether there are any children of the family to whom this section applies; and

(b) where there are any such children, whether (in the light of the arrangements which have been, or are proposed to be, made for their upbringing and welfare) it should exercise any of its powers under the Children Act 1989 with respect to any of them.

(2) Where, in any case to which this section applies, it appears to the court that—

(a) the circumstances of the case require it, or are likely to require it, to exercise any of its powers under the Act of 1989 with respect to any such child;

(b) it is not in a position to exercise that power or (as the case may be) those powers without giving further consideration to the case; and

(c) there are exceptional circumstances which make it desirable in the interests of the child that the court should give a direction under this section,

it may direct that the decree of divorce or nullity is not to be made absolute, or that the decree of judicial separation is not to be granted, until the court orders otherwise.

(3) This section applies to—

(a) any child of the family who has not reached the age of sixteen at the date when the court considers the case in accordance with the requirements of this section; and

(b) any child of the family who has reached that age at that date and in relation to whom the court directs that this section shall apply.

(B) Inheritance (Provision for Family and Dependants) Act 1975

1 Application for financial provision from deceased's estate

(1) Where after the commencement of this Act a person dies domiciled in England and Wales and is survived by any of the following persons—

(a) the spouse or civil partner of the deceased;

(b) a former spouse or former civil partner of the deceased, but not one who has formed a subsequent marriage or civil partnership;

(ba) any person (not being a person included in paragraph (a) or (b) above) to whom subsection (1A) or (1B) below applies;

(c) a child of the deceased;

(d) any person (not being a child of the deceased) who, in the case of any marriage or civil partnership to which the deceased was at any time a party, was treated by the deceased as a child of the family in relation to that marriage or civil partnership;

(e) any person (not being a person included in the foregoing paragraphs of this subsection) who immediately before the death of the deceased was being maintained, either wholly or partly, by the deceased;

that person may apply to the court for an order under section 2 of this Act on the ground that the disposition of the deceased's estate affected by his will or the law relating to intestacy, or the combination of his will and that law, is not such as to make reasonable financial provision for the applicant.

(1A) This subsection applies to a person if the deceased died on or after 1st January 1996 and, during the whole of the period of two years ending immediately before the date when the deceased died, the person was living—

(a) in the same household as the deceased, and

(b) as the husband or wife of the deceased.

(1B) This subsection applies to a person if for the whole of the period of two years ending immediately before the date when the deceased died the person was living—

(a) in the same household as the deceased, and

(b) as the civil partner of the deceased.

(2) In this Act 'reasonable financial provision'—

(a) in the case of an application made by virtue of subsection (1)(a) above by the husband or wife of the deceased (except where the marriage with the deceased was the subject of a decree of judicial separation and at the date of death the decree was in force and the separation was continuing), means such financial provision as it would be reasonable in all the circumstances of the case for a husband or wife to receive, whether or not that provision is required for his or her maintenance;

(aa) in the case of an application made by virtue of subsection (1)(a) above by the civil partner of the deceased (except where, at the date of death, a separation order under Chapter 2 of Part 2 of the Civil Partnership Act 2004 was in force in relation to the civil partnership and the separation was continuing), means such financial provision as would be reasonable in all the circumstances of the case for a civil partner to receive, whether or not that provision is required for his or her maintenance;

(b) in the case of any other application made by virtue of subsection (1) above, means such financial provision as it would be reasonable in all the circumstances of the case for the applicant to receive for his maintenance.

(3) For the purposes of subsection (1)(e) above, a person shall be treated as being maintained by the deceased, either wholly or partly, as the case may be, if the deceased,

otherwise than for full valuable consideration, was making a substantial contribution in money or money's worth towards the reasonable needs of that person.

2 Powers of court to make orders

(1) Subject to the provisions of this Act, where an application is made for an order under this section, the court may, if it is satisfied that the disposition of the deceased's estate effected by his will or the law relating to intestacy, or the combination of his will and that law, is not such as to make reasonable financial provision for the applicant, make any one or more of the following orders—

(a) an order for the making to the applicant out of the net estate of the deceased of such periodical payments and for such term as may be specified in the order;

(b) an order for the payment to the applicant out of that estate of a lump sum of such amount as may be so specified;

(c) an order for the transfer to the applicant of such property comprised in that estate as may be so specified;

(d) an order for the settlement for the benefit of the applicant of such property comprised in that estate as may be so specified;

(e) an order for the acquisition out of property comprised in that estate of such property as may be so specified and for the transfer of the property so acquired to the applicant or for the settlement thereof for his benefit;

(f) an order varying any ante-nuptial or post-nuptial settlement (including such a settlement made by will) made on the parties to a marriage to which the deceased was one of the parties, the variation being for the benefit of the surviving party to that marriage, or any child of that marriage, or any person who was treated by the deceased as a child of the family in relation to that marriage;

(g) an order varying any settlement made—

(i) during the subsistence of a civil partnership formed by the deceased, or

(ii) in anticipation of the formation of a civil partnership by the deceased, on the civil partners (including such a settlement made by will), the variation being for the benefit of the surviving civil partner, or any person who was treated by the deceased as a child of the family in relation to the civil partnership.

(2)–(4) (not reproduced)

15 Restriction imposed in divorce proceedings etc on application under this Act

(1) On the grant of a decree of divorce, a decree of nullity of marriage or a decree of judicial separation or at any time thereafter the court, if it considers it just to do so, may, on the application of either party to the marriage, order that the other party to the marriage shall not on the death of the applicant be entitled to apply for an order under section 2 of this Act.

In this subsection 'the court' means the High Court or, where a county court has jurisdiction by virtue of Part V of the Matrimonial and Family Proceedings Act 1984, a county court.

(2) In the case of a decree of divorce or nullity of marriage an order may be made under subsection (1) above before or after the decree is made absolute, but if it is made before the decree is made absolute it shall not take effect unless the decree is made absolute.

(3) Where an order made under subsection (1) above on the grant of a decree of divorce or nullity of marriage has come into force with respect to a party to a marriage, then, on the death of the other party to that marriage, the court shall not entertain any application for an order under section 2 of this Act made by the first-mentioned party.

(4) Where an order made under subsection (1) above on the grant of a decree of judicial separation has come into force with respect to any party to a marriage, then, if the other

party to that marriage dies while the decree is in force and the separation is continuing, the court shall not entertain any application for an order under section 2 of this Act made by the first-mentioned party.

15ZA Restriction imposed in proceedings for the dissolution etc. of a civil partnership on application under this Act

(1) On making a dissolution order, nullity order, separation order or presumption of death order under Chapter 2 of Part 2 of the Civil Partnership Act 2004, or at any time after making such an order, the court if it considers it just to do so, may, on the application of either of the civil partners, order that the other civil partner shall not on the death of the applicant be entitled to apply for an order under section 2 of this Act.

(2) In subsection (1) above 'the court' means the High Court, or where a county court has jurisdiction by virtue of Part 5 of the Matrimonial and Family Proceedings Act 1984, a county court.

(3) In the case of a dissolution order, nullity order or presumption of death order ('the main order') an order may be made under subsection (1) above before (as well as after) the main order is made final, but if made before the main order is made final it shall not take effect unless the main order is made final.

(4) Where an order under subsection (1) above made in connection with a dissolution order, nullity order or presumption of death order has come into force with respect to a civil partner, then, on the death of the other civil partner, the court shall not entertain any application for an order under section 2 of the Act made by the surviving civil partner.

(5) Where an order under subsection (1) above made in connection with a separation order has come into force with respect to a civil partner, then, if the other civil partner dies while the separation order is in force and the separation is continuing, the court shall not entertain any application for an order under section 2 of this Act made by the surviving civil partner.

(C) Domestic Proceedings and Magistrates' Courts Act 1978

1 Grounds of application for financial provision

Either party to a marriage may apply to a magistrates' court for an order under section 2 of this Act on the ground that the other party to the marriage ...—

(a) has failed to provide reasonable maintenance for the applicant; or

(b) has failed to provide, or to make a proper contribution towards, reasonable maintenance for any child of the family; or

(c) has behaved in such a way that the applicant cannot reasonably be expected to live with the respondent; or

(d) has deserted the applicant.

2 Powers of court to make orders for financial provision

(1) Where on an application for an order under this section the applicant satisfies the court of any ground mentioned in section 1 of this Act, the court may, subject to the provisions of this Part of this Act, make any one or more of the following orders, that is to say—

- (a) an order that the respondent shall make to the applicant such periodical payments, and for such term, as may be specified in the order;
- (b) an order that the respondent shall pay to the applicant such lump sum as may be so specified;
- (c) an order that the respondent shall make to the applicant for the benefit of a child of the family to whom the application relates, or to such a child, such periodical payments, and for such term, as may be so specified;
- (d) an order that the respondent shall pay to the applicant for the benefit of a child of the family to whom the application relates, or to such a child, such lump sum as may be so specified.

(2) Without prejudice to the generality of subsection (1)(b) or (d) above, an order under this section for the payment of a lump sum may be made for the purpose of enabling any liability or expenses reasonably incurred in maintaining the applicant, or any child of the family to whom the application relates, before the making of the order to be met.

(3) The amount of any lump sum required to be paid by an order under this section shall not exceed £1,000 or such larger amount as the Lord Chancellor may from time to time by order fix for the purposes of this subsection.

...

(4) An order made by the Lord Chancellor under this section—

- (a) shall be made only after consultation with the Lord Chief Justice;
- (b) shall be made by statutory instrument and be subject to annulment in pursuance of a resolution of either House of Parliament.

(5) The Lord Chief Justice may nominate a judicial office holder (as defined in section 109(4) of the Constitutional Reform Act 2005) to exercise his functions under this section.

3 Matters to which court is to have regard in exercising its powers under s 2

(1) Where an application is made for an order under section 2 of this Act, it shall be the duty of the court, in deciding whether to exercise its powers under that section and, if so, in what manner, to have regard to all the circumstances of the case, first consideration being given to the welfare while a minor of any child of the family who has not attained the age of eighteen.

(2) As regards the exercise of its powers under subsection (1)(a) or (b) of section 2, the court shall in particular have regard to the following matters—

(a) the income, earning capacity, property and other financial resources which each of the parties to the marriage has or is likely to have in the foreseeable future, including in the case of earning capacity any increase in that capacity which it would in the opinion of the court be reasonable to expect a party to the marriage to take steps to acquire;

(b) the financial needs, obligations and responsibilities which each of the parties to the marriage has or is likely to have in the foreseeable future;

(c) the standard of living enjoyed by the parties to the marriage before the occurrence of the conduct which is alleged as the ground of the application;

(d) the age of each party to the marriage and the duration of the marriage;

(e) any physical or mental disability of either of the parties to the marriage;

(f) the contributions which each of the parties has made or is likely in the foreseeable future to make to the welfare of the family, including any contribution by looking after the home or caring for the family;

(g) the conduct of each of the parties, if that conduct is such that it would in the opinion of the court be inequitable to disregard it.

(3) As regards the exercise of its power under subsection (1)(c) or (d) of section 2, the court shall in particular have regard to the following matters—

(a) the financial needs of the child;

(b) the income, earning capacity (if any), property and other financial resources of the child;

(c) any physical or mental disability of the child;

(d) the standard of living enjoyed by the family before the occurrence of the conduct which is alleged as the ground of the application;

(e) the manner in which the child was being and in which the parties to the marriage expected him to be educated or trained;

(f) the matters mentioned in relation to the parties to the marriage in paragraphs (a) and (b) of subsection (2) above.

(4) As regards the exercise of its power under section 2 in favour of a child of the family who is not the child of the respondent, the court shall also have regard—

(a) to whether the respondent has assumed any responsibility for the child's maintenance and, if he did, to the extent to which, and the basis on which, he assumed that responsibility and to the length of time during which he discharged that responsibility;

(b) to whether in assuming and discharging that responsibility the respondent did so knowing that the child was not his own child;

(c) to the liability of any other person to maintain the child.

(D) Child Abduction Act 1984

1 Offence of abduction of child by parent, etc

(1) Subject to subsections (5) and (8) below, a person connected with a child under the age of sixteen commits an offence if he takes or sends the child out of the United Kingdom without the appropriate consent.

(2) A person is connected with a child for the purposes of this section if—

(a) he is a parent of the child; or

(b) in the case of a child whose parents were not married to each other at the time of his birth, there are reasonable grounds for believing that he is the father of the child; or

(c) he is a guardian of the child; or

(ca) he is a special guardian of the child; or

(d) he is a person in whose favour a residence order is in force with respect to the child; or

(e) he has custody of the child.

(3) In this section 'the appropriate consent', in relation to a child, means—

(a) the consent of each of the following—

(i) the child's mother;

(ii) the child's father, if he has parental responsibility for him;

(iii) any guardian of the child;

(iiia) any special guardian of the child;

(iv) any person in whose favour a residence order is in force with respect to the child;

(v) any person who has custody of the child; or

(b) the leave of the court granted under or by virtue of any provision of Part II of the Children Act 1989; or

(c) if any person has custody of the child, the leave of the court which awarded custody to him.

(4) A person does not commit an offence under this section by taking or sending a child out of the United Kingdom without obtaining the appropriate consent if—

(a) he is a person in whose favour there is a residence order in force with respect to the child, and he takes or sends him out of the United Kingdom for a period of less than one month; or

(b) he is a special guardian of the child and he takes or sends the child out of the United Kingdom for a period of less than three months.

(4A) Subsection (4) above does not apply if the person taking or sending the child out of the United Kingdom does so in breach of an order under Part II of the Children Act 1989.

(5) A person does not commit an offence under this section by doing anything without the consent of another person whose consent is required under the foregoing provisions if—

(a) he does it in the belief that the other person—

(i) has consented; or

(ii) would consent if he was aware of all the relevant circumstances; or

(b) he has taken all reasonable steps to communicate with the other person but has been unable to communicate with him; or

(c) the other person has unreasonably refused to consent, …

(5A) Subsection (5)(c) above does not apply if—

(a) the person who refused to consent is a person—

(i) in whose favour there is a residence order in force with respect to the child; ...

(ia) who is a special guardian of the child; or

(ii) who has custody of the child; or

(b) the person taking or sending the child out of the United Kingdom is, by so acting, in breach of an order made by a court in the United Kingdom.

(6) Where, in proceedings for an offence under this section, there is sufficient evidence to raise an issue as to the application of subsection (5) above, it shall be for the prosecution to prove that that subsection does not apply.

(7) For the purposes of this section—

(a) 'guardian of a child', 'special guardian', 'residence order' and 'parental responsibility' have the same meaning as in the Children Act 1989; and

(b) a person shall be treated as having custody of a child if there is in force an order of a court in the United Kingdom awarding him (whether solely or jointly with another person) custody, legal custody or care and control of the child.

(8) This section shall have effect subject to the provisions of the Schedule to this Act in relation to a child who is in the care of a local authority detained in a place of safety, remanded to a local authority accommodation or the subject of proceedings or an order relating to adoption.

2 Offence of abduction of child by other persons

(1) Subject to subsection (3) below, a person, other than one mentioned in subsection (2) below, commits an offence if, without lawful authority or reasonable excuse, he takes or detains a child under the age of sixteen—

(a) so as to remove him from the lawful control of any person having lawful control of the child; or

(b) so as to keep him out of the lawful control of any person entitled to lawful control of the child.

(2) The persons are—

(a) where the father and mother of the child in question were married to each other at the time of his birth, the child's father and mother;

(b) where the father and mother of the child in question were not married to each other at the time of his birth, the child's mother; and

(c) any other person mentioned in section 1(2)(c) to (e) above.

(3) In proceedings against any person for an offence under this section, it shall be a defence for that person to prove—

(a) where the father and mother of the child in question were not married to each other at the time of his birth—

(i) that he is the child's father; or

(ii) that, at the time of the alleged offence, he believed, on reasonable grounds, that he was the child's father; or

(b) that, at the time of the alleged offence, he believed that the child had attained the age of sixteen.

3 Construction of references to taking, sending and detaining

For the purposes of this Part of this Act—

(a) a person shall be regarded as taking a child if he causes or induces the child to accompany him or any other person or causes the child to be taken;

(b) a person shall be regarded as sending a child if he causes the child to be sent; ...

(c) a person shall be regarded as detaining a child if he causes the child to be detained or induces the child to remain with him or any other person; and

(d) references to a child's parents and to a child whose parents were (or were not) married to each other at the time of his birth shall be construed in accordance with section 1 of the Family Law Reform Act 1987 (which extends their meaning).

(E) Children Act 1989

1 Welfare of the child

(1) When a court determines any question with respect to—

(a) the upbringing of a child; or

(b) the administration of a child's property or the application of any income arising from it,

the child's welfare shall be the court's paramount consideration.

(2) In any proceedings in which any question with respect to the upbringing of a child arises, the court shall have regard to the general principle that any delay in determining the question is likely to prejudice the welfare of the child.

(3) In the circumstances mentioned in subsection (4), a court shall have regard in particular to—

(a) the ascertainable wishes and feelings of the child concerned (considered in the light of his age and understanding);

(b) his physical, emotional and educational needs;

(c) the likely effect on him of any change in his circumstances;

(d) his age, sex, background and any characteristics of his which the court considers relevant;

(e) any harm which he has suffered or is at risk of suffering;

(f) how capable each of his parents, and any other person in relation to whom the court considers the question to be relevant, is of meeting his needs;

(g) the range of powers available to the court under this Act in the proceedings in question.

(4) The circumstances are that—

(a) the court is considering whether to make, vary or discharge a section 8 order, and the making, variation or discharge of the order is opposed by any party to the proceedings; or

(b) the court is considering whether to make, vary or discharge a special guardianship order or an order under Part IV.

(5) Where a court is considering whether or not to make one or more orders under this Act with respect to a child, it shall not make the order or any of the orders unless it considers that doing so would be better for the child than making no order at all.

2 Parental responsibility for children

(1) Where a child's father and mother were married to each other at the time of his birth, they shall each have parental responsibility for the child.

(1A) Where a child—

(a) has a parent by virtue of section 42 of the Human Fertilisation and Embryology Act 2008; or

(b) has a parent by virtue of section 43 of that Act and is a person to whom section 1(3) of the Family Law Reform Act 1987 applies,

the child's mother and the other parent shall each have parental responsibility for the child.

(2) Where a child's father and mother were not married to each other at the time of his birth—

(a) the mother shall have parental responsibility for the child;

(b) the father shall have parental responsibility for the child if he has acquired it (and has not ceased to have it) in accordance with the provisions of this Act.

(2A) Where a child has a parent by virtue of section 43 of the Human Fertilisation and Embryology Act 2008 and is not a person to whom section 1(3) of the Family Law Reform Act 1987 applies—

(a) the mother shall have parental responsibility for the child;

(b) the other parent shall have parental responsibility for the child if she has acquired it (and has not ceased to have it) in accordance with the provisions of this Act.

(3) References in this Act to a child whose father and mother were, or (as the case may be) were not, married to each other at the time of his birth must be read with section 1 of the Family Law Reform Act 1987 (which extends their meaning).

(4) The rule of law that a father is the natural guardian of his legitimate child is abolished.

(5) More than one person may have parental responsibility for the same child at the same time.

(6) A person who has parental responsibility for a child at any time shall not cease to have that responsibility solely because some other person subsequently acquires parental responsibility for the child.

(7) Where more than one person has parental responsibility for a child, each of them may act alone and without the other (or others) in meeting that responsibility; but nothing in this Part shall be taken to affect the operation of any enactment which requires the consent of more than one person in a matter affecting the child.

(8) The fact that a person has parental responsibility for a child shall not entitle him to act in any way which would be incompatible with any order made with respect to the child under this Act.

(9) A person who has parental responsibility for a child may not surrender or transfer any part of that responsibility to another but may arrange for some or all of it to be met by one or more persons acting on his behalf.

(10) The person with whom any such arrangement is made may himself be a person who already has parental responsibility for the child concerned.

(11) The making of any such arrangement shall not affect any liability of the person making it which may arise from any failure to meet any part of his parental responsibility for the child concerned.

3 Meaning of 'parental responsibility'

(1) In this Act 'parental responsibility' means all the rights, duties, powers, responsibilities and authority which by law a parent of a child has in relation to the child and his property.

(2) It also includes the rights, powers and duties which a guardian of the child's estate (appointed, before the commencement of section 5, to act generally) would have had in relation to the child and his property.

(3) The rights referred to in subsection (2) include, in particular, the right of the guardian to receive or recover in his own name, for the benefit of the child, property of whatever description and wherever situated which the child is entitled to receive or recover.

(4) The fact that a person has, or does not have, parental responsibility for a child shall not affect—

(a) any obligation which he may have in relation to the child (such as a statutory duty to maintain the child); or

(b) any rights which, in the event of the child's death, he (or any other person) may have in relation to the child's property.

(5) A person who—

(a) does not have parental responsibility for a particular child; but

(b) has care of the child,

may (subject to the provisions of this Act) do what is reasonable in all the circumstances of the case for the purpose of safeguarding or promoting the child's welfare.

4 Acquisition of parental responsibility by father

(1) Where a child's father and mother were not married to each other at the time of his birth, the father shall acquire parental responsibility for the child if—

(a) he becomes registered as the child's father under any of the enactments specified in subsection (1A);

(b) he and the child's mother make an agreement (a 'parental responsibility agreement') providing for him to have parental responsibility for the child; or

(c) the court, on his application, orders that he shall have parental responsibility for the child.

(1A) The enactments referred to in subsection (1)(a) are—

(a) paragraphs (a), (b) and (c) of section 10(1) and of section 10A(1) of the Births and Deaths Registration Act 1953;

(b) paragraphs (a), (b)(i) and (c) of section 18(1), and sections 18(2)(b) and 20(1)(a) of the Registration of Births, Deaths and Marriages (Scotland) Act 1965; and

(c) sub-paragraphs (a), (b) and (c) of Article 14(3) of the Births and Deaths Registration (Northern Ireland) Order 1976.

(1B) The Secretary of State may by order amend subsection (1A) so as to add further enactments to the list in that subsection.

(2) No parental responsibility agreement shall have effect for the purposes of this Act unless—

(a) it is made in the form prescribed by regulations made by the Lord Chancellor; and

(b) where regulations are made by the Lord Chancellor prescribing the manner in which such agreements must be recorded, it is recorded in the prescribed manner.

(2A) A person who has acquired parental responsibility under subsection (1) shall cease to have that responsibility only if the court so orders.

(3) The court may make an order under subsection (2A) on the application—

(a) of any person who has parental responsibility for the child; or

(b) with the leave of the court, of the child himself,

subject, in the case of parental responsibility acquired under subsection (1)(c), to section 12(4).

(4) The court may only grant leave under subsection (3)(b) if it is satisfied that the child has sufficient understanding to make the proposed application.

4ZA Acquisition of parental responsibility by second female parent

(1) Where a child has a parent by virtue of section 43 of the Human Fertilisation and Embryology Act 2008 and is not a person to whom section 1(3) of the Family Law Reform Act 1987 applies, that parent shall acquire parental responsibility for the child if—

(a) she becomes registered as a parent of the child under any of the enactments specified in subsection (2);

(b) she and the child's mother make an agreement providing for her to have parental responsibility for the child; or

(c) the court, on her application, orders that she shall have parental responsibility for the child.

(2) The enactments referred to in subsection (1)(a) are—

(a) paragraphs (a), (b) and (c) of section 10(1B) and of section 10A(1B) of the Births and Deaths Registration Act 1953;

(b) paragraphs (a), (b) and (d) of section 18B(1) and sections 18B(3)(a) and 20(1)(a) of the Registration of Births, Deaths and Marriages (Scotland) Act 1965; and

(c) sub-paragraphs (a), (b) and (c) of Article 14ZA(3) of the Births and Deaths Registration (Northern Ireland) Order 1976.

(3) The Secretary of State may by order amend subsection (2) so as to add further enactments to the list in that subsection.

(4) An agreement under subsection (1)(b) is also a 'parental responsibility agreement', and section 4(2) applies in relation to such an agreement as it applies in relation to parental responsibility agreements under section 4.

(5) A person who has acquired parental responsibility under subsection (1) shall cease to have that responsibility only if the court so orders.

(6) The court may make an order under subsection (5) on the application—

(a) of any person who has parental responsibility for the child; or

(b) with the leave of the court, of the child himself,

subject, in the case of parental responsibility acquired under subsection (1)(c), to section 12(4).

(7) The court may only grant leave under subsection (6)(b) if it is satisfied that the child has sufficient understanding to make the proposed application.

4A Acquisition of parental responsibility by step-parent

(1) Where a child's parent ('parent A') who has parental responsibility for the child is married to, or a civil partner of, a person who is not the child's parent ('the step-parent')—

(a) parent A, or if the other parent of the child also has parental responsibility for the child, both parents may by agreement with the step-parent provide for the step-parent to have parental responsibility for the child; or

(b) the court may, on the application of the step-parent, order that the step-parent shall have parental responsibility for the child.

(2) An agreement under subsection (1)(a) is also a 'parental responsibility agreement', and section 4(2) applies in relation to such agreements as it applies in relation to parental responsibility agreements under section 4.

(3) A parental responsibility agreement under subsection (1)(a), or an order under subsection (1)(b), may only be brought to an end by an order of the court made on the application—

(a) of any person has parental responsibility for the child; or

(b) with the leave of the court, of the child himself.

(4) The court may only grant leave under subsection (3)(b) if it is satisfied that the child has sufficient understanding to make the proposed application.

5 Appointment of guardians

(1) Where an application with respect to a child is made to the court by any individual, the court may by order appoint that individual to be the child's guardian if—

(a) the child has no parent with parental responsibility for him; or

(b) a residence order has been made with respect to the child in favour of a parent, guardian or special guardian of his who has died while the order was in force; or

(c) paragraph (b) does not apply, and the child's only or last surviving special guardian dies.

(2) The power conferred by subsection (1) may also be exercised in any family proceedings if the court considers that the order should be made even though no application has been made for it.

(3) A parent who has parental responsibility for his child may appoint another individual to be the child's guardian in the event of his death.

(4) A guardian of a child may appoint another individual to take his place as the child's guardian in the event of his death; and a special guardian of a child may appoint another individual to be the child's guardian in the event of his death.

(5) An appointment under subsection (3) or (4) shall not have effect unless it is made in writing, is dated and is signed by the person making the appointment or—

(a) in the case of an appointment made by a will which is not signed by the testator, is signed at the direction of the testator in accordance with the requirements of section 9 of the Wills Act 1837; or

(b) in any other case, is signed at the direction of the person making the appointment, in his presence and in the presence of two witnesses who each attest the signature.

(6) A person appointed as a child's guardian under this section shall have parental responsibility for the child concerned.

(7) Where—

(a) on the death of any person making an appointment under subsection (3) or (4), the child concerned has no parent with parental responsibility for him; or

(b) immediately before the death of any person making such an appointment, a residence order in his favour was in force with respect to the child, or he was the child's only (or last surviving) special guardian

the appointment shall take effect on the death of that person.

(8) Where, on the death of any person making an appointment under subsection (3) or (4)—

(a) the child concerned has a parent with parental responsibility for him; and

(b) subsection (7)(b) does not apply,

the appointment shall take effect when the child no longer has a parent who has parental responsibility for him.

(9) Subsections (1) and (7) do not apply if the residence order referred to in paragraph (b) of those subsections was also made in favour of a surviving parent of the child.

(10) Nothing in this section shall be taken to prevent an appointment under subsection (3) or (4) being made by two or more persons acting jointly.

(11) Subject to any provision made by rules of court, no court shall exercise the High Court's inherent jurisdiction to appoint a guardian of the estate of any child.

(12) Where the rules of court are made under subsection (11) they may prescribe the circumstances in which, and conditions subject to which, an appointment of such a guardian may be made.

(13) A guardian of a child may only be appointed in accordance with the provisions of this section.

7 Welfare reports

(1) A court considering any question with respect to a child under this Act may—

(a) ask an officer of the Service or a Welsh family proceedings officer; or

(b) ask a local authority to arrange for—

(i) an officer of the authority; or

(ii) such other person (other than an officer of the Service or a Welsh family proceedings officer) as the authority considers appropriate, to report to the court on such matters relating to the welfare of that child as are required to be dealt with in the report.

(2) The Lord Chancellor may, after consulting the Lord Chief Justice, make regulations specifying matters which, unless the court orders otherwise, must be dealt with in any report under this section.

(3) The report may be made in writing, or orally, as the court requires.

(4) Regardless of any enactment or rule of law which would otherwise prevent it from doing so, the court may take account of—

(a) any statement contained in the report; and

(b) any evidence given in respect of the matters referred to in the report,

in so far as the statement or evidence is, in the opinion of the court, relevant to the question which it is considering.

(5) It shall be the duty of the authority or officer of the Service or a Welsh family proceedings officer to comply with any request for a report under this section.

(6) The Lord Chief Justice may nominate a judicial office holder (as defined in section 109(4) of the Constitutional Reform Act 2005) to exercise his functions under subsection (2).

8 Residence, contact and other orders with respect to children

(1) In this Act—

'a contact order' means an order requiring the person with whom a child lives, or is to live, to allow the child to visit or stay with the person named in the order, or for that person and the child otherwise to have contact with each other;

'a prohibited steps order' means an order that no step which could be taken by a parent in meeting his parental responsibility for a child, and which is of a kind specified in the order, shall be taken by any person without the consent of the court;

'a residence order' means an order settling the arrangements to be made as to the person with whom a child is to live; and

'a specific issue order' means an order giving directions for the purpose of determining a specific question which has arisen, or which may arise, in connection with any aspect of parental responsibility for a child.

(2) In this Act 'a section 8 order' means any of the orders mentioned in subsection (1) and any order varying or discharging such an order.

(3) For the purposes of this Act 'family proceedings' means any proceedings—

(a) under the inherent jurisdiction of the High Court in relation to children; and

(b) under the enactments mentioned in subsection (4),

but does not include proceedings on an application for leave under section 100(3).

(4) The enactments are—

(a) Parts I, II and IV of this Act;

(b) the Matrimonial Causes Act 1973;

(ba) Schedule 5 to the Civil Partnership Act 2004;

(c) …

(d) the Adoption and Children Act 2002;

(e) the Domestic Proceedings and Magistrates' Courts Act 1978;

(ea) Schedule 6 to the Civil Partnership Act 2004;

(f) …

(g) Part III of the Matrimonial and Family Proceedings Act 1984;

(h) the Family Law Act 1996;

(i) sections 11 and 12 of the Crime and Disorder Act 1998.

9 Restrictions on making section 8 orders

(1) No court shall make any section 8 order, other than a residence order, with respect to a child who is in the care of a local authority.

(2) No application may be made by a local authority for a residence order or contact order and no court shall make such an order in favour of a local authority.

(3) A person who is, or was at any time within the last six months, a local authority foster parent of a child may not apply for leave to apply for a section 8 order with respect to the child unless—

(a) he has the consent of the authority;

(b) he is relative of the child; or

(c) the child has lived with him for at least one year preceding the application.

(4) . . .

(5) No court shall exercise its powers to make a specific issue order or prohibited steps order—

(a) with a view to achieving a result which could be achieved by making a residence or contact order; or

(b) in any way which is denied to the High Court (by section 100(2)) in the exercise of its inherent jurisdiction with respect to children.

(6) No court shall make a specific issue order, contact order or prohibited steps order which is to have effect for a period which will end after the child has reached the age of sixteen unless it is satisfied that the circumstances of the case are exceptional.

(7) No court shall make any section 8 order, other than one varying or discharging such an order, with respect to a child who has reached the age of sixteen unless it is satisfied that the circumstances of the case are exceptional.

10 Power of court to make section 8 orders

(1) In any family proceedings in which a question arises with respect to the welfare of any child, the court may make a section 8 order with respect to the child if—

(a) an application for the order has been made by a person who—

(i) is entitled to apply for a section 8 order with respect to the child; or

(ii) has obtained the leave of the court to make the application; or

(b) the court considers that the order should be made even though no such application has been made.

(2) The court may also make a section 8 order with respect to any child on the application of a person who—

(a) is entitled to apply for a section 8 order with respect to the child; or

(b) has obtained the leave of the court to make the application.

(3) This section is subject to the restrictions imposed by section 9.

(4) The following persons are entitled to apply to the court for any section 8 order with respect to a child—

(a) any parent, guardian or special guardian of the child;

(aa) any person who by virtue of section 4A has parental responsibility for the child;

(b) any person in whose favour a residence order is in force with respect to the child.

(5) The following persons are entitled to apply for a residence or contact order with respect to a child—

(a) any party to a marriage (whether or not subsisting) in relation to whom the child is a child of the family;

(aa) any civil partner in a civil partnership (whether or not subsisting) in relation to whom the child is a child of the family;

(b) any person with whom the child has lived for a period of at least three years;

(c) any person who—

(i) in any case where a residence order is in force with respect to the child, has the consent of each of the persons in whose favour the order was made;

(ii) in any case where the child is in the care of a local authority, has the consent of that authority; or

(iii) in any other case, has the consent of each of those (if any) who have parental responsibility for the child.

(5A) A local authority foster parent is entitled to apply for a residence order with respect to a child if the child has lived with him for a period of at least one year immediately preceding the application.

(5B) A relative of a child is entitled to apply for a residence order with respect to the child if the child has lived with the relative for a period of at least one year immediately preceding the application.

(6) A person who would not otherwise be entitled (under the previous provisions of this section) to apply for the variation or discharge of a section 8 order shall be entitled to do so if—

(a) the order was made on his application; or

(b) in the case of a contact order, he is named in the order.

(7) Any person who falls within a category of person prescribed by rules of court is entitled to apply for any such section 8 order as may be prescribed in relation to that category of person.

(7A) If a special guardianship order is in force with respect to a child, an application for a residence order may only be made with respect to him, if apart from this subsection the leave of the court is not required, with such leave.

(8) Where the person applying for leave to make an application for a section 8 order is the child concerned, the court may only grant leave if it is satisfied that he has sufficient understanding to make the proposed application for the section 8 order.

(9) Where the person applying for leave to make an application for a section 8 order is not the child concerned, the court shall, in deciding whether or not to grant leave, have particular regard to—

(a) the nature of the proposed application for the section 8 order;

(b) the applicant's connection with the child;

(c) any risk there might be of that proposed application disrupting the child's life to such an extent that he would be harmed by it; and

(d) where the child is being looked after by a local authority—

(i) the authority's plans for the child's future; and

(ii) the wishes and feelings of the child's parents.

(10) The period of three years mentioned in subsection (5)(b) need not be continuous but must not have begun more than five years before, or ended more than three months before, the making of the application.

11 General principles and supplementary provisions

(1) In proceedings in which any question of making a section 8 order, or any other question with respect to such an order, arises, the court shall (in the light of any rules made by virtue of subsection (2))—

(a) draw up a timetable with a view to determining the question without delay; and

(b) give such directions as it considers appropriate for the purpose of ensuring, so far as is reasonably practicable, that that timetable is adhered to.

(2) Rules of court may—

(a) specify periods within which specified steps must be taken in relation to proceedings in which such questions arise; and

(b) make other provision with respect to such proceedings for the purpose of ensuring, so far as is reasonably practicable, that such questions are determined without delay.

(3) Where a court has power to make a section 8 order, it may do so at any time during the course of the proceedings in question even though it is not in a position to dispose finally of those proceedings.

(4) Where a residence order is made in favour of two or more persons who do not themselves all live together, the order may specify the periods during which the child is to live in the different households concerned.

(5) Where—

(a) a residence order has been made with respect to a child; and

(b) as a result of the order the child lives, or is to live, with one of two parents who each have parental responsibility for him,

the residence order shall cease to have effect if the parents live together for a continuous period of more than six months.

(6) A contact order which requires the parent with whom a child lives to allow the child to visit, or otherwise have contact with, his other parent shall cease to have effect if the parents live together for a continuous period of more than six months.

(7) A section 8 order may—

(a) contain directions about how it is to be carried into effect;

(b) impose conditions which must be complied with by any person—

(i) in whose favour the order is made;

(ii) who is a parent of the child concerned;

(iii) who is not a parent of his but who has parental responsibility for him; or

(iv) with whom the child is living,

and to whom the conditions are expressed to apply;

(c) be made to have effect for a specified period, or contain provisions which are to have effect for a specified period;

(d) make such incidental, supplemental or consequential provision as the court thinks fit.

11A Contact activity directions

(1) This section applies in proceedings in which the court is considering whether to make provision about contact with a child by making—

(a) a contact order with respect to the child, or

(b) an order varying or discharging a contact order with respect to the child.

(2) The court may make a contact activity direction in connection with that provision about contact.

(3) A contact activity direction is a direction requiring an individual who is a party to the proceedings to take part in an activity that promotes contact with the child concerned.

(4) The direction is to specify the activity and the person providing the activity.

(5) The activities that may be so required include, in particular—

(a) programmes, classes and counselling or guidance sessions of a kind that—

(i) may assist a person as regards establishing, maintaining or improving contact with a child;

(ii) may, by addressing a person's violent behaviour, enable or facilitate contact with a child;

(b) sessions in which information or advice is given as regards making or operating arrangements for contact with a child, including making arrangements by means of mediation.

(6) No individual may be required by a contact activity direction—

(a) to undergo medical or psychiatric examination, assessment or treatment;

(b) to take part in mediation.

(7) A court may not on the same occasion—

(a) make a contact activity direction, and

(b) dispose finally of the proceedings as they relate to contact with the child concerned.

(8) Subsection (2) has effect subject to the restrictions in sections 11B and 11E.

(9) In considering whether to make a contact activity direction, the welfare of the child concerned is to be the court's paramount consideration.

11B Contact activity directions: further provision

(1) A court may not make a contact activity direction in any proceedings unless there is a dispute as regards the provision about contact that the court is considering whether to make in the proceedings.

(2) A court may not make a contact activity direction requiring an individual who is a child to take part in an activity unless the individual is a parent of the child in relation to whom the court is considering provision about contact.

(3) A court may not make a contact activity direction in connection with the making, variation or discharge of a contact order, if the contact order is, or would if made be, an excepted order.

(4) A contact order with respect to a child is an excepted order if—

(a) it is made in proceedings that include proceedings on an application for a relevant adoption order in respect of the child; or

(b) it makes provision as regards contact between the child and a person who would be a parent or relative of the child but for the child's adoption by an order falling within subsection (5).

(5) An order falls within this subsection if it is—

(a) a relevant adoption order;

(b) an adoption order, within the meaning of section 72(1) of the Adoption Act 1976, other than an order made by virtue of section 14 of that Act on the application of a married couple one of whom is the mother or the father of the child;

(c) a Scottish adoption order, within the meaning of the Adoption and Children Act 2002, other than an order made—

(i) by virtue of section 14 of the Adoption (Scotland) Act 1978 on the application of a married couple one of whom is the mother or the father of the child, or

(ii) by virtue of section 15(1)(aa) of that Act; or

(iii) by virtue of an application under section 30 of the Adoption and Children (Scotland) Act 2007 where subsection (3) of that section applies; or

(d) a Northern Irish adoption order, within the meaning of the Adoption and Children Act 2002, other than an order made by virtue of Article 14 of the Adoption (Northern Ireland) Order 1987 on the application of a married couple one of whom is the mother or the father of the child.

(6) A relevant adoption order is an adoption order, within the meaning of section 46(1) of the Adoption and Children Act 2002, other than an order made—

(a) on an application under section 50 of that Act by a couple (within the meaning of that Act) one of whom is the mother or the father of the person to be adopted, or

(b) on an application under section 51(2) of that Act.

(7) A court may not make a contact activity direction in relation to an individual unless the individual is habitually resident in England and Wales; and a direction ceases to have effect if the individual subject to the direction ceases to be habitually resident in England and Wales.

11C Contact activity conditions

(1) This section applies if in any family proceedings the court makes—

(a) a contact order with respect to a child, or

(b) an order varying a contact order with respect to a child.

(2) The contact order may impose, or the contact order may be varied so as to impose, a condition (a 'contact activity condition') requiring an individual falling within subsection (3) to take part in an activity that promotes contact with the child concerned.

(3) An individual falls within this subsection if he is—

(a) for the purposes of the contact order so made or varied, the person with whom the child concerned lives or is to live;

(b) the person whose contact with the child concerned is provided for in that order; or

(c) a person upon whom that order imposes a condition under section 11(7)(b).

(4) The condition is to specify the activity and the person providing the activity.

(5) Subsections (5) and (6) of section 11A have effect as regards the activities that may be required by a contact activity condition as they have effect as regards the activities that may be required by a contact activity direction.

(6) Subsection (2) has effect subject to the restrictions in sections 11D and 11E.

11D Contact activity conditions: further provision

(1) A contact order may not impose a contact activity condition on an individual who is a child unless the individual is a parent of the child concerned.

(2) If a contact order is an excepted order (within the meaning given by section 11B(4)), it may not impose (and it may not be varied so as to impose) a contact activity condition.

(3) A contact order may not impose a contact activity condition on an individual unless the individual is habitually resident in England and Wales; and a condition ceases to have effect if the individual subject to the condition ceases to be habitually resident in England and Wales.

11E Contact activity directions and conditions: making

(1) Before making a contact activity direction (or imposing a contact activity condition by means of a contact order), the court must satisfy itself as to the matters falling within subsections (2) to (4).

(2) The first matter is that the activity proposed to be specified is appropriate in the circumstances of the case.

(3) The second matter is that the person proposed to be specified as the provider of the activity is suitable to provide the activity.

(4) The third matter is that the activity proposed to be specified is provided in a place to which the individual who would be subject to the direction (or the condition) can reasonably be expected to travel.

(5) Before making such a direction (or such an order), the court must obtain and consider information about the individual who would be subject to the direction (or the condition) and the likely effect of the direction (or the condition) on him.

(6) Information about the likely effect of the direction (or the condition) may, in particular, include information as to—
   (a) any conflict with the individual's religious beliefs;
   (b) any interference with the times (if any) at which he normally works or attends an educational establishment.

(7) The court may ask an officer of the Service or a Welsh family proceedings officer to provide the court with information as to the matters in subsections (2) to (5); and it shall be the duty of the officer of the Service or Welsh family proceedings officer to comply with any such request.

(8) In this section 'specified' means specified in a contact activity direction (or in a contact activity condition).

11F Contact activity directions and conditions: financial assistance

(1) The Secretary of State may by regulations make provision authorising him to make payments to assist individuals falling within subsection (2) in paying relevant charges or fees.

(2) An individual falls within this subsection if he is required by a contact activity direction or condition to take part in an activity that promotes contact with a child, not being a child ordinarily resident in Wales.

(3) The National Assembly for Wales may by regulations make provision authorising it to make payments to assist individuals falling within subsection (4) in paying relevant charges or fees.

(4) An individual falls within this subsection if he is required by a contact activity direction or condition to take part in an activity that promotes contact with a child who is ordinarily resident in Wales.

(5) A relevant charge or fee, in relation to an activity required by a contact activity direction or condition, is a charge or fee in respect of the activity payable to the person providing the activity.

(6) Regulations under this section may provide that no assistance is available to an individual unless—
   (a) the individual satisfies such conditions as regards his financial resources as may be set out in the regulations;
   (b) the activity in which the individual is required by a contact activity direction or condition to take part is provided to him in England or Wales;
   (c) where the activity in which the individual is required to take part is provided to him in England, it is provided by a person who is for the time being approved by the Secretary of State as a provider of activities required by a contact activity direction or condition;
   (d) where the activity in which the individual is required to take part is provided to him in Wales, it is provided by a person who is for the time being approved by the National Assembly for Wales as a provider of activities required by a contact activity direction or condition.

(7) Regulations under this section may make provision—
   (a) as to the maximum amount of assistance that may be paid to or in respect of an individual as regards an activity in which he is required by a contact activity direction or condition to take part;
   (b) where the amount may vary according to an individual's financial resources, as to the method by which the amount is to be determined;
   (c) authorising payments by way of assistance to be made directly to persons providing activities required by a contact activity direction or condition.

11G Contact activity directions and conditions: monitoring

(1) This section applies if in any family proceedings the court—

(a) makes a contact activity direction in relation to an individual, or

(b) makes a contact order that imposes, or varies a contact order so as to impose, a contact activity condition on an individual.

(2) The court may on making the direction (or imposing the condition by means of a contact order) ask an officer of the Service or a Welsh family proceedings officer—

(a) to monitor, or arrange for the monitoring of, the individual's compliance with the direction (or the condition);

(b) to report to the court on any failure by the individual to comply with the direction (or the condition).

(3) It shall be the duty of the officer of the Service or Welsh family proceedings officer to comply with any request under subsection (2).

11H Monitoring contact

(1) This section applies if in any family proceedings the court makes—

(a) a contact order with respect to a child in favour of a person, or

(b) an order varying such a contact order.

(2) The court may ask an officer of the Service or a Welsh family proceedings officer—

(a) to monitor whether an individual falling within subsection (3) complies with the contact order (or the contact order as varied);

(b) to report to the court on such matters relating to the individual's compliance as the court may specify in the request.

(3) An individual falls within this subsection if the contact order so made (or the contact order as so varied)—

(a) requires the individual to allow contact with the child concerned;

(b) names the individual as having contact with the child concerned; or

(c) imposes a condition under section 11(7)(b) on the individual.

(4) If the contact order (or the contact order as varied) includes a contact activity condition, a request under subsection (2) is to be treated as relating to the provisions of the order other than the contact activity condition.

(5) The court may make a request under subsection (2)—

(a) on making the contact order (or the order varying the contact order), or

(b) at any time during the subsequent course of the proceedings as they relate to contact with the child concerned.

(6) In making a request under subsection (2), the court is to specify the period for which the officer of the Service or Welsh family proceedings officer is to monitor compliance with the order; and the period specified may not exceed twelve months.

(7) It shall be the duty of the officer of the Service or Welsh family proceedings officer to comply with any request under subsection (2).

(8) The court may order any individual falling within subsection (3) to take such steps as may be specified in the order with a view to enabling the officer of the Service or Welsh family proceedings officer to comply with the court's request under subsection (2).

(9) But the court may not make an order under subsection (8) with respect to an individual who is a child unless he is a parent of the child with respect to whom the order falling within subsection (1) was made.

(10) A court may not make a request under subsection (2) in relation to a contact order that is an excepted order (within the meaning given by section 11B(4)).

11I Contact orders: warning notices

Where the court makes (or varies) a contact order, it is to attach to the contact order (or the order varying the contact order) a notice warning of the consequences of failing to comply with the contact order.

11J Enforcement orders

(1) This section applies if a contact order with respect to a child has been made.

(2) If the court is satisfied beyond reasonable doubt that a person has failed to comply with the contact order, it may make an order (an 'enforcement order') imposing on the person an unpaid work requirement.

(3) But the court may not make an enforcement order if it is satisfied that the person had a reasonable excuse for failing to comply with the contact order.

(4) The burden of proof as to the matter mentioned in subsection (3) lies on the person claiming to have had a reasonable excuse, and the standard of proof is the balance of probabilities.

(5) The court may make an enforcement order in relation to the contact order only on the application of—

- (a) the person who is, for the purposes of the contact order, the person with whom the child concerned lives or is to live;
- (b) the person whose contact with the child concerned is provided for in the contact order;
- (c) any individual subject to a condition under section 11(7)(b) or a contact activity condition imposed by the contact order; or
- (d) the child concerned.

(6) Where the person proposing to apply for an enforcement order in relation to a contact order is the child concerned, the child must obtain the leave of the court before making such an application.

(7) The court may grant leave to the child concerned only if it is satisfied that he has sufficient understanding to make the proposed application.

(8) Subsection (2) has effect subject to the restrictions in sections 11K and 11L.

(9) The court may suspend an enforcement order for such period as it thinks fit.

(10) Nothing in this section prevents a court from making more than one enforcement order in relation to the same person on the same occasion.

(11) Proceedings in which any question of making an enforcement order, or any other question with respect to such an order, arises are to be regarded for the purposes of section 11(1) and (2) as proceedings in which a question arises with respect to a section 8 order.

(12) In Schedule A1—

- (a) Part 1 makes provision as regards an unpaid work requirement;
- (b) Part 2 makes provision in relation to the revocation and amendment of enforcement orders and failure to comply with such orders.

(13) This section is without prejudice to section 63(3) of the Magistrates' Courts Act 1980 as it applies in relation to contact orders.

11K Enforcement orders: further provision

(1) A court may not make an enforcement order against a person in respect of a failure to comply with a contact order unless it is satisfied that before the failure occurred the person had been given (in accordance with rules of court) a copy of, or otherwise informed of the terms of—

(a) in the case of a failure to comply with a contact order that was varied before the failure occurred, a notice under section 11I relating to the order varying the contact order or, where more than one such order has been made, the last order preceding the failure in question;

(b) in any other case, a notice under section 11I relating to the contact order.

(2) A court may not make an enforcement order against a person in respect of any failure to comply with a contact order occurring before the person attained the age of 18.

(3) A court may not make an enforcement order against a person in respect of a failure to comply with a contact order that is an excepted order (within the meaning given by section 11B(4)).

(4) A court may not make an enforcement order against a person unless the person is habitually resident in England and Wales; and an enforcement order ceases to have effect if the person subject to the order ceases to be habitually resident in England and Wales.

11L Enforcement orders: making

(1) Before making an enforcement order as regards a person in breach of a contact order, the court must be satisfied that—

(a) making the enforcement order proposed is necessary to secure the person's compliance with the contact order or any contact order that has effect in its place;

(b) the likely effect on the person of the enforcement order proposed to be made is proportionate to the seriousness of the breach of the contact order.

(2) Before making an enforcement order, the court must satisfy itself that provision for the person to work under an unpaid work requirement imposed by an enforcement order can be made in the local justice area in which the person in breach resides or will reside.

(3) Before making an enforcement order as regards a person in breach of a contact order, the court must obtain and consider information about the person and the likely effect of the enforcement order on him.

(4) Information about the likely effect of the enforcement order may, in particular, include information as to—

(a) any conflict with the person's religious beliefs;

(b) any interference with the times (if any) at which he normally works or attends an educational establishment.

(5) A court that proposes to make an enforcement order may ask an officer of the Service or a Welsh family proceedings officer to provide the court with information as to the matters in subsections (2) and (3).

(6) It shall be the duty of the officer of the Service or Welsh family proceedings officer to comply with any request under this section.

(7) In making an enforcement order in relation to a contact order, a court must take into account the welfare of the child who is the subject of the contact order.

11M Enforcement orders: monitoring

(1) On making an enforcement order in relation to a person, the court is to ask an officer of the Service or a Welsh family proceedings officer—

(a) to monitor, or arrange for the monitoring of, the person's compliance with the unpaid work requirement imposed by the order;

(b) to report to the court if a report under paragraph 8 of Schedule A1 is made in relation to the person;

(c) to report to the court on such other matters relating to the person's compliance as may be specified in the request;

(d) to report to the court if the person is, or becomes, unsuitable to perform work under the requirement.

(2) It shall be the duty of the officer of the Service or Welsh family proceedings officer to comply with any request under this section.

11N Enforcement orders: warning notices

Where the court makes an enforcement order, it is to attach to the order a notice warning of the consequences of failing to comply with the order.

11O Compensation for financial loss

(1) This section applies if a contact order with respect to a child has been made.

(2) If the court is satisfied that—

(a) an individual has failed to comply with the contact order, and

(b) a person falling within subsection (6) has suffered financial loss by reason of the breach,

it may make an order requiring the individual in breach to pay the person compensation in respect of his financial loss.

(3) But the court may not make an order under subsection (2) if it is satisfied that the individual in breach had a reasonable excuse for failing to comply with the contact order.

(4) The burden of proof as to the matter mentioned in subsection (3) lies on the individual claiming to have had a reasonable excuse.

(5) An order under subsection (2) may be made only on an application by the person who claims to have suffered financial loss.

(6) A person falls within this subsection if he is—

(a) the person who is, for the purposes of the contact order, the person with whom the child concerned lives or is to live;

(b) the person whose contact with the child concerned is provided for in the contact order;

(c) an individual subject to a condition under section 11(7)(b) or a contact activity condition imposed by the contact order; or

(d) the child concerned.

(7) Where the person proposing to apply for an order under subsection (2) is the child concerned, the child must obtain the leave of the court before making such an application.

(8) The court may grant leave to the child concerned only if it is satisfied that he has sufficient understanding to make the proposed application.

(9) The amount of compensation is to be determined by the court, but may not exceed the amount of the applicant's financial loss.

(10) In determining the amount of compensation payable by the individual in breach, the court must take into account the individual's financial circumstances.

(11) An amount ordered to be paid as compensation may be recovered by the applicant as a civil debt due to him.

(12) Subsection (2) has effect subject to the restrictions in section 11P.

(13) Proceedings in which any question of making an order under subsection (2) arises are to be regarded for the purposes of section 11(1) and (2) as proceedings in which a question arises with respect to a section 8 order.

(14) In exercising its powers under this section, a court is to take into account the welfare of the child concerned.

11P Orders under section 11O(2): further provision

(1) A court may not make an order under section 11O(2) requiring an individual to pay compensation in respect of a failure by him to comply with a contact order unless it is satisfied that before the failure occurred the individual had been given (in accordance with rules of court) a copy of, or otherwise informed of the terms of—

(a) in the case of a failure to comply with a contact order that was varied before the failure occurred, a notice under section 11I relating to the order varying the contact order or, where more than one such order has been made, the last order preceding the failure in question;

(b) in any other case, a notice under section 11I relating to the contact order.

(2) A court may not make an order under section 11O(2) requiring an individual to pay compensation in respect of a failure by him to comply with a contact order where the failure occurred before the individual attained the age of 18.

(3) A court may not make an order under section 11O(2) requiring an individual to pay compensation in respect of a failure by him to comply with a contact order that is an excepted order (within the meaning given by section 11B(4)).

12 Residence orders and parental responsibility

(1) Where the court makes a residence order in favour of the father of a child it shall, if the father would not otherwise have parental responsibility for the child, also make an order under section 4 giving him that responsibility.

(1A) Where the court makes a residence order in favour of a woman who is a parent of a child by virtue of section 43 of the Human Fertilisation and Embryology Act 2008 it shall, if that woman would not otherwise have parental responsibility for the child, also make an order under section 4ZA giving her that responsibility.

(2) Where the court makes a residence order in favour of any person who is not the parent or guardian of the child concerned that person shall have parental responsibility for the child while the residence order remains in force.

(3) Where a person has parental responsibility for a child as a result of subsection (2), he shall not have the right—

(a) . . .

(b) to agree, or refuse to agree, to the making of an adoption order, or an order under section 84 of the Adoption and Children Act 2002, with respect to the child; or

(c) to appoint a guardian for the child.

(4) Where subsection (1) or (1A) requires the court to make an order under section 4 or 4ZA in respect of the parent of a child, the court shall not bring that order to an end at any time while the residence order concerned remains in force.

(5), (6) . . .

13 Change of child's name or removal from jurisdiction

(1) Where a residence order is in force with respect to a child, no person may—

(a) cause the child to be known by a new surname; or

(b) remove him from the United Kingdom;

without either the written consent of every person who has parental responsibility for the child or the leave of the court.

(2) Subsection (1)(b) does not prevent the removal of a child, for a period of less than one month, by the person in whose favour the residence order is made.

(3) In making a residence order with respect to a child the court may grant the leave required by subsection (1)(b), either generally or for specified purposes.

14A Special guardianship orders

(1) A 'special guardianship order' is an order appointing one or more individuals to be a child's 'special guardian' (or special guardians).

(2) A special guardian—

(a) must be aged eighteen or over; and

(b) must not be a parent of the child in question,

and subsections (3) to (6) are to be read in that light.

(3) The court may make a special guardianship order with respect to any child on the application of an individual who—

(a) is entitled to make such an application with respect to the child; or

(b) has obtained the leave of the court to make the application,

or on the joint application of more than one such individual.

(4) Section 9(3) applies in relation to an application for leave to apply for a special guardianship order as it applies in relation to an application for leave to apply for a section 8 order.

(5) The individuals who are entitled to apply for a special guardianship order with respect to a child are—

(a) any guardian of the child;

(b) any individual in whose favour a residence order is in force with respect to the child;

(c) any individual listed in subsection (5)(b) or (c) of section 10 (as read with subsection (10) of that section);

(d) a local authority foster parent with whom the child has lived for a period of at least one year immediately preceding the application;

(e) a relative with whom the child has lived for a period of at least one year immediately preceding the application.

(6) The court may also make a special guardianship order with respect to a child in any family proceedings in which a question arises with respect to the welfare of the child if—

(a) an application for the order has been made by an individual who falls within subsection (3)(a) or (b) (or more than one such individual jointly); or

(b) the court considers that a special guardianship order should be made even though no such application has been made.

(7) No individual may make an application under subsection (3) or (6)(a) unless, before the beginning of the period of three months ending with the date of the application, he has given written notice of his intention to make the application—

(a) if the child in question is being looked after by a local authority, to that local authority, or

(b) otherwise, to the local authority in whose area the individual is ordinarily resident.

(8) On receipt of such a notice, the local authority must investigate the matter and prepare a report for the court dealing with—

(a) the suitability of the applicant to be a special guardian;

(b) such matters (if any) as may be prescribed by the Secretary of State; and

(c) any other matter which the local authority consider to be relevant.

(9) The court may itself ask a local authority to conduct such an investigation and prepare such a report, and the local authority must do so.

(10) The local authority may make such arrangements as they see fit for any person to act on their behalf in connection with conducting an investigation or preparing a report referred to in subsection (8) or (9).

(11) The court may not make a special guardianship order unless it has received a report dealing with the matters referred to in subsection (8).

(12) Subsections (8) and (9) of section 10 apply in relation to special guardianship orders as they apply in relation to section 8 orders.

(13) This section is subject to section 29(5) and (6) of the Adoption and Children Act 2002.

14B Special guardianship orders: making

(1) Before making a special guardianship order, the court must consider whether, if the order were made—

(a) a contact order should also be made with respect to the child, . . .

(b) any section 8 order in force with respect to the child should be varied or discharged,

(c) where a contact order made with respect to the child is not discharged, any enforcement order relating to that contact order should be revoked, and

(d) where a contact activity direction has been made as regards contact with the child and is in force, that contact activity direction should be discharged.

(2) On making a special guardianship order, the court may also—

(a) give leave for the child to be known by a new surname;

(b) grant the leave required by section 14C(3)(b), either generally or for specified purposes.

14C Special guardianship orders: effect

(1) The effect of a special guardianship order is that while the order remains in force—

(a) a special guardian appointed by the order has parental responsibility for the child in respect of whom it is made; and

(b) subject to any other order in force with respect to the child under this Act, a special guardian is entitled to exercise parental responsibility to the exclusion of any other person with parental responsibility for the child (apart from another special guardian).

(2) Subsection (1) does not affect—

(a) the operation of any enactment or rule of law which requires the consent of more than one person with parental responsibility in a matter affecting the child; or

(b) any rights which a parent of the child has in relation to the child's adoption or placement for adoption.

(3) While a special guardianship order is in force with respect to a child, no person may—

(a) cause the child to be known by a new surname; or

(b) remove him from the United Kingdom,

without either the written consent of every person who has parental responsibility for the child or the leave of the court.

(4) Subsection (3)(b) does not prevent the removal of a child, for a period of less than three months, by a special guardian of his.

(5) If the child with respect to whom a special guardianship order is in force dies, his special guardian must take reasonable steps to give notice of that fact to—

(a) each parent of the child with parental responsibility; and

(b) each guardian of the child,

but if the child has more than one special guardian, and one of them has taken such steps in relation to a particular parent or guardian, any other special guardian need not do so as respects that parent or guardian.

(6) This section is subject to section 29(7) of the Adoption and Children Act 2002.

14D Special guardianship orders: variation and discharge

(1) The court may vary or discharge a special guardianship order on the application of—

(a) the special guardian (or any of them, if there are more than one);

(b) any parent or guardian of the child concerned;

(c) any individual in whose favour a residence order is in force with respect to the child;

(d) any individual not falling within any of paragraphs (a) to (c) who has, or immediately before the making of the special guardianship order had, parental responsibility for the child;

(e) the child himself; or

(f) a local authority designated in a care order with respect to the child.

(2) In any family proceedings in which a question arises with respect to the welfare of a child with respect to whom a special guardianship order is in force, the court may also vary or discharge the special guardianship order if it considers that the order should be varied or discharged, even though no application has been made under subsection (1).

(3) The following must obtain the leave of the court before making an application under subsection (1)—

(a) the child;

(b) any parent or guardian of his;

(c) any step-parent of his who has acquired, and has not lost, parental responsibility for him by virtue of section 4A;

(d) any individual falling within subsection (1)(d) who immediately before the making of the special guardianship order had, but no longer has, parental responsibility for him.

(4) Where the person applying for leave to make an application under subsection (1) is the child, the court may only grant leave if it is satisfied that he has sufficient understanding to make the proposed application under subsection (1).

(5) The court may not grant leave to a person falling within subsection (3)(b)(c) or (d) unless it is satisfied that there has been a significant change in circumstances since the making of the special guardianship order.

15 Orders for financial relief with respect to children

(1) Schedule 1 (which consists primarily of the re-enactment, with consequential amendments and minor modifications, of provisions of section 6 of the Family Law Reform Act 1969, the Guardianship of Minors Acts 1971 and 1973, the Children Act 1975 and of sections 15 and 16 of the Family Law Reform Act 1987) makes provision in relation to financial relief for children.

(2) The powers of a magistrates' court under section 60 of the Magistrates' Courts Act 1980 to revoke, revive or vary an order for the periodical payment of money and the power of a clerk of a magistrates' court to vary such an order shall not apply in relation to an order made under Schedule 1.

16 Family assistance orders

(1) Where, in any family proceedings, the court has power to make an order under this Part with respect to any child, it may (whether or not it makes such an order) make an order requiring—

(a) an officer of the Service or a Welsh family proceedings officer to be made available; or

(b) a local authority to make an officer of the authority available,

to advise, assist and (where appropriate) befriend any person named in the order.

(2) The persons who may be named in an order under this section ('a family assistance order') are—

(a) any parent, guardian or special guardian of the child;

(b) any person with whom the child is living or in whose favour a contact order is in force with respect to the child;

(c) the child himself.

(3) No court may make a family assistance order unless—

(a) . . .

(b) it has obtained the consent of every person to be named in the order other than the child.

(4) A family assistance order may direct—

(a) the person named in the order; or

(b) such of the persons named in the order as may be specified in the order,

to take such steps as may be so specified with a view to enabling the officer concerned to be kept informed of the address of any person named in the order and to be allowed to visit any such person.

(4A) If the court makes a family assistance order with respect to a child and the order is to be in force at the same time as a contact order made with respect to the child, the family assistance order may direct the officer concerned to give advice and assistance as regards establishing, improving and maintaining contact to such of the persons named in the order as may be specified in the order.

(5) Unless it specifies a shorter period, a family assistance order shall have effect for a period of twelve months beginning with the day on which it is made.

(6) If the court makes a family assistance order with respect to a child and the order is to be in force at the same time as a section 8 order made with respect to the child, the family assistance order may direct the officer concerned to report to the court on such matters relating to the section 8 order as the court may require (including the question whether the section 8 order ought to be varied or discharged).

(7) A family assistance order shall not be made so as to require a local authority to make an officer of theirs available unless—

(a) the authority agree; or

(b) the child concerned lives or will live within their area.

(8), (9) ...

17 Provision of services for children in need, their families and others

(1) It shall be the general duty of every local authority (in addition to the other duties imposed on them by this Part)—

(a) to safeguard and promote the welfare of children within their area who are in need; and

(b) so far as is consistent with that duty, to promote the upbringing of such children by their families,

by providing a range and level of services appropriate to those children's needs.

(2) For the purpose principally of facilitating the discharge of their general duty under this section, every local authority shall have the specific duties and powers set out in Part I of Schedule 2.

(3) Any service provided by an authority in the exercise of functions conferred on them by this section may be provided for the family of a particular child in need or for any member of his family, if it is provided with a view to safeguarding or promoting the child's welfare.

(4) The appropriate national authority may by order amend any provision of Part I of Schedule 2 or add any further duty or power to those for the time being mentioned there.

(4A) Before determining what (if any) services to provide for a particular child in need in the exercise of functions conferred on them by this section, a local authority shall, so far as is reasonably practicable and consistent with the child's welfare—

(a) ascertain the child's wishes and feelings regarding the provision of those services; and

(b) give due consideration (having regard to his age and understanding) to such wishes and feelings of the child as they have been able to ascertain.

(5) Every local authority—

(a) shall facilitate the provision by others (including in particular voluntary organisations) of services which it is a function of the authority to provide by virtue of this section, or section 18, 20, 22A to 22C, 23B to 23D, 24A or 24B; and

(b) may make such arrangements as they see fit for any person to act on their behalf in the provision of any such service.

(6) The services provided by a local authority in the exercise of functions conferred on them by this section may include providing accommodation and giving assistance in kind or . . . in cash.

(7) Assistance may be unconditional or subject to conditions as to the repayment of the assistance or of its value (in whole or in part).

(8) Before giving any assistance or imposing any conditions, a local authority shall have regard to the means of the child concerned and of each of his parents.

(9) No person shall be liable to make any repayment of assistance or of its value at any time when he is in receipt of income support under Part VII of the Social Security Contributions and Benefits Act 1992, of any element of child tax credit other than the family element, of working tax credit, of an income-based jobseeker's allowance or of an income-related employment and support allowance.

(10) For the purposes of this Part a child shall be taken to be in need if—

(a) he is unlikely to achieve or maintain, or to have the opportunity of achieving or maintaining, a reasonable standard of health or development without the provision for him of services by a local authority under this Part;

(b) his health or development is likely to be significantly impaired, or further impaired, without the provision for him of such services; or

(c) he is disabled,

and 'family,' in relation to such a child, includes any person who has parental responsibility for the child and any other person with whom he has been living.

(11) For the purposes of this Part, a child is disabled if he is blind, deaf or dumb or suffers from mental disorder of any kind or is substantially and permanently handicapped by illness, injury or congenital deformity or such other disability as may be prescribed; and in this Part—

'development' means physical, intellectual, emotional, social or behavioural development; and

'health' means physical or mental health.

(12) The Treasury may by regulations prescribe circumstances in which a person is to be treated for the purposes of this Part (or for such of those purposes as are prescribed) as

in receipt of any element of child tax credit other than the family element or of working tax credit.

20 Provision of accommodation for children: general

(1) Every local authority shall provide accommodation for any child in need within their area who appears to them to require accommodation as a result of—

(a) there being no person who has parental responsibility for him;

(b) his being lost or having been abandoned; or

(c) the person who has been caring for him being prevented (whether or not permanently, and for whatever reason) from providing him with suitable accommodation or care.

(2) Where a local authority provide accommodation under subsection (1) for a child who is ordinarily resident in the area of another local authority, that other local authority may take over the provision of accommodation for the child within—

(a) three months of being notified in writing that the child is being provided with accommodation; or

(b) such other longer period as may be prescribed.

(3) Every local authority shall provide accommodation for any child in need within their area who has reached the age of sixteen and whose welfare the authority consider is likely to be seriously prejudiced if they do not provide him with accommodation.

(4) A local authority may provide accommodation for any child within their area (even though a person who has parental responsibility for him is able to provide him with accommodation) if they consider that to do so would safeguard or promote the child's welfare.

(5) A local authority may provide accommodation for any person who has reached the age of sixteen but is under twenty-one in any community home which takes children who have reached the age of sixteen if they consider that to do so would safeguard or promote his welfare.

(6) Before providing accommodation under this section, a local authority shall, so far as is reasonably practicable and consistent with the child's welfare—

(a) ascertain the child's wishes and feelings regarding the provision of accommodation; and

(b) give due consideration (having regard to his age and understanding) to such wishes and feelings of the child as they have been able to ascertain.

(7) A local authority may not provide accommodation under this section for any child if any person who—

(a) has parental responsibility for him; and

(b) is willing and able to—

(i) provide accommodation for him; or

(ii) arrange for accommodation to be provided for him,

objects.

(8) Any person who has parental responsibility for a child may at any time remove the child from accommodation provided by or on behalf of the local authority under this section.

(9) Subsections (7) and (8) do not apply while any person—

(a) in whose favour a residence order is in force with respect to the child; ...

(aa) who is a special guardian of the child; or

(b) who has care of the child by virtue of an order made in the exercise of the High Court's inherent jurisdiction with respect to children,

agrees to the child being looked after in accommodation provided by or on behalf of the local authority.

(10) Where there is more than one such person as is mentioned in subsection (9), all of them must agree.

(11) Subsections (7) and (8) do not apply where a child who has reached the age of sixteen agrees to being provided with accommodation under this section.

22 General duty of local authority in relation to children looked after by them

(1) In this Act, any reference to a child who is looked after by a local authority is a reference to a child who is—

(a) in their care; or

(b) provided with accommodation by the authority in the exercise of any functions (in particular those under this Act) which are social services functions within the meaning of the Local Authority Social Services Act 1970, apart from functions under sections 17, 23B and 24B.

(2) In subsection (1) 'accommodation' means accommodation which is provided for a continuous period of more than 24 hours.

(3) It shall be the duty of a local authority looking after any child—

(a) to safeguard and promote his welfare; and

(b) to make such use of services available for children cared for by their own parents as appears to the authority reasonable in his case.

(3A) The duty of a local authority under subsection (3)(a) to safeguard and promote the welfare of a child looked after by them includes in particular a duty to promote the child's educational achievement.

(4) Before making any decision with respect to a child whom they are looking after, or proposing to look after, a local authority shall, so far as is reasonably practicable, ascertain the wishes and feelings of—

(a) the child;

(b) his parents;

(c) any person who is not a parent of his but who has parental responsibility for him; and

(d) any other person whose wishes and feelings the authority consider to be relevant,

regarding the matter to be decided.

(5) In making any such decision a local authority shall give due consideration—

(a) having regard to his age and understanding, to such wishes and feelings of the child as they have been able to ascertain;

(b) to such wishes and feelings of any person mentioned in subsection (4)(b) to (d) as they have been able to ascertain; and

(c) to the child's religious persuasion, racial origin and cultural and linguistic background.

(6) If it appears to a local authority that it is necessary, for the purposes of protecting members of the public from serious injury, to exercise their powers with respect to a child whom they are looking after in a manner which may not be consistent with their duties under this section, they may do so.

(7) If the appropriate national authority considers it necessary, for the purpose of protecting members of the public from serious injury, to give directions to a local authority with respect to the exercise of their powers with respect to a child whom they are looking after, the appropriate national authority may give such directions to the local authority.

(8) Where any such directions are given to an authority they shall comply with them even though doing so is inconsistent with their duties under this section.

23 Provision of accommodation and maintenance by local authority for children whom they are looking after

(1) It shall be the duty of any local authority looking after a child—

(a) when he is in their care, to provide accommodation for him; and

(b) to maintain him in other respects apart from providing accommodation for him.

(2) A local authority shall provide accommodation and maintenance for any child whom they are looking after by—

(a) placing him (subject to subsection (5) and any regulations made by the appropriate national authority) with—

(i) a family;

(ii) a relative of his; or

(iii) any other suitable person,

on such terms as to payment by the authority and otherwise as the authority may determine (subject to section 49 of the Children Act 2004);

(aa) maintaining him in an appropriate children's home; or

(f) making such other arrangements as—

(i) seem appropriate to them; and

(ii) comply with any regulations made by the appropriate national authority.

(2A) Where under subsection (2)(aa) a local authority maintains a child in a home provided, equipped and maintained by an appropriate national authority under section 82(5), it shall do so on such terms as that national authority may from time to time determine.

(3) Any person with whom a child has been placed under subsection (2)(a) is referred to in this Act as a local authority foster parent unless he falls within subsection (4).

(4) A person falls within this subsection if he is—

(a) a parent of the child;

(b) a person who is not a parent of the child but who has parental responsibility for him; or

(c) where the child is in care and there was a residence order in force with respect to him immediately before the care order was made, a person in whose favour the residence order was made.

(5) Where a child is in the care of a local authority, the authority may only allow him to live with a person who falls within subsection (4) in accordance with regulations made by the appropriate national authority.

(5A) For the purposes of subsection (5) a child shall be regarded as living with a person if he stays with that person for a continuous period of more than 24 hours.

(6) Subject to any regulations made by the appropriate national authority for the purposes of this subsection, any local authority looking after a child shall make arrangements to enable him to live with—

(a) a person falling within subsection (4); or

(b) a relative, friend or other person connected with him,

unless that would not be reasonably practicable or consistent with his welfare.

(7) Where a local authority provide accommodation for a child whom they are looking after, they shall, subject to the provisions of this Part and so far as is reasonably practicable and consistent with his welfare, secure that—

(a) the accommodation is near his home; and

(b) where the authority are also providing accommodation for a sibling of his, they are accommodated together.

(8) Where a local authority provide accommodation for a child whom they are looking after and who is disabled, they shall, so far as is reasonably practicable, secure that the accommodation is not unsuitable to his particular needs.

(9) Part II of Schedule 2 shall have effect for the purposes of making further provision as to children looked after by local authorities and in particular as to the regulations that may be made under subsections (2)(a) and (f) and (5).

(10) In this Act—

'appropriate children's home' means a children's home in respect of which a person is registered under Part II of the Care Standards Act 2000; and

'children's home' has the same meaning as in that Act.

26 Review of cases and inquiries into representations

(1) The appropriate national authority may make regulations requiring the case of each child who is being looked after by a local authority to be reviewed in accordance with the provisions of the regulations.

(2) The regulations may, in particular, make provision—

(a) as to the manner in which each case is to be reviewed;

(b) as to the considerations to which the local authority are to have regard in reviewing each case;

(c) as to the time when each case is first to be reviewed and the frequency of subsequent reviews;

(d) requiring the authority, before conducting any review, to seek the views of—

(i) the child;

(ii) his parents;

(iii) any person who is not a parent of his but who has parental responsibility for him; and

(iv) any other person whose views the authority consider to be relevant,

including, in particular, the views of those persons in relation to any particular matter which is to be considered in the course of the review;

(e) requiring the authority ..., in the case of a child who is in their care—

(i) to keep the section 31A plan for the child under review and, if they are of the opinion that some change is required, to revise the plan, or make a new plan, accordingly,

(ii) to consider whether an application should be made to discharge the care order;

(f) requiring the authority ..., in the case of a child in accommodation provided by the authority—

(i) if there is no plan for the future care of the child, to prepare one,

(ii) if there is such a plan for the child, to keep it under review and, if they are of the opinion that some change is required, to revise the plan or make a new plan, accordingly,

(iii) to consider whether the accommodation accords with the requirements of this Part;

(g) requiring the authority to inform the child, so far as is reasonably practicable, of any steps he may take under this Act;

(h) requiring the authority to make arrangements, including arrangements with such other bodies providing services as it considers appropriate, to implement any decision which they propose to make in the course, or as a result, of the review;

(i) requiring the authority to notify details of the result of the review and of any decision taken by them in consequence of the review to—

(i) the child;

(ii) his parents;

(iii) any person who is not a parent of his but who has parental responsibility for him; and

(iv) any other person whom they consider ought to be notified;

(j) requiring the authority to monitor the arranangements which they have made with a view to ensuring that they comply with the regulations;

(k) . . .

(2A)–(2D) . . .

(3) Every local authority shall establish a procedure for considering any representations (including any complaint) made to them by—

(a) any child who is being looked after by them or who is not being looked after by them but is in need;

(b) a parent of his;

(c) any person who is not a parent of his but who has parental responsibility for him;

(d) any local authority foster parent;

(e) such other person as the authority consider has a sufficient interest in the child's welfare to warrant his representations being considered by them,

about the discharge by the authority of any of their qualifying functions in relation to the child.

(3A) The following are qualifying functions for the purposes of subsection (3)—

(a) functions under this Part,

(b) such functions under Part 4 or 5 as are specified by the appropriate national authority in regulations.

(3B) The duty under subsection (3) extends to representations (including complaints) made to the authority by—

(a) any person mentioned in section 3(1) of the Adoption and Children Act 2002 (persons for whose needs provision is made by the Adoption Service) and any other person to whom arrangements for the provision of adoption support services (within the meaning of that Act) extend,

(b) such other person as the authority consider has sufficient interest in a child who is or may be adopted to warrant his representations being considered by them,

about the discharge by the authority of such functions under the Adoption and Children Act 2002 as are specified by the appropriate national authority in regulations.

(3C) The duty under subsection (3) extends to any representations (including complaints) which are made to the authority by—

(a) a child with respect to whom a special guardianship order is in force,

(b) a special guardian or a parent of such a child,

(c) any other person the authority consider has a sufficient interest in the welfare of such a child to warrant his representations being considered by them, or

(d) any person who has applied for an assessment under section 14F(3) or (4),

about the discharge by the authority of such functions under section 14F as may be specified by the appropriate national authority in regulations.

(4) The procedure shall ensure that at least one person who is not a member or officer of the authority takes part in—

(a) the consideration; and

(b) any discussions which are held by the authority about the action (if any) to be taken in relation to the child in the light of the consideration,

but this subsection is subject to subsection (5A).

(4A) Regulations may be made by the appropriate national authority imposing time limits on the making of representations under this section.

(5) In carrying out any consideration of representations under this section a local authority shall comply with any regulations made by the appropriate national authority for the purpose of regulating the procedure to be followed.

(5A) Regulations under subsection (5) may provide that subsection (4) does not apply in relation to any consideration or discussion which takes place as part of a procedure for which provision is made by the regulations for the purpose of resolving informally the matters raised in the representations.

(6) The appropriate national authority may make regulations requiring local authorities to monitor the arrangements that they have made with a view to ensuring that they comply with any regulations made for the purposes of subsection (5).

(7) Where any representation has been considered under the procedure established by a local authority under this section, the authority shall—

(a) have due regard to the findings of those considering the representation; and

(b) take such steps as are reasonably practicable to notify (in writing)—

(i) the person making the representation;

(ii) the child (if the authority consider that he has sufficient understanding); and

(iii) such other persons (if any) as appear to the authority to be likely to be affected,

of the authority's decision in the matter and their reasons for taking that decision and of any action which they have taken, or propose to take.

(8) Every local authority shall give such publicity to their procedure for considering representations under this section as they consider appropriate.

31 Care and supervision orders

(1) On the application of any local authority or authorised person, the court may make an order—

(a) placing the child with respect to whom the application is made in the care of a designated local authority; or

(b) putting him under the supervision of a designated local authority. ...

(2) A court may only make a care order or supervision order if it is satisfied—

(a) that the child concerned is suffering, or is likely to suffer, significant harm; and

(b) that the harm, or likelihood of harm, is attributable to—

(i) the care given to the child, or likely to be given to him if the order were not made, not being what it would be reasonable to expect a parent to give to him; or

(ii) the child's being beyond parental control.

(3) No care order or supervision order may be made with respect to a child who has reached the age of seventeen (or sixteen, in the case of a child who is married).

(3A) No care order made by made with respect to a child until the court has considered a section 31A care plan.

(4) An application under this section may be made on its own or in any other family proceedings.

(5) The court may—

(a) on an application for a care order, make a supervision order;

(b) on an application for a supervision order, make a care order.

(6) Where an authorised person proposes to make an application under this section he shall—

(a) if it is reasonably practicable to do so; and

(b) before making the application,

consult the local authority appearing to him to be the authority in whose area the child concerned is ordinarily resident.

(7) An application made by an authorised person shall not be entertained by the court if, at the time when it is made, the child concerned is—

(a) the subject of an earlier application for a care order, or supervision order, which has not been disposed of; or

(b) subject to—

(i) a care order or supervision order;

(ii) a youth rehabilitation order within the meaning of Part 1 of the Criminal Justice and Immigration Act 2008;

(iii) (applies to Scotland only)

(8) The local authority designated in a care order must be—

(a) the authority within whose area the child is ordinarily resident; or

(b) where the child does not reside in the area of a local authority, the authority within whose area any circumstances arose in consequence of which the order is being made.

(9) In this section—

'authorised person' means—

(a) the National Society for the Prevention of Cruelty to Children and any of its officers; and

(b) any person authorised by order of the Secretary of State to bring proceedings under this section and any officer of a body which is so authorised;

'harm' means ill-treatment or the impairment of health or development including, for example, impairment suffered from seeing or hearing the ill-treatment of another;

'development' means physical, intellectual, emotional, social or behavioural development;

'health' means physical or mental health; and

'ill-treatment' includes sexual abuse and forms of ill-treatment which are not physical.

(10) Where the question of whether harm suffered by a child is significant turns on the child's health or development, his health or development shall be compared with that which could reasonably be expected of a similar child.

(11) In this Act—

'a care order' means (subject to section 105(1)) an order under subsection (1)(a) and (except where express provision to the contrary is made) includes an interim care order made under section 38; and

'a supervision order' means an order under subsection (1)(b) and (except where express provision to the contrary is made) includes an interim supervision order made under section 38.

31A Care orders: care plans

(1) Where an application is made on which a care order might be made with respect to a child, the appropriate local authority must, within such time as the court may direct, prepare a plan ('a care plan') for the future care of the child.

(2) While the application is pending, the authority must keep any care plan prepared by them under review and, if they are of the opinion some change is required, revise the plan, or make a new plan, accordingly.

(3) A care plan must give any prescribed information and do so in the prescribed manner.

(4) For the purposes of this section, the appropriate local authority, in relation to a child in respect of whom a care order might be made, is the local authority proposed to be designated in the order.

(5) In section 31(3A) and this section, references to a care order do not include an interim care order.

(6) A plan prepared, or treated as prepared, under this section is referred to in this Act as a 'section 31A care plan'.

33 Effect of care order

(1) Where a care order is made with respect to a child it shall be the duty of the local authority designated by the order to receive the child into their care and to keep him in their care while the order remains in force.

(2) Where—

(a) a care order has been made with respect to a child on the application of an authorised person; but

(b) the local authority designated by the order was not informed that that person proposed to make the application,

the child may be kept in the care of that person until received into the care of the authority.

(3) While a care order is in force with respect to a child, the local authority designated by the order shall—

(a) have parental responsibility for the child; and

(b) have the power (subject to the following provisions of this section) to determine the extent to which—

(i) a parent, guardian or special guardian of the child; or

(ii) a person who by virtue of section 4A has parental responsibility for the child,

may meet his parental responsibility for him.

(4) The authority may not exercise the power in subsection (3)(b) unless they are satisfied that it is necessary to do so in order to safeguard or promote the child's welfare.

(5) Nothing in subsection (3)(b) shall prevent a person mentioned in that provision who has care of the child from doing what is reasonable in all the circumstances of the case for the purpose of safeguarding or promoting his welfare.

(6) While a care order is in force with respect to a child, the local authority designated by the order shall not—

(a) cause the child to be brought up in any religious persuasion other than that in which he would have been brought up if the order had not been made; or

(b) have the right—

(i) . . .

(ii) to agree or refuse to agree to the making of an adoption order, or an order under section 84 of the Adoption and Children Act 2002, with respect to the child; or

(iii) to appoint a guardian for the child.

(7) While a care order is in force with respect to a child, no person may—

(a) cause the child to be known by a new surname; or

(b) remove him from the United Kingdom,

without either the written consent of every person who has parental responsibility for the child or the leave of the court.

(8) Subsection (7)(b) does not—

(a) prevent the removal of such a child, for a period of less than one month, by the authority in whose care he is; or

(b) apply to arrangements for such a child to live outside England and Wales (which are governed by paragraph 19 of Schedule 2).

(9) The power in subsection (3)(b) is subject (in addition to being subject to the provisions of this section) to any right, duty, power, responsibility or authority which a person mentioned in that provision has in relation to the child and his property by virtue of any other enactment.

34 Parental contact etc with children in care

(1) Where a child is in the care of a local authority, the authority shall (subject to the provisions of this section) allow the child reasonable contact with—

(a) his parents;

(b) any guardian or special guardian of his;

(ba) any person who by virtue of section 4A has parental responsibility for him;

(c) where there was a residence order in force with respect to the child immediately before the care order was made, the person in whose favour the order was made; and

(d) where, immediately before the care order was made, a person had care of the child by virtue of an order made in the exercise of the High Court's inherent jurisdiction with respect to children, that person.

(2) On an application made by the authority or the child, the court may make such order as it considers appropriate with respect to the contact which is to be allowed between the child and any named person.

(3) On an application made by—

(a) any person mentioned in paragraphs (a) to (d) of subsection (1); or

(b) any person who has obtained the leave of the court to make the application,

the court may make such order as it considers appropriate with respect to the contact which is to be allowed between the child and that person.

(4) On an application made by the authority or the child, the court may make an order authorising the authority to refuse to allow contact between the child and any person who is mentioned in paragraphs (a) to (d) of subsection (1) and named in the order.

(5) When making a care order with respect to a child, or in any family proceedings in connection with a child who is in the care of a local authority, the court may make an order under this section, even though no application for such an order has been made with respect to the child, if it considers that the order should be made.

(6) An authority may refuse to allow the contact that would otherwise be required by virtue of subsection (1) or an order under this section if—

(a) they are satisfied that it is necessary to do so in order to safeguard or promote the child's welfare; and

(b) the refusal—

(i) is decided upon as a matter of urgency; and

(ii) does not last for more than seven days.

(7) An order under this section may impose such conditions as the court considers appropriate.

(8) The Secretary of State may by regulations make provision as to—

(a) the steps to be taken by a local authority who have exercised their powers under subsection (6);

(b) the circumstances in which, and conditions subject to which, the terms of any order under this section may be departed from by agreement between the local authority and the person in relation to whom the order is made;

(c) notification by a local authority of any variation or suspension of arrangements made (otherwise than under an order under this section) with a view to affording any person contact with a child to whom this section applies.

(9) The court may vary or discharge any order made under this section on the application of the authority, the child concerned or the person named in the order.

(10) An order under this section may be made either at the same time as the care order itself or later.

(11) Before making a care order with respect to any child the court shall—

(a) consider the arrangements which the authority have made, or propose to make, for affording any person contact with a child to whom this section applies; and

(b) invite the parties to the proceedings to comment on those arrangements.

35 Supervision orders

(1) While a supervision order is in force it shall be the duty of the supervisor—

(a) to advise, assist and befriend the supervised child;

(b) to take such steps as are reasonably necessary to give effect to the order; and

(c) where—

(i) the order is not wholly complied with; or

(ii) the supervisor considers that the order may no longer be necessary,

to consider whether or not to apply to the court for its variation or discharge.

(2) Parts I and II of Schedule 3 make further provision with respect to supervision orders.

37 Powers of court in certain family proceedings

(1) Where, in any family proceedings in which a question arises with respect to the welfare of any child, it appears to the court that it may be appropriate for a care or supervision order to be made with respect to him, the court may direct the appropriate authority to undertake an investigation of the child's circumstances.

(2) Where the court gives a direction under this section the local authority concerned shall, when undertaking the investigation, consider whether they should—

(a) apply for a care order or for a supervision order with respect to the child;

(b) provide services or assistance for the child or his family; or

(c) take any other action with respect to the child.

(3) Where a local authority undertake an investigation under this section, and decide not to apply for a care order or supervision order with respect to the child concerned, they shall inform the court of—

(a) their reasons for so deciding;

(b) any service or assistance which they have provided, or intend to provide, for the child and his family; and

(c) any other action which they have taken, or propose to take, with respect to the child.

(4) The information shall be given to the court before the end of the period of eight weeks beginning with the date of the direction, unless the court otherwise directs.

(5) The local authority named in a direction under subsection (1) must be—

(a) the authority in whose area the child is ordinarily resident; or

(b) where the child is not ordinarily resident in the area of a local authority, the authority within whose area any circumstances arose in consequence of which the direction is being given.

(6) If, on the conclusion of any investigation or review under this section, the authority decide not to apply for a care order or supervision order with respect to the child—

(a) they shall consider whether it would be appropriate to review the case at a later date; and

(b) if they decide that it would be, they shall determine the date on which that review is to begin.

38 Interim orders

(1) Where—

(a) in any proceedings on an application for a care order or supervision order, the proceedings are adjourned; or

(b) the court gives a direction under section 37(1),

the court may make an interim care order or an interim supervision order with respect to the child concerned.

(2) A court shall not make an interim care order or interim supervision order under this section unless it is satisfied that there are reasonable grounds for believing that the circumstances with respect to the child are as mentioned in section 31(2).

(3) Where, in any proceedings on an application for a care order or supervision order, a court makes a residence order with respect to the child concerned, it shall also make an interim supervision order with respect to him unless satisfied that his welfare will be satisfactorily safeguarded without an interim order being made.

(4) An interim order made under or by virtue of this section shall have effect for such period as may be specified in the order, but shall in any event cease to have effect on whichever of the following events first occurs—

(a) the expiry of the period of eight weeks beginning with the date on which the order is made;

(b) if the order is the second or subsequent such order made with respect to the same child in the same proceedings, the expiry of the relevant period;

(c) in a case which falls within subsection (1)(a), the disposal of the application;

(d) in a case which falls within subsection (1)(b), the disposal of an application for a care order or supervision order made by the authority with respect to the child;

(e) in a case which falls within subsection (1)(b) and in which—

(i) the court has given a direction under section 37(4), but

(ii) no application for a care order or supervision order has been made with respect to the child,

the expiry of the period fixed by that direction.

(5) In subsection (4)(b) 'the relevant period' means—

(a) the period of four weeks beginning with the date on which the order in question is made; or

(b) the period of eight weeks beginning with the date on which the first order was made if that period ends later than the period mentioned in paragraph (a).

(6) Where the court makes an interim care order, or interim supervision order, it may give such directions (if any) as it considers appropriate with regard to the medical or psychiatric examination or other assessment of the child; but if the child is of sufficient understanding to make an informed decision he may refuse to submit to the examination or other assessment.

(7) A direction under subsection (6) may be to the effect that there is to be—

(a) no such examination or assessment; or

(b) no such examination or assessment unless the court directs otherwise.

(8) A direction under subsection (6) may be—

(a) given when the interim order is made or at any time while it is in force; and

(b) varied at any time on the application of any person falling within any class of person prescribed by rules of court for the purposes of this subsection.

(9) Paragraphs 4 and 5 of Schedule 3 shall not apply in relation to an interim supervision order.

(10) Where a court makes an order under or by virtue of this section it shall, in determining the period for which the order is to be in force, consider whether any party who was, or might have been, opposed to the making of the order was in a position to argue his case against the order in full.

38A Power to include exclusion requirement in interim care order

(1) Where—

(a) on being satisfied that there are reasonable grounds for believing that the circumstances with respect to a child are as mentioned in section 31(2)(a) and (b)(i), the court makes an interim care order with respect to a child, and

(b) the conditions mentioned in subsection (2) are satisfied,

the court may include an exclusion requirement in the interim care order.

(2) The conditions are—

(a) that there is reasonable cause to believe that, if a person ('the relevant person') is excluded from a dwelling-house in which the child lives, the child will cease to suffer, or cease to be likely to suffer, significant harm, and

(b) that another person living in the dwelling-house (whether a parent of the child or some other person)—

(i) is able and willing to give to the child the care which it would be reasonable to expect a parent to give him, and

(ii) consents to the inclusion of the exclusion requirement.

(3) For the purposes of this section an exclusion requirement is any one or more of the following—

(a) a provision requiring the relevant person to leave a dwelling-house in which he is living with the child,

(b) a provision prohibiting the relevant person from entering a dwelling-house in which the child lives, and

(c) a provision excluding the relevant person from a defined area in which a dwelling-house in which the child lives is situated.

(4) The court may provide that the exclusion requirement is to have effect for a shorter period than the other provisions of the interim care order.

(5) Where the court makes an interim care order containing an exclusion requirement, the court may attach a power of arrest to the exclusion requirement.

(6) Where the court attaches a power of arrest to an exclusion requirement of an interim care order, it may provide that the power of arrest is to have effect for a shorter period than the exclusion requirement.

(7) Any period specified for the purposes of subsection (4) or (6) may be extended by the court (on one or more occasions) on an application to vary or discharge the interim care order.

(8) Where a power of arrest is attached to an exclusion requirement of an interim care order by virtue of subsection (5), a constable may arrest without warrant any person whom he has reasonable cause to believe to be in breach of the requirement.

(9) Sections 47(7), (11) and (12) and 48 of, and Schedule 5 to, the Family Law Act 1996 shall have effect in relation to a person arrested under subsection (8) of this section as they have effect in relation to a person arrested under section 47(6) of that Act.

(10) If, while an interim care order containing an exclusion requirement is in force, the local authority have removed the child from the dwelling-house from which the relevant person is excluded to other accommodation for a continuous period of more than 24 hours, the interim care order shall cease to have effect in so far as it imposes the exclusion requirement.

38B Undertakings relating to interim care orders

(1) In any case where the court has power to include an exclusion requirement in an interim care order, the court may accept an undertaking from the relevant person.

(2) No power of arrest may be attached to any undertaking given under subsection (1).

(3) An undertaking given to a court under subsection (1)—

(a) shall be enforceable as if it were an order of the court, and

(b) shall cease to have effect if, while it is in force, the local authority have removed the child from the dwelling-house from which the relevant person is excluded to other accommodation for a continuous period of more than 24 hours.

(4) This section has effect without prejudice to the powers of the High Court and county court apart from this section.

(5) In this section 'exclusion requirement' and 'relevant person' have the same meaning as in section 38A.

39 Discharge and variation etc of care orders and supervision orders

(1) A care order may be discharged by the court on the application of—

(a) any person who has parental responsibility for the child;

(b) the child himself; or

(c) the local authority designated by the order.

(2) A supervision order may be varied or discharged by the court on the application of—

(a) any person who has parental responsibility for the child;

(b) the child himself; or

(c) the supervisor.

(3) On the application of a person who is not entitled to apply for the order to be discharged, but who is a person with whom the child is living, a supervision order may be varied by the court in so far as it imposes a requirement which affects that person.

(3A) On the application of a person who is not entitled to apply for the order to be discharged, but who is a person to whom an exclusion requirement contained in the order applies, an interim care order may be varied or discharged by the court in so far as it imposes the exclusion requirement.

(3B) Where a power of arrest has been attached to an exclusion requirement of an interim care order, the court may, on the application of any person entitled to apply for the discharge of the order so far as it imposes the exclusion requirement, vary or discharge the order in so far as it confers a power of arrest (whether or not any application has been made to vary or discharge any other provision of the order).

(4) Where a care order is in force with respect to a child the court may, on the application of any person entitled to apply for the order to be discharged, substitute a supervision order for the care order.

(5) When a court is considering whether to substitute one order for another under subsection (4) any provision of this Act which would otherwise require section 31(2) to

be satisfied at the time when the proposed order is substituted or made shall be disregarded.

44 Orders for emergency protection of children

(1) Where any person ('the applicant') applies to the court for an order to be made under this section with respect to a child, the court may make the order if, but only if, it is satisfied that—

(a) there is reasonable cause to believe that the child is likely to suffer significant harm if—

(i) he is not removed to accommodation provided by or on behalf of the applicant; or

(ii) he does not remain in the place in which he is then being accommodated;

(b) in the case of an application made by a local authority—

(i) enquiries are being made with respect to the child under section 47(1)(b); and

(ii) those enquiries are being frustrated by access to the child being unreasonably refused to a person authorised to seek access and that the applicant has reasonable cause to believe that access to the child is required as a matter of urgency; or

(c) in the case of an application made by an authorised person—

(i) the applicant has reasonable cause to suspect that a child is suffering, or is likely to suffer, significant harm;

(ii) the applicant is making enquiries with respect to the child's welfare; and

(iii) those enquiries are being frustrated by access to the child being unreasonably refused to a person authorised to seek access and the applicant has reasonable cause to believe that access to the child is required as a matter of urgency.

(2) In this section—

(a) 'authorised person' means a person who is an authorised person for the purposes of section 31; and

(b) 'a person authorised to seek access' means—

(i) in the case of an application by a local authority, an officer of the local authority or a person authorised by the authority to act on their behalf in connection with the enquiries; or

(ii) in the case of an application by an authorised person, that person.

(3) Any person—

(a) seeking access to a child in connection with enquiries of a kind mentioned in subsection (1); and

(b) purporting to be a person authorised to do so,

shall, on being asked to do so, produce some duly authenticated document as evidence that he is such a person.

(4) While an order under this section ('an emergency protection order') is in force it—

(a) operates as a direction to any person who is in a position to do so to comply with any request to produce the child to the applicant;

(b) authorises—

(i) the removal of the child at any time to accommodation provided by or on behalf of the applicant and his being kept there; or

(ii) the prevention of the child's removal from any hospital, or other place, in which he was being accommodated immediately before the making of the order; and

(c) gives the applicant parental responsibility for the child.

(5) Where an emergency protection order is in force with respect to a child, the applicant—

(a) shall only exercise the power given by virtue of subsection (4)(b) in order to safeguard the welfare of the child;

(b) shall take, and shall only take, such action in meeting his parental responsibility for the child as is reasonably required to safeguard or promote the welfare of the child (having regard in particular to the duration of the order); and

(c) shall comply with the requirements of any regulations made by the Secretary of State for the purposes of this subsection.

(6) Where the court makes an emergency protection order, it may give such directions (if any) as it considers appropriate with respect to—

(a) the contact which is, or is not, to be allowed between the child and any named person;

(b) the medical or psychiatric examination or other assessment of the child.

(7) Where any direction is given under subsection (6)(b), the child may, if he is of sufficient understanding to make an informed decision, refuse to submit to the examination or other assessment.

(8) A direction under subsection (6)(a) may impose conditions and one under subsection (6)(b) may be to the effect that there is to be—

(a) no such examination or assessment; or

(b) no such examination or assessment unless the court directs otherwise.

(9) A direction under subsection (6) may be—

(a) given when the emergency protection order is made or at any time while it is in force; and

(b) varied at any time on the application of any person falling within any class of person prescribed by rules of court for the purposes of this subsection.

(10) Where an emergency protection order is in force with respect to a child and—

(a) the applicant has exercised the power given by subsection (4)(b)(i) but it appears to him that it is safe for the child to be returned; or

(b) the applicant has exercised the power given by subsection (4)(b)(ii) but it appears to him that it is safe for the child to be allowed to be removed from the place in question,

he shall return the child or (as the case may be) allow him to be removed.

(11) Where he is required by subsection (10) to return the child the applicant shall—

(a) return him to the care of the person from whose care he was removed; or

(b) if that is not reasonably practicable, return him to the care of—

(i) a parent of his;

(ii) any person who is not a parent of his but who has parental responsibility for him; or

(iii) such other person as the applicant (with the agreement of the court) considers appropriate.

(12) Where the applicant has been required by subsection (10) to return the child, or to allow him to be removed, he may again exercise his powers with respect to the child (at any time while the emergency protection order remains in force) if it appears to him that a change in the circumstances of the case makes it necessary for him to do so.

(13) Where an emergency protection order has been made with respect to a child, the applicant shall, subject to any direction given under subsection (6), allow the child reasonable contact with—

(a) his parents;

(b) any person who is not a parent of his but who has parental responsibility for him;

(c) any person with whom he was living immediately before the making of the order;

(d) any person in whose favour a contact order is in force with respect to him;

(e) any person who is allowed to have contact with the child by virtue of an order under section 34; and

(f) any person acting on behalf of any of those persons.

(14) Wherever it is reasonably practicable to do so, an emergency protection order shall name the child; and where it does not name him it shall describe him as clearly as possible.

(15) A person shall be guilty of an offence if he intentionally obstructs any person exercising the power under subsection (4)(b) to remove, or prevent the removal of, a child.

(16) A person guilty of an offence under subsection (15) shall be liable on summary conviction to a fine not exceeding level 3 on the standard scale.

46 Removal and accommodation of children by police in cases of emergency

(1) Where a constable has reasonable cause to believe that a child would otherwise be likely to suffer significant harm, he may—

(a) remove the child to suitable accommodation and keep him there; or

(b) take such steps as are reasonable to ensure that the child's removal from any hospital, or other place, in which he is then being accommodated is prevented.

(2) For the purposes of this Act, a child with respect to whom a constable has exercised his powers under this section is referred to as having been taken into police protection.

(3) As soon as is reasonably practicable after taking a child into police protection, the constable concerned shall—

(a) inform the local authority within whose area the child was found of the steps that have been, and are proposed to be, taken with respect to the child under this section and the reasons for taking them;

(b) give details to the authority within whose area the child is ordinarily resident ('the appropriate authority') of the place at which the child is being accommodated;

(c) inform the child (if he appears capable of understanding)—

(i) of the steps that have been taken with respect to him under this section and of the reasons for taking them; and

(ii) of the further steps that may be taken with respect to him under this section;

(d) take such steps as are reasonably practicable to discover the wishes and feelings of the child;

(e) secure that the case is inquired into by an officer designated for the purposes of this section by the chief officer of the police area concerned; and

(f) where the child was taken into police protection by being removed to accommodation which is not provided—

(i) by or on behalf of a local authority; or

(ii) as a refuge, in compliance with the requirements of section 51,

secure that he is moved to accommodation which is so provided.

(4) As soon as is reasonably practicable after taking a child into police protection, the constable concerned shall take such steps as are reasonably practicable to inform—

(a) the child's parents;

(b) every person who is not a parent of his but who has parental responsibility for him; and

(c) any other person with whom the child was living immediately before being taken into police protection,

of the steps that he has taken under this section with respect to the child, the reasons for taking them and the further steps that may be taken with respect to him under this section.

(5) On completing any inquiry under subsection (3)(e), the officer conducting it shall release the child from police protection unless he considers that there is still reasonable cause for believing that the child would be likely to suffer significant harm if released.

(6) No child may be kept in police protection for more than 72 hours.

(7) While a child is being kept in police protection, the designated officer may apply on behalf of the appropriate authority for an emergency protection order to be made under section 44 with respect to the child.

(8) An application may be made under subsection (7) whether or not the authority know of it or agree to its being made.

(9) While a child is being kept in police protection—

(a) neither the constable concerned nor the designated officer shall have parental responsibility for him; but

(b) the designated officer shall do what is reasonable in all the circumstances of the case for the purpose of safeguarding or promoting the child's welfare (having regard in particular to the length of the period during which the child will be so protected).

(10) Where a child has been taken into police protection, the designated officer shall allow—

(a) the child's parents;

(b) any person who is not a parent of the child but who has parental responsibility for him;

(c) any person with whom the child was living immediately before he was taken into police protection;

(d) any person in whose favour a contact order is in force with respect to the child;

(e) any person who is allowed to have contact with the child by virtue of an order under section 34; and

(f) any person acting on behalf of any of those persons,

to have such contact (if any) with the child as, in the opinion of the designated officer, is both reasonable and in the child's best interests.

(11) Where a child who has been taken into police protection is in accommodation provided by, or on behalf of, the appropriate authority, subsection (10) shall have effect as if it referred to the authority rather than to the designated officer.

47 Local authority's duty to investigate

(1) Where a local authority—

(a) are informed that a child who lives, or is found, in their area—

(i) is the subject of an emergency protection order; or

(ii) is in police protection; . . .

(iii) . . .

(b) have reasonable cause to suspect that a child who lives, or is found, in their area is suffering, or is likely to suffer, significant harm,

the authority shall make, or cause to be made, such enquiries as they consider necessary to enable them to decide whether they should take any action to safeguard or promote the child's welfare.

. . .

(2) Where a local authority have obtained an emergency protection order with respect to a child, they shall make, or cause to be made, such enquiries as they consider necessary to enable them to decide what action they should take to safeguard or promote the child's welfare.

(3) The enquiries shall, in particular, be directed towards establishing—

(a) whether the authority should make any application to the court, or exercise any of their other powers under this Act or section 11 of the Crime and Disorder Act 1998 (child safety orders), with respect to the child;

(b) whether, in the case of a child—

(i) with respect to whom an emergency protection order has been made; and

(ii) who is not in accommodation provided by or on behalf of the authority,

it would be in the child's best interests (while an emergency protection order remains in force) for him to be in such accommodation; and

(c) whether, in the case of a child who has been taken into police protection, it would be in the child's best interests for the authority to ask for an application to be made under section 46(7).

(4) Where enquiries are being made under subsection (1) with respect to a child, the local authority concerned shall (with a view to enabling them to determine what action, if any, to take with respect to him) take such steps as are reasonably practicable—

(a) to obtain access to him; or

(b) to ensure that access to him is obtained, on their behalf, by a person authorised by them for the purpose,

unless they are satisfied that they already have sufficient information with respect to him.

(5) Where, as a result of any such enquiries, it appears to the authority that there are matters connected with the child's education which should be investigated, they shall consult the local authority (as defined in section 579(1) of the Education 1996), if different, specified in subsection (5ZA).

(5ZA)The local authority referred to in subsection (5) is—

(a) the local authority who—

(i) maintain any school at which the child is a pupil, or

(ii) make arrangements for the provision of education for the child otherwise than at school pursuant to section 19 of the Education Act 1996, or

(b) in a case where the child is a pupil at a school which is not maintained by a local authority, the local authority in whose area the school is situated.

(5A) For the purposes of making a determination under this section as to the action to be taken with respect to a child, a local authority shall, so far as is reasonably practicable and consistent with the child's welfare—

(a) ascertain the child's wishes and feelings regarding the action to be taken with respect to him; and

(b) give due consideration (having regard to his age and understanding) to such wishes and feelings of the child as they have been able to ascertain.

(6) Where, in the course of enquiries made under this section—

(a) any officer of the local authority concerned; or

(b) any person authorised by the authority to act on their behalf in connection with those enquiries—

(i) is refused access to the child concerned; or

(ii) is denied information as to his whereabouts,

the authority shall apply for an emergency protection order, a child assessment order, a care order or a supervision order with respect to the child unless they are satisfied that his welfare can be satisfactorily safeguarded without their doing so.

(7) If, on the conclusion of any enquiries or review made under this section, the authority decide not to apply for an emergency protection order, a care order, a child assessment order or a supervision order they shall—

(a) consider whether it would be appropriate to review the case at a later date; and

(b) if they decide that it would be, determine the date on which that review is to begin.

(8) Where, as a result of complying with this section, a local authority conclude that they should take action to safeguard or promote the child's welfare they shall take that action (so far as it is both within their power and reasonably practicable for them to do so).

(9) Where a local authority are conducting enquiries under this section, it shall be the duty of any person mentioned in subsection (11) to assist them with those enquiries (in particular by providing relevant information and advice) if called upon by the authority to do so.

(10) Subsection (9) does not oblige any person to assist a local authority where doing so would be unreasonable in all the circumstances of the case.

(11) The persons are—

(a) any local authority;

(b) . . .

(c) any local housing authority;

(d) any Local Health Board, Special Health Authority, Primary Care Trust, National Health Service trust or NHS Foundation trust; and

(e) any person authorised by the Secretary of State for the purposes of this section.

(12) Where a local authority are making enquiries under this section with respect to a child who appears to them to be ordinarily resident within the area of another authority, they shall consult that other authority, who may undertake the necessary enquiries in their place.

SCHEDULE 2
LOCAL AUTHORITY SUPPORT FOR CHILDREN AND FAMILIES

Sections 17, 23, 29

PART I
PROVISION OF SERVICES FOR FAMILIES

Identification of children in need and provision of information

1.— (1) Every local authority shall take reasonable steps to identify the extent to which there are children in need within their area.

(2) Every local authority shall—

(a) publish information—

(i) about services provided by them under sections 17, 18, 20, 23B to 23D, 24A and 24B; and

(ii) where they consider it appropriate, about the provision by others (including, in particular, voluntary organisations) of services which the authority have power to provide under those sections; and

(b) take such steps as are reasonably practicable to ensure that those who might benefit from the services receive the information relevant to them.

. . .

Maintenance of a register of disabled children

2.— (1) Every local authority shall open and maintain a register of disabled children within their area.

(2) The register may be kept by means of a computer.

Assessment of children's needs

3. Where it appears to a local authority that a child within their area is in need, the authority may assess his needs for the purposes of this Act at the same time as any assessment of his needs is made under—

(a) the Chronically Sick and Disabled Persons Act 1970;

(b) Part IV of the Education Act 1996;

(c) the Disabled Persons (Services, Consultation and Representation) Act 1986; or

(d) any other enactment.

Prevention of neglect and abuse

4.— (1) Every local authority shall take reasonable steps, through the provision of services under Part III of this Act, to prevent children within their area suffering ill-treatment or neglect.

(2) Where a local authority believe that a child who is at any time within their area—

(a) is likely to suffer harm; but

(b) lives or proposes to live in the area of another local authority they shall inform that other local authority.

(3) When informing that other local authority they shall specify—

(a) the harm that they believe he is likely to suffer; and

(b) (if they can) where the child lives or proposes to live.

Provision of accommodation in order to protect child

5.— (1) Where—

(a) it appears to a local authority that a child who is living on particular premises is suffering, or is likely to suffer, ill treatment at the hands of another person who is living on those premises; and

(b) that other person proposes to move from the premises,

the authority may assist that other person to obtain alternative accommodation.

(2) Assistance given under this paragraph may be in cash.

(3) Subsections (7) to (9) of section 17 shall apply in relation to assistance given under this paragraph as they apply in relation to assistance given under that section.

Provision for disabled children

6.— (1) Every local authority shall provide services designed—

(a) to minimise the effect on disabled children within their area of their disabilities; . . .

(b) to give such children the opportunity to lead lives which are as normal as possible; and

(c) to assist individuals who provide care for such children to continue to do so, or to do so more effectively, by giving them breaks from caring.

(2) The duty imposed by sub-paragraph (1)(c) shall be performed in accordance with regulations made by the appropriate national authority.

Provision to reduce need for care proceedings etc

7. Every local authority shall take reasonable steps designed—

(a) to reduce the need to bring—

(i) proceedings for care or supervision orders with respect to children within their area;

(ii) criminal proceedings against such children;

(iii) any family or other proceedings with respect to such children which might lead to them being placed in the authority's care; or

(iv) proceedings under the inherent jurisdiction of the High Court with respect to children;

(b) to encourage children within their area not to commit criminal offences; and

(c) to avoid the need for children within their area to be placed in secure accommodation.

Provision for children living with their families

8. Every local authority shall make such provision as they consider appropriate for the following services to be available with respect to children in need within their area while they are living with their families—

(a) advice, guidance and counselling;

(b) occupational, social, cultural, or recreational activities;

(c) home help (which may include laundry facilities);

(d) facilities for, or assistance with, travelling to and from home for the purpose of taking advantage of any other service provided under this Act or of any similar service;

(e) assistance to enable the child concerned and his family to have a holiday.

Provision for accommodated children

8A.— (1) Every local authority shall make provision for such services as they consider appropriate to be available with respect to accommodated children.

(2) 'Accommodated children' are those children in respect of whose accommodation the local authority have been notified under section 85 or 86.

(3) The services shall be provided with a view to promoting contact between each accommodated child and that child's family.

(4) The services may, in particular, include—

(a) advice, guidance and counselling;

(b) services necessary to enable the child to visit, or to be visited by, members of the family;

(c) assistance to enable the child and members of the family to have a holiday together.

(5) Nothing in this paragraph affects the duty imposed by paragraph 10.

Family centres

9.— (1) Every local authority shall provide such family centres as they consider appropriate in relation to children within their area.

(2) 'Family centre' means a centre at which any of the persons mentioned in sub-paragraph (3) may—

(a) attend for occupational, social, cultural or recreational activities;

(b) attend for advice, guidance or counselling; or

(c) be provided with accommodation while he is receiving advice, guidance or counselling.

(3) The persons are—

(a) a child;

(b) his parents;

(c) any person who is not a parent of his but who has parental responsibility for him;

(d) any other person who is looking after him.

Maintenance of the family home

10. Every local authority shall take such steps as are reasonably practicable, where any child within their area who is in need and whom they are not looking after is living apart from his family—

(a) to enable him to live with his family; or

(b) to promote contact between him and his family,

if, in their opinion, it is necessary to do so in order to safeguard or promote his welfare.

Duty to consider racial groups to which children in need belong

11. Every local authority shall, in making any arrangements—

(a) for the provision of day care within their area; or

(b) designed to encourage persons to act as local authority foster parents, have regard to the different racial groups to which children within their area who are in need belong.

PART II

CHILDREN LOOKED AFTER BY LOCAL AUTHORITIES

Regulations as to conditions under which child in care is allowed to live with parent, etc

12A. Regulations under section 22C may, in particular, impose requirements on a local authority as to—

(a) the making of any decision by a local authority to allow a child in their care to live with any person falling within section 22C(3) (including requirements as to those who must be consulted before the decision is made and those who must be notified when it has been made);

(b) the supervision or medical examination of the child concerned;

(c) the removal of the child, in such circumstances as may be prescribed, from the care of the person with whom the child has been allowed to live;

(d) the records to be kept by local authorities.

Regulations as to placements of a kind specified in section 22C(6)(d)

12B. Regulations under section 22C as to placements of the kind specified in section 22C(6)(d) may, in particular, make provision as to—

(a) the persons to be notified of any proposed arrangements;

(b) the opportunities such persons are to have to make representations in relation to the arrangements proposed;

(c) the persons to be notified of any proposed changes in arrangements;

(d) the records to be kept by local authorities;

(e) the supervision by local authorities of any arrangements made.

Placements out of area

12C. Regulations under section 22C may, in particular, impose requirements which a local authority must comply with—

(a) before a child looked after by them is provided with accommodation at a place outside the area of the authority; or

(b) if the child's welfare requires the immediate provision of such accommodation, within such period of the accommodation being provided as may be prescribed.

Avoidance of disruption in education

12D.—(1) Regulations under section 22C may, in particular, impose requirements which a local authority must comply with before making any decision concerning a child's placement if he is in the fourth key stage.

(2) A child is 'in the fourth key stage' if he is a pupil in the fourth key stage for the purposes of Part 6 or 7 of the Education 2002 (see section 82 and 103 of that Act).

Regulations as to placing of children with local authority foster parents

12E. Regulations under section 22C may, in particular, make provision—

(a) with regard to the welfare of children placed with local authority foster parents;

(b) as to the arrangements to be made by local authorities in connection with the health and education of such children;

(c) as to the records to be kept by local authorities;

(d) for securing that where possible the local authority foster parent with whom a child is to be placed is—

(i) of the same religious persuasion as the child; or

(ii) gives an undertaking that the child will be brought up in that religious persuasion;

(e) for securing the children placed with local authority foster parents, and the premises in which they are accommodated, will be supervised and inspected by a local authority and that the children will be removed from those premises if their welfare appears to require it.

12F.—(1) Regulations under section 22C may, in particular, also make provision—

(a) for securing that a child is not placed with a local authority foster parent unless that person is for the time being approved as a local authority foster parent by such local authority as may be prescribed;

(b) establishing a procedure under which any person in respect of whom a qualifying determination has been made may apply to the appropriate national authority for a review of that determination by a panel constituted by that national authority.

(2) A determination is a qualifying determination if—

(a) it relates to the issue of whether a person should be approved, or should continue to be approved, as a local authority foster parent; and

(b) it is of a prescribed description.

(3) Regulations made by virtue of sub-paragraph (1)(b) may include provision as to—

(a) the duties and powers of a panel;

(b) the administration and procedures of a panel;

(c) the appointment of members of a panel (including the number, or any limit on the number, of members who may be appointed and any conditions for appointment);

(d) the payment of fees to members of a panel;

(e) the duties of any person in connection with a review conducted under the regulations;

(f) the monitoring of any such reviews.

(4) Regulations made by virtue of sub-paragraph (3)(e) may impose a duty to pay to the appropriate national authority such sum as that national authority may determine; but such a duty may not be imposed upon a person who has applied for a review of a qualifying determination.

(5) The appropriate national authority must secure that, taking one financial year with another, the aggregate of the sums which become payable to it under regulations made by virtue of sub-paragraph (4) does not exceed the cost to it of performing its independent review functions.

(6) The appropriate national authority may make an arrangement with an organisation under which independent review functions are performed by the organisation on the national authority's behalf.

(7) If the appropriate national authority makes such an arrangement with an organisation, the organisation is to perform its functions under the arrangement in accordance with any general or special directions given by that national authority.

(8) The arrangement may include provision for payments to be made to the organisation by the appropriate national authority.

(9) Payments made by the appropriate national authority in accordance with such provision shall be taken into account in determining (for the purpose of sub-paragraph (5)) the cost to that national authority of performing its independent review functions.

(10) Where the Welsh Ministers are the appropriate national authority, sub-paragraphs (6) and (8) also apply as if references to an organisation included references to the Secretary of State.

(11) In this paragraph—

'financial year' means a period of twelve months ending with 31st March;

'independent review function' means a function conferred or imposed on a national authority by regulations made by virtue of sub-paragraph (1)(b);

'organisation' includes a public body and a private or voluntary organisation.

12G. Regulations under section 22C may, in particular, also make provision as to the circumstances in which local authorities may make arrangements for duties imposed on them by the regulations to be discharged on their behalf.

Promotion and maintenance of contact between child and family

15.— (1) Where a child is being looked after by a local authority, the authority shall, unless it is not reasonably practicable or consistent with his welfare, endeavour to promote contact between the child and—

(a) his parents;

(b) any person who is not a parent of his but who has parental responsibility for him; and

(c) any relative, friend or other person connected with him.

(2) Where a child is being looked after by a local authority—

(a) the authority shall take such steps as are reasonably practicable to secure that—

(i) his parents; and

(ii) any person who is not a parent of his but who has parental responsibility for him,

are kept informed of where he is being accommodated; and

(b) every such person shall secure that the authority are kept informed of his or her address.

(3) Where a local authority ('the receiving authority') take over the provision of accommodation for a child from another local authority ('the transferring authority') under section 20(2)—

(a) the receiving authority shall (where reasonably practicable) inform—

(i) the child's parents; and

(ii) any person who is not a parent of his but who has parental responsibility for him;

(b) sub-paragraph (2)(a) shall apply to the transferring authority, as well as the receiving authority, until at least one such person has been informed of the change; and

(c) sub-paragraph (2)(b) shall not require any person to inform the receiving authority of his address until he has been so informed.

(4) Nothing in this paragraph requires a local authority to inform any person of the whereabouts of a child if—

(a) the child is in the care of the authority; and

(b) the authority has reasonable cause to believe that informing the person would prejudice the child's welfare.

(5) Any person who fails (without reasonable excuse) to comply with sub-paragraph (2)(b) shall be guilty of an offence and liable on summary conviction to a fine not exceeding level 2 on the standard scale.

(6) It shall be a defence in any proceedings under sub-paragraph (5) to prove that the defendant was residing at the same address as another person who was the child's parent or had parental responsibility for the child and had reasonable cause to believe that the other person had informed the appropriate authority that both of them were residing at that address.

Visits to or by children: expenses

16.— (1) This paragraph applies where—

(a) a child is being looked after by a local authority; and

(b) the conditions mentioned in sub-paragraph (3) are satisfied.

(2) The authority may—

(a) make payments to—

(i) a parent of the child;

(ii) any person who is not a parent of his but who has parental responsibility for him; or

(iii) any relative, friend or other person connected with him,

in respect of travelling, subsistence or other expenses incurred by that person in visiting the child; or

(b) make payments to the child, or to any person on his behalf, in respect of travelling, subsistence or other expenses incurred by or on behalf of the child in his visiting—

(i) a parent of his;

(ii) any person who is not a parent of his but who has parental responsibility for him; or

(iii) any relative, friend or other person connected with him.

(3) The conditions are that—

(a) it appears to the authority that the visit in question could not otherwise be made without undue financial hardship; and

(b) the circumstances warrant the making of the payments.

...

Power to guarantee apprenticeship deeds etc

18.— (1) While a child is being looked after by a local authority, or is a person qualifying for advice and assistance, the authority may undertake any obligation by way of guarantee under any deed of apprenticeship or articles of clerkship which he enters into.

(2) Where a local authority have undertaken any such obligation under any deed or articles they may at any time (whether or not they are still looking after the person concerned) undertake the like obligation under any supplemental deed or articles.

Arrangements to assist children to live abroad

19.— (1) A local authority may only arrange for, or assist in arranging for, any child in their care to live outside England and Wales with the approval of the court.

(2) A local authority may, with the approval of every person who has parental responsibility for the child arrange for, or assist in arranging for, any other child looked after by them to live outside England and Wales.

(3) The court shall not give its approval under sub-paragraph (1) unless it is satisfied that—

(a) living outside England and Wales would be in the child's best interests;

(b) suitable arrangements have been, or will be, made for his reception and welfare in the country in which he will live;

(c) the child has consented to living in that country; and

(d) every person who has parental responsibility for the child has consented to his living in that country.

(4) Where the court is satisfied that the child does not have sufficient understanding to give or withhold his consent, it may disregard sub-paragraph (3)(c) and give its approval if the child is to live in the country concerned with a parent, guardian, special guardian, or other suitable person.

(5) Where a person whose consent is required by sub-paragraph (3)(d) fails to give his consent, the court may disregard that provision and give its approval if it is satisfied that that person—

(a) cannot be found;

(b) is incapable of consenting; or

(c) is withholding his consent unreasonably.

(6) Section 85 of the Adoption and Children Act 2002 (which imposes restrictions on taking children out of the United Kingdom) shall not apply in the case of any child who is to live outside England and Wales with the approval of the court given under this paragraph.

(7) Where a court decides to give its approval under this paragraph it may order that its decision is not to have effect during the appeal period.

(8) In sub-paragraph (7) 'the appeal period' means—

(a) where an appeal is made against the decision, the period between the making of the decision and the determination of the appeal; and

(b) otherwise, the period during which an appeal may be made against the decision.

(9) This paragraph does not apply to a local authority placing a child for adoption with prospective adopters.

Preparation for ceasing to be looked after

19A. It is the duty of the local authority looking after a child to advise, assist and befriend him with a view to promoting his welfare when they have ceased to look after him.

19B.—(1) A local authority shall have the following additional functions in relation to an eligible child whom they are looking after.

(2) In sub-paragraph (1) 'eligible child' means, subject to sub-paragraph (3), a child who—

(a) is aged sixteen or seventeen; and

(b) has been looked after by a local authority for a prescribed period, or periods amounting in all to a prescribed period, which began after he reached a prescribed age and ended after he reached the age of sixteen.

(3) The appropriate national authority may prescribe—

(a) additional categories of eligible children; and

(b) categories of children who are not to be eligible children despite falling within sub-paragraph (2).

(4) For each eligible child, the local authority shall carry out an assessment of his needs with a view to determining what advice, assistance and support it would be appropriate for them to provide him under this Act—

(a) while they are still looking after him; and

(b) after they cease to look after him,

and shall then prepare a pathway plan for him.

(5) The local authority shall keep the pathway plan under regular review.

(6) Any such review may be carried out at the same time as a review of the child's case carried out by virtue of section 26.

(7) The appropriate national authority may by regulations make provision as to assessments for the purposes of sub-paragraph (4).

(8) The regulations may in particular provide for the matters set out in section 23B(6).

Personal advisers

19C. A local authority shall arrange for each child whom they are looking after who is an eligible child for the purposes of paragraph 19B to have a personal adviser.

Death of children being looked after by local authorities

20.— (1) If a child who is being looked after by a local authority dies, the authority—

(a) shall notify the appropriate national authority and (in the case of a local authority in England) Her Majesty's Chief Inspector of Education, Children's Services and Skills;

(b) shall, so far as is reasonably practicable, notify the child's parents and every person who is not a parent of his but who has parental responsibility for him;

(c) may, with the consent (so far as it is reasonably practicable to obtain it) of every person who has parental responsibility for the child, arrange for the child's body to be buried or cremated; and

(d) may, if the conditions mentioned in sub-paragraph (2) are satisfied, make payments to any person who has parental responsibility for the child, or any relative, friend or other person connected with the child, in respect of travelling, subsistence or other expenses incurred by that person in attending the child's funeral.

(2) The conditions are that—

(a) it appears to the authority that the person concerned could not otherwise attend the child's funeral without undue financial hardship; and

(b) that the circumstances warrant the making of the payments.

(3) Sub-paragraph (1) does not authorise cremation where it does not accord with the practice of the child's religious persuasion.

(4) Where a local authority have exercised their power under sub-paragraph (1)(c) with respect to a child who was under sixteen when he died, they may recover from any parent of the child any expenses incurred by them.

(5) Any sums so recoverable shall, without prejudice to any other method of recovery, be recoverable summarily as a civil debt.

(6) Nothing in this paragraph affects any enactment regulating or authorising the burial, cremation or anatomical examination of the body of a deceased person.

PART III

CONTRIBUTIONS TOWARDS MAINTENANCE OF CHILDREN LOOKED AFTER BY LOCAL AUTHORITIES

Liability to contribute

21.— (1) Where a local authority are looking after a child (other than in the cases mentioned in sub-paragraph (7)) they shall consider whether they should recover contributions towards the child's maintenance from any person liable to contribute ('a contributor').

(2) An authority may only recover contributions from a contributor if they consider it reasonable to do so.

(3) The persons liable to contribute are—

(a) where the child is under sixteen, each of his parents;

(b) where he has reached the age of sixteen, the child himself.

(4) A parent is not liable to contribute during any period when he is in receipt of income support under Part VII of the Social Security Contributions and Benefits Act 1992, of any element of child tax credit other than the family element, of working tax credit, of an income-based jobseeker's allowance or of an income-related employment and support allowance.

(5) A person is not liable to contribute towards the maintenance of a child in the care of a local authority in respect of any period during which the child is living with, under arrangements made by the authority in accordance with section 22C, a parent of his.

(6) A contributor is not obliged to make any contribution towards a child's maintenance except as agreed or determined in accordance with this Part of this Schedule.

(7) The cases are where the child is looked after by a local authority under—

(a) section 21;

(b) an interim care order;

(c) section 92 of the Powers of Criminal Courts (Sentencing) Act 2000.

Agreed contributions

22.— (1) Contributions towards a child's maintenance may only be recovered if the local authority have served a notice ('a contribution notice') on the contributor specifying—

(a) the weekly sum which they consider that he should contribute; and

(b) arrangements for payment.

(2) The contribution notice must be in writing and dated.

(3) Arrangements for payment shall, in particular, include—

(a) the date on which liability to contribute begins (which must not be earlier than the date of the notice);

(b) the date on which liability under the notice will end (if the child has not before that date ceased to be looked after by the authority); and

(c) the date on which the first payment is to be made.

(4) The authority may specify in a contribution notice a weekly sum which is a standard contribution determined by them for all children looked after by them.

(5) The authority may not specify in a contribution notice a weekly sum greater than that which they consider—

(a) they would normally be prepared to pay if they had placed a similar child with local authority foster parents; and

(b) it is reasonably practicable for the contributor to pay (having regard to his means).

(6) An authority may at any time withdraw a contribution notice (without prejudice to their power to serve another).

(7) Where the authority and the contributor agree—

(a) the sum which the contributor is to contribute; and

(b) arrangements for payment,

(whether as specified in the contribution notice or otherwise) and the contributor notifies the authority in writing that he so agrees, the authority may recover summarily as a civil debt any contribution which is overdue and unpaid.

(8) A contributor may, by serving a notice in writing on the authority, withdraw his agreement in relation to any period of liability falling after the date of service of the notice.

(9) Sub-paragraph (7) is without prejudice to any other method of recovery.

Contribution orders

23.— (1) Where a contributor has been served with a contribution notice and has—

(a) failed to reach any agreement with the local authority as mentioned in paragraph 22(7) within the period of one month beginning with the day on which the contribution notice was served; or

(b) served a notice under paragraph 22(8) withdrawing his agreement,

the authority may apply to the court for an order under this paragraph.

(2) On such an application the court may make an order ('a contribution order') requiring the contributor to contribute a weekly sum towards the child's maintenance in accordance with arrangements for payment specified by the court.

(3) A contribution order—

(a) shall not specify a weekly sum greater than that specified in the contribution notice; and

(b) shall be made with due regard to the contributor's means.

(4) A contribution order shall not—

(a) take effect before the date specified in the contribution notice; or

(b) have effect while the contributor is not liable to contribute (by virtue of paragraph 21); or

(c) remain in force after the child has ceased to be looked after by the authority who obtained the order.

(5) An authority may not apply to the court under sub-paragraph (1) in relation to a contribution notice which they have withdrawn.

(6) Where—

(a) a contribution order is in force;

(b) the authority serve another contribution notice; and

(c) the contributor and the authority reach an agreement under paragraph 22(7) in respect of that other contribution notice,

the effect of the agreement shall be to discharge the order from the date on which it is agreed that the agreement shall take effect.

(7) Where an agreement is reached under sub-paragraph (6) the authority shall notify the court—

(a) of the agreement; and

(b) of the date on which it took effect.

(8) A contribution order may be varied or revoked on the application of the contributor or the authority.

(9) In proceedings for the variation of a contribution order, the authority shall specify—

(a) the weekly sum which, having regard to paragraph 22, they propose that the contributor should contribute under the order as varied; and

(b) the proposed arrangements for payment.

(10) Where a contribution order is varied, the order—

(a) shall not specify a weekly sum greater than that specified by the authority in the proceedings for variation; and

(b) shall be made with due regard to the contributor's means.

(11) An appeal shall lie in accordance with rules of court from any order made under this paragraph.

Enforcement of contribution orders etc

24.— (1) A contribution order made by a magistrates' court shall be enforceable as a magistrates' court maintenance order (within the meaning of section 150(1) of the Magistrates' Courts Act 1980).

(2) Where a contributor has agreed, or has been ordered, to make contributions to a local authority, any other local authority within whose area the contributor is for the time being living may—

(a) at the request of the local authority who served the contributions notice; and

(b) subject to agreement as to any sum to be deducted in respect of services rendered,

collect from the contributor any contributions due on behalf of the authority who served the notice.

(3) In sub-paragraph (2) the reference to any other local authority includes a reference to—

(a) a local authority within the meaning of section 1(2) of the Social Work (Scotland) Act 1968; and

(b) a Health and Social Services Board established under Article 16 of the Health and Personal Social Services (Northern Ireland) Order 1972.

(4) The power to collect sums under sub-paragraph (2) includes the power to—

(a) receive and give a discharge for any contributions due; and

(b) (if necessary) enforce payment of any contributions,

even though those contributions may have fallen due at a time when the contributor was living elsewhere.

(5) Any contribution collected under sub-paragraph (2) shall be paid (subject to any agreed deduction) to the local authority who served the contribution notice.

(6) In any proceedings under this paragraph, a document which purports to be—

(a) a copy of an order made by a court under or by virtue of paragraph 23; and

(b) certified as a true copy by the designated officer for the court,

shall be evidence of the order.

(7) In any proceedings under this paragraph, a certificate which—

(a) purports to be signed by the clerk or some other duly authorised officer of the local authority who obtained the contribution order; and

(b) states that any sum due to the authority under the order is overdue and unpaid,

shall be evidence that the sum is overdue and unpaid.

Regulations

25. The appropriate national authority may make regulations—

(a) as to the considerations which a local authority must take into account in deciding—

(i) whether it is reasonable to recover contributions; and

(ii) what the arrangements for payment should be;

(b) as to the procedures a local authority must follow in reaching agreements with—

(i) contributors (under paragraphs 22 and 23); and

(ii) any other local authority (under paragraph 23).

(F) Child Support Act 1991

1 The duty to maintain

(1) For the purposes of this Act, each parent of a qualifying child is responsible for maintaining him.

(2) For the purposes of this Act, a non-resident parent shall be taken to have met his responsibility to maintain any qualifying child of his by making periodical payments of maintenance with respect to the child of such amount, and at such intervals, as may be determined in accordance with the provisions of this Act.

(3) Where a maintenance calculation made under this Act requires the making of periodical payments, it shall be the duty of the non-resident parent with respect to whom the calculation was made to make those payments.

2 Welfare of children: the general principle

Where, in any case which falls to be dealt with under this Act, the Commission ... is considering the exercise of any discretionary power conferred by this Act, it shall have regard to the welfare of any child likely to be affected by its decision.

3 Meaning of certain terms used in this Act

(1) A child is a 'qualifying child' if—

(a) one of his parents is, in relation to him, a non-resident parent; or

(b) both of his parents are, in relation to him, non-resident parents.

(2) The parent of any child is a 'non-resident parent', in relation to him, if—

(a) that parent is not living in the same household with the child; and

(b) the child has his home with a person who is, in relation to him, a person with care.

(3) A person is a 'person with care', in relation to any child, if he is a person—

(a) with whom the child has his home;

(b) who usually provides a day to day care for the child (whether exclusively or in conjunction with any other person); and

(c) who does not fall within a prescribed category of person.

(4) The Secretary of State shall not, under subsection (3)(c), prescribe as a category—

(a) parents;

(b) guardians;

(c) persons in whose favour residence orders under section 8 of the Children Act 1989 are in force;

(d) (not reproduced)

(5) For the purposes of this Act there may be more than one person with care in relation to the same qualifying child.

(6) Periodical payments which are required to be paid in accordance with a maintenance calculation are referred to in this Act as 'child support maintenance'.

(7) Expressions are defined in this section only for the purposes of this Act.

4 Child support maintenance

(1) A person who is, in relation to any qualifying child or any qualifying children, either the person with care or the non-resident parent may apply to the Commission for a maintenance calculation to be made under this Act with respect to that child, or any of those children.

(2) Where a maintenance calculation has been made in response to an application under this section the Commission may, if the person with care or non-resident parent with

respect to whom the calculation was made applies to it under this subsection, arrange for—

(a) the collection of the child support maintenance payable in accordance with the calculation;

(b) the enforcement of the obligation to pay child support maintenance in accordance with the calculation.

(3) Where an application under subsection (2) for the enforcement of the obligation mentioned in subsection (2)(b) authorises the Commission to take steps to enforce that obligation whenever it considers it necessary to do so, the Commission may act accordingly.

(4) A person who applies to the Commission under this section shall, so far as that person reasonably can, comply with such regulations as may be made by the Secretary of State with a view to the Commission ... being provided with the information which is required to enable—

(a) the non-resident parent to be identified or traced (where that is necessary);

(b) the amount of child support maintenance payable by the non-resident parent to be calculated; and

(c) that amount to be recovered from the non-resident parent.

(5) Any person who has applied to the Commission under this section may at any time request it to cease acting under this section.

(6) It shall be the duty of the Commission to comply with any request made under subsection (5) (but subject to any regulations made under subsection (8)).

(7) The obligation to provide information which is imposed by subsection (4)—

(a) shall not apply in such circumstances as may be prescribed; and

(b) may, in such circumstances as may be prescribed, be waived by the Commission.

(8) The Secretary of State may by regulations make such incidental, supplemental or transitional provision as he thinks appropriate with respect to cases in which he is requested to cease to act under this under this section.

(9) . . .

(10) No application may be made at any time under this section with respect to a qualifying child or any qualifying children if—

(a) there is in force a written maintenance agreement made before 5 April 1993, or a maintenance order made before a prescribed date, in respect of that child or those children and the person who is, at that time, the non-resident parent; or

(aa) a maintenance order made on or after the date prescribed for the purposes of paragraph (a) is in force in respect of them, but has been so for less than the period of one year beginning with the date on which it was made; or

(ab) a maintenance agreement—

(i) made on or after the date prescribed for the purposes of paragraph (a); and

(ii) registered for execution in the Books of Council and Session or the sheriff court books,

is in force in respect of them, but has been so for less than the period of one year beginning with the date on which it was made; ...

(11) . . .

5 Child support maintenance: supplemental provisions

(1) Where—

(a) there is more than one person with care of a qualifying child; and

(b) one or more, but not all, of them have parental responsibility for ... the child;

no application may be made for a maintenance calculation with respect to the child by any of those persons who do not have parental responsibility for ... the child.

(2) Where more than one application for a maintenance calculation is made with respect to the child concerned, only one of them may be proceeded with.

(3) The Secretary of State may by regulation make provision as to which of two or more applications for a maintenance calculation with respect to the same child is to be proceeded with.

8 Role of the courts with respect to maintenance for children

(1) This subsection applies in any case where the Commission would have jurisdiction to make a maintenance calculation with respect to a qualifying child and a non-resident parent of his on an application duly made . . . by a person entitled to apply for such a calculation with respect to that child.

(2) Subsection (1) applies even though the circumstances of the case are such that the Commission would not make a calculation if it were applied for.

(3) Except as provided in subsection (3A), in any case where subsection (1) applies, no court shall exercise any power which it would otherwise have to make, vary or revive any maintenance order in relation to the child and non-resident parent concerned.

(3A) Unless a maintenance calculation has been made with respect to the child concerned, subsection (3) does not prevent a court from varying a maintenance order in relation to that child and the non-resident parent concerned—

(a) if the maintenance order was made on or after the date prescribed for the purposes of section 4(10)(a) or 7(10)(a); or

(b) where the order was made before then, in any case in which section 4(10) or 7(10) prevents the making of an application for a maintenance calculation with respect to or by that child.

(4) Subsection (3) does not prevent a court from revoking a maintenance order.

(5) The Lord Chancellor . . . may by order provide that, in such circumstances as may be specified by the order, this section shall not prevent a court from exercising any power which it has to make a maintenance order in relation to a child if—

(a) a written agreement (whether or not enforceable) provides for the making, or securing, by a non-resident parent of the child of periodical payments to or for the benefit of the child; and

(b) the maintenance order which the court makes is, in all material respects, in the same terms as that agreement.

(5A) The Lord Chancellor may make an order under subsection (5) only with the concurrence of the Lord Chief Justice.

(6) This section shall not prevent a court from exercising any power which it has to make a maintenance order in relation to a child if—

(a) a maintenance calculation is in force with respect to the child;

(b) the non-resident parent's net weekly income exceeds the figure referred to in paragraph 10(3) of Schedule 1 (as it has effect from time to time pursuant to regulations made under paragraph 10A(1)(b)); and

(c) the court is satisfied that the circumstances of the case make it appropriate for the non-resident parent to make or secure the making of periodical payments under a maintenance order in addition to the child support maintenance payable by him in accordance with the maintenance calculation.

(7) This section shall not prevent a court from exercising any power which it has to make a maintenance order in relation to a child if—

(a) the child is, will be or (if the order were to be made) would be receiving instruction at an educational establishment or undergoing training for a trade, profession or vocation (whether or not while in gainful employment); and

(b) the order is made solely for the purposes of requiring the person making or securing the making of periodical payments fixed by the order to meet some or all of the expenses incurred in connection with the provision of the instruction or training.

(8) This section shall not prevent a court from exercising any power which it has to make a maintenance order in relation to a child if—

(a) a disability living allowance is paid to or in respect of him; or

(b) no such allowance is paid but he is disabled,

and the order is made solely for the purpose of requiring the person making or securing the making of periodical payments fixed by the order to meet some or all of any expenses attributable to the child's disability.

(9) For the purposes of subsection (8), a child is disabled if he is blind, deaf or dumb or is substantially and permanently handicapped by illness, injury, mental disorder or congenital deformity or such other disability as may be prescribed.

(10) This section shall not prevent a court from exercising any power which it has to make a maintenance order in relation to a child if the order is made against a person with care of the child.

(11) In this Act 'maintenance order', in relation to any child, means an order which requires the making or securing of periodical payments to or for the benefit of the child and which is made under—

(a) Part II of the Matrimonial Causes Act 1973;

(b) the Domestic Proceedings and Magistrates' Courts Act 1978;

(c) Part III of the Matrimonial and Family Proceedings Act 1984;

. . .

(e) Schedule 1 to the Children Act 1989; ...

(ea) Schedule 5, 6 or 7 of the Civil Partnership Act 2004; or

(f) any other prescribed enactment,

and includes any order varying or reviving such an order.

(12) The Lord Chief Justice may nominate a judicial office holder (as defined in section 109(4) of the Constitutional Reform Act 2005) to exercise his functions under this section.

9 Agreements about maintenance

(1) In this section 'maintenance agreement' means any agreement for the making, or for securing the making, of periodical payments by way of maintenance, or in Scotland aliment, to or for the benefit of any child.

(2) Nothing in this Act shall be taken to prevent any person from entering into a maintenance agreement.

(3) Subject to section 4(10)(a) and (ab) and section 7(10), the existence of a maintenance agreement shall not prevent any party to the agreement, or any other person, from applying for a maintenance calculation with respect to any child to or for whose benefit periodical payments are to be made or secured under the agreement.

(4) Where any agreement contains a provision which purports to restrict the right of any person to apply for a maintenance calculation, that provision shall be void.

(5) Where section 8 would prevent any court from making a maintenance order in relation to a child and a non-resident parent of his, no court shall exercise any power that it has to vary any agreement so as—

(a) to insert a provision requiring that non-resident parent to make or secure the making of periodical payments by way of maintenance, or in Scotland aliment, to or for the benefit of that child; or

(b) to increase the amount payable under such a provision.

(6) In any case in which section 4(10) or 7(10) prevents the making of an application for a maintenance calculation, . . .

subsection (5) shall have effect with the omission of paragraph (b).

10 Relationship between maintenance calculations and certain court orders and related matters

(1) Where an order of a kind prescribed for the purposes of this subsection is in force with respect to any qualifying child with respect to whom a maintenance calculation is made, the order—

(a) shall, so far as it relates to the making or securing of periodical payments, cease to have effect to such extent as may be determined in accordance with regulations made by the Secretary of State; or

(b) where the regulations so provide, shall, so far as it so relates, have effect subject to such modifications as may be so determined.

(2) Where an agreement of a kind prescribed for the purposes of this subsection is in force with respect to any qualifying child with respect to whom a maintenance calculation is made, the agreement—

(a) shall, so far as it relates to the making or securing of periodical payments, be unenforceable to such extent as may be determined in accordance with regulations made by the Secretary of State; or

(b) where the regulations so provide, shall, so far as it so relates, have effect subject to such modifications as may be so determined.

(3) Any regulations under this section may, in particular, make such provision with respect to—

(a) any case where any person with respect to whom an order or agreement of a kind prescribed for the purposes of subsection (1) or (2) has effect applies to the prescribed court, before the end of the prescribed period, for the order or agreement to be varied in the light of the maintenance calculation and of the provisions of this Act;

(b) the recovery of any arrears under the order or agreement which fell due before the coming into force of the maintenance calculation,

as the Secretary of State considers appropriate and may provide that, in prescribed circumstances, an application to any court which is made with respect to an order of a prescribed kind relating to the making or securing of periodical payments to or for the benefit of a child shall be treated by the court as an application for the order to be revoked.

(4) The Secretary of State may by regulations make provision for—

(a) notification to be given by the Commission concerned to the prescribed person in any case where it considers that the making of a maintenance calculation has affected, or is likely to affect, any order of a kind prescribed for the purposes of this subsection;

(b) notification to be given by the prescribed person to the Commission in any case where a court makes an order which it considers has affected, or is likely to affect, a maintenance calculation.

(5) Rules may be made under section 144 of the Magistrates' Courts Act 1980 (rules of procedure) requiring any person who, in prescribed circumstances, makes an application to a magistrates' court for a maintenance order to furnish the court with a

statement in a prescribed form, and signed by an officer of the Commission, as to whether or not, at the time when the statement is made, there is a maintenance calculation in force with respect to that person or the child concerned.

In this subsection—

'maintenance order' means an order of a prescribed kind for the making or securing of periodical payments to or for the benefit of a child; and

'prescribed' means prescribed by the rules.

11 Maintenance calculations

(1) An application for a maintenance calculation made to the Commission shall be dealt with by it in accordance with the provision made by or under this Act.

(2) The Commission shall (unless it decides not to make a maintenance calculation in response to the application, or makes a decision under section 12) determine the application by making a decision under this section about whether any child support maintenance is payable and, if so, how much.

(3), (5) . . .

(6) The amount of child support maintenance to be fixed by a maintenance calculation shall be determined in accordance with Part I of Schedule 1 unless an application for a variation has been made and agreed.

(7) If the Commission has agreed to a variation, the amount of child support maintenance to be fixed shall be determined on the basis it determines under section 28F(4).

(8) Part II of Schedule 1 makes further provision with respect to maintenance calculations.

44 Jurisdiction

(1) The Commission shall have jurisdiction to make a maintenance calculation with respect to a person who is—

(a) a person with care;

(b) a non-resident parent; or

(c) a qualifying child,

only if that person is habitually resident in the United Kingdom, except in the case of a non-resident parent who falls within subsection (2A).

(2) Where the person with care is not an individual, subsection (1) shall have effect as if paragraph (a) were omitted.

(2A) A non-resident parent falls within this subsection if he is not habitually resident in the United Kingdom, but is—

(a) employed in the civil service of the Crown, including Her Majesty's Diplomatic Service and Her Majesty's Overseas Civil Service;

(b) a member of the naval, military or air forces of the Crown, including any person employed by an ssociation established for the purposes of Part XI of the Reserves Forces Act 1996;

(c) employed by a company of a prescribed description registered under the Companies Act 2006; or

(d) employed by a body of a prescribed description.

(3) (not reproduced)

(4) The Commission does not have jurisdiction under this section if the exercise of jurisdiction would be contrary to the jurisdictional requirements of the Maintenance Regulation.

(5) In subsection (4) 'the Maintenance Regulation' means Council Regulation (EC) No. 4/2009 including as applied in relation to Denmark by virtue of the Agreement made on 19th October 2005 between the European Community and the Kingdom of Denmark.

Schedule 1
Maintenance Calculations

Part I
Calculation of Weekly Amount of Child Support Maintenance

1 General rule

(1) The weekly rate of child support maintenance is the basic rate unless a reduced rate, a flat rate or the nil rate applies.

(2) Unless the nil rate applies, the amount payable weekly to a person with care is—

(a) the applicable rate, if paragraph 6 does not apply; or

(b) if paragraph 6 does apply, that rate as apportioned between the persons with care in accordance with paragraph 6,

as adjusted, in either case, by applying the rules about shared care in paragraph 7 or 8.

2 Basic rate

(1) The basic rate is the following percentage of the non-resident parent's net weekly income—

15% where he has one qualifying child;

20% where he has two qualifying children;

25% where he has three or more qualifying children.

(2) If the non-resident parent also has one or more relevant other children, the appropriate percentage referred to in sub-paragraph (1) is to be applied instead to his net weekly income less—

15% where he has one relevant other child;

20% where he has two relevant other children;

25% where he has three or more relevant other children.

3 Reduced rate

(1) A reduced rate is payable if—

(a) neither a flat rate nor the nil rate applies; and

(b) the non-resident parent's net weekly income is less than £200 but more than £100.

(2) The reduced rate payable shall be prescribed in, or determined in accordance with, regulations.

(3) The regulations may not prescribe, or result in, a rate of less than £5.

4 Flat rate

(1) Except in a case falling within sub-paragraph (2), a flat rate of £5 is payable if the nil rate does not apply and—

(a) the non-resident parent's net weekly income is £100 or less; or

(b) he receives any benefit, pension or allowance prescribed for the purposes of this paragraph of this sub-paragraph; or

(c) he or his partner (if any) receives any benefit prescribed for the purposes of this paragraph of this sub-paragraph.

(2) A flat rate of a prescribed amount is payable if the nil rate does not apply and—

(a) the non-resident parent has a partner who is also a non-resident parent;

(b) the partner is a person with respect to whom a maintenance calculation is in force; and

(c) the non-resident parent or his partner receives any benefit prescribed under sub-paragraph (1)(c).

(3) The benefits, pensions and allowances which may be prescribed for the purposes of sub-paragraph (1)(b) include ones paid to the non-resident parent under the law of a place outside the United Kingdom.

5 Nil rate

The rate payable is nil if the non-resident parent—

(a) is of a prescribed description; or

(b) has a net weekly income of below £5.

6 Apportionment

(1) If the non-resident parent has more than one qualifying child and in relation to them there is more than one person with care, the amount of child support maintenance payable is (subject to paragraph 7 or 8) to be determined by apportioning the rate between the persons with care.

(2) The rate of maintenance liability is to be divided by the number of qualifying children, and shared among the persons with care according to the number of qualifying children in relation to whom each is a person with care.

7 Shared care—basic and reduced rate

(1) This paragraph applies only if the rate of child support maintenance payable is the basic rate or a reduced rate.

(2) If the care of a qualifying child is shared between the non-resident parent and the person with care, so that the non-resident parent from time to time has care of the child overnight, the amount of child support maintenance which he would otherwise have been liable to pay the person with care, as calculated in accordance with the preceding paragraphs of this Part of this Schedule, is to be decreased in accordance with this paragraph.

(3) First, there is to be a decrease according to the number of such nights which the Commission determines there to have been, or expects there to be, or both during a prescribed twelve-month period.

(4) The amount of that decrease for one child is set out in the following Table—

Number of nights	Fraction to subtract
52 to 103	One-seventh
104 to 155	Two-sevenths
156 to 174	Three-sevenths
175 or more	One half

(5) If the person with care is caring for more than one qualifying child of the non-resident parent, the applicable decrease is the sum of the appropriate fractions in the Table divided by the number of such qualifying children.

(6) If the applicable fraction is one-half in relation to any qualifying child in the care of the person with care, the total amount payable to the person with care is then to be further decreased by £7 for each such child.

(7) If the application of the preceding provisions of this paragraph would decrease the weekly amount of child support maintenance (or the aggregate of all such amounts) payable by the non-resident parent to the person with care (or all of them) to less than

£5, he is instead liable to pay child support maintenance at the rate of £5 a week, apportioned (if appropriate) in accordance with paragraph 6.

8 Shared care—flat rate

(1) This paragraph applies only if—

(a) the rate of child support maintenance payable is a flat rate; and

(b) that rate applies because the non-resident parent falls within paragraph 4(1)(b) or (c) or 4(2).

(2) If the care of a qualifying child is shared as mentioned in paragraph 7(2) for at least 52 nights during a prescribed 12-month period, the amount of child support maintenance payable by the non-resident parent to the person with care of that child is nil.

9 Regulations about shared care

The Secretary of State may by regulations provide—

(a) for which nights are to count for the purposes of shared care under paragraphs 7 and 8, or for how it is to be determined whether a night counts;

(b) for what counts, or does not count, as 'care' for those purposes; and

(c) for paragraph 7(3) or 8(2) to have effect, in prescribed circumstances, as if the period mentioned there were other than 12 months, and in such circumstances for the Table in paragraph 7(4) (or that Table as modified pursuant to regulations made under paragraph 10A(2)(a)), or the period mentioned in paragraph 8(2), to have effect with prescribed adjustments.

10 Net weekly income

(1) For the purposes of this Schedule, net weekly income is to be determined in such manner as is provided for in regulations.

(2) The regulations may, in particular, provide for the Commission to estimate any income or make an assumption as to any fact where, in his view, the information at its disposal is unreliable, insufficient, or relates to an atypical period in the life of the non-resident parent.

(3) Any amount of net weekly income (calculated as above) over £2,000 is to be ignored for the purposes of this Schedule.

10A Regulations about rates, figures, etc

(1) The Secretary of State may by regulations provide that—

(a) paragraph 2 is to have effect as if different percentages were substituted for those set out there;

(b) paragraph 3(1) or (3), 4(1), 5, 7(7) or 10(3) is to have effect as if different amounts were substituted for those set out there.

(2) The Secretary of State may by regulations provide that—

(a) the Table in paragraph 7(4) is to have effect as if different numbers of nights were set out in the first column and different fractions were substituted for those set out in the second column;

(b) paragraph 7(6) is to have effect as if a different amount were substituted for that mentioned there, or as if the amount were an aggregate amount and not an amount for each qualifying child, or both.

10B Regulations about income

The Secretary of State may by regulations provide that, in such circumstances and to such extent as may be prescribed—

(a) where the Commission is satisfied that a person has intentionally deprived himself of a source of income with a view to reducing the amount of his net weekly income, his net weekly income shall be taken to include income from that source of an amount estimated by the Commission;

(b) a person is to be treated as possessing income which he does not possess;

(c) income which a person does possess is to be disregarded.

10C References to various terms

(1) References in this Part of this Schedule to 'qualifying children' are to those qualifying children with respect to whom the maintenance calculation falls to be made.

(2) References in this Part of this Schedule to 'relevant other children' are to—

  (a) children other than qualifying children in respect of whom the non-resident parent or his partner receives child benefit under Part IX of the Social Security Contributions and Benefits Act 1992; and

  (b) such other description of children as may be prescribed.

(3) In this Part of this Schedule, a person 'receives' a benefit, pension, or allowance for any week if it is paid or due to be paid to him in respect of that week.

(4) In this Part of this Schedule, a person's 'partner' is—

  (a) if they are a couple, the other member of that couple;

  (b) if the person is a husband or wife by virtue of a marriage entered into under a law which permits polygamy, another party to the marriage who is of the opposite sex and is a member of the same household.

(5) In sub-paragraph (4)(a), 'couple' means—

  (a) a man and a woman who are married to each other and are members of the same household,

  (b) a man and a woman who are not married to each other but are living together as husband and wife,

  (c) two people of the same sex who are civil partners of each other and are members of the same household, or

  (d) two people of the same sex who are not civil partners of each other but are living together as if they were civil partners.

(6) For the purposes of this paragraph, two people of the same sex are to be regarded as living together as if they were civil partners if, but only if, they would be regarded as living together as husband and wife were they instead two people of the opposite sex.

Part II
General Provisions about Maintenance Calculations

11 Effective date of calculation

(1) A maintenance calculation shall take effect on such date as may be determined in accordance with regulations made by the Secretary of State.

(2) That date may be earlier than the date on which the calculation is made.

12 Form of calculation

Every maintenance calculation shall be made in such form and contain such information as the Commission may direct.

13 (not reproduced)

14 Consolidated applications and calculations

The Secretary of State may by regulations provide—

(a) for two or more applications for maintenance calculations to be treated, in prescribed circumstances, as a single application; and

(b) for the replacement, in prescribed circumstances, of a maintenance calculation made on the application of one person by a later maintenance calculation made on the application of that or any other person.

15 Separate calculations for different periods

Where the Commission is satisfied that the circumstances of a case require different amounts of child support maintenance to be calculated in respect of different periods, it may make separate maintenance calculations each expressed to have effect in relation to a different specified period.

16 Termination of calculations

(1) A maintenance calculation shall cease to have effect—

- (a) on the death of the non-resident parent, or of the person with care, with respect to whom it was made;
- (b) on there no longer being any qualifying child with respect to whom it would have effect;
- (c) on the non-resident parent with respect to whom it was made ceasing to be a parent of—
  - (i) the qualifying child with respect to whom it was made; or
  - (ii) where it was made with respect to more than one qualifying child, all of the qualifying children with respect to whom it was made;
- (d), (e) (not reproduced)

(2)–(9) (not reproduced)

(10) A person with care with respect to whom a maintenance calculation is in force shall provide the Commission with such information, in such circumstances, as may be prescribed, with a view to assisting the Commission ... in determining whether the calculation has ceased to have effect ...

(11) The Secretary of State may by regulations make such supplemental, incidental or transitional provision as he thinks necessary or expedient in consequence of the provisions of this paragraph.

(G) Family Law Act 1996

30 Rights concerning home where one spouse or civil partner has no estate, etc.

(1) This section applies if—

(a) one spouse or civil partner ('A') is entitled to occupy a dwelling-house by virtue of—

(i) a beneficial estate or interest or contract; or

(ii) any enactment giving A the right to remain in occupation; and

(b) the other spouse or civil partner ('B') is not so entitled.

(2) Subject to the provisions of this Part, B has the following rights ('home rights')—

(a) if in occupation, a right not to be evicted or excluded from the dwelling-house or any part of it by A except with the leave of the court given by an order under section 33;

(b) if not in occupation, a right with the leave of the court so given to enter into and occupy the dwelling-house.

(3) If B is entitled under this section to occupy a dwelling-house or any part of a dwelling-house, any payment or tender made or other thing done by B in or towards satisfaction of any liability of A in respect of rent, mortgage payments or other outgoings affecting the dwelling-house is, whether or not it is made or done in pursuance of an order under section 40, as good as if made or done by A.

(4) B's occupation by virtue of this section—

(a) is to be treated, for the purposes of the Rent (Agriculture) Act 1976 and the Rent Act 1977 (other than Part V and sections 103 to 106 of that Act), as occupation by A as A's residence, and

(b) if B occupies the dwelling-house as B's only or principal home, is to be treated, for the purposes of the Housing Act 1985, Part I of the Housing Act 1988 and Chapter I of Part V of the Housing Act 1996, as occupation by A as A's only or principal home.

(5) If B—

(a) is entitled under this section to occupy a dwelling-house or any part of a dwelling-house, and

(b) makes any payment in or towards satisfaction of any liability of A in respect of mortgage payments affecting the dwelling-house,

the person to whom the payment is made may treat it as having been made by A, but the fact that that person has treated any such payment as having been so made does not affect any claim of B against A to an interest in the dwelling-house by virtue of the payment.

(6) If B is entitled under this section to occupy a dwelling-house or part of a dwelling-house by reason of an interest of A under a trust, all the provisions of subsections (3) to (5) apply in relation to the trustees as they apply in relation to A.

(7) This section does not apply to a dwelling-house which—

(a) in the case of spouses, has at no time been, and which was at the time intended by them to be, a matrimonial home of theirs, and

(b) in the case of civil partners, has at no time been, and was at no time intended to be, a civil partnership home of theirs.

(8) B's home rights continue—

(a) only so long as the marriage or civil partnership subsists, except to the extent that an order under section 33(5) otherwise provides; and

(b) only so long as A is entitled as mentioned in subsection (1) to occupy the dwelling-house, except where provision is made by section 31 for those rights to be a charge on an estate or interest in the dwelling-house.

(9) It is hereby declared that a person—

(a) who has an equitable interest in a dwelling-house or in its proceeds of sale, but

(b) is not a person in whom there is vested (whether solely or as joint tenant) a legal estate in fee simple or a legal term of years absolute in the dwelling-house,

is to be treated, only for the purpose of determining whether he has home rights, as not being entitled to occupy the dwelling-house by virtue of that interest.

33 Occupation orders where applicant has estate or interest etc or has home rights

(1) If—

(a) a person ('the person entitled')—

(i) is entitled to occupy a dwelling-house by virtue of a beneficial estate or interest or contract or by virtue of any enactment giving him the right to remain in occupation, or

(ii) has home rights in relation to a dwelling-house, and

(b) the dwelling-house—

(i) is or at any time has been the home of the person entitled and of another person with whom he is associated, or

(ii) was at any time intended by the person entitled and any such other person to be their home,

the person entitled may apply to the court for an order containing any of the provisions specified in subsections (3), (4) and (5).

(2) If an agreement to marry is terminated, no application under this section may be made by virtue of section 62(3)(e) by reference to that agreement after the end of the period of three years beginning with the date on which it is terminated.

(2A) If a civil partnership agreement (as defined by section 73 of the Civil Partnership Act 2004) is terminated, no application under this section may be made by virtue of section 62(3)(eza) by reference to that agreement after the period of three years beginning with the day on which it is terminated.

(3) An order under this section may—

(a) enforce the applicant's entitlement to remain in occupation as against the other person ('the respondent');

(b) require the respondent to permit the applicant to enter and remain in the dwelling-house or part of the dwelling-house;

(c) regulate the occupation of the dwelling-house by either or both parties;

(d) if the respondent is entitled as mentioned in subsection (1)(a)(i), prohibit, suspend or restrict the exercise by him of his right to occupy the dwelling-house;

(e) if the respondent has home rights in relation to the dwelling-house and the applicant is the other spouse or civil partner, restrict or terminate those rights;

(f) require the respondent to leave the dwelling-house or part of the dwelling-house; or

(g) exclude the respondent from a defined area in which the dwelling-house is included.

(4) An order under this section may declare that the applicant is entitled as mentioned in subsection (1)(a)(i) or has home rights.

(5) If the applicant has home rights and the respondent is the other spouse or civil partner, an order under this section made during the marriage or civil partnership may provide that those rights are not brought to an end by—

(a) the death of the other spouse or civil partner; or

(b) the termination (otherwise than by death) of the marriage or civil partnership.

(6) In deciding whether to exercise its powers under subsection (3) and (if so) in what manner, the court shall have regard to all the circumstances including—

(a) the housing needs and housing resources of each of the parties and of any relevant child;

(b) the financial resources of the parties;

(c) the likely effect of any order, or of any decision by the court not to exercise its powers under subsection (3), on the health, safety or well-being of the parties and of any relevant child; and

(d) the conduct of the parties in relation to each other and otherwise.

(7) If it appears to the court that the applicant or any relevant child is likely to suffer significant harm attributable to conduct of the respondent if an order under this section containing one or more of the provisions mentioned in subsection (3) is not made, the court shall make the order unless it appears to the court that—

(a) the respondent or any relevant child is likely to suffer significant harm if the order is made; and

(b) the harm likely to be suffered by the respondent or child in that event is as great as, or greater than, the harm attributable to conduct of the respondent which is likely to be suffered by the applicant or child if the order is not made.

(8) The court may exercise its powers under subsection (5) in any case where it considers that in all the circumstances it is just and reasonable to do so.

(9) An order under this section—

(a) may not be made after the death of either of the parties mentioned in subsection (1); and

(b) except in the case of an order made by virtue of subsection (5)(a), ceases to have effect on the death of either party.

(10) An order under this section may, in so far as it has continuing effect, be made for a specified period, until the occurrence of a specified event or until further order.

34 Effect of order under s 33 where rights are charge on dwelling-house

(1) If B's home rights are a charge on the estate or interest of A or of trustees for A—

(a) an order under section 33 against A has, except so far as a contrary intention appears, the same effect against persons deriving title under A or under the trustees and affected by the charge, and

(b) sections 33(1), (3), (4) and (10) and 30(3) to (6) apply in relation to any person deriving title under A or under the trustees and affected by the charge as they apply in relation to A.

(2) The court may make an order under section 33 by virtue of subsection (1)(b) if it considers that in all the circumstances it is just and reasonable to do so.

35 One former spouse or former civil partner with no existing right to occupy

(1) This section applies if—

(a) one former spouse or former civil partner is entitled to occupy a dwelling-house by virtue of a beneficial estate or interest or contract, or by virtue of any enactment giving him the right to remain in occupation;

(b) the other former spouse or former civil partner is not so entitled; and

(c) the dwelling-house—

(i) in the case of former spouses, was at any time their matrimonial home or was at any time intended by them to be their matrimonial home, or

(ii) in the case of former civil partners, was at any time their civil partnership home or was at any time intended by them to be their civil partnership home.

(2) The former spouse or former civil partner not so entitled may apply to the court for an order under this section against the other former spouse or former civil partner ('the respondent').

(3) If the applicant is in occupation, an order under this section must contain provision—

(a) giving the applicant the right not to be evicted or excluded from the dwelling-house or any part of it by the respondent for the period specified in the order; and

(b) prohibiting the respondent from evicting or excluding the applicant during that period.

(4) If the applicant is not in occupation, an order under this section must contain provision—

(a) giving the applicant the right to enter into and occupy the dwelling-house for the period specified in the order; and

(b) requiring the respondent to permit the exercise of that right.

(5) An order under this section may also—

(a) regulate the occupation of the dwelling-house by either or both of the parties;

(b) prohibit, suspend or restrict the exercise by the respondent of his right to occupy the dwelling-house;

(c) require the respondent to leave the dwelling-house or part of the dwelling-house; or

(d) exclude the respondent from a defined area in which the dwelling-house is included.

(6) In deciding whether to make an order under this section containing provision of the kind mentioned in subsection (3) or (4) and (if so) in what manner, the court shall have regard to all the circumstances including—

(a) the housing needs and housing resources of each of the parties and of any relevant child;

(b) the financial resources of each of the parties;

(c) the likely effect of any order, or of any decision by the court not to exercise its powers under subsection (3) or (4), on the health, safety or well-being of the parties and of any relevant child;

(d) the conduct of the parties in relation to each other and otherwise;

(e) the length of time that has elapsed since the parties ceased to live together;

(f) the length of time that has elapsed since the marriage or civil partnership was dissolved or annulled; and

(g) the existence of any pending proceedings between the parties—

(i) for an order under section 23A or 24 of the Matrimonial Causes Act 1973 (property adjustment orders in connection with divorce proceedings etc);

(ia) for a property adjustment order under Part 2 of Schedule 5 to the Civil Partnership Act 2004;

(ii) for an order under paragraph 1(2)(d) or (e) of Schedule 1 to the Children Act 1989 (orders for financial relief against parents); or

(iii) relating to the legal or beneficial ownership of the dwelling-house.

(7) In deciding whether to exercise its power to include one or more of the provisions referred to in subsection (5) ('a subsection (5) provision') and (if so) in what manner, the court shall have regard to all the circumstances including the matters mentioned in subsection (6)(a) to (e).

(8) If the court decides to make an order under this section and it appears to it that, if the order does not include a subsection (5) provision, the applicant or any relevant child is likely to suffer significant harm attributable to conduct of the respondent, the court shall include the subsection (5) provision in the order unless it appears to the court that—

(a) the respondent or any relevant child is likely to suffer significant harm if the provision is included in the order; and

(b) the harm likely to be suffered by the respondent or child in that event is as great as or greater than the harm attributable to conduct of the respondent which is likely to be suffered by the applicant or child if the provision is not included.

(9) An order under this section—

(a) may not be made after the death of either of the former spouses or former civil partners; and

(b) ceases to have effect on the death of either of them.

(10) An order under this section must be limited so as to have effect for a specified period not exceeding six months, but may be extended on one or more occasions for a further specified period not exceeding six months.

(11) A former spouse or former civil partner who has an equitable interest in the dwelling-house or in the proceeds of sale of the dwelling-house but in whom there is not vested (whether solely or as joint tenant) a legal estate in fee simple or a legal term of years absolute in the dwelling-house is to be treated (but only for the purpose of determining whether he is eligible to apply under this section) as not being entitled to occupy the dwelling-house by virtue of that interest.

(12) Subsection (11) does not prejudice any right of such a former spouse or former civil partner to apply for an order under section 33.

(13) So long as an order under this section remains in force, subsections (3) to (6) of section 30 apply in relation to the applicant—

(a) as if he were B (the person entitled to occupy the dwelling-house by virtue of that section); and

(b) as if the respondent were A (the person entitled as mentioned in subsection (1)(a) of that section).

36 One cohabitant or former cohabitant with no existing right to occupy

(1) This section applies if—

(a) one cohabitant or former cohabitant is entitled to occupy a dwelling-house by virtue of a beneficial estate or interest or contract or by virtue of any enactment giving him the right to remain in occupation;

(b) the other cohabitant or former cohabitant is not so entitled; and

(c) that dwelling-house is the home in which they cohabit or a home in which they at any time cohabited or intended to cohabit.

(2) The cohabitant or former cohabitant not so entitled may apply to the court for an order under this section against the other cohabitant or former cohabitant ('the respondent').

(3) If the applicant is in occupation, an order under this section must contain provision—

(a) giving the applicant the right not to be evicted or excluded from the dwelling-house or any part of it by the respondent for the period specified in the order, and

(b) prohibiting the respondent from evicting or excluding the applicant during that period.

(4) If the applicant is not in occupation, an order under this section must contain provision—

(a) giving the applicant the right to enter into and occupy the dwelling-house for the period specified in the order; and

(b) requiring the respondent to permit the exercise of that right.

(5) An order under this section may also—

(a) regulate the occupation of the dwelling-house by either or both of the parties;

(b) prohibit, suspend or restrict the exercise by the respondent of his right to occupy the dwelling-house;

(c) require the respondent to leave the dwelling-house or part of the dwelling-house; or

(d) exclude the respondent from a defined area in which the dwelling-house is included.

(6) In deciding whether to make an order under this section containing provision of the kind mentioned in subsection (3) or (4) and (if so) in what manner, the court shall have regard to all the circumstances including—

(a) the housing needs and housing resources of each of the parties and of any relevant child;

(b) the financial resources of each of the parties;

(c) the likely effect of any order, or of any decision by the court not to exercise its powers under subsection (3) or (4), on the health, safety or well-being of the parties and of any relevant child;

(d) the conduct of the parties in relation to each other and otherwise;

(e) the nature of the parties' relationship and in particular the level of commitment involved in it;

(f) the length of time during which they have cohabited;

(g) whether there are or have been any children who are children of both parties or for whom both parties have or have had parental responsibility;

(h) the length of time that has elapsed since the parties ceased to live together; and

(i) the existence of any pending proceedings between the parties—

(i) for an order under paragraph 1(2)(d) or (e) of Schedule 1 to the Children Act 1989 (orders for financial relief against parents), or

(ii) relating to the legal or beneficial ownership of the dwelling-house.

(7) In deciding whether to exercise its powers to include one or more of the provisions referred to in subsection (5) ('a subsection (5) provision') and (if so) in what manner, the court shall have regard to all the circumstances including—

(a) the matters mentioned in subsection (6)(a) to (d); and

(b) the questions mentioned in subsection (8).

(8) The questions are—

(a) whether the applicant or any relevant child is likely to suffer significant harm attributable to conduct of the respondent if the subsection (5) provision is not included in the order; and

(b) whether the harm likely to be suffered by the respondent or child if the provision is included is as great as or greater than the harm attributable to conduct of the respondent which is likely to be suffered by the applicant or child if the provision is not included.

(9) An order under this section—

(a) may not be made after the death of either of the parties; and

(b) ceases to have effect on the death of either of them.

(10) An order under this section must be limited so as to have effect for a specified period not exceeding six months, but may be extended on one occasion for a further specified period not exceeding six months.

(11) A person who has an equitable interest in the dwelling-house or in the proceeds of sale of the dwelling-house but in whom there is not vested (whether solely or as joint tenant) a legal estate in fee simple or a legal term of years absolute in the dwelling-house is to be treated (but only for the purpose of determining whether he is eligible to apply under this section) as not being entitled to occupy the dwelling-house by virtue of that interest.

(12) Subsection (11) does not prejudice any right of such a person to apply for an order under section 33.

(13) So long as the order remains in force, subsections (3) to (6) of section 30 apply in relation to the applicant—

(a) as if he were B (the person entitled to occupy the dwelling-house by virtue of that section); and

(b) as if the respondent were A (the person entitled as mentioned in subsection (1)(a) of that section).

37 Neither spouse or civil partner entitled to occupy

(1) This section applies if—

(a) one spouse or former spouse and the other spouse or former spouse occupy a dwelling-house which is or was the matrimonial home; but

(b) neither of them is entitled to remain in occupation—

(i) by virtue of a beneficial estate or interest or contract; or

(ii) by virtue of any enactment giving him the right to remain in occupation.

(1A) This section applies if—

(a) the civil partner or former civil partner and the other civil partner or former civil partner occupy a dwelling-house which is or was the civil partnership home; but

(b) neither of them is entitled to remain in occupation—

(i) by virtue of a beneficial estate or contract; or

(ii) by virtue of any enactment giving him the right to remain in occupation.

(2) Either of the parties may apply to the court for an order against the other under this section.

(3) An order under this section may—

(a) require the respondent to permit the applicant to enter and remain in the dwelling-house or part of the dwelling-house;

(b) regulate the occupation of the dwelling-house by either or both of the parties;

(c) require the respondent to leave the dwelling-house or part of the dwelling-house; or

(d) exclude the respondent from a defined area in which the dwelling-house is included.

(4) Subsections (6) and (7) of section 33 apply to the exercise by the court of its powers under this section as they apply to the exercise by the court of its powers under subsection (3) of that section.

(5) An order under this section must be limited so as to have effect for a specified period not exceeding six months, but may be extended on one or more occasions for a further specified period not exceeding six months.

38 Neither cohabitant or former cohabitant entitled to occupy

(1) This section applies if—

(a) one cohabitant or former cohabitant and the other cohabitant or former cohabitant occupy a dwelling-house which is the home in which they cohabit or cohabited; but

(b) neither of them is entitled to remain in occupation—

(i) by virtue of a beneficial estate or interest or contract; or

(ii) by virtue of any enactment giving him the right to remain in occupation.

(2) Either of the parties may apply to the court for an order against the other under this section.

(3) An order under this section may—

(a) require the respondent to permit the applicant to enter and remain in the dwelling-house or part of the dwelling-house;

(b) regulate the occupation of the dwelling-house by either or both of the parties;

(c) require the respondent to leave the dwelling-house or part of the dwelling-house; or

(d) exclude the respondent from a defined area in which the dwelling-house is included.

(4) In deciding whether to exercise its powers to include one or more of the provisions referred to in subsection (3) ('a subsection (3) provision') and (if so) in what manner, the court shall have regard to all the circumstances including—

(a) the housing needs and housing resources of each of the parties and of any relevant child;

(b) the financial resources of each of the parties;

(c) the likely effect of any order, or of any decision by the court not to exercise its powers under subsection (3), on the health, safety or well-being of the parties and of any relevant child;

(d) the conduct of the parties in relation to each other and otherwise; and

(e) the questions mentioned in subsection (5).

(5) The questions are—

(a) whether the applicant or any relevant child is likely to suffer significant harm attributable to conduct of the respondent if the subsection (3) provision is not included in the order; and

(b) whether the harm likely to be suffered by the respondent or child if the provision is included is as great as or greater than the harm attributable to conduct of the respondent which is likely to be suffered by the applicant or child if the provision is not included.

(6) An order under this section shall be limited so as to have effect for a specified period not exceeding six months, but may be extended on one occasion for a further specified period not exceeding six months.

39 Supplementary provisions

(1) In this Part an 'occupation order' means an order under section 33, 35, 36, 37 or 38.

(2) An application for an occupation order may be made in other family proceedings or without any other family proceedings being instituted.

(3) If—

(a) an application for an occupation order is made under section 33, 35, 36, 37 or 38, and

(b) the court considers that it has no power to make the order under the section concerned, but that it has power to make an order under one of the other sections,

the court may make an order under that other section.

(4) The fact that a person has applied for an occupation order under sections 35 to 38, or that an occupation order has been made, does not affect the right of any person to claim a legal or equitable interest in any property in any subsequent proceedings (including subsequent proceedings under this Part).

40 Additional provisions that may be included in certain occupation orders

(1) The court may on, or at any time after, making an occupation order under section 33, 35 or 36—

(a) impose on either party obligations as to—

(i) the repair and maintenance of the dwelling-house; or

(ii) the discharge of rent, mortgage payments or other outgoings affecting the dwelling-house;

(b) order a party occupying the dwelling-house or any part of it (including a party who is entitled to do so by virtue of a beneficial estate or interest or contract or by virtue of any enactment giving him the right to remain in occupation) to make periodical payments to the other party in respect of the accommodation, if the other party would (but for the order) be entitled to occupy the dwelling-house by virtue of a beneficial estate or interest or contract or by virtue of any such enactment;

(c) grant either party possession or use of furniture or other contents of the dwelling-house;

(d) order either party to take reasonable care of any furniture or other contents of the dwelling-house;

(e) order either party to take reasonable steps to keep the dwelling-house and any furniture or other contents secure.

(2) In deciding whether and, if so, how to exercise its powers under this section, the court shall have regard to all the circumstances of the case including—

(a) the financial needs and financial resources of the parties; and

(b) the financial obligations which they have, or are likely to have in the foreseeable future, including financial obligations to each other and to any relevant child.

(3) An order under this section ceases to have effect when the occupation order to which it relates ceases to have effect.

42 Non-molestation orders

(1) In this Part a 'non-molestation order' means an order containing either or both of the following provisions—

(a) provision prohibiting a person ('the respondent') from molesting another person who is associated with the respondent;

(b) provision prohibiting the respondent from molesting a relevant child.

(2) The court may make a non-molestation order—

(a) if an application for the order has been made (whether in other family proceedings or without any other family proceedings being instituted) by a person who is associated with the respondent; or

(b) if in any family proceedings to which the respondent is a party the court considers that the order should be made for the benefit of any other party to the proceedings or any relevant child even though no such application has been made.

(3) In subsection (2) 'family proceedings' includes proceedings in which the court has made an emergency protection order under section 44 of the Children Act 1989 which includes an exclusion requirement (as defined in section 44A(3) of that Act).

(4) Where an agreement to marry is terminated, no application under subsection (2)(a) may be made by virtue of section 62(3)(e) by reference to that agreement after the end of the period of three years beginning with the day on which it is terminated.

(4A) A court considering whether to make an occupation order shall also consider whether to exercise the power conferred by subsection (2)(b).

(4B) In this Part 'the applicant', in relation to a non-molestation order, includes (where the context permits) the person for whose benefit such an order would be or is made in exercise of the power conferred by subsection (2)(b).

(5) In deciding whether to exercise its powers under this section and, if so, in what manner, the court shall have regard to all the circumstances including the need to secure the health, safety and well-being—

(a) of the applicant . . .; and

(b) of any relevant child.

(6) A non-molestation order may be expressed so as to refer to molestation in general, to particular acts of molestation, or to both.

(7) A non-molestation order may be made for a specified period or until further order.

(8) A non-molestation order which is made in other family proceedings ceases to have effect if those proceedings are withdrawn or dismissed.

42A Offence of breaching non-molestation order

(1) A person who without reasonable excuse does anything that he is prohibited from doing by a non-molestation order is guilty of an offence.

(2) In the case of a non-molestation order made by virtue of section 45(1), a person can be guilty of an offence under this section only in respect of conduct engaged in at a time when he was aware of the existence of the order.

(3) Where a person is convicted of an offence under this section in respect of any conduct, that conduct is not punishable as a contempt of court.

(4) A person cannot be convicted of an offence under this section in respect of any conduct which has been punished as a contempt of court.

(5) A person guilty of an offence under this section is liable—

(a) on conviction on indictment, to imprisonment for a term not exceeding five years, or a fine, or both;

(b) on summary conviction, to imprisonment for a term not exceeding 12 months, or a fine not exceeding the statutory maximum, or both.

(6) A reference in any enactment to proceedings under this Part, or to an order under this Part, does not include a reference to proceedings for an offence under this section or to an order made in such proceedings.

45 Ex parte orders

(1) The court may, in any case where it considers that it is just and convenient to do so, make an occupation order or a non-molestation order even though the respondent has not been given such notice of the proceedings as would otherwise be required by rules of court.

(2) In determining whether to exercise its powers under subsection (1), the court shall have regard to all the circumstances including—

(a) any risk of significant harm to the applicant or a relevant child, attributable to conduct of the respondent, if the order is not made immediately;

(b) whether it is likely that the applicant will be deterred or prevented from pursuing the application if an order is not made immediately; and

(c) whether there is reason to believe that the respondent is aware of the proceedings but is deliberately evading service and that the applicant or a relevant child will be seriously prejudiced by the delay involved—

(i) where the court is a magistrates' court, in effecting service of proceedings; or

(ii) in any other case, in effecting substituted service.

(3) If the court makes an order by virtue of subsection (1) it must afford the respondent an opportunity to make representations relating to the order as soon as just and convenient at a full hearing.

(4) If, at a full hearing, the court makes an occupation order ('the full order'), then—

(a) for the purposes of calculating the maximum period for which the full order may be made to have effect, the relevant section is to apply as if the period for which the full order will have effect began on the date on which the initial order first had effect; and

(b) the provisions of section 36(10) or 38(6) as to the extension of orders are to apply as if the full order and the initial order were a single order.

(5) In this section—

'full hearing' means a hearing of which notice has been given to all the parties in accordance with rules of court;

'initial order' means an occupation order made by virtue of subsection (1); and

'relevant section' means section 33(10), 35(10), 36(10), 37(5) or 38(6).

46 Undertakings

(1) In any case where the court has power to make an occupation order or non-molestation order, the court may accept an undertaking from any party to the proceedings.

(2) No power of arrest may be attached to any undertaking given under subsection (1).

(3) The court shall not accept an undertaking under subsection (1) instead of making an occupation order in any case where apart from this section a power of arrest would be attached to the order.

(3A) The court shall not accept an undertaking under subsection (1) instead of making a non-molestation order in any case where it appears to the court that—

(a) the respondent has used or threatened violence against the applicant or a relevant child; and

(b) for the protection of the applicant or child it is necessary to make a non-molestation order so that any breach may be punishable under section 42A.

(4) An undertaking given to a court under subsection (1) is enforceable as if the court had made an occupation order or a non-molestation order in terms corresponding to those of the undertaking.

(5) This section has effect without prejudice to the powers of the High Court and the county court apart from this section.

47 Arrest for breach of order

(2) If—

(a) the court makes an occupation order; and

(b) it appears to the court that the respondent has used or threatened violence against the applicant or a relevant child,

it shall attach a power of arrest to one or more provisions of the order unless the court is satisfied that in all the circumstances of the case the applicant or child will be adequately protected without such a power of arrest.

(3) Subsection (2) does not apply in any case where the occupation order is made by virtue of section 45(1), but in such a case the court may attach a power of arrest to one or more provisions of the order if it appears to it—

(a) that the respondent has used or threatened violence against the applicant or a relevant child; and

(b) that there is a risk of significant harm to the applicant or child, attributable to conduct of the respondent, if the power of arrest is not attached to those provisions immediately.

(4) If, by virtue of subsection (3), the court attaches a power of arrest to any provisions of an occupation order, it may provide that the power of arrest is to have effect for a shorter period than the other provisions of the order.

(5) Any period specified for the purposes of subsection (4) may be extended by the court (on one or more occasions) on an application to vary or discharge the occupation order.

(6) If, by virtue of subsection (2) or (3), a power of arrest is attached to certain provisions of an order, a constable may arrest without warrant a person whom he has reasonable cause for suspecting to be in breach of any such provision.

(7) If a power of arrest is attached under subsection (2) or (3) to certain provisions of the order and the respondent is arrested under subsection (6)—

(a) he must be brought before the relevant judicial authority within the period of 24 hours beginning at the time of his arrest; and

(b) if the matter is not then disposed of forthwith, the relevant judicial authority before whom he is brought may remand him.

In reckoning for the purposes of this subsection any period of 24 hours, no account is to be taken of Christmas Day, Good Friday or any Sunday.

(8) If the court—

(a) has made a non-molestation order, or

(b) has made an occupation order but has not attached a power of arrest under subsection (2) or (3) to any provision of the order, or has attached that power only to certain provisions of the order,

then, if at any time the applicant considers that the respondent has failed to comply with the order, he may apply to the relevant judicial authority for the issue of a warrant for the arrest of the respondent.

(9) The relevant judicial authority shall not issue a warrant on an application under subsection (8) unless—

(a) the application is substantiated on oath; and

(b) the relevant judicial authority has reasonable grounds for believing that the respondent has failed to comply with the order.

(10) If a person is brought before a court by virtue of a warrant issued under subsection (9) and the court does not dispose of the matter forthwith, the court may remand him.

(11) Schedule 5 (which makes provision corresponding to that applying in magistrates' courts in civil cases under sections 128 and 129 of the Magistrates' Courts Act 1980) has effect in relation to the powers of the High Court and a county court to remand a person by virtue of this section.

(12) If a person remanded under this section is granted bail (whether in the High Court or a county court under Schedule 5 or in a magistrates' court under section 128 or 129 of the Magistrates' Courts Act 1980), he may be required by the relevant judicial authority to comply, before release on bail or later, with such requirements as appear to that authority to be necessary to secure that he does not interfere with witnesses or otherwise obstruct the course of justice.

62 Meaning of 'cohabitants', 'relevant child' and 'associated persons'

(1) For the purposes of this Part—

(a) 'cohabitants' are two persons who are neither married to each other nor civil partners of each other but are living together as husband and wife or as if they were civil partners; and

(b) 'cohabit' and 'former cohabitants' are to be read accordingly, but the latter expression does not include cohabitants who have subsequently married each other or become civil partners of each other.

(2) In this Part, 'relevant child', in relation to any proceedings under this Part, means—

(a) any child who is living with or might reasonably be expected to live with either party to the proceedings;

(b) any child in relation to whom an order under the Adoption Act 1976, the Adoption and Children Act 2002 or the Children Act 1989 is in question in the proceedings; and

(c) any other child whose interests the court considers relevant.

(3) For the purposes of this Part, a person is associated with another person if—

(a) they are or have been married to each other;

(aa) they are or have been civil partners of each other;

(b) they are cohabitants or former cohabitants;

(c) they live or have lived in the same household, otherwise than merely by reason of one of them being the other's employee, tenant, lodger or boarder;

(d) they are relatives;

(e) they have agreed to marry one another (whether or not that agreement has been terminated);

(eza) they have entered into a civil partnership agreement (as defined by section 73 of the Civil Partnership Act 2004) (whether or not that agreement has been terminated);

(ea) they have or have had an intimate personal relationship with each other which is or was of significant duration;

(f) in relation to any child, they are both persons falling within subsection (4); or

(g) they are parties to the same family proceedings (other than proceedings under this Part).

(4) A person falls within this subsection in relation to a child if—

(a) he is a parent of the child; or

(b) he has or has had parental responsibility for the child.

(5) If a child has been adopted or falls within subsection (7), two persons are also associated with each other for the purpose of this Part if—

(a) one is a natural parent of the child or a parent of such a natural parent; and

(b) the other is the child or any person—

(i) who has become a parent of the child by virtue of an adoption order or has applied for an adoption order, or

(ii) with whom the child has at any time been placed for adoption.

(6) A body corporate and another person are not, by virtue of subsection (3)(f) or (g), to be regarded for the purposes of this Part as associated with each other.

(7) A child falls within this section if—

(a) an adoption agency, within the meaning of section 2 of the Adoption and Children Act 2002, has power to place him for adoption under section 19 of that Act (placing children with parental consent) or he has become the subject of an order under section 21 of that Act (placement orders); or

(b) he is freed for adoption by virtue of an order made—

(i) in England and Wales, under section 18 of the Adoption Act 1976,

(ii) . . .

(iii) in Northern Ireland, under Article 17(1) or 18(1) of the Adoption (Northern Ireland) Order 1987, or

(c) he is the subject of a Scottish permanence order which includes provision granting authority to adopt.

(8) In subsection (7)(c) 'Scottish permanence order' means a permanence order under section 80 of the Adoption and Children (Scotland) Act 2007 (asp 4) (including a deemed permanence order having effect by virtue of article 13(1), 14(2), 17(1) or 19(2) of the Adoption and Children (Scotland) Act 2007 (Commencement No. 4, Transitional and Savings Provisions) Order 2009 (SSI 2009/267)).

(H) Trusts of Land and Appointment of Trustees Act 1996

14 Applications for order

(1) Any person who is a trustee of land or has an interest in property subject to a trust of land may make an application to the court for an order under this section.

(2) On an application for an order under this section the court may make any such order—

(a) relating to the exercise by the trustees of any of their functions (including an order relieving them of any obligation to obtain the consent of, or to consult, any person in connection with the exercise of any of their functions), or

(b) declaring the nature or extent of a person's interest in property subject to the trust,

as the court thinks fit.

(3) The court may not under this section make any order as to the appointment or removal of trustees.

(4) The powers conferred on the court by this section are exercisable on an application whether it is made before or after the commencement of this Act.

15 Matters relevant in determining applications

(1) The matters to which the court is to have regard in determining an application for an order under section 14 include—

(a) the intentions of the person or persons (if any) who created the trust,

(b) the purposes for which the property subject to the trust is held,

(c) the welfare of any minor who occupies or might reasonably be expected to occupy any land subject to the trust as his home, and

(d) the interests of any secured creditor of any beneficiary.

(2) In the case of an application relating to the exercise in relation to any land of the powers conferred on the trustees by section 13, the matters to which the court is to have regard also include the circumstances and wishes of each of the beneficiaries who is (or apart from any previous exercise by the trustees of those powers would be) entitled to occupy the land under section 12.

(3) In the case of any other application, other than one relating to the exercise of the power mentioned in section 6(2), the matters to which the court is to have regard also include the circumstances and wishes of any beneficiaries of full age and entitled to an interest in possession in property subject to the trust or (in case of dispute) of the majority (according to the value of their combined interests).

(4) This section does not apply to an application if section 335A of the Insolvency Act 1986 (which is inserted by Schedule 3 and relates to applications by a trustee of a bankrupt) applies to it.

(I) Family Procedure Rules 2010 (SI 2010/2955)

Part 1
Overriding Objective

1.1 The overriding objective

(1) These rules are a new procedural code with the overriding objective of enabling the court to deal with cases justly, having regard to any welfare issues involved.

(2) Dealing with a case justly includes, so far as is practicable—

- (a) ensuring that it is dealt with expeditiously and fairly;
- (b) dealing with the case in ways which are proportionate to the nature, importance and complexity of the issues;
- (c) ensuring that the parties are on an equal footing;
- (d) saving expense; and
- (e) allotting to it an appropriate share of the court's resources, while taking into account the need to allot resources to other cases.

1.2 Application by the court of the overriding objective

The court must seek to give effect to the overriding objective when it—

(a) exercises any power given to it by these rules; or

(b) interprets any rule.

1.3 Duty of the parties

The parties are required to help the court to further the overriding objective.

1.4 Court's duty to manage cases

(1) The court must further the overriding objective by actively managing cases.

(2) Active case management includes—

- (a) encouraging the parties to co-operate with each other in the conduct of the proceedings;
- (b) identifying at an early stage—
  - (i) the issues; and
  - (ii) who should be a party to the proceedings;
- (c) deciding promptly—
  - (i) which issues need full investigation and hearing and which do not; and
  - (ii) the procedure to be followed in the case;
- (d) deciding the order in which issues are to be resolved;
- (e) encouraging the parties to use an alternative dispute resolution procedure if the court considers that appropriate and facilitating the use of such procedure;
- (f) helping the parties to settle the whole or part of the case;
- (g) fixing timetables or otherwise controlling the progress of the case;
- (h) considering whether the likely benefits of taking a particular step justify the cost of taking it;
- (i) dealing with as many aspects of the case as it can on the same occasion;
- (j) dealing with the case without the parties needing to attend at court;
- (k) making use of technology; and
- (l) giving directions to ensure that the case proceeds quickly and efficiently.

Part 3
Alternative Dispute Resolution: the Court's Powers

3.1 Scope of this Part

(1) This Part contains the court's powers to encourage the parties to use alternative dispute resolution and to facilitate its use.

(2) The powers in this Part are subject to any powers given to the court by any other rule or practice direction or by any other enactment or any powers it may otherwise have.

3.2 Court's duty to consider alternative dispute resolution

The court must consider, at every stage in proceedings, whether alternative dispute resolution is appropriate.

3.3 When the court will adjourn proceedings or a hearing in proceedings

(1) If the court considers that alternative dispute resolution is appropriate, the court may direct that the proceedings, or a hearing in the proceedings, be adjourned for such specified period as it considers appropriate—

  (a) to enable the parties to obtain information and advice about alternative dispute resolution; and

  (b) where the parties agree, to enable alternative dispute resolution to take place.

(2) The court may give directions under this rule on an application or of its own initiative.

(3) Where the court directs an adjournment under this rule, it will give directions about the timing and method by which the parties must tell the court if any of the issues in the proceedings have been resolved.

(4) If the parties do not tell the court if any of the issues have been resolved as directed under paragraph (3), the court will give such directions as to the management of the case as it considers appropriate.

(5) The court or court officer will—

  (a) record the making of an order under this rule; and

  (b) arrange for a copy of the order to be served as soon as practicable on the parties.

  (6) Where the court proposes to exercise its powers of its own initiative, the procedure set out in rule 4.3(2) to (6) applies.

(By rule 4.1(7), any direction given under this rule may be varied or revoked.)

PRACTICE DIRECTION 3A

PRE-APPLICATION PROTOCOL FOR MEDIATION INFORMATION AND ASSESSMENT

This Practice Direction supplements FPR Part 3

Introduction

1.1 This Practice Direction applies where a person is considering applying for an order in family proceedings of a type specified in Annex B (referred to in this Direction as 'relevant family proceedings').

1.2 Terms used in this Practice Direction and the accompanying Pre-action Protocol have the same meaning as in the FPR.

1.3 This Practice Direction is supplemented by the following Annexes—

  (i) Annex A: The Pre-application Protocol ('the Protocol'), which sets out steps which the court will normally expect an applicant to follow before an application is made to the court in relevant family proceedings;

(ii) Annex B: Proceedings which are 'relevant family proceedings' for the purposes of this Practice Direction; and

(iii) Annex C: Circumstances in which attendance at a Mediation Information and Assessment Meeting is not expected.

Aims

2.1 The purpose of this Practice Direction and the accompanying Protocol is to—

(a) supplement the court's powers in Part 3 of the FPR to encourage and facilitate the use of alternative dispute resolution;

(b) set out good practice to be followed by any person who is considering making an application to court for an order in relevant family proceedings; and

(c) ensure, as far as possible, that all parties have considered mediation as an alternative means of resolving their disputes.

Rationale

3.1 There is a general acknowledgement that an adversarial court process is not always best-suited to the resolution of family disputes, particularly private law disputes between parents relating to children, with such disputes often best resolved through discussion and agreement, where that can be managed safely and appropriately.

3.2 Litigants who seek public funding for certain types of family proceedings are (subject to some exceptions) already required to attend a meeting with a mediator as a pre-condition of receiving public funding.

3.3 There is growing recognition of the benefits of early information and advice about mediation and of the need for those wishing to make an application to court, whether publicly-funded or otherwise, to consider alternative means of resolving their disputes, as appropriate.

3.4 In private law proceedings relating to children, the court is actively involved in helping parties to explore ways of resolving their dispute. The Private Law Programme, set out in Practice Direction 12B, provides for a first hearing dispute resolution appointment ('FHDRA'), at which the judge, legal advisor or magistrates, accompanied by an officer from Cafcass (the Children and Family Court Advisory and Support Service), will discuss with parties both the nature of their dispute and whether it could be resolved by mediation or other alternative means and can give the parties information about services which may be available to assist them. The court should also have information obtained through safeguarding checks carried out by Cafcass, to ensure that any agreement between the parties, or any dispute resolution process selected, is in the interests of the child and safe for all concerned.

3.5 Against that background, it is likely to save court time and expense if the parties take steps to resolve their dispute without pursuing court proceedings. Parties will therefore be expected to explore the scope for resolving their dispute through mediation before embarking on the court process.

The Pre-application Protocol

4.1 To encourage this approach, all potential applicants for a court order in relevant family proceedings will be expected, before making their application, to have followed the steps set out in the Protocol. This requires a potential applicant except in certain specified circumstances, to consider with a mediator whether the dispute may be capable of being resolved through mediation. The court will expect all applicants to have complied with the Protocol before commencing proceedings and (except where any of the circumstances in Annex C applies) will expect any respondent to have attended a Mediation Information and Assessment Meeting, if invited to do so. If court proceedings are taken, the court will wish to know at the first hearing whether mediation has been considered by the parties. In considering the conduct of any relevant family proceedings, the court will take into account any failure to comply with the Protocol and may refer the parties to a meeting with a mediator before the proceedings continue further.

4.2 Nothing in the Protocol is to be read as affecting the operation of the Private Law Programme, set out in Practice Direction 12B, or the role of the court at the first hearing in any relevant family proceedings.

Annex A
The Pre-application Protocol

1. This Protocol applies where a person ('the applicant') is considering making an application to the court for an order in relevant family proceedings.

2. Before an applicant makes an application to the court for an order in relevant family proceedings, the applicant (or the applicant's legal representative) should contact a family mediator to arrange for the applicant to attend an information meeting about family mediation and other forms of alternative dispute resolution (referred to in this Protocol as 'a Mediation Information and Assessment Meeting').

3. An applicant is not expected to attend a Mediation Information and Assessment Meeting where any of the circumstances set out in Annex C applies.

4. Information on how to find a family mediator may be obtained from local family courts, from the Community Legal Advice Helpline – CLA Direct (0845 345 4345) or at www.direct.gov.uk.

5. The applicant (or the applicant's legal representative) should provide the mediator with contact details for the other party or parties to the dispute ('the respondent(s)'), so that the mediator can contact the respondent(s) to discuss that part"s willingness and availability to attend a Mediation Information and Assessment Meeting.

6. The applicant should then attend a Mediation Information and Assessment Meeting arranged by the mediator. If the parties are willing to attend Together, the meeting may be conducted jointly, but where necessary separate meetings may be held. If the applicant and respondent(s) do not attend a joint meeting, the mediator will invite the respondent(s) to a separate meeting unless any of the circumstances set out in Annex C applies.

7. A mediator who arranges a Mediation Information and Assessment Meeting with one or more parties to a dispute should consider with the party or parties concerned whether public funding may be available to meet the cost of the meeting and any subsequent mediation. Where none of the parties is eligible for, or wishes to seek, public funding, any charge made by the mediator for the Mediation Information and Assessment Meeting will be the responsibility of the party or parties attending, in accordance with any agreement made with the mediator.

8. If the applicant then makes an application to the court in respect of the dispute, the applicant should at the same time file a completed Family Mediation Information and Assessment Form (Form FM1) confirming attendance at a Mediation Information and Assessment Meeting or giving the reasons for not attending.

9. The Form FM1, must be completed and signed by the mediator, and countersigned by the applicant or the applicant's legal representative, where either—

   (a) the applicant has attended a Mediation Information and Assessment Meeting; or

   (b) the applicant has not attended a Mediation Information and Assessment Meeting and

(i) the mediator is satisfied that mediation is not suitable because another party to the dispute is unwilling to attend a Mediation Information and Assessment Meeting and consider mediation;

(ii) the mediator determines that the case is not suitable for a Mediation Information and Assessment Meeting; or

(iii) a mediator has made a determination within the previous four months that the case is not suitable for a Mediation Information and Assessment Meeting or for mediation.

10. In all other circumstances, the Form FM1 must be completed and signed by the applicant or the applicant's legal representative.

11. The form may be obtained from magistrates' courts, county courts or the High Court or from www.direct.gov.uk.

Annex B
Proceedings which are 'relevant family proceedings' for the purposes of this Practice Direction

1. Private law proceedings relating to children, except—
   - proceedings for an enforcement order, a financial compensation order or an order under paragraph 9 or Part 2 of Schedule Al to the Children Act 1989;
   - any other proceedings for enforcement of an order made in private law proceedings; or
   - where emergency proceedings have been brought in respect of the same child(ren) and have not been determined.

   ('Private law proceedings' and 'emergency proceedings' are defined in Rule 12.2)

2. Proceedings for a financial remedy, except—
   - Proceedings for an avoidance of disposition order or an order preventing a disposition;
   - Proceedings for enforcement of any order made in financial remedy proceedings.

   ('Financial remedy' is defined in Rule 2.3(1) and 'avoidance of disposition order' and 'order preventing a disposition' are defined in Rule 9.3(1))

Annex C
A person considering making an application to the court in relevant family proceedings is not expected to attend a Mediation Information and Assessment Meeting before doing so if any of the following circumstances applies:

1. The mediator is satisfied that mediation is not suitable because another party to the dispute is unwilling to attend a Mediation Information and Assessment Meeting and consider mediation.
2. The mediator determines that the case is not suitable for a Mediation Information and Assessment Meeting.
3. A mediator has made a determination within the previous four months that the case is not suitable for a Mediation Information and Assessment Meeting or for mediation.

Domestic abuse

4. Any party has, to the applicant's knowledge, made an allegation of domestic Violence against another party and this has resulted in a police investigation or the issuing of civil proceedings for the protection of any party within the last 12 months.

Bankruptcy

5. The dispute concerns financial issues and the applicant or another party is bankrupt.
6. The parties are in agreement and there is no dispute to mediate.
7. The whereabouts of the other party are unknown to the applicant.
8. The prospective application is for an order in relevant family proceedings which are already in existence and are continuing.
9. The prospective application is to be made without notice to the other party.

Urgency

10. The prospective application is urgent, meaning—
    (a) there is a risk to the life, liberty or physical safety of the applicant or his or her family or his or her home; or
    (b) any delay caused by attending a Mediation Information and Assessment Meeting would cause a risk of significant harm to a child, a significant risk of a miscarriage of justice, unreasonable hardship to the applicant or irretrievable problems in dealing with the dispute (such as an irretrievable loss of significant evidence).
11. There is current social services involvement as a result of child protection concerns in respect of any child who would be the subject of the prospective application.
12. A child would be a party to the prospective application by virtue of Rule 12.3(1).
13. The applicant (or the applicant's legal representative) contacts three mediators within 15 miles of the applicant's home and none is able to conduct a Mediation Information and Assessment Meeting within 15 working days of the date of contact.

Family Procedure Rules 2010 (SI 2010/2955)

Part 7
Procedure for Applications in Matrimonial and Civil Partnership Proceedings

Chapter 2
Rules about Starting and Responding to Proceedings

7.8 Service of application

(1) After an application for a matrimonial or civil partnership order has been issued by the court, a copy of it must be served on the respondent and on any co-respondent.

(Rule 6.4 provides for who may serve an application for a matrimonial or civil partnership order.)

(2) When the application is served on a respondent it must be accompanied by—
- (a) a form for acknowledging service;
- (b) a notice of proceedings; and
- (c) where applicable, a copy of the statement of arrangements for children.

7.12 What the respondent and co-respondent should do on receiving the application

(1) The respondent, and any co-respondent, must file an acknowledgment of service within 7 days beginning with the date on which the application for a matrimonial or civil partnership order was served.

(2) This rule is subject to rule 6.42 (which specifies how the period for filing an acknowledgment of service is calculated where the application is served out of the jurisdiction).

(3) The acknowledgment of service must—

(a) subject to paragraph (4), be signed by the respondent or the respondent's legal representative or, as the case may be, the co respondent or the co respondent's legal representative;

(b) include the respondent's or, as the case may be, the co respondent's address for service; and

(c) where it is filed by the respondent, indicate whether or not the respondent intends to defend the case.

(4) Where paragraph (5) or (6) applies, the respondent must sign the acknowledgment of service personally.

(5) This paragraph applies where—

(a) the application for a matrimonial order alleges that the respondent has committed adultery; and

(b) the respondent admits the adultery.

(6) This paragraph applies where—

(a) the application for a matrimonial or civil partnership order alleges that the parties to the marriage or civil partnership concerned have been separated for more than 2 years; and

(b) the respondent consents to the making of the matrimonial or civil partnership order.

(7) Where the respondent does not agree with the proposals set out in the applicant's statement of arrangements for children, the respondent may file a statement of arrangements for children under section 41(1) of the 1973 Act or section 63(1) of the 2004 Act.

(8) A respondent who wishes to defend the case must file and serve an answer within 21 days beginning with the date by which the acknowledgment of service is required to be filed.

(9) An answer is not required where the respondent does not object to the making of the matrimonial or civil partnership order but objects to paying the costs of the application or to the applicant's statement of arrangements for children.

(10) A respondent may file an answer even if the intention to do so was not indicated in the acknowledgment of service.

(11) Where the application is for nullity of marriage under section 12(d) of the 1973 Act or for nullity of civil partnership under section 50(1)(b) of the 2004 Act and the respondent files an answer containing no more than a simple denial of the facts stated in the application, the respondent must, if intending to rebut the matters stated in the application, give notice to the court of that intention when filing the answer.

(12) A respondent to an application for a matrimonial or civil partnership order alleging 2 years' separation and the respondent's consent may—

(a) indicate consent to the making of the matrimonial or civil partnership order in writing at any time after service of the application, whether in the acknowledgment of service or otherwise;

(b) indicate lack of consent to the making of that order, or withdraw any such consent already given, by giving notice to the court.

(13) Where a respondent gives a notice under paragraph (12)(b) and no other relevant fact is alleged, the proceedings must be stayed[(GL)], and notice of the stay[(GL)] given to the parties by the court officer.

(14) In this rule, a 'relevant fact' is—

(a) in matrimonial proceedings, one of the facts mentioned in section (1)(2) of the 1973 Act; and

(b) in civil partnership proceedings, one of the facts mentioned in section 44(5) of the 2004 Act.

(The form of the answer is referred to in Practice Direction 5A.)

Chapter 3
How the Court Determines Matrimonial and Civil Partnership Proceedings

7.20 What the court will do on an application for a decree nisi, a conditional order, a decree of judicial separation or a separation order

(1) This rule applies where an application is made under rule 7.19.

(2) If at the relevant time the case is an undefended case, the court must—

(a) if satisfied that the applicant is entitled to—

(i) in matrimonial proceedings, a decree nisi or a decree of judicial separation (as the case may be); or

(ii) in civil partnership proceedings, a conditional order or a separation order (as the case may be),

so certify and direct that the application be listed before a district judge for the making of the decree or order at the next available date;

(b) if not so satisfied, direct—

(i) that any party to the proceedings provide such further information, or take such other steps, as the court may specify; or

(ii) that the case be listed for a case management hearing.

(3) If the applicant has applied for costs, the court may, on making a direction under paragraph (2)(a)—

(a) if satisfied that the applicant is entitled to an order for costs, so certify; or

(b) if not so satisfied, make no direction about costs.

(4) If at the relevant time the case is a defended case, the court must direct that the case be listed for a case management hearing.

(5) The court may, when giving a direction under paragraph (2)(b), direct that the further information provided be verified by an affidavit.

(6) The court must not give directions under this rule unless at the relevant time it is satisfied—

(a) that a copy of each application for a matrimonial or civil partnership order or answer (including any amended application or answer) has been properly served on each party on whom it is required to be served; and

(b) that—

(i) in matrimonial proceedings, the application for a decree nisi or a decree of judicial separation; or

(ii) in civil partnership proceedings, the application for a conditional order or separation order,

was made at a time permitted by rule 7.19(1).

(7) In this rule, 'the relevant time' means the time at which the court is considering an application made under rule 7.19(1).

Chapter 4
Court Orders

7.32 Making decrees nisi absolute or conditional orders final by giving notice

(1) Unless rule 7.33 applies—

(a) in matrimonial proceedings, a spouse in whose favour a decree nisi has been made may give notice to the court that he or she wishes the decree nisi to be made absolute; or

(b) in civil partnership proceedings, a civil partner in whose favour a conditional order has been made may give notice to the court that he or she wishes the conditional order to be made final.

(2) Subject to paragraphs (3) and (4), where the court receives a notice under paragraph (1) it will make the decree nisi absolute or the conditional order final (as the case may be) if it is satisfied that—

(a) no application for rescission of the decree nisi or the conditional order is pending;

(b) no appeal against the making of the decree nisi or the conditional order is pending;

(c) no order has been made by the court extending the time for bringing an appeal of the kind mentioned in sub-paragraph (b), or if such an order has been made, that the time so extended has expired;

(d) no application for an order of the kind mentioned in sub-paragraph (c) is pending;

(e) no application to prevent the decree nisi being made absolute or the conditional order being made final is pending;

(f) the court has complied with section 41(1) of the 1973 Act or section 63(1) of the 2004 Act, as the case may be, and has not given any direction under subsection (2) of either of those sections;

(g) the provisions of section 10(2) to (4) of the 1973 Act or section 48(2) to (4) of the 2004 Act do not apply or have been complied with;

(h) any order under section 10A(2) of the 1973 Act has been complied with; and

(i) where the decree nisi was made on the ground in section 12(g) of, or paragraph 11(1)(e) of Schedule 1 to, the 1973 Act, or the conditional order was made under section 50(1)(d) of the 2004 Act—

(i) there is not pending a reference under section 8(5) of the Gender Recognition Act 2004 in respect of the application on which the interim gender recognition certificate to which the application relates was granted;

(ii) that interim certificate has not been revoked under section 8(6)(b) of that Act; and

(iii) no appeal is pending against an order under section 8(6)(a) of that Act.

(3) Where the notice is received more than 12 months after the making of the decree nisi or the conditional order, it must be accompanied by an explanation in writing stating—

(a) why the application has not been made earlier;

(b) whether the applicant and respondent have lived together since the decree nisi or the conditional order was made, and, if so, between what dates;

(c) if the applicant is female, whether she has given birth to a child since the decree nisi or the conditional order was made and whether it is alleged that the child is or may be a child of the family;

(d) if the respondent is female, whether the applicant has reason to believe that she has given birth to a child since the decree nisi or the conditional order was made and whether it is alleged that the child is or may be a child of the family.

(4) Where paragraph (3) applies, the court may—

(a) require the applicant to file an affidavit verifying the explanation; and

(b) make such order on the application as it thinks fit, but where it orders the decree nisi to be made absolute or the conditional order to be made final that order is not to take effect until the court is satisfied that none of the matters mentioned in paragraph (2)(a) to (i) applies.

Part 9
Applications for a Financial Remedy

9.7 Application for interim orders

(1) A party may apply at any stage of the proceedings for—

(a) an order for maintenance pending suit;

(b) an order for maintenance pending outcome of proceedings;

(c) an order for interim periodical payments;

(d) an interim variation order; or

(e) any other form of interim order.

(2) The Part 18 procedure applies to an application for an interim order.

(3) Where a party makes an application before filing a financial statement, the written evidence in support must—

(a) explain why the order is necessary; and

(b) give up to date information about that party's financial circumstances.

(4) Unless the respondent has filed a financial statement, the respondent must, at least 7 days before the court is to deal with the application, file a statement of his means and serve a copy on the applicant.

(5) An application for an order mentioned in paragraph (1)(e) may be made without notice.

9.12 Duties of the court and the applicant upon issuing an application

(1) When an application under this Part is issued in the High Court or in a county court—

(a) the court will fix a first appointment not less than 12 weeks and not more than 16 weeks after the date of the filing of the application; and

(b) subject to paragraph (2), within 4 days beginning with the date on which the application was filed, a court officer will—

(i) serve a copy of the application on the respondent; and

(ii) give notice of the date of the first appointment to the applicant and the respondent.

(2) Where the applicant wishes to serve a copy of the application on the respondent and on filing the application so notifies the court—

(a) paragraph (1)(b) does not apply;

(b) a court officer will return to the applicant the copy of the application and the notice of the date of the first appointment; and

(c) the applicant must,—

(i) within 4 days beginning with the date on which the copy of the application is received from the court, serve the copy of the application and notice of the date of the first appointment on the respondent; and

(ii) file a certificate of service at or before the first appointment.

(Rule 6.37 sets out what must be included in a certificate of service.)

(3) The date fixed under paragraph (1), or for any subsequent appointment, must not be cancelled except with the court's permission and, if cancelled, the court must immediately fix a new date.

(4) In relation to an application to which the Maintenance Regulation applies, where the applicant does not already know the address of the respondent at the time the application is issued, paragraph (2) does not apply and the court will serve the application in accordance with paragraph (1).

9.13 Service of application on mortgagees, trustees etc

(1) Where an application for a financial remedy includes an application for an order for a variation of settlement, the applicant must serve copies of the application on—

(a) the trustees of the settlement;

(b) the settlor if living; and

(c) such other persons as the court directs.

(2) In the case of an application for an avoidance of disposition order, the applicant must serve copies of the application on the person in whose favour the disposition is alleged to have been made.

(3) Where an application for a financial remedy includes an application relating to land, the applicant must serve a copy of the application on any mortgagee of whom particulars are given in the application.

(4) Any person served under paragraphs (1), (2) or (3) may make a request to the court in writing, within 14 days beginning with the date of service of the application, for a copy of the applicant's financial statement or any relevant part of that statement.

(5) Any person who—

(a) is served with copies of the application in accordance with paragraphs (1), (2) or (3); or

(b) receives a copy of a financial statement, or a relevant part of that statement, following an application made under paragraph (4),

may within 14 days beginning with the date of service or receipt file a statement in answer.

(6) Where a copy of an application is served under paragraphs (1), (2) or (3), the applicant must file a certificate of service at or before the first appointment.

(7) A statement in answer filed under paragraph (5) must be verified by a statement of truth.

9.14 Procedure before the first appointment

(1) Not less than 35 days before the first appointment both parties must simultaneously exchange with each other and file with the court a financial statement in the form referred to in Practice Direction 5A.

(2) The financial statement must—

(a) be verified by an affidavit; and

(b) accompanied by the following documents only—

(i) any documents required by the financial statement;

(ii) any other documents necessary to explain or clarify any of the information contained in the financial statement; and

(iii) any documents provided to the party producing the financial statement by a person responsible for a pension arrangement, either following a request under rule 9.30 or as part of a relevant valuation; and

(iv) any notification or other document referred to in rule 9.37(2), (4) or (5) which has been received by the party producing the financial statement.

(2A) Where the application is made under Article 56 of, using the form in Annex VII to, the Maintenance Regulation, and the relief sought is limited to relief of a type to which that Regulation applies, the requirement of paragraph (2)(a) relating to verification by affidavit does not apply.

(3) Where a party was unavoidably prevented from sending any document required by the financial statement, that party must at the earliest opportunity—

(a) serve a copy of that document on the other party; and

(b) file a copy of that document with the court, together with a written explanation of the failure to send it with the financial statement.

(4) No disclosure or inspection of documents may be requested or given between the filing of the application for a financial remedy and the first appointment, except—

(a) copies sent with the financial statement, or in accordance with paragraph (3); or

(b) in accordance with paragraphs (5) and (6).

(Rule 21.1 explains what is meant by disclosure and inspection.)

(5) Not less than 14 days before the hearing of the first appointment, each party must file with the court and serve on the other party—

(a) a concise statement of the issues between the parties;

(b) a chronology;

(c) a questionnaire setting out by reference to the concise statement of issues any further information and documents requested from the other party or a statement that no information and documents are required; and

(d) a notice stating whether that party will be in a position at the first appointment to proceed on that occasion to a FDR appointment.

(6) Not less than 14 days before the hearing of the first appointment, the applicant must file with the court and serve on the respondent confirmation—

(a) of the names of all persons served in accordance with rule 9.13(1) to (3); and

(b) that there are no other persons who must be served in accordance with those paragraphs.

9.15 Duties of the court at the first appointment

(1) The first appointment must be conducted with the objective of defining the issues and saving costs.

(2) At the first appointment the court must determine—

(a) the extent to which any questions seeking information under rule 9.14(5)(c) must be answered; and

(b) what documents requested under rule 9.14(5)(c) must be produced,

and give directions for the production of such further documents as may be necessary.

(3) The court must give directions where appropriate about—

(a) the valuation of assets (including the joint instruction of joint experts);

(b) obtaining and exchanging expert evidence, if required;

(c) the evidence to be adduced by each party; and

(d) further chronologies or schedules to be filed by each party.

(4) If the court decides that a referral to a FDR appointment is appropriate it must direct that the case be referred to a FDR appointment.

(5) If the court decides that a referral to a FDR appointment is not appropriate it must direct one or more of the following—

(a) that a further directions appointment be fixed;

(b) that an appointment be fixed for the making of an interim order;

(c) that the case be fixed for a final hearing and, where that direction is given, the court must determine the judicial level at which the case should be heard.

(By rule 3.3 the court may also direct that the case be adjourned if it considers that alternative dispute resolution is appropriate.)

(6) In considering whether to make a costs order under rule 28.3(5), the court must have particular regard to the extent to which each party has complied with the requirement to send documents with the financial statement and the explanation given for any failure to comply.

(7) The court may—

(a) where an application for an interim order has been listed for consideration at the first appointment, make an interim order;

(b) having regard to the contents of the notice filed by the parties under rule 9.14(5)(d), treat the appointment (or part of it) as a FDR appointment to which rule 9.17 applies;

(c) in a case where a pension sharing order or a pension attachment order is requested, direct any party with pension rights to file and serve a Pension Inquiry Form, completed in full or in part as the court may direct; and

(d) in a case where a pension compensation sharing order or a pension compensation attachment order is requested, direct any party with PPF compensation rights to file and serve a Pension Protection Fund Inquiry Form, completed in full or in part as the court may direct.

(8) Both parties must personally attend the first appointment unless the court directs otherwise.

9.16 After the first appointment

(1) Between the first appointment and the FDR appointment, a party is not entitled to the production of any further documents except—

(a) in accordance with directions given under rule 9.15(2); or

(b) with the permission of the court.

(2) At any stage—

(a) a party may apply for further directions or a FDR appointment;

(b) the court may give further directions or direct that parties attend a FDR appointment.

9.17 The FDR appointment

(1) The FDR appointment must be treated as a meeting held for the purposes of discussion and negotiation.

(2) The judge hearing the FDR appointment must have no further involvement with the application, other than to conduct any further FDR appointment or to make a consent order or a further directions order.

(3) Not less than 7 days before the FDR appointment, the applicant must file with the court details of all offers and proposals, and responses to them.

(4) Paragraph (3) includes any offers, proposals or responses made wholly or partly without prejudice (GL), but paragraph (3) does not make any material admissible as evidence if, but for that paragraph, it would not be admissible.

(5) At the conclusion of the FDR appointment, any documents filed under paragraph (3), and any filed documents referring to them, must, at the request of the party who filed them, be returned to that party and not retained on the court file.

(6) Parties attending the FDR appointment must use their best endeavours to reach agreement on matters in issue between them.

(7) The FDR appointment may be adjourned from time to time.

(8) At the conclusion of the FDR appointment, the court may make an appropriate consent order.

(9) If the court does not make an appropriate consent order as mentioned in paragraph (8), the court must give directions for the future course of the proceedings including, where appropriate—

(a) the filing of evidence, including up to date information; and

(b) fixing a final hearing date.

(10) Both parties must personally attend the FDR appointment unless the court directs otherwise.

9.26 Applications for consent orders for financial remedy

(1) Subject to paragraph (5) and to rule 35.2, in relation to an application for a consent order—

(a) the applicant must file two copies of a draft of the order in the terms sought, one of which must be endorsed with a statement signed by the respondent to the application signifying agreement; and

(b) each party must file with the court and serve on the other party, a statement of information in the form referred to in Practice Direction 5A.

(2) Where each party's statement of information is contained in one form, it must be signed by both the applicant and respondent to certify that they have read the contents of the other party's statement.

(3) Where each party's statement of information is in a separate form, the form of each party must be signed by the other party to certify that they have read the contents of the statement contained in that form.

(4) Unless the court directs otherwise, the applicant and the respondent need not attend the hearing of an application for a consent order.

(5) Where all or any of the parties attend the hearing of an application for a financial remedy the court may—

(a) dispense with the filing of a statement of information; and

(b) give directions for the information which would otherwise be required to be given in such a statement in such a manner as it thinks fit.

(6) In relation to an application for a consent order under Part 3 of the 1984 Act or Schedule 7 to the 2004 Act, the application for permission to make the application may be heard at the same time as the application for a financial remedy if evidence of the respondent's consent to the order is filed with the application.

(The following rules contain provision in relation to applications for consent orders - rule 9.32 (pension sharing order), rule 9.34 (pension attachment order), rule 9.41 (pension compensation sharing orders) and rule 9.43 (pension compensation attachment orders.)

9.26A Questions as to the court's jurisdiction or whether the proceedings should be stayed

(1) This rule applies to applications for maintenance where a question as to jurisdiction arises under—

(a) the 1968 Convention;

(b) the 1988 Convention;

(c) the Lugano Convention; or

(d) the Maintenance Regulation.

(2) If at any time after the issue of the application it appears to the court that it does not or may not have jurisdiction to hear an application, or that under the instruments referred to in paragraph (1) it is or may be required to stay the proceedings or to decline jurisdiction, the court must—

(a) stay the proceedings, and

(b) fix a date for a hearing to determine jurisdiction or whether there should be a stay or other order.

(3) The court officer will serve notice of the hearing referred to at paragraph (2)(b) on the parties to the proceedings.

(4) The court must, in writing—

(a) give reasons for its decision under paragraph (2), and

(b) where it makes a finding of fact, state such finding.

(5) The court may with the consent of all the parties deal with any question as to the jurisdiction of the court, or as to whether the proceedings should be stayed, without a hearing.

(6) In this rule—

(a) 'the 1968 Convention' has the meaning given to it in the Civil Jurisdiction and Judgments Act 1982;

(b) 'the 1988 Convention' and 'the Lugano Convention' have the meanings given to them in rule 34.1(2).

Chapter 7
Estimates of Costs

9.27 Estimates of Costs

(1) Subject to paragraph (2), at every hearing or appointment each party must produce to the court an estimate of the costs incurred by that party up to the date of that hearing or appointment.

(2) Not less than 14 days before the date fixed for the final hearing of an application for a financial remedy, each party ('the filing party') must (unless the court directs otherwise) file with the court and serve on each other party a statement giving full particulars of all costs in respect of the proceedings which the filing party has incurred or expects to incur, to enable the court to take account of the parties' liabilities for costs when deciding what order (if any) to make for a financial remedy.

(3) This rule does not apply to magistrates' courts.

(Rule 28.3 makes provision for orders for costs in financial remedy proceedings.)

9.28 Duty to make open proposals

(1) Not less than 14 days before the date fixed for the final hearing of an application for a financial remedy, the applicant must (unless the court directs otherwise) file with the court and serve on the respondent an open statement which sets out concise details, including the amounts involved, of the orders which the applicant proposes to ask the court to make.

(2) Not more than 7 days after service of a statement under paragraph (1), the respondent must file with the court and serve on the applicant an open statement which sets out concise details, including the amounts involved, of the orders which the respondent proposes to ask the court to make.

Chapter 8
Pensions

9.29 Application and interpretation of this Chapter

(1) This Chapter applies

(a) where an application for a financial remedy has been made; and

(b) the applicant or respondent is the party with pension rights.

(2) In this Chapter—

(a) in proceedings under the 1973 Act and the 1984 Act, all words and phrases defined in sections 25D(3) and (4) of the 1973 Act have the meaning assigned by those subsections;

(b) in proceedings under the 2004 Act—

(i) all words and phrases defined in paragraphs 16(4) to (5) and 29 of Schedule 5 to that Act have the meanings assigned by those paragraphs; and

(ii) 'the party with pension rights' has the meaning given to 'civil partner with pension rights' by paragraph 29 of Schedule 5 to the 2004 Act;

(c) all words and phrases defined in section 46 of the Welfare Reform and Pensions Act 1999 have the meanings assigned by that section.

9.30 What the party with pension rights must do when the court fixes a first appointment

(1) Where the court fixes a first appointment as required by rule 9.12(1)(a) the party with pension rights must request the person responsible for each pension arrangement under which the party has or is likely to have benefits to provide the information referred to in regulation 2(2) of the Pensions on Divorce etc (Provision of Information) Regulations 2000.

(The information referred to in regulation 2 of the Pensions on Divorce etc (Provision of Information) Regulations 2000 relates to the valuation of pension rights or benefits.)

(2) The party with pension rights must comply with paragraph (1) within 7 days beginning with the date on which that party receives notification of the date of the first appointment.

(3) Within 7 days beginning with the date on which the party with pension rights receives the information under paragraph (1) that party must send a copy of it to the other party, together with the name and address of the person responsible for each pension arrangement.

(4) A request under paragraph (1) need not be made where the party with pension rights is in possession of, or has requested, a relevant valuation of the pension rights or benefits accrued under the pension arrangement in question.

9.31 Applications for pension sharing orders

Where an application for a financial remedy includes an application for a pension sharing order, or where a request for such an order is added to an existing application for a financial remedy, the applicant must serve a copy of the application on the person responsible for the pension arrangement concerned.

9.32 Applications for consent orders for pension sharing

(1) This rule applies where—

(a) the parties have agreed on the terms of an order and the agreement includes a pension sharing order;

(b) service has not been effected under rule 9.31; and

(c) the information referred to in paragraph (2) has not otherwise been provided.

(2) The party with pension rights must—

(a) request the person responsible for the pension arrangement concerned to provide the information set out in Section C of the Pension Inquiry Form; and

(b) on receipt, send a copy of the information referred to in sub-paragraph (a) to the other party.

9.33 Applications for pension attachment orders

(1) Where an application for a financial remedy includes an application for a pension attachment order, or where a request for such an order is added to an existing application for a financial remedy, the applicant must serve a copy of the application on the person responsible for the pension arrangement concerned and must at the same time send—

(a) an address to which any notice which the person responsible is required to serve on the applicant is to be sent;

(b) an address to which any payment which the person responsible is required to make to the applicant is to be sent; and

(c) where the address in sub-paragraph (b) is that of a bank, a building society or the Department of National Savings, sufficient details to enable the payment to be made into the account of the applicant.

(2) A person responsible for a pension arrangement who receives a copy of the application under paragraph (1) may, within 21 days beginning with the date of service of the application, request the party with the pension rights to provide that person with the information disclosed in the financial statement relating to the party's pension rights or benefits under that arrangement.

(3) If the person responsible for a pension arrangement makes a request under paragraph (2), the party with the pension rights must provide that person with a copy of the section of that party's financial statement that relates to that party's pension rights or benefits under that arrangement.

(4) The party with the pension rights must comply with paragraph (3)—

(a) within the time limited for filing the financial statement by rule 9.14(1); or

(b) within 21 days beginning with the date on which the person responsible for the pension arrangement makes the request, whichever is the later.

(5) A person responsible for a pension arrangement who receives a copy of the section of a financial statement as required pursuant to paragraph (4) may, within 21 days beginning with the date on which that person receives it, send to the court, the applicant and the respondent a statement in answer.

(6) A person responsible for a pension arrangement who files a statement in answer pursuant to paragraph (5) will be entitled to be represented at the first appointment, or such other hearing as the court may direct, and the court must within 4 days, beginning with the date on which that person files the statement in answer, give the person notice of the date of the first appointment or other hearing as the case may be.

9.34 Applications for consent orders for pension attachment

(1) This rule applies where service has not been effected under rule 9.33(1).

(2) Where the parties have agreed on the terms of an order and the agreement includes a pension attachment order, then they must serve on the person responsible for the pension arrangement concerned—

(a) a copy of the application for a consent order;

(b) a draft of the proposed order, complying with rule 9.35; and

(c) the particulars set out in rule 9.33(1).

(3) No consent order that includes a pension attachment order must be made unless either—

(a) the person responsible for the pension arrangement has not made any objection within 21 days beginning with the date on which the application for a consent order was served on that person; or

(b) the court has considered any such objection, and for the purpose of considering any objection the court may make such direction as it sees fit for the person responsible to attend before it or to furnish written details of the objection.

9.35 Pension sharing orders or pension attachment orders

An order for a financial remedy, whether by consent or not, which includes a pension sharing order or a pension attachment order, must—

(a) in the body of the order, state that there is to be provision by way of pension sharing or pension attachment in accordance with the annex or annexes to the order; and

(b) be accompanied by a pension sharing annex or a pension attachment annex as the case may require, and if provision is made in relation to more than one pension arrangement there must be one annex for each pension arrangement.

9.36 Duty of the court upon making a pension sharing order or a pension attachment order

(1) A court which varies or discharges a pension sharing order or a pension attachment order, must send, or direct one of the parties to send—

(a) to the person responsible for the pension arrangement concerned; or

(b) where the Board has assumed responsibility for the pension scheme or part of it, the Board;

the documents referred to in paragraph (4).

(2) A court which makes a pension sharing order or pension attachment order, must send, or direct one of the parties to send to the person responsible for the pension arrangement concerned, the documents referred to in paragraph (4).

(3) Where the Board has assumed responsibility for the pension scheme or part of it after the making of a pension sharing order or attachment order but before the documents have been sent to the person responsible for the pension arrangement in accordance with paragraph (2), the court which makes the pension sharing order or the pension attachment order, must send, or direct one of the parties to send to the Board the documents referred to in paragraph (4).

(4) The documents to be sent in accordance with paragraph (1) to (3) are—

(a) in the case of—

(i) proceedings under the 1973 Act, a copy of the decree of judicial separation;

(ii) proceedings under Schedule 5 to the 2004 Act, a copy of the separation order;

(iii) proceedings under Part 3 of the 1984 Act, a copy of the document of divorce, annulment or legal separation;

(iv) proceedings under Schedule 7 to the 2004 Act, a copy of the document of dissolution, annulment or legal separation;

(b) in the case of divorce or nullity of marriage, a copy of the decree absolute under rule 7.31 or 7.32; or

(c) in the case of dissolution or nullity of civil partnership, a copy of the order making the conditional order final under rule 7.31 or 7.32; and

(d) a copy of the pension sharing order or the pension attachment order, or as the case may be of the order varying or discharging that order, including any annex to that order relating to that pension arrangement but no other annex to that order.

(5) The documents referred to in paragraph (1) must be sent—

(a) in proceedings under the 1973 Act and the 1984 Act, within 7 days beginning with the date on which—

(i) the relevant pension sharing or pension attachment order is made; or

(ii) the decree absolute of divorce or nullity or decree of judicial separation is made,

whichever is the later; and

(b) in proceedings under the 2004 Act, within 7 days beginning with the date on which—

(i) the relevant pension sharing or pension attachment order is made; or

(ii) the final order of dissolution or nullity or separation order is made, whichever is the later.

9.37 Procedure where Pension Protection Fund becomes involved with the pension scheme

(1) This rule applies where—

(a) rules 9.30 to 9.34 or 9.36 apply; and

(b) the party with the pension rights ('the member') receives or has received notification in compliance with the Pension Protection Fund (Provision of Information) Regulations 2005 ('the 2005 Regulations')—

(i) from the trustees or managers of a pension scheme, that there is an assessment period in relation to that scheme; or

(ii) from the Board that it has assumed responsibility for the pension scheme or part of it.

(2) If the trustees or managers of the pension scheme notify or have notified the member that there is an assessment period in relation to that scheme, the member must send to the other party, all the information which the Board is required from time to time to provide to the member under the 2005 Regulations including—

(a) a copy of the notification; and

(b) a copy of the valuation summary,

in accordance with paragraph (3).

(3) The member must send the information or any part of it referred to in paragraph (2)—

(a) if available, when the member sends the information received under rule 9.30(1); or

(b) otherwise, within 7 days of receipt.

(4) If the Board notifies the member that it has assumed responsibility for the pension scheme, or part of it, the member must—

(a) send a copy of the notification to the other party within 7 days of receipt; and

(b) comply with paragraph (5).

(5) Where paragraph (4) applies, the member must—

(a) within 7 days of receipt of the notification, request the Board in writing to provide a forecast of the member's compensation entitlement as described in the 2005 Regulations; and

(b) send a copy of the forecast of the member's compensation entitlement to the other party within 7 days of receipt.

(6) In this rule—

(a) 'assessment period' means an assessment period within the meaning of Part 2 of the Pensions Act 2004; and

(b) 'valuation summary' has the meaning assigned to it by the 2005 Regulations.

Chapter 9
Pension Protection Fund Compensation

9.38 Application and interpretation of this Chapter

(1) This Chapter applies—

(a) where an application for a financial remedy has been made; and

(b) the applicant or respondent is, the party with compensation rights.

(2) In this Chapter 'party with compensation rights'—

(a) in proceedings under the 1973 Act and the 1984 Act, has the meaning given to it by section 25G(5) of the 1973 Act;

(b) in proceedings under the 2004 Act, has the meaning given to 'civil partner with compensation rights' by paragraph 37(1) of Schedule 5 to the 2004 Act.

9.39 What the party with compensation rights must do when the court fixes a first appointment

(1) Where the court fixes a first appointment as required by rule 9.12(1)(a) the party with compensation rights must request the Board to provide the information about the valuation of entitlement to PPF compensation referred to in regulations made by the Secretary of State under section 118 of the Pensions Act 2008.

(2) The party with compensation rights must comply with paragraph (1) within 7 days beginning with the date on which that party receives notification of the date of the first appointment.

(3) Within 7 days beginning with the date on which the party with compensation rights receives the information under paragraph (1) that party must send a copy of it to the other party, together with the name and address of the trustees or managers responsible for each pension scheme.

(4) Where the rights to PPF Compensation are derived from rights under more than one pension scheme, the party with compensation rights must comply with this rule in relation to each entitlement.

9.40 Applications for pension compensation sharing orders

Where an application for a financial remedy includes an application for a pension compensation sharing order or where a request for such an order is added to an existing application for a financial remedy, the applicant must serve a copy of the application on the Board.

9.41 Applications for consent orders for pension compensation sharing

(1) This rule applies where—

(a) the parties have agreed on the terms of an order and the agreement includes a pension compensation sharing order;

(b) service has not been effected under rule 9.40; and

(c) the information referred to in paragraph (2) has not otherwise been provided.

(2) The party with compensation rights must—

(a) request the Board to provide the information set out in Section C of the Pension Protection Fund Inquiry Form; and

(b) on receipt, send a copy of the information referred to in sub-paragraph (a) to the other party.

9.42 Applications for pension compensation attachment orders

Where an application for a financial remedy includes an application for a pension compensation attachment order or where a request for such an order is added to an existing application for a financial remedy, the applicant must serve a copy of the application on the Board and must at the same time send—

(a) an address to which any notice which the Board is required to serve on the applicant is to be sent;

(b) an address to which any payment which the Board is required to make to the applicant is to be sent; and

(c) where the address in sub-paragraph (b) is that of a bank, a building society or the Department of National Savings, sufficient details to enable the payment to be made into the account of the applicant.

9.43 Applications for consent orders for pension compensation attachment

(1) This rule applies where service has not been effected under rule 9.42.

(2) Where the parties have agreed on the terms of an order and the agreement includes a pension compensation attachment order, then they must serve on the Board—

(a) a copy of the application for a consent order;

(b) a draft of the proposed order, complying with rule 9.44; and

(c) the particulars set out in rule 9.42.

9.44 Pension compensation sharing orders or pension compensation attachment orders

An order for a financial remedy, whether by consent or not, which includes a pension compensation sharing order or a pension compensation attachment order, must—

(a) in the body of the order, state that there is to be provision by way of pension compensation sharing or pension compensation attachment in accordance with the annex or annexes to the order; and

(b) be accompanied by a pension compensation sharing annex or a pension compensation attachment annex as the case may require, and if provision is made in relation to entitlement to PPF compensation that derives from rights under more than one pension scheme there must be one annex for each such entitlement.

9.45 Duty of the court upon making a pension compensation sharing order or a pension compensation attachment order

(1) A court which makes, varies or discharges a pension compensation sharing order or a pension compensation attachment order, must send, or direct one of the parties to send, to the Board—

(a) in the case of—

(i) proceedings under Part 3 of the 1984 Act, a copy of the document of divorce, annulment or legal separation;

(ii) proceedings under Schedule 7 to the 2004 Act, a copy of the document of dissolution, annulment or legal separation;

(b) in the case of—

(i) divorce or nullity of marriage, a copy of the decree absolute under rule 7.32 or 7.33;

(ii) dissolution or nullity of civil partnership, a copy of the order making the conditional order final under rule 7.32 or 7.33;

(c) in the case of separation—

(i) in the matrimonial proceedings, a copy of the decree of judicial separation;

(ii) in civil partnership proceedings, a copy of the separation order; and

(d) a copy of the pension compensation sharing order or the pension compensation attachment order, or as the case may be of the order varying or discharging that order, including any annex to that order relating to that PPF compensation but no other annex to that order.

(2) The documents referred to in paragraph (1) must be sent—

(a) in proceedings under the 1973 Act and the 1984 Act, within 7 days beginning with the date on which—

(i) the relevant pension compensation sharing or pension compensation attachment order is made; or

(ii) the decree absolute of divorce or nullity or the decree of judicial separation is made,

whichever is the later; and

(b) in proceedings under the 2004 Act, within 7 days beginning with the date on which—

(i) the relevant pension compensation sharing or pension compensation attachment order is made; or

(ii) the final order of dissolution or nullity or separation order is made,

whichever is the later.

PRACTICE DIRECTION 9A
APPLICATION FOR A FINANCIAL REMEDY

This Practice Direction supplements FPR Part 9

Introduction

1.1 Part 9 of the Family Procedure Rules sets out the procedure applicable to the financial proceedings that are included in the definition of a 'financial remedy'.

1.2 The procedure is applicable to a limited extent to applications for financial remedies that are heard in magistrates' courts (namely, those under section 35 of the Matrimonial Causes Act 1973, paragraph 69 of Schedule 5 to the Civil Partnership Act 2004, Part I of the Domestic Proceedings and Magistrates' Courts Act 1978, Schedule 1 to the Children Act 1989 and Schedule 6 to the Civil Partnership Act 2004). However, unless the context otherwise requires, this Practice Direction does not apply to proceedings in a magistrates' court.

1.3 Where an application for a financial remedy includes an application relating to land, details of any mortgagee must be included in the application.

Pre-application protocol

2.1 The 'pre-application protocol' annexed to this Direction outlines the steps parties should take to seek and provide information from and to each other prior to the commencement of any application for a financial remedy. The court will expect the parties to comply with the terms of the protocol.

Costs

3.1 Rule 9.27 applies in the High Court and county court. The rule requires each party to produce to the court, at every hearing or appointment, an estimate of the costs incurred by the party up to the date of that hearing or appointment.

3.2 The purpose of this rule is to enable the court to take account of the impact of each party's costs liability on their financial situations. Parties should ensure that the information contained in the estimate is as full and accurate as possible and that any sums already paid in respect of a party's financial remedy costs are clearly set out. Where relevant, any liability arising from the costs of other proceedings between the parties should continue to be referred to in the appropriate section of a party's financial statement; any such costs should not be included in the estimates under rule 9.27.

3.3 Rule 28.3 provides that the general rule in financial remedy proceedings is that the court will not make an order requiring one party to pay the costs of another party. However the court may make such an order at any stage of the proceedings where it considers it appropriate to do so because of the conduct of a party in relation to the proceedings.

3.4 Any breach of this practice direction or the pre-application protocol annexed to it will be taken into account by the court when deciding whether to depart from the general rule as to costs.

Procedure before the first appointment

4.1 In addition to the matters listed at rule 9.14(5), the parties should, if possible, with a view to identifying and narrowing any issues between the parties, exchange and file with the court—

(a) a summary of the case agreed between the parties;

(b) a schedule of assets agreed between the parties; and

(c) details of any directions that they seek, including, where appropriate, the name of any expert they wish to be appointed.

4.2 Where a party is prevented from sending the details referred to in (c) above, the party should make that information available at the first appointment.

Financial Statements and other documents

5.1 Practice Direction 22A (Written Evidence) applies to any financial statement filed in accordance with rules 9.14 or 9.19 and to any exhibits to a financial statement. In preparing a bundle of documents to be exhibited to or attached to a financial statement, regard must be had in particular to paragraphs 11.1 to 11.3 and 13.1 to 13.4 of that Direction. Where on account of their bulk, it is impracticable for the exhibits to a financial statement to be retained on the court file after the First Appointment, the court may give directions as to their custody pending further hearings.

5.2 Where the court directs a party to provide information or documents by way of reply to a questionnaire or request by another party, the reply must be verified by a statement of truth. Unless otherwise directed, a reply to a questionnaire or request for information and shall not be filed with the court.

(Part 17 and Practice Direction 17A make further provision about statements of truth)

Financial Dispute Resolution (FDR) Appointment

6.1 A key element in the procedure is the Financial Dispute Resolution (FDR) appointment. Rule 9.17 provides that the FDR appointment is to be treated as a meeting held for the purposes of discussion and negotiation. Such meetings have been developed as a means of reducing the tension which inevitably arises in family disputes and facilitating settlement of those disputes.

6.2 In order for the FDR to be effective, parties must approach the occasion openly and without reserve. Non-disclosure of the content of such meetings is vital and is an essential prerequisite for fruitful discussion directed to the settlement of the dispute between the parties. The FDR appointment is an important part of the settlement process. As a consequence of *Re D (Minors) (Conciliation: Disclosure of Information)* [1993] Fam 231, evidence of anything said or of any admission made in the course of an FDR appointment will not be admissible in evidence, except at the trial of a person for an offence committed at the appointment or in the very exceptional circumstances indicated in *Re D*.

6.3 Courts will therefore expect—

(a) parties to make offers and proposals;

(b) recipients of offers and proposals to give them proper consideration; and

(c) (subject to paragraph 6.4), that parties, whether separately or together, will not seek to exclude from consideration at the appointment any such offer or proposal.

6.4 Paragraph 6.3(c) does not apply to an offer or proposal made during alternative dispute resolution.

6.5 In order to make the most effective use of the first appointment and the FDR appointment, the legal representatives attending those appointments will be expected to have full knowledge of the case.

6.6 The rules do not provide for FDR appointments to take place during proceedings in magistrates' courts.

(Provision relating to experts in financial remedy proceedings is contained in the Practice Direction supplementing Part 25 of the FPR relating to Experts and Assessors in Family Proceedings)

Consent orders

7.1 Rule 9.26 (1)(a) requires an application for a consent order to be accompanied by two copies of the draft order in the terms sought, one of which must be endorsed with a statement signed by the respondent to the application signifying the respondent's agreement. The rule is considered to have been properly complied with if the endorsed statement is signed by solicitors on record as acting for the respondent; but where the consent order applied for contains undertakings, it should be signed by the party giving the undertakings as well as by that party's solicitor.

(Provision relating to the enforcement of undertakings is contained in the Practice Direction 33A supplementing Part 33 of the FPR)

7.2 Rule 9.26(1)(b) requires each party to file with the court and serve on the other party a statement of information. Where this is contained in one form, both parties must sign the statement to certify that each has read the contents of the other's statement.

7.3 Rule 35.2 deals with applications for a consent order in respect of a financial remedy where the parties wish to have the content of a written mediation agreement to which the Mediation Directive applies made the subject of a consent order.

Section 10(2) of the Matrimonial Causes Act 1973 and section 48(2) of the Civil Partnership Act 2004

8.1 Where a respondent who has applied under section 10(2) of the Matrimonial Causes Act 1973, or section 48(2) of the Civil Partnership Act 2004, for the court to consider his or her financial position after a divorce or dissolution elects not to proceed with the application, a notice of withdrawal of the application signed by the respondent or by the respondent's solicitor may be filed without leave of the court. In this event a formal order dismissing or striking out the application is unnecessary. Notice of withdrawal should also be given to the applicant's solicitor.

8.2 An application under section 10(2) or section 48(2) which has been withdrawn is not a bar to making in matrimonial proceedings, the decree absolute and in civil partnership proceedings, the final order.

Maintenance Orders—registration in magistrates' courts

9.1 Where periodical payments are required to be made to a child under an order registered in a magistrates' court, section 62 of the Magistrates' Courts Act 1980 permits the payments to be made instead to the person with whom the child has his home. That person may proceed in his own name for variation, revival or revocation of the order and may enforce payment either in his own name or by requesting the designated officer of the court to do so.

9.2 The registration in a magistrates' court of an order made direct to a child entails a considerable amount of work. Accordingly, when the court is considering the form of an order where there are children, care should be taken not to make orders for payment direct where such orders would be of no benefit to the parties.

Pensions

10.1 The phrase 'party with pension rights' is used in FPR Part 9, Chapter 8. For matrimonial proceedings, this phrase has the meaning given to it by section 25D(3) of the Matrimonial Causes Act 1973 and means 'the party to the marriage who has or is likely to have benefits under a pension arrangement'. There is a definition of 'civil partner with pension rights' in paragraph 29 of Schedule 5 to the Civil Partnership Act 2004 which mirrors the definition of 'party with pension rights' in section 25D(3) of the 1973 Act. The phrase 'is likely to have benefits' in these definitions refers to accrued rights to pension benefits which are not yet in payment.

PPF Compensation

11.1 The phrase 'party with compensation rights' is used in FPR Part 9,Chapter 9.For matrimonial proceedings, the phrase has the meaning given to it by section 25G(5) of the Matrimonial Causes Act 1973 and means the party to the marriage who is or is likely to be entitled to PPF compensation. There is a definition of 'civil partner with compensation rights' in paragraph 37(1) of Schedule 5 to the Civil Partnership Act 2004 which mirrors the definition of 'party with compensation rights' in section 25G(5).The phrase 'is likely to be entitled to PPF Compensation' in those definitions refers to statutory entitlement to PPF Compensation which is not yet in payment.

Annex
Pre-application protocol
Notes of guidance

Scope of the Protocol

1. This protocol is intended to apply to all applications for a financial remedy as defined by rule 2.3. It is designed to cover all classes of case, ranging from a simple application for periodical payments to an application for a substantial lump sum and property adjustment order. The protocol is designed to facilitate the operation of the procedure for financial remedy applications.
2. In considering the options of pre-application disclosure and negotiation, solicitors should bear in mind the advantage of having a court timetable and court managed process. There is sometimes an advantage in preparing disclosure before proceedings are commenced. However, solicitors should bear in mind the objective of controlling costs and in particular the costs of discovery and that the option of pre-application disclosure and negotiation has risks of excessive and uncontrolled expenditure and delay. This option should only be encouraged where both parties agree to follow this route and disclosure is not likely to be an issue or has been adequately dealt with in mediation or otherwise.
3. Solicitors should consider at an early stage and keep under review whether it would be appropriate to suggest mediation and/or collaborative law to the clients as an alternative to solicitor negotiation or court based litigation.
4. Making an application to the court should not be regarded as a hostile step or a last resort, rather as a way of starting the court timetable, controlling disclosure and endeavouring to avoid the costly final hearing and the preparation for it.

First letter

5. The circumstances of parties to an application for a financial remedy are so various that it would be difficult to prepare a specimen first letter. The request for information will be different in every case. However, the tone of the initial letter is important and the guidelines in paragraphs 14 and 15 should be followed. It should be approved in advance by the client. Solicitors writing to an unrepresented party should always recommend that he seeks independent legal advice and enclose a second copy of the letter to be passed to any solicitor instructed. A reasonable time limit for an answer may be 14 days.

Negotiation and Settlement

6. In the event of pre-application disclosure and negotiation, as envisaged in paragraph 12 an application should not be issued when a settlement is a reasonable prospect.

Disclosure

7. The protocol underlines the obligation of parties to make full and frank disclosure of all material facts, documents and other information relevant to the issues. Solicitors owe their clients a duty to tell them in clear terms of this duty and of the possible consequences of breach of the duty, which may include criminal sanctions under the Fraud Act 2006. This duty of disclosure is an ongoing obligation and includes the duty to disclose any material changes after initial disclosure has been given. Solicitors are referred to the Good Practice Guide for Disclosure produced by Resolution (obtainable from the Administrative Director, 366A Crofton Road, Orpington, Kent BR2 8NN) and can also contact the Law Society's Practice Advice Service on 0870 606 2522.

The Protocol

General principles

8. All parties must always bear in mind the overriding objective set out at rules 1.1 to 1.4 and try to ensure that applications should be resolved and a just outcome achieved as speedily as possible without costs being unreasonably incurred. The needs of any children should be addressed and safeguarded. The procedures which it is appropriate to follow should be conducted with minimum distress to the parties and in a manner designed to promote as good a continuing relationship between the parties and any children affected as is possible in the circumstances.

9. The principle of proportionality must be borne in mind at all times. It is unacceptable for the costs of any case to be disproportionate to the financial value of the subject matter of the dispute.

10. Parties should be informed that where a court is considering whether to make an order requiring one party to pay the costs of another party, it will take into account pre-application offers to settle and conduct of disclosure.

Identifying the issues

11. Parties must seek to clarify their claims and identify the issues between them as soon as possible. So that this can be achieved, they must provide full, frank and clear disclosure of facts, information and documents, which are material and sufficiently accurate to enable proper negotiations to take place to settle their differences. Openness in all dealings is essential.

Disclosure

12. If parties carry out voluntary disclosure before the issue of proceedings the parties should exchange schedules of assets, income, liabilities and other material facts, using the financial statement as a guide to the format of the disclosure. Documents should only be disclosed to the extent that they are required by the financial statement. Excessive or disproportionate costs should not be incurred.

Correspondence

13. Any first letter and subsequent correspondence must focus on the clarification of claims and identification of issues and their resolution. Protracted and unnecessary correspondence and 'trial by correspondence' must be avoided.

14. The impact of any correspondence upon the reader and in particular the parties must always be considered. Any correspondence which raises irrelevant issues or which

might cause the other party to adopt an entrenched, polarised or hostile position is to be discouraged.

Summary

15. The aim of all pre-application proceedings steps must be to assist the parties to resolve their differences speedily and fairly or at least narrow the issues and,should that not be possible, to assist the court to do so.

Family Procedure Rules 2010 (SI 2010/2955)

Part 21
Miscellaneous Rules about Disclosure and Inspection of Documents

21.2 Orders for disclosure against a person not a party

(1) This rule applies where an application is made to the court under any Act for disclosure by a person who is not a party to the proceedings.

(2) The application—
- (a) may be made without notice; and
- (b) must be supported by evidence.

(3) The court may make an order under this rule only where disclosure is necessary in order to dispose fairly of the proceedings or to save costs.

(4) An order under this rule must—
- (a) specify the documents or the classes of documents which the respondent must disclose; and
- (b) require the respondent, when making disclosure, to specify any of those documents—
  - (i) which are no longer in the respondent's control; or
  - (ii) in respect of which the respondent claims a right or duty to withhold inspection.

(5) Such an order may—
- (a) require the respondent to indicate what has happened to any documents which are no longer in the respondent's control; and
- (b) specify the time and place for disclosure and inspection.

(6) An order under this rule must not compel a person to produce any document which that person could not be compelled to produce at the final hearing.

(7) This rule does not limit any other power which the court may have to order disclosure against a person who is not a party to proceedings.

(Rule 35.3 contains provisions in relation to the disclosure and inspection of evidence arising out of mediation of cross-border disputes.)

Part 28
Costs

28.1 Costs

The court may at any time make such order as to costs as it thinks just.

28.2 Application of other rules

(1) Subject to rule 28.3 and to paragraph (2), Parts 43, 44 (except rules 44.3(2) and (3), 44.9 to 44.12C, 44.13(1A) and (1B) and 44.18 to 20), 47 and 48 and rule 45.6 of the CPR apply to costs in proceedings, with the following modifications—

(a) in rule 43.2(1)(c)(ii), 'district judge' includes a district judge of the principal registry;

(b) in rule 48.7(1) after 'section 51(6) of the Senior Courts Act 1981' insert 'or section 145A of the Magistrates' Courts Act 1980';

(c) in accordance with any provisions in Practice Direction 28A; and

(d) any other necessary modifications.

(2) Part 47 and rules 44.3C and 45.6 of the CPR do not apply to proceedings in a magistrates' court.

28.3 Costs in financial remedy proceedings

(1) This rule applies in relation to financial remedy proceedings.

(2) Rule 44.3(1), (4) and (5) of the CPR do not apply to financial remedy proceedings.

(3) Rule 44.3(6) to (9) of the CPR apply to an order made under this rule as they apply to an order made under rule 44.3 of the CPR.

(4) In this rule—

(a) 'costs' has the same meaning as in rule 43.2(1)(a) of the CPR; and

(b) 'financial remedy proceedings' means proceedings for—

(i) a financial order except an order for maintenance pending suit, an order for maintenance pending outcome of proceedings, an interim periodical payments order or any other form of interim order for the purposes of rule 9.7(1)(a), (b), (c) and (e);

(ii) an order under Part 3 of the 1984 Act;

(iii) an order under Schedule 7 to the 2004 Act;

(iv) an order under section 10(2) of the 1973 Act;

(v) an order under section 48(2) of the 2004 Act.

(5) Subject to paragraph (6), the general rule in financial remedy proceedings is that the court will not make an order requiring one party to pay the costs of another party.

(6) The court may make an order requiring one party to pay the costs of another party at any stage of the proceedings where it considers it appropriate to do so because of the conduct of a party in relation to the proceedings (whether before or during them).

(7) In deciding what order (if any) to make under paragraph (6), the court must have regard to—

(a) any failure by a party to comply with these rules, any order of the court or any practice direction which the court considers relevant;

(b) any open offer to settle made by a party;

(c) whether it was reasonable for a party to raise, pursue or contest a particular allegation or issue;

(d) the manner in which a party has pursued or responded to the application or a particular allegation or issue;

(e) any other aspect of a party's conduct in relation to proceedings which the court considers relevant; and

(f) the financial effect on the parties of any costs order.

(8) No offer to settle which is not an open offer to settle is admissible at any stage of the proceedings, except as provided by rule 9.17.

Part 30
Appeals

30.3 Permission

(1) An appellant or respondent requires permission to appeal—

(a) against a decision in proceedings where the decision appealed against was made by a district judge or a costs judge, unless paragraph (2) applies; or

(b) as provided by Practice Direction 30A.

(2) Permission to appeal is not required where the appeal is against—

(a) a committal order; or

(b) a secure accommodation order under section 25 of the 1989 Act.

(3) An application for permission to appeal may be made—

(a) to the lower court at the hearing at which the decision to be appealed was made; or

(b) to the appeal court in an appeal notice.

(Rule 30.4 sets out the time limits for filing an appellant's notice at the appeal court. Rule 30.5 sets out the time limits for filing a respondent's notice at the appeal court. Any application for permission to appeal to the appeal court must be made in the appeal notice (see rules 30.4(1) and 30.5(3).)

(4) Where the lower court refuses an application for permission to appeal, a further application for permission to appeal may be made to the appeal court.

(5) Where the appeal court, without a hearing, refuses permission to appeal, the person seeking permission may request the decision to be reconsidered at a hearing.

(6) A request under paragraph (5) must be filed within 7 days beginning with the date on which the notice that permission has been refused was served.

(7) Permission to appeal may be given only where—

(a) the court considers that the appeal would have a real prospect of success; or

(b) there is some other compelling reason why the appeal should be heard.

(8) An order giving permission may—

(a) limit the issues to be heard; and

(b) be made subject to conditions.

(9) In this rule 'costs judge' means a taxing master of the Senior Courts.

30.4 Appellant's notice

(1) Where the appellant seeks permission from the appeal court it must be requested in the appellant's notice.

(2) Subject to paragraph (3), the appellant must file the appellant's notice at the appeal court within—

(a) such period as may be directed by the lower court (which may be longer or shorter than the period referred to in sub-paragraph (b)); or

(b) where the court makes no such direction, 21 days after the date of the decision of the lower court against which the appellant wishes to appeal.

(3) Where the appeal is against an order under section 38(1) of the 1989 Act, the appellant must file the appellant's notice within 7 days beginning with the date of the decision of the lower court.

(4) Unless the appeal court orders otherwise, an appellant's notice must be served on each respondent and the persons referred to in paragraph (5)—

(a) as soon as practicable; and

(b) in any event not later than 7 days,

after it is filed.

(5) The persons referred to in paragraph (4) are—

(a) any children's guardian, welfare officer, or children and family reporter;

(b) a local authority who has prepared a report under section 14A(8) or (9) of the 1989 Act;

(c) an adoption agency or local authority which has prepared a report on the suitability of the applicant to adopt a child;

(d) a local authority which has prepared a report on the placement of the child for adoption; and

(e) where the appeal is from a magistrates' court, the court officer.

30.5 Respondent's notice

(1) A respondent may file and serve a respondent's notice.

(2) A respondent who—

(a) is seeking permission to appeal from the appeal court; or

(b) wishes to ask the appeal court to uphold the order of the lower court for reasons different from or additional to those given by the lower court,

must file a respondent's notice.

(3) Where the respondent seeks permission from the appeal court it must be requested in the respondent's notice.

(4) A respondent's notice must be filed within—

(a) such period as may be directed by the lower court; or

(b) where the court makes no such direction, 14 days beginning with the date referred to in paragraph (5).

(5) The date referred to in paragraph (4) is—

(a) the date on which the respondent is served with the appellant's notice where—

(i) permission to appeal was given by the lower court; or

(ii) permission to appeal is not required;

(b) the date on which the respondent is served with notification that the appeal court has given the appellant permission to appeal; or

(c) the date on which the respondent is served with notification that the application for permission to appeal and the appeal itself are to be heard together.

(6) Unless the appeal court orders otherwise, a respondent's notice must be served on the appellant, any other respondent and the persons referred to in rule 30.4(5)—

(a) as soon as practicable; and

(b) in any event not later than 7 days,

after it is filed.

(7) Where there is an appeal against an order under section 38(1) of the 1989 Act—

(a) a respondent may not, in that appeal, bring an appeal from the order or ask the appeal court to uphold the order of the lower court for reasons different from or additional to those given by the lower court; and

(b) paragraphs (2) and (3) do not apply.

30.6 Grounds of appeal

The appeal notice must state the grounds of appeal.

30.7 Variation of time

(1) An application to vary the time limit for filing an appeal notice must be made to the appeal court.

(2) The parties may not agree to extend any date or time limit set by—

(a) these rules;

(b) Practice Direction 30A; or

(c) an order of the appeal court or the lower court.

(Rule 4.1(3)(a) provides that the court may extend or shorten the time for compliance with a rule, practice direction or court order (even if an application for extension is made after the time for compliance has expired).)

(Rule 4.1(3)(c) provides that the court may adjourn or bring forward a hearing.)

30.8 Stay

Unless the appeal court or the lower court orders otherwise, an appeal does not operate as a stay (GL) of any order or decision of the lower court.

30.9 Amendment of appeal notice

An appeal notice may not be amended without the permission of the appeal court.

30.10 Striking outappeal notices and setting aside or imposing conditions on permission to appeal

(1) The appeal court may—

(a) strike out (GL) the whole or part of an appeal notice;

(b) set aside (GL) permission to appeal in whole or in part;

(c) impose or vary conditions upon which an appeal may be brought.

(2) The court will only exercise its powers under paragraph (1) where there is a compelling reason for doing so.

(3) Where a party was present at the hearing at which permission was given that party may not subsequently apply for an order that the court exercise its powers under paragraphs (1)(b) or (1)(c).

30.11 Appeal court's powers

(1) In relation to an appeal the appeal court has all the powers of the lower court.

(Rule 30.1(4) provides that this Part is subject to any enactment that sets out special provisions with regard to any particular category of appeal.)

(2) The appeal court has power to—

(a) affirm, set aside (GL) or vary any order or judgment made or given by the lower court;

(b) refer any application or issue for determination by the lower court;

(c) order a new hearing;

(d) make orders for the payment of interest;

(e) make a costs order.

(3) The appeal court may exercise its powers in relation to the whole or part of an order of the lower court.

(Rule 4.1 contains general rules about the court's case management powers.)

(4) If the appeal court—

(a) refuses an application for permission to appeal;

(b) strikes out an appellant's notice; or

(c) dismisses an appeal,

and it considers that the application, the appellant's notice or the appeal is totally without merit, the provisions of paragraph (5) must be complied with.

(5) Where paragraph (4) applies—

(a) the court's order must record the fact that it considers the application, the appellant's notice or the appeal to be totally without merit; and

(b) the court must at the same time consider whether it is appropriate to make a civil restraint order.

30.12 Hearing of appeals

(1) Every appeal will be limited to a review of the decision of the lower court unless—

(a) an enactment or practice direction makes different provision for a particular category of appeal; or

(b) the court considers that in the circumstances of an individual appeal it would be in the interests of justice to hold a re-hearing.

(2) Unless it orders otherwise, the appeal court will not receive—

(a) oral evidence; or

(b) evidence which was not before the lower court.

(3) The appeal court will allow an appeal where the decision of the lower court was—

(a) wrong; or

(b) unjust because of a serious procedural or other irregularity in the proceedings in the lower court.

(4) The appeal court may draw any inference of fact which it considers justified on the evidence.

(5) At the hearing of the appeal a party may not rely on a matter not contained in that party's appeal notice unless the appeal court gives permission.

Part 33
Enforcement

33.3 How to apply

(1) Except where a rule or practice direction otherwise requires, an application for an order to enforce an order for the payment of money must be made in a notice of application accompanied by a statement which must—

(a) state the amount due under the order, showing how that amount is arrived at; and

(b) be verified by a statement of truth.

(2) The notice of application may either—

(a) apply for an order specifying the method of enforcement; or

(b) apply for an order for such method of enforcement as the court may consider appropriate.

(3) If an application is made under paragraph (2)(b), an order to attend court will be issued and rule 71.2 (6) and (7) of the CPR will apply as if the application had been made under that rule.

Appendix 2 – Code of Practice for Resolution Members

Membership of Resolution commits family lawyers to resolving disputes in a non-confrontational way.

We believe that family law disputes should be dealt with in a constructive way designed to preserve people's dignity and to encourage agreements.

Members of Resolution are required to:

- Conduct matters in a constructive and non-confrontational way
- Avoid use of inflammatory language both written and spoken
- Retain professional objectivity and respect for everyone involved
- Take into account the long term consequences of actions and communications as well as the short term implications
- Encourage clients to put the best interests of the children first
- Emphasise to clients the importance of being open and honest in all dealings
- Make clients aware of the benefits of behaving in a civilised way
- Keep financial and children issues separate
- Ensure that consideration is given to balancing the benefits of any steps against the likely costs – financial or emotional
- Inform clients of the options eg counselling, family therapy, round table negotiations, mediation, collaborative law and court proceedings
- Abide by the Resolution Guides to Good Practice

This Code should be read in conjunction with the Law Society's Family Law Protocol.

All solicitors are subject to the Solicitors Practice Rules

Reproduced with kind permission of Resolution.

Appendix 3 – Court Forms

(A) Divorce petition

Divorce/dissolution/ (judicial) separation petition

To be completed by the Court	
Name of court	
Case No.	
Date received by the court	
Date issued	
Time issued	

Notes to Petitioners

- This form should be used if you are making an application to the court for divorce/dissolution to end your marriage or civil partnership or (judicial) separation from your spouse or civil partner.
- Before completing this form, please read the supporting notes for guidance on completing the form.
- Please answer all questions. If you are unsure of the answer to any question, or you do not think that it applies to you, please indicate this on the form.
- If there is not enough room on the form, you may continue on a separate sheet. Please put your name, the Respondent's (your spouse/civil partner) name, and the number of the Part the information relates to, at the top of your continuation sheet.
- If completing this form by hand, please use **black ink and BLOCK CAPITAL LETTERS** and tick the boxes that apply.

See the supporting notes for guidance

I, [ ] (please state your full name)

apply for a ☐ divorce
☐ dissolution
☐ (judicial) separation

in respect of my ☐ marriage
☐ civil partnership

and give the following details in support of my application.

continued over the page ➩

Part 1 About you (the Petitioner) and the Respondent (your spouse/civil partner)

See the supporting notes for guidance

Petitioner

My current name is
First name(s) (in full)

Last name

My address is (including postcode)

Postcode

My date of birth is

D D / M M / Y Y Y Y

My occupation is

I am

☐ male ☐ female

Respondent

The Respondent's current name is
First name(s) (in full)

Last name

The Respondent's address is (including postcode)

Postcode

The Respondent's date of birth is

D D / M M / Y Y Y Y

The Respondent's occupation is

The Respondent is

☐ male ☐ female

Part 2 Details of marriage or civil partnership

See the supporting notes for guidance

On the day of [19] [20]

(insert your name exactly as it appears on your marriage/civil partnership certificate)

☐ married ☐ formed a civil partnership with

(insert the name of the Respondent exactly as it appears on your marriage/civil partnership certificate)

at

(insert the place where the marriage/civil partnership was formed, exactly as it appears on your marriage/civil partnership certificate)

A certified copy of your marriage/civil partnership certificate must be sent to the court with this completed petition (see supporting notes for guidance).

Part 3 Jurisdiction

See the supporting notes for guidance

The Respondent and I last lived together as ☐ husband and wife ☐ civil partners at

Address

The court has jurisdiction to hear this case under

☐ Article 3(1) of the Council Regulation (EC) No 2201/2003 of 27 November 2003

or

☐ the Civil Partnership (Jurisdiction and Recognition of Judgments) Regulations 2005

on the following grounds

☐ The Petitioner and Respondent are both habitually resident in England and Wales

☐ Other (please state any other connection(s) on which you wish to rely)

or

☐ The court has jurisdiction other than under the Council Regulation on the basis that no court of a Contracting State has jurisdiction under the Council Regulation and the ☐ Petitioner ☐ Respondent is domiciled in England and Wales on the date when this application is issued

or

☐ The court has jurisdiction other than under the Civil Partnership (Jurisdiction and Recognition of Judgments) Regulations on the basis that no court has, or is recognised as having jurisdiction as set out in the Regulations, and

either:

☐ the ☐ Petitioner ☐ and/or the Respondent is domiciled in England or Wales

or

☐ the Petitioner and Respondent registered as civil partners of each other in England or Wales and it would be in the interests of justice for the court to assume jurisdiction in this case.

continued over the page ⇨

Part 4 Other proceedings or arrangements

See the supporting notes for guidance

☐ There are and/or have been

☐ proceedings in any court in England and Wales or elsewhere with reference to the

☐ marriage
☐ civil partnership
☐ or to any child of the family
☐ or between the Petitioner and Respondent with reference to any property of either or both of them

(please enter details below)

or

☐ no other proceedings in any court in England and Wales or elsewhere.

☐ This is an application based on five years' separation and

☐ agreement has been made or is proposed to be made between the parties for the support of the Petitioner (and any child of the family)

(please enter details below)

or

☐ no agreement has been made or is proposed to be made.

Part 5 The fact(s)

See the supporting notes for guidance

I apply for a

☐ divorce on the ground that the marriage has broken down irretrievably, or
☐ dissolution on the ground that the civil partnership has broken down irretrievably, or
☐ (judicial) separation

and

I rely on the following fact(s) in support of my application:

☐ The Respondent has committed adultery and the Petitioner finds it intolerable to live with the Respondent (this fact is not applicable in relation to a civil partnership)

☐ The Respondent has behaved in such a way that the Petitioner cannot reasonably be expected to live with the Respondent

☐ The Respondent has deserted the Petitioner for a continuous period of at least two years immediately preceding the presentation of this petition

☐ The parties to the marriage/civil partnership have lived apart for a continuous period of at least two years immediately preceding the presentation of the petition and the Respondent consents to a decree/order being granted

☐ The parties to the marriage/civil partnership have lived apart for a continuous period of at least five years immediately preceding the presentation of the petition.

Part 6 Statement of case

See the supporting notes for guidance

(in all cases, please state briefly any relevant details about the fact(s) on which you rely)

Part 7 Details of the children

See the supporting notes for guidance

Children of the family

Full names of the children of the family	Gender male	Gender female	Date of birth (or state if over 18)	Over 16 but under 18 and in education, training or working full time	(a) Child of both parties	(b) Other child of the family
	☐	☐	D D / M M / Y Y Y Y	☐	☐	☐
	☐	☐	D D / M M / Y Y Y Y	☐	☐	☐
	☐	☐	D D / M M / Y Y Y Y	☐	☐	☐
	☐	☐	D D / M M / Y Y Y Y	☐	☐	☐
	☐	☐	D D / M M / Y Y Y Y	☐	☐	☐
	☐	☐	D D / M M / Y Y Y Y	☐	☐	☐

Statement of arrangements for children

See the supporting notes for guidance

☐ I attach a completed statement of arrangements in respect of those children of the family who are either aged under 16, or aged under 18 and at school, college, or in training for a trade, profession or vocation

or

☐ No statement of arrangements is attached, because there are no children of the family, or no children of the family are either aged under 16 or aged under 18 and at school, college, or in training for a trade, profession or vocation.

Children of either party who are not children of the family

Full names of the children of either party who are not children of the family	Gender male	Gender female	Date of birth (or state if over 18)	Born to or adopted by Petitioner	Born to or adopted by Respondent
	☐	☐	DD/MM/YYYY	☐	☐
	☐	☐	DD/MM/YYYY	☐	☐
	☐	☐	DD/MM/YYYY	☐	☐
	☐	☐	DD/MM/YYYY	☐	☐
	☐	☐	DD/MM/YYYY	☐	☐
	☐	☐	DD/MM/YYYY	☐	☐

Part 8 Special assistance or facilities if you attend court

See the supporting notes for guidance

If you are required to attend court during these proceedings will you need any special assistance or facilities?

☐ Yes (please supply details below) ☐ No

continued over the page ➪

Part 9 Service details

See the supporting notes for guidance

- ☐ I am not represented by a solicitor in these proceedings
- ☐ I am not represented by a solicitor in these proceedings but am receiving advice from a solicitor
- ☐ I am represented by a solicitor in these proceedings and all documents for my attention should be sent to my solicitor whose details are as follows:

Box 1 Solicitor's details

Name of solicitor			
Name of firm			
Address to which all documents should be sent for service		Telephone no.	
		Fax no.	
		DX no.	
Postcode		Your ref.	

E-mail	

Box 2 Petitioner's address for service

Address (including postcode)

Postcode

Box 3 Respondent's address for service

Address (including postcode)

Postcode

Box 4 Co-Respondent's details, if any

- ☐ There is no Co-Respondent
- ☐ There is a Co-Respondent whose details are as follows:

First Name	
Last Name	
Address (including postcode)	
Postcode	

Part 10

See the supporting notes for guidance

Prayer

The Petitioner therefore prays

(1) **The application**

☐ That the ☐ marriage ☐ civil partnership be dissolved

or

☐ That the Petitioner be (judicially) separated from the Respondent.

(2) **Costs (if you wish to claim costs from the Respondent or Co-Respondent)**

☐ That the ☐ Respondent ☐ Co-Respondent shall be ordered to pay the costs of this application

(3) **Financial Order (if you wish to make an application for a Financial Order)**

☐ (a) That the Petitioner may be granted the following Financial Order(s):

- ☐ an order for maintenance pending suit
- ☐ periodical payments order
- ☐ secured provision order
- ☐ lump sum order
- ☐ property adjustment order
- ☐ order under section 24B, 25B or 25C of the Act of 1973 (Pension Sharing/Attachment Order)

☐ (b) **For the children**

- ☐ a periodical payments order
- ☐ a secured provision order
- ☐ a lump sum order
- ☐ a property adjustment order

Signed ☐ Dated D D / M M / Y Y Y Y

(B) Statement of arrangements for children

Statement of arrangements for children

To be completed by the parties	
Name of court	Case No. (if known)
Name of Petitioner	
Name of Respondent	

To the Petitioner

You must complete this form if you or the Respondent have any children under 16 or any children under 18 who are at school or college or are training for a trade, profession or vocation.

The Petitioner is only required to complete Parts 1, 2, 3 and the Statement of Truth. Please use **black ink and BLOCK CAPITAL LETTERS**.

Before you issue a divorce/dissolution/(judicial) separation or nullity petition try to reach an agreement with your spouse or civil partner over the proposals for the children's future. There is space for them to sign at the end of this form if agreement is reached.

If your spouse/civil partner does not agree with the proposals, they will have the opportunity at a later stage to state why they do not agree and will be able to make their own proposals.

You should take or send the completed form together with a copy to the court when you issue your divorce/dissolution/(judicial) separation or nullity petition.

To the Respondent

The Petitioner has completed Part 1, 2 and 3 of this form.

Please read all parts of the form carefully.

If you agree with the arrangements and proposals for the children you should sign Part 4 of the form. If completing this form by hand, please use **black ink and BLOCK CAPITAL LETTERS** and tick the boxes that apply. You should return the form to the Petitioner or their solicitor.

If you do not agree with all or some of the proposals, **do not sign this form**. You will be given the opportunity of explaining your position when you receive the divorce/dissolution/(judicial) separation or nullity petition.

To the Petitioner and Respondent

If you wish to apply for any of the orders which may be available to you under Part I or II of the Children Act 1989 please see leaflet CB1 'Making an application - children and the family courts'. If you are unsure of which application you require, you are advised to see a solicitor or go to a Citizens Advice Bureau.

Addresses of solicitors and advice agencies can be obtained from the Yellow Pages and the Solicitors' Regional Directory which can be found at Citizens Advice Bureaux, Law Centres and any local library.

The Court will only make an order if it considers that an order will be better for the child(ren) than no order.

Part 1 Details of the children

1. Are the details of the children as stated in Part 7 of the divorce/dissolution/(judicial) separation or nullity petition correct?

   ☐ Yes ☐ No

   If No, please give further information in the box below

Part 2 Arrangements for the children of the family

Please give details for each child, if arrangements are different. If necessary, continue on another sheet and attach it to this form.

Living arrangements

2. Where and with whom do the children live?

Name of child(ren)	Resides with	At address

3. Is this arrangement agreed by both the Petitioner and Respondent?

   ☐ Yes ☐ No

   If No, please give details in the box below.

4. What are the contact arrangements between the child(ren) and the non-resident parent?

5. Have you (the Petitioner) and Respondent agreed to these contact arrangements?

   ☐ Yes ☐ No

   If No, please give details in the box below.

6. Who will care for the child(ren) on a day to day basis?

7. Have you (the Petitioner) and Respondent agreed to who will care for the child(ren) on a daily basis?

☐ Yes ☐ No

If No, please give details in the box below.

Education

8. Give the name(s) of the school, college or place of training attended by the child(ren).

Name of child	Name of school, college or place of training

9. Will there be any change in these arrangements as a result of your divorce/dissolution/(judicial) separation or annulment?

☐ Yes ☐ No

If Yes, please give details in the box below (include any changes to payment of school fees).

10. Do any of the children have any special educational needs?

☐ Yes ☐ No

If Yes, please give details in the box below.

continued over the page

Details of health

11. Are the children generally in good health and do not have any special health needs?

☐ Yes ☐ No

If No, please give details of any serious disability, chronic illness, or the care needed and how it is to be provided, in the box below.

12. Do any of the children have any special health needs?

☐ Yes ☐ No

If Yes, please give details of the care needed and how it is to be provided, in the box below.

Details of care and other court proceedings

13. Are the children in the care of the local authority, or under the supervision of a social worker or probation officer?

☐ Yes ☐ No

If Yes, please give details in the box below. Please include information about any current proceedings in the youth or family courts.

14. Are any of the children the subject of a Child Protection Plan?

☐ Yes ☐ No

If Yes, please give details in the box below, including the name of the local authority and the date of registration.

15. Are there, or have there been, any proceedings in any court involving the children, for example;

a) residence or contact proceedings?
b) care or supervision?
c) adoption or wardship?

☐ Yes ☐ No

If Yes, please give details in the box below and attach a copy of any order(s) which you have.

☐ A maintenance calculation has been made under the Child Support Act 1991, or, an application has been made for a maintenance calculation, but it has not yet been determined, and the details are as follows:

☐ The following agreement has been reached in relation to child maintenance:

☐ No agreement has been reached and no application has been made for a maintenance calculation.

16. Are there, or have there been, any proceedings in any court which may impact on the children, for example non-molestation orders, or criminal proceedings relating to domestic violence?

☐ Yes ☐ No

If Yes, please give details in the box below.

Part 3 To the Petitioner

Mediation

17. If you are not agreed as to the arrangements for the children, are you intending to:

- seek to resolve matters with the Respondent directly?

  ☐ Yes ☐ No

- propose the use of Alternative Dispute Resolution such as mediation?

  ☐ Yes ☐ No

  If No, would you agree to do so?

  ☐ Yes ☐ No

- make an application to the court?

  ☐ Yes ☐ No

Statement of Truth

I believe that the facts stated in this statement of arrangements for children are true

Print full name

Signed (Petitioner) Dated D D / M M / Y Y Y Y

Proceedings for contempt of court may be brought against a person who makes or causes to be made, a false statement in a document verified by a statement of truth.

Part 4 Agreement of Respondent

☐ I agree with the arrangements and proposals contained in Part 1 and 2 of this form.

☐ I do not agree with the arrangements and proposals contained in Part 1 and 2 of this form.
If you do not agree would you be prepared to see a mediator?

☐ Yes ☐ No

Signed (Respondent) Dated D D / M M / Y Y Y Y

(C) Form FM1 (Family mediation information and assessment)

Family Mediation Information and Assessment Form (FM1)

<u>**Family Mediation Information and Assessment Form FM1**</u>

This form is to be used in connection with family proceedings to which Practice Direction 3A applies. It should be completed in accordance with the Pre-application Protocol annexed to the Practice Direction and be filed with the court with any application made in proceedings to which the Practice Direction applies.

Where either Part 1 or Part 2 applies, the form must be completed and signed by the mediator concerned and counter-signed by the applicant or the applicant's solicitor.

Where either Part 3 or Part 4 applies, the form must be completed and signed by the applicant or the applicant's solicitor

Part 1

☐ **The applicant has attended a Mediation Information and Assessment meeting**

Part 2

The applicant has not attended a Mediation Information and Assessment meeting because:

☐ **The mediator is satisfied that mediation is not suitable because another party to the dispute is unwilling to attend a Mediation Information and Assessment Meeting and consider mediation.**

☐ **The mediator determines that the case is not suitable for a Mediation Information and Assessment Meeting.**

☐ **A mediator has made a determination within the previous four months that the case is not suitable for a Mediation Information and Assessment Meeting or for mediation.**

Part 3

The applicant has not attended a Mediation Information and Assessment meeting because:

☐ **A party has, to the applicant's knowledge, made an allegation of domestic violence against another party and this has resulted in a police investigation or the issuing of civil proceedings for the protection of any party within the last 12 months.**

(Please attach evidence confirming the date of any civil proceedings or police investigation)

☐ **The dispute concerns financial issues and the applicant or another party is bankrupt.**

☐ **The parties are in agreement and there is no dispute to mediate.**

☐ **The whereabouts of the other party are unknown to the applicant.**

☐ **The prospective application is for an order in relevant family proceedings which are already in existence and are continuing.**

☐ **The prospective application is to be made without notice to the other party.**

☐ **The prospective application is urgent, meaning:**
(a) there is a risk to the life, liberty or physical safety of the applicant or his or her family or his or her home; or
(b) any delay caused by attending a Mediation Information and Assessment Meeting would cause a risk of significant harm to a child, a significant risk of a miscarriage of justice, unreasonable hardship to the applicant or irretrievable problems in dealing with the dispute (such as an irretrievable loss of significant evidence).

Please give details here:

☐ **There is current social services involvement as a result of child protection concerns in respect of any child who would be the subject of the prospective application.**

☐ **A child would be a party to the prospective application by virtue of the Family Procedure Rules 2010, r 12.3(1).**

The applicant (or the applicant's solicitor) has contacted three mediators within 15 miles of the applicant's home and none has been able to conduct a Mediation Information and Assessment Meeting within 15 working days of the date of contact.

Part 4

☐ **The applicant has not complied with the Pre-application Protocol and has not attended a Mediation Information and Assessment meeting for the following reason (not being a reason specified in Parts 2 or 3 of this Form).**

Please state reason here:

Signed.................................[solicitor for] the applicant

Signed.................................mediator

Address..

2

(D) Form A (Application for a financial order)

Notice of [intention to proceed with] an application for a financial order

To be completed by the Applicant	
Name of court	Case No.
Name of Applicant	
Name of Respondent	

Respondent('s Solicitor(s)) name and address

Please note that this form should only be completed if you are applying for a financial order.

If you are applying for a financial remedy other than a financial order in the county court please complete Form A1.

If you are applying for a financial remedy in the magistrates court please complete Form A2.

(please tick the appropriate boxes)

The Applicant intends:

☐ **to apply** to the Court for:

☐ **to proceed** with the application in the [application][answer] for:

☐ **to apply to vary**:

☐ an order for maintenance pending suit/ outcome of proceedings

☐ a secured provision order

☐ a lump sum order

☐ a property adjustment order (please provide address)

☐ a periodical payments order

☐ a pension sharing order

☐ a pension attachment order

☐ a pension compensation sharing order

☐ a pension compensation attachment order

continued over the page

Please tick the appropriate box below if an application is made for any periodical payments or secured periodical payments for children:

- ☐ and there is a written agreement made before 5 April 1993 about maintenance for the benefit of children
- ☐ and there is a written agreement made on or after 5 April 1993 about maintenance for the benefit of children
- ☐ but there is no agreement, tick any of the boxes below to show if you are applying for payment:

  ☐ for a stepchild or stepchildren

  ☐ in addition to child support maintenance already paid under a Child Support Agency assessment

  ☐ to meet expenses arising from a child's disability

  ☐ to meet expenses incurred by a child in being educated or training for work

  ☐ when either the child **or** the person with care of the child **or** the absent parent of the child is not habitually resident in the United Kingdom

  ☐ Other (please state)

Have you attended a mediation information/assessment meeting as suggested in the pre-action protocol and/or attached Form FM1? ☐ Yes ☐ No

Signed ________________ Dated D D / M M / Y Y Y Y

(Applicant) (Applicant's solicitor)

(E) Form E (Statement for a financial order)

Financial statement for a financial order or for financial relief after an overseas divorce or dissolution etc

of

☐ Husband ☐ Wife ☐ Civil partner

Dated D D / M M / Y Y Y Y

To be completed by the relevant party	
Name of court	Case No.
Name of Applicant	
Name of Respondent	

(please tick appropriate boxes)

The parties are

and

Who is the	Who is the
☐ husband ☐ wife ☐ civil partner	☐ husband ☐ wife ☐ civil partner
☐ Petitioner ☐ Applicant ☐ Respondent in the	☐ Petitioner ☐ Applicant ☐ Respondent in the
☐ divorce ☐ dissolution ☐ nullity	☐ divorce ☐ dissolution ☐ nullity
☐ (judicial) separation ☐ financial relief application	☐ (judicial) separation ☐ financial relief application
Applicant in this matter	Respondent in this matter

This form should only be completed in applications for a financial order or for financial relief after an overseas divorce/dissolution etc. If the application is for any other financial remedy in the county court please complete Form E1. If the application is for a financial remedy in the magistrates court please complete Form E2.

Please fill in this form fully and accurately. Where any box is not applicable, write 'N/A'.

You have a duty to the court to give a full, frank and clear disclosure of all your financial and other relevant circumstances.

A failure to give full and accurate disclosure may result in any order the court makes being set aside.

If you are found to have been deliberately untruthful, criminal proceedings may be brought against you for fraud under the Fraud Act 2006.

The information given in this form must be confirmed by an affidavit. Proceedings for perjury may be brought against a person who makes or causes to be made, a false statement in a document confirmed by an affidavit.

You must attach documents to the form where they are specifically sought and you may attach other documents where it is necessary to explain or clarify any of the information that you give.

Essential documents that must accompany this statement are detailed in the form.

If there is not enough room on the form for any particular piece of information, you may continue on an attached sheet of paper.

If you are in doubt about how to complete any part of this form you should seek legal advice.

This statement is filed by

Name and address of solicitor

1 General Information

1.1 Full name

1.2 Date of birth

Date	Month	Year

1.3 Date of the marriage/ civil partnership

Date	Month	Year

1.4 Occupation

1.5 Date of the separation

Date	Month	Year

Tick here if not applicable ☐

1.6 Date of the

Petition for divorce/ dissolution/nullity/ (judicial) separation			Decree nisi/ conditional order/ (judicial) separation order			Decree absolute/ final order (if applicable)		
Date	Month	Year	Date	Month	Year	Date	Month	Year

1.7 If you have subsequently married or formed a civil partnership, or will do so, state the date

Date	Month	Year

1.8 Are you living with a new partner? Yes ☐ No ☐

1.9 Do you intend to live with a new partner within the next six months? Yes ☐ No ☐

1.10 Details of any children of the family

Full names	Date of birth			With whom does the child live?
	Date	Month	Year	

1.11 Details of the state of health of yourself and the children if you think this should be taken into account

Yourself	Children

1.12 Details of the present and proposed future educational arrangements for the children.

Present arrangements	Future arrangements

1.13 Details of any child support maintenance calculation or any maintenance order or agreement made in respect of any children of the family. If no calculation, order or agreement has been made, give an estimate of the liability of the non-resident parent in respect of the children of the family under the Child Support Act 1991.

1.14 If this application is to vary an order, attach a copy of the order and give details of the part that is to be varied and the changes sought. You may need to continue on a separate sheet.

1.15 Details of any other court cases between you and your spouse/civil partner, whether in relation to money, property, children or anything else.

Case No	Court	Type of proceedings

1.16 Your present residence and the occupants of it and on what terms you occupy it (e.g. tenant, owner-occupier).

Address	Occupants	Terms of occupation

2 Financial Details

Part 1 Real Property (land and buildings) and Personal Assets

2.1 Complete this section in respect of the family home (the last family home occupied by you and your spouse/civil partner) if it remains unsold.

> Documentation required for attachment to this section:
> a) A copy of any valuation of the property obtained within the last six months. If you cannot provide this document, please give your own realistic estimate of the current market value
> b) A recent mortgage statement confirming the sum outstanding on **each** mortgage

Property name and address	
Land Registry title number	
Mortgage company name(s) and address(es) and account number(s)	
Type of mortgage	
Details of who owns the property and the extent of your legal and beneficial interest in it (i.e. state if it is owned by you solely or jointly owned with your spouse/civil partner or with others)	
If you consider that the legal ownership as recorded at the Land Registry does not reflect the true position, state why	
Current market value of the property	
Balance outstanding on any mortgage(s)	
If a sale at this stage would result in penalties payable under the mortgage, state amount	
Estimate the costs of sale of the property	
Total equity in the property (i.e. market value less outstanding mortgage(s), penalties if any and the costs of sale)	

TOTAL value of your interest in the family home: Total A | £

2.2 Details of your interest in any other property, land or buildings. Complete one page for each property you have an interest in.

Documentation required for attachment to this section:

a) A copy of any valuation of the property obtained within the last six months. If you cannot provide this document, please give your own realistic estimate of the current market value

b) A recent mortgage statement confirming the sum outstanding on **each** mortgage

Property name and address	
Land Registry title number	
Mortgage company name(s) and address(es) and account number(s)	
Type of mortgage	
Details of who owns the property and the extent of your legal and beneficial interest in it (i.e. state if it is owned by you solely or jointly owned with your spouse/civil partner or with others)	
If you consider that the legal ownership as recorded at the Land Registry does not reflect the true position, state why	
Current market value of the property	
Balance outstanding on any mortgage(s)	
If a sale at this stage would result in penalties payable under the mortgage, state amount	
Estimate the costs of sale of the property	
Total equity in the property (i.e. market value less outstanding mortgage(s), penalties if any and the costs of sale)	
Total value of your interest in this property	

TOTAL value of your interest in ALL other property: Total B | **£**

2.3 Details of all personal bank, building society and National Savings Accounts that you hold or have held at any time in the last twelve months and which are or were either in your own name or in which you have or have had any interest. This applies whether any such account is in credit or in debit. For joint accounts give your interest and the name of the other account holder. If the account is overdrawn, show a minus figure.

Documentation required for attachment to this section:
For each account listed, all statements covering the last 12 months.

Name of bank or building society, including branch name	Type of account (e.g. current)	Account number	Name of other account holder (if applicable)	Balance at the date of this statement	Total current value of your interest

TOTAL value of your interest in ALL accounts: (C1) £ 0.00

2.4 Details of all investments, including shares, PEPs, ISAs, TESSAs, National Savings Investments (other than already shown above), bonds, stocks, unit trusts, investment trusts, gilts and other quoted securities that you hold or have an interest in. (Do not include dividend income as this will be dealt with separately later on.)

Documentation required for attachment to this section:
Latest statement or dividend counterfoil relating to each investment.

Name	Type of Investment	Size of Holding	Current value	Name of any other account holder (if applicable)	Total current value of your interest

TOTAL value of your interest in ALL holdings: (C2) £ 0.00

2.5 Details of all life insurance policies including endowment policies that you hold or have an interest in. Include those that do not have a surrender value. Complete one page for each policy.

Documentation required for attachment to this section: A surrender valuation of each policy that has a surrender value.

Name of company			
Policy type			
Policy number			
If policy is assigned, state in whose favour and amount of charge			
Name of any other owner and the extent of your interest in the policy			
Maturity date (if applicable)	Date	Month	Year
Current surrender value (if applicable)			
If policy includes life insurance, the amount of the insurance and the name of the person whose life is insured			
Total current surrender value of your interest in this policy			

TOTAL value of your interest in ALL policies: (C3) £

2.6 Details of all monies that are OWED TO YOU. Do not include sums owed in director's or partnership accounts which should be included at section 2.11.

Brief description of money owed and by whom	Balance outstanding	Total current value of your interest

TOTAL value of your interest in ALL debts owed to you: (C4) £ 0.00

2.7 Details of all cash sums held in excess of £500. You must state where it is held and the currency it is held in.

Where held	Amount	Currency	Total current value of your interest
		TOTAL value of your interest in ALL cash sums: (C5)	£ 0.00

2.8 Details of personal belongings individually worth more than £500.

INCLUDE:

- Cars (gross value)
- Collections, pictures and jewellery
- Furniture and house contents

Brief description of item	Total current value of your interest
TOTAL value of your interest in ALL personal belongings: (C6)	£ 0.00
Add together all the figures in boxes C1 to C6 to give the TOTAL current value of your interest in personal assets: TOTAL C	**£** 0.00

2 Financial Details Part 2 Capital: Liabilities and Capital Gains Tax

2.9 Details of any liabilities you have.

EXCLUDE liabilities already shown such as:

- Mortgages
- Any overdrawn bank, building society or National Savings accounts

INCLUDE:

- Money owed on credit cards and store cards
- Bank loans
- Hire purchase agreements

List all credit and store cards held including those with a nil or positive balance. Where the liability is not solely your own, give the name(s) of the other account holder(s) and the amount of your share of the liability.

Liability	Name(s) of other account holder(s) (if applicable)	Total liability	Total current value of your interest in the liability
		TOTAL value of your interest in ALL liabilities: (D1)	£ 0.00

2.10 If any Capital Gains Tax would be payable on the disposal now of any of your real property or personal assets, give your estimate of the tax liability.

Asset	Total Capital Gains Tax liability
TOTAL value of ALL your potential Capital Gains Tax liabilities: (D2)	£
Add together D1 and D2 to give the TOTAL value of your liabilities: TOTAL D	**£** 0.00

2 Financial Details — Part 3 Capital: Business assets and directorships

2.11 Details of all your business interests. Complete one page for each business you have an interest in.

Documentation required for attachment to this section:
a) Copies of the business accounts for the last two financial years
b) Any documentation, if available at this stage, upon which you have based your estimate of the current value of your interest in this business, for example a letter from an accountant or a formal valuation.
It is not essential to obtain a formal valuation at this stage

Name of the business	
Briefly describe the nature of the business	
Are you (please tick appropriate box)	☐ Sole trader ☐ Partner in a partnership with others ☐ Shareholder in a limited company
If you are a partner or a shareholder, state the extent of your interest in the business (i.e. partnership share or the extent of your shareholding compared to the overall shares issued)	
State when your next set of accounts will be available	
If any of the figures in the last accounts are not an accurate reflection of the current position, state why. For example, if there has been a material change since the last accounts, or if the valuations of the assets are not a true reflection of their value (e.g. because property or other assets have not been re-valued in recent years or because they are shown at a book value)	
Total amount of any sums owed to you by the business by way of a director's loan account, partnership capital or current accounts or the like. Identify where these appear in the business accounts	
Your estimate of the current value of your business interest. Explain briefly the basis upon which you have reached that figure	
Your estimate of any Capital Gains Tax that would be payable if you were to dispose of your business now	
Net value of your interest in this business after any Capital Gains Tax liability	

TOTAL value of ALL your interests in business assets: TOTAL E | £

2.12 List any directorships you hold or have held in the last 12 months (other than those already disclosed in Section 2.11).

2 Financial Details

Part 4 Capital: Pensions and Pension Protection Fund (PPF) Compensation

2.13 Give details of all your pension rights and all PPF compensation entitlements, including prospective entitlements. Complete a separate page for each pension or PPF compensation entitlement.

EXCLUDE:

- Basic State Pension

INCLUDE (complete a separate page for each one):

- Additional State Pension (SERPS and State Second Pension (S2P))
- Free Standing Additional Voluntary Contribution Schemes (FSAVC) separate from the scheme of your employer
- Membership of ALL pension plans or schemes
- PPF compensation entitlement for each scheme you were a member of which has transferred to PPF

Documentation required for attachment to this section:

a) A recent statement showing the cash equivalent (CE) provided by the trustees or managers of each pension arrangement; for the additional state pension, a valuation of these rights or for PPF a valuation of PPF compensation entitlement

b) If any valuation is not available, give the estimated date when it will be available and attach a copy of your letter to the pension company, administrators, or PPF Board from whom the information was sought and/or state the date on which an application for a valuation of an Additional State Pension was submitted to the Department of Work and Pensions

Name and address of pension arrangement or PPF Board			
Your National Insurance Number			
Number of pension arrangement or reference number or PPF compensation reference number			
Type of scheme e.g. occupational or personal, final salary, money purchase, additional state pension, PPF or other (if other, please give details)			
Date the CE, PPF compensation or additional state pension was calculated	Date	Month	Year
Is the pension in payment or drawdown? (please answer Yes or No)	☐ Yes ☐ No		
State the CE quotation, the additional state pension valuation or PPF valuation of those rights			
If the arrangement is an occupational pension arrangement that is paying reduced CEs, please quote what the CE would have been if not reduced. If this is not possible, please indicate if the CE quoted is a reduced CE			
Is the PPF compensation capped? (please answer Yes or No)	☐ Yes ☐ No		

TOTAL value of ALL your pension assets: TOTAL F | £

2 Financial Details Part 5 Capital: Other assets

2.14 Give details of any other assets not listed in Parts 1 to 4 above.

INCLUDE (the following list is not exhaustive):

- Any personal or business assets not yet disclosed
- Unrealisable assets
- Share option schemes, stating the estimated net sale proceeds of the shares if the options were capable of exercise now, and whether Capital Gains Tax or income tax would be payable
- Business expansion schemes
- Futures
- Commodities
- Trust interests (including interests under a discretionary trust), stating your estimate of the value of the interest and when it is likely to become realisable. If you say it will never be realisable, or has no value, give your reasons
- Any asset that is likely to be received in the foreseeable future
- Any asset held on your behalf by a third party
- Any asset not disclosed elsewhere on this form even if held outside England and Wales

You are reminded of your obligation to disclose all your financial assets and interests of ANY nature.

Type of asset	Value	Total NET value of your interest
	TOTAL value of ALL your other assets: TOTAL G	£

2 Financial Details **Part 6 Income: Earned income from employment**

2.15 Details of earned income from employment. Complete one page for each employment.

Documentation required for attachment to this section:

a) P60 for the last financial year (you should have received this from your employer shortly after the last 5th April)

b) Your last three payslips

c) Your last Form P11D if you have been issued with one

Name and address of your employer	
Job title and brief details of the type of work you do	
Hours worked per week in this employment	
How long have you been with this employer?	
Explain the basis of your income i.e. state whether it is based on an annual salary or an hourly rate of pay and whether it includes commissions or bonuses	
Gross income for the last financial year as shown on your P60	
Net income for the last financial year i.e. gross income less income tax and national insurance	
Average net income for the last three months i.e. total income less income tax and national insurance divided by three	
Briefly explain any other entries on the attached payslips other than basic income, income tax and national insurance	
If the payslips attached for the last three months are not an accurate reflection of your normal income briefly explain why	
Details and value of any bonuses or other occasional payments that you receive from this employment not otherwise already shown, including the basis upon which they are paid	
Details and value of any benefits in kind, perks or other remuneration received from this employer in the last year (e.g. provision of a car, payment of travel, accommodation, meal expenses, etc.)	
Your estimate of your net income from this employment for the next 12 months. If this differs significantly from your current income explain why in box 4.1.2	

Estimated TOTAL of ALL net earned income from employment for the next 12 months: TOTAL H | £

2 Financial Details

Part 7 Income: Income from self-employment or partnership

2.16 You will have already given details of your business and provided the last two years accounts at section 2.11. Complete this section giving details of your income from your business. Complete one page for each business.

Documentation required for attachment to this section:

a) A copy of your last tax assessment or, if that is not available, a letter from your accountant confirming your tax liability

b) If net income from the last financial year and estimated net income for the next 12 months is significantly different, a copy of management accounts for the period since your last account

Name of the business	
Date to which your last accounts were completed	
Your share of gross business profit from the last completed accounts	
Income tax and national insurance payable on your share of gross business profit above	
Net income for that year (using the two figures directly above, gross business profit less income tax and national insurance payable)	
Details and value of any benefits in kind, perks or other remuneration received from this business in the last year e.g. provision of a car, payment of travel, accommodation, meal expenses, etc.	
Amount of any regular monthly or other drawings that you take from this business	
If the estimated figure directly below is different from the net income as at the end date of the last completed accounts, briefly explain the reason(s)	
Your estimate of your net annual income for the next 12 months	

Estimated TOTAL of ALL net income from self-employment or partnership for the next 12 months: TOTAL I £

2 Financial Details

Part 8 Income: Income from investments e.g. dividends, interest or rental income

2.17 Details of income received in the last financial year (the year ended last 5th April), and your estimate of your income for the current financial year. Indicate whether the income was paid gross or net of income tax. You are not required to calculate any tax payable that may arise.

Nature of income and the asset from which it derived	Paid gross or net	Income received in the last financial year	Estimated income for the next 12 months

Estimated TOTAL investment income for the next 12 months: TOTAL J £

2 Financial Details

Part 9 Income: Income from state benefits (including state pension and child benefit)

2.18 Details of all state benefits that you are currently receiving.

Name of benefit	Amount paid	Frequency of payment	Estimated income for the next 12 months

Estimated TOTAL benefit income for the next 12 months: TOTAL K £

2 Financial Details Part 10 Income: Any other income

2.19 Details of any other income not disclosed above.

INCLUDE:

Any source including a Pension (excluding State Pension), and Pension Protection Fund (PPF) compensation

- from which income has been received during the last 12 months (even if it has now ceased)
- from which income is likely to be received during the next 12 months

You are reminded of your obligation to give full disclosure of your financial circumstances

Nature of income	Paid gross or net	Income received in the last financial year	Estimated income for the next 12 months

Estimated TOTAL other income for the next 12 months: TOTAL L £

2 Financial Details Summaries

2.20 Summary of your capital (Parts 1 to 5).

Description	Reference of the section on this statement	Value
Current value of your interest in the family home	A	
Current value of your interest in all other property	B	
Current value of your interest in personal assets	C	0.00
Current value of your liabilities	D	0.00
Current value of your interest in business assets	E	
Current value of your pension and PPF compensation assets	F	
Current value of all your other assets	G	

TOTAL value of your assets (Totals A to G less D): £ 0.00

2.21 Summary of your estimated income for the next 12 months (Parts 6 to 10).

Description	Reference of the section on this statement	Value
Estimated net total of income from employment	H	
Estimated net total of income from self-employment or partnership	I	
Estimated net total of investment income	J	
Estimated state benefit receipts	K	
Estimated net total of all other income	L	

Estimated TOTAL income for the next 12 months (Totals H to L): £ 0.00

3 Financial Requirements Part 1 Income needs

3.1 Income needs for yourself and for any children living with you or provided for by you. ALL figures should be annual, monthly or weekly (state which). You ***must not*** use a combination of these periods. State your current income needs and, if these are likely to change in the near future, explain the anticipated change and give an estimate of the future cost.

The income needs below are: (delete those not applicable)	Weekly	Monthly	Annual
I anticipate my income needs are going to change because			

3.1.1 Income needs for yourself.

INCLUDE:

- All income needs for yourself
- Income needs for any children living with you or provided for by you only if these form part of your total income needs (e.g. housing, fuel, car expenses, holidays, etc)

Item	Current cost	Estimated future cost
	SUB-TOTAL your income needs	£

3.1.2 Income needs for children living with you or provided for by you.

INCLUDE:

- Only those income needs that are different to those of your household shown above

Item	Current cost	Estimated future cost
	SUB-TOTAL children's income needs:	£
	TOTAL of ALL income needs:	**£** 0.00

3 Financial Requirements Part 2 Capital needs

3.2 Set out below the reasonable future capital needs for yourself and for any children living with you or provided for by you.

3.2.1 Capital needs for yourself.

INCLUDE:

- All capital needs for yourself
- Capital needs for any children living with you or provided for by you only if these form part of your total capital needs (e.g. housing, car, etc.)

Item	Cost
SUB-TOTAL your capital needs:	£

3.2.2 Capital needs for children living with you or provided for by you.

INCLUDE:

- Only those capital needs that are different to those of your household shown above

Item	Cost
SUB-TOTAL your children's capital needs	£
TOTAL of ALL capital needs:	**£** 0.00

4 Other Information

4.1 Details of any significant changes in your assets or income.

At both sections 4.1.1 and 4.1.2, INCLUDE:

- ALL assets held both within and outside England and Wales
- The disposal of any asset

4.1.1 Significant changes in assets or income during the LAST 12 months.

4.1.2 Significant changes in assets or income likely to occur during the NEXT 12 months.

4.2 Brief details of the standard of living enjoyed by you and your spouse/civil partner during the marriage/civil partnership.

4.3 Are there any particular contributions to the family property and assets or outgoings, or to family life, or the welfare of the family that have been made by you, your partner or anyone else that you think should be taken into account? If there are any such items, briefly describe the contribution and state the amount, when it was made and by whom.

INCLUDE:

- Contributions already made
- Contributions that will be made in the foreseeable future

4.4 Bad behaviour or conduct by the other party will only be taken into account in very exceptional circumstances when deciding how assets should be shared after divorce/dissolution. If you feel it should be taken into account in your case, identify the nature of the behaviour or conduct below.

4.5 Give details of any other circumstances that you consider could significantly affect the extent of the financial provision to be made by or for you or any child of the family.

INCLUDE (the following list is not exhaustive):

- Earning capacity
- Disability
- Inheritance prospects
- Redundancy
- Retirement
- Any agreement made between you and your spouse/civil partner before or after your marriage/civil partnership stating whether or not you rely upon the agreement giving your reasons
- Any plans to marry, form a civil partnership or live with a new partner
- Any contingent liabilities

4.6 If you have subsequently married or formed a civil partnership (or intend to) or are living with another person (or intend to), give brief details, so far as they are known to you, of his or her income, assets and liabilities.

Annual Income		Assets and Liabilities	
Nature of income	Value (if known, state whether gross or net)	Item	Value (if known)
Total income:	£	Total assets/liabilities:	£

5 Order Sought

5.1 If you are able at this stage, specify what kind of orders you are asking the court to make. Even if you cannot be specific at this stage, if you are able to do so, indicate:

a) If the family home is still owned, whether you are asking for it to be transferred to yourself or your spouse/civil partner or whether you are saying it should be sold

b) Whether you consider this is a case for continuing spousal maintenance/maintenance for your civil partner or whether you see the case as being appropriate for a 'clean break' *(A 'clean break' means a settlement or order which provides amongst other things, that neither you nor your spouse/civil partner will have any further claim against the income or capital of the other party. A 'clean break' does not terminate the responsibility of a parent to a child.)*

c) Whether you are seeking a

i) pension sharing order

ii) pension attachment order

iii) pension compensation sharing order

iv) pension compensation attachment order

d) If you are seeking a transfer or settlement of any property or assets, identify the property or assets in question

5.2 If you are seeking a variation of an ante-nuptial or post-nuptial settlement or a relevant settlement made during, or in anticipation of, a civil partnership, identify the settlement, by whom it was made, its trustees and beneficiaries and state why you allege it is a settlement which the court can vary.

5.3 If you are seeking an avoidance of disposition order, or if you have already applied for such an order, identify the property to which the disposition relates and the person or body in whose favour the disposition is alleged to have been made.

Sworn confirmation of the information

I, [ ] Enter your full name

of [ ] Enter your full residential address

The above named ☐ Applicant
☐ Respondent

☐ make oath
☐ affirm

and confirm that the information given above is a full, frank, clear and accurate disclosure of my financial and other relevant circumstances.

SWORN/AFFIRMED at [ ]

in the County of [ ]

on D D / M M / Y Y Y Y

[ ]

Before me, [ ]

☐ A Commissioner for Oaths
☐ Officer of the Court appointed by the Judge to take Affidavits

---

Address all communications to the Court Manager of the Court and quote the case number. If you do not quote this number, your correspondence may be returned.

Schedule of Documents to accompany Form E

The following list shows the documents you must attach to your Form E if applicable. You may attach other documents where it is necessary to explain or clarify any of the information that you give in the Form E.

Form E paragraph	Document	Please tick		
		Attached	Not applicable	To follow
1.14	**Application to vary an order:** if applicable, attach a copy of the relevant order.	☐	☐	☐
2.1	**Matrimonial home valuation:** a copy of any valuation relating to the matrimonial home that has been obtained in the last six months.	☐	☐	☐
2.1	**Matrimonial home mortgage(s):** a recent mortgage statement in respect of each mortgage on the matrimonial home confirming the amount outstanding.	☐	☐	☐
2.2	**Any other property:** a copy of any valuation relating to each other property disclosed that has been obtained in the last six months.	☐	☐	☐
2.2	**Any other property:** a recent mortgage statement in respect of each mortgage on each other property disclosed confirming the amount outstanding.	☐	☐	☐
2.3	**Personal bank, building society and National Savings accounts:** copies of statements for the last 12 months for each account that has been held in the last twelve months, either in your own name or in which you have or have had any interest.	☐	☐	☐
2.4	**Other investments:** the latest statement or dividend counterfoil relating to each investment as disclosed in paragraph 2.4.	☐	☐	☐
2.5	**Life insurance (including endowment) policies:** a surrender valuation for each policy that has a surrender value as disclosed under paragraph 2.5.	☐	☐	☐
2.11	**Business interests:** a copy of the business accounts for the last two financial years for each business interest disclosed.	☐	☐	☐
2.11	**Business interests:** any documentation that is available to confirm the estimate of the current value of the business, for example, a letter from an accountant or formal valuation if that has been obtained.	☐	☐	☐
2.13	**Pension and PPF compensation:** a recent statement showing the cash equivalent (CE) provided by the trustees or managers of each pension arrangement or valuation of each PPF entitlement provided by the PPF Board that you have disclosed (or, in the case of the additional state pension, a valuation of these rights). If not yet available, attach a copy of the letter sent to the pension company, administrators or the PPF Board requesting the information.	☐	☐	☐
2.15	**Employment income:** your P60 for the last financial year in respect of each employment that you have.	☐	☐	☐
2.15	**Employment income:** your last three payslips in respect of each employment that you have.	☐	☐	☐
2.15	**Employment income:** your last form P11D if you have been issued with one.	☐	☐	☐
2.16	**Self-employment or partnership income:** a copy of your last tax assessment or if that is not available, a letter from your accountant confirming your tax liability.	☐	☐	☐
2.16	**Self-employment or partnership income:** if net income from the last financial year and the estimated income for the next twelve months is significantly different, a copy of the management accounts for the period since your last accounts.	☐	☐	☐
State relevant Form E paragraph	Description of other documents attached:	☐	☐	☐

(F) Form D81 (Statement of information for a consent order)

Statement of information for a consent order in relation to a financial remedy

To be completed by the parties	
Name of court	Case No.
Name of Petitioner/Applicant	
Name of Respondent	

If completing this form by hand, please use **black ink and BLOCK CAPITAL LETTERS** and tick the boxes that apply.

You may complete separate forms if you wish. However both parties must confirm they have read the contents of each statement of information.

Details of the marriage/civil partnership

1. Please give the date of the ☐ marriage ☐ civil partnership   DD/MM/YYYY

2. On what date did you separate?   DD/MM/YYYY

3. On what date was your decree nisi/conditional order of divorce/ dissolution/nullity or (judicial) separation decree/order pronounced?   DD/MM/YYYY

   (Please note that a consent order cannot be made until the court has pronounced a decree nisi/conditional order unless it is a consent order for maintenance pending suit.)

4. On what date was your decree absolute/final order of divorce/ dissolution/nullity granted?   DD/MM/YYYY

   If this has not yet been pronounced please write 'not applicable'

Dates of birth of the parties

5. Please give the date of birth of the parties along with the date of birth of any child(ren) of the family aged under 18, or any other child(ren) dependant upon the family.

	Date of birth		
Petitioner/ Applicant	DD/MM/YYYY		
Respondent	DD/MM/YYYY		
Child(ren) (if applicable)	DD/MM/YYYY	DD/MM/YYYY	DD/MM/YYYY
	DD/MM/YYYY	DD/MM/YYYY	DD/MM/YYYY

Financial agreements

6. Please state how the attached proposed consent order was reached e.g. discussions between parties, negotiations through solicitors, Mediation, Collaborative Process or other out of court dispute resolution process.

Summary of means

The information in this section should so far as possible be correct as at the time this statement is signed.

The information should therefore be stated before implementation of the proposed consent order.

If the application is made only for an order for interim periodical payments or for variation of an order for periodical payments, you need only give details of 'net income'.

Capital

7. Please give the following information for each party and the child(ren) (if applicable). Use additional sheets if necessary. Jointly owned capital should be divided as appropriate and listed below. If no agreement has been reached regarding shares, it should be divided equally.

Type of capital	Petitioner/Applicant	Respondent	Child(ren) if applicable
a. Property (net of any mortgage(s))	£	£	£
b. Other capital e.g. savings, investments, ISAs etc	£	£	£
c. Gross capital (a. plus b.)	£	£	£
d. c. less liabilities (excluding mortgages deducted at a.) e.g. loans and overdrafts	£	£	£
e. Net capital excluding pensions and Pension Protection Fund (PPF) compensation (c. less d.)	£	£	£
f. Pensions valuation including the Additional State Pension (cash equivalent)	£	£	£
g. PPF compensation valuation	£	£	£
h. Total capital (e. plus f. plus g.)	£	£	£

Income

8. Please state for each party, their total **net** (after deductions for tax and NI contributions only) monthly income from all sources e.g. wages, state benefits, child support and maintenance payments, pension or PPF compensation payments, interest from bank accounts, tips etc.

Petitioner/Applicant	£
Respondent	£
Child(ren) (if applicable)	£

9. Are there any other matters relating to the proposed consent order that the court should consider e.g. medical conditions, change of employment, any significant change in circumstances, any prior agreement reached between the parties etc?

Where the parties and the children will live

10. Please give details of where the named parties will live and the basis on which you will occupy the property e.g. owner, tenant etc.

	Address	Basis of occupation in property
Petitioner/Applicant		
Respondent		
Child(ren) (if applicable)		

New relationships

11. Please tick the appropriate box below

Petitioner/Applicant

- ☐ I have no intention at present to remarry/enter into a new civil partnership or cohabit.
- ☐ I have remarried/formed a civil partnership.
  The date of the marriage/civil partnership was D D / M M / Y Y Y Y
- ☐ I intend to remarry/form a civil partnership.
  The date of the intended marriage/civil partnership is D D / M M / Y Y Y Y
- ☐ I am in a cohabiting relationship with another person.
- ☐ I intend to cohabit.

Respondent

- ☐ I have no intention at present to remarry/enter into a new civil partnership or cohabit.
- ☐ I have remarried/formed a civil partnership.
  The date of the marriage/civil partnership was D D / M M / Y Y Y Y
- ☐ I intend to remarry/form a civil partnership.
  The date of the intended marriage/civil partnership is D D / M M / Y Y Y Y
- ☐ I am in a cohabiting relationship with another person.
- ☐ I intend to cohabit.

continued over the page ➪

Notice to mortgagee

These questions are to be answered by the Petitioner/Applicant where the terms of the order provide for a transfer of property.

12. Has every mortgagee (if any) of the property been served with notice of the application?

☐ Yes ☐ No

13. Has any objection to a transfer of property been made by any mortgagee, within 14 days from the date when the notice of the application was served?

☐ Yes ☐ No

Notice to pension arrangement/PPF Board

These questions are to be answered by the Petitioner/Applicant where the terms of an order include provision for a pension attachment order and/or a PPF pension compensation attachment order.

(Please note that if you wish to include provision relating to a pension or to PPF compensation in your consent order you should first seek legal advice as this area of law is complex. Court staff are unable to assist, as they are not trained to give legal advice.)

14. Has notice been served on every person responsible for any pension arrangement under Rules 9.33(1) or 9.34, and/or the PPF Board under 9.42 or 9.43 of the Family Procedure Rules 2010

☐ Yes ☐ No

15. Has any objection to an attachment order been made by the person responsible for the pension arrangements within 21 days from the date when the notice of the application was served?

☐ Yes ☐ No

Pension sharing on divorce, dissolution or nullity

These questions are to be answered by the Petitioner/Applicant where the terms of an order include provision for a PPF compensation sharing order.

(Please note that if you wish to include provision relating to a PPF compensation in your consent order you should first seek legal advice. Court staff are unable to assist, as they are not trained to give legal advice.)

16. Has the PPF Board provided the information required by Regulation 5 of The Pension Protection Fund (Pension Compensation and Attachment on Divorce etc) Regulations 2011?

☐ Yes ☐ No

17. Does it appear from that information that there is power to make an order for compensation sharing?

☐ Yes ☐ No

Proposed consent order

Please ensure that you attach the proposed consent order with this completed form when lodging at court, and if appropriate, any pension sharing/attachment annex or compensation sharing/annex.

Petitioner/Applicant's Statement of Truth *delete as appropriate

*I ____________________ (Petitioner/Applicant's full name)

believe that the facts stated in this Statement of information for a consent order are true.

I confirm that I have read a fully completed Statement of information for a consent order from the Respondent and that I have made full disclosure of all relevant facts.

*I am duly authorised by the Petitioner/Applicant to sign this statement

Print full name ____________________

Name of Petitioner/ Applicant's solicitor's firm ____________________

Signed ____________________ Dated D D / M M / Y Y Y Y

*Petitioner/Applicant('s solicitor)('s litigation friend)

Position or office held (if signing on behalf of firm or company) ____________________

Proceedings for contempt of court may be brought against a person who makes or causes to be made, a false statement in a document verified by a statement of truth.

Respondent's Statement of Truth *delete as appropriate

*I ____________________ (Respondent's full name)

believe that the facts stated in this Statement of information for a consent order are true.

I confirm that I have read a fully completed Statement of information for a consent order from the Petitioner/Applicant and that I have made full disclosure of all relevant facts.

*I am duly authorised by the Respondent to sign this statement

Print full name ____________________

Name of Respondent's solicitor's firm ____________________

Signed ____________________ Dated D D / M M / Y Y Y Y

*(Respondent('s solicitor)('s litigation friend)

Position or office held (if signing on behalf of firm or company) ____________________

Proceedings for contempt of court may be brought against a person who makes or causes to be made, a false statement in a document verified by a statement of truth.

6

(G) Parental responsibility agreement (1)

Parental Responsibility Agreement
Section 4(1)(b) Children Act 1989

Keep this form in a safe place
Date recorded at the Principal Registry of the Family Division:

Read the notes on the other side before you make this agreement.

This is a Parental Responsibility Agreement regarding

the Child — *Full Name* ______________________

Gender ________ *Date of birth* ________ *Date of 18th birthday* ________

Between the Mother
Name
Address

and the Father
Name
Address

We declare that
we are the mother and father of the above child and we agree that the child's father shall have parental responsibility for the child (in addition to the mother having parental responsibility).

Signed **(Mother)**	Signed **(Father)**
Date	Date

Certificate of witness

The following evidence of identity was produced by the person signing above:	The following evidence of identity was produced by the person signing above:
Signed in the presence of: *Name of Witness*	Signed in the presence of: *Name of Witness*
Address	*Address*
Signature of Witness	*Signature of Witness*
[A Justice of the Peace] [Justices' Clerk] [An assistant to a justices' clerk] [An officer of the court authorised by the judge to administer oaths]	[A Justice of the Peace] [Justices' Clerk] [An assistant to a justices' clerk] [An Officer of the Court authorised by the judge to administer oaths]

C(PRA1) (09.09)

Notes about the Parental Responsibility Agreement

Read these notes before you make the agreement.

About the Parental Responsibility Agreement

The making of this agreement will affect the legal position of the mother and the father. You should both seek legal advice before you make the Agreement. You can obtain the name and address of a solicitor from the Children Panel (020 7242 1222)

or from
- your local family proceedings court, or county court
- a Citizens Advice Bureau
- a Law Centre
- a local library.

You may be eligible for public funding.

When you fill in the Agreement

Please use black ink (the Agreement will be copied). Put the name of one child only. If the father is to have parental responsibility for more than one child, fill in a separate form for each child. **Do not sign the Agreement.**

When you have filled in the Agreement

Take it to a local family proceedings court, or county court, or the Principal Registry of the Family Division (the address is below).

A justice of the peace, a justices' clerk, an assistant to a justices' clerk, or a court official who is authorised by the judge to administer oaths, will witness your signature and he or she will sign the certificate of the witness. **A solicitor cannot witness your signature.**

To the mother: When you make the declaration you will have to prove that you are the child's mother so take to the court the child's full birth certificate.

You will also need evidence of your identity showing a photograph and signature (for example, a photocard, official pass or passport). **Please note that the child's birth certificate cannot be accepted as sufficient proof of your identity.**

To the father: You will need evidence of your identity showing a photograph and signature (for example, a photocard, official pass or passport).

When the Certificate has been signed and witnessed

Make 2 copies of the Agreement form. You do not need to copy these notes.

Take, or send, this form and the copies to **The Principal Registry of the Family Division, First Avenue House, 42-49 High Holborn, London, WC1V 6NP**.

The Registry will record the Agreement and keep this form. The copies will be stamped and sent back to each parent at the address on the Agreement. The Agreement will not take effect until it has been received and recorded at the Principal Registry of the Family Division.

Ending the Agreement

Once a parental responsibility agreement has been made it can only end
- by an order of the court made on the application of any person who has parental responsibility for the child
- by an order of the court made on the application of the child with permission of the court
- when the child reaches the age of 18.

C(PRA1) (Notes) (12.05)

(H) Parental responsibility agreement (2)

Step-Parent Parental Responsibility Agreement

Section 4A(1)(a) Children Act 1989

Keep this form in a safe place

Date recorded at the Principal Registry of the Family Division:

Read the notes on the other side before you make this agreement.

This is a Step-Parent Parental Responsibility Agreement regarding

the Child — *Full Name* ______________________

Gender ______ *Date of birth* ______ *Date of 18th birthday* ______

Between

Parent A — *Name*

Address

and

*the other parent (with parental responsibility) — *Name*

Address

and

the step-parent — *Name*

Address

We declare that — we are the parents and step-parent of the above child and we agree that the above mentioned step-parent shall have parental responsibility for the child (in addition to those already having parental responsibility).

	Signed **(Parent A)**	*Signed **(Other Parent)**	Signed **(Step-Parent)**
	Date	Date	Date
Certificate of witness	The following evidence of identity was produced by the person signing above:	The following evidence of identity was produced by the person signing above:	The following evidence of identity was produced by the person signing above:
	Signed in the presence of: *Name of Witness*	Signed in the presence of: *Name of Witness*	Signed in the presence of: *Name of Witness*
	Address	*Address*	*Address*
*If there is only one parent with parental responsibility, please delete this section.	*Signature of Witness*	*Signature of Witness*	*Signature of Witness*
	[A Justice of the Peace] [Justices' Clerk] [An assistant to a justices' clerk] [An Officer of the Court authorised by the judge to administer oaths]	[A Justice of the Peace] [Justices' Clerk] [An assistant to a justices' clerk] [An Officer of the Court authorised by the judge to administer oaths]	[A Justice of the Peace] [Justices' Clerk] [An assistant to a justices' clerk] [An Officer of the Court authorised by the judge to administer oaths]

C(PRA2) (09.09)

Notes about the Step-Parent Parental Responsibility Form

Read these notes before you make the Agreement

About the Step-Parent Parental Responsibility Agreement

The making of this agreement will affect the legal position of the parent(s) and the step-parent. You should seek legal advice before you make the Agreement. You can obtain the name and address of a solicitor from the Children Panel (020 7242 1222) or from:

- your local family proceedings court, or county court,
- a Citizens Advice Bureau,
- a Law Centre,
- a local library.

You may be eligible for public funding.

When you fill in the Agreement

Please use black ink (the Agreement will be copied). Put the name of one child only. If the step-parent is to have parental responsibility for more than one child, fill in a separate form for each child. **Do not sign the Agreement.**

When you have filled in the Agreement

Take it to a local family proceedings court, or county court, or the Principal Registry of the Family Division (the address is below).

A justice of the peace, a justices' clerk, an assistant to a justices' clerk, or a court official who is authorised by the judge to administer oaths, will witness your signature and he or she will sign the certificate of the witness. **A solicitor cannot witness your signature.**

To Parent A and the Other Parent with parental responsibility:

When you make the declaration you will have to prove that you have parental responsibility for the child. You should therefore take with you to the court one of the following documents:

- the child's full birth certificate and a marriage certificate or civil partnership certificate to show that the parents were married to each other or were in a civil partnership with each other at the time of birth or subsequently,
- a court order granting parental responsibility,
- a registered Parental Responsibility Agreement Form between the child's mother and father or other parent
- if the birth was registered after the 1 December 2003, the child's full birth certificate showing that the parents jointly registered the child's birth.

You will also require evidence of your (both parents') identity showing a photograph and signature (for example, a photocard, official pass or passport) **(Please note that the child's birth certificate cannot be accepted as sufficient proof of your identity.)**

To the step-parent: When you make the declaration you will have to prove that you are married to, or the civil partner of, a parent of the child so take to the court your marriage certificate or certificate of civil partnership.

You will also need evidence of your identity showing a photograph and signature (for example, a photocard, official pass or passport).

When the Certificate has been signed and witnessed

Make sufficient copies of the Agreement Form for each person who has signed the form. You do not need to copy these notes.

Take, or send, the original form and the copies to: **The Principal Registry of the Family Division, First Avenue House, 42-49 High Holborn, London, WC1V 6NP.**

The Registry will record the Agreement and retain the original form. The copies will be stamped with the seal of the court and sent back to every person with parental responsibility who has signed the Agreement Form and to the step-parent. The Agreement will not take effect until it has been received and recorded at the Principal Registry of the Family Division.

Ending the Agreement

Once a step-parent parental responsibility agreement has been made it can only end:

- by an order of the court made on the application of any person who has parental responsibility for the child,
- by an order of the court made on the application of the child with permission of the court,
- when the child reaches the age of 18.

(I) Form C1 (Children Act application)

Application for an order

Form C1

Children Act 1989

The court	To be completed by the court
	Date issued
	Case number
The full name(s) of the child(ren)	Child(ren)'s number(s)

Important Note

You should only answer question 7 if you are asking the court to make one of the following orders: **a Contact Order, a Residence Order, a Prohibited Steps Order, a Specific Issue Order or a Parental Responsibility Order.**

1 About you (the person completing this form known as 'the applicant')

State:

- *your title, full name, address, telephone number, date of birth and relationship to each child above*
- *your solicitor's name, address, reference, telephone, FAX and DX numbers.*

2 The child(ren) and the order(s) you are applying for

For each child state:

- *the full name, date of birth and sex*
- *the type of order(s) you are applying for (for example, residence order, contact order, supervision order).*

3 Other cases which concern the child(ren)

If there have ever been, or there are pending, any court cases which concern:
- *a child whose name you have put in paragraph 2*
- *a full, half or step brother or sister of a child whose name you have put in paragraph 2*
- *a person in this case who is or has been, involved in caring for a child whose name you have put in paragraph 2*

attach a copy of the relevant order and give:
- *the name of the court*
- *the name and contact address (if known) of the children's guardian, if appointed*
- *the name and contact address (if known) of the children and family reporter, if appointed*
- *the name and contact address (if known) of the welfare officer, if appointed*
- *the name and contact address (if known) of the solicitor appointed for the child(ren).*

4 The respondent(s)

Appendix 3 Family Proceedings Rules 1991; Schedule 2 Family Proceedings Courts (Children Act 1989) Rules 1991

For each respondent state:
- *the title, full name and address*
- *the date of birth (if known) or the age*
- *the relationship to each child.*

5 Others to whom notice is to be given

Appendix 3 Family Proceedings Rules 1991; Schedule 2 Family Proceedings Courts (Children Act 1989) Rules 1991

For each person state:

- *the title, full name and address*
- *the date of birth (if known) or the age*
- *the relationship to each child.*

6 The care of the child(ren)

For each child in paragraph 2 state:

- *the child's current address and how long the child has lived there*
- *whether it is the child's usual address and who cares for the child there*
- *the child's relationship to the other children (if any).*

7 Domestic abuse, violence or harm

Do you believe that the child(ren) named above have suffered or are at risk of suffering any harm from any of the following:

- *any form of domestic abuse*
- *violence within the household*
- *child abduction*
- *other conduct or behaviour*

by any person who is or has been involved in caring for the child(ren) or lives with, or has contact with, the child(ren)?

	Yes	No
Please tick the box which applies	☐	☐

If you tick the Yes box,* you must *also fill in Supplemental Information Form (form C1A). *You can obtain a copy of this from a court office if one has not been enclosed with the papers served on you.*

8 Social Services

For each child in paragraph 2 state:

- *whether the child is known to the Social Services. If so, give the name of the social worker and the address of the Social Services department.*
- *whether the child is, or has been, on the Child Protection Register. If so, give details of registration.*

9 The education and health of the child(ren)

For each child state:

- *the name of the school, college or place of training which the child attends*
- *whether the child is in good health. Give details of any serious disabilities or ill health.*
- *whether the child has any special needs.*

10 The parents of the child(ren)

For each child state:

- *the full name of the child's parents*
- *whether the parents are, or have been, married to each other or civil partners of each other*
- *whether the parents live together. If so, where.*
- *whether, to your knowledge, either of the parents have been involved in a court case concerning a child. If so, give the date and the name of the court.*

11 The family of the child(ren) (other children)

For any other child not already mentioned in the family (for example, a brother or half sister) state:

- *the full name and address*
- *the date of birth (if known) or age*
- *the relationship of the child to you.*

12 Other adults

State:

- *the full name of any other adults (for example, lodgers) who live at the same address as any child named in paragraph 2*
- *whether they live there all the time*
- *whether, to your knowledge, the adult has been involved in a court case concerning a child. If so, give the date and the name of the court.*

13 Your reason(s) for applying and any plans for the child(ren)

State briefly your reasons for applying and what you want the court to order.

- ***Do not** give a full statement if you are applying for an order under Section 8 of Children Act 1989. You may be asked to provide a full statement later.*
- ***Do not** complete this section if this form is accompanied by a supplementary form.*

14 Attending the court

State:

- *whether you will need an interpreter at court. If so, please indicate what language interpreter you will use. If you require an interpreter you must notify the court immediately so that one can be arranged.*
- *whether you have a disability for which you require special assistance or special facilities. If so, please say what your needs are. The court staff will get in touch with you about your requirements.*

15 Parenting Information – Arrangements after Separation

	Yes	No
Have you received a Parenting Plan booklet? (If No, you may obtain a copy from a court office, a citizen's advice bureau or other family advice service.)	☐	☐
Have you agreed to a Parenting Plan? (If Yes, please include a copy of the Plan when you send your application to the court)	☐	☐
If you did agree a Parenting Plan, has the Plan broken down?	☐	☐

If Yes, please explain briefly why the Plan broke down –

Signed
(Applicant)

Date

C1

(J) Form C100 (Application for a s 8 order)

C100

Application under the Children Act 1989 for a residence, contact or other section 8 order

To be completed by the court	
Name of court	
Date issued	
Case number	
Child(ren)'s name(s)	Child(ren)'s number(s)

Before completing this application please read the booklet **'CB1 – Making an application – Children and the Family Courts'**. You can get a copy of all the forms and leaflets from your local court or they can be found at www.hmcourts-service.gov.uk

Cafcass/CAFCASS CYMRU will carry out checks as it considers necessary.

Cafcass - Children and Family Court Advisory and Support Service (in England); CAFCASS CYMRU - Children and Family Court Advisory and Support Service Wales.

Summary of application

Some people need permission to apply - See Section C of the booklet CB1

Have you applied to the court for permission to make this application? ☐ Yes ☐ Permission not required

Your name (the applicant(s))

The respondent's name(s)
See Sections G and H of the booklet CB1.

Please list the name(s) of the child(ren) and the type(s) of order you are applying for, starting with the oldest. To understand which order to apply for read the booklet CB1 Section D.

Name of child(ren)	Date of birth	Order(s) applied for
	D D / M M / Y Y Y Y	
	D D / M M / Y Y Y Y	
	D D / M M / Y Y Y Y	
	D D / M M / Y Y Y Y	
	D D / M M / Y Y Y Y	
	D D / M M / Y Y Y Y	

1. About you (the applicant)

Your first name

Middle name(s)

Surname

Previous surnames (if any)

Date of birth D D / M M / Y Y Y Y   Sex ☐ Male ☐ Female

Place of birth (town/county/country)

If you do not wish your address to be made known to the respondent, leave the address details blank and complete Confidential Address Form C8.

Address

Postcode

Home telephone number

Mobile telephone number

Have you lived at this address for more than 5 years? ☐ Yes ☐ No

If No, please provide details of all previous addresses you have lived at for the last 5 years.

Your solicitor's details

Do you have a solicitor acting for you? ☐ Yes ☐ No

If Yes, please give the following details

Your solicitor's name

Name of firm

Address

Postcode

Telephone number

Fax number

DX number

Solicitor's Reference

Applicant 2 (if applicable)

Your first name

Middle name(s)

Surname

Previous surnames (if any)

Date of birth D D / M M / Y Y Y Y Sex ☐ Male ☐ Female

Place of birth (town/county/country)

If your address details and those of your solicitor are different from the first applicant please provide details of these on a separate sheet.

What is your relationship to the applicant listed above?

2. The child(ren)

Please give details of the child(ren) and the order(s) you are applying for. If there are more than 4 children please continue on a separate sheet.

Child 1

Child's first name

Middle name(s)

Surname

Sex ☐ Male ☐ Female

What is your relationship to the child?

Applicant 1	Applicant 2

Is the child known by the Local Authority children's services? ☐ Yes ☐ No ☐ Don't know

If Yes, what is the name of the:

Local Authority

Social worker (If known)

Is the child subject of a child protection plan? ☐ Yes ☐ No ☐ Don't know

Who are the child's parents?

Who does the child live with?

Please give the full names of any other adults living at the same address and their relationship to the child.

Child 2

Child's first name

Middle name(s)

Surname

Sex ☐ Male ☐ Female

What is your relationship to the child?

Applicant 1	Applicant 2

Is the child known by the Local Authority children's services? ☐ Yes ☐ No ☐ Don't know

If Yes, what is the name of the:

Local Authority

Social worker (If known)

Is the child subject of a child protection plan? ☐ Yes ☐ No ☐ Don't know

Who are the child's parents?

Who does the child live with?

Please give the full names of any other adults living at the same address and their relationship to the child.

Child 3

Child's first name

Middle name(s)

Surname

Sex ☐ Male ☐ Female

What is your relationship to the child?

Applicant 1	Applicant 2

Is the child known by the Local Authority children's services? ☐ Yes ☐ No ☐ Don't know

If Yes, what is the name of the:

Local Authority

Social worker (If known)

Is the child subject of a child protection plan? ☐ Yes ☐ No ☐ Don't know

Who are the child's parents?

Who does the child live with?

Please give the full names of any other adults living at the same address and their relationship to the child.

Child 4

Child's first name

Middle name(s)

Surname

Sex ☐ Male ☐ Female

What is your relationship to the child?

Applicant 1	Applicant 2

Is the child known by the Local Authority children's services? ☐ Yes ☐ No ☐ Don't know

If Yes, what is the name of the:

Local Authority

Social worker (If known)

Is the child subject of a child protection plan? ☐ Yes ☐ No ☐ Don't know

Who are the child's parents?

Who does the child live with?

Please give the full names of any other adults living at the same address and their relationship to the child.

3. Why are you making this application?

Please give brief details about why you are making this application. You should include details of:

- any previous agreements (formal or informal), and how they have broken down
- your reasons for bringing this application to the court
- what you want the court to do.

Do not give a full statement, please provide a summary. You may be asked to provide a full statement later.

4. Agreements about residence and/or contact

Have you received a copy of the 'Parenting Plan: Putting your children first: A guide for separating parents', booklet?

☐ Yes ☐ No

If No, you can get a copy free of charge from your local court or you can download a copy from the website www.tso.co.uk

Have you used family mediation to attempt to agree arrangements for your children?

☐ Yes ☐ No

If you would like to find out more about mediation please ask at your local court or see the website www.familymediationhelpline.co.uk.

Please give brief details about:

- If you attended family mediation what was the outcome?
- If you did not use mediation please explain why?

5. Risk

Do you believe that the child(ren) named at Section 2 have suffered or are at risk of suffering any harm from any of the following:

- any form of domestic abuse
- violence within the household
- child abduction
- other conduct or behaviour

by any person who has had contact with the child?

☐ Yes ☐ No ☐ Other

If Yes, please complete form C1A (Supplemental information form).

If Other, please give details

6. Other court cases which concern the child(ren) listed at Section 2

Are you aware of any other court cases now, or at any time in the past, which concern any of the child(ren) at Section 2?

☐ Yes — If Yes, please **attach a copy of any relevant order** and give additional details below

☐ No — If No, please **go to Section 7**

Additional details

Name of child(ren)

Name of the court where proceedings heard

Case no.

Date/year (if known)

Name of Cafcass/CAFCASS CYMRU officer

Name and address of child's solicitor, if known

Postcode

If the above details are different for each child please provide details on additional sheets.

Please tick if additional sheets are attached. ☐

7. The respondents

Sections G and H of the the booklet **'CB1 - Making an application - Children and the Family Courts'** explain who a respondent is.

If there are more than 2 respondents please continue on a separate sheet.

Respondent 1

Respondent's first name

Middle name(s)

Surname

Previous surnames (if known)

Date of birth D D / M M / Y Y Y Y   Sex ☐ Male ☐ Female

Place of birth (town/county/country, if known)

Address

Postcode

Have they lived at this address for more than 5 years? ☐ Yes ☐ No ☐ Don't know

If No, please provide all previous addresses for the last 5 years below, if known.

Relationship to the child(ren)

Name of child	Relationship

Respondent 2

Respondent's first name

Middle name(s)

Surname

Previous surnames (if known)

Date of birth D D / M M / Y Y Y Y   Sex ☐ Male ☐ Female

Place of birth (town/county/country, if known)

Address

Postcode

Have they lived at this address for more than 5 years? ☐ Yes ☐ No ☐ Don't know

If No, please provide all previous addresses for the last 5 years below, if known.

Relationship to the child(ren)

Name of child	Relationship

8. Others who should be given notice

There may be other people who should be notified of your application, for example, someone who cares for the child but is not a parent. Sections G and I of the the booklet **'CB1 - Making an application - Children and the Family Courts'** explain who others are.

Person 1

Person's first name

Surname

Date of birth D D / M M / Y Y Y Y   Sex ☐ Male ☐ Female

Address

Postcode

Relationship to the child(ren)

Name of child	Relationship

Person 2

Person's first name

Surname

Date of birth D D / M M / Y Y Y Y   Sex ☐ Male ☐ Female

Address

Postcode

Relationship to the child(ren)

Name of child	Relationship

9. Signature

Print full name

Signed

Applicant

Date D D / M M / Y Y Y Y

10. Attending the court

Section N of the the booklet **'CB1 - Making an application - Children and the Family Courts'** provides information about attending court.

If you require an interpreter, you must tell the court now so that one can be arranged.

Do you or any of the parties need an interpreter at court?

☐ Yes ☐ No

If Yes, please specify the language and dialect:

If attending the court, do you or any of the parties involved have a disability for which you require special assistance or special facilities?

☐ Yes ☐ No

If Yes, please say what the needs are

Please say whether the court needs to make any special arrangements for you to attend court (e.g. providing you with a separate waiting room from the respondent or other security provisions).

Court staff may get in touch with you about the requirements

continued over the page ⇨

What to do now

- ☐ Check you have attached copies of any **relevant orders** (as per Section 6).
- ☐ Check you have **signed** the form Section 9.
- ☐ You must provide a **copy** of the application and attached documents for each of the respondents and one for the Children and Family Court Advisory and Support Service (Cafcass or CAFCASS CYMRU).
- ☐ Is Form C1A attached (if applicable)?
- ☐ Details of the additional children if there are more than 4 in Section 2
- ☐ Details of the additional respondents if there are more than 2 in Section 7
- ☐ Check you have attached the correct fee. The leaflet 'EX50 County court fees' provides information about court fees you will have to pay.

Now take or send your application with the correct fee and correct number of copies to the court.

Court fees

You may be exempt from paying all or part of the fee. The combined booklet and application form 'EX160A Court Fees - Do you have to pay them' gives more information. You can get a copy from the court or download a copy from our website at www.hmcourts-service.gov.uk

(K) Form C1A (Supplemental information)

Supplemental Information Form

Form C1A

Children Act 1989

The court	To be completed by the court
	Date issued
	Case number
The full name(s) of the child(ren)	Child(ren)'s number(s)

Important Note
Please read the C1A Notes for Guidance before completing this form.

Section 1 About you (the person completing this form)

1 **Personal details**

Full Name (including any title):

Date of Birth:

*Do not state your address if you have asked the court to withhold your address

Address*:

Day time telephone number:

Your relationship to each child named above:

2 **Your solicitor's details**

Name:

Address:

Reference:

Telephone Number:

Fax Number:

DX Number:

C1A (01.05) *Designed by Publications Branch*

Section 2 Respondent's comments on allegations made by the Applicant

About this section:

- **Go straight to Section 3 (Further information) if:**
  - (a) you are the **Applicant**; or
  - (b) you are the **Respondent** and the Applicant has not filed form C1A Supplemental Information Form with his or her application.
- This section of the form should only be completed **by the Respondent** where the Applicant has served a completed form C1A with his or her application for an order.
- **You do not have to complete this section unless you wish to comment on any of the information given by the Applicant in his or her form C1A.** This section should not be used to comment on any other information given by the Applicant in his or her application.
- **Please comment in summary form only.** You will have an opportunity to make a more detailed statement later in the proceedings.

Comments on allegations made by the Applicant:

Section 3 Further Information

1 **Involvement with outside authorities and organisations**

If as a result of any incidence of domestic abuse, other harm or risk of harm to you or the child(ren) there is, has been or there is pending any known involvement with the police, social services, mental health services or other support services in respect of:

- *any child(ren)whose name(s) is/are given at the top of this form*
- *a full, half or step brother or sister of a child(ren) whose name(s) is/are given at the top of this form, or*
- *a person who is or has been involved in caring for the child(ren) or is having or has had contact with the child(ren) whose name(s) is/are given at the top of this form*

please provide details and identify:

- *which agency or service has been involved*
- *the name of the person who has been the main contact in that agency or service*
- *the date or dates of any involvement*
- *whether there is any current or continuing involvement*
- *whether or not you have any documents, reports or correspondence relating to the agency or service's involvement.*

2

Incidents of abuse, violence or harm

For each alleged incidence of violence, domestic abuse or harm, please provide in summary form the following information:

Note: You shall have an opportunity later in the proceedings to provide a more substantial statement

- *the date(s) on which the incident occurred*
- *the nature and seriousness of the alleged abuse, violence or harm*
- *by whom and against whom it was directed*
- *how frequently the alleged abuse, harm or violence occurred and the date(s) of the most recent occurrence(s)*
- *whether any hospital or medical treatment has been sought by the child(ren) whose name(s) is/are given at the top of this form, the applicant or other person in respect of any injuries sustained, and*
- *whether you consider there is a likelihood of further harm, abuse or violence occurring.*

3

Involvement of the child(ren)

If the child(ren) whose name(s) is/are given at the top of this form have seen or heard any of the alleged incident(s) of abuse within the household or been aware of any alleged abuse and its impact on the family, please give details and in particular state how you believe the child(ren) have been affected by this experience:

---

4 **Witnesses**

Has anyone else seen, heard or had reported to them any alleged incidence of violence, domestic abuse or harm? If Yes, would that person be able to provide supporting evidence?

5 **Medical treatment or other assessment of the child(ren)**

If any child(ren) whose name(s) is/are given at the top of this form have been referred for treatment or psychiatric or psychological assessment, by any medical or health service relating to his/her emotional, social or behavioural development (or where any such treatment or referral is pending), please state:

- *when and to whom such a referral was made*
- *details of any treatment or assessment recommended*
- *whether there is any continuing involvement with the relevant service in relation to the referral, and*
- *whether you are aware of or have in your possession any reports or other correspondence in relation to any treatment or assessment recommended.*

6 **Abduction**

If you feel the child(ren) whose name(s) is/are given at the top of this form are at real risk of being abducted please give the following information:

- *your reason for believing that the child(ren) may be abducted*
- *whether the child(ren) have previously been the subject of a threatened abduction, an attempted abduction or have been abducted*
- *whether the police or any other organisation has been involved in any alleged previous incident identified above, and*
- *whether each child has their own passport and who has that passport at the moment?*

7 **Steps or orders required to protect you and the children**
Please indicate what steps or orders you believe the court should take or make in order to protect the safety of the child(ren) whose name(s) is/are given at the top of this form and/or yourself.

8 **Attending the Court**
Please also indicate whether the court needs to make any special arrangements for you to attend court (e.g. providing you with a separate waiting room from the respondent or other security provision). Do you consider the court should give consideration to any special measures for you or any witnesses to give evidence at the hearing (e.g. use of video link equipment where available)? If Yes, please explain why.

Signed
(Applicant/Respondent)

Date

C1A

(L) Form C110 (Application for a care or supervision order)

C110

Application under the Children Act 1989 for a care or supervision order

To be completed by the court	
Name of court	
Date issued	
Case number	
Child(ren)'s name(s)	Child(ren)'s number(s)

Summary of application

Name of applicant	
Name of respondent(s)	

Child 1 - Name of child	Date of birth	Order(s) applied for (including interim orders)
	/ /	
Name of mother	Name of father	Parental Responsibility
		Yes No

Child 2 - Name of child	Date of birth	Order(s) applied for (including interim orders)
	/ /	
Name of mother	Name of father	Parental Responsibility
		Yes No

Child 3 - Name of child	Date of birth	Order(s) applied for (including interim orders)
	/ /	
Name of mother	Name of father	Parental Responsibility
		Yes No

Child 4 - Name of child	Date of birth	Order(s) applied for (including interim orders)
	/ /	
Name of mother	Name of father	Parental Responsibility
		Yes No

1. The applicant

Name of applicant
(local authority or authorised person)

Name of contact

Job title

Address

Postcode

Contact telephone number

Mobile telephone number

Fax number

Email

DX number

Solicitor's details

Solicitor's name

Address

Postcode

Telephone number

Mobile telephone number

Fax number

Email

DX number

Solicitor's Reference

2. The child(ren)

Please give details of the child(ren) and the order(s) you are applying for.
If there are more than 4 children please continue on a separate sheet.

Child 1

Child's first name

Middle name(s)

Surname

Date of birth ☐☐/☐☐/☐☐☐☐ Gender ☐ Male ☐ Female

Name of Social worker and telephone number

Is the child subject of a child protection plan? ☐ Yes ☐ No

Are there any health or disability issues relating to the child? ☐ Yes ☐ No

If Yes, please give details

Who does the child live with?

At which address does the child live?

Postcode

Please give the full names of any other adults living at the same address and their relationship to the child.

Are there any contact arrangements in place for this child? ☐ Yes ☐ No

If Yes, please give details

Name of person	Frequency of contact	Supervised contact
		☐ Yes ☐ No
		☐ Yes ☐ No
		☐ Yes ☐ No
		☐ Yes ☐ No

Child 2

Child's first name

Middle name(s)

Surname

Date of birth / / Gender Male Female

Name of Social worker and telephone number

Is the child subject of a child protection plan? Yes No

Are there any health or disability issues relating to the child? Yes No

If Yes, please give details

Who does the child live with?

At which address does the child live?

Postcode

Please give the full names of any other adults living at the same address and their relationship to the child.

Are there any contact arrangements in place for this child? Yes No

If Yes, please give details

Name of person	Frequency of contact	Supervised contact
		Yes No
		Yes No
		Yes No
		Yes No

Child 3

Child's first name

Middle name(s)

Surname

Date of birth ☐☐/☐☐/☐☐☐☐ Gender ☐ Male ☐ Female

Name of Social worker and telephone number

Is the child subject of a child protection plan? ☐ Yes ☐ No

Are there any health or disability issues relating to the child? ☐ Yes ☐ No

If Yes, please give details

Who does the child live with?

At which address does the child live?

Postcode

Please give the full names of any other adults living at the same address and their relationship to the child.

Are there any contact arrangements in place for this child? ☐ Yes ☐ No

If Yes, please give details

Name of person	Frequency of contact	Supervised contact
		☐ Yes ☐ No
		☐ Yes ☐ No
		☐ Yes ☐ No
		☐ Yes ☐ No

Child 4

Child's first name

Middle name(s)

Surname

Date of birth ☐☐/☐☐/☐☐☐☐ Gender ☐ Male ☐ Female

Name of Social worker and telephone number

Is the child subject of a child protection plan? ☐ Yes ☐ No

Are there any health or disability issues relating to the child? ☐ Yes ☐ No

If Yes, please give details

Who does the child live with?

At which address does the child live?

Postcode

Please give the full names of any other adults living at the same address and their relationship to the child.

Are there any contact arrangements in place for this child? ☐ Yes ☐ No

If Yes, please give details

Name of person	Frequency of contact	Supervised contact
		☐ Yes ☐ No
		☐ Yes ☐ No
		☐ Yes ☐ No
		☐ Yes ☐ No

3. The respondents

If there are more than 2 respondents please continue on a separate sheet.

Respondent 1

Respondent's first name

Middle name(s)

Surname

Date of birth ☐☐/☐☐/☐☐☐☐ Gender ☐ Male ☐ Female

Place of birth (town/county/country, if known)

Current address

Postcode

Telephone number

Are you aware of any relevant family court proceedings involving the respondent? ☐ Yes ☐ No

If Yes, give details (include type of order, date, name of court and case no.)

Relationship to the child(ren)

Name of child(ren)	Relationship	Parental Responsibility
		☐ Yes ☐ No
		☐ Yes ☐ No
		☐ Yes ☐ No
		☐ Yes ☐ No

Respondent 2

Respondent's first name

Middle name(s)

Surname

Date of birth __/__/____ Gender ☐ Male ☐ Female

Place of birth (town/county/country, if known)

Current address

Postcode

Telephone number

Are you aware of any relevant family court proceedings involving the respondent? ☐ Yes ☐ No

If Yes, give details (include type of order, date, name of court and case no.)

Relationship to the child(ren)

Name of child(ren)	Relationship	Parental Responsibility
		☐ Yes ☐ No
		☐ Yes ☐ No
		☐ Yes ☐ No
		☐ Yes ☐ No

4. Grounds for the application

The grounds for the application are that the child(ren) is suffering or is likely to suffer, significant harm and the harm or likelihood of harm is because the child is:

- ☐ not receiving care that would be reasonably expected from a parent
- ☐ beyond parental control

5. Why are you making this application?

Please give a brief summary of why you are making this application. You should include:

- the background circumstances
- the precipitating circumstances

In this summary it is not sufficient just to refer to existing or future documents.

6. Factors affecting ability to participate in proceedings

Do you have any reason to believe that any respondent or other person to be given notice of the application may lack capacity to conduct proceedings?

☐ Yes ☐ No

If Yes, please give details

Provide details of any referral to or assessment by the Adult Learning Disability team, together with the outcome

Are you aware of any other factors which may affect the ability of the person concerned to take part in the proceedings?

7. Plans for the child(ren)

Please give a brief summary of the plans for the child(ren).

- **for supervision orders only**, any requirements which you will invite the court to impose under Part 1 of Schedule 3 Children Act 1989

In this summary it is not sufficient just to refer to or repeat the Care Plan.

8. Timetable for the child(ren)

The timetable for the child will be set by the court to take account of dates of the significant steps in the child's life that are likely to take place during the proceedings. Those steps include not only legal steps but also social, care, health and education steps.

Please give any relevant dates/events in relation to the child(ren)

- it may be necessary to give different dates for each child.

Are you aware of any significant event in the timetable, before which the case should be concluded?

☐ Yes ☐ No

If Yes, please give a date

☐☐/☐☐/☐☐☐☐

and give your reasons

9. Your allocation proposal

You need to provide the court with your proposal for allocation of this case.

Please select from the following:

☐ magistrates' court

☐ county court (Care Centre)

☐ High Court

and give your reasons

10. Other court cases which concern the child(ren)

Are you aware of any other court cases, including cases concerning the children, which are relevant to this application?

☐ Yes

☐ No If No, **go to section 11**

If Yes, give details (include type of order, date, name of court and case no.) and in cases where the child was represented the name of any guardian and solicitor for the child.

11. Others who should be given notice

Person 1

Person's first name

Middle name(s)

Surname

Date of birth ☐☐/☐☐/☐☐☐☐ Gender ☐ Male ☐ Female

Address

Postcode ☐☐☐☐ ☐☐☐☐

Relationship to the child(ren)

Name of child	Relationship	Parental Responsibility
		☐ Yes ☐ No
		☐ Yes ☐ No
		☐ Yes ☐ No
		☐ Yes ☐ No

Relationship to the respondents

Name of respondent	Relationship

Person 2

Person's first name

Middle name(s)

Surname

Date of birth ☐☐/☐☐/☐☐☐☐ Gender ☐ Male ☐ Female

Address

Postcode ☐☐☐☐ ☐☐☐☐

Relationship to the child(ren)

Name of child	Relationship	Parental Responsibility
		☐ Yes ☐ No
		☐ Yes ☐ No
		☐ Yes ☐ No
		☐ Yes ☐ No

Relationship to the respondents

Name of respondent	Relationship

12. Signature

Print full name

Your role/position held

Signed

Applicant

Date D D / M M / Y Y Y Y

13. Attending the court

If an interpreter will be required, you must tell the court now so that one can be arranged.

Are you aware of whether an interpreter will be required?

☐ Yes ☐ No

If Yes, please specify the language and dialect:

If attending the court, do any of the parties involved have a disability for which special assistance or special facilities would be required?

☐ Yes ☐ No

If Yes, please specifiy what the needs are:

Please state whether the court needs to make any special arrangements for the parties attending court (e.g. providing a separate waiting room or other security requirements).

Court staff may get in contact with you about the requirements

continued over the page

Annex

This annex must be completed by the applicant with any application for a care order or supervision order.
The documents specified in this annex must be filed with the application if available.
If any relevant document is not filed with the application, the reason and any expected date of filing must be stated.
All documents filed with the application must be clearly marked with their title and numbered consecutively.

1. Social Work Chronology
(A succinct summary)

☐ attached ☐ to follow

If **to follow** please give reasons why not included and the date when the document will be sent to the court.

2. Initial Social Work Statement

☐ attached ☐ to follow

If **to follow** please give reasons why not included and the date when the document will be sent to the court.

3. Initial and Core Assessments

☐ attached ☐ to follow

If **to follow** please give reasons why not included and the date when the document will be sent to the court.

4. Letters Before Proceedings

☐ attached ☐ to follow

If **to follow** please give reasons why not included and the date when the document will be sent to the court.

5. Schedule of Proposed Findings

☐ attached ☐ to follow

If **to follow** please give reasons why not included and the date when the document will be sent to the court.

6. Care Plan

☐ attached ☐ to follow

If **to follow** please give reasons why not included and the date when the document will be sent to the court.

What to do once you have completed this form

Ensure that you have:

- ☐ attached copies of any **relevant** documents.
- ☐ **signed** the form at Section 12.
- ☐ provided a **copy** of the application and attached documents for each of the respondents, and for Cafcass or CAFCASS CYMRU.
- ☐ given details of the additional children if there are more than 4 in Section 2.
- ☐ given details of the additional respondents if there are more than 2 in Section 3.
- ☐ the correct fee.

It is good practice to inform Cafcass or CAFCASS CYMRU that you are making this application. The court will expect the local authority to have informed Cafcass or CAFCASS CYMRU that proceedings are being issued.

Have you notified Cafcass - Children and Family Court Advisory and Support Service (for England)

or

CAFCASS CYMRU - Children and Family Court Advisory and Support Service Wales.

☐ Yes ☐ No

If Yes, please give the date of notification

☐☐/☐☐/☐☐☐☐

Now take or send your application with the correct fee and correct number of copies to the court.

(M) Form FL401 (Family Law Act application)

Application for:
a non-molestation order
an occupation order

Family Law Act 1996 (Part IV)

The court

To be completed by the court
Date issued
Case number

Please read the accompanying notes as you complete this form.

1 About you (the applicant)

State your title (Mr, Mrs etc), full name, address, telephone number and date of birth (if under 18):

State your solicitor's name, address, reference, telephone, FAX and DX numbers:

2 About the respondent

State the respondent's name, address and date of birth (if known):

3 The Order(s) for which you are applying

This application is for:

☐ a non-molestation order

☐ an occupation order

☐ Tick this box if you wish the court to hear your application without notice being given to the respondent. The reasons relied on for an application being heard without notice must be stated in the statement in support.

4 Your relationship to the respondent (the person to be served with this application)

Your relationship to the respondent is:

(Please tick only one of the following)

1 ☐ Married

2 ☐ Civil Partners

3 ☐ Were married

4 ☐ Former civil partners

5 ☐ Cohabiting

6 ☐ Were cohabiting

7 ☐ Both of you live or have lived in the same household

8 ☐ Relative
State how related:

9 ☐ Agreed to marry.
Give the date the agreement was made.
If the agreement has ended, state when.

10 ☐ Agreed to form a civil partnership.
Give the date the agreement was made.
If the agreement has ended, state when.

11 ☐ Both of you are parents of, or have parental responsibility for, a child

12 ☐ One of you is a parent of a child and the other has parental responsibility for that child

13 ☐ One of you is the natural parent or grandparent of a child adopted, placed or freed for adoption, and the other is:

(i) the adoptive parent

or (ii) a person who has applied for an adoption order for the child

or (iii) a person with whom the child has been placed for adoption

or (iv) the child who has been adopted, placed or freed for adoption.

State whether (i), (ii), (iii) or (iv):

14 ☐ Both of you are the parties to the same family proceedings (see also Section 11 below).

5 Application for a non-molestation order

If you wish to apply for a non-molestation order, state briefly in this section the order you want.

Give full details in support of your application in your supporting evidence.

6 Application for an occupation order

If you do not wish to apply for an occupation order, please go to section 9 of this form.

(A) State the address of the dwelling-house to which your application relates:

(B) State whether it is occupied by you or the respondent now or in the past, or whether it was intended to be occupied by you or the respondent:

(C) State whether you are entitled to occupy the dwelling-house: ☐ Yes ☐ No

If yes, explain why:

(D) State whether the respondent is entitled to occupy the dwelling-house: ☐ Yes ☐ No

If yes, explain why:

On the basis of your answers to (C) and (D) above, tick one of the boxes 1 to 6 below to show the category into which you fit

1 ☐ a spouse or civil partner who has home rights in the dwelling-house, or a person who is entitled to occupy it by virtue of a beneficial estate or interest or contract or by virtue of any enactment giving him or her the right to remain in occupation.

If you tick box 1, state whether there is a dispute or pending proceedings between you and the respondent about your right to occupy the dwelling-house.

2 ☐ a former spouse or former civil partner with no existing right to occupy, where the respondent spouse or civil partner is so entitled.

3 ☐ a cohabitant or former cohabitant with no existing right to occupy, where the respondent cohabitant or former cohabitant is so entitled.

4 ☐ a spouse or former spouse who is not entitled to occupy, where the respondent spouse or former spouse is also not entitled.

5 ☐ a civil partner or former civil partner who is not entitled to occupy, where the respondent civil partner or former civil partner is also not entitled.

6 ☐ a cohabitant or former cohabitant who is not entitled to occupy, where the respondent cohabitant or former cohabitant is also not entitled.

Home Rights

If you do have home rights please:

State whether the title to the land is registered or unregistered (if known):

If registered, state the Land Registry title number (if known):

If you wish to apply for an occupation order, state briefly here the order you want. Give full details in support of your application in your supporting evidence:

7 Application for additional order(s) about the dwelling-house

If you want to apply for any of the orders listed in the notes to this section, state what order you would like the court to make:

8 Mortgage and rent

Is the dwelling-house subject to a mortgage?

☐ Yes ☐ No

If yes, please provide the name and address of the mortgagee:

Is the dwelling-house rented?

☐ Yes ☐ No

If yes, please provide the name and address of the landlord:

9 At the court

Will you need an interpreter at court?

☐ Yes ☐ No

If yes, specify the language:

If you require an interpreter, you must notify the court immediately so that one can be arranged.

If you have a disability for which you require special assistance or special facilities, please state what your needs are. The court staff will get in touch with you about your requirements.

10 Other information

State the name and date of birth of any child living with or staying with, or likely to live with or stay with, you or the respondent:

State the name of any other person living in the same household as you and the respondent, and say why they live there:

11 Other Proceedings and Orders

If there are any other current family proceedings or orders in force involving you and the respondent, state the type of proceedings or orders, the court and the case number. This includes any application for an occupation order or non-molestation order against you by the respondent.

This application is to be served upon the respondent

Signed: Date:

Index

access to justice
bank loans 18
lump sum orders 18
maintenance pending suit 17–18
public funding *see* **public funding**
Sears Tooth agreement 17
acknowledgement of service
divorce petition 39
section 8 orders 191
adultery
co-respondent 24
cohabitation after 24–5
confession of 23
intolerability 24
meaning 23
proof 23
agreements *see individual types eg* cohabitation agreements
alternative dispute resolution 6
arbitration 7
collaborative law 7
mediation *see* **mediation**
ancillary relief *see* financial provisions
annulment *see* nullity
appeals
financial orders 152
maintenance assessments 152
welfare benefits 152–3
arbitration 7
arrangements for children
divorce 35–6, 40–1, 417–22
arrest
domestic abuse order enforcement 249, 250
power of 50, 249
warrant of 249
attachment of earnings 148, 149

bank loans 18
bankruptcy
ancillary relief 116
financial provision 115–16
matrimonial home 115–16
behaviour in divorce
cohabitation and 25–6
respondent's 25
'big money' cases
capital tied up 99
fairness 53
lump sums 113–15
Brussels II Revised 20, 22
budgeting loans 81

capital assets
'big money' cases 113–15
lump sums 113–15
pensions 115
protection of

capital assets – *continued*
injunctions 112–13
in joint names 110
matrimonial home rights 111
pending land action 111–12
in sole name 111–13
see also **matrimonial home**
capital gains tax
disposal of assets 71
marriage breakdown 69–71
matrimonial home
deferred charge 71, 104, 108, 133
deferred trust of land 71, 104, 105–6, 133
extra-statutory concession 70
future sale 70–1
private residence exemption 70
sale to third party 70
transfer between spouses 70
capital orders
clean break 63–4
homes *see* **matrimonial home**
lump sums 47, 50, 63–4, 65, 66, 82, 113–15, 132
orders for sale 47, 51, 103–5, 134, 148–9
pension sharing compensation orders 48, 51, 65
pension sharing orders 47, 51
property adjustment orders 47, 50–1, 67, 109, 132–4, 152, 263
care orders
application 211
application form 225, 461–6, 465–70, 491–507
availability to court 213
care plans 213–14, 231
case management conference 229
causation of harm 212–13
children's guardian 226–7
choice of court 223
choice of order 218
concurrent applications 213
contact 215–16, 220
discharge 216–17
discharge of contact order by 214
disclosure 229
effect 200, 214–15
evidence
admissibility 228
disclosure 229
expert evidence 229
witness statements 228
exclusion requirement 219–20
final hearing 230
first appointment
attendance 228
timetable for proceedings 227–8
grounds 211
human rights 215, 230–1
independence of child 217
interim 218–20

care orders – *continued*
'is likely to suffer' 212
'is suffering' 212
issue of application 225
issues resolution hearing 229
judgment 230
jurisdiction 223
kinship assessments 224
letter before proceedings 224–5
meeting with parents 225
name change 214
parental responsibility 214
parties to application 225–6
'pathway plan' 217
pre-proceedings action 224–5
procedure 223–30
checklist 233
public funding 224
related proceedings 224
service of application 226
significant harm 211
solicitor appointment 227
stage 1 225–6
transfer of cases 223
welfare principle 213, 231
care plan 213–14, 231
case management conferences 229
change of name
care orders and 214
residence orders 172
charging order 149
child abduction
Child Abduction Act 1984 197–8
criminal offences 197–8
Family Law Act 1986 197
international 198–9
passports
preventing issue 198
surrender 198–9
'port alert' procedure 198
practical advice 199
prohibited steps orders 178–9
recovery of child 199
section 8 orders 197
Child Abduction Act 1984
text 292–4
child assessment orders 200
emergency assessment 222–3
child benefit 73
Child Contact Centre 174
child of the family 29, 61
Child Maintenance and Enforcement Commission 85–6, 87, 150, 151–2
see also **Child Support Agency**
child protection
abduction *see* **child abduction**
care orders *see* **care orders**
care plan 213–14, 231
conferences 210
contact
application to court 215–16
initial considerations 215
local authority duties 215
child protection – *continued*
refusal 216
emergency assessment orders 222–3
emergency protection orders 200, 220–3
general 199–200
investigation
court-directed 209–10
local authorities 181, 210
local authorities *see* **children, public law**
neglect or abuse 209–11
police protection 222
registers 210–11
supervision orders *see* **supervision orders**
wardship 200
child protection conferences 210
child protection register 210–11
Child Support Act 1991
text 348–58
Child Support Agency 81, 200
adult children 87
apportionment 92
assessable income 91
calculation of maintenance 90–6
application 146
apportionment 92
basic rate 91
capital transfers 94
existing court orders 92
flat rate 91
formula 91
formula under CMOPA 2008 92
nil rate 91
property transfers 94
reduced rate 91
shared care 92–3
special cases 92–3
special expenses 94
variations 94
downwards 94–5
voluntary payments 96
capital orders 87
capital transfers 94
child
with disability 88
meaning 86
clean break and 94, 105
collection by 150–2
default maintenance decision 95
educational expenses 87–8
enforcement 150–2
financial provision during marriage 68
habitual residence 86
interim maintenance decision 95
jurisdiction of court 86–7
legislation 85
lump sum orders 87
maintenance assessment *see* calculation of maintenance
naming of father 86
non-resident parent 86, 87
parent 86
parentage determination 86
periodical payments 87

Child Support Agency – *continued*
person with care 86
property adjustment orders 87
property transfers 94
qualifying child 86, 87
shared care 92–3
step-children 87
step-parents 86
supplementary maintenance 87
voluntary payments 96
children
abduction *see* **child abduction**
child of the family 29, 61
consent orders 88–9
contact orders
conditions 174
directions 174
domestic violence 175–6
enforcement 177–8
grandparents 175
letters, email or telephone contact 174
monitoring contact 177
physical contact 174
Practice Direction 176
step-parents 175
delay avoidance 186
with disability 61, 88
divorce and
child of the family 29
child protection 29–30
delay to decree absolute 30
service of petition 39
family assistance order 179–80
financial provision
child with disability 61
child of the family 61
Child Support Agency *see* **Child Support Agency**
Children Act 1989 relief 201–3
'Christmas' orders 89
consent orders 88–9
during marriage 201
flowchart 89–90
jurisdiction 200
maintenance agreements 88, 160
matrimonial breakdown and 60–1
matrimonial proceedings 201
property orders 263
reform 96
Segal orders 89, 96
separation agreements 88
step-children 61
unmarried parents 201, 263
see also **Child Support Agency**
guardianship 168–9
human rights 182
legislation 165
local authority and *see* **children, public law**
maintenance agreements 88
matrimonial home and 104
name change
care orders 214
residence orders 172
children – *continued*
'no order' presumption 186
nullity of marriage and 31
parental responsibility
agreement 166–7
civil partners 169
cohabitants 261–2
delegation of 170
exercise of 170
guardianship 168–9
human rights 262–3
local authority 169
loss of 169–70
meaning 166
order 167–8
refusal 167–8
termination 168
persons with 166
removal 262
same-sex couples 262
special guardianship orders 180–1, 232
step-parents 169
supervision orders 218
unmarried fathers 166–9, 261–2
refusal of order 167–8
as party to proceedings 190
passports
preventing issue 198
surrender 198–9
prohibited steps orders 178–9
protection *see* **child protection**; **children, public law**
residence orders 172, 262
change of surname 172
conditions 171–2
directions 171–2
domestic violence 176
interim 218–20
leaving UK 172–3
relocation within UK 174
section 8 orders *see* **section 8 orders** *and individual orders eg* residence orders
separation agreements and 161
special guardianship orders 180–1, 232
special guardianship support services 181
specific issues order 179
step-children 61, 87
of unmarried parents
appointment of guardian 262
financial provision orders 263
guardianship 262
human rights 262–3
occupation of home 260
parental responsibility 261–2
removal 262
property orders 263
residence order 262
s.8 orders 262
same sex couples 262
welfare principle *see* **welfare principle**
Children Act 1989
text 295–347

Children and Family Court Advisory and Support Service (Cafcass) **165–6**
children, public law **205–33**
accommodation provision
duty 207
limits 207
preventing removal 207
care orders
application 211
application form 225, 465–70, 491–507
availability to court 213
care plans 213–14, 231
case management conference 229
causation of harm 212–13
children's guardian 226–7
choice of court 223
choice of order 218
concurrent applications 213
contact 215–16, 220
discharge 216–17
discharge of contact order by 214
disclosure 229
effect 214–15
evidence
admissibility 228
disclosure 229
expert evidence 229
witness statements 228
exclusion requirement 219–20
final hearing 230
first appointment
attendance 228
timetable for proceedings 227–8
grounds 211, 233
human rights 215, 230–1
independence of child 217
interim 218–20
'is likely to suffer' 212
'is suffering' 212
issue of application 225
issues resolution hearing 229
judgment 230
jurisdiction 223
kinship assessments 224
letter before proceedings 224–5
meeting with parents 225
name change 214
parental responsibility 214
parties to application 225–6
'pathway plan' 217
pre-proceedings action 224–5
procedure 223–30
procedure checklist 233
public funding 224
related proceedings 224
service of application 226
significant harm 211
solicitor appointment 227
stage 1 225–6
transfer of cases 223
welfare principle 213, 231
care plans 213–14, 231
challenging local authority
children, public law – *continued*
complaints 208–9
judicial review 209
child assessment orders 200, 222–3
child protection conferences 210
child protection register 210–11
child support 206–9
children in need
definition 206
duty to 206–7
children 'looked after' 208
compensation for failures 232
contact
application to court 215–16
emergency protection orders 221
Independent Reviewing Officer 215
initial considerations 215
interim care order 220
local authorities and 215, 220, 221
public funding 224
refusal 216
delay 206
emergency assessment orders 222–3
emergency protection orders 200, 220–3
human rights 230–1
Independent Reviewing Officer 215
investigation
court-directed 209–10
local authority 181, 210
issue of application 225
issues resolution hearing 229
kinship assessments 224
letter before proceedings 224–5
meeting with parents 225
neglect or abuse
child protection conferences 210
child protection register 210–11
court-directed investigation 209–10
local authority investigation 181, 210
parties to application 226
pre-proceedings action 224–5
prevention of harm 206
protection of child 200
provision of services 208
Public Law Outline 206, 223
related proceedings 224
stage 1 225–6
supervision orders
application 211
application form 225, 465–70, 491–507
availability to court 213
case management conference 229
causation of harm 212–13
children's guardian 226–7
choice of court 223
choice of 218
concurrent applications 213
disclosure 229
duration 218
duties of supervisor 217
effect of 217–18
evidence
admissibility 228

children, public law – *continued*
disclosure 229
expert evidence 229
witness statements 228
final hearing 230
first appointment
attendance 228
timetable for proceedings 227–8
grounds 211, 233
human rights implications 230–1
interim 218–20
'is likely to suffer' 212
issue of application 225
issues resolution hearing 229
judgment 230
jurisdiction 223
kinship assessments 224
letter before proceedings 224–5
meeting with parents 225
parental responsibility 218
parties to application 225–6
pre-proceedings action 224–5
procedure 223–30
procedure checklist 233
public funding 224
related proceedings 224
service of application 226
significant harm 211
'is suffering' 212
solicitor appointment 227
stage 1 225–6
transfer of cases 223
welfare principle 213, 231
welfare principle 213, 231
children's guardian 221
appointment 226–7
duties 226–7
children's tax credit
amount 77
eligibility 77
income 77
maintenance and 81
means testing 77–8
passport benefits 78–9
'Christmas' orders 89
civil partnership 253
dissolution 23
parental responsibility 169
see also **matrimonial home**
clean break
capital orders 63–4
Child Support Agency and 94, 105
deferred 63
drafting order 134–5
duty to consider 62
income orders 62–3
matrimonial home 104
principle 62
co-respondent 24
service of divorce petition on 38
cohabitation
after adultery 24–5
after desertion 26
cohabitation – *continued*
after separation (2 years) 27
after separation (5 years) 29
agreements *see* **cohabitation agreements**
bankruptcy 263
breaking up 256–61
occupation of home 259–60
ownership of home 256–9
sale of property 260–1
tenancies 261
children
appointment of guardian 262
financial provision orders 263
guardianship 262
human rights 262–3
parental responsibility 261–2
removal 262
same-sex couples 262
property orders 263
residence order 262
s.8 orders 262
civil partnerships 253
death of cohabitant
family provision 263–4
intestacy 263
ownership rights 263
domestic abuse 236
life insurance 254
'Living Together' (Dept of Constitutional Affairs 2004) 253
occupation of home
breaking up 259–60
children and 260
contractual licence 259
Family Law Act 1996 260
licence by estoppel 260
ownership of home
acting to detriment 258
breaking up and 256–9
common intention 258
conduct of parties 258
constructive trust 258–9
contribution 258–9
declaration of interests 254
detrimental reliance 259
duty of buyers' solicitor 254
jointly owned 254, 256–7
mortgages 254
proprietary estoppel 259
resulting trust 257–8
sole legal ownership 257–9
sale of property 260–1
same-sex couples 253
setting up home together 254–6
tenancies 261
wills 255
cohabitation agreements 159
certainty 255
consideration 256
enforcement 256
intention 255
matters to be covered 256
public policy 255

cohabitation agreements – *continued*
- undue influence 255
- validity 255–6

cold weather payments 80

collaborative law 7

committal to prison
- enforcement 149–50

community care grant 80–1

consent orders
- attendance at court 146
- financial provision 130
- procedures 145–6
- statement of information 455–9

contact, local authorities and
- application to court 215–16
- emergency protection orders 221
- Independent Reviewing Officer 215
- initial considerations 215
- interim care order 220
- local authority duties 215
- public funding 224
- refusal 216

contact orders
- activities 176–7
- conditions 174
- contact activity conditions 176
- contact activity directions 176
- directions 174
- domestic violence 175–6
- duration 194–5
- enforcement 177–8
- grandparents 175
- letters, email or telephone contact 174
- monitoring contact 177
- physical contact 174
- Practice Direction 176
- step-parents 175

costs
- cost rules 128–9
- divorce 43
- drafting orders 135
- financial provision proceedings 128–9
  - conduct of party 129
  - offers to settle 129
- offers to settle 129
- public funding 14–15
- solicitor's 15

council tax benefit 75
- amount 80
- eligibility 79
- maintenance and 81

counselling 5–6

county court orders
- enforcement 147–9

county courts 7
- divorce courts 189
- domestic abuse 245
- non-divorce courts 189
- section 8 orders 189
  - checklist 196
- variation of orders 155–7

court forms 121, 122, 127, 190, 225, 409–514

crisis loans 81

death
- of cohabitant
  - family provision 263–4
  - intestacy 263
  - ownership rights 263
- presumption of 32

decree absolute
- petitioner's application 41–2
- religious marriages 42–3
- respondent's application 42

decree nisi 41
- application 39

defended divorce
- filing an answer 43
- notice of intent 43
- procedure 43

delay
- children and 186, 206

desertion
- cohabitation after 26
- elements 26

directions for hearing
- divorce 39–40

disabilities, persons with *see* person under disability

disclosure
- care and supervision orders 229
- financial provision procedure 123

discretionary housing payments 80

distress, warrant of 150

divorce
- acknowledgement of service 39
- adultery
  - co-respondent 24
  - cohabitation after 24–5
  - confession of 23
  - intolerability 24
  - meaning 23
  - proof 23
- arrangements for children 35–6, 40–1, 417–22
- behaviour
  - cohabitation and 25–6
  - respondent's 25
- checklist 45
- child protection
  - child of the family 29
  - delay to decree absolute 30
  - protection 29–30
- choice of nullity or 31
- co-respondent 24
- costs 43
- decree absolute
  - delay and child protection 30
  - petitioner's application 41–2
  - religious marriages 42–3
  - respondent's application 42
- decree nisi 41
- defended
  - filing an answer 43
  - notice of intent 43
  - procedure 43
- desertion
  - cohabitation and 26

divorce – *continued*
elements 26
directions for hearing 39–40
exemption from fees 36
family help (higher) 32
fees 36
filing of petition 36
first interview 33
five facts *see individual facts eg* adultery
future law reform 43
irretrievable breakdown ground 22–3
jurisdiction of courts
Brussels II Revised 20, 22
choice of forum 22
domicile 21–2
habitual residence 21
recognition of foreign decrees 22
legal help 32
legal representation 32
notice of acting 32
nullity *see* **nullity**
one-year rule 20
pensions and 64–6
petition *see* **divorce petition**
public funding 32
section 41 certificates 40–1
separation (2 years) with consent
calculation of period 27
cohabitation after 27
consent 27
financial position 27–8
mental element 27
separation 27
separation (5 years)
cohabitation after 29
financial hardship 28–9
grave hardship 28–9
meaning 28
service of petition *see* **divorce petition**
summary 43–4
divorce petition
acknowledgement of service 39
affidavit in support 39
amendments 35
arrangements for children 35–6, 40–1, 417–22
exemption from fees 36
fees 36
form 405–12
marriage certificate 36
minor corrections 35
prescribed form 33–5
reconciliation certificate 36
service 36
alternative methods 37–8
children 39
co-respondent 38
deemed service 37
dispensing with 38
finding respondent 38
outside England and Wales 38
person under disability 39
personal service 37
usual method 36–7
divorce petition – *continued*
supporting documents 35–6
domestic abuse
applicants 237
child applicants 237
choice of court 244–5
cohabitants 236
county courts 245
distressed client 235
Domestic Violence Protection Notice 235–6
Domestic Violence Protection Order 235–6
emergency applications 244
emergency legal representation 245
enforcement of orders
penalty available 249–50
power of arrest 50, 249
warrant of arrest 249
Family Law Act 1996 protection 236–50
family proceedings court 245
human rights issues 250
legal representation 245
legislation 236
local authority housing 82
non-molestation orders *see* **non-molestation orders**
occupation orders *see* **occupation orders**
orders available 236
procedure 244–8
checklist 248
protection from harassment 251
public funding 245
refuges 236
transfer of cases 245
undertakings 244
with notice application 247–8
without notice application 245–7
Domestic Proceedings and Magistrates' Courts Act 1978
text 290–1
Domestic Violence Protection Notice 235–6
Domestic Violence Protection Order 235–6
domicile
of choice 22
of dependence 22
divorce 21–2
of origin 21
drafting financial provisions
clean break orders 134–5
form of order 130–1
lump sums 132
orders for sale 134
pensions 134
periodical payments 132
property adjustment orders 132–4
undertakings 131

emergency applications
domestic abuse 244
emergency assessment orders 222–3
emergency legal representation
domestic abuse 245
emergency protection orders 200
application 220–1

emergency protection orders – *continued*
children's guardian 221
contact during currency of 221
duration 222
effect of order 221
examination or assessment 222
grounds 220
police protection 222
enforcement
attachment of earnings 148, 149
charging order 149
Child Support Agency 150–2
cohabitation agreements 256
committal to prison 149–50
contact orders 177–8
in county court 147–9
domestic abuse orders 248–50
family proceedings court 149–50
judgment summons 149
non-molestation orders 248–50
occupation orders 248–50
order for sale 148
power of arrest 249, 250
preliminary steps 147–8
property adjustment orders 152
registration of maintenance orders 150
separation/maintenance agreements 162
third party debt order 148
warrant of arrest 249
warrant of distress 150
warrant of execution 148
evidence
care and supervision orders 228–9
expert 192–3, 228–9
financial provision procedure 123–5
section 8 proceedings 192–3
expert evidence
care and supervision procedure 229
section 8 proceedings 192–3

Family Advocacy Scheme 14
family assistance order 179–80
family client 1–2
family courts 7–8
transparency of proceedings 8
family help (higher) 119
alternative sources 13
care and supervision orders 224
cost benefit test 13
divorce 32
financial eligibility 13
mediation and 13–14
prospect of success 14–15
family help (lower) 119
care and supervision orders 224
cost benefit test 13
financial eligibility 13
family home (cohabitants)
bankruptcy of cohabitant 263
breaking up partnership 256–61
death of cohabitant 263–4
married couples *see* **matrimonial home**
occupation
family home (cohabitants) – *continued*
breaking up 259–60
children and 260
contractual licence 259
Family Law Act 1996 260
licence by estoppel 260
ownership
acting to detriment 258
breaking up and 256–9
common intention 258
conduct of parties 258
constructive trust 258–9
contribution 258–9
declaration of interests 254
detrimental reliance 259
duty of buyers' solicitor 254
jointly owned 254, 256–7
mortgages 254
proprietary estoppel 259
resulting trust 257–8
sole legal ownership 257–9
sale of property 260–1
tenancies 261
Family Justice Review 9
Family Law Act 1986
child abduction 197
Family Law Act 1996
domestic abuse protection
236–50
text 359–72
family practitioner
advisory role 3
emotions of client 4–5
interviewing skills 4
long-term objectives 3–4
negotiation skills 4
professional conduct 3
vulnerability of clients 3
Family Procedure Rules 2010 374–405
family proceedings court 8
domestic abuse 245
enforcement 149–50
section 8 orders 189
transparency 8
variation of orders 157
final hearing
care and supervision orders 230
financial provision 127–8
section 8 orders 193–4
Financial Dispute Resolution (FDR) appointment 126–7
financial provisions
appeals *see* **appeals**
application 143–5
at early stage 121–2
dismissal 134
filing 122
form A 121, 122, 421–2
making application 121
pre-application protocol 120–1
remarriage trap 120–1
service on respondent 122–3
bankruptcy 115–16

financial provision – *continued*
capital assets *see* **capital assets; matrimonial home**
capital orders 47–8, 50–1, 82
clean break 63–4
children
child of the family 61
Child Support Agency *see* **Child Support Agency**
Children Act 1989 relief 201–3
'Christmas' orders 89
consent orders 88–9
during marriage 201
flowchart 89–90
jurisdictions 200
maintenance agreements 88, 160
matrimonial breakdown and 60–1
matrimonial proceedings 201
property orders 263
reform 96
Segal orders 89, 96
separation agreements 88
step-children 61
unmarried parents 201, 263
with disability 61
choice of order 52–61
clean break *see* **clean break**
consent orders 130
costs 128–9
drafting orders 135
offers to settle 129
council tax benefit 81
dismissal of application 134
diversion procedure 75, 81
drafting
clean break orders 134–5
costs 135
form of order 130–1
'liberty to apply' 135
lump sums 132
orders for sale 134
pensions 134
periodical payments 132
property adjustment orders 132–4
side-letters 135
specimen orders 136–42
undertakings 131
final hearing 127–8
first appointment 125–6
form A 121, 122, 425–6
form E 127, 427–53
form H1 127
hearings
FDR appointment 126–7
final 127–8
first appointment 125–6
housing benefit 81
income orders 47, 48–50
clean break 62–3
income support 81, 101, 102
interim orders 128
jobseeker's allowance 81, 101, 102

financial provision – *continued*
lump sum orders 47, 50, 63–4, 65, 66, 82, 113–15, 132
maintenance pending suit 47, 48–9
marriage 66–8
agreed applications 67
Child Support Agency and 68
contested applications 67
duration of periodic payments 67–8
failure to make reasonable provision 67
family proceedings court 67–8
MCA 1973 67
matrimonial breakdown 52–60
age of parties 56–7
'big money' cases 53, 99
children 60–1
conduct 58–60
contributions to family 52, 57–8
disability 57
duration of marriage 56–7
earning capacity 52, 54
equal sharing principle 53
factors to be considered 52
fairness 53
high income families 99
human rights 60
inherited assets 54
low income families 101–2
middle income families 100–1
misconduct 58–60
needs 55–6
negative contribution 58
non-matrimonial assets 54–5
pension rights 60
potential financial loss 60
reasonable requirements 53
resources 54–5
second family 55, 56, 120–1, 125–6
second spouse's income 55
spouses 99–102
standard of living 56
welfare benefits 54
yardstick of equality 53
negotiations 129
new partners 55, 56, 125–6
orders available *see individual orders eg* periodical payments
orders for sale 47, 51, 134
pensions 126, 134
information required 123, 126
pension sharing compensation orders 48, 51, 65
see also **pensions**
periodical payments 47, 49, 62–3, 67–8, 132, 161
powers of court 47–8
procedure
application *see* application
consent orders 130, 145–6
costs 128–9
court hearings *see* hearings
disclosure 123
dismissal of application 134
documentation required 124–5

financial provision – *continued*
first appointment 125–6
negotiations 129
obtaining evidence 123–5
overview 119–20
pre-application protocol 120–1
public funding 119
summary of procedure 143–6
property adjustment orders 47, 50–1, 67, 109, 132–4, 152, 263
reform 66
remarriage trap 120–1
school fees 94
second marriages 55, 56, 120–1, 125–6
secured periodical payments 47, 49–50, 51
setting aside orders 153–4
tax credits 81
working tax credit 102
term maintenance 63
undertakings 131
valuation
of business 125
of home 125
variation of orders
county court orders 155–7
family proceedings court orders 157
welfare benefits and 81–2, 101–2
when orders available 48
first appointment
care and supervision orders 227–8
first hearing
financial provision 125–6
First Hearing Dispute Resolution Appointment (FHDRA) 191–4
first interview
divorce 33
forced marriage 251–2
Funding Code 11
funeral grants 80

grandparents
contact orders 175
leave to apply for section 8 order 188
guardianship 168–9, 262
children of cohabitants 262

habitual residence
child support 86
divorce 21
harassment *see* **domestic abuse; protection from harassment**
***Harvey* order 107–8**
hearings
care and supervision orders
final 230
first 227–8
financial provision
directions 126
FDR appointment 126–7
final 127–8
first appointment 125–6
High Court 8
section 8 orders 189
Hildebrand rules 123
homelessness
domestic abuse 82
intentional 83
local authority housing 82–3
homes
married couples *see* **matrimonial home**
unmarried partners *see* **family home (cohabitants)**
housing benefit 75
amount 79
eligibility 79
maintenance and 81
housing payments, discretionary 80
human rights
care orders 215
care and supervision orders 230–1
children 182
domestic abuse orders 250
European Convention 8–9, 17
Human Rights Act 1998 8–9, 17
marriage 19
non-molestation orders 250
occupation orders 250
public funding 17
unmarried fathers 262–3

in work credit 75
income orders
clean break 62–3
maintenance pending suit 47, 48–9
periodical payments 47, 49, 62–3, 67–8
secured periodical payments 47, 49–50, 51
term maintenance 63
income support 101, 102
applicable amount 74
eligibility 74
getting a job 75
income 74–5
in work credit 75
lone parent job grant 75
lump sum payments 82
maintenance and 81
passport benefits 75
income tax
marriage breakdown 69
Inheritance (Provision for Family and Dependants) Act 1975
text 287–9
inheritance tax 71–2
dispositions
family maintenance 72
without donative intent 72
spouse exemption 71
intentional homelessness 83
interim orders 128
care orders 218–20
residence orders 218–20
supervision orders 218–20
international issues
jurisdiction *see* **jurisdiction**
service of divorce petition 38
intimidation *see* **domestic abuse**

investigations, child protection
court-directed 209–10
local authorities 181, 210
issues resolution hearing 229

jobseeker's allowance 101, 102
applicable amount 76
eligibility 76
income 76
in work credit 76
lump sum payments 82
maintenance and 81
passport benefits 76
judgment
care and supervision orders 230
section 8 orders 194
judgment summons 149
judicial review
local authority services 209
judicial separation 31
effect of decree 32
grounds 31–2
reasons for seeking 32
jurisdiction
divorce
Brussels II Revised 20, 22
choice of forum 22
domicile 21–2
habitual residence 21
recognition of foreign decrees 22
relocation within UK 174
section 8 orders 187
taking child from UK 172–3

legal help
advice 12
divorce 32
financial eligibility 12
financial order 119
sufficient benefit test 12
legal representation 14
care and supervision orders 224
divorce 32
domestic abuse 245
Legal Services Commission 11
see also **public funding**
lenders
property adjustment orders 109
'put on inquiry' 109
undue influence 108–9
life insurance
cohabitants 254
'Living Together' (Dept of Constitutional Affairs 2004) 253
local authorities, child protection
accommodation provision
duty 207
limits 207
preventing removal 207
care orders
application 211
application form 225, 465–70, 491–507
availability to court 213

local authorities, child protection – *continued*
care plans 213–14, 231
case management conference 229
causation of harm 212–13
children's guardian 226–7
choice of court 223
choice of order 218
concurrent applications 213
contact 215–16, 220
discharge 217
discharge of contact order by 214
disclosure 229
effect 214–15
evidence
admissibility 228
disclosure 229
expert evidence 229
witness statements 228
exclusion requirement 219–20
final hearing 230
first appointment
attendance 228
timetable for proceedings 227–8
grounds 211, 233
human rights 215, 230–1
independence of child 217
interim 218–20
'is likely to suffer' 212
'is suffering' 212
issue of application 225
issues resolution hearings 229
judgment 230
jurisdiction 223
kinship assessments 224
letter before proceedings 224–5
meeting with parents 225
name change 214
parental responsibility 214
parties to application 225–6
'pathway plan' 217
pre-proceedings action 224–5
procedure 223–30
procedure checklist 233
public funding 224
related proceedings 224
service of application 226
significant harm 211
solicitor appointment 227
stage 1 225–6
transfer of cases 223
welfare principle 213, 231
care plans 213–14, 231
challenging local authority
complaints 208–9
judicial review 209
child assessment orders 200
child protection conferences 210
child protection register 210–11
child support 206–9
children 'looked after' 208
children in need
definition 206
duty to 206–7

local authorities, child protection – *continued*
compensation for failures 232
contact
application to court 215–16
emergency protection orders 221
initial considerations 215
interim care order 220
local authorities and 220, 221
local authority duties 215
public funding 224
refusal 216
delay 206
emergency assessment orders 222–3
emergency protection orders 200, 220–3
human rights, care and supervision orders 230–1
investigation
court-directed 209–10
local authority 181, 210
neglect or abuse
child protection conferences 210
child protection register 210–11
court-directed investigation 209–10
local authority investigation 181, 210
parental responsibility 169
prevention of harm 206
protection of child 200
provision of services 208
special guardianship orders 181, 232
supervision orders
application 211
application form 225, 465–70, 491–507
availability to court 213
case management conference 229
causation of harm 212–13
children's guardian 226–7
choice of court 223
choice of 218
concurrent applications 213
disclosure 229
duration 218
duties of supervisor 217
effect of 217–18
evidence
admissibility 228
disclosure 229
expert evidence 229
witness statements 228
final hearing 230
first appointment
attendance 228
timetable for proceedings 227–8
grounds 211, 233
human rights 230–1
interim 218–20
'is likely to suffer' 212
issue of application 225
issues resolution hearings 229
judgment 230
jurisdiction 223
kinship assessments 224
letter before proceedings 224–5
meeting with parents 225

local authorities, child protection – *continued*
parental responsibility 218
parties to application 225–6
pre-proceedings action 224–5
procedure 223–30
procedure checklist 233
public funding 224
related proceedings 224
service of application 226
significant harm 211
'is suffering' 212
solicitor appointment 227
stage 1 225–6
transfer of cases 223
welfare principle 213, 231
welfare principle 213, 231
local authority housing
domestic abuse 82
duties of local authority 83
homelessness 82–3
intentional homelessness 83
local connection provision 83–4
priority need 83
tenancies 84
local connection 83–4
lump sums 47, 50, 63–4, 65, 66
'big money' cases 113–15
Child Support Agency 87
drafting orders 132
income support 81
jobseeker's allowance 81
orders 18, 87
pensions 115
welfare benefits and 81

maintenance
child support *see* **Child Support Agency**
marriage breakdown *see* **financial provisions**
term 63
maintenance agreements 160–1
advantages 161–2
agreement to separate 161
children 160
disadvantages 162
enforceability 162
finality 162
flexibility 162
periodical payments 161
property 161
speed 161
variation 162–3
court jurisdiction 162–3
maintenance pending suit 17–18, 47, 48–9
marriage
annulment *see* **nullity**
divorce *see* **divorce**
forced marriage 251–2
judicial separation *see* **judicial separation**
presumption of death 32
religious 42–3
void 30
voidable 30–1

marriage breakdown
ancillary orders *see* **financial provisions**
capital gains tax 69–71
income tax 69
inheritance tax 71–2
stamp duty land tax 72
taxation *see individual taxes*
welfare benefits and 81–2
see also **divorce**; **nullity**
***Martin* order 107**
maternity grants 80
Matrimonial Causes Act 1973
text 267–86
matrimonial home 64
bankruptcy 115–16
'buy out' 105
capital gains tax
deferred charge 71, 104, 108, 133
deferred trust of land 71, 104, 105–6, 133
extra-statutory concession 70
future sale 70–1
private residence exemption 70
sale to third party 70
transfer between spouses 70
clean break 104
deferred charge 71, 104, 108, 133
deferred trust of land 71, 104, 105–6, 133
Harvey order 107–8
injunctions
avoiding enforcement 112
preventing disposal 112
setting aside disposition 112
joint names 110
lenders
mortgages 108–9
property adjustment orders 109
undue influence 108–9
Martin order 107
Mesher order 106–7
minor children and 104
mortgages 104, 108–9
redemption from sale 104
order for sale 103–5, 134
pending land action 111–12
property adjustment orders 109
registration of charge 111
rented 110
retention by one party 105
rights of non-owning spouse 111–13
separation agreements 161
in sole name 111–13
statutory tenancies 110
third parties
co-owners 108
lenders 108–9
transfer between spouses
CSA payments and 105
outright transfer 105, 133
transfer of tenancy 110, 133–4
unmarried partners *see* **family home (cohabitants)**
mediation 6–7
appointment before public funding 119
mediation – *continued*
family help (higher) and 13–14
Form FM1 120, 423–24
pre-application protocol 120
***Mesher* order**
triggering events 106
use 107
misconduct
financial provision and 58–60
relating to proceedings 59
mortgages 104
cohabitants 254
matrimonial home 108–9
occupation orders and payment 242
redemption from sale 104
see also **lenders**

name of child, changing
care orders 214
residence orders 172
negotiation skills 4
negotiations
financial provision 129
'no order' presumption 186
non-molestation orders
applicants 237
application form 509–14
breach 249
duration 237
emergency applications 244
enforcement 248–50
factors to consider 237
human rights 250
penalties 249–50
pestering 237
power of arrest 249, 250
procedure checklist 248
undertakings 244
warrant of arrest 249
with notice application 247–8
without notice application 245–6
nullity
ancillary orders 31
children 31
choice of divorce or 31
consequences of decree 31
void marriage 30
voidable marriage 30–1
wills 31

occupation orders
additional provisions 242
applicants 237
cohabitant 240
with existing occupation right 237–9
flowchart 243
former cohabitant 240
former spouse 239–40
neither party with rights 241
with no existing right 239–41
application form 505–10
balance of harm test 238, 240
breach 249–50

occupation orders – *continued*
duration 239–40, 241
emergency applications 244
enforcement 242, 248–50
examples 241–2
human rights 250
mortgage payments 242
penalties 249–50
power of arrest 249, 250
procedure checklist 248
undertakings 244
warrant of arrest 249
with notice application 247–8
without notice application 245–6
off-setting pensions 64, 66
offers to settle
costs 129
one-year rule 20
orders for sale 47, 51, 103–5, 148–9
drafting 134
jointly owned property 51

parentage, determination 86
parental responsibility
agreement 166–7, 461–4
civil partners 169
cohabitants 261–2
delegation of 170
exercise of 170
guardianship 168–9
local authority 169
loss of 169–70
meaning 166
order 167–8
refusal 167–8
termination 168
paternity disputes 167
persons with 166
removal 262
s.8 orders 262
same-sex couples 262
special guardianship orders 180–1, 232
step-parents 169, 459–60
supervision orders 218
unmarried fathers 166–9, 261–2
refusal of order 167–8
passport benefits
food vouchers 75, 79
free school meals 75, 78–9
free vitamins 75, 79
housing and council tax benefits 75
income support 75
interest-free loans 75
jobseeker's allowance 76
NHS charge exemption 75, 78
tax credits 78–9
paternity disputes 167
'pathway plan' 217
pensions
ancillary relief applications 123, 126
cash equivalent transfer value 66
court powers 64
divorce and 64–6
pensions – *continued*
external transfer 66
future benefits 64
internal transfer 66
loss of rights on matrimonial breakdown 60
lump sums 115
payable on retirement 65, 66
off-setting 64, 66
'pension attachments' 65, 66
pension credit 65
pension debit 65
pension sharing 65–6, 134
compensation order 48, 51, 65
order 47, 51, 65–6
types of pension 66
traditional approach 64
valuation 66, 115
periodical payments 47, 49
Child Support Agency 87
clean breaks 62–3
drafting orders 132
during marriage 67–8
maintenance agreements 161
secured 47, 49–50, 51
person under disability
children 61, 88
service of divorce petition 39
spouse 57
pestering 237
police protection 222
'port alert' procedure 198
power of arrest 249, 250
pre-application protocol
financial orders 120–1
mediation information and assessment 120
pre-marital agreements 159–60
general contract principles 160
law reform 163
private residence exemption 70
professional conduct 3
prohibited steps orders 178–9
duration 194–5
property adjustment orders 47, 51, 67, 103
Child Support Agency 87
children 263
deferred charge 71, 104, 108, 133
deferred trusts of land 104, 105–6, 133
drafting 132–4
enforcement 152
lenders and 109
outright transfers 105, 133
preliminary considerations 132–3
transfer of tenancies 110, 133–4
welfare benefits 82
protection from harassment 251
public funding
care orders 224
contact orders 224
contracting 11
costs 14–15
domestic abuse 245
emergency legal representation 245
Family Advocacy Scheme 14

public funding – *continued*
family help (higher) 119, 224
alternative sources 13
cost benefit test 14
divorce 32
financial eligibility 13
mediation and 13–14
prospect of success 14–15
family help (lower) 119, 224
cost benefit test 13
financial eligibility 13
financial provisions 119
Funding Code 11
human rights 17
legal help
advice 12
divorce 32
financial eligibility 12
financial order 119
sufficient benefit test 12
legal representation 14, 224, 225, 245
divorce 32
levels of service 12–14
mediation 119
family help (higher) and 13–14
notification duty 14
section 8 orders 187, 188
solicitor-client relationship 14
statutory charge 15
supervision orders 224
Public Law Outline 206, 223

refuges 236
religious marriage 42–3
relocation within UK 174
residence orders 171–4
children of cohabitants 262
conditions 171–2
directions 171–2
domestic violence 176
duration 194–5
interim 218–20
leaving UK 172–3
name change 172
relocation within UK 174
Resolution Code of Practice 4, 407
Revised Private Law Programme 190–4
Revised Public Law Outline 225

same-sex couples 253
parental responsibility 262
see also **cohabitation**
***Sears Tooth* agreement 17**
section 8 orders
acknowledgement of service 191
applicants
child 188–9
leave to apply 187–9
application
acknowledgement of service 191
child as party 190
forms 190, 471–90
service 190–1
section 8 orders – *continued*
without notice 191
child abduction 197
child applicant 188–9
leave of court 188
merits of case 189
public funding 188
solicitor to act 188
choice of court 189–90
contact orders
conditions 174
directions 174
domestic violence 175–6
enforcement 177–8
grandparents 175
letters, email or telephone contact 174
monitoring contact 177
physical contact 174
Practice Direction 176
step-parents 175
costs 194
county court 189
checklist 196
duration 194–5
emergency protection 197
family proceedings court 189
final hearing 193–4
First Hearing Dispute Resolution Appointment (FHDRA) 191–4
case management 193–4
consent orders 192
dispute resolution 192
expert evidence 192–3
orders 194
safeguarding 192
timetable 193–4
transfer to family proceedings court 194
welfare reports 192
wishes and feelings of child 193
witness statements 193
High Court 189
judgment 194
jurisdiction 187
leave to apply 187–9
no further application without leave of court 194
parental responsibility 262
procedure 187–95
prohibited steps orders 178–9, 194–5
public funding 187, 188
residence orders 171–4
conditions 171–2
directions 171–2
domestic violence 176
duration 194–5
interim 218–20
leaving UK 172–3
name change 172
relocation within UK 174
risk assessments 191
safety checks 191
service of application 190–1
acknowledgement 192

section 8 orders – *continued*
specific issues order 179
transfer of cases 189
witness statements 193
filing 193
hearsay evidence in 193
secured periodical payments 47, 49–50, 51
***Segal* orders 89, 96**
separation (2 years) with consent
calculation of period 27
cohabitation after 27
consent 27
financial position 27–8
mental element 27
separation 27
separation (5 years)
cohabitation after 29
financial hardship 28–9
grave hardship 28–9
meaning 28
separation agreements 160–3
advantages 161–2
agreement to separate 161
children 161
disadvantages 162
enforceability 162
finality 162
flexibility 162
periodical payments 161
property 161
speed 161
variation 162–3
court jurisdiction 162–3
service
care order application 226
divorce petition 36
alternative methods 37–8
children 39
co-respondent 38
deemed service 37
dispensing with 38
finding respondent 38
outside England and Wales 38
person under disability 39
personal service 37
usual method 36–7
financial provision application 122–3
section 8 order application 190–1
supervision order application 226
setting aside orders
grounds 153–4
subsequent maintenance assessment 154
side-letters
drafting 135
social fund
budgeting loans 81
cold weather payments 80
community care grant 80–1
crisis loans 81
discretionary 80–1
funeral grants 80
regulated 80
sure start maternity grants 80
social fund – *continued*
winter fuel payments 80
solicitor's costs 15
special guardianship orders 180–1, 232
application 180–1
procedure 181
special guardianship support services 181
specific issues order 179, 262
duration 194–5
stamp duty land tax 72
statutory charge
exemptions 16
operation of 15–16
postponement 16
step-children 61
Child Support Agency 87
step-parents
child support 87
contact orders 175
parental responsibility 169
supervision orders
application 211
application form 225, 465–70, 491–507
availability to court 213
case management conference 229
causation of harm 212–13
children's guardian 226–7
choice of court 223
choice of 218
concurrent applications 213
disclosure 229
duration 218
duties of supervisor 217
effect of 200, 217–18
evidence
admissibility 228
disclosure 229
expert evidence 229
witness statements 228
final hearing 230
first appointment
attendance 228
timetable for proceedings 227–8
grounds 211, 233
human rights implications 230–1
interim 218–20
'is likely to suffer' 212
issue of application 225
issue resolution hearings 229
judgment 230
jurisdiction 223
kinship assessments 224
letter before proceedings 224–5
meetings with parents 225
parental responsibility 218
parties to application 225–6
pre-proceedings action 224–5
procedure 223–30
procedure checklist 233
public funding 224
related proceedings 224
service of application 226
significant harm 211

supervision orders – *continued*
'is suffering' 212
solicitor appointment 227
stage 1 225–6
transfer of cases 223
welfare principle 213, 231

tax credits
children's tax credit 77–8, 81
maintenance and 81
working tax credit 76–7, 81, 102
term maintenance 63
third party debt order 148
Trusts of Land and Appointment of Trustees Act 1996
text 373

undertakings
domestic abuse 244
financial provision 131
undue influence
cohabitation agreements 255
matrimonial home lenders 108–9
unmarried families *see* cohabitation
unmarried fathers
human rights 262–3
parental responsibility 166–9, 261–2
refusal of order 167–8

violence *see* domestic abuse
void marriage 30
wills 31
voidable marriage 30–1
wills 31

wardship 200
warrant of arrest 249
warrant of distress 150
warrant of execution 148
welfare benefits
appeals 152–3
child benefit 73
children's tax credit 77–8, 81
council tax benefit 75, 79–80, 81
discretionary housing payments 80
financial provision 101–2
housing benefit 79
income support 73–5, 101, 102
jobseeker's allowance 76, 101, 102

welfare benefits – *continued*
lump sum payments and 82
maintenance payments and 81–2
marriage breakdown and 81–2
property adjustment 82
social fund 80–1
working tax credit 76–7, 81, 102
see also **local authority housing**
welfare principle 181–2
age of child 184
background of child 184–5
capability of parent or carer 185
care orders 213
care and supervision orders 231
change of circumstances, effect of 184
characteristics of child 184–5
checklist 182–6
delay 186
educational needs 184
emotional needs 184
feelings of child 183
harm, past or future 185
human rights 182
'no order' presumption 186
physical needs 184
powers of court 185–6
sex of child 184
supervision orders 213
wishes of child 183
Welfare Reform Bill 96
welfare reports
section 8 proceedings 192
wills
cohabitants 255
void marriage and 31
voidable marriage and 31
winter fuel payments 80
witness statements
care and supervision orders 228
section 8 proceedings 193
working tax credit 102
amount 77
eligibility 76
income 77
maintenance and 81
means testing 77–8
passport benefits 78–9

yardstick of equality 53